The Gift of the Church

The Gift of the Church

A Textbook on Ecclesiology in Honor of
Patrick Granfield, O.S.B.

Peter C. Phan

Editor

A Michael Glazier Book
THE LITURGICAL PRESS
Collegeville, Minnesota

www.litpress.org

A Michael Glazier Book published by Liturgical Press

Cover design by David Manahan, O.S.B.

ISBN 13: 978-0-8146-5931-1
ISBN 10: 0-8146-5931-4

	5	6	7	8	9

Library of Congress Cataloging-in-Publication Data

The gift of the church : a textbook on ecclesiology in honor of Patrick Granfield,
O.S.B. / Peter C. Phan, editor.
     p.   cm.
  Includes bibliographical references and index.
  ISBN 0-8146-5931-4 (alk. paper)
  1. Church. 2. Catholic Church—Doctrines. I. Granfield, Patrick. II. Phan,
Peter C., 1943–

BX1746 .G48 2000
262'.02—dc21

                                                           00-021485

To

Pope John Paul II

For his notable contributions to the theology of the Church

"In the Jubilee Year Christians will stand
with the renewed wonder of faith before
the love of the Father who gave his Son. With
a profound sense of commitment, they will
likewise express their gratitude for
the gift of the Church."

—*Tertio millennio adveniente*, 32

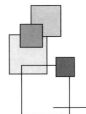

Contents

PART III
A North American Ecclesiology:
The Theological Achievement of Patrick Granfield

Abbreviations

AA	*Apostolicam actuositatem*
AAS	*Acta Apostolicae Sedis*
AG	*Ad gentes*
ARCIC	Anglican–Roman Catholic International Commission
CA	*Centesimus annus*
CCEO	*Codex Canonum Ecclesiarum Orientalium*
CCL	*Corpus Christianorum, Series Latina*
CD	*Christus Dominus*
CELAM	Council of Latin American Episcopacies
CL	*Christifideles laici*
CSEL	*Corpus scriptorum ecclesiasticorum Latinorum*
D&V	*Dominum et vivificantem*
DB	H. Denzinger, C. Bannwart, and I. B. Umbert, *Enchiridion symbolorum, definitionum et declarationum de rebus fidei et morum,* 28th edition (1952).
DOL	ICEL, *Documents of the Liturgy 1963–1979: Conciliar, Papal, and Curial Texts*
DP	Pontifical Council for Interreligious Dialogue and the Congregation for the Evangelization of Peoples, *Dialogue and Proclamation*
DS	H. Denzinger and A. Schönmetzer, eds., *Enchiridion symbolorum, definitionum et declarationum de rebus fidei et morum,* 36th edition (1976)
DV	*Dei verbum*
ELA	*Evangelization in Latin America's Present and Future*
EN	*Evangelii nuntiandi*
EV	*Evangelium vitae*

FC	*Familiaris consortio*
GS	*Gaudium et spes*
JBL	*Journal of Biblical Literature*
JW	1971 Synod of Bishops, *Justice in the World*
LG	*Lumen gentium*
LTK	*Lexikon für Theologie und Kirche*, 3rd edition
MD	*Mulieris dignitatem*
MM	*Mater et magistra*
NA	*Nostra aetate*
OE	*Orientalium ecclesiarum*
OT	*Optatum totius*
PDV	*Pastores dabo vobis*
PG	J. P. Migne, *Patrologia Graeca*
PL	J. P. Migne, *Patrologia Latina*
PO	*Presbyterorum ordinis*
PP	*Populorum progressio*
PT	*Pacem in terris*
QA	*Quadragesimo anno*
R&P	*Reconciliatio et paenitentia*
RH	*Redemptor hominis*
RMis	*Redemptoris missio*
RN	*Rerum novarum*
SC	*Sacrosanctam concilium*
ST	Thomas Aquinas, *Summa Theologiae*
TMA	*Tertio millennio adveniente*
UR	*Unitatis redintegratio*
UUS	*Ut unum sint*
VC	*Vita consecrata*
VS	*Veritas splendor*

Patrick Granfield, O.S.B.

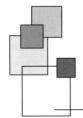

Introduction

Peter C. Phan

Had Patrick Granfield been fortunate enough to be born in Vietnam, he would upon reaching the age of seventy be covered with honors and marks of respect. He would be given the title of "Revered Sir." At public festivities he would sit at the head table with other dignitaries and be given attentive service. Since he is also a professor, he would be addressed by everyone as "Master," and his students would forever call him by this title, with reverence and affection, even if they have gone on to occupy high positions in society. And being a priest, he would always be greeted by the laity with elaborate salutations (e.g., "I beg the permission to greet you, venerable Father"), and never, *horribile dictu,* with the casual "Hi, Pat!"

But since divine providence has disposed otherwise with Reverend Professor Granfield's birth, the next best thing his friends and colleagues can do for him, at least in academe, is to honor him with a *Festschrift* to celebrate his accomplishments and to show him gratitude for the service he has rendered to theology and to the Church.

However, this book is no *Festschrift* in the usual mold, that is, a collection of disparate and highly specialized essays whose destiny is to gather dust on the library shelf. The editor has planned it as a textbook for upper undergraduate and graduate classes in ecclesiology. It is also hoped that those engaged in various ministries in the Church will find it a useful tool to update themselves on the theology of different aspects of the Church. The choice of ecclesiology as the focus of the book is highly appropriate, both because it is the field in which Granfield has distinguished himself and also because it has been the central theme of theological reflections since the Second Vatican Council and will presumably continue to be in the next century.

The purpose of the book dictates not only the style of its essays, which is intended to be clear and readable, but also its comprehensive character. The essays attempt to present the current state of ecclesiology and deal with all the most important aspects of the Church. The book is divided into three parts: the first discusses ecclesiology in its historical development as well as its methodology; the second examines various aspects of the Church; and the third presents the life and work of Patrick Granfield.

It is my pleasure to thank first of all the contributors to the volume. Their kindness and generosity as well as their conscientious keeping of the deadline made my editorial labor much lighter than I had expected. I am also deeply grateful to two of my students, Jonathan Tan and Pham Thi Van, for their assistance in preparing the manuscript. Lastly, my heartfelt thanks to Annette Kmitch, editor at The Liturgical Press, for her careful editorial work, and to Colleen Stiller, production manager at The Liturgical Press, for supervising the publication of this book.

In his account of the first seventy-five years of the *American Ecclesiastical Review* in 1964, Granfield tells us that the motto that the founder, Fr. Hermann Heuser, chose for the journal is: *"Ut ecclesia aedificationem accipiat"* (1 Cor 14:5). He also tells us that the symbol of the dolphin and anchor, which appeared for so many years on the cover of the journal, was a favorite of Father Heuser. The dolphin, Father Heuser explains, is an ancient and appropriate symbol for Christ since dolphins are found only in purest waters, have great strength, and are known for their attraction for humans. The anchor, too, is found in antiquity and, as a symbol of the Church, it connotes solidarity, confidence, and hope.

Consciously or unconsciously, Patrick Granfield has made the building up of the Church the central task of his life and work. The emblem of the dolphin winding itself around the anchor, symbolizing the unity of Christ and the Church, is also a fitting summary of his achievements. May the love and light of Christ and the hope and security that the Church offers accompany him and us in our pilgrimage to the kingdom of God of which the Church is a sacrament.

As we celebrate you with this *Festschrift*, we greet you, Pat, with affection, as the Vietnamese would: "Revered Sir," "Master," and "Venerable Father."

Peter C. Phan
The Catholic University of America

PART I

Ecclesiology in Historical Context

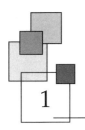

1

Theologies of the Church in the New Testament

Frank J. Matera

The Church plays a central role in the New Testament, even when it is not mentioned.[1] The reason for this is quite simple. The authors of the New Testament wrote for communities of believers. Thus, the Church preceded and gave birth to the New Testament. But having brought forth the New Testament, the Church must continually return to this foundational document as it reflects upon its origins and identity.

Such reflection can proceed in several ways. For example, one could employ these writings as historical sources to investigate how the Church came into being. Or one could view them in light of contemporary social theory to study the Church as a social phenomenon of the first century. Or, as the title of this essay suggests, one could employ these writings to uncover their theologies of the Church.

Today most New Testament exegetes acknowledge that the New Testament contains a variety of theologies, not all of which can be harmonized with each other since the New Testament consists of diverse writings composed by several authors for differing circumstances. Thus, there are many ecclesiologies in the New Testament. This essay accepts that premise as it investigates these writings in the following order: (1) the Four Gospels; (2) the Acts of the Apostles; (3) the Pauline Letters; (4) 1 Peter, Hebrews, and Revelation.[2]

A Community of Disciples

Although *ekklēsia* ("church") only occurs three times in the Gospels (Matt 16:18; 18:17 [twice]), these writings are not bereft of ecclesiology.

[1] The point is made by Rudolf Schnackenburg, *The Church in the New Testament* (New York: Herder and Herder, 1965) 9.

[2] Since Paul's nondisputed correspondence was written before the Synoptic Gospels, it is evident that this grouping is not based on chronological considerations. But it does have the advantage of beginning with Jesus, to whom the Church owes its origin.

To be sure, their primary purpose is to proclaim the gospel by narrating the story of Jesus, but each of them presupposes and implies an ecclesiology.

The Gospel of Mark was probably written for a community of Gentile Christians in Rome during the period of the Jewish War (66–70 C.E.). It views the Church as a community of disciples in which service defines leadership. This community was scattered at Jesus' death (14:27, 50), but then reconstituted by the risen Lord (16:7). It has now become a missionary congregation that preaches the gospel to all nations (13:10) as it awaits the imminent return of the Son of Man (13:32-37). It is a spiritual temple, the fruit of the Messiah's saving death upon the cross, as suggested by the tearing of the temple veil at Jesus' death (15:38).[3]

At the beginning of the Gospel, Jesus calls his first disciples (1:16-20). Later he summons twelve men whom he constitutes as "the Twelve."[4] Among them, Peter, James, John (and sometimes Andrew) form an inner circle (5:37; 9:2; 13:3). Throughout the Gospel Jesus teaches the Twelve that greatness consists in service to others rather than in the exercise of power and authority (10:41-44). Therefore, the Church must pattern itself on the Son of Man who did not come to be served but to serve (10:45). Its members must take up the cross (8:34) and serve the needs of each other (9:33-37).

The Gospel of Matthew employs Mark's Gospel as its primary source and shares many of its ecclesiological themes. Written for a community of Jewish and Gentile Christians in Antioch of Syria about 85 C.E., the Gospel exhibits a more developed ecclesiology than does the Gospel of Mark, especially in terms of ecclesial discipline and structure.

The most distinctive aspect of Matthew's Gospel is a series of discourses that Jesus addresses to his disciples: the Sermon on the Mount (5–7); the Missionary Discourse (10); the Parable Discourse (13); the Discourse on Church Life (18); and the Eschatological Discourse on the return of the Son of Man (24–25). The intended audience of these discourses is the Matthean community, and they function as the risen Lord's instructions to the Church of Matthew's day. As such, they disclose a great deal about Matthean ecclesiology.

---

[3] There is an ironic dimension to the false charge that Jesus would destroy the temple and build another not made by human hands (Mark 14:58), for, since Jesus gives his life as a ransom for many (Mark 10:45), his death calls into question any further need for the old temple cult and suggests that the community of believers is the new temple not made by hands.

[4] While some manuscripts identify the Twelve as "apostles," the best manuscripts do not. On the question of the Twelve, see John P. Meier, "The Circle of the Twelve: Did It Exist During Jesus' Public Ministry?" *JBL* 116 (1997) 635–72.

The Sermon on the Mount, for example, shows that Matthew understands the Church as a community of disciples which fulfills the Mosaic Law as interpreted by Jesus the Messiah. Because it has been taught by the Messiah, the Church bears fruit and practices a righteousness that surpasses that of the scribes and Pharisees (5:20). Accordingly, Jesus identifies his disciples as the salt of the earth and the light of the world (5:13-16).

In the Missionary Discourse, Matthew discloses the missionary character of the Church, and it is evident that the instructions are intended for the missionaries of Matthew's day.[5] Although Jesus limited his own mission and that of his disciples to the lost sheep of the house of Israel (10:5-6; 15:24), the risen Lord commissions the Church to make disciples of all nations (28:18-20).

In the Parable Discourse, the parable of the weeds (13:24-30, 36-43) and the parable of the great net (13:47-50) suggest that not all is well in the Matthean congregation. The Church is like a field in which there are weeds as well as wheat. It is like a net that has collected fish of every kind, bad as well as good. As Jesus warned at the end of the Sermon on the Mount, there are false prophets in the Church who call him "Lord" but do not do his words (7:15-23). While some members of the community may be tempted to expel such evildoers from the community now, the Matthean Jesus cautions them to wait patiently for the moment of judgment when the Son of Man will send his angels to separate the bad from the good (13:30, 40-42, 49).

Because there are failures within the Church, the Matthean Jesus establishes a community rule for dealing with disciples who have sinned or gone astray (18:1-35). In the case of a serious offense, one should deal privately with the offending party first (18:15). If this fails, then one should gather two or three others (18:16). Should this fail, one should tell the Church (*ekklēsia;* 18:17). If even this fails, then the Church has the authority to deal with the sinful person, for whatever it binds or looses on earth will be bound or loosed in heaven (18:18).

Jesus' Eschatological Discourse instructs the Church how to live in the time between his resurrection and his return as the royal Son of Man. The Church must not be deceived by false prophets or surprised by persecution. Rather, it must preach the gospel of the kingdom until the Son of Man appears (24:14). The Church must be as vigilant as bridesmaids awaiting the bridegroom (25:1-13) and as industrious as servants awaiting their master's return (25:14-30).

---

[5] A reading of the discourses will show that its instructions fit the circumstances of Matthew's day better than those of Jesus' day. For example, see Matt 10:23.

In sum, the discourses show that Matthew views the Church as a community instructed in all righteousness, missionary in nature, empowered to discipline its members as it waits for the Son of Man who will separate the bad from the good.

The most distinctive aspect of Matthew's ecclesiology, however, is the beatitude Jesus pronounces upon Peter, and which is only found in Matthew's Gospel.

> Blessed are you, Simon son of Jonah! For flesh and blood has not revealed this to you, but my Father in heaven. And I tell you, you are Peter, and on this rock I will build my church *[ekklēsian]*, and the gates of Hades will not prevail against it. I will give you the keys of the kingdom of heaven, and whatever you bind on earth will be bound in heaven, and whatever you loose on earth will be loosed in heaven (16:17-19, NRSV).

In this text, Matthew portrays Jesus as the founder of the *ekklēsia* that has emerged in communities such as his own, with Peter as its rock foundation. As regards this *ekklēsia,* Jesus identifies it as his own ("my church") since he is the one who calls it into being. It is eschatological in nature because not even the powers of death ("the gates of Hades") can prevail against it. As regards Peter, he is the one upon whom the building is constructed, Christ being its founder. Therefore, Jesus grants him the keys of the kingdom so that what Peter binds and looses on earth will be bound and loosed in heaven. While the community is given similar authority (18:18-19), only Peter is granted the power of the keys, indicating that he holds a unique and authoritative role within the Church.

But what is the relationship of Jesus' *ekklēsia* to Israel? On the one hand, Matthew sees continuity between Israel and the Church since Jesus the Messiah established it. On the other hand, Matthew is keenly aware that the larger portion of Israel has not accepted Jesus as Messiah. Therefore, in the Matthean version of the parable of the tenants, Jesus warns the religious leaders that the kingdom of God will be taken from them and given to a nation that will produce fruit (21:43). Accordingly, Matthew thinks of the Church as both distinct from, and in continuity with, historic Israel. It is in continuity with Israel because its founder is the Messiah, and yet it is distinct because, without excluding Israel, it now embraces all nations.

The Gospel of Luke shares many of the ecclesiological traits found in the Gospel of Mark since it employs Mark's Gospel as one of its sources. Written for a predominantly Gentile readership about 85 C.E., it presents the Church as a community of disciples, a "little flock" (12:32) that is missionary in nature and distinguished by its humble service. However, Luke develops his ecclesiology in a new manner since his Gospel is the first part of a two-volume work, Luke-Acts.

Writing as a historian who has carefully investigated the sources available to him, Luke promises to set forth an orderly account so that believers will have assurance about what has transpired from the time of Jesus to the time of the Church (1:1-4). Thus, Luke presents the origins of the Church within a broader perspective and makes a clearer distinction between the time of Jesus and the time of the Church than does Mark.

The Gospel focuses upon the time of Jesus, which Luke clearly portrays as the fulfillment of Israel's messianic hopes (1:5–2:40). But since Luke writes with his second volume in view, his story of Jesus foreshadows the time of the Church. For example, since he will present the apostles as the eschatological rulers of the reestablished Israel, Luke explicitly identifies them with the Twelve (6:12-16). At the Last Supper, after Jesus teaches his followers the importance of humble service (22:24-27), he confers rulership upon them and promises that they will sit on thrones and judge the twelve tribes of Israel (22:28-30). Jesus then highlights the central role of Peter who, after he has repented, will strengthen his brethren (22:31-34). Later, the risen Lord appears to the apostles and constitutes them as his witnesses to preach repentance for the forgiveness of sins to all nations (24:46-49). By the conclusion of the Gospel, then, the community of Jesus' disciples is poised to become the Church.

Although Luke wrote for a primarily Gentile audience, he emphasizes the continuity between Israel and the community of those who believe in Jesus. For example, his infancy narrative demonstrates how the God of Israel discloses the fulfillment of his promises to holy and righteous Israelites such as Zechariah and Elizabeth, Mary and Joseph, Simeon and Anna. In Acts, Luke will explain how and why Gentiles came to populate the Church.

The Gospel of John is primarily interested in christology. Nevertheless, exegetes have been able to determine a great deal about its ecclesiology from the story it tells.[6] Written independently of the Synoptics, the present form of the Gospel was composed toward the end of the first century, after several earlier editions, for a community that coalesced around a figure identified as the disciple whom Jesus loved (13:23; 19:26; 20:2; 21:7, 20).

[6] Raymond E. Brown, *The Community of the Beloved Disciple: The Life, Loves, and Hates of an Individual Church in the New Testament* (New York: Paulist Press, 1979); J. Louis Martyn, *History and Theology in the Fourth Gospel*, rev. and enlarged ed. (Nashville: Abingdon Press, 1979).

Although the Fourth Gospel alludes to the Twelve (6:70), there is no account of Jesus calling them, and this suggests that they did not play a central role in John's view of the Church. Peter, however, plays an important role in 6:67-69, and in 21:15-19 Jesus instructs him to feed his sheep. Most exegetes, however, view chapter 21 as a later edition to the Gospel.[7] If this is so, it may indicate a later stage in the community's life when certain members found it necessary to build bridges to other communities for whom Peter's ecclesial role was more significant.

Two images dominate Johannine ecclesiology: the sheepfold and the vine. In 10:1-18 Jesus employs the metaphors of the gate and the good shepherd to describe his relationship to his disciples. He is the gate by which the sheep enter the fold (10:7, 9), and the disciples are his sheep. He is the Good Shepherd who lays down his life for the sheep (10:11, 15). Jesus also has other sheep who do not belong to *this* fold (10:16). Read from the point of view of the Johannine community, this verse may be referring to believers who do not belong to the Johannine circle.

In 15:1-10, the Gospel employs the metaphor of the vine and the branches to describe the intimate relationship between Jesus and his disciples. He is the true vine, his Father the vine grower, and his disciples the branches. Only if they abide in him, and he abides in them, will they bear fruit. On the basis of this metaphor, one could describe the Johannine church as a community of mystical participation.[8]

In addition to mystical participation, however, there are other elements of Johannine ecclesiology. For example, the community is guided by the Paraclete *(paraklētos)*, the Holy Spirit, whom the Father sends in Jesus' name (14:26). The Paraclete teaches the community and reminds it of everything that Jesus taught (14:26). The community views the world *(kosmos)* as hostile to it and does not identify itself with the world. Nonetheless, it is aware that it is *in* the world, even though it is not *of* the world, for Jesus sent his disciples into the world just as the Father sent him (17:18). Thus the Church is missionary in nature, open to Gentiles (12:20-23), Samaritans (4:35-42), and Jews, indeed, to all who believe that Jesus came from the Father. Finally, the community sees itself as worshiping in spirit and in truth (4:21-24). The old cult no longer satisfies its needs, for the risen Christ has become the temple of the living God (2:13-22).

Although each of the Gospels views the Church from a slightly different vantage point, the Fourth Gospel being the most distinctive, it is

[7] Since there is no manuscript evidence for this, this judgment is made on the basis of the chapter's theology and style.

[8] Howard Clark Kee, *Who Are the People of God? Early Christian Models of Community* (New Haven, Conn.: Yale University Press, 1995) 157–78.

possible to draw some general conclusions from their theologies of the Church. First, the Church is a community of disciples that Jesus called into being. While the earthly Lord called the first disciples, the community of disciples that is the Church has been called into being through the death and resurrection of Christ. Second, the Church is the eschatological community of those who wait for the imminent return of their Lord. As an eschatological community, the Church is a new temple where believers worship in spirit and in truth. Third, the Church is missionary in nature, for Jesus commissioned it to preach to all nations. Fourth, the Church defines its authority in terms of service after the example of Christ's self-giving death. Finally, Peter and the Twelve play a prominent ecclesial role in the Synoptic Gospels, and the Beloved Disciple in the Fourth Gospel.

The Reestablished Israel

The Church plays a more central role in Acts than in the Gospels since Acts narrates how the gospel spread after the death and resurrection of Jesus through the witness of the apostles and those who believed in Jesus. Accordingly, *ekklēsia* occurs frequently in Acts.[9] But it is not the only way that Luke designates the early Christian community.[10]

According to Acts, the Church is a creation of the Spirit and comes into existence on Pentecost (2:1-42). But it is not until 5:11 that Acts identifies the community of believers as the Church.[11] The reason may be Luke's desire to present the Church first as that portion of Israel which has repented and been baptized in the name of Jesus for the forgiveness of sins and has received the Holy Spirit (2:37-39). The Church, then, is the reestablished Israel whose eschatological rulers are the twelve apostles; it is not a new Israel or a community separated from Israel. In the early chapters of Acts, therefore, Luke is content to describe the Church as a community of believers who devote themselves to the teaching of the apostles, life in common *(koinōnia)*, the breaking of the bread, and prayer (2:42). Holding all things in common (2:44), no

---

[9] *Ekklēsia* occurs twenty-three times in Acts. In 7:38 it refers to the community of Israel in the wilderness, and in three instances to an unruly mob (Acts 19:32, 39, 40). In the remaining nineteen instances, it refers to the Church (5:11; 8:1, 3; 9:31; 11:22, 26; 12:1, 5; 13:1; 14:23, 27; 15:3, 4, 22, 41; 16:5; 18:22; 20:17, 28).

[10] Other terms that he employs are: the brethren, the disciples, the saints, Christians, people, those who believe.

[11] After narrating the story of Ananias and Sapphira, Acts says, "And great fear seized the whole church and all who heard of these things" (5:11, NRSV).

one was needy among them (4:32-35). Accordingly, the early Church fulfills the perfect ideal of communal life.

The Twelve stand at the center of this community witnessing to the Lord's resurrection and calling Israel to repentance (1:8, 21-22; 3:15; 5:33; 10:42). When conflicts arise between the Hebrew- and Greek-speaking factions of the Jerusalem community, it is the Twelve who resolve them (6:1-6). And when the Twelve hear that Samaria accepts the word of God, they send Peter and John to investigate (8:14).

Having established that the community of believers is the reestablished Israel,[12] Luke focuses upon the distinctive nature of the new community and its surprising growth among Gentiles. In doing so, he uses *ekklēsia* with greater frequency. For example, after the death of Stephen, he notes that a severe persecution afflicted the church in Jerusalem and that Saul was ravaging it house by house (8:1-3). Here, *ekklēsia* clearly refers to the Jerusalem community that Luke has already portrayed as the reestablished Israel. After his account of Paul's conversion, however, he speaks of the Church "throughout Judea, Galilee, and Samaria" (9:31), suggesting something more than a local congregation.

In most instances, however, Acts applies *ekklēsia* to the local community, with the community of Jerusalem holding pride of place. Thus, when the church of Jerusalem hears that the word has spread among the Gentiles in Antioch, it sends Barnabas to investigate (11:22). The Gentile congregation of Antioch, however, is also called a church, and Barnabas and Paul play central roles in its life and mission (11:26).

The church at Antioch, like its Jerusalem counterpart, is guided by the Spirit; and Barnabas and Paul are numbered among its prophets and teachers (13:1-3). Sent out by the Holy Spirit (13:4), they undertake a missionary journey among the Gentiles on behalf of the church at Antioch (13:4–14:28), and the communities they establish are also called churches, each with its own elders *(presbyteroi)* appointed by Barnabas and Paul (14:23). Thus, Acts first applies *ekklēsia* to the church at Jerusalem, then to the believers of Judea, Samaria, and Galilee, next to the Gentile congregation of Antioch, and finally to the communities established by Barnabas and Paul.

The missionary journey of Barnabas and Paul, however, confronts the church at Jerusalem with a crisis. On what basis should the Gentile congregations of the Pauline mission be admitted into communion with the church of Jerusalem? Sent by the church at Antioch (15:3), Paul

---

[12] Notice the frequent references to the growth of the Church among the Jerusalemites (2:41; 4:4; 5:14; 6:1, 7; 9:31) which culminate in James' statement that there are now thousands of believers, all zealous observers of the law (21:20).

and Barnabas present the case for Gentile believers to the church at Jerusalem, the apostles, and the elders (15:4). Agreeing not to trouble the Gentiles further by requiring circumcision and full observance of the Mosaic Law, they send delegates with Paul and Barnabas to the church of Antioch to announce this good news (15:22). Thus, the Jerusalem church opens the way for further missionary activity among the Gentiles.

Luke describes Paul's missionary activity in 15:36–19:20 (Paul's second and third missionary journeys), but he rarely identifies the communities that Paul establishes as churches. Instead, he refers to "the brethren," "the disciples," "the saints," "those who had come to believe," "those who followed the way." This is not to say that Luke does not view these congregations as churches since he does speak of the elders of the Ephesian church (20:17). Rather, he alters his vocabulary to remind readers that the Church is a community of disciples who believe in the Lord, following a "way" that leads to salvation for those who call upon the name of the Lord. Moreover, to show that the Gentile communities of Asia and Greece are in communion with the church of Jerusalem, Luke mentions Paul's visits to the church of Jerusalem after Paul's second and third missionary journeys (18:22; 21:17).

The final use of *ekklēsia* in Acts occurs during Paul's farewell to the elders of the Ephesian church and is, perhaps, the most important (20:18-35). Recalling his ministry among them, and warning them of what will happen after his departure, Paul reminds the elders to keep watch over the flock of which the Holy Spirit has made them overseers (*episkopous*), for it is "the Church of God" obtained through the blood of his own Son (20:28).[13] Here, "the Church of God" refers to something more than the local community of Jerusalem, Antioch, or Ephesus; it is the Church spread throughout the world. Moreover, Luke emphasizes that God acquired the Church at the cost of his Son's death.[14] Thus, while the Church is born at Pentecost, the death of Christ makes its existence possible.

The theology of the Church in Acts is narrative and descriptive. It is narrative because it tells the story of the Church from its birth in Jerusalem to its growth among the Gentiles of Asia Minor and Greece. It is descriptive because it describes the Church in a variety of ways: as a community of disciples and brethren who live a common life, and as a

[13] The Greek reads *dia tou haimatos tou idiou* ("through his own blood") and could refer to the blood of God. Or, the Greek could be construed "through the blood of his own"; that is, the blood of his own Son.

[14] This statement is remarkable since Luke does not otherwise focus upon the salvific dimension of Christ's death.

people who call upon the name of the Lord and follow a way that leads to salvation. The Church is the reestablished Israel in which God's promises are fulfilled (2:16-21). But as the story unfolds and Gentiles play a greater role, it becomes apparent that there is a serious division between the reestablished Israel and that portion of Israel which has not believed in Jesus as the Messiah, especially Israel's leaders.[15]

Finally, the churches of Acts are both structured and charismatic. On the one hand, there are elders in the church of Jerusalem and the congregations of the Pauline mission,[16] and in the initial stages of the Church's growth the apostles play an indispensable role. But, on the other hand, the Church is also a charismatic community guided by the Spirit who inaugurates the Gentile mission (13:2) and guides its missionary activity (16:7).

Ekklēsia, Body of Christ, Temple of God

The Pauline writings provide a rich theological reflection on the Church. Not only was Paul one of the most original thinkers of the New Testament, the very nature of his ministry compelled him to write on issues dealing with the nature of the Church and its implications for the Christian life. Consequently, it is not surprising that *ekklēsia* occurs sixty-two times in the letters attributed to him, whereas it only occurs three times in the Gospels.[17] But in addition to the frequent use of *ekklēsia*, the Pauline letters employ other concepts to develop the theology of the Church. Primary among these are the metaphor of the body of Christ, the identification of the community as the temple of God, and the use of familial and election language to describe the Christian community.[18]

The study of Pauline ecclesiology, however, presents a difficulty since Paul did not write all of the letters attributed to him.[19] Moreover,

[15] Note the frequent controversies between the apostles and the religious leaders in the first five chapters of Acts and Paul's statements in Jewish synagogues that he will turn to the Gentiles (13:46; 18:6; 28:28).

[16] 11:30; 14:23; 15:2, 4, 6, 22, 23; 16:4; 20:17, 18.

[17] Rom 16:1, 4, 5, 16, 23; 1 Cor 1:2; 4:17; 6:4; 7:17; 10:32; 11:16, 18, 22; 12:28; 14:4, 5, 12, 19, 23, 28, 33, 34, 35; 15:9; 16:1, 19 (twice); 2 Cor 1:1; 8:1, 18, 19, 23, 24; 11:8, 28; 12:13; Gal 1:2, 13, 22; Eph 1:22; 3:10, 21; 5:24, 25, 27, 29, 32; Phil 3:6; 4:15; Col 1:18, 24; 4:15, 16; 1 Thess 1:1; 2:14; 2 Thess 1:1, 4; 1 Tim 3:5, 15; 5:16; Philemon 2.

[18] Election language identifies believers as God's holy ones, the called, chosen, and beloved of God. Familial language refers to members of the Church as brothers and sisters and to the founding apostle as their father in Christ.

[19] Paul is surely the author of Romans, 1 and 2 Corinthians, Galatians, Philippians, 1 Thessalonians, and Philemon. There is disagreement about his authorship of

since he wrote in response to problems and questions, he did not have the luxury of developing a full-fledged ecclesiology. Nonetheless, the Pauline writings presuppose a rather profound ecclesiology that begins with the word *ekklēsia.*

In secular Greek literature, *ekklēsia* designated an assembly of free men entitled to vote, long before it attained a religious meaning in the writings of the New Testament. This, for example, is how it is used in Acts 19:29, 32. But in the Greek Bible, the Septuagint, *ekklēsia* is often translated *qāhāl*, the Hebrew word that designated the congregation of Israel that YHWH assembled during the wilderness period. The New Testament phrase "the Church of God" *(hē ekklēsia tou theou)* invites a comparison between this wilderness congregation and the community of those called in Christ.

Paul employs *ekklēsia* in a variety of ways. In most instances, the term clearly refers to a local assembly of Christians in a city or province. For example, Paul speaks of "the church of Cenchreae" (Rom 16:1), "the churches of Galatia" (Gal 1:2; 1 Cor 16:1), "the churches of Asia" (1 Cor 16:19), and "the churches of Macedonia" (2 Cor 8:1). At other times his language is more general, and he speaks of "*all* the churches of the Gentiles" (Rom 16:4), "*all* the churches in Christ" (Rom 16:16), "*all* the churches of the saints" (1 Cor 14:33), or simply of "*all* the churches" (2 Cor 8:18; 11:28). But in these instances, he clearly has local communities in view.

At other times, he writes of the church in a particular house. Thus, he is acquainted with the church in the house of Prisca and Aquila (Rom 16:1-5; 1 Cor 16:19). And, at the end of Romans, he speaks of Gaius, "who is host to me and to the whole church" (Rom 16:23). Gaius was Paul's host at Corinth (where Paul wrote Romans) and may have hosted gatherings of the whole Corinthian church which probably consisted of several house churches, such as the one that met in the home of Prisca and Aquila.

Several Pauline texts highlight the Church as an assembly. For example, when discussing abuses at the Eucharist Paul writes, "when you *come together* as a church" (1 Cor 11:18). Later, when addressing the question of charisms, he notes, "If, therefore, the whole church *comes together* and all speak in tongues . . ." (1 Cor 14:23). Still later, when considering the role of women in the assembly, he commands, "let them be silent in church and speak to themselves and to God" (1 Cor 14:28). In all of these texts, *ekklēsia* refers to a gathering or assembly of God's holy ones rather than a place or institution. *Ekklēsia* is the local

---

2 Thessalonians and Colossians, and something approaching a consensus that he did not author Ephesians or the Pastorals (1 and 2 Timothy, Titus).

assembly in which the Spirit is active, dispensing gifts for building up the church understood as a local congregation (1 Cor 14:4, 5, 12).

On several occasions, Paul speaks of "the church of God," "the churches of God," or simply "the church," and he still has the local congregation in view. In 1 Cor 15:9 and Gal 1:13, for example, he describes himself as someone who persecuted "the church of God," probably referring to the original Jerusalem community. But in 1 Cor 1:1 and 2 Cor 1:2, he addresses his letters to "the church of God that is in Corinth," thereby bestowing upon his Gentile congregation a title of honor that originally belonged to the church of Jerusalem. This title also stands behind the shorter formula, "the church" (1 Cor 6:4; 12:28; 14:5, 12; Phil 3:6).

In 1 Cor 10:32 and 11:22, "the church of God" probably still refers to the local community at Corinth, but one begins to detect the beginnings of a different usage whereby "the church of God" has a more general sense.[20] The authors of Colossians and Ephesians may have sensed this. For, when they unite the Pauline notion of the Church with that of the body of Christ, they clearly portray the Church as universal in scope.[21]

The Body of Christ metaphor, which plays such a prominent role in Colossians and Ephesians, only appears in two other Pauline writings, 1 Corinthians and Romans. But since Colossians and Ephesians were probably written by others in Paul's name, they develop the concept of the Church as the body of Christ on the basis of what is found in 1 Corinthians and Romans.

The "body of Christ" can refer to the crucified body of Christ (Rom 7:4) or to the eucharistic body of Christ (1 Cor 10:16), but in 1 Cor 12:27 Paul clearly relates it to the Corinthian church ("Now you are the body of Christ and individually members of it," NRSV), as the next verse (1 Cor 12:28, NRSV) indicates, "And God has appointed in the church first apostles, second prophets, third teachers . . ."[22]

Paul does not develop an abstract theology of the Church as the body of Christ. Rather, he employs the concept as he responds to a number of problems plaguing the Corinthian community. For example, in 1 Cor 10:14-22 he warns his audience that participation in the table of

---

[20] This is the suggestion of Joseph A. Fitzmyer, *Paul and His Theology: A Brief Sketch* (Englewood Cliffs, N.J.: Prentice Hall, 1989) 96.

[21] In Ephesians and Colossians, *ekklēsia* has all but lost its local sense. See Eph 1:22; 3:10, 21; 5:23, 24, 25, 27, 29, 32; Col 1:18, 24. Col 4:15, 16, however, refer to a local congregation.

[22] The Greek text of 1 Cor 12:27 does not have a definite article *(hymeis de este soma Christou)* and could be translated, "you are a body belonging to Christ."

the Lord (the Eucharist) and the table of demons (idol worship) are mutually exclusive. In making his argument, he reminds the Corinthians that the Eucharist is a sharing in the "body of Christ," and then notes, "Because there is one bread, *we who are many are one body*" (10:17, NRSV).

In 1 Cor 12:12-26, Paul employs an extended metaphor of the body to remind the Corinthians that just as there are many members in a human body, each with its own role, so there are many spiritual gifts in the Church.

> For just as the body is one and has many members, and all the members of the body, though many, are one body, so it is with Christ. For in the one Spirit we were all baptized into *one body*—Jews or Greeks, slaves or free—and we were all made to drink of one Spirit (1 Cor 12:12-13, NRSV).

After explaining the need for diversity in the human body (12:14-26), Paul tells the Corinthians that they are the body of Christ (12:27). Then, using *ekklēsia* for the first time with this image, he lists the different ministries and gifts God has appointed for the Church (12:27-31).

In 1 Cor 12:12-31 and Rom 12:3-8, Paul has the local community in view when he speaks of the body of Christ, and he clearly employs the image to emphasize the different gifts and functions within the local congregation. But the Church is not merely *like* a body. Rather, it has become one body in Christ because its members participate in the one eucharistic body of Christ (10:16-17). Paul presupposes that the local *ekklēsia* participates in and belongs to the body of Christ because its members have been baptized into Christ's body (12:13) and share his eucharistic body (10:16). As members of Christ's body, each has a different function intended for the common good.

Therefore, when Paul asks the factious Corinthian community, "Has Christ been divided?" (1 Cor 1:13, NRSV), he is speaking of the church at Corinth. And when he tries to dissuade the Corinthians from immorality by reminding them that their bodies are members of Christ (1 Cor 6:15), he is speaking to them as members of the church whose bodies are members of Christ.

Colossians and Ephesians develop Paul's imagery of the body in new ways. First, whereas Paul speaks of the *body* of Christ, the authors of these writings speak of Christ as the head *(kephalē)* of the body, which is the Church (Col 1:18; 2:19; Eph 1:22-23; 4:15-16; 5:23). This new image allows Colossians and Ephesians to explain the relationship between Christ and his Church more clearly than Paul did in Romans 12 and 1 Corinthians 12. For example, Colossians notes that the Church is nourished by the head, who is Christ, and grows with a growth that comes from God (2:19). In a similar vein, Ephesians exhorts its audience to grow into Christ who is the head, from whom the whole body grows (4:15-16). Ephesians also combines the head and body metaphor with the metaphor of marriage (5:22-33). Comparing the relationship of Christ and his Church to the relationship of husband and wife, Ephesians describes Christ as the head of the Church, his body, of which he is the Savior. Because Christ loved the Church and handed himself over for her to make her holy, the Church should be subject to Christ who nourishes and cares for his body, the Church.

Second, when Colossians and Ephesians identify the Church as the body of Christ, they understand *ekklēsia* in a more general sense than Paul did. *Ekklēsia* now refers to the Church universally spread throughout the world. Accordingly, God has subjected all things to Christ and made him head over all things for the sake of the Church, which is Christ's body (Eph 1:22-23). Christ, in turn, has created a new humanity in himself so that he might reconcile Gentile and Jew *in one body* through the cross (Eph 2:15-16). Accordingly, the Church is the showpiece of Christ's work of reconciliation. It is filled with the "fullness" of Christ who is filling all things with the fullness of God (1:23).[23] In it, God reveals the mystery hidden for ages, but now revealed to the holy apostles and prophets that "the Gentiles have become fellow heirs, *members of the same body*, and sharers in the promise in Christ Jesus through the Gospel" (3:6, NRSV).

To summarize, as the body of Christ metaphor focuses ever more intensely upon the relationship of Christ and his Church in Ephesians and Colossians, the center of gravity shifts from the local to the universal Church.

The temple of God is akin to the body of Christ metaphor. Aware that those who are in Christ have been called, elected, sanctified, and set apart for worship in the Spirit, Paul views the Christian community as the temple of God. Thus, he reminds the Corinthian community that they are God's holy temple because God's Spirit dwells in them (1 Cor 3:16-17). As the temple of the living God, believers are as different from unbelievers as light is from darkness (2 Cor 6:16). Employing similar imagery, the author of Ephesians reminds his Gentile audience that they are now "citizens with the saints and also members of the household of God" (2:19, NRSV). Built on the foundation of the apostles and prophets, Christ being the cornerstone, they are growing into a *holy temple* in the Lord (2:21).

Pauline ecclesiology could be developed in other ways. For example, Paul describes those who believe in Christ as descendants of Abraham (Gal 3:29), the true circumcision (Phil 3:3), the Israel of God

---

[23] Here, "fullness" *(plērōma)* refers to the very being of God.

(Gal 6:16). He also employs kinship language to reinforce the notion that the believing community is a new family in Christ (1 Thess 2:11). But the images discussed above (*ekklēsia*, body of Christ, temple of God) are the most powerful and enduring of the Pauline legacy.

Persecuted Pilgrim People of God

Although there is no literary relationship between 1 Peter, Hebrews, and Revelation, each of these writings functions as a moral exhortation to communities of believers to persevere in faith despite the threat of persecution. Consequently, they present an ecclesiology that focuses upon the Church as the People of God in exile (1 Peter), a pilgrim community seeking to enter God's Sabbath rest (Hebrews), and a persecuted community that will participate in the heavenly Jerusalem after it has borne witness to the Lamb who was slain (Revelation).

First Peter never employs the word *ekklēsia*, but the idea of the Church as the People of God is ever in the background. For example, the author describes the Gentile recipients of this letter in language that was once applied to Israel of old.[24] They are "a chosen race, a royal priesthood, a holy nation, God's own people" (1 Pet 2:9, NRSV, alluding to Exod 19:6 and Isa 43:20-21). At one time, they were not a people, but now they have become God's people (1 Pet 2:10, alluding to Hos 1:9; 2:23).

The reason for their new status is Christ's redemptive death. As the People of God they have been sprinkled with Christ's blood (1:2), just as Israel was sprinkled with blood when it entered into covenant with God at Sinai (Exod 24:7-8). Thus, they have been ransomed by "the precious blood of Christ, . . . a lamb without defect or blemish" (1 Pet 1:19, NRSV). Indeed, their status as the People of God is so central that, in prophesying Christ's sufferings, Israel's prophets were serving them (1:10-12).

The author exhorts the recipients of this letter to let themselves be built into a spiritual house (*oikos pneumatikos*), a holy priesthood, so that they can offer spiritual sacrifices to God through Christ (2:5). The cornerstone of this house is Christ, and they, like "living stones," must allow themselves to be built into this spiritual house. Although 1 Peter never uses the word "temple," it seems to view the Church as a temple of the living God, as do 1 Cor 3:16-17 and Eph 2:21.

---

[24] Written in Peter's name, this letter was probably sent from Rome (5:13) to Gentile Christians in Asia Minor (1:1) by someone closely associated with a Petrine circle of believers.

First Peter's ecclesiology, however, is in the service of moral exhortation. It refers to its recipients as exiles (1:1; 2:11) and the present as the time of their exile (1:17). During this period of exile, they must suffer as Christ suffered if they hope to attain the glory he now enjoys (3:13-18; 4:1, 12-16). First Peter, then, implies that although the Church is presently in exile, it is ultimately the priestly People of God and a spiritual house that offers spiritual sacrifices to God.

Hebrews is also a "word of exhortation" (Heb 13:22, NRSV).[25] But in this case, it appears that the community has lost some of its original fervor (10:32-39; 12:3-13). Consequently, Hebrews undertakes one of the most sophisticated christological discussions of the New Testament to remind its audience that Christ, a high priest according to the order of Melchizedek, has effected a perfect sacrifice for sins, once and for all, and established a new covenant (4:14–10:18). Consequently, there is no second repentance for those who willfully reject God's eschatological offer of salvation (6:4-8; 10:26-31; 12:15-17).

Although Hebrews is primarily concerned with moral exhortation and christological exposition, it contains an implicit ecclesiology that views the Church as a community of believers similar to Israel of old, which sought to enter God's Sabbath rest. That community, however, failed to enter God's rest because it hardened its heart and did not heed God's voice (3:7–4:13). More importantly, the Levitical priesthood could not bring the community to perfection (7:11), nor could its sacrifices adequately deal with sin (10:4).

The community of the Church, however, has approached the city of the living God and the heavenly Jerusalem (12:22) because its high priest has entered the heavenly sanctuary (9:12) and become the mediator of a new covenant that effects the forgiveness of sins (9:15). Jesus, the pioneer and perfecter of faith (12:2), has shown the Church how to enter the heavenly sanctuary where it will finally attain God's Sabbath rest.

For Hebrews the Church is like the wilderness congregation of Israel inasmuch as it has not yet attained God's Sabbath rest. But inasmuch as its "great Shepherd" (13:20) is an eternal high priest according to the order of Melchizedek, the Church is the eschatological community of the new covenant and already experiences the forgiveness of sins.

Revelation recounts a vision of the risen Christ to John, while he was on the island of Patmos (1:9). Addressed to "the seven churches that are

[25] The author of this writing is anonymous, and it is not clear from where, or to whom, the author is writing. The designation "to the Hebrews" does not belong to the original text.

in Asia" (1:4), it functions as a prophetic work in which the risen Lord admonishes the seven churches (2:1–3:22) and then, through John, provides them with a vision of what is and what will be. Consequently, Revelation focuses on two aspects of the Church's life: its present struggle with the power of evil and the eschatological victory that the Lamb has obtained for it through his death.

The messages to the churches of Ephesus, Smyrna, Pergamum, Thyatira, Sardis, Philadelphia, and Laodicea are akin to royal edicts, and they indicate that the risen Christ "knows" what is happening in his churches (2:2, 9, 13, 19; 3:1, 8, 15). They present the churches in all of their human frailty as the risen Christ reviews their conduct. But in every instance, they conclude with a promise of reward for those who will be victorious in the struggle the churches are now enduring (2:7, 11, 17, 26; 3:5, 12, 21). Because the risen Christ has already won this victory, he sits with his Father on the throne, and those who are victorious will sit with him (3:21). According to Revelation, then, the Church must participate in the struggle of the Lamb if it wishes to share in his victory.

The struggle that the Church must endure is described when John is taken into the throne room of heaven, and the Lamb opens the scroll with its seven seals, resulting in the seven trumpets and the seven bowls (4:1–16:21). The defeat of Satan and the beasts (17:1–20:15) then leads to a description of the Holy City, the new Jerusalem, the bride, the wife of the Lamb (21:9). The book of Revelation never explicitly identifies the Church as the bride of Christ, as does Ephesians. Indeed, all twenty references to *ekklēsia* in Revelation are in the plural and refer to the seven churches of Asia.[26] The narrative line of Revelation, however, suggests that the heavenly Jerusalem will be inhabited by those who have conquered with the Lamb. Thus, it is the destiny of the Church to be the bride of the Lamb.

Revelation, Hebrews, and 1 Peter are neglected documents in the study of the Church. Each of them, however, witnesses to the struggle that the Church must endure if it is to enter into its glory.

Conclusion

There are several theologies of the Church in the New Testament. Among the more significant are those that present the Church as a community of disciples, the reestablished Israel, the Church of God, the body of Christ, the bride of Christ, the temple of God, and the pilgrim

---

[26] Rev 1:4, 11, 20 (twice); 2:1, 7, 8, 11, 12, 17, 18, 23, 29; 3:1, 6, 7, 13, 14, 22; 22:16.

People of God. As rich as each of these images is, however, no one of them adequately expresses the mystery of the Church. But when they are held together in a creative tension, they truly reflect the splendor of the Church.

For Further Reading

Banks, Robert. *Paul's Idea of Community.* Rev. ed. Peabody, Mass.: Hendrickson, 1994.

Bockmuehl, Markus, and Michael B. Thompson, eds. *A Vision for the Church: Studies in Early Christian Ecclesiology.* Edinburgh: T. & T. Clark, 1997.

Brown, Raymond E. *The Churches the Apostles Left Behind.* New York: Paulist Press, 1984.

_____. *The Community of the Beloved Disciple: The Life, Loves, and Hates of an Individual Church in the New Testament Times.* New York, Paulist Press, 1979.

Brown, Raymond E., and John P. Meier. *Antioch and Rome: New Testament Cradles of Catholic Christianity.* New York: Paulist Press, 1982.

Cerfaux, Lucien. *The Church in the Theology of St. Paul.* Trans. Geoffrey Webb and Adrian Walker. New York: Herder and Herder, 1959.

Cwiekowski, Frederick H. *The Beginnings of the Church.* New York: Paulist Press, 1988.

Denaux, Adelbert. "Did Jesus Found the Church?" *Louvain Studies* 21 (1996) 25–45.

Doohan, Helen. *Paul's Vision of Church.* Good News Studies 31. Wilmington, Del.: Michael Glazier, 1989.

Dunn, James D. G. *The Theology of Paul the Apostle.* Grand Rapids, Mich.: Eerdmans, 1998.

Harrington, Daniel J. *God's People in Christ: New Testament Perspectives on the Church and Judaism.* Overtures to Biblical Theology. Philadelphia: Fortress Press, 1980.

_____. *Light of All Nations: Essays on the Church in New Testament Research.* Good News Studies 3. Wilmington, Del.: Michael Glazier, 1982.

Hanson, Paul D. *The People Called: The Growth of Community in the Bible.* San Francisco: Harper & Row, 1986.

Kee, Howard Clark. *Who Are the People of God? Early Christian Models of Community.* New Haven, Conn.: Yale University Press, 1995.

Meeks, Wayne. *The First Urban Christians: The Social World of the Apostle Paul.* New Haven, Conn.: Yale University Press, 1983.

Meier, John P. "The Circle of the Twelve: Did It Exist During Jesus' Public Ministry?" *JBL* 116 (1997) 635–72.

_____. *The Mission of Christ and His Church: Studies in Christology and Ecclesiology.* Good News Studies 30. Wilmington, Del.: Michael Glazier, 1990.

Schnackenburg, Rudolf. *The Church in the New Testament.* New York: Herder and Herder, 1965.

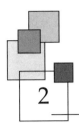

The Development of Ecclesiology: Early Church to the Reformation[1]

2

Eric Plumer

Not until the beginning of the fourteenth century do we find treatises in "ecclesiology" in the technical sense of a distinct subdiscipline of theology dealing with the nature and mission of the Church.[2] Before that time the idea of the Church is generally a presupposition of theological speculation rather than its primary focus, so that our evidence for the Church's self-understanding tends to be partial and indirect. The following essay will survey the leading images, concepts, and beliefs that were used to express the Church's self-understanding during the first sixteen centuries of its existence. The point of view will be Roman Catholic, so that the questions of how the Church became "Roman," how it became "Catholic," and so on, will receive concentrated attention in a way that they would not if the point of view were Eastern Orthodox, for example. Other churches will be examined mainly, though not exclusively, for the role they played in the Roman Catholic Church's process of self-definition. As an aid to reflection we will frequently ask how the evidence under consideration relates to the four "marks of the Church" spoken of in the Nicene Creed: the Church is "one, holy, catholic, and apostolic."

The Apostolic Fathers

The earliest Christian writings outside the New Testament to win general acceptance in the Church are those of the Apostolic Fathers. Though diverse in content and form, these writings display a common

[1] I would like to thank John T. Ford, C.S.C., for a number of very helpful suggestions and comments on an earlier version of this essay.

[2] James of Viterbo's *On Christian Government* of 1301–02 is often cited as the earliest treatise in ecclesiology in this technical sense. The work usually cited as the earliest *systematic* treatise in ecclesiology is even later: John of Torquemada's *Summa on the Church* of 1436 [published in 1489].

concern for the unity of the Church as it faced threats of heresy, schism, and persecution.[3] A vivid illustration of this concern appears in a work of great importance for the development of Roman Catholic ecclesiology, *1 Clement*, a letter written about 96 C.E. by Clement of Rome on behalf of "the Church of God which sojourns in Rome to the Church of God which sojourns in Corinth." This opening formula is itself instructive, implying that there is one "Church of God," whether localized in Rome or in Corinth, and that it is merely "sojourning" until it arrives at its true homeland in heaven. Thus in some mysterious sense, the Church's nature and destiny transcend history. For the present, however, this Church exists visibly and concretely in the world and must deal with present problems.

In this letter the church of Rome admonishes the church of Corinth to reinstate the men it had wrongfully removed from liturgical office, explaining:

> Our Apostles also knew, through our Lord Jesus Christ, that there would be contention over the bishop's office. So, for this reason, having received complete foreknowledge, they appointed the above mentioned men, and afterwards gave them a permanent character, so that, as they died, other approved men should succeed to the ministry.[4]

This is the earliest articulation of the idea of apostolic succession, and it is clearly analogous to the Jewish idea of a hereditary Levitical priesthood. Indeed, Clement views the Church as a hierarchical society after the pattern of Israel, in which Christ, the apostles, and the bishops and deacons are comparable to the high priest, priests, and Levites.[5] It should be noted that the titles "bishop" (Greek: *episkopos*) and "presbyter" (Greek: *presbyteros*) are used interchangeably in *1 Clement* for the same office. Moreover, that office appears to have been exercised collegially rather than by a single individual acting alone. Thus monarchical episcopacy (the rule of a church by a single bishop) was probably a later development for both the church of Corinth and the church of Rome.[6]

---

[3] Thus Robert M. Grant has noted that "the most important aspect of the Church for the Apostolic Fathers is its unity" (*The Apostolic Fathers* [New York: Thomas Nelson & Sons, 1964] 1:137).

[4] *1 Clement* 44, as translated in Thomas Halton, *The Church*, Message of the Fathers of the Church 4 (Wilmington, Del.: Michael Glazier, 1985) 101–2.

[5] *1 Clement* 40:5; 42.

[6] This is not to deny that Clement could have been the leading bishop-presbyter of the Roman church in an unofficial sense, and indeed such an informal arrangement may well have been the way in which monarchical episcopacy developed. See Raymond E. Brown and John P. Meier, *Antioch and Rome: New Testament Cradles of Catholic Christianity* (New York: Paulist Press, 1983) 163–4.

In calling for unity and order Clement appeals to apostolic authority in another way by citing Paul's own letter to the Corinthians.[7] *1 Clement* is thus from one perspective a continuation of Paul's pastoral care for the Corinthian church.[8] Yet it is also a development, since we see the older, charismatic structure of apostles, prophets, and teachers (1 Cor 12:28) giving way to a more stable structure characterized by permanent offices.

Along with images of the Church familiar to us from the New Testament, such as the new Israel[9] and the body of Christ,[10] Clement uses another image to emphasize ecclesiastical unity and order: the Church under Christ's command is like the Roman army under the emperor's command.[11] Thus, as Raymond Brown has observed: "In resisting the deposition of the presbyters by the Corinthians, the author has appealed to two authoritative models: the Jerusalem levitical priesthood and the imperial political and military organization."[12] By making such an appeal Clement provides a striking example of that power to assimilate elements from different cultures which is one aspect of the Church's catholicity.

Further evidence of the development of church order is found ca. 110 in the letters of Ignatius, bishop of Antioch, who wrote to various churches in Asia Minor while being taken under armed guard to Rome to be executed for his faith. These letters reveal Ignatius' deep concern about divisions in the churches and his firm conviction that church unity must be rooted in the bishop. Although we do not find the idea of apostolic succession in Ignatius, we do find the idea of the episcopate as divinely willed.[13] These letters also furnish the earliest unmistakable evidence of monarchical episcopacy:

> Nobody must do anything that has to do with the Church without the bishop's approval. You should regard that Eucharist as valid which is celebrated either by the bishop or by someone he authorizes. Where the bishop is present, there let the congregation gather, just as where Jesus Christ is, there is the Catholic Church.[14]

[7] References to 1 Corinthians appear in *1 Clement* 37; 47; and 49.

[8] See Brown and Meier, *Antioch and Rome,* 165–6.

[9] *1 Clement* 29.

[10] *1 Clement* 37–8.

[11] *1 Clement* 37:1-4.

[12] Brown and Meier, *Antioch and Rome,* 175.

[13] See Ignatius, *Letter to the Philadelphians* 7.

[14] Ignatius, *Letter to the Smyrnaeans* 8, Cyril C. Richardson, ed. and trans., *Early Christian Fathers* (New York: Macmillan, 1970) 115. The expression "the Catholic Church" occurs here for the first time in Christian literature.

The bishop is assisted by presbyters and deacons, so that there is a threefold ministry in the church. This form of ministry will become dominant in the course of the second century. Even as he insists on the importance of church office, however, Ignatius is emphatic that it is nothing in comparison with faith and love.[15]

In a letter written after Ignatius' death by a fellow bishop, Polycarp of Smyrna, Ignatius is numbered among the martyrs,[16] as Polycarp himself would be many years later.[17] The idea of the Church as "the Church of the Martyrs," following in the footsteps of Christ, would remain central even after official persecution of the Church ended in 313.

The Apologists

While Clement and Ignatius address an audience within the Church, the Apologists of the second and third centuries address an audience of "outsiders."[18] The need for Christian apologetics became acute as Christianity spread through the empire and found itself in conflict with the religion of the state. Although Christians were willing to pay tribute to Caesar, they refused to worship him, and this refusal, together with the secrecy of their rites, gave rise to hostility and persecution. In the face of this, writers such as Justin Martyr (ca. 100–ca. 165) attempted to explain and defend the gospel as the definitive answer to humanity's ancient religious and philosophical quest for truth. Moreover, Christianity's proclamation of a universal fellowship met one of the strongest desires of the age, of which the Roman Empire itself had been one expression. Thus the Apologists envisaged a Church that was "catholic" in the breadth of its appeal.

Heretical Movements

In the second century competing interpretations of Christianity vied for dominance. Gnostics claimed to offer initiates superior knowledge (Greek: *gnosis*) handed down by the apostles in secret traditions.

---

[15] Ignatius, *Letter to the Smyrnaeans* 6.

[16] Polycarp, *Letter to the Philippians* 9:1.

[17] *The Martyrdom of Polycarp*, which gives an eyewitness account of Polycarp's trial and execution, is the oldest account of Christian martyrdom outside the New Testament.

[18] Such, at least, is the impression given by the literary form of their writings. These writers probably hoped, however, that their arguments would also serve to strengthen the faith of "insiders."

Marcion (fl. ca. 150), though similar to the Gnostics in some of his doctrines, differed from them in the openness of his evangelism, publishing his own canon of Scripture and establishing a worldwide church that rivaled the Catholic Church for centuries. A third movement, Montanism, takes its name from its founder, Montanus (fl. ca. 170), who claimed to be uniquely inspired by the Holy Spirit and prophesied the imminent end of all things. What the Spirit demanded, the Montanists maintained, was a rekindling of the moral zeal that had been lost when the Church became institutional.

Irenaeus and Hippolytus

In response to such challenges, the Catholic Church insisted that the true Church is characterized by apostolicity. Irenaeus, bishop of Lyons (fl. 190), defined the three criteria of apostolicity in classical terms. The first criterion is the episcopate which, founded by the apostles and continued by their duly appointed successors, guarantees the validity of church doctrine. The second criterion is the New Testament which, written by the apostles, represents the authoritative and definitive witness to God's saving act in Jesus Christ. The third criterion is the "canon of truth" which, handed down by the apostles, provides a concise statement of the essentials of the faith in the form of a creed. These criteria are in force in all the churches:

> The churches founded in Germany believe and hand down no differently, nor do those among the Iberians, among the Celts, in the Orient, in Egypt, or in Libya, or those established in the middle of the world. As the sun, God's creature, is one and the same in the whole world, so the light, the preaching of truth, shines everywhere and illuminates all men who wish to come to the knowledge of truth.[19]

For Irenaeus, the unity and uniformity of Catholic doctrine stands in vivid contrast with the mutual contradictions of the competing Gnostic systems.

While Irenaeus and others emphasize the bishops' teaching authority, Hippolytus of Rome emphasizes their sacramental power to ordain. In his *Apostolic Tradition* (ca. 215), which contains the earliest known rite of ordination, Hippolytus speaks of episcopal ordination as being carried out by the bishops of the neighboring churches—a sign both of

---

[19] Irenaeus, *Against Heresies* 1.10.2, Robert M. Grant, ed. and trans., *Irenaeus of Lyons* (London and New York: Routledge, 1997) 71.

sacramental power and of communion. Hippolytus is also notable as an early exponent, along with Tertullian (ca. 160–ca. 225), of the rigorist view of the Church as a kind of training camp for saints rather than a convalescent home for sinners.

The Christian Platonists of Alexandria

Clement of Alexandria (ca. 150–ca. 215) and Origen (184–254), his successor as head of the catechetical school there, were deeply influenced by Neoplatonism and tended to view the Church on earth as merely an imperfect imitation of the true Church in heaven. Neoplatonism also colored their idea of salvation. Viewing intellectual and spiritual enlightenment as humanity's highest end, they conceived of the historical Church as a school designed to help the soul on its path toward enlightenment. Within the Church so conceived the distinction between clergy and laity fades into insignificance before the distinction between those who have attained enlightenment and those who have not. Origen seems to have thought that since perfect enlightenment was not possible in this life, there must be worlds beyond this world where spiritual growth could continue and all might ultimately be saved. Thus in Origen's thought the importance of the historical Church is further relativized.

Cyprian, Augustine, and the North African Tradition

Very different in tone from the Alexandrians are the representatives of the North African tradition, with their intense concern for practical matters of Church discipline. Cyprian became bishop of Carthage shortly before the outbreak of the Decian persecution (250–251), in which many Christians lapsed from the faith. When the persecution ended, there was deep division in the Carthaginian church over the question of readmitting the lapsed. Against rigorists, Cyprian maintained that the Church had the power to reconcile even those guilty of apostasy; against laxists he argued that such reconciliation could be granted only by the bishop and only after satisfactory penance had been done. For Cyprian the decisions of the local bishop (or, for a region, those of an episcopal conference) were the legitimate basis of unity and order in the Church.

Later Cyprian was involved in a bitter dispute with Pope Stephen I over the latter's acceptance of the validity of baptism by heretics. Cyprian rejected this view, insisting that valid baptism required ministers who were within the Church. Anyone not in communion with the bishop is outside the Church, he said, and "outside the Church there is no salvation."[20]

The unity and holiness of the Church become a central concern in North Africa again following the persecution under Diocletian (303–311). The Donatists maintained that those who had surrendered copies of the Scriptures to the persecuting authorities had forfeited their membership in the Church and needed to be rebaptized. Viewing the Catholic Church as having compromised its holiness, the Donatists set up a separate church of their own. Against them Augustine of Hippo (354–430), elaborating arguments put forward by Optatus, bishop of Milev (fl. 370), contended that the holiness of the Church and its sacraments was dependent upon God, not upon its members—not even upon its clergy. He maintained that the Church is a mixed body *(corpus permixtum)* of saints and sinners whose interior motives can be known with certainty only by God, who will be their judge. For mere mortals to presume to judge is the height of pride.

Augustine also criticized Donatism for its lack of catholicity (it was limited to North Africa) and especially for the utter lack of charity it displayed in shattering the unity of the Church. Augustine long sought peaceful reconciliation with the Donatists but finally and reluctantly accepted the necessity of calling upon the state to end the Donatist schism. Some of the themes elaborated in controversy with the Donatists reappear in *The City of God,* where Augustine explores the ambiguities surrounding not only the Church's relation to the state but also its relation to the kingdom of God.

In Pelagianism Augustine detected another form of spiritual elitism and pride. According to him, Pelagius (ca. 350–ca. 425) and his followers so stressed humanity's natural capacity to live without sin that they had lost sight of the lifelong need for grace. In response Augustine elaborated a view of human nature as deeply wounded as the result of sin. Thus, in Augustine's allegorical interpretation of the parable of the Good Samaritan, the Good Samaritan is Christ, the wounded man is the Christian, and the inn in which the man convalesces is the Church.

Augustine's ecclesiology is linked with his understanding of Trinity: as the Spirit is the bond of love between the Father and the Son, so the Spirit is the bond of love between believers, and thus the unity of

---

[20] *"Salus extra ecclesiam non est" (Letter* 73.21.2). Similar is another often-quoted line of his: "He cannot have God for his Father who does not have the Church for his mother" *("Habere non potest Deum patrem qui ecclesiam non habet matrem").* The latter quotation appears in the sixth chapter of Cyprian's *On the Unity of the Catholic Church,* a work which, though quite limited in scope, comes as near as any work from the patristic era to being an essay in ecclesiology.

the Church is a reflection of and a participation in the unity of the Triune God. This reflection and participation are signified and realized most fully in this life in the celebration of the Eucharist, in which the faithful join together with one another and with Christ in his sacrificial self-offering. In these matters as in so many others Augustine's influence on the development of Western Christian thought has been momentous.

The Constantinian Revolution

The Constantinian revolution is often regarded as the greatest turning point in the history of the Church. When the emperor Constantine converted to Christianity in 312 and then forged the Edict of Milan (313), the persecution which had dogged the Church since its inception came to an end. For the first time in its history Christianity was a religion recognized by law, and by 381 it had become the only religion recognized by law. The end of persecution created a crisis of its own, however, for Christians whose identity was bound up with "the Church of the Martyrs." One way the crisis was alleviated was by remembering and identifying with the martyrs through special liturgies and private devotions. Another way, illustrated supremely by the writings of the Church historian Eusebius of Caesarea (ca. 260–ca. 339), was to see the empire and especially Constantine's conversion as the providential means by which Christianity would finally be carried to the ends of the earth.

For some, however, most notably the founders of Christian monasticism, Constantine symbolized the contamination of the Church by the world. In order to preserve the purity of the faith monks separated themselves from the world. The name of Antony of Egypt (ca. 251–356) is associated with the origins of eremitic (solitary) monasticism, while that of Pachomius (ca. 290–346) is associated with the origins of cenobitic (communal) monasticism. That this separation from the world did not mean schism with the Church is attributable in part to the mediation of sympathetic bishops such as Athanasius of Alexandria (ca. 296–373) and Basil of Caesarea (ca. 330–379), who were also crucial in transmitting monastic ideals to the wider Church. In the fifth century, Egyptian monastic ideals were reinterpreted and adapted for the West by John Cassian (ca. 360–435). In the sixth century, Western monastic traditions received their most influential expression in the Rule of Benedict of Nursia (ca. 480–ca. 550). For both East and West monasticism would prove to be a vital source of renewal and reform in the Church in the centuries to come.

The Emergence of Ecumenical Councils

Councils in some form or other were in use in the Church since the Council of Jerusalem (Acts 15). The earliest councils for which there is evidence after the Council of Jerusalem are those gatherings of the bishops of Asia Minor in the second century to address the problem of Montanism. But it was only with the conversion of Constantine that the possibility of a worldwide council was realized. Constantine saw religion as a means of unifying his empire. When dissension arose over Arianism he called a council of all the bishops in the empire to resolve the dispute. Held at the imperial residence of Nicaea with Constantine presiding, the First Ecumenical Council (325) is said to have adopted Constantine's own formula to express its faith in the divinity of Christ: Christ is "one in being [Greek: *homoousios*] with the Father." Further doctrinal conflict led to the Second Ecumenical Council, held in Constantinople in 381. The creed promulgated by this council made the four marks of the Church ("one, holy, catholic, and apostolic") official Church doctrine. These and later ecumenical councils sought to define and eliminate heresy and thus to bring unity to the Church's doctrine and belief. Such councils also fostered a sense of the Church as being not merely local or regional but universal in its scope.

The Development of the Papacy to Gregory the Great

The traditional Roman Catholic view of Peter as the first pope is an anachronism: the papacy emerged only gradually in the history of the Church. In Newman's words: "While Apostles were on earth, there was the display neither of Bishop nor Pope; their power had no prominence, as being exercised by Apostles. In course of time, first the power of the Bishop displayed itself, and then the power of the Pope."[21] Indeed, there is no clear evidence of rule by a single bishop in Rome before Pius I (ca. 142–ca. 155).[22]

The papacy considered as a historical phenomenon appears to have arisen as the result of a combination of factors, including the following: the primacy of Peter among the Twelve; the fact that Rome was the place where both Peter and Paul were martyred and buried; the fact that Rome was the only church in the West to claim apostolic foundation

[21] John Henry Newman, *An Essay on the Development of Christian Doctrine,* 7th ed. (London: Sheed and Ward, 1960) 109.

[22] In this essay the dates given after the name of a pope refer not to his birth and death but to the beginning and end of his pontificate.

(whereas the East had Jerusalem, Alexandria, and Antioch); the symbolism of Rome as the hub of the empire and Rome's practical usefulness as a center of communications. Notably absent, however, is any claim earlier than the middle of the third century that Matt 16:18-19 is the charter of the papacy.[23]

The evidence of Peter's primacy among the Twelve is clear from the New Testament.[24] Peter and Paul were the greatest missionaries among the apostles insofar as the former had been given the mission to the circumcised and the latter the mission to the uncircumcised (Gal 2:7). Since Rome could claim to have links with both apostles, the Bishop of Rome came to be regarded as the heir to their twofold apostolate and thus to a ministry embracing the entire Church. It is true that Rome was not the only city that could claim Peter and Paul: both men also had connections with Jerusalem, Antioch, and Corinth.[25] But precedence was inevitably given to Rome as the place where both apostles had borne definitive witness to Christ in martyrdom.[26]

The rise of Rome to a position of eminence in the Church coincided with the eclipse of Jerusalem as a Christian center following the destruction of the city in 70. Rome's leadership initially took the form of giving guidance. Such is the case with *1 Clement*, as we have seen. Can we go further and see *1 Clement* as our earliest evidence of Roman primacy? The question is intricate, but most scholars would now regard *1 Clement* as an impressive example of fraternal correction rather than an authoritative intervention. More authoritative were the condemnations issued by Rome against Marcion ca. 144 and against the Montanists ca. 180. At other times appeals were made to Rome concerning disputed matters, such as those made by Polycarp of Smyrna ca. 155, by Dionysius of Corinth ca. 170, and by Irenaeus of Lyons ca. 177. By the end of the second century we find the teaching authority of Rome being praised in lofty terms. Irenaeus says that "it is necessary for every church—that is, the believers from everywhere—to agree with [the Roman] church,

[23] The earliest such claim for which there is evidence is that of Pope Stephen I (254–257).

[24] For New Testament evidence see Frank Matera's article, "Theologies of the Church in the New Testament," in this volume.

[25] For Peter and Paul at Antioch see Gal 2:11-14. For the possibility that Peter had been at Corinth see 1 Cor 9:5. At the very least there was a Petrine faction at Corinth (1 Cor 1:12; 3:22).

[26] Thus Clement refers to their trials at Rome (*1 Clement* 5), Ignatius implies that they had exercised special authority over the church of Rome (*Romans* 4), and Irenaeus speaks of them as having "founded" the church of Rome (*Against Heresies* 3.3.2).

in which the tradition from the apostles has always been preserved by those who are from everywhere, because of its more excellent origin."[27] Similarly Tertullian speaks of

> Rome, from which there comes even into our own hands the very authority of the apostles themselves. How happy is its church, on which the apostles poured forth all their doctrine along with their blood! where Peter endures a passion like his Lord's! where Paul wins his crown in a death like John's![28]

Not everyone praised Rome so highly. We have already noted Cyprian's direct challenge to Rome's authority in his dispute with Pope Stephen over the question of rebaptism. But even though Cyprian disagreed with Stephen's actual position, he elsewhere spoke of "the chair of Peter" as "the primordial church, the very source of episcopal unity."[29] Stephen's views on rebaptism ultimately triumphed over those of Cyprian. And in the fourth and fifth centuries the papacy was consistently orthodox in its teaching in a way that no other great see could claim to have been.[30]

To an unparalleled record of orthodoxy was added an imperial aura as the papacy began to fill the void created by the removal of the imperial capital from Rome to Constantinople in 330. Popes received official inquiries from faraway places, just as emperors had done, and answered them by means of quasi-imperial decretals. Another sign of the imperial aura of the papacy was the title "Pontifex Maximus." Formerly

[27] Irenaeus, *Against Heresies* 3.3.2, Robert M. Grant, trans., *Irenaeus of Lyons* (London and New York: Routledge, 1997) 125 [modified]. The original meaning of this passage has been the subject of much scholarly dispute. In a nuanced statement Robert Eno has observed:

> The context of Irenaeus' argument does not claim that the Roman church is literally unique, the one and only in its class; rather, he argues that the Roman church is the outstanding example of its class, the class in question being apostolic sees. While he chose to speak primarily of Rome for brevity's sake, in fact, before finishing, he also referred to Ephesus and Smyrna (*The Rise of the Papacy* [Wilmington, Del.: Michael Glazier, 1990] 39).

[28] *On Prescription against Heretics* 36, A. Roberts and J. Donaldson, eds.; P. Holmes, trans., *The Ante-Nicene Fathers* (New York: Charles Scribner's Sons, 1926) 3:260.

[29] "*Petri cathedram . . . ecclesiam principalem unde unitas sacerdotalis exorta est*" (Letter 59.14.1 [addressed to Pope Cornelius], G. W. Clarke, trans., *The Letters of St. Cyprian of Carthage*, vol. 3, Ancient Christian Writers 46 [New York/Mahwah, N.J.: Newman Press, 1983] 82).

[30] A celebrated example of Rome's orthodoxy was its welcoming of Athanasius after he had been deposed as bishop of Alexandria by Arian opponents.

a title of the Roman emperor, Leo I made it a title of the pope. The most memorable image of the imperial papacy in antiquity is that of Pope Leo persuading Attila the Hun not to sack Rome in 452.

More explicit than these signs and images was the elaboration of the doctrine of papal primacy in the century extending from the reign of Damasus I (366–384) to that of Leo I (440–461). As Leo represents the culmination of this development, we will look at his teaching in some detail. From the outset of his pontificate Leo appealed explicitly to the three passages of Scripture that have since become the classic proof texts of papal primacy: Matt 16:13-19, Luke 22:31-32, and John 21:15-19. This is no mere primacy of honor. Leo taught that the pope as successor of Peter possesses the same fullness of power *(plenitudo potestatis)* over the entire Church as Christ bestowed upon Peter. Indeed, Leo goes so far as to say that it is Peter himself who speaks and acts through the pope. Even though the pope might personally be an "unworthy heir" of Peter, this does not negate his office. Leo's careful distinction between person and office would subsequently enable the papacy to retain its authority despite some dubious incumbents.

Leo's importance for the development of the papacy can also be gauged from the influential role his *Tome* played at the Fourth Ecumenical Council, held at Chalcedon in 451. When this document, with its clear and balanced statement of the relation of the divine and human in Christ, was read aloud at the council, the bishops in attendance cried out, "The voice of Peter has spoken through Leo!" The christology of Leo's *Tome* has been regarded as the standard of orthodoxy ever since.

The stature of the papacy was further enhanced during the pontificate of Gregory the Great (590–604), not merely because of the claims he made for the office but also and especially because of the heroism with which he carried it out. At a time when Rome was in a state of near-total collapse, Gregory took charge of the civil and military administration and saved the city from going under. He proved equally proficient in administering the Roman church and in strengthening its connections with other churches both Eastern and Western. He displayed particular sensitivity and foresight in the mission he sent to England to convert the Anglo-Saxons. Gregory combined the deeply contemplative spirit of a monk (he was the first monk to hold papal office) with the vigorous activity of a humane Roman administrator. These qualities are reflected in his *Pastoral Rule,* which has had an enormous influence on bishops and other leaders throughout the subsequent history of the Church. Finally we may note that it was characteristic of him to have rejected the title of "ecumenical patriarch" and to have chosen instead that of "servant of the servants of God" *(servus servorum Dei).*

The Making of Western Christendom (600–1300)

The pontificate of Damasus (366–384) had coincided with the begin-ning of the barbarian invasions and the collapse of the Western empire. In 378 the Emperor Valens died in battle against the Goths. In 410 Rome itself was sacked. Although the capital of the empire had long since moved to Constantinople, what happened to the Eternal City sent psy-chic shock waves throughout the empire, for it was the first time in a thousand years that the walls of Rome had been breached. For the next six hundred years such invasions by Germanic and other tribes would continue to change the face of the former Western empire.

Part of Gregory the Great's achievement at the end of the sixth cen-tury had been to lay the foundations of a new social and political order in Europe, centered on the papacy, to replace that of the Western em-pire. As we have noted, Gregory was a monk, and throughout his pon-tificate monks played a leading role. After Gregory's death it would also be monks who contributed most to the formation of Christendom. Their monasteries in the countryside became hubs of missionary activ-ity to rural populations. Celtic monks were conspicuous in this regard, carrying their own brand of Christianity throughout Europe during the sixth and seventh centuries. The work of these monks was followed by that of the Benedictines, who brought organization and stability to Christendom. They also strengthened Christendom's links with the papacy, as in the case of Boniface (680–754), an Anglo-Saxon monk who was sent by the Pope as a missionary to Germany and who helped the Frankish king to reform his church. When in 754 Pope Stephen II needed assistance to ward off Lombard invaders he was able to call upon the Frankish King Pepin III, who agreed to secure the Italian territories that had long been under papal supervision. But with Pepin's military backing, papal supervision now became papal sovereignty. Pepin's gift, known as "the Donation of Pepin," marks the beginning of the Papal States and the beginning of temporal rule by popes.

After Pepin's death, his son Charlemagne renewed the pledge to the pope and brought much of the remainder of Western Europe to the Catholic faith by force. His achievement was acknowledged by Pope Leo III, who crowned him "Emperor of the Romans" on Christmas Day 800 in the Basilica of St. Peter in Rome. Charlemagne's coronation sym-bolized the union of the religious and political orders in Europe and the formation of Western Christendom. At the same time, by proclaim-ing Charlemagne emperor the papacy had clearly separated itself from the Byzantine emperor's sphere of influence.

Charlemagne initiated a reform of Church and society that would be continued by his successors. But while the "Carolingian reform"

was a powerful means of unification for Western society, it also dangerously blurred the line between Church and state.

The Monastic Revival and the Gregorian Reform

The tenth century witnessed the emergence of centers of monastic
renewal and reform, the most influential of which was the French
Benedictine monastery of Cluny. Founded in 909, by the mid-twelfth
century Cluny had become the heart of a system comprising more than
three hundred monasteries. This centralization enabled Cluniac monasticism to enjoy a notable freedom from the influence of local lords.
But as the Cluniac monasteries began to accumulate vast property and
wealth, they themselves became the target of criticism from other Benedictines, who proceeded to initiate their own movements of renewal
(e.g., the Cistercians).

The Gregorian reform, which takes its name from its most famous
champion, Pope Gregory VII (1073–85), was inspired in part by the monastic revival. It too was intent on securing ecclesiastical independence
from the state. Gregory considered that such independence required a
strong papacy, so he had past church decrees supporting papal authority gathered and organized to form a watertight legal case against the
possibility of encroachment by the state. This juridical emphasis may
have been necessary at the time, but it brought unintended consequences along with it. For one thing, a corporate concept of the Church
began to eclipse the ancient, sacramental concept, as may be seen in the
way in which the term "Mystical Body," which had previously referred
to the Eucharist, now began to refer mainly to the Church as a social
body. Likewise, the authority of priests and bishops, which had been
viewed chiefly as a moral authority flowing from the grace of ordination, began to be viewed more and more as a juridical authority.

Nevertheless, Gregory had succeeded in lifting the papacy to new
eminence and establishing its canonical authority in a convincing way.
From now on monarchs would have to regard the papacy as having
monarchical power of its own. Internally the government of the Catholic Church became increasingly centralized and bureaucratic. Bishops
began to show a level of obedience to the pope which was without parallel in earlier times.

The work of canonists that had marked Gregory's pontificate continued afterwards, culminating in the publication of Gratian's *Decretum*
(ca. 1140), providing the Catholic Church with a brilliant systematic
presentation of its vast legal traditions. A century later the papal decretals were brought together and codified under Pope Gregory IX. Thus a

juridical conception of the Church as a visible, hierarchical society attained predominance in the West.

With a highly centralized ecclesiastical polity, Pope Innocent III (1198–1216) was able to exercise the power of his office widely and confidently, and his reign is considered the zenith of the medieval papacy. Although he regularly intervened in the affairs of sovereigns, his most enduring work lay in the area of church reform, especially his convening of the Fourth Lateran Council (1215), the most important council of the Middle Ages. It was Innocent who approved of the new mendicant orders of Franciscans and Dominicans, which brought new energy and vision to the Western Church.

The Divergence of the Eastern and Western Churches

The divergence of the Eastern and Western churches,[31] leading ultimately to the East-West Schism, was a process of many centuries, influenced by a host of political, cultural, and theological factors. From the point of view of ecclesiology, the question of authority in the Church was acute, with the relative standings of Rome and Constantinople a recurrent source of tension. When the Council of Chalcedon (451) decreed in its twenty-eighth canon that Constantinople, as "New Rome," enjoyed honor equal to that of Rome, Pope Leo I refused to endorse that canon. The ninth-century patriarch Photius of Constantinople came into conflict with Pope Nicholas I (858–867) by denying papal supremacy. In 1054 conflict broke out between papal legates in Constantinople and Patriarch Michael Cerularius, resulting in mutual excommunications. Finally, in 1204 the armies of the Fourth Crusade sacked Constantinople—including its churches. The resentment caused by this Crusade was deep and lasting, and foredoomed to failure attempts at reconciliation made by the councils of Lyons in 1274 and Florence in 1439.

The most notorious theological disagreement arose over the Western alteration of the Nicene-Constantinopolitan Creed of 381. Where the Creed originally said that the Spirit "proceeds from the Father," the phrase "and the Son" (Latin: *filioque*) was added in sixth-century Spain and gradually gained acceptance in the West over a period of centuries. Apart from the theological questions which it raised, the addition also raised in an acute form the question of authority in the Church, with

---

[31] In discussing Eastern churches it has been necessary to omit the Oriental Orthodox churches from consideration and to concentrate exclusively on the Byzantine Orthodox churches.

the East insisting that the West had no authority to change a creed ratified by an ecumenical council.

In general the Eastern Orthodox churches accept papal primacy
only in the limited sense of a primacy of honor and reject the Catholic
view that the pope enjoys of a primacy of jurisdiction over the entire
Church. Rather, the pope is viewed in the East as possessing only the
limited jurisdiction that attaches to the Patriarchate of the West. Universal jurisdiction is unthinkable without Rome, Alexandria, Antioch,
Jerusalem, and Constantinople being taken together. Even so, this jurisdiction is considered more a matter of ecclesiastical organization than
of divine right. Ultimate authority in the Church is held to reside in
ecumenical councils as representing the Church in its entirety.

A focus on the universal church, however, has been more characteristic of Roman Catholicism, especially since the Gregorian reform, than
of Eastern Orthodoxy, which has concentrated most of its attention on
the local church as the quintessential worshiping community. Such a
concentration has meant that the idea of the episcopal order as being
above all a eucharistic ministry has remained central since it was first
articulated by the earliest of the Eastern Fathers, Ignatius of Antioch.[32]
By contrast, Western juridical notions stemming from the Middle Ages
have sometimes seemed to grant the episcopate a raison d'être independent of the Eucharist. Moreover, the Eastern Orthodox understanding of the eucharistic community accords to the laity an importance
that tended to be lost sight of in the medieval West.

Eastern Orthodoxy is also distinguished by the prominent place
given to icons of Christ and the saints in both public and private worship. Icons are believed to be sacramental, mediating an earthly encounter with heavenly reality. Made out of earthly matter yet disclosing
the glory of God, an icon is analogous to the incarnation itself.

Thomas Aquinas and Scholasticism

Scholasticism is viewed with suspicion by Eastern Orthodoxy as
veering dangerously close to rationalism. Yet scholasticism's influence
not only on the Catholic Church but on the whole subsequent development of Western Europe perhaps exceeds that of any other achievement of the Middle Ages. The product of the emerging universities of
the twelfth and thirteenth centuries, scholasticism at its best and especially in the work of Thomas Aquinas (ca. 1225–74) embodied a truly
catholic spirit in its broad embrace not only of the Scripture and tradi-

---

[32] See, for example, the quotation from Ignatius given above on pg. 25.

tion of the Church but also of the truths expressed by Jewish, Muslim, and pagan thinkers. Of the scholastics only Aquinas will be considered here, partly because his ecclesiology may be regarded as typical of the scholastics,[33] partly because his theology in general enjoys a uniquely magisterial status in the Catholic Church.

Aquinas's ecclesiology follows from his teaching on grace. It is the grace of the Spirit that summons people to believe and unites them in faith in the Mystical Body, the Church. Our new life through the Spirit is the life of Christ in us, who enables us to perform acts of faith, hope, and love, which in turn enable us to experience ever closer union with God. The inner nature of the Church is made visible in its institutional aspects as a diversified and organized society. These aspects include the ministry of faith and of the sacraments of faith, especially the Eucharist, by which the body of Christ grows and thrives.

In his *Exposition of the Apostles' Creed* Aquinas comments upon the marks of the Church. The Church is "one" in faith, hope, and love. The Church is "holy" insofar as it is the temple of God. The Church is "catholic" in reaching out to all humanity through space and time and indeed beyond time, since the Church in heaven endures forever. Finally it is "apostolic" because it has the apostles as its foundation.

Opposition to the Idea of the Papal Monarchy

The "two-swords theory" first formulated by Pope Gelasius I (492–496), according to which God has given spiritual authority to the Church and temporal authority to the state, received two historic interpretations at the beginning of the fourteenth century. The first, put forward by the Dominican theologian John of Paris in 1302–03, argued for the autonomy of each power except in the case of a conflict between Church and state, when the spiritual power should take precedence. This interpretation was marked by balance and moderation. The same cannot be said, however, of the second interpretation, that of Pope Boniface VIII (1294–1303) in his papal bull *Unam sanctam* (1302). Boniface, provoked by the insolent behavior of King Philip IV of France, declared that the temporal sword of the state could only be wielded at the command and with the permission of the Church. Furthermore, he insisted that submission to the pope was necessary for salvation. Boniface misjudged the effect his words would have, however. Far from being cowed into submission, Philip promptly had the Pope arrested. Within a month Boniface was dead.

[33] See Yves Congar, *The Mystery of the Church*, trans. A. V. Littledale, 2nd rev. ed. (Baltimore and Dublin: Helicon Press, 1965) 54.

In 1309, at Philip's insistence, the papacy was transferred to Avignon, where it remained in a kind of exile (the "Babylonian Captivity of the Papacy") until 1377. In this period the papal prerogatives suffered encroachment not only by the French monarchy but even by the College of Cardinals. This blow to papal prestige was followed almost immediately by the Great Western Schism (1378–1417), during which there were two and at one point even three rival claimants to the papal throne. The Council of Constance (1414–18) resolved the crisis and proposed frequent meetings of church councils to ensure that such a crisis never arose again. In support of this proposal the council noted that an ecumenical council, by representing the Church in its entirety, enjoyed an authority superior to that of the pope alone.

Voices of Opposition to the Monarchical Papacy

The monarchical papacy also faced opposition from several notable intellectuals of the time. The political theorist Marsilius of Padua (ca. 1275–1342), often regarded as the founder of conciliarism, had argued that authority in the Church resided in the Christian community as a whole. Another even more notable figure was the Czech priest and reformer Jan Hus (ca. 1372–1415). Following the lead of Oxford theologian John Wycliffe (ca. 1329–84), Hus drew a sharp distinction between the visible church under the rule of the pope and the invisible but authentic church under the rule of Christ. The latter was made up of those predestined by God. When excommunicated for this and other teachings, Hus decided to appeal to a council. Although he had been promised safe-conduct, upon his arrival at the Council of Constance he was arrested, tried and condemned for heresy, and burned at the stake. Nevertheless, his followers carried on in a separate church, thus anticipating the Reformation by a full century.

Martin Luther and the Protestant Reformation

Martin Luther (1483–1546) was inspired by the teaching and example of men such as Hus and shared their longing for a return to the authenticity of the primitive church. Luther's original intention was not to create a new church but to restore the existing one to pristine purity. As he saw it, the true Church of the apostles had been obscured by a heavy overlay of ecclesiastical bureaucracy and popular piety symbolized by the practice of indulgences. Above all, the visible, hierarchical Church had lost sight of the central doctrine of grace as set forth by

Paul in his letter to the Romans. Of Luther and of the reformers in general it has been said that "what they saw in the teaching of the Roman Catholic Church was the undue stress upon works, and the answer to this was the justification of the sinner by divine grace through faith alone."[34]

A direct corollary of Luther's doctrine of justification was his conception of the Church as essentially the congregation of those who have justifying faith. The faith of believers is evoked and sustained by the word of God. In Luther's thought, the word of God and particularly the Bible assume an authority greater than and even in conflict with the authority of tradition, the magisterium, and the pope. From this it follows that the genuine sacraments of Christ are not the seven proclaimed by the pope but only those whose institution by Christ is explicit in the Gospels: baptism and the Eucharist. Luther never went so far as some of the radical reformers would do in discarding the institutional idea of the Church altogether. Indeed he insisted against them that the Church was truly instituted by God as a means of grace: it was the Church's task to preach the gospel and administer the sacraments. Nevertheless, the common core of the Protestant Reformation, despite the bewildering variety of forms that it took, was the rejection of the Roman Catholic idea of the Church and above all its insistence upon the clerical hierarchy as mediating salvation. Against the idea of a clerical hierarchy Luther stressed the notion of the priesthood of *all* believers—including the laity—who are called to be ministers of the Word to one another.

The Catholic Reformation and Counter-Reformation

Meanwhile the Roman Catholic Church was undergoing a reformation of its own. Although often referred to simply as "the Counter-Reformation," this designation is inaccurate to the extent that it implies that the Catholic Reformation was only a reaction to the Protestant Reformation, when in fact the Catholic Church had begun a process of renewal and reform much earlier. Nevertheless, for the purposes of this essay it will be necessary to concentrate on those aspects of the Catholic Reformation which were intended as a response to Protestantism. That response did not become fully organized and visible until the Council of Trent (1545–63), which reaffirmed traditional Catholic teachings that had been repudiated by the Reformers: the hierarchical authority of the

---

[34] Jaroslav Pelikan, *The Riddle of Roman Catholicism* (New York and Nashville: Abingdon Press, 1959) 49.

Church; the seven sacraments, including ordination; the necessity of receiving both Scripture and tradition "with equal reverence." Trent also instituted numerous reforms, including the establishment of seminaries to provide priests, who until then had not been given formal training, with both general education and specific instruction in priestly ministry.

In spreading the ideals of the Catholic Reformation a leading role was played by the newly established Society of Jesus, founded in 1534 by Ignatius of Loyola (1491–1556). An outstanding Jesuit theologian, Robert Bellarmine (1542–1621), defended the Catholic faith against Protestantism and became the most influential Catholic ecclesiologist until Yves Congar (1904–95). Because Protestantism had attacked the visible, hierarchical structure of the Catholic Church, Bellarmine made that structure the focal point of his defense, as may be inferred from his famous definition of the one true Church as "the community of men brought together by the profession of the same Christian faith and conjoined in the communion of the same sacraments, under the government of the legitimate pastors and especially the one vicar of Christ on earth, the Roman pontiff."[35] In the same passage Bellarmine states that as a visible society the Church may be compared to the kingdom of France, for example, or the republic of Venice. Bellarmine's stress on visibility meant that there was little room in his ecclesiology for the idea of the Church as a mystery—"a reality imbued with the hidden presence of God."[36] Thus in the very effort to retrieve an important aspect of Catholic ecclesiology, Bellarmine neglected another aspect that was even more important.

Conclusion

The development of the Church's self-understanding over a period of a millennium and a half cannot be adequately treated in a brief essay such as this. Nevertheless it is hoped that a sketch of that development and of the historical factors that influenced it most decisively has been provided and will be of use. Much of the discussion has concentrated on the structure of the Roman Catholic Church and especially the papacy. These are undoubtedly central to its identity and self-understanding.

---

[35] *De controversiis*, tom. 2, liber 3, *De ecclesia militante*, cap. 2, "De definitione Ecclesiae" (Naples: Giuliano, 1857) 2:75; trans. and quoted by Avery Dulles in *Models of the Church*, expanded ed. (New York: Doubleday, 1987) 16.

[36] The quotation is from Pope Paul VI's opening address at the second session of Vatican Council II.

At the same time, however, it must be said that the vital essence of the Church lies not in these but in its invisible, intangible elements—"the riches of the glory of this mystery among the Gentiles; it is Christ in you, the hope for glory" (Col 1:27). These elements have eluded this author's powers of expression.

Bearing in mind these limitations, we may summarize the history of the Church and its self-understanding as follows. From its beginnings as a seemingly insignificant sect within Judaism, Christianity spread rapidly through the Roman Empire, quickly becoming predominantly Gentile in membership and assimilating many elements of Roman civilization and culture. In the second century internal threats of heresy and schism elicited a movement toward greater uniformity of structure and belief and away from the relative pluralism that had marked the earliest Church. In its relations with the pagan world the Church encountered frequent opposition and harsh persecution for its refusal to participate in the worship of the emperor. The conversion of Constantine ended this persecution and by leading the way to the establishment of Christianity as the official religion of the empire did much to make the Church more Roman and more Catholic. With the Germanic invasions across Europe beginning in the fourth century, the need for strong leadership to preserve the heritage of Roman civilization and culture became acute. The papacy rose to the occasion magnificently. The subsequent commingling of Roman and Germanic elements gave a distinctive cast to the Church in Western Europe and caused its development to diverge from that of the East until finally, owing to a series of tragic events, schism separated East from West. Further crisis in the Western Church soon followed, culminating in the Protestant Reformation. But there had been movement toward reform and renewal earlier (the Catholic Reformation) and there would be further movement after (the Counter-Reformation).

Despite the reform, renewal, and missionary expansion of the Catholic Church throughout the sixteenth century, this was a time of loss of incalculable proportions. The unity of Western Christendom had been shattered, even as its unity with Eastern Christendom had been shattered earlier, so that now more than ever the idea of the Church as "one" and "catholic" seemed unreal and even a mockery. Established Christianity, which had held sway in Europe for more than twelve hundred years, began a long process of collapse in the face of forces of disintegration within and forces of secularization without. The latter, which included nationalism, capitalism, rationalism, and the rise of modern science, would transform European civilization and culture in the centuries to come. In response to this crisis, official Catholic ecclesiology tended to assume a defensive posture too often marked by rigidity and narrowness. Nevertheless, the limitations of official ecclesiology could not extinguish the spontaneity, vitality, and creativity of the Spirit in the Church.

For Further Reading

Bouyer, Louis. *The Church of God.* Trans. Charles Underhill Quinn. Chicago: Franciscan Herald Press, 1982.

Brown, Raymond E., and John P. Meier. *Antioch and Rome: New Testament Cradles of Catholic Christianity.* New York: Paulist Press, 1983.

Congar, Yves. *L'ecclésiologie de S. Augustin à l'époque moderne.* Paris: Cerf, 1970.

_____. *The Mystery of the Church.* Trans. A. V. Littledale. 2nd rev. ed. Baltimore and Dublin: Helicon Press, 1965.

Eno, Robert B. *The Rise of the Papacy.* Wilmington, Del.: Michael Glazier, 1990.

Granfield, Patrick. *The Papacy in Transition.* Garden City, N.Y.: Doubleday & Company, 1980.

Halton, Thomas. *The Church.* Message of the Fathers of the Church Series 4. Wilmington, Del.: Michael Glazier, 1985.

Jay, Eric G. *The Church: Its Changing Image Through Twenty Centuries.* Volume 1: *The First Seventeen Centuries.* London: SPCK, 1977.

Küng, Hans. *The Church.* Trans. Ray and Rosaleen Ockenden. New York: Sheed and Ward, 1967.

Le Guillou, M. J. *Christ and Church: A Theology of the Mystery.* Trans. Charles E. Schaldenbrand. New York: Desclee, 1966.

Pelikan, Jaroslav. *The Christian Tradition: A History of the Development of Doctrine.* Vols. 1–4. Chicago and London: University of Chicago Press, 1971–83.

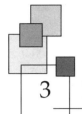

3 | The Development of Ecclesiology: Modernity to the Twentieth Century

Michael J. Himes

In the four hundred years between the close of the Council of Trent and the beginning of the Vatican Council II the Church became a question to itself. The dimension of this change can be seen if we consider that the great medieval texts from which students learned theology—Peter Lombard's *IV Libri sententiarum* and Thomas Aquinas's *Summa Theologiae*—had contained no section specifically devoted to the Church and now it is unthinkable that one could study systematic theology without attending to ecclesiology. These centuries can be conveniently divided into four periods: (1) the Counter-Reformation (1563–1650), (2) early Modernity (1650–1800), (3) the nineteenth century, and (4) the period from Vatican I to Vatican II (1870–1960). In the first two periods ecclesiology was primarily concerned with questions of Church polity and the relationship of the Church to civil governments. Beginning in the nineteenth century there emerged a systematic ecclesiology, that is, an ecclesiology which considered the connections between the Church and the central doctrinal areas of the Christian faith, such as Trinity, incarnation, Holy Spirit, creation, grace, eschatology, etc.

The Counter-Reformation (1563–1650)

Three factors were especially important in shaping Catholic ecclesiology in this period: (1) anti-Reformation polemics, (2) scholastic theological method and epistemology, and (3) the emergence of the unified state.

Today many historians prefer to use the term "Catholic Reformation" rather than "Counter-Reformation" in order to emphasize the positive reorganization and revitalization of the Catholic Church in the century following the Council of Trent. But while it is true that the period saw an extraordinary burst of energy in evangelization, preaching, liturgy, theology, popular spirituality and devotional life, art, music, and architecture, it is also undeniably true that "Counter-Reformation" does capture an important aspect of the period. For this rebirth of Catholicism had a polemical edge; it was always experienced and understood in *opposition* to an alternative. When the Council of Trent opened in 1545, the Catholic Church had been losing one land after another to the Reformation in its various forms for almost thirty years. By 1600 it had not only stopped the steady advance of Protestantism in Europe but had actually rolled it back in Germany, France, and Poland and had begun to see the fruits of its new missionary efforts in Asia and the Americas. The vitality of the Counter-Reformation and the confident joy of the Baroque were marked by the sense that a great threat had been met and survived.

The polemical edge of Counter-Reformation theology shaped the period's understanding of the Church. The Council of Trent (1545–63) had three goals: reformation, correction, and clarification. The call for greater purity in Christian life and the concomitant institutional reform of the Church had been heard repeatedly since the High Middle Ages but became urgent in order to respond to the criticisms of the Reformers. The fathers of Trent charged that the Reformers based their theologies on erroneous doctrines and false readings of Scripture and set out to expose, correct, and reject these errors, especially those of Luther and Zwingli, the former having died when the council had barely begun and the latter fourteen years before its first meeting. But Reformation was already a generation old before Trent met; the council finally held its first session twenty-eight years after Luther posted his ninety-five theses. Catholic pastors and congregations alike were confused about what the Church taught, what it permitted, and what it rejected. The council needed to clarify what Catholic doctrine was on the disputed questions regarding grace and salvation, Scripture and doctrine, Church and sacraments. In achieving its three goals—reformation, correction, and clarification—the Council of Trent was remarkably successful.

But these clearly-defined goals meant that Trent had a limited doctrinal agenda which was, in an odd way, set by the Reformers. The council only treated doctrinal issues on which it understood the Reformers to differ from Catholic tradition. On those doctrines where there was no disagreement, such as the Trinity or the incarnation, Trent was silent. This set the tone for much of the polemical and apologetical theology of the post-Tridentine period. Theologians emphasized the differences between Catholics and Protestants and among the various Protestant communions. For Catholic ecclesiology this meant that what must be taught about the Church was what the Reformation either denied or undervalued: visibility.

Counter-Reformation Catholic theologians understood the Lutheran teaching on the Church to be that the true Church was invisible, that is, its membership was known only to God. Article 7 of the Augsburg Confession (1530) defined the Church as the congregation of the saints. Article 8 explained that the Church consists properly of saints and true believers. Luther had cautioned that "the church is hidden and the saints are unknown"[1] and on occasion expressed his insistence on the word of God as the *sole* authority in the Church by denouncing canon law and hierarchical authority, especially that of the papacy and episcopacy. Read unsympathetically, such statements seemed to lead to the conclusion that there are two quite different meanings of the word "church": one, the true Church known by God and revealed at the final judgment, and the other, the earthly institution whose membership might or (more likely) might not coincide with the true Church. Even read sympathetically, it remains true that Luther's understanding of the Church has little room for an institution exercising its authority and pursuing its purposes sometimes in conjunction and sometimes in conflict with other institutional communities. Catholic scholars concluded that the Lutheran doctrine of the Church taught that the visible community of baptized persons on earth is not the true Church but only a helpful means by which persons might enter into the true Church of the justified elect. Not surprisingly in the highly polemical context of post-Reformation theology, much of Catholic ecclesiology in the decades following the Council of Trent insisted that the true and only Church is a visible institution, a *societas perfecta*; that is, a society having within it all the means necessary for the attainment of its ends.

This insistence is best seen in the classic post-Tridentine definition of the Church given by Robert Bellarmine (1542–1621): the Church is "an assembly of persons united by the profession of the same faith and communion in the same sacraments under the governance of legitimate pastors and especially of the one vicar of Christ on earth, the Roman pontiff."[2] This definition, which was still being quoted in manuals of theology as late as World War I, is remarkable both for what it includes and what it omits. First, the Church is "an assembly of persons" with no restriction about the character of those persons. The Church is not a congregation of saints; Bellarmine specifically noted that it includes sinners, heretics, and *de facto* unbelievers (although he adds that such people are not fully members). Second, far from its members being known only to God, they are recognizable by their unity not through one faith but through the *profession* of one faith, not through belief in the same sacraments but through *communion* in them. Only

---

[1] *De servo arbitrio, D. Martin Luthers Werke* (Weimar, 1883–) 18:652.
[2] *Disputationes de controversiis Christianae fidei adversus huius temporis haereticos*, 3 vols. (Ingolstadt, 1586–93) 4.3.2.

God can know what one believes, but other people can know what one professes; only God knows whether one truly believes in baptism or the Eucharist, but one's name in a baptismal register or one's presence at Mass are bonds of unity which, Bellarmine pointedly observed, are matters available to our sense knowledge. Third, these Church members are governed by *legitimate* pastors, that is, pastors appointed by due institutional process not by popular discernment of charisms, and who are hierarchically ordered, at least in that the Roman pontiff is uniquely the Vicar of Christ. So definite was Bellarmine on the institutional nature of the Church that he did not hesitate to add that it is as "visible and palpable as the assembly of the Roman people or the kingdom of France or the republic of Venice." Bellarmine was far too acute a theologian not to know that his definition was a limited one. He recognized that it defined the Church externally and omitted its deepest internal characteristics. Thus, immediately after his definition, he distinguished between the body and the soul of the Church, noting that one might belong to the body but not to the soul which is the grace of the Holy Spirit. Nevertheless, his influential definition authorized describing the Church in terms that were essentially visible, organizational, and institutional and, in doing so, it was perfectly in accord with the polemical theological formulae of Counter-Reformation Catholicism.[3]

The very way in which theology was taught and written reinforced this emphasis on the Church as a visible institutional society. The century following the Council of Trent saw an extraordinary development of positive theology or, as it was sometimes called, historical theology. The charge constantly hurled back and forth between Protestants and Catholics was that of innovation. Both sides agreed that everything necessary for salvation had been revealed by Jesus to his disciples. Consequently, any addition to this deposit of faith could only be a corruption or distortion. To be an innovator was thus tantamount to being a heretic. Starting with Luther's *Babylonian Captivity of the Church*

---

[3] Bellarmine's definition was by no means idiosyncratic. Jacques Duperron (1556–1618), convert from Calvinism and cardinal archbishop of Sens, who was greatly influenced by Bellarmine, defined the Church as "those whom God has called to salvation through the profession of the true faith, sincere administration of the sacraments, and adherence to legitimate pastors"; *Réplique à la réponse du sérénissime roy de la Grande-Bretagne* (Paris, 1620) 36. Francis de Sales (1567–1622) followed the same pattern in his definition of the Church as "a holy universal community or general company of persons united and gathered in the profession of one and the same Christian faith, in participation in the same sacraments and sacrifice, and in obedience to one and the same vicar and general lieutenant of our Savior Jesus Christ and successor of Peter, under the charge of legitimate bishops"; *Opera omnia*, 26 vols. (Annecy, 1892–1932) 1:43.

(1520), the Protestant charge was that the Church had been corrupted by new doctrines and practices throughout the Middle Ages, all of them aimed at supporting hierarchical and especially papal pretensions. The Reformers called for the Church to be purged of these medieval accretions and returned to its pristine state as founded by Christ. The Catholic response was that the Church's doctrine and polity had remained unchanged from the apostolic age and that the Reformers were introducing novelties. In opposition to the Reformation principle of *sola scriptura* the Catholic tradition insisted on both Scripture and tradition as sources of revelation. Counter-Reformation positive or historical theology had as its task the demonstration from Scripture or patristic and ecclesiastical documents that the Church as it existed in the sixteenth century was identical with the Church of the first century. Armed with the critical tools honed by Renaissance humanists for the recovery of classical texts, Catholic and Protestant scholars of the sixteenth and seventeenth centuries diligently worked at biblical exegesis, patristics, Church history, and canonical history.[4]

Positive theology supplied both historical and documentary support for Church teaching and matter for subsequent elaboration and organization by speculative theology. The sixteenth century saw the appearance of a revived scholasticism, purified of the excesses of its decadent period in the preceding century. Theologians confidently assumed an essential harmony between divine revelation and human reason rightly employed. Clarity, discrimination, and organization were the hallmarks of this theology. The conjunction of the scholastic revival with the emergence of a polemically directed positive theology gave rise to an ecclesiology primarily concerned with visible forms in an institutional society.

The placement of the treatment of the Church in the course of theological study—its position in the system of theology—furthered this institutional ecclesiology. Until the beginning of the sixteenth century the standard text for students in theology had been the *Sentences* of Peter Lombard. In Dominican houses of study Thomas Aquinas's *Summa Theologiae* had long been the basic text, but gradually in the years before and during the Council of Trent the *Summa* began to be used in other schools as well, especially in Jesuit faculties. The most creative and influential center of Thomistic theology in the sixteenth and early seventeenth centuries was in Salamanca. Although there is no tract on

---

[4] For a brief but useful account of the emergence of positive theology in this period, see Hubert Jedin, "The Rise of Positive Theology," *Reformation and Counter Reformation,* ed. Erwin Iserloh, Joseph Glazik, and Hubert Jedin, *History of the Church,* 10 vols. (New York: Seabury Press, 1980) 5:546–55.

the Church in the *Summa Theologiae*, the custom was to discuss certain ecclesiological issues in commenting on *ST* II-II, q. 1, a. 10, on whether the pope has the authority to draw up a symbol of faith. Starting in 1562 in Rome the Jesuit Francisco de Toledo (1532–96), former student and teacher at Salamanca, treated questions of Church authority and especially the rights of popes and councils in relation to this passage in the *Summa*. Others, like his student Robert Bellarmine, continued to do so. Indeed, the Dominican Domingo Bañez (1528–1604) elaborated a considerable tract on the Church from the same text. But locating the teaching of ecclesiology in relation to the article in the *Summa* on papal authority over the formulae of faith necessarily narrowed the field of questions considered. The context of the discussion tended to limit the treatment of the Church to issues of institutional authority and the relative prerogatives of magisterial organs.

In the century following the Council of Trent the unified nation state replaced the older feudal monarchies in Western Europe. In Spain, France, and England political power became increasingly centralized in the monarch who ruled through an ever growing number of agencies and offices of government. This meant a transfer of power from the semi-independent feudal aristocracy who governed their own estates to royal servants and intendants acting in the name of the monarch. The new centralized states were no longer patchworks of overlapping fiefs but unified national communities embodied in the persons of their kings. Not surprisingly, this development was paralleled in the Church. The Church has often understood itself as a society by analogy to the dominant forms of social organization in the world around it. As the post-Constantinian Church had borrowed and adapted features of imperial organization and the medieval Church had incorporated elements of feudal society, now the Church of the sixteenth and seventeenth century understood itself as a community united and expressed in the pope who governs it through local delegates, the bishops. For example, in Bellarmine's definition of the Church it is noteworthy that he reserved the title "Vicar of Christ" to the Roman pontiff; fifty years before in debates at Trent that title had been accorded to every bishop in his own diocese. Just as the centralization of the state was contested by the feudal nobility and local interests, however, so the centralization of the Church in the Roman pontiff did not go unchallenged.

Early Modernity (1650–1800)

The Counter-Reformation stress on the Church as a visible society like "the assembly of the Roman people or the kingdom of France or the republic of Venice" inevitably raised an old question in a new key: What is the relationship of this society to the kingdom of France or the republic of Venice? At the same time, the strong emphasis in the period following the Council of Trent on the Church as a hierarchically organized society under legitimate pastors raised in a new way another old question: How are the rights and responsibilities of these pastors ordered? The cultural and political impact of the growth of nation-states in Western Europe provided a context in which one could respond in two ways: one might understand the Church as a highly centralized society with authority placed primarily in a papacy modeled on the absolute monarchies of the period, or one might cast the Church as itself determined by national boundaries and so emphasize the role of national hierarchies. Thus, in the period from the Peace of Westphalia ending the Thirty Years' War (1618–48), the last and worst of the post-Reformation wars of religion, to the end of the eighteenth century when the French Revolution and the Napoleonic wars radically altered Europe politically and socially, ecclesiological discussion centered on (1) the intertwined issues of Church polity (e.g., "episcopal" Gallicanism) and Church-state relations (e.g., "royal" Gallicanism). Outside France, the clearest instance of the former was (2) Febronianism and of the latter was (3) Josephinism.

"Gallicanism" is a complex phenomenon with long roots. The claim that the church in France was more or less free from papal authority because of various privileges attaching to the French crown had been asserted with varying degrees of strength since the High Middle Ages. It had taken on greater insistence at the time of the Great Western Schism in conjunction with conciliarist doctrines. Jean Gerson (1363–1429), Pierre d'Ailly (1350–1420), and later Jacques Almain (ca. 1480–1515) and John Major (1470–1550) defended the position that authority belongs first to the faithful as a whole and is only derived to the pope for certain purposes. In the early seventeenth century Jean Launoy (1603–78) criticized Robert Bellarmine for including making the papal office an element in his definition of the Church and for attributing the title "Vicar of Christ" only to the pope. Paolo Sarpi (1552–1623) and Marco Antonio de Dominis (1566–1624) attacked the centralization of authority in the papacy as an obstacle to reconciliation with Protestant communities. Pierre Pithou (1539–96), Edmond Richer (1560–1631), and Pierre de Marca (1594–1662) elaborated historical and canonical defenses of the Gallican claims. At the same time as the theory of episcopal Gallicanism was being formulated, practical measures of royal Gallicanism sought to limit the power of the Roman see in the French church. The Pragmatic Sanction of Bourges (1438), in which the French clergy asserted that church property in France and nominations of bishops to French sees were not subject to papal jurisdiction, had been superseded by the still more sweeping Concordat of Bologna (1516) which recognized the right of the French crown to appoint virtually all bishops and abbots in its dominions. Because the decrees of the Council of Trent conflicted with the provisions of the Concordat, the French monarchy had not permitted their publication in France. Cardinal Richelieu (1585–1642) found that the "Gallican liberties" were both a useful theoretical support for his program of centralizing power in the monarchy and a handy weapon with which to intimidate the Holy See into falling into line with his anti-Hapsburg foreign policy. By the close of his career, he was floating the idea of the formation of a Patriarchate of France, equivalent in authority to the eastern patriarchates, which would have rendered the French church virtually independent of the Roman church. Later Louis XIV (1638–1715) advanced or retracted Gallican claims as suited his relations with the papacy. In 1663 the faculty of the Sorbonne, with royal prompting, issued a declaration affirming the freedom of the crown from papal authority, asserting the supremacy of ecumenical councils to the papacy, and rejecting papal infallibility.

The simplest formulation of Gallican claims are the four Gallican Articles written by Jacques Bénigne Bossuet (1627–1704) and accepted by an assembly of the French clergy in 1682. The Articles held that the pope has no power over temporal matters and that therefore kings are not subject to ecclesiastical authority in such matters; that the papacy can neither depose a monarch nor absolve his subjects from their allegiance to him; that a general council is of greater authority than a pope; that the traditional Gallican liberties are inviolable; and that, until ratified by a general council, papal decrees are reformable. Thus two strands of Gallicanism—royal, that is, asserting the independence of monarchs from ecclesiastical and especially papal authority, and episcopal, that is, affirming the rights of individual bishops and national hierarchies over against Roman centralization—were brought together in the Articles and reinforced one another. Although the Gallican Articles were eventually condemned by Rome in 1690 and withdrawn by Louis XIV in 1693, their substance continued to be widely taught in French schools and seminaries throughout the eighteenth century and, thanks to the largely French-educated faculties of seminaries in the United States, in this country well into the nineteenth century.

The episcopal strand of Gallicanism found its clearest expression in the movement known as Febronianism in the eighteenth century in the German-speaking lands. The name comes from Justinus Febronius, the pseudonym of Johann Nioklaus von Hontheim (1701–90), a suffragan bishop of Trier who in 1763 published a treatise on the proper relationship between the local bishops and the papacy.[5] In fact, his position had long been held by many of the great metropolitans of Germany and Austria. Following the Gallican canonists with whom he had studied in Belgium, Hontheim held that Christ had conferred the power of the keys on the whole Church, although it is exercised by the bishops sometimes individually but especially when gathered in general council. Papal primacy is purely a primacy of honor; the papal role is that of a coordinator seeking peace and harmony within the universal Church. Episcopal approval, either individually or in council, is required for the validity of any papal directive. The pope has no authority to nominate or even confirm bishops and certainly not to depose them, nor can he appoint diocesan officials anywhere save in Rome. Hontheim suggested a plan of action by which the German bishops might force Roman recognition of what he regarded as the proper order of the Church: the bishops should refuse approval of papal pronouncements, summon on their own authority local synods, and collaborate with secular princes in the reform of local churches. At a meeting in 1786 at Bad Ems representatives of the major German metropolitan sees issued a statement consisting of twenty-three articles, the Punctation of Ems, which essentially embodies the Febronian program, and invited the emperor to summon a council of all the German bishops. Because local bishops were unwilling to exchange the authority of a distant pope for that of a neighboring metropolitan, the Ems initiative met with no success. But the mainlines of Febronian ecclesiology continued to be taught in various areas of the German-speaking world well into the nineteenth century.

The most notable attempt at systematically implementing royal Gallicanism was Josephinism, named for the emperor Joseph II (1741–90). An "enlightened despot" deeply marked by the values and views of the *Aufklärung*, Joseph set out to modernize and reform Austria in 1780 once the death of his mother, Maria Theresa, left him as sole ruler. Determined not to allow the Church to stand in the way of changes in education, the promotion of religious toleration, and relaxation of censorship, he took as his operational principle that the Church and its ministers were subordinate to civil authority in all matters which did not directly affect doctrine. The reformation of liturgical practices, the disciplining of the clergy, the regulation of Church schools, the redrawing of diocesan and parish boundaries, all were not specifically doctrinal issues and were therefore to be governed by the state. Although

---

[5] *De statu Ecclesiae et legitima potestate Romani Pontificis liber singularis* (Bouillon, 1763). Not only did Hontheim use a pseudonym, he disguised the place of publication; the book was actually published in Frankfurt-am-Main.

Joseph's successor, his brother Leopold II (1747–92), reached an accommodation with Rome and officially repealed most of the Josephinist legislation, Leopold had previously as Grand Duke of Tuscany carried his brother's program into effect with great thoroughness. Scipione de'Ricci (1741–1810), appointed by Leopold as bishop of Pistoia, presided at a synod in 1786 which formally adopted the Gallican Articles of 1682 and most of the positions espoused by Hontheim.

The ecclesiological attitude of the *Aufklärung* was that the Church was a necessary and useful instrument in bringing about the order and peace of the human community. Its mission was preeminently educational: it taught virtuous living and supported its teaching with divine sanctions. Thus it formed good, honest, and law-abiding members of society. The state, increasingly seen as omnicompetent, naturally had an interest in the formation of its members and so had a directive power over the Church. The medieval ideal of Christendom had been shattered by the divisions of the Reformation period, and consequently the notion that the universal Church was ultimately subordinate to the Christian princes taken as a whole or to the Holy Roman Emperor as the theoretical head of Christendom was manifestly impractical in the new world of independent nation-states. Therefore, enlightened thinkers tended to accord less attention to the universal Church and much more to the Church within the state. This meant that the bishops were seen as civil administrators for spiritual concerns, and the Bishop of Rome could have, at most, a primacy of honor. The Church was indeed a visible society but not a *societas perfecta*; that description belonged to the state.

The Nineteenth Century

The key issues to be noticed in this especially rich theological period are: (1) the emergence of ecclesiology as a field within systematic theology, (2) the recovery of a rich understanding of tradition, (3) Ultramontanism, and (4) the heightened centralization of authority in the papacy culminating at Vatican I.

In the first decades of the nineteenth century Catholicism in the German-speaking lands was marked by two quite different ways of understanding the Church and its mission. *Aufklärung* Catholicism with its Febronian and Josephinist views on Church polity was by no means dead. Some bishops and many pastors had been formed in and continued to preach a theology which envisioned the Church primarily as an ethical instructor and which tended to dismiss ideas of the Church as communion in the Holy Spirit, the sacramental community of worship, or participation in trinitarian life by the pejorative term "mysticism." But new currents of Romantic Catholicism sought for a deeper grounding of the Church in the economy of salvation. Often this was supported by a return to patristic sources for an "internal" understanding of the Church (as opposed to the Counter-Reformation definition of the Church *ab externis*) and vision of its mission which was more than merely educative. As theology influenced by the *Aufklärung* sometimes ended as dry-as-dust rationalism, so Romantic theology ran the danger of becoming merely pious effusions or, in its insistence on inner religious experience, bizarrely sectarian. But the tension between the two currents created a fertile field for fresh theological approaches.

Nowhere was this more true than in the Catholic theological faculty at the University of Tübingen. Founded in 1812 at Ellwangen and moved to Tübingen in 1817, the Catholic faculty numbered several distinguished members in its first thirty years. Two who had a particular impact on ecclesiology were Johann Sebastian Drey (1777–1853), the "father" of the Catholic Tübingen school, and his student and then colleague, Johann Adam Möhler (1796–1838), perhaps the most famous member of the school.

Although Drey seldom dealt with specifically ecclesiological questions, his outline and methodology for theology as a field of study gave a central place to the Church which he described as "fundamental with regard both to [Christianity's] outward organization and to its inward elaboration of a scientific construction."[6] The reason that Drey gave why the Church is fundamental for theology was quite different from that which had been familiar to Counter-Reformation Catholic theologians. Previously the indispensable role played by the Church was that of transmitter and guarantor of tradition, the carrier of the material on which the theologian worked. But Drey taught that the Church was itself that material. "The church is for the theologian what the state is for political science, what the animal organism is for medicine: the concrete expression of the science itself, that through which it becomes positive."[7] The theologian's task was to give theoretical systematic form to the life of the Church, that is, its worship, preaching, and practice. This meant that the Church's history was not simply illustrative of its doctrine, it was doctrine embodied. The necessary implication was that doctrine itself had a history, a development, and that intrinsic to the theological task was *both* the tracing of that development and its furtherance.

[6] Johann Sebastian Drey, *Brief Introduction to the Study of Theology with Reference to the Scientific Standpoint and the Catholic System,* trans. Michael J. Himes (Notre Dame, Ind.: University of Notre Dame Press, 1994) 30.

[7] Ibid., 22.

> A unified system of ideas which is not to be thought of as the dead tradition of a bygone age but as the development of a living reality has within it two elements—a *fixed* and a *mutable* one. The first is that which has been closed by development up to now, the second as that which is still *being understood* as it develops.[8]

Drey gave theologians a new role of ecclesial leadership when he insisted that "it is characteristic of Christian doctrine to unfold itself ever more clearly and the theologian as a teacher of his church is called to participate in this."[9] The goal of theology is not only the maintenance of the tradition but its furtherance, and the ground, the goal, and the test of this furtherance is the common life of the Church. One cannot do theology without studying the multidimensional reality which is the Church.

Throughout his brief career Möhler was much more directly engaged with ecclesiology than Drey. In fact, he deserves to be regarded as the creator of ecclesiology as a field within systematic (or, as he would have said, scientific) theology. His first book, *Unity in the Church*, was a patristic study of the principle of unity within the Church as the product and sign of the Holy Spirit. "The Church exists through a life directly and continually moved by the divine Spirit, and is maintained and continued by the loving mutual exchange of believers."[10] This strongly pneumatic direction produced an ecclesiology very different from that of the Counter-Reformation and Enlightenment theologians. To be sure, Bellarmine had written of the grace of the Holy Spirit as the "soul" of the Church. But his definition of the Church had emphasized its "body," that is, its external nature. "Visibility," in opposition to the Reformers' "invisible" Church, had been the hallmark of Counter-Reformation ecclesiology. For Möhler, the interior life of the members of the Church generated in them by the Spirit through their participation in community with one another was the key to understanding the Church. Thus the Church was defined first of all by its "soul," not its "body," *ab internis* rather than *ab externis*.[11] His definition of the Church in his first book stood in sharp contrast to Bellarmine's: "Because the

---

[8] Ibid., 116f.

[9] Ibid., 117.

[10] Johann Adam Möhler, *Unity in the Church or The Principle of Catholicism Presented in the Spirit of the Church Fathers of the First Three Centuries*, ed. and trans. Peter C. Erb (Washington, D.C.: Catholic University of America Press, 1996) 93.

[11] This was apparent even from the structure of Möhler's *Unity in the Church*. It was divided into two parts; the first and longer was entitled "Unity of the Spirit of the Church," while the second bore the title "Unity of the Body of the Church."

Spirit fills her, the Church, the totality of believers that the Spirit forms, is the unconquerable treasure of the new life principle, ever renewing and rejuvenating herself, the uncreated source of nourishment for all."[12]

Employing the model of a biological organism so dear to Romantic social theory, Möhler attempted to show how the external forms of ecclesiastical polity developed out of and gave expression to the growth of the community's internal life by tracing the development of the offices of bishop and metropolitan, the episcopal college, and finally papal primacy as necessary crystallizations of internal needs of the community. All these developments are the work of the Spirit: "On the one hand, the need for a bishop is brought about by the Holy Spirit and, on the other, this need is satisfied by the same Holy Spirit."[13] Whereas in his early essays and reviews he had described the evolution of Church offices as an unfortunate necessity brought about by the cooling of the primitive community's ardor over time, in *Unity in the Church* Möhler stressed that these offices and structures were concrete expressions of the community's love and desire for union. It is noteworthy, however, that he traced the Church's polity to the action of the Spirit through the Church's history and not to the will of Christ expressed at the community's founding.

By 1832, when he published *Symbolism,* the book for which he was best remembered throughout the rest of the nineteenth century, Möhler had moved to a quite different ecclesiological position. *Unity in the Church* had been strongly influenced by the great Reformed theologian Friedrich Schleiermacher (1768–1834). Over the course of the seven years which separated it from the first edition of *Symbolism,* Möhler had critically distanced himself from Schleiermacher, first in trinitarian theology, then in theological anthropology and the understanding of the relationship of grace and nature. *Symbolism* sparked a debate with several distinguished Protestant scholars, most notably Ferdinand Christian Baur (1792–1860). This debate caused Möhler to refine and clarify his positions further in the four subsequent revised editions which followed. As he matured his thought in these other areas, he found that his ecclesiology necessarily altered as well. He became increasingly concerned about finding a way to maintain the need for divine grace while asserting the reality of human freedom. The Reformers' inability to hold both these poles in tension was, he thought, the tragic root of Protestantism as a whole. Obviously, the Church is the great test case in which divine grace and human freedom meet. Möhler

---

[12] Möhler, *Unity in the Church,* 84.
[13] Ibid., 222.

was dissatisfied by his earlier pneumatocentric approach to understanding the Church because he had come to think that he had not sufficiently distinguished between the Spirit of God and the communal spirit *(Gemeingeist)* of the Church and that he had given too little scope to human freedom. He believed that he could better relate and distinguish both the divine and human elements in the Church by employing a christological model rather than a pneumatological one, so Möhler sought to build his ecclesiology on the base of the Chalcedonian formula for the incarnation. "Thus, the visible Church, from the point of view here taken, is the Son of God himself, everlastingly manifesting himself among men in a human form, perpetually renovated, and eternally young—the permanent incarnation of the same, as in Holy Writ, even the faithful are called 'the body of Christ.'"[14] Like the theologians of the Counter-Reformation, Möhler stressed the visibility of the Church in his treatment of the differences between Catholicism and Protestantism. Unlike his predecessors, however, he did not so much defend the legitimacy of institutional forms and ecclesiastical offices as to insist on the continuous presence of the incarnate Christ in history.

> By the Church on earth, Catholics understand the visible community of believers, founded by Christ, in which, by means of an enduring apostleship, established by him, and appointed to conduct all nations, in the course of ages, back to God, the works wrought by him during his earthly life, for the redemption and sanctification of mankind, are, under the guidance of his spirit, continued to the end of the world.[15]

Möhler is significant in the history of ecclesiology for three reasons. First, his early Spirit-centered understanding of the Church, although largely forgotten in the nineteenth century, did have an influence in the twentieth century, most notably on Yves Congar. Second, his mature incarnation-centered ecclesiology was an important moment in the recovery of the image of the Mystical Body of Christ for the Church; one can see its effect on Pius XII's *Mystici corporis*. But third and most importantly, the development of his ecclesiology in interaction with his christology and theological anthropology gradually affected the way in which subsequent theologians understood the Church. After him, the

---

[14] Johann Adam Möhler, *Symbolism: Exposition of the Doctrinal Differences Between Catholics and Protestants as Evidenced by Their Symbolical Writings,* trans. James Burton Robertson (New York: Crossroad, 1997) 259.

[15] Ibid., 258; the decision to translate Geist by the lowercase "spirit" rather than with a capital "S" was that of the nineteenth-century translator; it is—at least—debatable.

Church was no longer the bearer of the mystery of faith but was itself an aspect of that mystery. Ecclesiology grew from being primarily concerned with questions of institutional polity to treating of the Church's inner nature and external mission as a dimension of the economy of salvation.

Möhler's thought played a role in the ecclesiology of the influential Roman school. The principal figures of the school—Giovanni Perrone (1794–1876) and Carlo Passaglia (1827–87), their students Johannes Baptist Franzelin (1816–86) and Clemens Schrader (1820–75), and Franzelin's and Schrader's student Matthias Joseph Scheeben (1835–88)—were all, like Möhler, influenced by patristic study and sought to place the treatment of the Church within a wider systematic theology. Their common characteristic is the integration of the Church into a strongly incarnational and (especially with Scheeben) sacramental theological vision. This incarnational perspective allowed them to provide deep doctrinal grounds for the Church's institutional polity, which was a much greater concern for the Roman school than for the Tübingen theologians.

Drey, Möhler, and the other figures associated with the Catholic Tübingen school also played an important role in the recovery of a rich and nuanced notion of tradition. Möhler rejected the idea of a "two-source" theory of revelation, if that is understood to mean that Scripture and tradition each contain part of the deposit of revelation: "The Holy Scriptures are not thought of as something different from the living gospel, nor the living gospel, the oral tradition, as something different from the written Gospels, as a different source."[16] The deposit of faith was not to be regarded as a static set of doctrines and practices passed on from one generation to another, but rather as a "living gospel," a life-principle which grows and clarifies and is formed as the community grows. This was a shift from thinking of tradition as *tradita*, a content handed down from age to age, to *traditio*, an active transmission which is part of the living reality of the Church.

Typically the Tübingen theologians employed the model of organic life to describe tradition. In his idiosyncratic fashion, John Henry Newman (1801–90) contributed importantly to the renewal of tradition. Faced with the fact that no church in the nineteenth century simply corresponded point by point to the apostolic Church as described in the New Testament, he advanced his "hypothesis to account for a difficulty":[17] doctrine develops. But he avoided sweeping theories and

[16] Möhler, *Unity in the Church*, 114.
[17] John Henry Newman, *An Essay on the Development of Christian Doctrine* (Notre Dame, Ind.: University of Notre Dame Press, 1989) 30.

organic metaphors because of his keen awareness of the sheer abundance of historical data and their irreducible particularity which make of history "a vision to dizzy and appall."[18] He recognized the diversity of ways in which doctrine has developed and the variety of factors which have affected the transmission of the tradition. But precisely that hesitancy to advance a single embracing theory enabled him to perceive elements in the Church's life and the furtherance of its tradition which had been overlooked. Thus he recovered in a new and creative way the notion of the *sensus fidelium* as an element in the preservation and development of tradition and, based on patristic evidence, envisioned a lively interaction between the *ecclesia docens* and the *ecclesia discens*.[19] His rich and complex ecclesiological vision is best stated in the preface to the third edition of *The Via Media*, written in 1878. Describing the Church's mission as a continuance of the threefold mission of Christ —as priest, prophet, and king—Newman located the centers of energy of these three tasks in the local community, the theological schools, and the hierarchy respectively, and he maintained that they function best when in a creative tension with one another. Newman refused to reduce his theology of the Church to a formula or all-embracing system: "Whatever is great refuses to be reduced to human rule, and to be made consistent in its many aspects with itself."[20]

But a consistent Church polity was precisely what many sought in the wake of the upheavals of the French revolution and the Napoleonic era. The years between the Congress of Vienna (1815) and the mid-century were marked by efforts to reestablish and preserve a social and political system that would prevent the excesses which the revolutionary years had let loose. Ultramontanism was an attempt to ensure the unity and good order of the Church by creating a highly centralized, omnicompetent papacy exercising its authority through a hierarchical chain of command in which the bishops were the principal links. The

---

[18] John Henry Newman, *Apologia pro vita sua*, ed. Martin J. Svaglic (Oxford: Oxford University Press, 1967) 217.

[19] John Henry Newman, *On Consulting the Faithful in Matters of Doctrine*, ed. John Coulson (Kansas City, Mo.: Sheed and Ward, 1961) 106:

> I think certainly that the *Ecclesia docens* is more happy when she has such enthusiastic partisans about her as are here represented, than when she cuts off the faithful from the study of her divine doctrines and the sympathy of her divine contemplations, and requires from them a *fides implicita* in her word, which in the educated classes will terminate in indifference, and in the poorer in superstition.

[20] John Henry Newman, *The Via Media of the Anglican Church*, 3rd ed. (London: Longmans, Green, and Co., 1901) xciv.

papacy had emerged from the dark years of Napoleonic oppression with renewed prestige. Gallicanism, though not dead, had suffered a severe blow when Napoleon determined to establish a concordat with Rome over the heads of the French clergy and hierarchy. The movement now split by differing responses to the Civil Constitution of the Clergy (1790) into "juring" and "non-juring" parties. Gregory XVI (1765–1846; pope from 1831) and Pius IX (1792–1878; pope from 1846) were strong, determined, and, in the latter's case, charismatic leaders who centered decision-making in the papacy. Ultramontanism easily coalesced with a restorationist political agenda, as can be seen in the writings of Joseph de Maistre (1753–1821), Louis de Bonald (1754–1840), and François René de Chateaubriand (1768–1848). Often, especially in France, Ultramontane appeals to papal authority were intertwined with anti-rationalist traditionalism which insisted on the incapacity of the mind to attain certitude and its need for an infallible and permanent external guarantor of truth. Early in his brilliant and tragic career Félicité de Lamennais (1782–1854) was a defender of this kind of Ultramontanism, as was later Louis Veuillot (1813–83).

Although Vatican I (1869–70) is frequently treated today as an essentially reactionary and defensive moment in the history of the Church, the council brought together several strands of ecclesiological thought and produced the fullest specifically ecclesiological conciliar text prior to Vatican II. Certainly the Ultramontane elevation of the papal office played an important role both in the preconciliar preparations and at the council, and one of the shaping factors in the final declaration on papal primacy and infallibility was a desire on the part of the council finally to lay Gallicanism to rest. The Roman school's incarnational ecclesiology laid the theological groundwork and colored the actual language of *Pastor aeternus*, but unfortunately neither its patristic richness nor its systematic vision is reflected in the document. Although it is a testimony to the new position which ecclesiology had taken in Catholic theology that a conciliar document on the Church was regarded as necessary, what resulted was very different and very much more limited than what was originally planned.

The preconciliar commission had prepared two draft documents, one on the Church which also included a section on Church-state relations, and a second on the Roman pontiff which did not treat of infallibility. Both these draft documents drew heavily on the Syllabus of Errors (1864). Then it was decided to combine these two documents and to add a section on infallibility. Because some bishops argued that infallibility was a pressing issue, having been much discussed in the press prior to the council, two new schemas were produced. The first, *Pastor aeternus*, dealt with papal primacy and infallibility and the second with the Church as a whole. Since the council never reassembled after its first session, this second schema on the Church, which would have put *Pastor aeternus* into a larger context, was never discussed. Some members of the council feared that, by treating the pope in isolation from the college and the Church at large, the role and dignity of the episcopal office were undercut. In response to this additions were made to the draft noting explicitly that

> the power of the supreme pontiff by no means detracts from that ordinary and immediate power of episcopal jurisdiction, by which bishops, who have succeeded to the place of the apostles by appointment of the Holy Spirit, tend and govern individually the particular flocks which have been assigned to them.[21]

It should be noted that according to this conciliar statement bishops are divinely appointed successors of the apostles, although the "flocks" which they tend, that is, the actual extent of their jurisdiction, is assigned to them—presumably by the pope; the doctrine of Vatican II is foreshadowed here. Nevertheless it is undeniably and unfortunately true that the separation of the document on the pope from the treatment of the Church at large had the effect of seeming to place the pope apart from the episcopal college. So much attention was given to the definition of papal infallibility at the time of Vatican I and ever since that one may overlook the important statement that when the pope, addressing the whole Church, defines a doctrine of faith or morals *ex cathedra*, he speaks with "that infallibility which the divine Redeemer willed his church to enjoy in defining doctrine concerning faith and morals."[22] Thus infallibility is a grace, and its first recipient is the Church. The juridical tone of the definition and the absence of a full ecclesiological context have tended to obscure this. This juridical tone was in part due to the concern of Pius IX and others at the council to exclude Gallicanism finally and completely and led to the inclusion in the definition of the statement that those definitions proposed as infallible by the Roman pontiff "are of themselves, and not by the consent of the church, irreformable."[23] Unless this is correctly understood as a firm rejection of royal and episcopal Gallicanism, it can seem to make infallibility a personal charism of the pope rather than a divine gift to and for

---

[21] *Pastor aeternus*, c. 3; English translation, *Decrees of the Ecumenical Councils*, 2 vols., ed. Norman P. Tanner (London and Washington, D.C.: Sheed and Ward and Georgetown University Press, 1990) 2:814.

[22] *Pastor aeternus*, c. 4, 2:816.

[23] Ibid.

the Church which the Bishop of Rome, as head of the episcopal college, exercises on the Church's behalf.

From Vatican I to Vatican II (1870–1960)

The ninety years separating the two Vatican Councils are part of what has been called "the century of the church." To conclude this brief survey, we must notice three currents. (1) Neoscholasticism, which had emerged prior to Vatican I, became the main stream of Catholic theology with the encouragement of Leo XIII; it shaped the manuals from which many learned ecclesiology in the first half of the twentieth century. (2) The recovery of the image of the Mystical Body of Christ which had started with Möhler became the dominant motif within ecclesiology, thanks to Pius XII's *Mystici corporis*. But (3), in the wake of the Modernist disaster, reawakened biblical, patristic, liturgical, and ecumenical studies brought new or previously forgotten elements into Catholic thinking about the Church's nature and mission; these came to fruition in the years just before and during Vatican II and prepared the ground for the council's work.

Some nineteenth-century critics of modern philosophy (e.g., Matteo Liberatore [1810–92] and Joseph Kleutgen [1811–83]) had been convinced that post-Kantian epistemology offered no reliable ground for knowledge and therefore no sure footing for doctrine. They had urged a return to what they believed had been a medieval synthesis in which theology and philosophy had been allied in a truly fruitful way. This movement received papal support in the call of Leo XIII (1810–1903; pope from 1878) for a return to the thought of Thomas Aquinas as the reliable foundation for Catholic theology (*Aeterni Patris*, 1879). Neoscholasticism gave a new turn to ecclesiological trends which had already emerged in the decades prior to Vatican I. Gradually a standard apologetic line had emerged in the first half of the nineteenth century which demonstrated the necessity for a continuous authoritative witness to revelation from the desire of human beings for truth about our ultimate destiny and our moral duties. Thus the Church was shown to be the divinely willed witness corresponding to human hopes and needs. Unlike the earlier traditionalists who began by denigrating the capacity of human reason to arrive at any certainty about ultimate truths, the writers of neoscholastic theological manuals began with a natural theology which demonstrated that Christianity corresponds to human needs and hopes and so is the true religion. They then went on to show that Christianity requires an infallible teacher and so grounded the Church. Thus ecclesiology was placed within fundamental theology or apologetics. Dogmatic theology treated the structure of the Church, showing that it was a hierarchically structured visible society. True, the basis for this visible society was traced to the incarnation, and so the christological ecclesiology which had begun with the Tübingen school and continued in the Roman school was continued in the neoscholastic manuals. But the relationship between Christ and the Church was reduced to that of a founder to an institution, and the rich scriptural and patristic resonances of the Mystical Body ecclesiology were very muted.

A much richer development of the christological ecclesiology traceable to Scheeben and Perrone and ultimately to Möhler was to be found in *Mystici corporis* (1943), the encyclical of Pius XII (1876–1958; pope from 1939). The encyclical emphasized that the spiritual, charismatic community of grace and the institutional, hierarchically-ordered society are one and the same. In this, *Mystici corporis* was still in the line of Bellarmine and the Counter-Reformation theologians who had insisted so strongly on the identity of the "visible" and "invisible" churches. But Pius XII united the two through the image of the Mystical Body of Christ which, the encyclical maintained, cannot be thought of merely as a metaphor. The image of the body of Christ emphasizes the corporate unity of all the members of the Church with Christ and with one another in a real union which is mystical rather than physical. The body of Christ is the now-existing Roman Catholic Church, and only members of the Roman Catholic communion or those in some way ordered toward the Roman Catholic Church by desire, even if they do not know it, are members of the body of Christ (a position significantly altered by Vatican II two decades later.) The connecting links holding the body together are the pope and bishops; they are its first members, but all who assist them in their mission of spreading the kingdom of Christ—i.e., the laity—are members, too, albeit in subordinate positions.

On the one hand, Pius XII took up the incarnational theme which had been growing in importance among Catholic theologians for more than a century, protected it from some of the more extreme interpretations which later members of the Roman school had given it (e.g., those who literally extended the hypostatic union to all members of the body), and used it to bring together the two strands of ecclesiology, that which dealt with Church polity and that which sought to understand the Church in relation to other doctrines. His interpretation of the image of the Mystical Body, however, explained the image exclusively in terms of corporate societal unity and ignored contemporary biblical scholarship which placed the image within a context of the economy of salvation or sacramentality. Those contexts were to be developed much more fully in the years between World War II and Vatican II.

Catholic scholarship—biblical, historical, and theological—went through a traumatic experience at the beginning of the twentieth century. In the climate of suspicion and self-censorship which followed the condemnation of Modernism (1907), many young Catholic scholars looked to "safe" areas of research, fields like patristics and liturgical history which were less likely to incur ecclesiastical censures. Ironically, the results of this scholarship often prepared for Vatican II.

In ecclesiology the revival of patristic studies meant the recovery of images for the Church which complemented both hierarchical institution and body of Christ. Especially important for the Vatican II and the years following it was that of the Church as communion. Also patristic sources illuminated once again theological importance of the role of the bishop and of episcopal collegiality. Adding to this new context for ecclesiology were the remarkable results of the revival of liturgical scholarship. The historical, theological, and pastoral work of Lambert Beauduin (1873–1960), Romano Guardini (1885–1968), Odo Casel (1886–1948), and Joseph Jungmann (1889–1975), among others, made the liturgy into a *locus theologiae* once again and resuscitated in a new way the ancient principle that *lex orandi lex credendi*. At the same time, the striking development of Catholic biblical scholarship in the twentieth century, greatly encouraged by Pius XII's *Divino afflante Spiritu* (1943), immensely enriched ecclesiology by placing the Church within the encompassing frame of salvation history. The recognition of the distinction between the Church and the kingdom of God, often simply identified previously, and the gradual retrieval of eschatology—an almost totally neglected field within Catholic theology since the Reformation—caused a thorough revision of understanding of the Church's mission. This entailed reconsideration of the way in which the Church's structure was understood and gave needed theological support to the emerging lay movements before and after World War II. As regards systematic ecclesiology, Scripture and the Fathers both turned the attention of theologians to the role of the Holy Spirit and the gradual recovery of a pneumatological ecclesiology balancing and completing the dominant christological ecclesiology. New questions emerged as the place of the Church in the system of doctrines was considered; for example, the trinitarian question of the relationship in the economy of salvation of the missions of the Son and the Spirit, and the eschatological question of the relation of the Church to the kingdom.

Increasingly, in the years prior to Vatican II, the theme of salvation history and the image of the Church as sacrament intertwined in ecclesiology. These were important elements in the work of theologians in the years prior to Vatican II—some of the most prominent being Marie-Dominique Chenu (1895–1990), Henri de Lubac (1896–1991), Karl

Rahner (1904–84), Yves Congar (1904–95), and Edward Schillebeeckx (1914–)—who made enormous contributions to rethinking the nature, mission, and structure of the Church and who played important roles at the council.

Theologians after the Council of Trent had insisted that one cannot separate the invisible Church of engraced believers from the visible Church of established forms. In the nineteenth and twentieth centuries theologians sought to hold united the charismatically gifted assembly of God's people with the hierarchically structured historical institution founded by Christ. In the seventeenth and eighteenth centuries there had been differing positions about leadership and authority in the Church culminating at the Vatican Council I in the decisive supremacy of the papacy. Ninety years later on the eve of the Vatican Council II it was clear that the role of the episcopacy needed to be reconsidered and the balance between Rome and the local churches had to be righted. Early in the nineteenth century systematic ecclesiology had been born as theologians tried to discern how the doctrines of the Trinity and the incarnation, of grace and human freedom, could be harmonized with their understanding of the Church. By the 1960s the question would be how to hold together the Spirit-filled community with the Church founded by Christ and continuing his work. Gradually, as theologians took greater account of biblical and historical data and simultaneously became more aware of the full import of the nineteenth-century recognition that the Church is an aspect of the saving Mystery of God's self-gift, they came to see that there has never been and can never be one ecclesiology, any more than there has been or ever can be a single theology or christology. Mysteries preclude finished and absolute formulation. There must always be images and models of the Church held in creative tension with one another. As *Lumen gentium* was about to teach, "the inner nature of the church is revealed to us through a variety of images."[24]

---

[24] *LG*, 1, 6; English translation, *Decrees of the Ecumenical Councils*, 2:851.

For Further Reading

Aubert, Roger. "Le géographie ecclésiologique au XIXe siècle." *L'Ecclésiologie au XIXe siècle.* Ed. Maurice Nédoncelle, 11–55. Paris: Éditions du Cerf, 1960.

Congar, Yves. "L'ecclésiologie, de la Révolution française au Concile du Vatican, sous le signe de l'affirmation de l'autorité." *L'Ecclésiologie au XIXe siècle.* Ed. Maurice Nédoncelle, 77–114. Paris: Éditions du Cerf, 1960.

_____. *L'Église de saint Augustin à l'époque moderne.* Paris: Éditions du Cerf, 1970.

Fries, Heinrich, and Georg Schwaiger, eds. *Katholische Theologen Deutschlands im 19. Jahrhundert.* 3 vols. Munich: Kösel-Verlag, 1975.

Himes, Michael J. *Ongoing Incarnation: Johann Adam Möhler and the Beginnings of Modern Ecclesiology.* New York: Crossroad, 1997.

Iserloh, Erwin, ed. *Katholische Theologen der Reformationszeit.* 5 vols. Münster: Aschendorff, 1984–88.

Jedin, Hubert, ed. *History of the Church.* 10 vols. New York: Crossroad, 1981.

Pottmeyer, Hermann Josef. *Unfehlbarkeit und Souveränität: Die päpstliche Unfehlbarkeit im System der ultramontanen Ekklesiologie des 19. Jahrhunderts.* Mainz: Matthias-Grünewald-Verlag, 1975.

Schoof, T. M. *A Survey of Catholic Theology 1800–1970.* Trans. N. D. Smith. New York: Paulist Newman Press, 1970.

Swidler, Leonard. *Aufklärung Catholicism: 1780–1850: Liturgical and Other Reforms in the Catholic Aufklärung.* Missoula, Mont.: American Academy of Religion, Scholars Press, 1978.

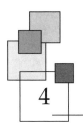

The Significance of
Vatican Council II for Ecclesiology

4

Joseph A. Komonchak

Ecclesiology, "talk about the Church," is usually considered to be a reflective discipline that makes the Church the object of inquiry and discourse. But there is another sense that can be given to the term "Church-talk," namely, the type of talk that makes the Church come to be in actuality. Thus, there is the proclamation of the gospel of Jesus Christ on the part of a preacher, and there is the "Amen" of faith, the fundamental genesis of the Church described in 1 John 1:1-4. Then there is the "we-language" which expresses the communion established among believers and between them and God, and there are the terms they use in speaking to and about one another, terms like brothers and sisters, father and children, etc. There also are the words they use of themselves: *"ekklesia"* (assembly), *"koinonia"* (communion, fellowship), *"congregatio fidelium"* (gathering of believers), "household of faith," etc. Finally, there are the terms which they use to describe the origin, nature, and purpose of their community: "People of God," "body of Christ," "temple of the Spirit," "bride of Christ," etc. All of this "Church-talk" expresses and mediates a community-consciousness in the everyday world, that is, a sense of what brings Christians together and makes them one, distinguishes them from other human groups, describes their relations with God and with one another, and orients them in the world. This first level of "Church-talk" might be called an implicit, lived ecclesiology, the living reality and sense of being the Church that is the subject on which the discipline of ecclesiology reflects critically and systematically.

A history of ecclesiology, then, cannot be solely a history of the reflective discipline, valuable as this is. It must also be a history of the first-level consciousness of the Church, of how Christians have understood and articulated their common lives and realized their mission in the successive worlds and in face of the historical challenges these posed. The life of the Church, its self-realization, is, therefore, a primary datum for the historian of ecclesiology.

All this is also true of the Second Vatican Council and of its significance for ecclesiology. The council is, of course, immensely important for what it said, for the sixteen documents it produced, all of which, Karl Rahner said, have to do with the Church.[1] But the council was also an event in the history of the Church, unusual in two senses: first, simply because ecumenical councils are relatively rare events, and, second, because the council represents a watershed event in the modern history of the Church. We will, therefore, have to consider the council under both respects, as a historic moment in the Church's self-constitution and as an expression of the Church's reflective self-consciousness.[2]

Preconciliar Catholicism and Its Ecclesiology

In his opening address to the council,[3] Pope John XXIII had a paragraph that is useful for interpreting the historic significance of the council. He said that in his daily ministry he often had to listen to people "who see only ruin and calamity in the present conditions of human society. They keep repeating that our times, if compared to past centuries, have been getting worse." On such people, who, he said, have not learned much from history and idealize the past, the pope added his judgment: "We believe We must quite disagree with these prophets of doom who are always forecasting disaster, as if the end of the world were at hand." The pope invited the bishops instead to consider that human society might be "entering a new order of things" and to have confidence in "the mysterious plans of divine Providence which through the passage of time and the efforts of men, and often beyond their expectation, are achieving their purpose and wisely dispos-

---

[1] Karl Rahner, "The New Image of the Church," *Theological Investigations,* vol. X (New York: Herder and Herder, 1973) 3.

[2] For the dialectic of experience, event, and documents at Vatican II, see Maria Teresa Fattori and Alberto Melloni, eds., *L'evento e le decisioni: Studi sulle dinamiche del Concilio Vaticano II* (Bologna: Il Mulino, 1997); John W. O'Malley, *Tradition and Transition: Historical Perspectives on Vatican II* (Wilmington, Del.: Michael Glazier, 1989).

[3] The official Latin text may be found in *Acta Apostolicae Sedis* 54 (1962) 786–95; a reconstruction of the textual history and variants of the speech is offered in Giuseppe Alberigo and Alberto Melloni, "L'allocuzione Gaudet Mater Ecclesia di Giovanni XXIII (11 ottobre 1962)," *Fede tradizione profezia: Studi su Giovanni XXIII e sul Vaticano II* (Brescia: Paideia, 1984) 187–283; an English translation is available in Walter M. Abbott, ed., *The Documents of Vatican II* (New York: America Press, 1966) 710–9.

ing of all things, even contrary human events, for the good of the Church."

Pope John was here critical of an attitude that has been described as "Catholic catastrophism," the view that the development that led to distinctive features of modernity was one long apostasy of Western society and culture from the ideal once achieved in medieval Christendom. The repudiation of Christ's reign, it was thought, had begun with the Reformation's destruction of the religious unity of the West, had then been spread into the realm of intellectual culture by the Enlightenment, and then through a series of revolutions had subtracted from the control and even the influence of Christ and his Church the realms of economics, politics, and culture. From the time of the French Revolution until the eve of Vatican II, this negative judgment, which at times, as the pope noticed, was even expressed apocalyptically, dominated official assessments of modernity given by popes and bishops.

This attitude not only determined the general interpretation of the modern world, but also provided the basic ideological justification for the construction of modern Roman Catholicism in the face of an apostate world. In its articulation of the ancient faith this distinctively modern form of Catholicism stressed the dogmas that stood in greatest contrast to the errors and heresies of modernity—original sin, the atonement, and the right of Christ to rule over society and culture. It encouraged devotions that would provide a popular reinforcement of this faith—the Immaculate Conception, the Sacred Heart of Jesus, the kingship of Christ. On the level of everyday social organization, it encouraged the multiplication of distinctively Catholic associations and movements to solidify a sense of identity among Catholics, to immunize them from contamination by the world, and to mobilize and energize them to restore the world to Christ. On a larger level, it promoted uniformity in the Church and an increasing centralization of authority in Rome by means of an exaltation of the person and role of the pope whose high-point was the definitions of papal primacy and infallibility at the First Vatican Council. The result was a distinctive Catholic subsociety whose ideology and organization reinforced one another.[4]

This new social form of Catholicism was justified by the ecclesiology that prevailed between the two Vatican Councils. It concentrated on the societal nature of the Church, that is, that Christ had established a visible institution of salvation with structures of juridical authority concentrated on the pope. A demonstration was offered that this was the one, holy, catholic, and apostolic Church founded by Christ and,

---

[4] See Joseph A. Komonchak, "Modernity and the Construction of Roman Catholicism," *Cristianesimo nella Storia* 18 (1997) 353–85.

according to his promise, still existing in the world and identifiable in the Roman Catholic Church. The only true members of this Church were those who were joined by the externally verifiable criteria of profession of the faith, sacramental participation, and subordination to rightful authority. The whole approach was institutional: the identification of the "one true Church," the distribution of authority, and the duties of submission to the hierarchy. The purpose of such treatises on the Church was to legitimize the solidly organized and ideologically self-confident institution that now lived in an apostate world.[5]

This vision of the Church and its effective expression in the life of the Catholic Church dominated in Roman circles right down to the eve of the council. When Pope John entrusted to a theological commission the preparation of texts for the Vatican Council II, it was natural for the commission to believe its purpose was to prepare documents that would simply repeat and reinforce the attitudes and strategies typical of modern Roman Catholicism, particularly as they had been articulated by the modern popes. Assuming that its role was primarily the defense of the faith against modern errors, the Theological Commission composed a set of documents that drew in large part upon the chief doctrinal interventions of the previous century and a half: the Syllabus of Errors (1864), Vatican I (1870), the condemnation of Modernism (1907), and the encyclicals of Pope Pius XII, particularly *Humani generis* (1950), so recently critical of what was disparaged as the "new theology."[6]

The Drama of the Council and the Need for a Renewed Ecclesiology

Among these official texts was one on the Church, which consisted of eleven chapters.[7] The first two established the institutional character of the Church and the visible criteria for membership. The next two

[5] For a good description of ecclesiology at the beginning of Vatican II, see Yves Congar, "Situation ecclésiologique au moment de 'Ecclesiam suam' et passage à une Église dans l'itinéraire des hommes," *Le Concile de Vatican II: Son Église, Peuple de Dieu et Corps du Christ* (Paris: Beauchesne, 1984) 7–32; Joseph A. Komonchak, "Concepts of Communion, Past and Present," *Cristianesimo nella Storia* 16 (1995) 321–40.

[6] See Joseph A. Komonchak, "The Struggle for the Council during the Preparation of Vatican II (1960–1962)," *History of Vatican II*, vol. 1, ed. Giuseppe Alberigo and Joseph A. Komonchak (Maryknoll, N.Y.: Orbis Books, 1995) 227–96.

[7] The text may be found in *Acta Synodalia Sacrosancti Oecumenici Concilii Vaticani II*, vol. 1:4 (Typis Polyglottis Vaticanis, 1971) 12–91.

were devoted to the episcopate and, although they were expected to balance the papally focused texts of Vatican I, they at every point reinforced papal prerogatives. A chapter on the laity reflected recent theological developments and the increasing role assigned to "Catholic Action." After a chapter on the religious life, largely devoted to vindicating their juridical place in the Church, two chapters addressed what was described as the crisis of authority in the Church. A chapter on Church and state repeated the modern "thesis" of the special favor that must be assigned to the Catholic Church. A chapter on the Church's missionary activity concentrated on the Church's right to evangelize. A final chapter on ecumenism concentrated on individuals and on their "return" to Mother Church and set out restrictive rules for common worship.

Three months before the council opened, the first set of texts for discussion (not including the draft on the Church, which was not yet finished) were sent out to the bishops. A number of bishops and their theological consultants began to express fears that the doctrinal texts would fall far short of the three purposes Pope John had assigned to the council: spiritual renewal, pastoral updating, and ecumenical unity. Several important cardinals registered these complaints strongly to the pope. It is likely that he was replying to these concerns when in his opening address he said that the council was not called simply in order to repeat what was already known but rather to preserve and to promote the Church's heritage faith in a pastorally effective way so as to meet the demands of the day. The council would refrain from condemnations and seek to correct error by "the medicine of mercy," that is, by a positive presentation of the faith. In a typically tactful way, Pope John was outlining a conciliar agenda quite different from the one reflected in the prepared texts and in effect authorizing the bishops, should they agree, to choose another direction for their work.

The bishops accepted the challenge. They overwhelmingly approved a draft-text on the liturgy which called for significant reforms over which local and regional episcopal bodies would have important responsibility. They were so critical of the doctrinal text On the Sources of Revelation that they were asked to vote on whether to retain it as the base text. Sixty-one percent of the bishops voted against the text, which Pope John then ordered withdrawn from the floor and remanded to a mixed commission for revision. These two votes revealed that the conciliar assembly shared the pope's vision and desired to produce texts that would authorize a serious review of the Church's pastoral activity and would state the faith in a language and with emphases quite different from those that had characterized the magisterial teaching of the previous century.

Meanwhile, the official text on the Church had been finished and distributed to the bishops. While the assembly was debating the other texts, efforts had already begun to prepare an alternate text. By the time Cardinal Ottaviani, head of the preparatory theological commission and now of the conciliar doctrinal commission, introduced the official text, the drama of the first session of the council had already been played out, and the few days of debate devoted to this document had an anticlimactic air; Ottaviani, and everyone else, knew that the text on the Church would also have to be significantly altered.[8]

The whole council, but particularly its first session, was the Church-in-act, and on the existential and historic level, important events were underway. On the structural level, there was a changing of the guard: those who had been at the margins during the preparation of the council were now replacing as leaders of the council those who had controlled the preparation. Bishops who had been expected obediently to follow the until-now normal direction of the central Roman authorities were now acting collegially and with a new sense of their own responsibility. And they had made it clear that what they wished to do and to say was often dramatically different in style, method, language, and substance from the mental attitudes, pastoral strategies, and creedal emphases that had marked modern Roman Catholicism. This ecclesiology-in-act displayed in the experiences and decisions of Vatican II required a cor-responding ecclesiology-in-theory.[9]

The conciliar process and the texts it produced were made possible by a series of theological and pastoral developments that had made their way, not without difficulty and opposition, in the decades before the council.[10] On the level of theological scholarship, we might point here to the biblical renewal which, after having been nearly smothered by the anti-Modernist reaction, had been re-animated by Pius XII's en-cyclical *Divino afflante Spiritu* (1943), to the recovery of the deep and rich Catholic tradition in the ages of the Fathers and the great medieval

[8] See Joseph A. Komonchak, "The Initial Debate about the Church," *Vatican II commence . . . Approches francophones,* ed. Étienne Fouilloux (Leuven: Bibliotheek van de Faculteit der Godgeleerdheid, 1993) 329–52; Alberto Melloni, "Ecclesiologie al Concilio Vaticano II (autunno 1962–estate 1963)," *Les commissions conciliaires à Vatican II,* ed. M. Lamberigts et al. (Leuven: Bibliotheek van de Faulteit Godgeleerd-heid, 1996) 91–179.

[9] For the drama of the first session of the council see Giuseppe Alberigo and Joseph A. Komonchak, eds., *History of Vatican II,* vol. 2 (Maryknoll, N.Y.: Orbis Books, 1998), especially, for the debate about the Church, 281–357.

[10] See Stanislas Jaki, *Les tendances nouvelles de l'ecclésiologie* (Rome: Herder, 1957); Avery Dulles, "A Half Century of Ecclesiology," *Theological Studies* 50 (1989) 419–42.

theologians, and to the reconstruction of the Church's liturgical tradition. On the level of the Church's life, we might invoke the liturgical renewal, the ecumenical movement, and the rethinking of the Church's relationship to the modern world reflected in Catholic action movements that inspired a theology of lay people, in efforts to elaborate theologies of history and of terrestrial realities, and in long-resisted attempts to reconceive and reform relations between Church and state. As might be expected, there was a dialectical relationship between what was happening on the level of Church life and what was being thought out on the level of scholarship and reflective theology.

In the course of these developments, fuller notions of the Church began to be elaborated and to demand a place in ecclesiology alongside the dominant institutional emphases. The late nineteenth and early twentieth centuries saw the recovery of the notion of the Church as the Mystical Body of Christ, endorsed and elaborated in the encyclical *Mystici corporis* (1943). The two decades before the council witnessed the emergence of the notion of the pilgrim People of God and the spread of the idea of the Church as sacrament. The relationship between Eucharist and Church, the subject of important historical studies, was also a major theme in liturgical theology. Ecumenically inspired investigations drew attention to the relations between Word and sacrament and between Scripture and tradition, to the problems of authority, and to the eschatological dimensions of the Church. The place and role of lay people was studied in terms both of their participation in the inner life of the Church and as bearers of the Church's mission in the world.

It was the small place of these notions in the official draft on the Church prepared for Vatican II that led to the general disappointment with the text. The redactional history that resulted in *Lumen gentium* and the other major ecclesiological texts of the council is largely the story of the effort to integrate the recent developments into a statement of the Church's awareness of itself.[11]

The final texts of Vatican II differ in genre, purpose, and doctrinal authority; they were elaborated over four years, during which the mind of the council itself developed; on many important subjects the council decided not to try to settle legitimately disputed theological questions but simply to set forth the elements that must be kept together, perhaps even in tension, and in the stating of these the council, as was centuries-old conciliar practice, worked by compromise and

---

[11] The best history of *Lumen gentium* remains Antonio Acerbi, *Due ecclesiologie: Ecclesiologia giuridica ed ecclesiologia di comunione nella "Lumen Gentium"* (Bologna: Dehoniane, 1975).

conciliation toward the greatest consensus possible. For all these reasons one should not expect to find a definitive and systematic treatise on the Church in the conciliar documents. An ecumenical council is not a theological seminar.

In the following analysis, I will identify major areas in the council's ecclesiology and explain their significance with regard to (1) developments beyond preconciliar emphases and (2) fruitfulness in the postconciliar period.

Basic Theological Notions of the Church

Some interpreters claim that there is no single ecclesiology in the council but only a variety of images or models of the Church. The council does, no doubt, employ many images; in fact, it devotes one paragraph to several biblical images and another to the development of the Pauline notion of the body of Christ (LG 6–7). On a more reflective level, the first chapter of *Lumen gentium* is devoted to the Church as mystery, and here the notions of "Church as sacrament" and as *communio* in the divine life are introduced; the second chapter discusses the Church as the People of God; and with the third the text turns to differentiations among the members of the Church, beginning with the hierarchy. This variety has led some people to speak of several distinct conciliar ecclesiologies and others to identify a single underlying notion that would capture the essence of Vatican II's view of the Church, some opting for "People of God," others for *"communio,"* and so forth.

The reason for the variety of images is to be found in the council's choice of a more biblical, patristic, and liturgical language. Images, precisely because of their concreteness, cannot be integrated as such. Integration can take place on the level of reflection or theory, but this too the council did not seek to achieve, being content with descriptive exposition rather than synthetic explanation. Notions such as "mystery," "communion," "sacrament," "body of Christ," "People of God," "temple of the Spirit," and so forth were introduced as a theme seemed to require. The council sought to set out the elements of the Church's life but it left it to theologians to construct a synthesis of them. These elements are many, but the council's ecclesiology includes them all and is, therefore, single in intention.

More unfortunate is the claim sometimes made, implicitly or explicitly, that one must choose among the conciliar notions. Thus one sometimes hears the suggestion that "People of God" and "body of Christ" are incompatible. Initial enthusiasm for "People of God," criticized as overly sociological or "democratic," has yielded lately to "communion" as the key conciliar idea, better able to set out the Church's dimensions of mystery. To make such choices is to betray the council's intentions and teaching. In explaining the structure of *Lumen gentium*, the doctrinal commission explained that with chapter two, "The People of God," the council was continuing the exposition of "The Mystery of the Church" begun in chapter one; only whereas the first chapter had discussed that mystery in the divine plan from creation to consummation, the second chapter would take up the same mystery in the time between ascension and parousia, that is, in history. A single mystery was being unfolded, first in its transcendent and then in its historical dimensions, and the commission had broken the material up into two chapters simply because a single chapter would be too long.[12]

Rather than thinking that a distinct ecclesiology flows from each of the major notions, this comment invites us to explore which dimensions of the one Church each concept expresses. A particularly important observation on this point is given in LG 8, where the council sets out the constitutive elements of the Church that a theological vision must integrate. It is at once a community of faith, hope, and love and a visible structure, a hierarchical society and the Mystical Body of Christ, a visible group and a spiritual community, existing on earth and endowed with heavenly gifts. These notions, which could be put in parallel columns, do not describe two distinct things but "a single complex reality composed of a divine and a human element." As in christology the systematic task is set by the attribution of both the divine and the human to "one and the same Jesus Christ," so ecclesiology attempts to understand the presence of both elements in the Church. To sacrifice or to ignore one or the other is to eliminate the mystery. Particular notions more fully than others illuminate one or another of the constitutive elements, but an integral ecclesiology must include them all.

Where Is the Church?

The council provides an answer to this question on three levels, all of which advance in significant ways beyond the common preconciliar ecclesiology. The easiest way to answer the question is to identify its members, who belong to the Church. The preparatory text on the Church, echoing a long tradition from Robert Bellarmine to Pius XII's *Mystici corporis*, had defined "true" members as those joined by the bonds of the external profession of the faith, the reception of the sacraments, and

---

[12] *Acta Synodalia Sacrosancti Concilii Oecumenici Vaticani II*, vol. 3:1 (Typis Polyglottis Vaticanis, 1973) 209–10.

submission to authority, particularly that of the pope. Since only Roman Catholics fulfilled all these criteria, it was possible for this draft, in answer to a second level of the question, simply to identify the Church of Christ with the Roman Catholic Church.

In the course of the conciliar discussions, however, it became clear that this was too simple an answer. Merely external criteria, which may suffice for some apologetical purposes, leave out of consideration the inner elements that constitute and animate the Church. Things are more complex when genuine faith, hope, and love, and the Spirit's grace that makes them possible, are taken into account. For, on the one hand, these gifts can be found outside the Catholic Church; on the other hand, they are not enjoyed by all Catholics. In addition, important constitutive features of the Church, such as the Holy Scriptures, the central creed, the sacraments, the apostolic ministry, are found in greater or less degree among non-Catholic churches and communities. The living body of Christ, then, cannot simply be identified with the Catholic Church.

On the first level of our question, then, a more flexible language had to be found than that of membership. The council chose instead to speak of degrees of communion with the Church. It began with full incorporation into the society of the Church which is enjoyed, it said,

> [by] those who, possessing the Holy Spirit, accept its entire organization and all the means of salvation established in it and within its visible structure are joined to Christ, who rules it through the Supreme Pontiff and the Bishops, by the bonds of the profession of faith, the sacraments, ecclesiastical governance, and communion (LG 14).

According to these last criteria, only Catholics can enjoy this full incorporation, but according to the first and most important of them, the life of the Spirit, not all Catholics are fully incorporated.

Lesser degrees of communion are then described in the following paragraph, which speaks of non-Catholic Christians, who enjoy a genuine but imperfect communion based upon an impressive set of elements found among them: the Scriptures, faith in God and Christ, union with Christ through baptism, other sacraments, the episcopate, the Eucharist, devotion to the Blessed Virgin, communion in prayer and spiritual blessings, a true union in the Holy Spirit, and martyrdom (LG 15). When the council considered non-Catholic Christian churches and communities in the Decree on Ecumenism *(Unitatis redintegratio),* it made the even stronger statement that

> some, even very many, of the most important elements or goods by which, taken together, the Church is built up and given life can exist

outside the visible boundaries of the Catholic Church: the written word of God, the life of grace, faith, hope, and charity and other inner gifts of the Holy Spirit, and visible elements.

In addition, the text went on, "more than a few of the sacred actions of the Christian religion are carried out among our separated brethren," actions that "can really generate the life of grace and must be said to be able to provide entrance into the communion of salvation" (UR 3).

These powerful and generous statements explain why, on the second level of our question, the council could not be content with a simple identification of the Church with the Catholic Church. Instead, making a significant change in the verb employed, the council said: "This Church [of Christ], established and organized as a society in this world, *subsists in* the Catholic Church, governed by the successor of Peter and by bishops in communion with him, even though many elements of sanctification and of truth are found outside its visible structure" (LG 8). The doctrinal commission explained that it had replaced the verb "is" (used in earlier drafts) with the term "subsists in," not because of a deep philosophical concept of "subsistence," but simply because the latter was a more appropriate phrase, given the council's affirmations, in the texts cited above, of the existence of ecclesial elements in other Christian communities.[13] A unique claim is being made, of course, of the Catholic Church, one that is explained in *Unitatis redintegratio* 3, where the council says that "it is only in the Catholic Church of Christ, the common help to salvation, that can be found all the fullness of the means of salvation." The council's claim, the concrete meaning of the "subsists in" formula, is that the means of salvation Christ wishes his Church to have—the Scriptures, the creed, the sacraments, the ministries—are found in their totality only in the Catholic Church. The claim remains a strong one and defines the object of ecumenical dialogue ever since the council as Catholics and other Christians discuss their differences over these various means of salvation and in particular whether they are all willed by Christ.

There remains a third level at which the question "Where is the Church?" can be asked. It concerns the relationship between the one

---

[13] "'Subsists in' is used here so that the phrase may better correspond to the statement that elements of the Church are present elsewhere"; *Acta Syndolia*, vol. 3:1, 177. The non-technical character of "subsists in" is revealed by the synonyms used in the doctrinal commission's explanation of the term: *"adest"* (is present) *"invenitur"* (is found). For the interpretation of the phrase, see Johannes Willebrands, "Vatican II's Ecclesiology of Communion," *Origins* 17 (1987) 27–33; Francis A. Sullivan, *The Church We Believe In* (New York: Paulist Press, 1988) 23–33.

universal Church and the many local or particular churches. For many centuries ecclesiology had developed in a universalistic perspective, perhaps above all because it devoted so much attention to the universal authority of the pope and because of the worldwide missionary expansion of the Church from Europe which not infrequently took the Western shape of the Church to be normative. The result, both in theory and in practice, was a highly centralized and uniform vision of the Church.

Three developments before the council began to qualify some of the assumptions of this view. The first was increased respect for the diverse cultures to which missionary efforts were directed, along with efforts by the popes to promote an indigenous clergy so that as missionary lands achieved political independence the Church would not be considered a foreign body. Second, conversations with the Orthodox East yielded a new appreciation of the diversity of spiritual, liturgical, and theological traditions within the one Church. Third, both theological scholarship on the relation between the Church and the Eucharist and liturgical emphasis on the role of the eucharistic assembly discovered points of contact with the eucharistic ecclesiologies of the East.

All of these movements concentrated attention on local realizations of the Church both in the form of the individual worshiping assembly and in distinct broad traditions of Church life. The conciliar texts reflected these developments and provided the basis for one of the most remarkable features of postconciliar ecclesiology, the new emphasis placed upon the local church.[14] Once again, one may not expect to find in the texts of Vatican II a full and coherent theology of the local Church, as is clear already from the inconsistency of its vocabulary. The council referred to both "local" and "particular" churches, but the referent of these terms (diocese, rite, patriarchal church, local congregation) varies from text to text.

A first dimension of the local churches is liturgical. The council stated that "the chief manifestation of the Church occurs in the full and active participation of the whole holy People of God in the same liturgical celebrations, particularly in the same Eucharist, in common prayer, at the same altar at which the bishop, surrounded by his presbyterate and ministers, presides." Local eucharists, as in parishes, "rep-

---

[14] See Jean-Marie Tillard, *Église d'Églises: L'ecclésiologie de communion* (Paris: Éditions du Cerf, 1987); Jean-Marie Tillard, *L'Église locale: Ecclésiologie de communion et catholicité* (Paris: Éditions du Cerf, 1995); Joseph A. Komonchak, "The Local Church and the Church Catholic: The Contemporary Theological Problematic," *The Jurist* 52 (1992) 416–45; Patrick Granfield, "The Priority-Debate: Universal or Local Church," *Ecclesia Tertii Millennii Advenientis: Omaggio al P. Angel Antón* (Casale Monferrato: Piemme, 1997) 152–61.

resent the visible Church established throughout the world" (SC 41–42). That this manifestation or representation is to be taken in a strong sense is indicated in LG 26:

> This Church of Christ is truly present in all legitimate local assemblies of the faithful, which, linked with their pastors, are themselves called Churches in the New Testament. For in their localities, these assemblies are the new People called by God in the Holy Spirit and in much fulness (see 1 Th 1:5). In them the faithful are gathered by the preaching of Christ's Gospel and the mystery of the Lord's Supper is celebrated "so that the whole fellowship is joined together through the flesh and blood of the Lord's body." In every altar-community, under the bishop's sacred ministry, is made manifest the symbol of that charity and "unity of the mystical body without which there can be no salvation." In these communities, although they be often small and poor and scattered, Christ is present by whose power the one, holy, catholic and apostolic church is brought together.

In these texts the particular, necessarily local, eucharistic assembly is described as an event of the one and catholic Church, whose whole mystery, generated out of the word of God and the sacrament, is realized there.

A similar focus is revealed in the Decree on the Pastoral Office of Bishops *(Christus Dominus)*, which offers a definition of the diocese that sees it as more than a merely administrative subdivision of a worldwide organization:

> A diocese is a portion of the People of God which is entrusted for shepherding to a bishop in cooperation with the presbyterate so that, united to their pastor and gathered by him into one flock in the Holy Spirit, they may constitute a particular Church in which is truly present and at work the one, holy, catholic and apostolic Church of Christ (CD 11).

That here, once again, the whole mystery of the Church is realized in the diocese is made clear in the very important statement found in *Lumen gentium:*

> The Roman Pontiff, as the successor of Peter, is the perpetual and visible principle and foundation of unity both of the bishops and of the multitude of the faithful. Individual bishops are the visible principle and foundation of unity in their own particular Churches, which are formed in the image of the universal Church and in and out of which the one and unique catholic Church exists (LG 23).

Two important statements are made here, in apparent tension with one another. On the one hand, the individual churches are said to be "formed in the image of the universal Church;" on the other, this latter is said to exist "in and out of" the individual churches. From the first statement it is clear that the individual local churches are not something distinct from the universal Church but represent it, realize it, bear its image in the sense that what makes the one Church the Church makes them churches. From the second statement it is clear that the universal Church is not something distinct from the individual churches but exists only in them and out of them. As Henri de Lubac said, apart from the individual local churches, the universal Church is only an *ens rationis,* an abstraction.[15] Taken together, the two statements represent one of the most important ecclesiological teachings of Vatican II, and a good deal of postconciliar reflection has been devoted to exploring it and its implications.

When this new orientation is taken seriously, attention focuses on the concrete circumstances in which the one Church comes to be and to act in and out of the many local churches. These are briefly alluded to in a number of paragraphs of the conciliar texts, particularly in its Decree on the Missionary Activity of the Church *(Ad gentes),* where the challenge of the Church's becoming genuinely at home in the various cultures of the world is described.[16] Such passages have inspired the considerable literature on inculturation and on local theologies that has been published in the decades since the council.

Such passages require that the catholicity of the Church be given concrete meaning. Once again the council led the way:

> This mark of universality which adorns the People of God is the gift of the Lord himself by which the Catholic Church effectively and constantly strives to recapitulate all of humanity with all its gifts under the headship of Christ and in the unity of his Spirit. In virtue of this catholicity, the individual parts bring their own gifts to the other parts and to the whole Church so that the whole and the individual parts grow through the mutual communication among all and their common desire for fullness in unity (LG 13).

Catholicity here appears as "fullness in unity," the fullness reflecting the many gifts given to the individual churches, the unity expressing and realizing the divine plan to bring scattered humanity back into unity under Christ and in his Spirit. This deep notion of catholicity is reflected later on in the same text when the council at once praises the diversity of discipline, liturgical usages, and theological and spiritual

---

[15] Henri de Lubac, *The Motherhood of the Church* (San Francisco: Ignatius Press, 1982) 207–8.

[16] See especially AG 4, 8, 15, 22.

patrimonies found in varied "matrices of faith" such as the ancient patriarchates, and insists that "this variety of local Churches, together aspiring to unity [*ecclesiarum localium in unum conspirans varietas*], more clearly demonstrates the catholicity of the undivided Church" (LG 23).

The Common Responsibility

The first draft on the Church, after initial chapters on the nature of the Church and on membership, had turned at once to its hierarchical structure. Before a revised draft was submitted to the second session of the council, it had been decided to place a chapter on the People of God before it entered upon differentiations within the Church. The doctrinal commission explained that this chapter focused on the whole body of believers, clergy, religious, and laity, to whom all that it said in its continued meditation on the mystery applied. If this explanation can prevent an understanding of the term "People of God" that applies it solely to the laity, it remains that this placement draws attention to another of the main contributions of Vatican II's ecclesiology, that the building up of the Church and the fulfillment of its mission in the world is the work of the whole body of believers. Historically, of course, this meant a rehabilitation of the laity, much neglected in typical preconciliar textbooks, which, as Yves Congar often commented, tended to turn ecclesiology into "hierarchology," treatises on the hierarchy.

Among the developments that led the council to this expanded vision was, first, the liturgical movement whose efforts Vatican II endorsed when it set down a primary intent of its Constitution on the Liturgy:

> Mother Church greatly desires that all the faithful be led to that full, conscious, and active participation in liturgical celebrations that is demanded by the nature of the liturgy itself and for which the Christian people, "a chosen race, a royal priesthood, a holy nation, a people God has purchased" (1 Pt 2:9; see 2:4-5), have a right and duty in virtue of their baptism (SC 14).

This was an important recognition that it is the whole community of faith that is the subject or agent of worship, so that the laity are not to be conceived as merely passive recipients or observers of liturgical actions performed by the clergy.

This particular application to the liturgy rests upon a more general statement:

> The chosen People of God is one: "one Lord, one faith, one baptism" (Eph 4:5); there is a common dignity as members deriving from their

rebirth in Christ, a common grace that makes them children [of God], one salvation, one hope and undivided charity. There is, therefore, no inequality in Christ and in the Church on the basis of nationality, social condition or sex, because "there is neither Jew nor Greek, slave nor free-man, male nor female. For you are all *one* in Christ Jesus" (Gal 3:28; see Col 3:11).

If all in Church do not walk along the same path, all are called to holiness and have received an equal faith in the righteousness of God (see 2 Pt 1:1). Although by Christ's will some are established as teach-ers, dispensers of the mysteries and pastors for others, still there is among all an equality in dignity and in the activity common to all the faithful with regard to the building up of the Body of Christ (LG 32).[17]

Within the Church this grounds the set of fundamental rights and duties of all Christians which have since been enshrined in the Code of Canon Law.[18] But these rights and duties do not mark only the inner life of the Church. The laity also have an apostolate, defined as "participa-tion in the saving mission of the Church," and to it, the council says, they "are commissioned by the Lord himself through baptism and con-firmation" (LG 33). To this sacramental call the Decree on the Aposto-late of the Laity *(Apostolicam actuositatem)* adds a charismatic basis:

From the reception of these charisms, even the simplest ones, arises the right and duty of any believer to exercise them in the Church and in the world for the good of men and for the building up of the Church, in the freedom of the Holy Spirit "who breathes where he will" (Jn 3:8) and at

[17] See also AA 2:

As in the structure of a living body no member is merely passive but shares both in the life and the activity of the body, so in the Body of Christ, which is the Church, the whole body "makes bodily growth when each part is work-ing properly" (Eph 4:16). Indeed, such is the connection and linkage of mem-bers in this body that a member which does not work according to its ability toward the growth of the body must be said to be useless to the Church and to itself. In the Church there is a diversity of ministry but a unity of mission.

[18] See *Codex Iuris Canonici*, canons 208–23. The only right mentioned in the concil-iar documents that is not included here is the one stated in the Decree on the Apos-tolate of the Laity *(Apostolicam actuositatem)* 3: "From the reception of these charisms, however simple they may be, there arises for every believer the right and duty to exercise them." This may be the place to recall what Pope John Paul II said in the apostolic constitution, *Sacrae disciplinae leges,* with which he promulgated the new code. After noting that the code is an effort to translate Vatican II's ecclesiology into canonical language, he said: "If, however, it is impossible to translate perfectly into canonical language the conciliar image of the Church, nevertheless the Code must always be referred to this image as the primary pattern whose outline the Code ought to express insofar as it can be by its very nature."

the same time in communion with his brethren in Christ, especially with his pastors (AA 3).

These vindications of the co-responsibility of all members of the Church have had their effect in the opening of new opportunities for lay people in the liturgy, in catechesis, and in the governance of the Church. While this is certainly a welcome realization of the council's intentions, the focus of the conciliar texts on the laity lies rather on their role in the world. This is clear in the very effort of the council, in LG 31, to provide a typical description of the layperson that would go beyond the banal sociological definition of them as all those who are not clergy or religious. Their basic Christian dignity is described when the council calls them Christians

> who, as incorporated into Christ by their baptism, constituted as the People of God, and made sharers in their own way in the priestly, prophetical, and royal office of Christ, have their own role to play in the mission of the whole Christian people in the Church and in the world.

But what is distinctive about the laity is their "secular character," that is, that they live their Christian lives and undertake their Christian responsibilities in the world as, typically, married and employed in secular occupations.

> It is there that they are called by God to exercise their own role, led by the spirit of the Gospel, working from within, like a leaven, for the sanctification of the world, and thus, especially by the witness of their lives, faith, hope, and love, they reveal Christ to others.

The council here places the distinctive and irreplaceable role of the laity in their daily efforts to redeem society, culture, and history. It is, in turn, precisely as those engaged in this activity in the world that they also have a right and duty to bring their experience and the wisdom gained in it as their necessary contribution to the inner life of the Church.

This effort to validate and encourage the participation of all in the life and work of the Church at all levels was reflected in the council's call for co-responsibility and for the establishment of structures to enable it. Thus, on the parish level, the council called for structures, such as parish councils, through which the laity could exercise their right, and even their duty, to make known their views on matters concerning the good of the Church (LG 37). Similarly, on the diocesan level, it endorsed senates or councils of priests and pastoral councils composed of priests, religious, and laity (CD 27). Finally, with regard to the governance of the whole Church, the council sought to restore a greater sense

of the collegial character of the episcopate, that is, of the common responsibility for the whole Church of the whole body of bishops, carried
out both by the faithful fulfillment of their responsibilities in their individual dioceses and by such forms of collective responsibility as episcopal conferences and the Synod of Bishops.

Once again, these emphases on participation and co-responsibility
reflect the council's renewed interest in the local churches in which the
mystery of the Church is realized. It does not see the Church as a vast
multinational religious corporation with central headquarters in Rome,
branch offices in major cities, and retail shops in parishes. The gathering of the People of God into communion in the mystery of God takes
place locally as the word of God is preached and faith is generated, as
the power of the Spirit renews hope, as the love of God creates love for
God in return and love of the brethren, as this new people, so defined
and so constituted, realizes an at least partial transformation of the world
in which it arises. Within this process there are different responsibilities,
variously grounded in the sacraments (baptism, confirmation, orders)
and in special gifts or charisms; but all make the Church come to be
and all help it to make a difference in the world. The Church that comes
from the Holy Trinity *(Ecclesia de Trinitate)* is the Church that arises
from among human beings *(Ecclesia ex hominibus)*; the one Church
whose constitutive principles make up the universal form of the churches
is the Church that arises in and out of the many local churches.

Primacy and Collegiality

Circumstances prevented the Vatican Council I, after its definition
of the jurisdictional primacy and of the infallible exercise of the teaching office of the pope, from moving on to a discussion of the role of
bishops. From the beginning it was expected that Vatican II would attempt to provide this necessary complement. The difficulty of this task,
which made the history of the third chapter of *Lumen gentium* one of
the most controversial in the whole course of Vatican II, lay, first, in the
need fully to respect the teaching of Vatican I and, second, in the fact
that between the two councils the papal role and an accompanying
mystique of the papacy had grown to such an extent that the impression could be gained that the whole Church was personified in the
pope and that its governance was a Roman monopoly.

The teaching of Vatican II, in LG 3, begins with the clear statement
that its teaching on the episcopate will be set out as a continuation of
the teaching of Vatican I on the governance and teaching authority of
the pope, which it again proposes for belief (LG 18). Paragraphs follow
on Christ's gathering of the apostles and on the continuation of their

ministry in their successors, the bishops. The important statement is then made that the three offices of the bishop (teaching, governing, and sanctifying) are radically communicated by episcopal ordination, an effort to overcome the dichotomy suggested by the common preconciliar teaching that only the third of these was communicated by the sacrament of orders while the first two were the result of papal delegation. The necessary unity with the pope this theory wished to defend was instead stated by the council in terms of "hierarchical communion with the head and members of the college" (LG 21). The three episcopal offices are later described at some length (LG 25–27).

The college of bishops embodies and makes still present the college of apostles represented by the Twelve. The council used a nontechnical and rather elastic notion of this "college." That the successors of the apostles constitute a "stable body" was proved by history, as in the ancient forms of communion among the bishops and with the pope, the holding of regional and general councils, the emergence of patriarchates, and, more recently, the establishment of conferences of bishops (LG 22–23). The delicate task the council faced was that of defining the authority of the episcopal college in such a way as not to infringe upon the primatial role of the pope. Rather than offering a speculative resolution of the difficulty, the council was content to set out the terms that any such theory must take into account (LG 23–24). On the one hand, the pope has "full, supreme, and universal power over the Church, which he may always freely exercise." On the other hand, "the order of bishops, . . . in union with its head, the Roman Pontiff, and never without this head, is also the subject of full and supreme power over the whole Church, a power which can only be exercised with the consent of the Roman Pontiff." During and after the council, theologians and canonists have debated how to reconcile and synthesize these two statements, which the council was content simply to state as the terms of the debate. These theoretical debates have been matched on more practical levels by discussions and even controversies about the relative authority of the pope, individual bishops, and regional forms of collegiality, such as episcopal conferences. As the council itself did not settle the theoretical debates then, so also its teachings, by themselves, do not provide answers to the practical controversies since. The chief challenge, then as now, is to reconcile the demands of unity and the requirements of diversity.

During the council, Joseph Ratzinger acutely distinguished two ways of approaching the question.[19] The one that came to dominate in

---

[19] Joseph Ratzinger, "Die bischöfliche Kollegialität nach der Lehre des Zweiten Vatikanischen Konzils," *Das neue Volk Gottes: Entwürfe zur Ekklesiologie* (Dusseldorf: Patmos, 1970) 184–7.

the modern era is universalistic and conceives the governance of the Church on the model of a central administration, monarchical under papalism, more corporate under one modern view of collegiality. The other view, typical of patristic ecclesiology, focuses on the realization of the full mystery of the one Church as a communion of the many local churches, and so derives the theology of the ministries of unity in the Church from a theology of communion rather than vice versa. Both views were represented in the debates on primacy and episcopacy and in the final texts of the council, and they continue to be defended today.[20]

The Church and the World

The council did not entitle its pastoral constitution The Church in the World, but The Church in the *Modern* World. With this effort, the council sought to provide general principles and guidelines for the task that Pope John XXIII had challenged it to undertake: to take a new look at the world in which the Church now lived, to offer an evaluation of its strengths and needs, to examine the appropriateness to this world of its pastoral attitudes, strategies, and institutions, to reform what was no longer appropriate, and to be willing at once to learn from the world even as it sought to teach it. The result was *Gaudium et spes*, the text in which, more than any other, the council agreed to follow the Pope in his rejection of "the prophets of doom."

The document begins with an expression of the Church's solidarity with "the joys and hopes and the sorrows and anxieties of people today" and then sets out upon an analysis of the strengths and weaknesses of the social and cultural transformations underway. The Church is now living in a more dynamic world, marked by the effort to increase human control over nature and "to establish a political, social and economic order that will be of ever greater service to people and will help individuals and groups to affirm and cultivate their own dignity" (GS 6–9). It is within this movement of conscious effort to transform and to direct human history that *Gaudium et spes* sets out the Christian understanding of the human person, the human community,

---

[20] See also Hervé Legrand, "Collégialité des évêques et communion des Églises dans la reception de Vatican II," *Revue des Sciences Philosophiques et Théologiques* 75 (1991) 545–67; for an example of the practical debates, see Joseph A. Komonchak, "The Roman Working Paper on Episcopal Conferences," *Episcopal Conferences: Historical, Canonical, and Theological Studies,* ed. Thomas J. Reese (Washington, D.C.: Georgetown University Press, 1989) 177–204.

and human history in order then to discuss the Church's task in the modern world (chs. 1–4). While sociologically informed, the approach has as its theological basis a christological anthropology nicely summed up in the statement that "it is only in the mystery of the Incarnate Word that the mystery of the human being is truly made clear" (GS 22). The intent throughout is to correct mistaken modern tendencies, found among both believers and unbelievers, to counterpose the sovereignty of the Creator and the self-responsibility of individuals and groups, what might be called their created autonomy. The classic Christian doctrine of freedom, sin, and redemption is here extended beyond the individual to include the collective human self-project.

There are at least two respects in which the method and the content of *Gaudium et spes* are significant for ecclesiology. The first is on the level of ecclesiology as lived, the basic attitudes and strategies that define the Church's activity in the world. Following Pope John's lead, the council largely refrained from the suspicious, negative, and defensive posture that had marked the Catholic subculture before; instead, it adopted a method of dialogue reflecting its judgment that the Spirit of God is not absent from modern developments (see GS 26) and enabling it to describe in paragraph 44 what the Church can learn from the world. While generally positive and hopeful, the presentation is not, as some would later complain, "naively optimistic"; it does not refrain from often quite critical remarks on imbalances and failures in the modern world and on the mistaken views of God and of humans that frequently lie behind them. But its response was a positive and confident statement of what the Church has to offer both through its message about Christ and through its own life of faith, hope, and love.

A particularly controversial example of the change in theory and practice that the council adopted is found in its teaching on religious freedom. As late as the mid-1950s, indeed even in the official schema on the Church prepared for the council, the ideal relation between Church and state was presented as one in which the Catholic Church is established as the official state religion, the state supports it financially and juridically, and the state may use its coercive power to prevent or to restrict the public activities of other religious bodies. The most that could be allowed would be "toleration" of mistaken religions in order to preserve public peace. Efforts to revise this theory and the corresponding practice were consistently resisted.

In its Declaration on Religious Freedom *(Dignitatis humanae)*, the council dethroned the preconciliar ideal. It asserted the right to religious freedom both of individuals and of religious bodies on the basis of the dignity of the human person, the freedom of the act of faith, and the juridical incompetence of the state in religious matters. While it did not utterly reject the possibility of a confessional state, this would have to allow other religions something more than mere "toleration," namely, genuine religious freedom and an equal share in the state's support. The freedom of the Church would be guaranteed in general constitutional and statutory guarantees of religious freedom. Paul VI put it well at the end of the council when in his remarks to leaders of governments he replied to his own question: "What does the Church ask of you? It asks only for freedom, the freedom to believe and to preach its faith, the freedom to live and to bring its message of life to people."[21] With this teaching, as some remarked at the time, the Church was leaving "the age of Constantine."

On the level of reflective ecclesiology, the method and teaching of *Gaudium et spes* are significant because they require that a theology of the Church include, and not simply as an afterthought, a consideration of the Church in the world. Certainly, an ecclesiology will have to consider the formal constituents of what *Lumen gentium* called "the image of the universal Church," that is, the generative principles, divine and human, that make the Church the distinctive reality that it is. But just as individuals become Christians in the concrete circumstances and under the concrete conditions that define and distinguish their particular lives, so the Church is never generated except in particular places, at particular times, and in face of particular historical challenges. The Church never comes to be except in the world, which means, of course, that the churches never come to be except in their particular worlds. In the concrete genesis of the Church in the churches, the world does not appear at some second moment and, as it were, "out there," as the object of redemptive concern. The genesis of the Church is a moment in, a dimension of, the genesis of the world. Its very existence is supposed to make the world different.

It would be a mistake, then, to imagine a tension, much less a dichotomy, between the texts of the council that, to use a not entirely happy distinction made at the time, speak of the *Ecclesia ad intra* and those that speak of the *Ecclesia ad extra,* to contrast a theological to a sociological or historical approach to the Church, or to divide the theological notions of the Church up between these two pretended oppositions. It is true, of course, that some notions direct attention more clearly than others to one or another of these dimensions, but it is a single dynamic historical agent that these dimensions constitute and these notions describe. The People of God that is the sacrament of Christ's redemptive presence in the world is the same Church that is

---

[21] See *Acta Apostolicae Sedis* 58 (1966) 10–11; Abbott, *Documents of Vatican II,* 729–30.

communion in the mystery of God, and the communion with God and among human beings that constitutes the Church's distinctive reality and that it celebrates in its central worship is what the pilgrim people are to bring to the world by proclaiming it in word and embodying it in life and service. The Church that the world needs is the Church that is most distinctively itself, and what distinguishes the Church is what most directly and immediately relates it to the world of human history. The mystery of the Church is realized in the history of the world.

For Further Reading

Acerbi, Antonio. *Due ecclesiologie: Ecclesiologia giuridica ed ecclesiologia di comunione nella "Lumen Gentium."* Bologna: Dehoniane, 1975.

Alberigo, Giuseppe, and Joseph A. Komonchak, eds. *History of Vatican II* (Maryknoll, N.Y.: Orbis Books, 1995– .

Antón, Angel. "Postconciliar Ecclesiology: Expectations, Results, and Prospects for the Future." *Vatican II: Assessments and Perspectives Twenty-five Years After (1962–1987)*, vol. I. Ed. René Latourelle (New York: Paulist Press, 1988) 407–38.

Baraúna, Guilherm, ed. *L'Église de Vatican II: Études autour de la Constitution conciliaire sur l'Église.* Paris: Éditions du Cerf, 1966.

Congar, Yves. *Le Concile de Vatican II: Son Église, Peuple de Dieu et Corps du Christ.* Paris: Beauchesne, 1984.

Kasper, Walter. "The Church as Communion: Reflections on the Guiding Ecclesiological Idea of the Second Vatican Council." *Theology and Church*, 148–65. New York: Crossroad, 1989.

McNamara, Kevin. *Vatican II: The Constitution on the Church. A Theological and Pastoral Commentary.* Chicago: Franciscan Herald Press, 1968.

Moeller, Charles. "History of *Lumen Gentium's* Structure and Ideas." *Vatican II: An Interfaith Appraisal.* Ed. John H. Miller, 133–52. Notre Dame, Ind.: University of Notre Dame Press, 1966.

O'Malley, John W. *Tradition and Transition: Historical Perspectives on Vatican II.* Wilmington, Del.: Michael Glazier, 1989.

Philips, Gérard. *L'Église et son mystère au IIe Concile du Vatican.* Paris: Desclée, 1967.

Rahner, Karl. "Basic Theological Interpretation of the Second Vatican Council." *Concern for the Church: Theological Investigations*, vol. XX, 77–89. New York: Crossroad, 1981.

_____. "The New Image of the Church." *Theological Investigations*, vol. X, 3–29. New York: Herder and Herder, 1973.

_____."The Sinful Church in the Decrees of Vatican II." *Theological Investigations*, vol. VI, 270–94. Baltimore: Helicon Press, 1966.

Ratzinger, Joseph. "The Ecclesiology of Vatican II." *Origins* 15 (1985) 370–6. This article also appears in *Church, Ecumenism and Politics: New Essays in Ecclesiology.* New York: Crossroad, 1988. 1–10.

Routhier, Gilles. *Le défi de la communion: Une relecture de Vatican II.* Montreal: Mediaspaul, 1994.

Tillard, Jean-Marie. *Église d'Églises: L'ecclésiologie de communion.* Paris: Éditions du Cerf, 1987.

_____. *L'Église locale: Ecclésiologie de communion et catholicité.* Paris: Éditions du Cerf, 1995.

Vorgrimler, Herbert, ed. *Commentary on the Documents of Vatican II.* 5 vols. New York: Herder and Herder, 1969.

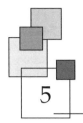

5 | The Ecclesiology of John Paul II

Avery Dulles

John Paul II, like Paul VI, is preeminently a pope of the Second Vatican Council, which he characterizes as "a providential event, whereby the Church began the more immediate preparation for the Jubilee of the Second Millennium" (TMA 18). As a young bishop, Karol Wojtyla participated energetically in all four sessions of the council. Of his twenty-three council interventions, six dealt with items that are treated in *Lumen gentium;* seven addressed topics pertinent to *Gaudium et spes*.[1]

As Cardinal Archbishop of Cracow, Wojtyla convened a Pastoral Synod involving the clergy and laity in the implementation of Vatican II. For the guidance of this synod he wrote a book, *Sources of Renewal* (Polish original, 1972),[2] which synthesizes the council's teaching with special reference to the consciousness of the Church. The Church's present self-awareness, he holds, is most fully expressed in two of the council's constitutions: *Lumen gentium,* which treats of the inner nature of the Church, and *Gaudium et spes,* which treats the Church in relation to the modern world. The latter constitution, says the Pope, complements the former.[3]

Cardinal Wojtyla's interpretation of Vatican II bears the imprint of his own personalistic phenomenology, which calls attention to personal subjectivity and the data of consciousness. The fundamental question to be answered by the council, Cardinal Wojtyla asserts, was: *"Ecclesia, quid dicis de teipsa?"* ("Church, what do you say of yourself?"). In requiring the Church to articulate its own identity, the council called for a new advance in ecclesial self-consciousness, corresponding to the

[1] These figures are my own, based on my study of the *Acta synodalia sacrosancti concilii oecumenici Vaticani II* (Vatican City: Typis polyglottis Vaticanis, 1970–77).

[2] Pope John Paul II, *Sources of Renewal: The Implementation of Vatican II* (San Francisco: Harper and Row, 1979).

[3] Ibid., 35.

present phase of human history. The Church, seen as the believing subject rather than simply the object of faith, is called to advance in maturity by taking personal responsibility for the faith it professes.[4]

Following the indications of Paul VI in his first encyclical, *Ecclesiam
suam,* Wojtyla makes the category of dialogue central to his understanding of the Church. The members are in dialogue with one another
and with God. Through a "dialogue of salvation," he asserts in *Sources
of Renewal,* the Church seeks to extend to all men and women the divine invitation to enter into a grace-filled communion with one another
and with the triune God. Conscious of the dignity of all human persons
and of the workings of grace beyond the visible borders of the Church,
Catholics are called upon to enter into dialogue with all groups of
people, believers and unbelievers, with full respect for the human personality and conscience of each individual.[5]

As pope, John Paul II has not issued any major documents on the
Church as such, but he has touched on aspects of the Church in many
of his important writings on missiology, ecumenism, priesthood, and
laity. He has dealt with ecclesiology most directly in the 137 catechetical lectures on the Church delivered at his weekly public audiences between July 1991 and August 1995.

The ecclesiology of John Paul II may perhaps be characterized in
terms of five familiar models: the Church as institution, mystical communion, sacrament, herald, and servant.[6] Elements of all five models
are present in the Pope's teaching, but with differing degrees of emphasis. In explaining what the Church is in itself, John Paul II attends
chiefly to its reality as communion, as institution, and as sacrament.
The remaining two models, however, are prominent in the Pope's treatment of the Church's mission to evangelize and to act as a leavening influence in secular society.

Church as Communion

John Paul II's preferred category for ecclesiology is evidently that of
communion. "The reality of the Church as communion," he writes, "is,
then, the integrating aspect, indeed the central content of the 'mystery,'
or rather, the divine plan for the salvation of humanity" (CL 19). A
communion, he explains, is more than a mere community. It cannot be
understood in merely sociological or psychological terms. Its bonds are

[4] Ibid., 38.
[5] Ibid., 29.
[6] Cf. Avery Dulles, *Models of the Church* (Garden City, N.Y.: Doubleday, 1974; expanded edition, 1987).

spiritual, since they arise from the Holy Spirit, who is poured forth on all the members. The Church may therefore be described as a community in which the members are brought into a supernatural relationship by their "reciprocal membership" in the body of Christ.[7] The supreme model for the Church, he explains, is the divine Trinity as a *communio personarum.*[8]

The foundations of this community were laid by Jesus Christ in his earthly life, when he molded his disciples into a community through their association with himself and with one another. This community began to pulsate with divine life after Pentecost, when the Holy Spirit came to animate it as a vital principle, a kind of soul. Already at Vatican II Wojtyla intervened to insist that the "Mystical Body of Christ is more than an image; for it is a determining aspect of Church's very nature under its Christological aspect and likewise under the aspect of the mysteries of the Incarnation and Redemption."[9] Although the Church in a mystical sense is the body of Christ, the term "body," suggesting organic unity, needs to be complemented by images of human society, which better indicate that the members preserve their distinct personalities. Thus the Second Vatican Council spoke especially of the Church as the People of God, God's household or family—images that reappear throughout the works of John Paul II.

Already in the Old Testament, the covenant between God and Israel established a quasi-familial relationship. This relationship is intensified under the "new and everlasting covenant" proclaimed at the Eucharist.[10] The image of God's household, according to the Pope, is fundamental:

> [This image] is in some way contained in all the others. It figures in the Pauline analogy of the body of Christ (cf. 1 Cor 12:13, 27; cf. Rom 12:5), to which Pope Pius XII referred in his historic encyclical *Mystici corporis.* It is also found in the notion of the people of God, to which the Council made reference. The Year of the Family is for all of us a call to make the Church ever more "the household of God, in which his family lives" (LG 6).[11]

[7] Pope John Paul II, *Sources of Renewal,* 120.

[8] Ibid., 121.

[9] *Acta synodalia* II/3, 857. This intervention was coauthored by Karol Wojtyla and John Jaroszewicz. See also John Paul II's General Audience talk of November 20, 1991, *L'Osservatore Romano* (English language edition), 25 November 1991, 3.

[10] Pope John Paul II, *Sign of Contradiction* (New York: Seabury Press/Crossroad, 1979) 25.

[11] John Paul II, Holy Thursday Letter "Priesthood and Pastoral Care of the Family," *Origins* 23 (March 31, 1994) 719–23, esp. 722.

In speaking of the Church as a people, family, or household, the Pope intends to accent the personal relationships by which it is constituted. What is distinctive to family relationships is the personal love and care extended to each member individually. Persons are not simply assigned to categories and treated as members of a class. The Church is a special kind of family because the members are bound together by a supernatural love that is poured into the hearts of the members by God. They love one another with a love that originates in the most holy Trinity.[12]

In his apostolic exhortation on Christian marriage, *Familiaris consortio,* John Paul II explores the analogies between the family and the Church. The Christian family, he says, is a "Church in miniature *(Ecclesia domestica)."* It represents the Church and participates in her saving mission. Just as the Church is animated and held together by the Holy Spirit, so the Spirit gathers the members of the Christian family into a mysterious fellowship with one another and with Christ in the unity of the Church (FC 21). As a fruit and sign of the supernatural fecundity of the Church, the Christian family is "a symbol, witness, and participant of the Church's motherhood" (FC 49).

Because the Church arises out of the trinitarian communion and brings its members to participate in that communion, the essential purpose of the Church must be understood in terms of its vertical relationship with God. Already at Vatican II, in a written communication of the fall of 1963, Bishop Wojtyla insisted upon this dimension, which he illustrated with references to John 17:18-19 and Eph 5:25-27. He went on to speak of the universal call of all members of the Church to holiness. The evangelical counsels, he said, ought to be explained in such a way that they may be seen as relevant to all Christians, not simply to those in the consecrated life. "Life in the spirit of the evangelical counsels is recommended by Christ to the faithful living in this age according to the circumstances of each person's state, so as best to attain their supernatural end."[13]

At times John Paul II expresses the finality of the Church in christological terms. "The Church wishes to serve this single end: that each person may be able to find Christ, in order that Christ may walk with each person the path of life" (RH 13).[14] Christ is the way of the Church, and the Church, from this point of view, is the community of disciples "each of whom in a different way—at times very consciously and con-

[12] General Audience of January 15, 1992, *L'Osservatore Romano* (English language edition), 22 January 1992, 11.
[13] *Acta synodalia* II/4, 341.
[14] See Pope John Paul II, *Sources of Renewal,* 66.

sistently, at other times not very consciously and very inconsistently—
is following Christ. This shows also the deeply 'personal' aspect and
dimension of this society" (RH 21).

In *Sources of Renewal* Cardinal Wojtyla devotes some ten pages
(189–200) to the holiness of the Church. Expressed by the term "communion of saints," holiness is the fundamental basis on which the
People of God is formed. Holiness is always personal; it is a response to
the divine gift of grace; and it finds in Christ its source and model. The
holiness of the Church on earth is imperfect; it is a vocation and aspiration rather than an achieved reality. Yet we find it realized in remarkable purity by the saints and especially by Mary. In the heavenly
kingdom the holiness of the Church will find its fulfillment.

The Church as Institution

The institutional structures of the Church are secondary in the sense
that they are intended to preserve and promote communion. It could
not long survive as a large and expanding body of persons unless it
had definite doctrines and stable sacramental and ministerial structures. Already in his public ministry, Jesus began to initiate the disciples into characteristic forms of prayer and rituals of worship. He laid
the foundations of a hierarchical style of leadership under Peter and
the Twelve. The appointment of the Twelve, according to the Pope, has
an institutional character,[15] as do the rituals whereby members of the
Church are baptized, absolved of their sins, and nourished with the Eucharist. The sacraments as institutions belong to the Church's visible
order, but they also signify and communicate divine life, thereby pertaining to the invisible dimension of the mystery of the Church.[16]

In the course of his ministry as a bishop and as pope, John Paul II
has had much to say about the episcopate and the papacy, which he describes as belonging to the hierarchical constitution given to the Church
by its divine founder. While recognizing the institutional responsibilities of the pope as successor of Peter and of bishops as successors of the
apostles, John Paul II frequently emphasizes the communal and spiritual dimensions of ecclesiastical office.

John Paul II speaks of the papal office in terms of his own ministry.
He is deeply conscious of his high responsibilities as Vicar of Christ for
the universal Church. Like Peter, he finds himself in need of conversion

---

[15] Pope John Paul II, *Jesus, Son and Savior: A Catechesis on the Creed,* vol. 2 (Boston: Pauline Press, 1996) 373–7.

[16] Ibid., 378–83.

and forgiveness.[17] He recognizes that the Church will always suffer opposition and persecution. The pope, he says, must serve unity first of all by bearing witness to the truth—that is to say, Jesus Christ, the living Truth, who will always remain the vital force of the Petrine ministry.[18]

Bishops likewise, according to John Paul II, must be personally responsive to the mysterious presence of Christ that they are mandated to communicate to their churches. "Bishops," he writes, "must become men of creative coordination because they are the 'meeting point' of Christ and the Church."[19]

As a participant in all the assemblies of the Synod of Bishops from 1969 through 1977, Cardinal Wojtyla became familiar with the problems of determining the precise meaning of collegiality. At the 1969 assembly he made an important speech that was designed to offset a movement that appeared to interpret collegiality as a restriction on the powers of the papacy. He insisted that collegiality and primacy, far from being opposed, sustain each other. Through their collegiate action the bishops come together to perfect and express their unity with one another under the presidency of the successor of Peter. In this way they give concrete form to the *communio* of their churches.[20] Again as Pope, in 1983, John Paul II pointed out that the primacy of the Bishop of Rome is at the service of the collegiality of the bishops, while their collegiality assists him in his primatial office.[21] Neither primacy nor collegiality can be rightly understood except in reference to the other.

Offices in the Church, as understood by John Paul II, are not ends in themselves. The sacred ministry is a gift or charism to be exercised for the benefit of others, thus upholding the Church in its complex diversity and helping to build it up in its fundamental reality as a *communio*.[22]

In the Church of our day, the relationships of the many local and regional churches to one another may be understood along the same

[17] Pope John Paul II, *Crossing the Threshold of Hope* (New York: Knopf, 1994) 8–14; see also *Ut unum sint* 4.

[18] General Audience of March 10, 1993, *L'Osservatore Romano* (English language edition), 17 March 1993, 11.

[19] Pope John Paul II, "Bishops as Servants of the Faith," *Irish Theological Quarterly* 43 (1978) 270–1.

[20] See Giovanni Caprile, *Il sinodo dei vescovi: prima assemblea straordinaria (11–28 ottobre 1969)* (Rome: Civiltà Cattolica, 1970) 121–2; also George H. Williams, *The Mind of John Paul II* (New York: Seabury Press, 1981) 228–9.

[21] John Paul II, "Ad Sodales Consilii Secretarii generalis Synodi Episcoporum," *Acta apostolicae Sedis* 75 (1983) 651.

[22] Pope John Paul II, *Sources of Renewal,* 137–40.

lines. As individuals in a family find themselves through mutual self-giving, so do the particular churches come to flower not by isolating themselves but by placing their distinctive gifts at the disposal of the other churches and of the Catholic Church in its entirety. *Communio* in this sense is the foundation of the Church's catholicity or universality.[23]

In the Church as a structured community the hierarchical leaders, succeeding to the office of the apostles, have the responsibility of maintaining unity and of discerning the authenticity of initiatives proposed or undertaken by the faithful. Charismatic gifts, which the Holy Spirit freely bestows upon all the members, are a benefit to the whole Church and must be acknowledged with gratitude. Claims to charismatic gifts, however, must be carefully scrutinized by those charged with pastoral leadership (CL 24).[24]

The institutional and the charismatic, therefore, are no more opposed to each other than are primacy and collegiality. Office does not take the place of charism or suppress it, but seeks to verify and foster the charismatic element in the Church. The institutional framework assists the charismatic element by preserving the space in which the charisms can effectively function; it also protects the faithful from being deluded by false claims to charismatic inspiration.

The Church as Sacrament

John Paul II's concern for the communal and institutional aspects of the Church should not be allowed to obscure the attention he has given to the third major aspect of the Church, that of being the sacrament of salvation. He frequently quotes from Vatican II's Constitution on the Church the statement that the Church is a kind of sacrament of the union of men and women with God and with one another in God (LG 1; cf. RH 3 and 18; D&V 63–4; CL 19). A sacrament by its nature is a visible and efficacious sign of an invisible grace. It confers grace precisely by signifying it. The Church as universal sacrament of salvation is both a visible sign and an efficacious instrument of the grace that saves and sanctifies men and women by bringing them into spiritual communion with God.

John Paul II explains the sacramentality of the Church in relation to the Holy Spirit and to Christ. In his encyclical on the Holy Spirit he writes: "The Church is the sign and instrument of the presence and

[23] Ibid., 136.

[24] For a discussion of criteria for evaluating charismatic gifts, see John Paul II's General Audience talk of June 24, 1992, *L'Osservatore Romano* (English language edition), 1 July 1992, 11.

action of the life-giving Spirit" (D&V 64). The term sacrament, he notes, is applied analogously to the Church as a whole and to the individual sacraments. "The Church is the visible dispenser of the sacred signs, while the Holy Spirit acts in them as the invisible dispenser of the life which they signify" (D&V 63).

In the power of the Spirit, Christ acts in the Church in such a way as to make it his own body (D&V 61). As the body of Christ, the Church is intimately united with its head, whom it visibly represents in the world. It carries on his work, or, more precisely, he continues to accomplish his work through it.

Just as Christ the head was prophet, priest, and king, so the Church carries on his work by exercising these three offices. By imprinting on the Church the features of his own threefold mission, Christ guides the supernatural development of the whole People of God.[25] The three offices of the Church, like those of Christ, interpenetrate, qualifying one another. The Church's prophetic work is priestly and royal; her priestly activity is prophetic and kingly; her royal functions are prophetic and priestly.[26]

As prophet, the Church speaks the message committed to her, so that those who hear her word hear Christ. She is, in a striking phrase of the pope, "the social subject of responsibility for divine truth" (RH 19). As priest, the Church continues his saving and sanctifying work, especially through the ministry of the sacraments, in which Christ himself is invisibly at work bestowing his graces. Especially through the Eucharist, the Church shares in the power of Christ's redeeming action (RH 20). Finally, as king the Church carries on the work of Christ in bringing creation into subjection to God, pressing forward to the day when God will be all in all. Paradoxically, it is through faithful service that the Church shares in the kingly function of Christ, who came not to be served but to serve (RH 21). Only Christ, says the Pope, is that king "whom to serve is to reign."[27] This glorious freedom shines forth in the martyrs, who most vividly live up to the Church's vocation to be a "sign of contradiction" (VS 93).

The sacramental representation of the Church is effected in different ways by the hierarchical priesthood and by the Church as a whole. Bishops and priests, in their different degrees, represent Christ by authoritatively proclaiming his word, presenting his offer of salvation, repeating his acts of forgiveness, and showing his loving concern for the flock to which they are called to give themselves. By the sacramental anointing of holy orders, the ordained ministers are configured in a

[25] Pope John Paul II, *Sources of Renewal*, 270.
[26] Ibid., 221.
[27] Ibid., 264.

new and special way to Christ the head and shepherd, so that they can act in his name and in his very person (PDV 15).

Ecclesial ministry, as we have already seen, is a means to an end. It achieves its purpose when the gifts of Christ are actively received by a process in which the whole body is built up in grace. In this receptive aspect, the Church may be understood as bride. Christ sanctified himself, according to Paul, so that he might present his bride to himself without spot or wrinkle (Eph 5:25-27). In its striving for holiness the Church seeks to follow in the footsteps of its most eminent member, Mary, the virginal bride who is fruitful as mother of all the faithful. With an explicit reference to the work of Hans Urs von Balthasar, John Paul II teaches that the Church has both an apostolic-Petrine dimension and a Marian dimension. Of the two, he says, the Marian dimension is the more fundamental and the more closely related to the purpose of the Church, which as we have said, is sanctification (MD 27).

The mystery and mission of the Church, according to John Paul II, shine forth with special brilliance in the consecrated life, which is deeply rooted in the example and teaching of Jesus (VC 1). The life of the counsels, present in the Church from the beginning, can never fail to be one of her essential and characteristic elements, for it expresses her very nature (VC 29; 105). Imitating the apostles, who left everything behind to be with the Lord and to serve the gospel, those who dedicate themselves through the profession of chastity, poverty, and obedience eloquently manifest the inmost nature of the Church as bride and her striving toward union with her one spouse (VC 3).

When speaking of the Church as sacrament, John Paul II emphasizes particularly the theme of reconciliation. The great reconciler, of course, is Christ, who was sent into the world "to reconcile to himself all things, whether on earth or in heaven, making peace by the blood of his cross" (Col 1:20). The Church carries on this ministry. She is the sacrament (i.e., the sign and means) of reconciliation in three principal ways. In the first place, she fulfills this role by her very existence as a reconciled community in which the walls of division between hostile groups have been broken down. Second, she is a sacrament of reconciliation insofar as she continues to proclaim the gospel of reconciliation to successive generations. And finally, she is a sacrament of reconciliation by her ministry of the sacraments, each of which, in one way or another, builds up the Church in unity. As the Church makes the sacraments, so too, conversely, the sacraments make the Church (R&P 11).

The name of reconciliation has come to be attached in a special way to the sacrament of penance, which brings sinful Christians back into communion with God through the Church. All the sacraments, however, are signs and instruments of reconciliation. Baptism, reenacting the death, burial, and resurrection of Christ, cleanses its recipients from sin and confusion, binding them together to form a reconciled people that represents Christ in a great variety of times and cultures. The Eucharist is the sacrament that most perfectly expresses and accomplishes the loving union that exists among the members, bringing them into the heart of the Mystical Body (R&P 27).

Necessity of the Church

The theology of John Paul II should be described not as ecclesiocentric but as christocentric. This difference appears in his discussion of salvation. "There is salvation," he writes, "only and exclusively in Christ. The Church, inasmuch as it is the body of Christ, is simply an instrument of salvation."[28] Later he writes: "People are saved *through* the Church, they are saved *in* the Church, but they are always saved *by the grace of Christ*."[29] Since there are many ways of being related to the Church, it is not unconditionally necessary for salvation that one be incorporated in the Church through formal membership.

In his *Sources of Renewal* Cardinal Wojtyla explains his interpretation of the teaching of Vatican II on this point. The council, he believes, taught the "objective necessity" of the Catholic Church for salvation, but balanced this doctrine by its recognition that the individual's relationship to the Church must be a matter of consciousness and choice. External membership and internal adherence do not automatically imply each other.[30] The council, as the Pope interprets it, allows for the possibility that some who are fully incorporated in an external way may lack inner adherence and the converse possibility that some who give no outward sign of being members of any religious community may be interiorly related to the Church in a salvific way. People's attitude toward moral values may express an aspiration toward God, even though they have not arrived at an explicit knowledge of God. Some theologians speak in this connection of "anonymous Christians."[31]

Aware of the complexity of the relationships to Christ and the Church, Vatican II carefully distinguished between those "belonging to the Catholic unity of the People of God" and those in one way or another "associated with it."[32] Catholics, non-Catholic Christians, Jews,

[28] Pope John Paul II, *Crossing the Threshold*, 136.
[29] Ibid., 140.
[30] Pope John Paul II, *Sources of Renewal*, 126–7.
[31] Ibid., 131.
[32] Ibid., 125.

Muslims, members of nontheistic religions, and persons without any religious affiliation are differently related to the Church. Those who lack the fullness of the means of salvation offered in the Catholic communion can be fruitfully related to the Church if they are not culpable for their separation. Vatican II, therefore,

> does not seek to obliterate the boundary between those who are related to the People of God and those who are not; but it defines the matter only as far as human judgment can reach, while leaving the verdict to God alone, who is the only *scrutator cordium* or searcher of hearts.[33]

Ecumenism

From what has been said it is evident that the mystery of the Church, as understood by John Paul II, is much larger than the visible structure of the Roman Catholic communion. Aware of the riches of other Christian traditions, he makes his own the saying of John XXIII: "What separates us as believers in Christ is much less than what unites us."[34] Although he seems optimistic about the possibilities of salvation of non-Catholic Christians, he does not look upon the existing divisions among the churches as acceptable. Expressing his deep commitment to the apostolate of Christian unity, in 1995 he published the first papal encyclical on the subject since Vatican II.

The title of the encyclical, *Ut unum sint* (That They May Be One), is taken from the prayer of Christ at the Last Supper (John 17:21). To the mind of John Paul II, that prayer makes it clear that ecumenism is a permanent priority of the Church, since the visible unity of Christians is emphatically the will of Christ. No Christian is justified in looking upon ecumenism as merely optional or as marginal to the mission of the Church. Divisions among the disciples of Christ are a scandal and a countersign because the Church by its very nature is a mystery of communion. It is a blessing, therefore, that the Holy Spirit has aroused in our century a vibrant ecumenical movement (UUS 1).

In his ecumenical theology John Paul II adheres to what may be called a *communio* model. Wherever there is faith or sacramental life, people are brought into that mysterious union that we have been describing as *communio*. All who believe in Christ and are baptized in his name exist in a measure of communion with one another, even though that communion may be imperfect. The task of the ecumenical movement is to recognize the *communio* that already exists and to foster its

---

[33] Ibid., 133.
[34] Pope John Paul II, *Crossing the Threshold*, 146; cf. UUS 20.

growth toward full communion in truth and charity (UUS 14), "which will be expressed in the common celebration of the Eucharist" (UUS 78). "The ultimate goal of the ecumenical movement is to reestablish full visible unity among all the baptized" (UUS 77). The catholic unity of the whole Church, understood in terms of *communio*, does not imply uniformity. As we have already noted, it allows for nondivisive differences and is in fact enriched by the complementary gifts of different cultural or geographical units.

The method of ecumenism, as described in *Ut unum sint*, is to build on the elements that the separated churches or communities have in common, to explore the potential of these common elements as a basis for closer unity, to identify limitations and distortions of the Christian message in particular ecclesial traditions, to reflect on the diverse gifts of each community, and to consider how these could be harmonized in a reunited Church. As a Roman Catholic faithful to the teaching of Vatican II, the Pope is of course convinced that the means of salvation instituted by Christ are not available in their totality except in Roman Catholicism (UUS 86; cf. UR 3). Other forms of Christianity are deficient to the extent that they lack some of these means—whether the full inheritance of apostolic doctrine, the fullness of sacramental life, or the fullness of the apostolic ministry. This does not mean that dialogue with other churches is simply a matter of persuading them to return to the Catholic fold. Through dialogue all the partners, including Roman Catholics, may come to recognize that they have committed sins against unity, and all may progress toward greater fidelity. The Pope does not hesitate to express his sorrow for the sins against unity committed by Catholics in times past (TMA 35; UUS 15, 88). Recognizing that the Holy Spirit has been active beyond the boundaries of Roman Catholicism, John Paul II favors an ecumenism of "mutual exchange" and "mutual enrichment" (UUS 87).

The ecumenical apostolate, as described by John Paul II, demands great faith and patience. It will take time for the resentments spawned by past brutalities to be healed. Theological dialogue must be preceded and accompanied by what this Pope, following Paul VI, calls a "dialogue of conversion," a dialogue of salvation and of charity (UUS 35). Admitting that the goal lies far beyond our human capacities, we must turn to the Lord in prayer. We can only dispose ourselves to receive the gifts which the Holy Spirit, in God's good time, may be pleased to confer.[35]

[35] Pope John Paul II, "Address for the Week of Prayer for Christian Unity" (1979) §2; text in Pope John Paul II, *Addresses and Homilies on Ecumenism 1978–1980* (Washington, D.C.: United States Catholic Conference, 1981) 7.

Evangelization

The ecclesiology of John Paul II is deeply influenced by his anthropology, which depicts the human person as constituting itself through action. The Church, analogously, constitutes itself by accepting and carrying out its divine mission to proclaim the gospel to every creature and to gather all peoples into communion with God and with one another.

On numerous occasions since 1983 John Paul II has called upon the Church to engage in a new evangelization—"new in its ardor, its methods, and its expression."[36] Seeking to offset a loss in interest in missionary outreach, he published in 1990 a major encyclical, *Redemptoris missio.* "I sense that the moment has come," he wrote, "to commit all of the Church's energies to a new evangelization and to the mission *ad gentes*" (RMis 3). The obligation to spread the gospel, he insisted, is essential to the mission of the Church as constituted by its divine founder. In answer to the question, "Why mission?" he replied that the love of Christ impels us to spread the knowledge and love of him who is our peace and who alone can deliver us from alienation, doubt, and the power of sin and death (RMis 11).

Echoing the thought of Paul VI, John Paul II maintains that evangelization is "the primary service which the Church can render to every individual and to all humanity in the modern world" (RMis 2). "No believer in Christ, no institution of the Church can avoid this supreme duty: to proclaim Christ to all peoples" (RMis 3).

Proclamation, which is the first priority of mission, is aimed at Christian conversion: "a complete and sincere adherence to Christ and his gospel through faith" (RMis 46). Since conversion takes individuals out of their isolation and brings them into the communion of the Church, it has a social dimension. Missionary activity in its ecclesial aspect involves the planting of young churches which themselves become centers of evangelization. Through these local churches the gospel becomes incarnated in a greater variety of cultures. The Church can be enriched by taking on forms consonant with the cultural traditions of different regions, but it must carefully assess to what extent these traditions are compatible with the objective requirements of the faith itself (RMis 53). As criteria for sound inculturation the Pope proposes compatibility with the gospel and communion with the universal Church (FC 10).

The *missio ad gentes* continues to be necessary and in fact takes on increased urgency in view of the mounting proportion of the human

---

[36] John Paul II, speech of March 9, 1983, at Port-au-Prince, Haiti, "The Task of the Latin American Bishop," *Origins* 12 (March 24, 1983) 661.

race who do not know Christ. Their number, says the Pope, has almost doubled since the end of Vatican II (RMis 3). Evangelization, therefore, must include a clear proclamation that salvation is offered to all in the name of Jesus, in whose name alone we can be saved (RMis 5; 44; cf. Acts 4:12). Even when evangelization does not achieve its desired fruit of faith in Christ, the Church may succeed in spreading certain gospel values, including "the rejection of violence and war; respect for the human person and for human rights; the desire for freedom, justice, and brotherhood; the surmounting of different forms of racism and na- tionalism; the affirmation of the dignity and role of women" (RMis 86). All of these objectives pertain to the worldwide mission of the Church.

In view of the mobility of peoples and the rapidity of communica- tions, the distinction between the *missio ad gentes* and the pastoral care of the faithful is less clear than in some previous centuries. Christian principles and values are in some degree known all over the world, but in many traditionally Christian countries, faith has grown cold. The "new evangelization" must therefore include redoubled efforts at reevangelization of people oblivious of their own Christian heritage. It must reach out to the new worlds of science, technology, and commu- nications that are opening up in every part of the world. Alluding to Paul's appearance at the cultural center of classical civilization, John Paul II calls for Christian proclamation in the modern "Areopagi," which are all too often antagonistic to the gospel (RMis 37–8).[37]

Interreligious Dialogue

As mentioned in the opening pages of this essay, John Paul II is con- vinced that the Church in our day must adopt by preference a dialogic style of discourse. It must treat other human associations with respect, seeking to propose the Christian message for free acceptance rather than to impose it by any kind of physical or psychological coercion. The Pope is strongly committed to the full implications of Vatican II's Declaration on Religious Freedom.

Turning to the theme of interreligious dialogue, the Pope calls at- tention to the teaching of the Greek Fathers that Christ has sown "seeds of the word" *(semina Verbi)* far and wide (RMis 55).[38] Faithful to the teaching of Vatican II that the Church respects all that is true and holy in other religions (NA 2), he exhorts Christians to seek out "rays of di- vine Truth" in the various religions of the world. He even speaks of a "common soteriological root present in all the religions" as a basis for

[37] See Pope John Paul II, *Crossing the Threshold*, 112.
[38] Ibid., 81.

respectful dialogue.[39] This soteriological foundation is of course much greater in religions that are theistic, and especially in Judaism, which rests upon the covenants given to Abraham, Moses, and David and the "rich heritage of the inspired prophets."[40]

Dialogue, however, is not an alternative to proclamation. On the contrary, sincere dialogue demands that the partners frankly declare their own convictions and seek to explain them in ways intelligible to their interlocutors. Dialogue, therefore, is one of the expressions of mission. "There must be no abandonment of principles nor false irenicism, but instead a witness given and received for mutual advancement on the road of religious inquiry and experience" (RMis 56).

Social Apostolate

In the thinking of John Paul II there is no sharp dichotomy between the herald and the servant functions of the Church. Because the gospel is a force for the renewal of society, the work of evangelization, which we have just considered, flows over into the reconstruction of the social order.

The keystone of John Paul II's social teaching is the dignity of the human person, created to the image and likeness of God and redeemed by the precious blood of the Son of God. Beginning with his first encyclical, *Redemptor hominis,* he has repeatedly endorsed the principles of the Universal Declaration of Human Rights, adopted by the United Nations in 1948. His longest encyclical, published in 1995, bears the significant title The Gospel of Life *(Evangelium vitae).* Human life, he argues, is the primary good that underlies all other rights. "Upon the recognition of this right [to life] every human community and the political community itself are founded" (EV 5). Under his supervision the Holy See in 1983 issued an important charter of family rights.[41] At various times the pope has spoken forcefully on the rights of women and the rights of nations.

All these rights, and the corresponding duties to respect them, have a theological foundation, since they stem ultimately from God the creator and redeemer. The Church consequently has a mission to call attention to the obligation of all human societies to implement these rights. When it sees human rights being violated, it may be obliged to utter a prophetic protest. By proclaiming Christ in an authentic and integral

[39] Ibid.
[40] Ibid., 100.
[41] Holy See, "Charter of the Rights of the Family," *Origins* 13 (December 15, 1983) 461–4.

manner, the Church makes itself a force for advancing human freedom and promoting the common good (RMis 39).

In his teaching on the relations between Church and state, John Paul II seeks to safeguard the biblical distinction between "what belongs to Caesar" and "what belongs to God" (cf. Matt 22:21).[42] In an important address to the European Parliament at Strasbourg in 1988 he argued against political totalitarianism. The competence of the state, he said, is only to administer the external aspects of the earthly city. It may not claim to teach the ultimate meaning of human existence, or to bring about final happiness, or to override the human conscience. It is not entitled to enforce atheism or to discriminate against citizens on the ground of their religion. The Church always retains the right to proclaim the gospel, to administer the sacraments, and to exercise pastoral care over its members.

Medieval Latin Christendom, according to the Pope, failed to distinguish sufficiently between the respective spheres of influence of faith and of civil life and thereby overstepped the boundary between the realms of Caesar and of God. Religious integralism, which still prevails in some parts of the world, identifies citizenship with a specific religious affiliation, and thereby exerts a pressure on consciences that violates the principle of religious freedom.[43]

The Church teaches its members to serve the common good of the secular society, to perform their civic duties, and to obey just laws (RH 17). The Church has no mandate to teach political or economic science, still less to exercise control over the civil society. She has no concrete models to present for the solution of social and economic problems (CA 43). "Her contribution to the political order is precisely her vision of the dignity of the person revealed in all its fullness in the mystery of the Incarnate Word" (CA 47).

The transformation of the social order in accordance with the gospel is a concern of the whole Church. It is for the hierarchy, in their exercise of the "social magisterium," to enunciate the authoritative Catholic teaching. The laity have as their special responsibility "to work towards the Christian animation of the temporal order," sanctifying the world from within (CA 36). As persons who live an ordinary life in the world, they are called to be a leaven, applying the gospel to their situations by their fulfillment of their particular duties (CL 15). The clergy, as stated above, must take care not to infringe on the laity's proper field of responsibility. The Christian laity have a unique contribution to make in building a civilization of love in which war and violence have no place.

---

[42] John Paul II, "The United Europe of Tomorrow," Strasbourg, October 11, 1988, §10; *Origins* 18 (October 27, 1988) 332.
[43] Ibid.

The Church and the Kingdom

In the secularization theology of the 1960s it became popular to pro-claim the autonomy of the secular sphere and to depict the Church as one of a number of service agencies working to bring about the "king-dom of God." Depicted as a human product marked by "peace, justice, freedom, brotherhood, etc." (RMis 17), the "kingdom" was described without reference to Christ and the Church. In opposition to this "re-ductive" theology John Paul II insists that the kingdom of God cannot be separated from Christ or the Church. The kingdom of God, he writes, "is not a concept, a doctrine, or a program subject to free inter-pretation, but it is before all else a person with the face and name of Jesus of Nazareth, the image of the invisible God" (RMis 18). The Church, for its part, is the seed, sign, and instrument of the kingdom. As the body of Christ and the dwelling place of the Holy Spirit, it has a special and necessary place in God's plan for the world. The kingdom, even in its temporal dimension, would be incomplete unless it were related to Christ as he abides in the Church (RMis 19–20).

The Church is a dynamic force in humankind's journey toward the eschatological kingdom (RMis 20). In seeking to dispose people to ac-cept the truth and values of the gospel, and to make the world more human, the Church "never loses sight of the priority of the transcen-dent and spiritual realities which are the premises of eschatological sal-vation" (RMis 20). In the end Jesus Christ, who is head of the Church and of all creation, will bring about a fulfillment in which both Church and world will find their glorious consummation.[44] The glory of God, which is the end of all creation, includes both the salvation of human beings and the renewal of the cosmos.[45]

Conclusion

While he possesses all the qualifications to rank as an original theo-logian in his own right, John Paul II, as a pastor, seeks to make himself above all else a spokesman for Vatican II. It is his mandate, he feels, to see that the council is rightly understood and duly implemented as the Church moves toward the great jubilee of the year 2000.

In his writings on the Church, occasional rather than systematic, John Paul II shows an awareness of the various ecclesial "models" op-erative in the council documents. Partly because of his philosophical background, he exhibits a marked preference for *communio* model, but he expounds it in a way that takes cognizance of the merits of other

[44] Pope John Paul II, *Sources of Renewal*, 186.
[45] Ibid., 187–8.

models, such as those depicting the Church as institution, sacrament, herald, and servant. With his personalistic orientation, Wojtyla clearly subordinates the institutional and the external to the communal and the spiritual. But he also uses the category of sacramentality to integrate the visible and invisible, the external and the internal. The visible Church is an effective instrument because she is, first of all, a sign of God's invisible grace. The ecumenical apostolate plays an important role in making the Church a sign of reconciliation and unity.

Because he is convinced of the inseparability of being from acting, and because he sees the entire Church in a state of mission, John Paul II attaches great importance to the action of the Church ad extra, including its functions of evangelization, dialogue, and social healing. All of these functions, he holds, overlap and interpenetrate. The Church evangelizes when it enters into dialogue; it transforms society when it proclaims the gospel.

Placed as she is in history, the Church is never static. Just as the human person achieves maturity by free and conscious commitment to the service of others, so the Church, as John Paul II understands it, comes to full self-realization in loving service to God and to the human family. Her self-realization within history is always incomplete, but she already anticipates by her striving for holiness the glory of the everlasting kingdom.

For Further Reading

Buttiglione, Rocco. *Karol Woityla: The Thought of the Man Who Became Pope John Paul II*. Grand Rapids, Mich.: Eerdmans, 1997.

John Paul II, Pope. "Ad Tuendam Fidem." *Origins* 28 (July 16, 1998) 113, 115–16.

_____. *Crossing the Threshold of Hope*. New York: Knopf, 1994.

_____. *Jesus, Son and Savior: A Catechesis on the Creed*. Boston: Pauline Books & Media, 1996.

_____. "Redemptoris Missio." *Origins* 20 (January 31, 1991) 541–68.

_____. *Sign of Contradiction*. New York: Seabury/Crossroad, 1979.

_____. *Sources of Renewal: The Implementation of Vatican II*. San Francisco: Harper and Row, 1979.

_____. "The Theological and Juridical Nature of Episcopal Conferences." *Origins* 28 (July 30, 1998) 152–8.

_____. "Ut Unum Sint." *Origins* 25 (June 8, 1995) 49, 51–72.

McDermott, John, ed. *The Thought of Pope John Paul II*. Rome: Editrice Pontificia Università Gregoriana, 1993.

Williams, George Huntston. *The Mind of John Paul II: Origins of His Thought and Action*. New York: Seabury Press, 1981.

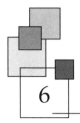

6   Ecumenical Ecclesiology

Michael A. Fahey

Although from the beginning Christians have had an acute sense of belonging to a reality larger than simply their local community of believers, it took over a millennium before individual Christian theologians began to write formal treatises on ecclesiology. St. Paul expressed Christians' concern not just for members of their local or house church but also for members of the worldwide Church across the Mediterranean world. When Paul wrote in 1 Cor 12:28 that "God has appointed in the church first apostles, second prophets" he was obviously referring to an entity more comprehensive than the local church of Corinth. A similar inclusive view of Church is reflected in the prayer recorded in the ancient *Didache:* "As this broken bread was scattered upon the mountains, but was brought together and become one, so let thy Church be gathered together from the ends of the earth, into thy kingdom, for thine is the glory and the power through Jesus Christ for ever" (9:4). That prayer for the Church scattered north, east, south, and west, continues: "Remember, Lord, thy Church, to deliver it from all evil and to make it perfect in thy love, and gather it together in its holiness from the four winds to thy kingdom which thou has prepared for it" (10:5). A similar concern for the wider Church is present in the description of an early Eucharist in Justin's *First Apology:*

> And on that day which is called after the sun, all who are in the towns and in the country gather together for a communal celebration. And then the memoirs of the Apostles or the writings of the Prophets are read, as long as time permits. . . . Then prayers in common are said . . . for ourselves, for the newly baptized and for all others wherever they may be (no. 67).

The broader Christian community was never forgotten during the first millennium. Communities remained united through the exchange of letters, synodal meetings, financial collections for the needy, exchanges

111

of hospitality, and even theological disputations. Other churches, often at considerable distance, were known to be reading and meditating the same scriptural texts and celebrating the same sacramental rituals of baptism and Eucharist.

Despite devout attachment to the wide community of believers and a sense of communion, oddly no formal theological treatises on the Church were composed during the first millennium. Theology remained first and foremost a *lectio divina*, meditative appropriation of the scriptural texts. When eventually systematic tractates on specific aspects of revelation began to appear, reflections on the mystery of the Church were subsumed into treatises on grace, christology, or redemption.

The earliest Western tractate treatises on Church date back to the fourteenth century. They were, in point of fact, more canonical studies exploring the rights and privileges of the Roman pontiff rather than comprehensive meditations on the mystery of the community of faith. Some of these treatises have come down to us, including *De regimine christiano* (ca. 1302) of James of Viterbo (Giacomo Capocci), identified as the oldest treatise on the Church; *De ecclesiastica potestate* of Giles of Rome (Egidio Colonna, ca. 1243–1316); *De potestate regia et papali* by John of Paris (Jean Quidort de Paris), who died in 1306; and eventually the *Summa de ecclesia* (1436) by John of Turrecremata. These early treatises concentrated on the institution, its structures, the rights of the hierarchy, the validity of the sacraments, and ministerial jurisdiction.

In writings on the Church in the West, Catholic authors did not explicitly reflect on the fact that what they were describing was in fact a divided Church, estranged in the first instance from Byzantium and other Eastern churches (at least since 1054 C.E., but actually much earlier), and separated from the various churches of the Reformation at least since the sixteenth century. From its earliest formulations through the polemics of Catholic Counter-Reformation, such as the writings of Roberto Bellarmino, *De controversiis christianae fidei,* theological expositions on the Church were highly confessional in character. Several useful studies on the slow development of the treatise *de Ecclesia* are available to us today.[1] The Western tractates in ecclesiology did not

---

[1] For the history of ecclesiology, see Yves Congar, "Kirche: dogmengeschichtlich," *Handbuch der theologischen Grundbegriffe*, vol. 1, ed. Heinrich Fries (Munich: Kösel, 1962) 801–12; M. J. Le Guillou, "Church: I. History of Ecclesiology," *Sacramentum Mundi*, vol. 1 (New York: Herder, 1968) 313–7; Eric Jay, *The Church: Its Changing Image through Twenty Centuries* (Atlanta: John Knox Press, 1980); Jon Nilson, *Nothing Beyond the Necessary: Roman Catholicism and the Ecumenical Future* (New York: Paulist Press, 1995).

grapple with the mystery of the entire Christian community of faith, nor of sinful divisions in the Church. Instead writings were typically confessional, apologetical, and isolationist.[2] Fortunately, in our lifetime, the phenomenon of separateness arising out of anathemas, real or psychological excommunications that has haunted the writings of the East and the West, produced by Orthodox, Catholic, or Protestant theologians, has begun to wane. In that sense, ecclesiology, meditation on the mystery of the Church, has begun to become ecumenically sensitive.

Ecumenical Ecclesiology?

The word "ecumenical" had been in common parlance among Christians since early times, but in a sense quite different from today's usage. Prior to the twentieth century, the word "ecumenical," related to the Greek word *oikoumene*, designated "the entire civilized world" and was roughly equivalent to our concept "universal." The word originally had come into usage while Alexander the Great was conquering the East. It suggested a dimension opposed to cultural isolation, something cosmopolitan by which people would enrich their humanity. When councils were held involving representatives of the major sees of the Christian community, they were "ecumenical." The term *oikoumene* occurs in the New Testament referring to the Roman Empire (e.g., Luke 2:1) or to the whole world (e.g., Matt 24:14). Eventually the term designated the whole Church as opposed to its divided segments, the faith of the worldwide Church as opposed to that of a small section of it.

Since the 1910 meeting of the Edinburgh Missionary Conference (a gathering of mostly English-speaking Protestant missionaries seeking to overcome in foreign countries the painful countersign of a divided Christendom), theologians began to use the term "ecumenical" to refer rather to activities designed to promote and achieve visible unity or reunion among the Christian churches. In today's usage, therefore, the term refers to the Christian concern for the unity and renewal of the Church and its relationship to God's reconciling mission. Unity efforts promoted by Edinburgh had, of course, roots earlier in the late nineteenth century (including such developments as the formation of the

---

[2] See especially Michael A. Fahey, "Church," *Systematic Theology: Roman Catholic Perspectives,* vol. 2, ed. Francis Schüssler Fiorenza and John Galvin (Minneapolis: Fortress Press, 1991) 3–74, esp. 6–8. The new appreciation for the need to reflect on the divided character of the Church is seen in several essays in *The Church in Fragments: Towards What Kind of Unity?* ed. Giuseppe Ruggieri and Miklós Tomka, *Concilium* 1997/3 (Maryknoll, N.Y.: Orbis Books, 1997).

YMCA and the Student Christian Movement), but the World Missionary Conference held in Edinburgh serves as a symbolic starting point.

Philip Potter, former general secretary of the World Council of
Churches, once described the "ecumenical" movement as follows:

> The ecumenical movement is, therefore, the means by which the churches
> which form the house, the *oikos* of God, are seeking so to live and wit-
> ness before all peoples that the whole *oikoumene* may become the *oikos*
> of God through the crucified and risen Christ in the power of the life-
> giving Spirit. The World Council of Churches was formed in 1948 pre-
> cisely to be a means of enabling this process to take place in the totality
> of the life and witness of the churches in response to the totality of God's
> claim on the life of the *oikoumene.*[3]

Inevitably the effort to promote "ecumenical" unity led to writings
on the Church that are neither introverted nor narrowly confessional.
Before this was possible, a preliminary stage took place in the Faith and
Order Movement, the theological arm of the World Council of Churches,
that concentrated on "comparative ecclesiology." At first, rather than
producing a common comprehensive description, each church articulated what was specific and unique to itself. Eventually, after this transitional stage, churches aimed at ecclesiological consensus which led to
"ecumenical ecclesiology," an expression that has appeared in the subtitles of several books on the Church.[4] These creative publications as
well as various consensus bilateral statements on the Church offer witness to the fact that theological reflection on the Church continues to be
further appropriated and broadened.

In this essay I avoid the expression "ecumenical ecclesiology" for
two reasons. Although I am sympathetic to what I understand is in-

---

[3] Cited in Michael Kinnamon and Brian E. Cope, eds., *The Ecumenical Movement:
An Anthology of Key Texts and Voices* (Grand Rapids, Mich.: Eerdmans; Geneva:
World Council of Churches, 1997) 55.

[4] Four books have made use of the expression "ecumenical ecclesiology" in their
subtitles: Christian Duquoc, *Provisional Churches: An Essay in Ecumenical Ecclesiology,*
trans. John Bowden (London: SCM Press, 1986); George Sabra, *Thomas Aquinas' Vision
of the Church: Fundamentals of an Ecumenical Ecclesiology,* Tübinger Theologische
Studien 27 (Mainz: Matthias-Grünewald Verlag, 1987); George H. Tavard, *The
Church, Community of Salvation: An Ecumenical Ecclesiology* (Collegeville: The Liturgical Press, 1992); Gillian Rosemary Evans, *The Church and the Churches: Toward an
Ecumenical Ecclesiology* (New York: Cambridge University Press, 1994). See also the
article by Anton Houtepen, "Kirche im Werden: Fundamentaltheologische Beiträge
zu einer ökumenischen Ekklesiologie," *Ökumenische Rundschau* 36 (1987) 397–420.
Also useful: Carl E. Braaten, *Mother Church: Ecclesiology and Ecumenism* (Minneapolis: Fortress Press, 1998).

tended by the term, I judge that using the singular noun "ecclesiology" rather than its plural form "ecclesiologies" obscures the rich and creative plurality of ecclesial self-understandings that the singular noun obscures. Given the broad range of nuances attached to the adjective "ecumenical," I prefer to speak of the Church's self-understanding in ecumenical perspectives. This suggests the multiplicity of legitimate approaches or models that are not incompatible but legitimately complementary, many of which are in fact rooted even in the New Testament.

Historians of the modern ecumenical movement usually identify the year 1952, associated with the Faith and Order meeting in Lund, Sweden, as the twilight of comparative ecclesiology before the dawn of ecclesiologies in ecumenical perspective.[5] With this shift the focus among Christians became not "this is what my church holds about this and that of the Church," but rather "this is what my church confesses and we sincerely ask you whether these descriptions correspond to your deepest convictions."

Acquired habits (especially bad ones) do not easily go away. Some writers, including Catholics, still continue to use the term "the Church" as a shorthand description for "the Catholic Church," even though it was explicitly stated at the Vatican Council II that the Church is a reality broader and more comprehensive than the Roman Catholic Church. Also problematic is the way that some Catholics still say "Church" when they intend to designate "the leadership or decision-makers of the Catholic Church." Now that Christians have moved into the third millennium, there is a growing awareness that they must learn to contemplate and conceive the Church not just as one's confessional family but as the wider community of all who believe in Christ whose number is known to God alone.

Why Changes in Attitude?

The change in attitude within the Catholic community regarding other churches came about for several reasons. First there is the obvious reason of God's outpouring of grace. In addition one can point to the pioneering work of specific Catholic theologians, increased interaction with Protestant and Orthodox theologians, the reformulation of Catholic

[5] See the preparatory study prepared prior to the Lund Faith and Order meeting: R. Newton Flew, ed., *The Nature of the Church: Papers Presented to the Theological Commission Appointed by the Continuation Committee of the World Conference on Faith and Order* (London: SCM Press, 1952).

self-understanding at Vatican II, and small but significant ecumenical initiatives that have had subtle but profound impact. In highlighting Catholic initiatives I in no way wish to ignore the many Protestant and several Orthodox leaders who preceded them. I simply wish to explain, especially to Catholics, how this change of attitude occurred within their own community.

The polemic Catholic literature in the post-Reformation era, despite occasional expressions of irenic literature, hardly suggests that eventually, by the late twentieth century, there could be a dramatic shift toward ecumenically sensitive discourse. Rome's official condemnation of Modernism, for instance, and its subsequent establishment of theological watchfulness scarcely offered a hint that, within several generations, paradigmatic changes in ecclesial self-understanding would occur. The shift among Catholics from a rigid "unionism" to modern "ecumenism" was not an easy one. With the possible exceptions of Johann Adam Möhler and John Henry Newman, the period extending from 1850 to 1950 was largely a period dominated by an ecclesiology that saw the Catholic Church as a "perfect society" rather than as a communion of communions.

Papal reaction to Modernism had also made the Catholics chary of ecumenical initiatives. Pius XI referred to ecumenists as "pan-Christians" in his encyclical *Mortalium animos* of 1928 published pointedly in reaction to the Faith and Order meeting the previous year in Lausanne:

> It is clear why this Apostolic See has never allowed its subjects to take part in the assemblies of non-Catholics. There is but one way in which the unity of Christians may be fostered, and that is by furthering the return to the one true Church of Christ of those who are separated from it; for from that one true Church of Christ they have in the past fallen away. The one Church of Christ is visible to all, and will remain, according to the will of its Author, exactly the same as He instituted it. The mystical Spouse of Christ has never in the course of centuries been contaminated, nor in the future can she ever be.[6]

The shift from isolation to tolerance, and then to admiration and collaboration, was influenced by the shared trauma of the two World Wars, especially World War II with its subsequent major population relocations. Other factors were the sympathetic adoption of historical-critical methods for interpreting Scripture and the growing appreciation of historical development of the Church's dogmas and doctrines. Catholics' lack of familiarity with the Protestant and Orthodox churches

---

[6] *Documents of Christian Unity: Selections from the First and Second Series, 1920–30,* ed. G.K.A. Bell (London: Oxford University Press, 1955) 198.

led them to think of their initiatives as original when clearly in many instances Protestant and Orthodox pioneers had preceded them. Modern students of ecumenism studying an anthology of key texts and voices from the twentieth century are surprised to find out that Catholic "discoveries" are actually ideas borrowed from others. One example is the appeal in 1962 by Pope John XXIII to St. Augustine's call for the Church to exhibit *"in dubiis libertas, in necessariis unitas,"* which was actually cited as early as 1920 by the Orthodox theologian Germanos of Thyateira.

Not surprisingly Catholics at first appealed to the importance of "spiritual" ecumenism (i.e., praying for Church reunification without attempting to iron out dogmatic or doctrinal issues). Little ecumenical leadership came from the popes or hierarchs.[7] However, one notable exception was the initiative of Cardinal Mercier of Malines, Belgium, who organized between 1921 and 1925 a series of unity conferences between Anglicans and Roman Catholics.[8]

Eventually there took place what one Protestant author has described as the "Catholic Rediscovery of Protestantism."[9] At first this shift of paradigm among Roman Catholics was largely the work of individual theologians. Yves Congar (1904–95), whose volume *Chrétiens désunis* was published in 1937, is properly identified as one of the key

---

[7] For the slow development of papal attitudes on ecumenism, see Gregory Baum, *That They May Be One: A Study of Papal Doctrine (Leo XIII–Pius XII)* (Westminster, Md.: Newman Press, 1958).

[8] *From Malines to ARCIC: The Malines Conversations Commemorated,* ed. Adelbert Denaux and John A. Dick (Leuven: Leuven University, 1997).

[9] Paul M. Minus Jr., *The Catholic Rediscovery of Protestantism: A History of Roman Catholic Ecumenical Pioneering* (New York: Paulist Press, 1976). See also Michael Fahey, "Twentieth Century Shifts in Roman Catholic Attitudes toward Ecumenism," *Catholic Perspectives on Baptism, Eucharist, and Ministry* (Lanham, Md.: University Press of America, 1986) 27–43. Other useful studies on the growth of ecumenism are: George H. Tavard, *Two Centuries of Ecumenism: The Search for Unity* (Notre Dame, Ind.: Fides Press, 1960); Barry Till, *The Churches Search for Unity* (Harmondsworth: Penguin, 1972); Geoffrey Wainwright, *The Ecumenical Moment: Crisis and Opportunity for the Church* (Grand Rapids, Mich.: Eerdmans, 1983); Mark Lowery, *Ecumenism: Striving for Unity amid Diversity* (Mystic, Conn.: Twenty-Third Publications, 1985). The most detailed historical account remains the comprehensive study: R. Rouse and S. C. Neill, eds., *History of the Ecumenical Movement 1517–1948,* 2d ed. (Philadelphia: Westminster Press, 1967); Harold Fey, ed., *History of the Ecumenical Movement 1948–1968* (Philadelphia: Westminster Press, 1970). A third volume is in preparation. For a critical bibliography see Michael A. Fahey, *Ecumenism: A Bibliographical Overview,* Bibliographies and Indexes in Religious Studies (Westport, Conn: Greenwood Press, 1992).

pioneering figures.[10] That his book was criticized and held in suspicion by the Roman Curial offices at the time illustrates how advanced it was for its age.

But other volumes by Catholic theologians had preceded Congar's book. Among early Catholic ecumenists were Victor de Buck (1817–76), Emilio de Augustinis (1829–99), Paul Watson (1863–1940), and Dom Lambert Beauduin (1873–1960), the founder of what became the Chevetogne monastery devoted to Christian unity between the East and the West.[11] Also important were the activities of two Frenchmen. The first was Paul Couturier (1881–1953), the father of the Week for Christian Unity and the founder of the ecumenical dialogue team known as the Groupe des Dombes whose importance continues to this day. The second was the Rome-based French Jesuit Charles Boyer (1884–1980), who cautiously but resolutely advised Pope Pius XII on matters of ecumenism and who founded *Unitas: International Quarterly Review of Ecumenism* in 1949, a journal that appeared in English, French, and Italian editions. Other individuals made contributions. In Germany, Max Pribilla (1874–1956) published an important work about the Life and Work movement and the Faith and Order organization entitled *Um kirchliche Einheit, Stockholm, Lausanne, Rom: Geschichtlich-theologische Darstellung der neueren Eininungsbestrebungen* (Freiburg: Herder, 1929).[12] In England in 1934 an anonymous "Father Jerome" (whose real identity was the British Jesuit priest Jerome Gille) published *A Catholic Plea for Reunion.*[13] Otto Karrer produced a pre-Vatican II study in German that anticipated in several ways the council's Decree on Ecumenism.[14] Other names could be listed too.

One of the groups to engage first in ecumenical reflection were biblical scholars. In conjointly studying the word of God, Protestant and Catholic professors of the Bible learned to discuss the implications of historical-critical method, especially the ramifications of form-critical method, and later redaction-critical analysis of the four Gospels. Not

---

[10] *Chrétiens désunis: Principes d'un oecuménisme catholique* (Paris: Cerf, 1937). The English title is: *Divided Christendom: A Catholic Study of the Problem of Reunion* (London: G. Bles, 1939).

[11] For a thorough discussion of the French-language pioneers in this early period of ecumenism, see Etienne Fouilloux, *Les catholiques et l'unité chrétienne du XIXe au XXe siècle: Itinéraires européens d'expression française* (Paris: Le Centurion, 1982).

[12] Max Pribilla, *Um kirchliche Einheit, Stockholm, Lausanne, Rom: Geschichtlich-theologische Darstellung der neueren Einigungsbestrebungen* (Freiburg: Herder, 1929).

[13] Jerome Gille (Father Jerome), *A Catholic Plea for Reunion* (London: Williams and Norgate, 1934).

[14] Otto Karrer, *Die christliche Einheit: Gabe und Aufgabe* (Lucerne: Räber, 1963).

surprisingly one of the leading ecumenists who became a standard bearer for Catholic ecumenism was the former professor of Scripture at the Pontifical Biblical Institute in Rome, the German Jesuit Augustin Bea (1881–1968), who was appointed by Pope John XXIII as the first cardinal prefect of the Secretariat for Promoting Christian Union (SPCU).[15]

Gradually among Catholics there emerged a greater sensitivity to Reformation perspectives regarding the theology of grace and Lutheran understanding of justification. A growing appreciation among Catholics strengthened the perspective that faith is God's pure and total gift which owes nothing to previous human quests or prayers of spiritual achievements. Also in the second half of the twentieth century the Catholic Church became committed to the idea that it was thoroughly evangelical to confess that *"ecclesia semper reformanda."* The Church asserted its need of reform, repentance, and humility, because of its sinfulness, its predilection for legalism, clericalism, and triumphalism.

Pope Pius XII's encyclical on the Church, *Mystici corporis Christi* (1943), had not satisfactorily settled the question of who are the "members" of the Mystical Body. Rather than attempting to formulate an answer to that question, the council promoted an ecclesiology inspired by the concept of the People of God. In the '80s and '90s this gradually developed into an ecclesiology inspired by the New Testament notion of *koinonia*, in Latin *communio*. The Church was described as a communion or participation in the communion of the Holy Spirit received by all in baptism. Besides the "vertical" relationship of Christians to the Spirit of God there exists also a "horizontal" relationship among all Christians even when their churches lack in full, visible unity. This emerging irenic theology was based too on solid historical studies by Catholic scholars that reassessed the events before, during, and after the schism between the East and West, or during the Protestant Reformation in Germany and England.

Obviously an important factor in developing the Catholic understanding of ecumenism was Vatican II, although it would be mistaken to see the council as a simple *creatio ex nihilo*. Although the council's preparatory stages did not point to reasons to anticipate dramatic changes in Catholicism's self-understanding as a Church,[16] eventually during

---

[15] See the biography, written by his long-time personal secretary, Stjepan Schmidt, *Augustin Bea: The Cardinal of Unity*, trans. Leslie Wearne (New York: New City Press, 1992). The original Italian edition was published in 1987.

[16] Important studies on the preparatory phase of Vatican II analyzed country by country have been begun especially under the inspiration of Giuseppe Alberigo and the Istituto per le Scienze religiose in Bologna. See *History of Vatican II*, vol. 1: *Announcing and Preparing Vatican Council II: Towards a New Era in Catholicism*, ed.

the council, especially because of close collaboration between bishops and theologians, some remarkable texts emerged. These included the Constitution on the Church *(Lumen gentium)*, the Decree on Ecumenism *(Unitatis redintegratio)*, and the Decree on the Eastern Catholic Churches *(Orientalium ecclesiarum)*.[17] Among the important insights contained in these documents on ecclesiology were affirmations about a hierarchy of truths in Christian revelation, the need for reconciliation with other Christians, the acceptance of other "churches and ecclesial communities," and emphasis on the presence of charisms in the faithful.

The notion that the Church of Christ could indeed be "holy" at the same time that it is "sinful" was a key notion in conciliar teaching. Just as God's kingdom or rule *(basileia)* could be "already here" but "still not yet" completely present, because of our unfulfilled yearning for eschatological realization, so too the Church's note of holiness (or catholicity, unity, apostolicity) is both a "given" but also "a reality still to be acquired in his fulness" (as German theologians described this, each one of the Church's four marks is both a *Gabe* and an *Aufgabe*—a given but also a challenge yet to be met). Describing the Church as a pilgrim Church en route toward fulfilment allowed for the possibility and the necessity of its daily conversion and openness to divine grace.

This notion of the Church's need for conversion or repentance has been specifically addressed by the Group of Les Dombes, the French-language Reformed/Roman Catholic team established by Paul Couturier.[18] One of its most profound agreed statements is its call to each confessional church to undergo a conversion or *metanoia* as a precondition for church unity.[19] The group's document on conversion stresses the need for confessional identity, but distinguishes that from

---

Giuseppe Alberigo, English version ed. Joseph A. Komonchak (Maryknoll, N.Y.: Orbis Books, 1995); Joseph Komonchak, "U.S. Bishops' Suggestions for Vatican II," *Cristianesimo nella Storia* 15 (1994) 313–71; and Michael A. Fahey, "A Vatican Request for Agenda Items Prior to Vatican II: Responses by English-Speaking Canadian Bishops," *L'Eglise canadienne et Vatican II*, ed. Gilles Routhier, Héritage et projet 58 (Québec: Fides Press, 1997) 61–71.

[17] See my "Commentary on the Dogmatic Constitution on the Church: Lumen gentium," *The Church Renewed: The Documents of Vatican II Reconsidered*, ed. George Schner (Lanham, Md.: University Press of America, 1986) 11–18.

[18] For an account of the achievements of this dialogue, see *Pour la communion des Eglises: L'apport du Groupe des Dombes 1937–1987* (Paris: Le Centurion, 1988).

[19] Groupe des Dombes, *Pour la conversion des Eglises: Identité et changement dans la dynamique de communion* (Paris: Le Centurion, 1991). See also the English version of the Group of Les Dombes, *For the Conversion of the Churches* (Geneva: World Council of Churches, 1993). For a summary of the document's thrust, see Ladislas Örsy, "The Conversion of the Churches: Condition of Unity. A Roman Catholic Perspec-

integrism or fundamentalism, both attitudes that harken back to the past and reflect interest in interior security, and that are prone to deny the rights of others and to suspect new ways of promoting evangelism.

One of the major factors promoting paradigm shifts and conversion of attitude among Catholics was its interaction with the World Council of Churches. This influence is somewhat paradoxical since Catholics are even now not officially members of the organization. Given the Catholic Church's own self-understanding and the way that the World Council of Churches member churches are represented on the basis of nation rather than international headquarters, this Catholic reluctance to join the World Council of Churches is understandable. Still, its impact on the development of Catholic ecclesiology can be richly documented, as has been done recently by Geoffrey Wainwright, the British Methodist professor of theology at Duke University.[20] Fortunately for the development of ecclesiology, a number of leading Catholic theologians have been appointed to "official" membership in the World Council of Churches' theological wing, the Faith and Order Commission. Catholics have also been asked by the Vatican to cooperate since 1965 with theologians of the World Council of Churches through the so-called Joint Working Group (JWG). The JWG has already produced a number of significant theological analyses, a fruit of this mutual interaction and enrichment.[21] It would be difficult to describe here even briefly the growth of understanding regarding ecclesiology that took place first within the World Council of Churches itself, much less the challenge of its interaction with Catholicism. Here I touch only on some salient moments.

Among the landmarks in the World Council of Churches' description of the nature of the Church is the "Toronto Statement" issued at the 1950 meeting of the World Council of Churches Central Committee (only a few years after the first world assembly in Amsterdam in 1948).

---

tive," *America* 166 (1992) 474–87. The village and monastery of Les Dombes, France, is located in Burgundy near the site of Cluny and the modern community of Taizé.

[20] Geoffrey Wainwright, "Church," *Dictionary of the Ecumenical Movement*, ed. Nicholas Lossky and others (Geneva: World Council of Churches, 1991) 159–67.

[21] For the period covering Amsterdam (1948) to the World Assembly meeting in Uppsala (1968), see Hildburg Wegener-Fueter, *Kirche und Ökumene: Das Kirchenbild des Ökumenischen Rates der Kirchen nach den Vollversammlungsdokumenten von 1948 bis 1968* (Göttingen: Vandenhoeck & Ruprecht, 1979); Heinrich Doring, *Grundriss der Ekklesiologie; Zentrale Aspekte des katholischen Selbstverstandnisses und ihre ökumenische Relevanz* (Darmstadt: Wissenschaftliche Buchgesellschaft, 1986). See also John J. McDonnell, *The World Council of Churches and the Catholic Church*, Toronto Studies in Theology 21 (New York: Edwin Mellen Press, 1985), which covers the period up to and including the General Assembly in Vancouver (1983).

The Toronto Statement, whose full title is "The Church, the Churches, and the World Council of Churches: The Ecclesiological Significance of the World Council of Churches," reasoned that the World Council of Churches is not based on any one particular conception of the Church, nor does it prejudge ecclesiological problems. Membership in the World Council of Churches, it asserts, does not imply that a confessional church treats its own self-understandings as relative. Finally, membership in the World Council of Churches does not imply the acceptance of a specific doctrine concerning the nature of Church unity.

Ecclesiological issues since the Toronto Statement were treated at first cautiously. At the World Assembly meeting in New Delhi (1961) it was stated that members would learn what the World Council of Churches was "by living together." Yet at the Faith and Order meeting of Montreal (1963) the delegates asked that the World Council devote greater attention to its ecclesiology. The World Assembly at Uppsala (1968) spoke of the World Council of Churches as a fellowship of churches seeking to express catholicity. In Nairobi (1975) the council described itself as "a conciliar fellowship of local churches which are themselves truly united."

A quantum leap in ecclesiology was the work done for the Fifth World Conference of the Faith and Order Commission held at Santiago de Compostela (1993) on communion ecclesiology entitled "Towards Koinonia in Faith, Life and Witness."[22] In many ways this study is the keystone to what is called "ecumenical ecclesiology." The roots of the document's preparatory work reach down into the work initiated in Toronto, but more immediately at the Faith and Order meeting of Lima, Peru, in 1982, that established the study program to explore "The Unity of the Church and the Renewal of Human Community," a project further pursued at Faith and Order meetings held in Stavanger, Norway (1985), and Budapest (1989).[23]

---

[22] The discussion paper "Towards Koinonia in Faith, Life and Witness," has been published in a number of places, perhaps most easily consulted in the appendix to *Fifth World Conference on Faith and Order: Santiago de Compostela 1993: Message, Section Reports, Discussion Paper,* Faith and Order Paper no. 164 (Geneva: World Council of Churches, 1993) 3–45.

[23] See Thomas F. Best, ed., *Faith and Renewal: Reports and Documents of the Commission on Faith and Order, Stavanger, Norway, 13–25 August 1985,* Faith and Order Paper no. 131 (Geneva: World Council of Churches, 1986); Thomas F. Best, ed., *Faith and Order 1985–1989: The Commission Meeting at Budapest, 1989,* Faith and Order Paper no. 148 (Geneva: World Council of Churches, 1990). The final document was eventually published as: *Church and World: The Unity of the Church and the Renewal of Human Community,* Faith and Order Paper no. 151 (Geneva: World Council of Churches, 1990). For a description of this period, see Paul A. Crow and Günther

Other Fruits of Ecumenical Commitment

Besides its association with the Faith and Order Commission, the Catholic Church has also been involved in a variety of ecumenical initiatives, some modest, some ambitious, that help to explain the irreversible change in its own understanding of other churches. After the first session of Vatican II, with the participation of Cardinal Bea, Catholics spoke at a historic symposium held in 1962 at Harvard University during which Bea, by then the prefect of the Vatican's newly established Secretariat for Promoting Christian Unity, gave several important addresses.[24]

Even before the Vatican's establishment of official international and national ecumenical bilateral consultations, Protestants and Catholics in the German-speaking world collaborated in a notable undertaking that culminated in a joint book-length document of the Christian faith. This was a creative, joint account of the Christian faith, a *Neues Glaubensbuch* (A New Book of the Faith) according to its original title, whose originality lost something in its subsequent translation into English as *The Common Catechism*.[25]

Beginning in 1965 the Catholic community, especially its theologians, developed ecumenical sensitivity through the experience of international and national official bilateral consultations coordinated by the Secretariat for Promoting Christian Unity. Many of these consultations have achieved notable results and have led to the publication of agreed statements or consensus documents, which often achieve a level of nuance and comprehensiveness superior even to the documents of Vatican II. Among those consultations whose impact has been most notable are the international Lutheran/Roman Catholic Consultation, the international Anglican/Roman Catholic Commission, and, despite some setbacks, the international Orthodox/Roman Catholic consultation. In various countries such as the United States, Canada, France, and Germany, there have also been bilateral consultations that have led

---

Gassmann, *Lausanne to Santiago de Compostela, 1927–1993: The Faith and Order World Conferences, and Issues and Results of the Working Period 1963–1993*, Faith and Order Paper no. 160 (Geneva: World Council of Churches, 1993).

[24] Samuel H. Miller and G. Ernest Wright, gen. eds., *Ecumenical Dialogue at Harvard: The Roman Catholic–Protestant Colloquium* (Cambridge, Mass.: Harvard University Press, 1964).

[25] Johannes Feiner and Lukas Vischer, eds., *The Common Catechism* (New York: Seabury Press, 1975). The German original published by Herder Verlag in 1973 had a more specific title: *Neues Glaubensbuch*. See especially the ecclesiology sections: "The Community of the Faithful" (322–47) and "The Church" (632–57).

to significant breakthroughs.[26] Precisely through "dialogue," as has been suggested, the Catholic Church has been able to respond more completely to its vocation *(Selbstvollzug).*[27]

Another factor that has contributed to the change toward ecclesiology in some parts of the world has been the relocation of previously isolated Catholic seminaries to settings in ecumenical clusters, which has promoted more academic and personal contacts with other Christians. Catholic schools of theology training persons for ministry have been active in the Association of Theological Schools of the United States and Canada, the ecumenical accrediting agency that oversees ministerial formation.

All of these factors, and preeminently the establishment of closer ties with the Faith and Order Commission, have brought it about that Roman Catholics had significant input into what arguably has been the major ecumenical achievement of the twentieth century, namely the Lima document on *Baptism, Eucharist, and Ministry.*[28] Catholics have responded to the question raised in the document's introduction that invites churches to state whether one's own community mirrored in the text is accurately described. The practice of intrachurch exchange during recent years has clearly helped in the emergence of an impressive group of studies on Catholic ecclesiology marked by ecumenical sensitivity.[29]

[26] These international and national documents are frequently difficult to locate, though Paulist Press has published five volumes in its series: *Ecumenical Documents: Doing the Truth in Charity* (1982), *Growth in Agreement* (1984), *Towards the Healing of Schism* (1987), *Building Unity* (1989), *Growing Consensus: U.S. 1962–1991* (1995). For a more comprehensive tracking of these documents and commentaries on them, consult the bi-annual newsletter *Centro Pro Unione Bulletin* (Via dell'Anima 30; I-00186 Rome, Italy).

[27] Gebhard Furst, ed., *Dialog als Selbstvollzug der Kirche?* Quaestiones disputatae 166 (Freiburg: Herder, 1997). See also earlier studies by Anton Houtepen, "L'ecclesiologia e l'ecumenismo: Alcune note provvisorie," *Studi Ecumenici* 10 (1992) 39–51; and Jos E. Vercruysse, "Chiesa in relazione ed in dialogo," *Studi Ecumenici* 11 (1993) 147–55. Agreeing with Konrad Reiser's assessments as outlined in *Ecumenism in Transition: A Paradigm Shift in the Ecumenical Movement* (Geneva: World Council of Churches, 1991), Jesuit professor Thomas Hughson comments that "ecumenical dialogue is a particular instance of a dynamic inherent in human existence and not an expedient transition en route to doctrinal consensus" ("Common Understanding of Ecumenism: A Present Need," *Ecumenical Review* 46 [1994] 340). See also more recently Konrad Raiser, "Fifty Years World Council of Churches," *Word and World* 18:2 (Spring 1998) 113–21.

[28] *Baptism, Eucharist and Ministry,* Faith and Order Paper no. 111 (Geneva: World Council of Churches, 1982). This work is frequently referred to as "the Lima Document" or "BEM."

[29] See articles by Joseph Hoffmann, Hervé Legrand, and J.-M.-R. Tillard, "Ecclésiologie," *Initiation à la pratique de la théologie. III: Dogmatique 2,* ed. Bernard Lauret and

The achievements of the International Orthodox/Roman Catholic Consultation, despite the many difficulties of this exchange, have opened new vistas for what might be deeply shared theological reflections on the nature of the Church and its structures.[30] The community of Church has only begun to appropriate the first three joint consensus statements on the Church worldwide, formulated by the Orthodox and Catholics in new theological language: "The Mystery of the Church and of the Eucharist in the Light of the Mystery of the Blessed Trinity" (Munich, 1982); "Faith, Sacraments and the Unity of the Church" (Bari, 1987); and "The Sacrament of Order in the Sacramental Structure of the Church with Particular Reference to the Importance of Apostolic Succession for the Sanctification and Unity of the People of God" (New Valamo, 1988).

Likewise, the learning process of the Anglican/Roman Catholic International Commissions (ARCIC I and II) shows the possibilities of assimilating a more profound notion of ecclesiology when done through joint efforts to rethink without the restrictions of archaic thought forms but in new categories.

Issues Resolved and Unresolved

The goal of ecclesiology and modern ecumenical efforts is not to develop or impose one "ecumenical ecclesiology," but to present common or converging lines of ecclesiological thinking. Several fine studies have helped to sketch what might be the outlines of an understanding of Church from ecumenical perspective.[31] This in no way intends to

---

François Refoulé (Paris: Cerf, 1983) 53–463; Avery Dulles, *Models of the Church*, 2d rev. ed. (Garden City, N.Y.: Doubleday, 1987, first ed. 1974); J.-M.-R. Tillard, *Eglise d'Eglises: L'ecclésiologie de communion* (Paris: Cerf, 1987), English translation: *Church of Churches: The Ecclesiology of Communion*, trans. R. C. De Peaux (Collegeville: The Liturgical Press, 1992) (the English translation of Tillard's book leaves much to be desired). Another recent Catholic ecclesiology study especially sensitive to Orthodox concerns is that of the late Basque ecclesiologist, professor at the University of Münster and director of its Center for Byzantine Studies, Miguel Garijo-Guembe, *Communion of the Saints: Foundation, Nature and Structure of the Church*, trans. Patrick Madigan (Collegeville: The Liturgical Press, 1994). For a brief account of communion ecclesiology, see the consensus statement of ARCIC-II: *Church as Communion* (London: Catholic Truth Society, 1991).

[30] See *The Quest for Unity: Orthodox and Catholics in Dialogue*, ed. John Borelli and John H. Erickson (Crestwood, N.Y.: St. Vladimir's Seminary Press; Washington, D.C.: USCC, 1996).

[31] See especially Colin Davey, "The Doctrine of the Church in International Bilateral Dialogues," *One in Christ* 22 (1986) 134–45; Johannes Willebrands, "Vatican II's

promote unbridled diversity, as Tillard insists in his study of communion ecclesiology when he states:

> Reactions to Faith and Order's Lima Document on *Baptism, Eucharist
> and Ministry* show in fact that some either dream of a unity very close to
> uniformity, or some cling to the defense of a pluralism that is almost
> without limits. But uniformity suffocates communion, whereas certain
> differences on fundamental points make it nonviable. Unity without di-
> versity makes the Church a dead body: pluralism without unity makes
> a body which is dismembered.[32]

Much remains to be done. Not only does the Catholic Church need
to promote the full "reception" of the conciliar teaching, a process that
may take a hundred years, but it also needs to deepen its understanding of the process of "recognition" of other churches in the light of the
way they formulate their creedal convictions.[33] This unfinished busi-
ness includes the question of how the Catholic Church would "recognize" the authenticity or "validity" of ordinations in other churches, a
process made especially complex given the Roman Catholic Church's
teaching on the nonadmissibility of women to priestly ordination. To
what extent also could the Catholic Church adjust its present teaching
on eucharistic hospitality or "intercommunion"?

Conclusion

In 1980 Professor Patrick Granfield, to whom this essay is cordially
dedicated, entitled one of his several important books on the Catholic
Church *The Papacy in Transition*. From our reflections here about the exchanges between the Catholic Church and its sister churches one could
appropriately describe this process as *The Church in Transition*. The task
in the twenty-first century will be to build on this and to interpret this
process to the faithful so they will see that what has happened is not a
falling away but a fidelity to Christian mission.

This will happen through prayerful assimilation of the fruits of renewal movements within the Catholic Church, many of which have
been promoted through its association with other committed Christians. Meditation on the Church will continue "in ecumenical perspec-

---

Ecclesiology of Communion," *One in Christ* 23 (1987) 179–91; and Anton Houtepan,
"Towards an Ecumenical Vision of the Church," *One in Christ* 25 (1989) 217–37.

[32] Tillard, *Church of Churches*, 320 (translation adjusted).

[33] Gerard Kelly, *Recognition: Advancing Ecumenical Thinking* (New York: P. Lang,
1996).

tive." In his study on Thomas Aquinas's ecclesiology, George Sabra has hinted at some of the characteristics of this future task. He writes:

> Only an ecclesiology that is primarily non-apologetical and non-juridical in intent and character, that emphasizes the radical primacy of grace and the communion in the effects of that grace, that is profoundly and consistently Christological, that does not overrate the institutional aspect but understands it functionally and in terms of service, and that presupposes and operates with a comprehensive and manifold conception of the church, in short, only a theological ecclesiology is ecumenically viable.[34]

This is the goal of all who daily meditate prayerfully on the mystery of the Church in ecumenical perspective.

---

[34] Sabra, *Thomas Aquinas' Vision of the Church*, 197.

For Further Reading

Braaten, Carl E. *Mother Church: Ecclesiology and Ecumenism.* Minneapolis: Fortress Press, 1998.

Duquoc, Christian. *Provisional Churches: An Essay in Ecumenical Ecclesiology.* Trans. John Bowden. London: SCM Press, 1986.

Evans, Gillian Rosemary. *The Church and the Churches: Toward an Ecumenical Ecclesiology.* New York: Cambridge University Press, 1994.

Garijo-Guembe, Miguel. *Communion of the Saints: Foundation, Nature and Structure of the Church.* Trans. Patrick Madigan. Collegeville: The Liturgical Press, 1994.

Kinnamon, Michael, and Brian E. Cope, eds. *The Ecumenical Movement: An Anthology of Key Texts and Voices.* Grand Rapids, Mich.: Eerdmans; Geneva: World Council of Churches, 1997.

Sabra, George. *Thomas Aquinas' Vision of the Church: Fundamentals of an Ecumenical Ecclesiology.* Tübinger Theologische Studien 27. Mainz: Matthias-Grünewald Verlag, 1987.

Tavard, George. *The Church, Community of Salvation: An Ecumenical Ecclesiology.* Collegeville: The Liturgical Press, 1992.

Tillard, J.-M.-R. *Church of Churches: The Ecclesiology of Communion.* Trans. R. C. De Peaux. Collegeville: The Liturgical Press, 1992.

VanderWilt, Jeffrey T. *A Church without Borders: The Eucharist and the Church in Ecumenical Perspective.* Collegeville: The Liturgical Press, 1998.

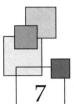

7 | Theological Method for Ecclesiology

Pedro Rodríguez

Under this title the essay will approach its theme in three points: (1) method in ecclesiology, (2) the service which the "images" of the Church render to method in ecclesiology, and (3) especially the concept of "People of God." We will begin with the first point mentioned above.

Method in Ecclesiology

One of the most challenging tasks for scholars of Saint Thomas's *Summa Theologiae* is to show why within the impressive architecture of this masterwork there is not a single question devoted to the issue at hand, namely, the Church.[1] The great treatises of dogmatic and moral theology of the following centuries show, in one way or another, a systematic dependence on the various treatises of Thomas's *Summa*. However, the same thing cannot be said of the tract *De Ecclesia* for the simple reason that the *Summa* does not contain ecclesiology as a treatise. I allude to this fact to highlight from the outset the peculiarity of dogmatic ecclesiology within the theological curriculum. This tract is one "under construction" which, from the point of view of systematics, lacks, as we shall see, a "classical" tradition assigning it a place, structure, and specific contents within dogmatic theology.

The search for a place within dogmatics for the tract *De Ecclesia*, which had been much in evidence in the two decades preceding Vatican II, became much more intense in the thirty years following the council. This was due to the impulses of the council itself, whose strong consciousness of the being and mission of the Church looked for an

---

[1] St. Thomas himself has a highly precise and extraordinarily rich understanding of the Church. See Yves Congar, "Traditio thomistica in materia ecclesiologica," *Angelicum* 43 (1966) 405–28.

adequate expression in systematic theology, that is, a theology that expounds and deepens "the mysteries of Christianity," to use an expression of Matthias J. Scheeben, and their mutual connections.[2]

This provisional state of the dogmatic tract on the Church was caused not only by the lack of an established tradition since the great theological syntheses in the Middle Ages. Other factors should also be noted which Michael Schmaus has already pointed out in his first dogmatic treatise[3] and which, according to Yves Congar, have given rise to the making of a tract on the Church as a reaction.[4]

To be mentioned in the first place is the autonomous growth of canon law with respect to theology. By its very nature this discipline investigates the relations of justice in the Church as an organization and visible institution, both in its more radical elements derived from the revelation proclaimed by Christ and the apostles *(de iure)* and in the historical developments arising from the needs of the times and cultures *(ius ecclesiasticum)*. Included among the first "autonomous" tracts on the Church are first of all the tracts "de postestate."[5] This legal matrix has been, already during the Middle Ages, the "humus" of academic discussions about the Church and has perdured down the centuries. Its traces on the ecclesiological mentality of Catholics are still visible, even though, from the theological point of view, they have to be regarded as a relic of the past.

Second, in intimate relation to the philosophical and cultural questions of modernity, another factor was at play, more important from the viewpoint of theological method. I refer to the concentration of various questions on the Church in a theological tract structured according to the apologetical method. Its structure can be seen, with more or less variations, in the manuals composed from the nineteenth century to almost the eve of Vatican II.[6] Whereas the methodological relation between the dogmatic tract *De Ecclesia* and canon law had basically been clarified several decades ago,[7] the demarcation between ecclesiology

---

[2] Matthias Josef Scheeben, *Mysteries of Christianity* (St. Louis, Mo.: Herder, 1961).

[3] Michael Schmaus, *Dogma*, vol. 4: *The Church: Its Origin and Structure* (New York: Sheed and Ward, 1972) 74.

[4] Yves Congar, *Lay People in the Church: A Study for a Theology and Laity,* 2d ed. (Westminster, Md.: Newman Press, 1965) 45.

[5] See Yves Congar, *Eclesiología desde San Agustín hasta nuestros días*, vol. 3 of *Historia de los Dogmas*, ed. M. Schmaus, A. Grillmeier, L. Scheffczyk (Madrid: Ed. BAC, 1976) 130–63; and Angel Antón, *El Misterio de la Iglesia* (Madrid: Ed. BAC, 1976) 97–118.

[6] See Avery Dulles, *A History of Apologetics* (New York: Corpus Books, 1971).

[7] Today we find ourselves rather before the inverse problem, namely, the attempt of canon law to rethink its foundations in relation to the ecclesiology elaborated in and from the point of view of Vatican II.

and fundamental theology and apologetics is still a live question under discussion by specialists of both disciplines. Consequently, it is logical that a good part of this essay will be devoted to the relation and distinction between dogmatic method and apologetical method. Hence, not only the legitimacy but also the necessity and the mutual complementarity of a double treatment of the issues concerning the Church.

Apologetical Method and Dogmatic Method

A classical tract or manual of fundamental theology used to comprise two parts: the first—usually called *De Revelatione* and beginning with a chapter or section called *De Religione*—studies and justifies revelation as a possibility and a historical fact. It culminates in the section titled *De Christo legato divino,* in which it is demonstrated that in Christ the historical self-manifestation of God has taken place and therefore one must listen to and follow him in order to reach the salvation offered by revelation.

How does this saving revelation which culminates in Christ reach us today? This question introduces the second part of classical fundamental theology which is precisely the apologetic tract *De Ecclesia:* It is argued that, in order to enable revelation and salvation to reach all human beings, Christ founded the Church. The purpose of the fundamental theology of the Church is to demonstrate that the present Roman Catholic Church was founded by Christ. It does so by demonstrating first that Christ truly wanted and founded a Church, and, second, that this community founded by him coincides with the Church that is in communion with the successor of Peter, the Roman Catholic Church. This is, of course, a question of decisive importance, since there are many communities claiming to be the Church of Christ. Fundamental theology seeks then to arrive at this conclusion: that the consciousness that the Church has of being the Church of Christ is well-founded and legitimate; that Christ authorizes the Church to demand from all a full and committed faith in the exposition of the Gospel which it presents, and that it—the Catholic Church—is the divinely instituted way to faith in, commitment to, and following after Christ.

The tracts of fundamental theology *De Ecclesia* are structured at the service of Vatican I's declaration: "In order that we may fulfill the duty of embracing the true faith and constantly persevere in it, God instituted the Church through his only-begotten Son and endowed it with clear proofs of its institution so that all can recognize it as guardian and teacher of the revealed Word" (DB 3012). Therefore, according to Vatican I (DB 3013), the Church appears as the "signum levatum in nationes" spoken of by Isaiah (11:12). This sign—visible and audible—precisely as sign, is explored scientifically by fundamental theology.

The starting point of the fundamental theologian is faith, the Catholic faith; otherwise, he or she would not be a theologian, nor would the result of his or her work be theology. Furthermore, without faith in the Church of Christ, there would be lacking the "existential interest" (Schmaus), so to speak, to walk the road of fundamental theology which otherwise would be no more than intellectual curiosity or mere history of religions. On the contrary, the theologian is accompanied by faith in each of the stages of his or her exploration. Nevertheless, the characteristic of the method of classical fundamental theology, which we can term apologetic in light of its principal, though not exclusive, aims, is that it is, in a strict sense, a movement of reason. True, faith is the starting point and goal of the entire itinerary (the mission of the theological labor is an apostolic goal), since its object is to provide an anthropological justification for, and in the process, to lead to faith. However, the itinerary itself seeks to be rational: to dialogue with the nonbelievers by means of speculative reason and, above all, of historical reason within their respective boundaries.

In the partners of this dialogue, and in the readers of the tract of fundamental theology, faith is not presupposed. What is required of them is that they use their "ratio" without prejudices and keep an "openness" to the transcendence, that is, an openness of spirit to God and, in questions regarding the Church, a recognition that Christ is the one sent by the Father. In this sense, the object of fundamental theology is to prepare a person reasonably and scientifically for the act of faith which in itself is a fruit of grace. (In another sense, already mentioned, the object of fundamental theology is to demonstrate the anthropological legitimacy, or the human *dignitas*, of the faith already possessed.)

It is necessary to note that in the last three decades profound reflections carried out by practitioners of fundamental theology have emphasized the dogmatic, strictly theological foundation of fundamental theology. This is particularly true in matters regarding revelation and faith as response of the human person mediated by the question of credibility. The apologetical method is without doubt valid and necessary, but today it no longer claims to be a "methodologically aseptic" discourse on revelation; on the contrary, its reason is shot through with the faith of the theologian. In this way it no doubt approaches the field of dogmatic proper.[8]

---

[8] See Rino Fisichella, ed., *La Teologia Fondamentale. Convergenze per il terzo millenio* (Cassato Monteferrato: Piemme, 1997); Joseph Doré, "L'évolution des manuels catholiques de théologie fondamentale de 1965 à 1995," *Gregorianum* 77 (1996) 617–

The dogmatic tract *De Ecclesia* moves within another methodological horizon. The mere fact of saying that it is dogmatic theology would be sufficient to describe what would be its method and object. However, it is necessary to go a little deeper, and for this purpose it would be useful not only to explain what a dogmatic method of ecclesiology is but also to compare it with the apologetical or fundamental method whose classical presuppositions we have just described.

Dogmatic theology studies in a direct way the contents of the Christian faith: the dogmas (hence its name), that is, the solemn declarations with which the ecclesiastical magisterium determines the contents of the revealed faith. Perhaps it would be more accurate to say that it studies the mysteries of faith manifested in and by divine revelation, in other words, as contained in tradition and Scripture. In this task the theologian is guided by the declarations of the magisterium which express the faithful understanding, the consciousness that the Church, as integral subject of the faith, has achieved of these mysteries. Dogmatics then treats the mystery of the triune God, the mystery of creation, the mystery of Jesus Christ, the mystery of the human person and the communication of grace, etc. Dogmatic theology *De Ecclesia* or dogmatic ecclesiology or, simply, ecclesiology in academic language treats as its proper object "the mystery of the Church," the Church as mystery. In summary, it may be said that ecclesiology, as someone has put it nicely, is "a gaze, methodically achieved, of the mystery of the Church."

This means in the first place that the Church is recognized by the theologian as an object of faith, as a reality only fully understandable in the light of divine revelation, and consequently as something—it is necessary to repeat here—which is manifested to us in Scripture and the living tradition and whose truth is arrived at under the guidance of the magisterium of apostolic origin. In this sense, the theologian is nothing but a believing Christian, a believer who develops methodically his or her *intellectus fidei*, connatural to the Christian, until it is transformed into a fuller and deeper knowledge, systematically ordered and unified, without, however, the mystery ever ceasing to be mystery or the knowledge transforming the theologian into a gnostic who can do without faith.

---

836. César Izquierdo, *Teología Fundamental* (Pamplona: Ed. Universidad de Navarra, 1998) 19, holds that "there is an agreement that the dogmatic element must be incorporated into fundamental theology, so that it is a treatment of the revelation of faith . . . but also there must be incorporated an apologetic character, however without its classical polemical and defensive presentation."

Here a first methodological difference from fundamental theology is apparent: in dogmatic theology, faith is not the point of departure and the goal, but also the road itself. Dogmatic theology develops within the bosom of faith and does not aim to go out of it; rather, it wants to reflect on it, understand it, deepen its implications by searching for the *nexus mysteriorum* of which Vatican I speaks (DB 3016) and observing the *hierarchia veritatum* mentioned by Vatican II (UR 11c). All this, of course, is the work of reason—*ratio fide illustrata*—but *intra fidem,* in the interior of faith: it is a faith which dwells within the human person and his or her faculties and seeks to understand *(fides quaerens intellectum).* Fundamental theology, especially in its apologetical perspective, does not argue from revelation as revelation but proves with rational arguments the legitimacy of the claims of the Church. Dogmatic theology presupposes these achievements; however, its reasonableness is not *ad fidem* but *in fide.* Also in dogmatics, reason makes use of the historical reason and speculative reason, since God reveals himself in history and appeals to human reason, but it integrates and unifies them in unfolding the intellectual and scientific implications of faith.

In the second place—and this is implicit in the foregoing—dogmatic ecclesiology intends to examine its object in all its aspects with a claim to totality. It does not select, as fundamental theology does, aspects connected with credibility in order to prove that the Church proceeds from Christ, or the visible and structural aspects, as canon law does. Instead it considers all aspects of the Church and tries to provide a unitary vision of the *realitas complexa* of the Church (LG 8a), gazing at it—if it is possible to use such an expression—from within the faith. Fundamental theology "leads" in a certain way to the Church by determining its place and significance in human history. The dogmatic theologian "enters" into the Church itself and, guided by faith which the same Church propounds, he or she explains the origin, nature, and structure of the Church and assumes, from this perspective, what fundamental theology has achieved.

From what has been said two conclusions of special interest may be deduced. First, the main difference between the two tracts of ecclesiology does not consist so much in different contents as in different approaches, that is, in the diverse methods and perspectives in which the contents are dealt with in one and the other discipline. Second, dogmatic theology, because of its claim to totality, also deals with the contents of faith that are of interest to fundamental theology, but it situates them in their proper and organic place within the mystery of the Church.

The reflections of dogmatic theology on the Church then are directed toward giving reasons for this mystery, presenting its various aspects and its beautiful unity which Vatican II has described as follows:

The society equipped with hierarchical structures and the mystical body of Christ, the visible society and the spiritual community, the earthly church and the church endowed with heavenly riches, are not to be thought of as two realities *(duas res)*. On the contrary, they form one complex reality comprising a human and a divine element. . . . This is the unique church of Christ, which in the creed we profess to be one, holy, catholic and apostolic which our Savior, after his resurrection, entrusted to Peter's pastoral care (John 21:17), commissioning him and the other apostles to extend and rule it (see Matthew 28:18, etc.), and which he raised up for all ages as the pillar and mainstay of the truth (see Timothy 3:15) (LG 8a–b).

Faith and Method in Ecclesiology

The exposition of the proper nature of the dogmatic tract on the Church has of course already treated this theme. Here the intention is to underline the double moment, the objective and subjective, of faith. Ecclesiology, as a scientific discipline inserted into the whole of dogmatics, has as its object the mystery of faith which is the Church. It is this object that determines the method and the scientific tools of ecclesiology, namely, Scripture and tradition, read in the Church "under the guidance of the sacred Magisterium" (LG 12a) and penetrated at the same time by "reason illumined by faith" (DB 3016). This celebrated expression—which we have already used above—opens up the subjective moment in the process of theological reflection, a moment which it is important to insist upon now. The faith required for doing good theology is not only the objective contents of the declarations of the magisterium. It is at the same time—and drawing upon it—the subjective faith of the theologian which animates his or her entire life, including his or her reason. Reason, strengthened by the virtue of faith which dwells in the soul of the theologian, projects itself on its object, that is, the mystery of the Church. It is this faith which seeks to understand with the help of reason.

Ecclesiology then is the intellectual manifestation of the *life* of faith lived in the Church. In other words, faith—and the ecclesiality of faith— is not extrinsic to the work of the theologian nor does it constitute a limit to the freedom of the Christian. On the contrary, it is the "habitat," the internal, essential, and constitutive dimension of theology, a true condition of its possibility. Without a living and ecclesial faith there is no theology. There might be something else, quite legitimate in itself, such as history of religions, religious sociology, and so on, but not theology. This has been affirmed by Luther as well as John Paul II. The latter has declared to the theologians at the University of Salamanca:

Faith is not only a necessary presupposition and a fundamental disposition of theology but there is also a profound and intimate connection between the two of them. Faith is the vital and permanent root of theology which sprouts from asking and searching, activities that are intrinsic to faith itself, that is, from its impulse to understand itself, both as a radically free option to personally adhere to Christ and as an assent to the contents of Christian revelation. To do theology, then, is a task exclusively proper to the believer as believer, a task vitally aroused and sustained in all its moments by faith, and therefore an unlimited questioning and searching.[9]

Ecclesiology, just as the whole of theology, and in a special way, dogmatics, is constructed therefore from the virtue of faith of the theologian which is "a radically free option to personally adhere to Christ," option that is inseparable from the delicate "assent to the contents of the Christian revelation."

THE TESTIMONY OF THE "SYMBOL OF FAITH"

The central affirmation of the Christian faith with regard to the Church is contained, as it could not have been otherwise, in the symbol of faith: "I believe the Church," *credo ecclesiam*.[10] Let us examine its implications for the method of ecclesiology.

The symbol of faith is in effect the most ancient and venerable comprehensive formulation of the faith produced by the Church. If dogmatics is a scientific reflection on faith, then it is clear why the creed is of paramount importance for the work of theology. In a certain sense, it may be said that the later declarations of the magisterium should be regarded as developments and concrete unfolding of the implications of this protoformulation of the ecclesial faith.[11] Hence, ecclesiology is in reality a meditation on the ninth article of the creed which says: "*Credo sanctam Ecclesiam catholicam, communionem sanctorum.*"[12]

To understand well the meaning of this statement, it is necessary to keep in mind that the structure of the creed is ternary: the faith of the Church is faith in God triune. The creed has three parts: (1) *Credo in Deum Patrem;* (2) *(Credo) et in Jesum Christum, Filium eius unicum;* (3) *Credo*

---

[9] Pope John Paul II, *Discurso a los teólogos,* Salamanca, November 1, 1982, no. 2.

[10] See Francis Sullivan, *The Church We Believe In: One, Holy, Catholic and Apostolic* (New York: Paulist Press, 1988).

[11] Thomas Aquinas has already proposed this view. See *ST* II-II, q. 1, a. 8.

[12] See DS 10–36 for the various forms and texts of the Apostles' Creed; also see the profound commentary by Henri de Lubac, *The Christian Faith: An Essay on the Structure of the Apostles' Creed* (San Francisco: Ignatius Press, 1986).

in Spiritum Sanctum. The twelve "articles" of the creed are internal "articulations" within the structure of the creed, which is a summary of the faith testified by Scripture, to use the phrase of Thomas Aquinas,[13] faith which is always theological, that is, *in Deum,* in each of the three divine persons.

The structure of the creed is not "systematic," but rather historical-salvific. It is a marvelous reflection of the history of salvation. It affirms that as Christians we believe in God the Father, creator of heaven and earth, who sends first his Son to save us, and then the Holy Spirit, to make fruitful the work of the Son. Having confessed faith in the Trinity, the last part of the creed confesses—especially in relation to the profession of faith in the Holy Spirit—the historical unfolding of the trinitarian economy of salvation. In the words of Alexander of Hales: "After the mention of the Holy Spirit, four general effects are posited: 1) the Catholic Church, communion of saints; 2) remission of sins; 3) resurrection of the flesh; 4) eternal life."[14]

This expression of Alexander of Hale, which recalls the patristic and traditional interpretation of the creed, is perfectly consistent with the exegesis which the Fathers gave to the various linguistic formulations of the faith in God and in the Church contained in the creed. There is a distinction of great methodological importance for ecclesiology. Faith in God is expressed by means of the preposition "in" followed by the accusative case: *"Credo in Deum (Patrem) . . . et in Filium, et in Spiritum Sanctum."* On the contrary, to express faith in the Church—in the "general effects" of which Alexander speaks—the direct accusative case is used without the preposition "in": *"Credo sanctam Ecclesiam, sanctorum communionem."* According to the Fathers, this linguistic difference of the expression of faith manifests the different ways in which God and the Church are constituted the object of faith.

The Roman Catechism (I, X, 22) recalls this tradition with the following words:

> We believe in the three persons of the Trinity, Father, Son, and Holy Spirit, in such a way that we place in them our faith. Now, however [as we confess our ecclesial faith], we change our way of speaking and do not say "I believe in the holy Church" *(in sanctam ecclesiam),* in order that, by a different form of expression *(ratio loquendi),* we distinguish God, creator of all things, from these same created things, and attribute

---

[13] *ST* II-II, q. 1, a. 9, ad 1.

[14] Alexander of Hales, *Summa Theologica,* Pars III, inq. II, tract. II, quaes. II, tit. III, litt. C (Ad Claras Aquas [Quaracchi] prope Florentiam: Ex Typographia Collegii S. Bonaventurae, 1924–48) vol. IV/2:1135.

to the goodness of God all the great gifts and benefits which he has given to the Church.

The Church is then the object of faith but as the effect of the saving action of God in whom we believe. St. Thomas Aquinas expresses this with his usual profundity when commenting on St. Anselm, who recalls the tradition of the Apostles' Creed with the less common form (*"credo in sanctam Ecclesiam"*). So writes Aquinas:

> If one prefers to say *in sanctam Ecclesiam*, it is necessary to take the expression to refer to the Holy Spirit who is, according to our faith, the one who sanctifies the Church, so that what is meant is that: I believe in the Holy Spirit *(in Spiritum Sanctum)* who sanctifies the Church *(sanctificantem Ecclesiam)*. Nevertheless, it is better to follow the traditional usage which does not add the preposition *in*.[15]

This is the interpretation of the Fathers which will be consecrated by the Roman Catechism which begins its exposition of the article on the Church as follows (I, X, 1): "This article [on the Church] depends on the previous article [on the Holy Spirit], because as there we have demonstrated that the Holy Spirit is the source and the splendid giver of all holiness, we confess here that the Church is sanctified by the Holy Spirit himself."[16]

The Apostles' Creed then presents to us the Church as mystery of faith within the framework of the total profession of faith, placing the emphasis on the origin of the Church in the Trinity. This will be the fundamental teaching of Vatican II, and at the same time it is also made clear how ecclesiology is inserted into the very heart of dogmatic theology.

"CREDO ECCLESIAM" AND METHOD IN ECCLESIOLOGY

The form of confessing faith in God and the Church which we have considered has another important consequence with respect to our theme: faith and theological method. The movement of the act of faith terminates in God—*in Deum*—and does not terminate in the Church: I do not believe *in Ecclesiam*, but *Ecclesiam*. I believe that the Church exists, that it is the Church of God, a great reality wholly referred to God. The Church's total reference to God and at the same time its total distinction from God (the distinction between God and the creatures)

---

[15] *ST*, II-II, q. 1, a. 9, ad 5.

[16] This suggestive interpretation of the Roman Catechism (I, 10, 22) has also been taken over by the *Catechism of the Catholic Church*, no. 750.

highlights the way the Church is a "mystery." The Church's being is being in history: The Church is a reality within the history of humanity which humans, including unbelievers, can observe and recognize, and within that which we call by the name "Church."[17] Therefore, the look of faith from which ecclesiology arises cannot be directed only to God and God's word, but also to humanity and its history: in this case, a look at the Church, at the concrete Church, as a reality which is there, "seen"—in their own way—by humans and "believed" in its mystery by Christians. In this sense, we Christians believe that the Church— whose historical vicissitudes we contemplate—has been created and is permanently recreated by the Lord and that its "mystery" derives from him. This is another way of expressing, from our own present sensibility, that which the ancients meant when they redacted articles 8 and 9 of the creed in the manner explained above.

What has been said above has repercussions for the theological method and the composition of a tract on the Church which attempts to give an account of its radical mysteriousness along the line indicated by Vatican II for dogmatic theology.[18] This means that the study of the origin of the Church in the history of Jesus and in the events of Easter and Pentecost—the first indispensable part of the tract *De Ecclesia*—is not something one studies "first" (for chronological-historical reasons) in order to pass next (for the same reasons) to the various historical forms of the Christian community, and finally to arrive at the description of the Church today in its social structures and in the functions (mission) by which it fulfills the "message" of Jesus. Instead, the mystery of the Church confessed in the creed becomes radical precisely in the fact that the divine, trinitarian origin of the Church is a permanent event which today determines the being of the Church. And this, not in the sense that we stand in front of an "institution" which there, in its founding, receives its rules by which it can perpetuate itself in history.

Rather, we stand in front of something much more profound. The historical "being" of the Church—of the concrete Church which today exists in history and in whom we Christians live—is not separable from its "origin." The reason for this is clear: the things that maintain the Church today in its being the Church of God are precisely the same christological and pneumatological realities which gave it origin. The mystery consists, if we may speak thus, in the fact that these christological and pneumatological realities referred to above do not stay "outside" but have been placed "inside" by God (sacramentally) in the

---

[17] See Severino Dianich, *Ecclesiologia: Questioni di metodo e una proposta* (Milano: Ed. Paoline, 1993) 8.

[18] See the decree *Optatam Totius*, 16c.

very bosom of the historical Church. These realities are words and sacraments: the words announcing the redeeming mystery of the Word made flesh and the gift of the Holy Spirit, and the sacraments conferring justifying grace. By means of words and sacraments the power of the Holy Spirit makes present in human history the mystery of Christ. Thus, the triune God in whom we believe *(credo "in" Deum)* creates and recreates the Church which we believe *(credo Ecclesiam)*.

In fact, the event of words and sacraments enables the Church to be reborn permanently as community and institution: the Church—according to Thomas's colorful phrase—is "fabricated" by means of the sacraments.[19] On the other hand, this service is also the very task of the Church, its mission: it is the Church that "makes" the sacraments *(sacramenta sunt Ecclesiae;* hence, the expression of Vatican II: *Ecclesia, sacramentum salutis).* In the historical phase of its existence, the mystery of the Church which we believe consists in being simultaneously fruit of salvation *(fructus salutis)* and instrument of salvation *(instrumentum salutis).* In words that introduce the fundamental concepts of Vatican II's ecclesiology, we say that the Church, as historical subject, is at the same time both *communio* and *sacramentum:* reality of communion and sacrament of this very same communion. It may be said that the object of the method or the road of dogmatic ecclesiology is to give an account of the mystery expressed in this binomial. The method consists substantially in studying the being and mission of the Church today from its historical and trinitarian origin. It is here that the theological effort should concentrate, even at the ecumenical level, as is clear from the Catholic/Lutheran document on the Church and justification.[20] Also, in this perspective the importance of understanding the Church as the new People of God becomes apparent.

The Names and Images of the Church

The revelation of the mystery of the Church is not a mere communication made by God of an idea, doctrine, or concept. It is, as we have said, the origination of a historical-salvific reality, that is, the Church, to which God, in his love, calls us by means of events and words, which are intertwined with each other and illumine each other. The words re-

[19] Thomas Aquinas, *In I Cor. 11:2* (Marietti), 269: *"Sacramenta, a quibus fabricata est Ecclesia."*

[20] See the Lutheran–Roman Catholic Joint Commission, *Church and Justification: Understanding the Church in the Light of the Doctrine of Justification* ([Geneva?]: Lutheran World Federation, 1994).

veal the events. That is why in the revelation about the Church an important place is occupied by "designations"—names, figures, images—with which the Scripture describes the community of salvation founded by Christ and animated by the Holy Spirit. A study of these designations is necessary in ecclesiology in order to penetrate into the "intimate essence" (Paul VI)[21] or the "intimate nature" (LG 6a) of the Church.

In its constitution *Lumen gentium* Vatican II has made a notable effort to explain the nature of the Church (LG 6a) by means of an exploration of the sacred Scripture and tradition. The results of this meditation are contained in nos. 6 and 7 of chapter 1 and the whole of chapter 2 with the doctrine of People of God. This magisterial patrimony provides an important help for a personal theological reading of biblical and patristic texts on the theme.

Numbers 2, 3, and 4 with which the constitution begins (after the proemium) are an exposition of the "origin of the Church" which is found in the triune God. Number 5 is dedicated to showing how this transcendent origin is made historical in the preaching of the reign of God by Jesus in whose preaching the Church is announced and originates. After explaining the origin of the Church in this way, the constitution moves on to expound its nature which, as we have shown, is inseparable from its origin. This it does by searching in the Scripture the revelation of the mystery. It finds it in a complex of designations (images, metaphors, figures) which point to this revelation. The council accomplishes this task in three phases:

(1) In no. 6 it gathers a numerous and varied series of significant explanations and subjects them to a sober and unified treatment.

(2) Number 7 also has the same descriptive nature, but it focuses on one single image of greatest importance in the revelation of the mystery: the Church as the body of Christ, which has been given a profound treatment in Pius XII's encyclical *Mystici corporis*.

(3) However, the exposition of the essence of the Church does not occur in nos. 6 and 7 of the constitution but continues in the whole text of chapter 2, especially in nos. 9 through 12, and more particularly in no. 9. We refer to the idea of "People of God," which is indisputably the axis of the constitution's exposition of the nature and mission of the Church. To this we now turn.

The most significant difference between the way of treating the images in no. 6 and the body of Christ in no. 7 on the one hand, and the theme of People of God in chapter 2 on the other, consists in the fact that in the former the "transcendent" reality of the Church appears in

---

[21] Pope Paul VI, "Discurso de promulgación de *Lumen gentium*," November 21, 1964, *AAS* 56 (1964) 1014.

the foreground, with the form of their historical realization remaining in the background. On the contrary, the chapter on the People of God approaches the life of this people as it unfolds itself in the pilgrimage of the Church and projects it forward to its eschatological consummation. Consequently we may say, in the wake of Monsignor Philips, that in the images of chapter 1 the mystery of unity and communion, which is the Church, is thrown into relief, whereas in the image of People of God, the plurality, the "historical catholicity" of the Church, is highlighted above all.[22] In my view, the post-Vatican II theology, in deepening the understanding of the trinitarian origin of the Church and its pneumatological dimension, has shown well that all the biblical images refer at the same time to both the pilgrim Church, in which we live and which we keep before our eyes, and the consummated Church, which is no other than the fullness of what has already been anticipated here on earth. So far then is the synthesis of Vatican I and Vatican II.

On the other hand, in addition to these biblical images and names, in order to explain the "intimate essence" of the Church and its "intimate nature," Vatican II and contemporary theology make use of certain ecclesiological concepts among which stand out *communio* (Church-communion) and *sacramentum* (Church-sacrament). *Lumen gentium* begins by saying that the Church "is in Christ as a sacrament" of the union of humans with God and among themselves. In no. 9 it is said of the new People of God that "it has been constituted in order to realize (in) the communion of life, charity and truth." And the Synod of Bishops of 1985 said that *communio* was "the central idea of the ecclesiology of Vatican II."[23]

The ecclesiology of the last decades has passed through various phases in search of a synthetic and comprehensive concept with which to organize its doctrinal exposition. A polemical confrontation has been set between *communio* and *sacramentum*, and between both of them and People of God *(populus Dei)*. Even the very designation of *mysterium* entered into competition with those other names as an alternative for an understanding of the Church.

It is neither possible nor necessary to study this complex of questions here. Nevertheless I submit that an ecclesiology that is faithful to the fundamental directions of Vatican II and at the same time receptive to the better developments of postconciliar theology is one that must retrieve the theme of "People of God" as the basic concept to understand the Church. An important trait of this ecclesiology is its decision

---

[22] Gérard Philips, *La Iglesia y su misterio en el Concilio Vaticano II*, vol. I (Barcelona: Herder, 1968) 162.

[23] "Relatio finalis," II, C. 1 (85), *Enchiridion Vaticanum* 9/1800.

to root itself in the Trinity. First, this is done to understand the origin of the Church as the saving plan of the Father, the redeeming incarnation of the Son, and the sanctifying mission of the Holy Spirit. Second, it is also done to understand the Church as the term of this trinitarian action, which is the Church itself considered as the People of God who are a pilgrim in history and will be consummated in glory, a people whose mystery consists in Easter (Church as body of Christ) and in Pentecost (Church as Temple of the Holy Spirit).[24]

In a good theology of the People of God the concepts of *communio* and *sacramentum* are not taken as mutually exclusive models or alternatives, but as complementary dimensions of the *mysterium* of this people and as ways to deepen our understanding of it.[25]

The Notion of People of God, "Method" of Ecclesiology

The notion of People of God is especially suited for the method of ecclesiology we have described. In fact, it gives rise to an ecclesiology which attempts to understand the Church in its historical-salvific reality, that is, as the new People of God sent into the world, "marked" trinitarianly, that is, christologically and pneumatologically, a people whose novelty is rooted in its essential and permanent origination in the love of the Father, the saving Easter of the Son, and in the gift of the Holy Spirit.

We will forgo an exposition of other names, images, and figures in order to concentrate on some essential aspects of the theology of People of God.

People of God and the Mystery of the Church

It is apparent for readers of the constitution *Lumen gentium* that the determining category of all its discourse is that of People of God. It is in function of this concept that all the other notions in the constitution are given their place and its materials are arranged. Of course, the reader will also perceive ruptures in the text, and if the reader is versed in these matters, she or he will see that there are traces of a previous option

---

[24] See Yves Congar, *I Believe in the Holy Spirit,* vol. 2 (New York: Seabury Press, 1983) 53–4.

[25] See Avery Dulles, *Models of the Church,* expanded edition (Garden City, N.Y.: Image Books, 1987). The author insists on the need to integrate various models. There remains the debate on the use of the concept of "model" in the field of theology.

(redactional and theological) of a quite different character. It will become apparent that the final text responds to a second option, rather deliberate, to take the category of People of God—and not, for example, body of Christ—as the starting point of its discourse on the Church. How and why the council took this course of action cannot be explained here.[26] Suffice it to say that in no way is this option contrary to the great ecclesiological patrimony included in the category of body of Christ. Rather, all this patrimony and its most profound perspective remained situated precisely in the ecclesiology of People of God.[27]

The preference that the council had for the concept of People of God shows its decision at the same time (1) to return to the style of biblical thinking; (2) to construct a "historical and concrete theology" (Paul VI) that takes account, in the language of the Church, of the unity of the saving plan of God, going back to its origins and unifying the two testaments, Israel and the Church; and (3) to show how the Church acts today in the history which we live and make and in whose bosom the People of God is present as a "historical subject."[28]

This "historical subject" which is the People of God concentrates in itself the "mystery of the Church." This is the first point that will be discussed and may be formulated in a form of an academic thesis as follows:

> The consideration of the Church as "People of God" can be carried out in a rigorous and formal way only within the theme of "mystery of the Church," a theme that envelops and involves theologically the theme of People of God.

[26] See G. Geremia, *I primi due capitoli della "Lumen gentium." Genesi ed elaborazione del testto conciliare* (Rome: Marianum, 1971); Antonio Acerbi, *Due ecclesiologie. Ecclesiologia giuridica e d ecclesiologia di comunione nella "Lumen gentium"* (Bologna: Dehoniane, 1974); Yves Congar, *Le Concile du Vatican II. Son Église, Peuple de Dieu et Corps du Christ* (Paris: Beauchèsne, 1984).

[27] This conviction is deeply indebted to the work of Lucien Cerfaux, particularly his famous *Théologie de l'Église suivant saint Paul* (Paris: Éditions du Cerf, 1942), where one reads: "La notion du Peuple de Dieu est le centre de la théologie paulinienne" (13). For St. Paul, "the image of Body of Christ is but another expression for the People of God and is not alternative notion." See Nils A. Dahl, *Das Volk Gottes. Eine Untersuchung zum Kirchenbewusstsein des Urchristentums* (Darmstadt: Wissenschaftliche Buchgesellschaft, 1969).

[28] This is the expression used by the International Theological Commission, *Themata selecta de Ecclesiologia*, October 8, 1985 (Rome: Libreria Editrice Vaticana, 1985), henceforth: ITC, *Themata selecta*, followed by the numbers of the chapter and the paragraph. See the title of chapter 3: "The Church as 'Mystery' and as 'Historical Subject.'" See also Giuseppe Colombo, "Il 'Popolo di Dio' e il 'misterio' della Chiesa nell'ecclesiologia post-conciliare," *Teologia* 10 (1985) 97–169. This long study offers one of the most suggestive analyses relative to our theme.

This is the fundamental doctrine of Vatican II which we have to seek to understand on the basis of its texts. The sequence of the two first chapters of *Lumen gentium* (1. The Mystery of the Church; 2. The People of God) has suggested to some that there is an opposition between the two, or at least—and this more frequently—that there is a change of theme in the transition from the one to the other, namely, the Church is considered as a mystery in chapter 1 and as People of God in chapter 2. The result is that chapter 2 is thought not to contemplate the Church as Church-Mystery but as a reality in the historical, social, and human perspective, that is, Church as a people among peoples.

It would be helpful to affirm, before going further, that the concepts of People of God and body of Christ strictly call for each other. The Church is People of God because and to the extent that it is the body of Christ.[29] The Church must be the body of Christ, that is, the community gathered by Christ insofar as its members believe in him and live for him, if it is the People of God, the People of the Father. Undoubtedly, the postconciliar debates on ecclesiology do seem at times to be a battle between the two chapters which are as it were the emblems of the opposition or tension between the Church as the People of God (receptive to history, attentive to social problems, and in permanent self-reform) and the Church as the body of Christ (invisible and transcendent mystery, intimate communion with God, and liturgy and life of prayer).

All this is contrary not only to the theological reality of things but also to the very intention of the council which underlines the thematic identity of chapters 1 and 2. This was explicitly affirmed by the relator when he presented chapter 2 to the assembly of the council: "The exposition on the People of God pertains in fact to the very mystery of the Church *(ad ipsum mysterium Ecclesiae)*, considered in itself . . . and cannot be separated from the fundamental teaching in chapter 1 on the end and intimate nature of the Church." In fact, the relator goes on to argue, they form a single chapter whose common title would be that of chapter 1: "The Mystery of the Church." The reason why the theme of *de Populo Dei* is not included in the one of *de Ecclesia mysterio*, said the relator, is purely material: "The first chapter would have been huge and disproportionate."[30]

---

[29] See Patrick Granfield's expression, "The Body of Christ established by God for his People," in his title *The Limits of the Papacy* (New York: Crossroad, 1987) 1.

[30] Giuseppe Alberigo and Franca Magistretti, eds., *Constitutionis dogmaticae "Lumen gentium" synopsis historica* (Bologna: Istituto per le Scienze Religiose, 1975) 441, ll. 44–7. The official text of the "Relatio" is found in *Acta Synodalia* III/1, 158–374.

This reflection is of the greatest importance for our theme. The concept of People of God (as is the case with other biblical concepts such as body of Christ and Temple of the Spirit, which show the trinitarian origin of the Church) highlights the *intima Ecclesiae natura* (LG 6a), the profound being of the Church, its mystery, without being a mere description of its social and visible aspects. The disaffection toward the concept of People of God in favor of that of *communio*, as occurred during the Extraordinary Synod of 1985,[31] is explained in good part by the deficient elaboration of the category of People of God provided in the '70s. Removed from the theme of "mystery," it was sliding in pastoral usage toward policies of a collectivistic and quasi-political type.[32]

Thus the International Theological Committee notes: "The concept of People of God, used insistently by the council in a perspective both new and faithful to the image of the Church as it appears in the New Testament and the Fathers, was transformed little by little into a slogan with rather superficial contents."[33] Precisely, the biblical and patristic concept of "mystery," which Vatican II retrieves in opposition to the modern meaning, so says the already quoted relator of *Lumen gentium,* "appears as very appropriate for designating the Church." And he gives the reason: the Church "is a divine transcendent and saving reality which reveals and manifests itself in a visible manner."[34]

It is therefore necessary, when studying the designations and images which Scripture proposes, to keep in mind that they always designate the whole—the mystery—even though from the peculiar perspective of each of them. The eminent services that the concept of People of God renders toward an understanding of the Church as "historical subject," a people among the peoples, could evaporate if it does not embrace adequately the "mystery" of this people. But if the People of God is understood as mystery, the theologian will be brought to see the basic and radical character of this notion which permits the integration of other notions in it. This brings us to the second point and thesis.

People of God as People of the Father

Let us consider the meaning of the genitive expression "of God" in the phrase "People of God." "It highlights the specific and definitive

---

[31] See Giuseppe Colombo, "Il Popolo di Dio," 107; Severino Dianich, *Ecclesiologia,* 201–30.

[32] M. Semaro, "Popolo di Dio. Una nozione ecclesiologica al Concilio e vent'anni dopo," *Rivista di Scienze Religiose* 2 (1988) 29–57, esp. 50–6.

[33] ITC, *Themata selecta,* praefatio (Cardinal Ratzinger).

[34] Giuseppe Alberigo, *Synopsis historica,* 436, ll. 75–7; *Acta Synodalia* III/1, 170 [18]. On the same theme, see Giuseppe Colombo, "Il Popolo di Dio."

range of the expression by situating it in the biblical context in which it appears and develops." The International Theological Commission, whose words have just been quoted, says that "of God" not only excludes any interpretation of the term "people" "in a merely biological, racial, cultural, political and ideological meaning," but also indicates that "the People of God proceeds from above, from the design of God, that is, from the election, covenant and mission." This argument is strengthened if one remembers that "*Lumen gentium* is not limited to propounding the Old Testament notion of people of God, but goes on to speak of the New People of God."[35] We can go further and formulate our second contribution to the theme in the form of a thesis:

> *The category "People of God" must be understood from the trinitarian and economic language of the New Testament, and hence as "People of the Father."*

We cannot of course remain in a merely human, organizational vision of the People of God which is the Church. Nor is it sufficient to make a generic reference to the divine origin of this people (People *of God*). The mystery of this people is made clear only in a trinitarian reading of its name: People *of the Father*. In fact, just as "Body" and "Temple" refer to the Son and the Holy Spirit, "people" in the expression "People of God" refers directly to the Father. It is the fruit of the Father's election, who gives being to his people by gathering it in Christ with the gift of the Spirit, gift that produces the Church and within the Christians the internal "christification" of its being and mission. In this way, the name "People of God," understood, according to the New Testament usage,[36] as the People of the Father, places us within a true trinitarian understanding of the origin, being, and mission of the Church. It cannot be otherwise: the Father, who at the "theological" level is the "origin" of the Son and the Spirit, is also, at the "economic" level, the "origin" of the Church. This reflection is that which, methodologically, indicates the way to a systematic reception of the contents of the concepts "body of Christ" and "Temple of the Spirit" within an ecclesiology of the People of God. This is of a piece with what has been said above: the consideration of the People of God as the People of the Father is the presupposition for affirming the christological and pneumatological origination of the People of God.

Both biblical exegesis and systematic theology have pointed toward this interpretation of the notion of People of God. In his exposition of

---

[35] ITC, *Themata selecta*, 2.2.

[36] See Karl Rahner, "*Theos* in the New Testament," *Theological Investigations*, vol. 1 (Baltimore: Helicon Press, 1961) 79–148.

the theme in St. Paul, Franz Mussner affirms that the novelty of the New Testament concept of People of God consists in the fact that the God of this people is and appears as the "Father of our Lord Jesus Christ."[37] On his part, Michael Schmaus, on the basis of the council, sees in this interpretation the foundation of the preeminence of the *Volkgottesbegriff* over other biblical concepts. This concept, explains Schmaus, designates the Church in its pertinence to God, pertinence realized through Jesus Christ, who is the only way to the Father. And he adds: "The New Testament never calls the Church the People of Christ but always the People of God. With this it means to say People of the heavenly Father whose Son is made flesh in the man Jesus."[38]

This is the climate of the constitution *Lumen gentium,* nos. 2, 3, and 4, which receives an explicit development in the decree *Ad gentes,* whose nos. 2, 3, and 4 have exercised a determining influence on the major postconciliar ecclesiologies.

The mission that the Church has is not added to it as to a Church already constituted; rather, it pertains to its very being: the Church is "missionary by nature" (AG 2a). The decree gives this reason: "because the Church has its origin in the mission of the Son and the mission of the Holy Spirit according to the plan of God the Father." The origin, nature, and mission of the Church are therefore only intelligible as historical-salvific projection of the mystery of God one and trine. The christological and pneumatological imprint of the Church and its mission will be discussed by the decree, in parallel to *Lumen gentium,* in nos. 3 and 4. This no. 2, like its counterpart in *Lumen gentium,* focuses on the design of the Father which appears as reflection of his intratrinitarian love. Concretely, the Church "derives from the originating love or charity of God the Father, Principle without principle *(Principium sine principio),* by whom the Son is generated *(ex quo Filius gignitur),* and from whom the Spirit proceeds by the Son."

From this radical origination, the person of the Father, eternal origin of the divine processions, is also, according to the decree,

> by his merciful goodness, the creator of humanity and the one who calls them to communion with himself in life and in glory, pouring out without ceasing and generously his divine goodness; and this in such a way that he who is the creator of all makes himself finally everything in all things, procuring at the same his glory and our happiness.

---

[37] Frans Mussner, "The People of God according to Eph. 1:3-14," *Concilium* 10 (1965) 96–109.

[38] Michael Schmaus, "Das gegenseitige Verhältnis von Leib Christi und Vilk Gottes im Kirchenverständnis," *Volk Gottes. Festgabe für Josef Höfer,* ed. R. Bäumer and H. Dolch (Freiburg: Herder, 1967) 26.

The divine plan of salvation, attributed to the Person of the Father, appears here in the anthropological key, and ends with the ecclesiology of the People of God as the People of the Father: "It has pleased God to call humans to participate in his life not only as individuals, excluding all relationships among them, but to constitute them into a people, so that his children, who were scattered, were congregated into unity." As is clear, the text of the decree leads the initial words of no. 9 of *Lumen gentium*, which it reproduces, to the idea of the people of the children of God. The reference that the decree makes to John 11:52 is unequivocal. The theme "children in the Son" (*filii in Filio*) and the christological dimension of this people are therefore intrinsically intertwined.

The same "patro-nomic" perspective is found in *Lumen gentium*, no. 2, which presents the design of the Father in a directly ecclesiological key: "The Eternal Father decided to assemble the believers in Christ into the Holy Church." After describing the historical stages and moments of this plan, the paragraph contemplates its eschatological consummation, when all the just (the firstborn Son and his many brothers and sisters) are gathered with the Father (*apud Patrem*) into a universal *ekklesia*. We meet this assembly of the children of God in the decree *Ad gentes* and the assembly of the just with the Father in the constitution *Lumen gentium*. But the theme is the same: the Church as the People of the Father. It is the theme of the eternal Sabbath of the People of God who celebrates its status, meaning, and mission as the people marching in the midst of history.

The idea of the People of God as the People of the Father is contained in the documents of Vatican II but was not developed systematically there nor even in the postconciliar ecclesiology. The points made by Mussner and Schmaus, at the closing of the council, found scarce echo in the subsequent ecclesiology. Why? Perhaps the Old Testament origin of the theme of the People of God and the idea of the continuity of the Church with Israel might have concealed its strictly trinitarian perspective. Perhaps the displacement of interest—from the theological to the organizational and the "popular"—might account for the interruption of the line of thought about the People of God initiated by the council. At any rate, this line must be retrieved and developed.[39]

[39] On this theme, see Pedro Rodríguez, ed., *Ecclesiología 30 años después de "Lumen gentium"* (Madrid: Rialp, 1994). Gerhard Müller, one of the contributors to the volume, writes in his recent work: "The essence of the Church is revealed through the trinitarian reality and from the historical-salvific and universal perspective of three basic, mutually related concepts: Church as the People of God the Father (LG 2), as the Body of Christ is the Church of the Son (LG 3), and as the Temple of the Holy Spirit (LG 4)." Gerhard Müller, *Katholische Dogmatik* (Freiburg: Herder, 1995) 612.

For this the key is what we have maintained in the first thesis: placing the category of People of God in the context of the mystery of the Church (by unifying chapters 1 and 2 of *Lumen gentium!*). Then, from its internal relation to the trinitarian mystery, it is possible to understand the "foundational" character corresponding to the notion of People of God in an ecclesiology inspired by the great options of the council.

Starting from this synthetic theology of the People of God it is possible to summarize the witness of revelation in the New Testament about the origin of the Church as follows:

> The People of God, which is the Church, has its origin in the Father through the double mission of the Son and the Holy Spirit.

Irenaeus, using the image of the two hands of God, expresses poetically—and profoundly—the idea that the Church was born in two missions, that of the Word and that of the Spirit.[40] As the council says: "To establish peace, that is, communion with himself [the Father], and to create thus the fraternal society of sinful humans among themselves, God decided to enter into human history in a new and definitive way by sending his Son in our flesh" (AG 3a).

> When the Son has accomplished the work the Father has assigned to him on earth (cf. John 17:4), the Holy Spirit was sent on the day of Pentecost so that he may sanctify the Church continually, and in this way, those who believe in Christ may have access to the Father in the same Spirit (Ephesians 2:18) (LG 4a).

Consequently, the Church appears as "a people gathered in and from the unity of the Father and the Son and the Holy Spirit" (St. Cyprian).[41]

But this people is a family. The People of God the Father is a family. In this sense it is important to note the thematic proximity between People of God and Family of God *(familia Dei)*. This last image focuses on the people as a family and clarifies the meaning of the fatherhood of God as Father of this people and the filial status of its members. They form a family, the family of the children of God. The constitution *Gaudium et spes* gives a special relevance to this theme:

> The Church has a saving and eschatological purpose which can be fully attained only in the next life. But it is now present here on earth and is composed of men and women; they, the members of the earthly city, are

---

[40] *Adversus Haereses*, V, 6, 1; V, 28, 4. See J. Mambrino, "Les deux mains du Père dans l'oeuvre de S. Irénée," *Nouvelle Revue Théologique* 79 (1957) 335–70.

[41] LG 4b: *"de unitate Patris et Filii et Sancti Spiritus plebs adunata."*

called to form the family of the children of God even in this present history of humankind and to increase it continually until the Lord comes (GS 40b).[42]

It has become clear how a "trinitarian" theology of the People of God, understood as a dimension of the design of God the Father, refers us immediately to Christ, the eternal Son of the Father made human. The Father, who is Father because of his relation to the Son, sent the Son to fulfill his plan, and the Son reveals him as Father, and the Father reveals him as the Son. Christ is the "mystery," the firstborn among many brothers and sisters, the center of the plan of God. In this perspective, all the forms of acting as the People of God (Israel) which preceded Jesus of Nazareth, the Son of God made human, are christological anticipations and prefigurations of what would be fully manifested when the Son of God came in human flesh. He came "to gather together, as Saint John says (11:52) the children of God who were scattered." The People and Family of God is the People of the brothers and sisters of Jesus, whom the Father calls and assembles in Christ and for the love for Christ.

This is the ecclesiological place to understand what the Mother of Christ is in the Family of God constituted by a multitude of brothers and sisters: she is at the same time daughter and mother, the Mother of the Church. As *Lumen gentium* affirms, "all of us who are children of God constitute the one family of God" (no. 51).

The gift of divine sonship and daughterhood and the life proper to the children of God are the fruit of the Word and sacraments with which the Church (the family of the children of God) "fabricates" itself, as we have seen. This is the same as saying that the Church lives off the gift and mission of the Holy Spirit, the other "hand" of the Father. The Father and the Son send the Holy Spirit so that he "christifies" the Church: the Spirit makes us into brothers and sisters of Christ and "children of the Father in the Son." In this way the Father creates and recreates in history the People and Family of God. That is why Christ says of the Holy Spirit: "I will send him to you."

Hence a double conclusion. First, the significance of the double mission of the Son and the Spirit for the understanding of the mystery of Church can be grasped only by seeing them from the unity of the Trinity and the unity of the plan of the Father. Second, the People of God as the plan of God, as the People of the Father and the Family of the

---

[42] "Christ ordered the Apostles to preach the evangelical message to all nations so that the human race may transform into the Family of God in which the fullness of the law would be love" (GS 32c).

children of God, is the methodological way to understand the Church in its relation to Christ and in its relation to the Holy Spirit.

Ekklesia *as Essential Designation of the People of God*

There is a consensus that among the many names with which the New Testament designates the group of followers of Jesus—besides the ones already mentioned such as the saints, the believers, the Christians, the Israel of God, the house of God, the children of Abraham, the disciples, etc.—the first generation of Christians preferred the term "Church" or *ekklesia*. Some thirty years ago Joseph Ratzinger had already written: "The primitive Church's own consciousness, which continues to be fundamentally normative for all the later developments of its being, given the normativity of the origins of Christianity, finds its fullest expression in the denomination *'ekklesia'* which the Christian community gave itself from the moment of its birth."[43] Here is the third opportunity to orient methodologically the ecclesiology we are considering. Let us formulate the principle in thesis form:

> *Church* (ekklesia, ekklesia tou theou), *the original denomination of the community of Jesus' disciples, concentrates in itself the novelty of the People of God as People of the Father, called and gathered in Christ.*

The term *ekklesia* is located in fact within the theology of the People of God. In this word the first disciples saw not only their profound connection with the Old Testament but also the new and gratuitous call coming from Jesus and creating a new people of Jews and Gentiles. On the other hand, the word was applied both to the universal community of Christians and, in the plural, to the local communities. It is important that we give some thought to why the first Christians of Greek language in general used the name *ekklesia* to designate the new reality of salvation which Jesus has brought to human history. It is significant for the theology of People of God that it has been so. Equally important is the observation coming from biblical exegesis: *ekklesia* comes into the Christian New Testament language from the biblical language of the Septuagint and not through an adaptation of the Hellenistic meaning of the term.

In the Greek world, *ekklesia* designates the assembly of the demos, the people in the sociopolitical sense. It appears in this profane meaning, for example, in Acts 19:32-40: that tumultuous meeting of the people

---

[43] J. Ratzinger, "Kirche," *Lexikon für Theologie und Kirche,* 2d ed., vol. VI (Freiburg: Herder, 1961) col. 174.

of Ephesus is an *ekklesia*. However, it is not this usage that gives rise to the Christian use of the term by which, down to our times, the result of Christ's saving work has been named. On the contrary, the word *ekklesia* connects immediately to the biblical theology of God and manifests in a surprising way the consciousness of novelty which the Christians had in understanding themselves.

In the Septuagint translation—from which the New Testament term comes—*ekklesia* designates the assembly convoked for a religious, usually cultic, purpose. It corresponds to the Hebrew *qahal*, which is used to refer to the meeting of the people in the desert (Deut 4:10; 31:30; Josh 8:35) or to later liturgical assemblies (1 Chr 28:8; Neh 8:2). *Ekklesia* is always the translation of *qahal*, though this word is sometimes translated with *synagoge* (Num 16:3; 20:4; Deut 5:22). They are in fact synonyms which do not oppose each other until the Christians reserved the latter for the unbelieving Jews. The biblical *ekklesia* evokes immediately for the Christians the idea of God who calls or convokes his people (*ek-klesia* = convoking) and establishes those who are called into a "sacred assembly," *kete hagia* (Exod 12:16; Lev 23:3). Thus they see themselves as the People of God convoked in a new manner, that is, by the blood of Christ poured out on the cross. The determining term becomes *ekklesia tou theou* (eleven times in St. Paul), the Church of God, which is the translation of *qahal Yahweh* of the Old Testament.

However, it must be asked why it was *ekklesia tou theou*, and not *laos tou theou*, that imposed itself on the vocabulary and in the Christian consciousness, in spite of the fact that in the Old Testament theology of People of God, *ekklesia* is intelligible only from *laos*. It seems to me that behind the triumph of this expression stands the whole christological and pneumatological novelty of the New Testament notion of People of God.

The *qahal Yahweh* was in the Old Testament the People of God insofar as it was gathered for worship and praise: the *qahal* was a "moment" of the pilgrimage. Once the sacred assembly is dismissed, the people would continue their journey: it was the People of God but not the "Church of God." The Israelites were dependent upon successive convocations.

In the New Testament the situation is different. Now the new people whom God convoked in Christ, even if its members were located and scattered throughout the city and the whole world, are always the *ekklesia tou theou*, a permanent, eschatological convocation of the Father in Christ and the Holy Spirit; an *ekklesia* which, through Christ and in the Holy Spirit, gives the Father honor and praise. The word "Church," in fact, bears witness to the consciousness that the apostles had, and with them the primitive Christian communities, of being the new and true People of God which is now permanently convoked by its Lord and gathered in a continuous and mysterious manner into a holy assembly, even though its members remain scattered throughout the city. Note that it is the permanent being of the Church that receives the name *qahal-ekklesia,* and not only the concrete assemblies and the liturgical meetings.[44] This is already clear in the first word of the first writing of the New Testament, that is, the first letter to the Thessalonians. St. Paul addresses himself to the Christians living in Thessalonica and calls them "the *ekklesia* . . . in God the Father and the Lord Jesus Christ" (1 Thess 1:1). The *ekklesia* is the people of God ransomed by Jesus Christ, scattered throughout the earth, but living, already now and always, in a mysterious and holy congregation. The plural *ekklesiai* (1 Thess 2:14; Gal 1:22) indicates that this people, wherever they are located, are always the one Church of God, the Holy People gathered together for praise in this or that location: "the Church of God which is in Corinth," according to the greetings in the letters to the Corinthians.

The mystery of this new people, in our perspective, consists in the fact that no new convocations are expected: it is always the *ekklesia,* the eschatological communion already present on earth, because they—the People whom Christ has convoked on the part of the Father—are for always the body of Christ and the Temple of the Holy Spirit. The believers have from the first moment understood the new People of God as the people whom the Father convoked through Christ and who gather around Christ "to go to the Father." Hence, the denominations "Church of God" and "Church of Christ" are interchangeable.[45]

The question, so often raised, of whether the word "Church" designates in the New Testament the local church or the universal Church has many times concealed this decisive reality to which I have been referring and which lies at the depth of the consciousness of the early Christians: that in the language of the Christians, *ekklesia* is, in both its universal and local dimensions, this mysterious and permanent convocation-congregation-communion of the believers in Christ which the Bible calls the body of Christ. Hence, this permanent congregation also refers essentially to the concrete cultic assembly in which the body of Christ is consecrated.

It is evident from what has been said about the continuous "recreation" of the Church through word and sacraments that the preeminent and paradigmatic meaning of the *ekklesia* of Christians is the liturgical

---

[44] "The cultic assembly is considered as the concrete realization of the being itself of the community." See Ratzinger, "Kirche," 175.

[45] See Dahl, *Das Volk Gottes,* 205: "The novelty of the new community consists in the fact that it is not only the *ekklesia* of God but also the *ekklesia* of Christ."

assembly, especially the celebration of the Eucharist, in which they are made into "the one body": *unum corpus multi sumus.* However, what the primitive communities have understood is that, through the gift of the Holy Spirit, they do not cease to be. Once the eucharistic assembly is terminated, they continue to be, precisely through the eucharistic communion, the body of Christ, the Church of Christ. The communion, the link of communion binding all as the body of Christ, was understood to be a reality accompanying all those who have been called in all parts of the world. Everywhere they are the Church.

The expressions so much in use today, "to be Church," "the laity are also the Church," with which Christians are urged to increase their responsibilities and mission in the world, are responses, in a rigorous manner, to this primitive self-consciousness which we have been studying. St. Paul's affirmation that the body of Christ is the Church is a summary of all this theology. The indisputable triumph of the term *ekklesia* to express the self-consciousness of Christians of who they are, points thus to the most profound reality of the mystery of the People of God.

It has been said with reason that the moderate use which St. Paul made of the expression *laos tou theou,* in contrast to the continuous use of *ekklesia tou theou,* shows that for him the concept of *laos tou theou* as such is not sufficiently expressive to embody the Christian reality.[46] On the contrary, the idea of the permanent and eschatological *qahal,* with which Christians designate their own community and not their assemblies, expresses with rare clarity the most profound novelty of the Church: to be the People of God which achieves already here on earth, and not only occasionally, the permanent communion of humanity with God in Christ. This shows once again that the foundational concept in a systematic ecclesiology is the People of God as the People of the Father.

Translated from the Spanish by Peter C. Phan.

[46] Ibid.

For Further Reading

Congar, Yves. *I Believe in the Holy Spirit.* 3 vols. New York: Seabury Press, 1983.

_____. *The Mystery of the Church.* 2d rev. ed. Baltimore: Helicon, 1965.

_____. *The Mystery of the Temple.* Westminster, Md.: Newman Press, 1962.

Dulles, Avery. *Models of the Church*. Expanded edition. Garden City, N.Y.: Image Books, 1987.

International Theological Commission. "Select Themes of Ecclesiology." *ITC, Texts and Documents, 1969–1985*. Ed. Michael Sharkey, 267–304. San Francisco: Ignatius Press, 1989.

Komonchak, Joseph A. *Foundations in Ecclesiology*. A supplementary issue of *Lonergan Workshop Journal* 11 (1995).

Küng, Hans. *The Church*. New York: Sheed & Ward, 1968.

Lennan, Richard. *The Ecclesiology of Karl Rahner*. Oxford: Clarendon Press, 1995.

Lubac, Henri de. *The Splendour of the Church*. New York: Sheed and Ward, 1956.

MacDonald, Timothy I. *The Ecclesiology of Yves Congar: Foundational Themes*. Lanham, Md.: University Press of America, 1984.

McCarthy, Timothy G. *The Catholic Tradition: The Church in the Twentieth Century*. 2d ed. Chicago: Loyola, 1997.

Schmaus, Michael. *Dogma*. Vol. 4: *The Church, Its Origin and Structure*. New York: Sheed and Ward, 1972.

Sullivan, Francis. *The Church We Believe In: One, Holy, Catholic and Apostolic*. New York: Paulist Press, 1988.

PART II

Contemporary Ecclesiology

8   The Church as Communion

Susan K. Wood

In the Apostles' Creed we confess that there is "one, holy, catholic and apostolic Church." Yet, even though there is one Church, the Church of Christ, there are many churches. A theology of the local church was one of the major achievements of the Second Vatican Council, even though this theology is not fully developed in the conciliar documents. Emmanuel Lanne calls the council's theology of the local church a "Copernican revolution."[1] The council retrieved an understanding of the universal Church as the sum and communion of the local churches and rediscovered the universal Church in the local church.[2] No longer is the local church seen to gravitate around the universal Church, but the Church of God is found present in each celebration of the local church.[3]

Prior to Vatican II, a strong theology of the universal Church was dominant. Even though this had been true since the High Middle Ages for a number of historical reasons, Vatican I contributed to this by defining the infallibility of the papacy without developing a corresponding theology of the episcopacy. This universal Church was characterized by great uniformity reinforced by a highly centralized form of government. Both Vatican I and the 1917 Code of Canon Law stressed the central authority of the pope and the Roman Curia. The local churches were patterned after the Roman church with respect to liturgical rites and disciplinary observances. Vatican II addressed a theology of the episcopacy and in doing so reasserted the importance of the particular churches. The particular churches are marked by a certain amount of diversity, inculturation, and decentralization.

---

[1] Emmanuel Lanne, "L'Eglise local et l'Eglise universelle: Actualité et portée du thème," *Irénikon* 43 (1970) 490.

[2] H. Vorgrimler, ed., *Commentary on the Documents of Vatican II*, vol. I (New York: Herder and Herder, 1967) 167.

[3] Hervé Legrand, "La réalisation de l'Eglise en un lieu," *Dogmatique II*, vol. 3 of *Initiation à la pratique de la théologie* (Paris: Éditions du Cerf, 1986) 150.

A struggle between those who emphasize the universal Church and those who prefer to emphasize the particular church represents one of the sources of polarization in the Church today. Ultimately, the two views need to remain in tension. The universal Church needs concrete expression in particular churches, and particular churches cannot be so caught up in particularity that they forget the church as a whole in its universality. A challenge in the Church today is to adjudicate the two views.

The 1985 Synod of Bishops affirmed that communion is the dominant image of the Church in the documents of Vatican II. "Communion ecclesiology," in contrast to ecclesiologies emphasizing the Church as the Mystical Body,[4] the People of God,[5] or perfect society,[6] emphasizes the local, particular church and its relationship to other local churches and the universal Church. Communion ecclesiology develops from the two biblical meanings of *koinonia:* the "common participation in the gifts of salvation won by Jesus Christ and bestowed by the Holy Spirit" and "the bond of fellowship or the community of Christians that results from our union with God."[7] Thus there is both a vertical and a horizontal dimension, a vertical communion in grace with the Father, Son, and Spirit modeled after the communion of the three persons of the Trinity, and a horizontal communion with companion Christians within the ecclesial community.

The soteriological relationship of vertical communion in grace with Father, Son, and Spirit is primarily realized through the proclamation of the Gospel and participation in the sacraments. For example, the sacrament of baptism is not merely a sign of faith or incorporation into a human organization, but a real participation in the death and resurrection of Christ. In the Eucharist we commune with the body of Christ. These sacramental means of bringing us into community with God also create ecclesial communion. In baptism we are incorporated into the Church; in the Eucharist we not only commune with the sacramental Christ, but, in communion with one another and with Christ, we are constituted Church as Christ's Mystical Body. The primary emphasis of communion consists in the elements of grace and sacrament that ultimately identify ecclesial communities in terms of their relationship to Christ. Organizational structure or the comradeship of good will among church members is secondary within communion ecclesiology.

[4] Pope Pius XII, *Mystici corporis,* 1943.
[5] LG 2.
[6] Robert Bellarmine, *De controversiis christianae fidei.*
[7] Patrick Granfield, "The Church Local and Universal: Realization of Communion," *The Jurist* 49 (1989) 451.

When viewed in its horizontal dimension, communion ecclesiology in its most recent developments furnishes a model for ecclesial governance. Here the Church is conceived as a communion of particular churches. Each particular church is in communion with the other churches and the church of Rome, which exercises the ministry of safeguarding the unity and communion of the particular churches. This bondedness of particular churches constitutes the plenitude of the Church according to a Western view.

The term "communion" occurs frequently in the Decree on Ecumenism. An ecclesiology of communion is proving to be fruitful within ecumenical dialogues today because it conceives of Church unity as a communion of churches.[8] Even though Church unity is yet to be achieved, this category allows for partial and incomplete, but nonetheless real, relationships of communion among Christian churches. This partial unity is realized through the written word of God, faith in Christ and in the Trinity, baptism, and the life of grace.

Conciliar Texts

Key conciliar texts supporting a theology of the particular church include:

> 1. Constitution on the Sacred Liturgy: "The principal manifestation of the church consists in the full, active participation of all God's holy people in the same liturgical celebrations, especially in the same Eucharist, in one prayer, at one altar, at which the bishop presides, surrounded by the college of priests and by his ministers" (SC 41).[9]
>
> 2. Dogmatic Constitution on the Church: "Individual bishops are the visible source and foundation of unity in their own particular churches, which are modeled on the universal church; it is

[8] See "*Communio/Koinonia:* A New Testament–Early Christian Concept and Its Contemporary Appropriation and Significance," a study by the Institute for Ecumenical Research, Strasbourg, 1990, in *A Commentary on "Ecumenism: The Vision of the ELCA,"* ed. William G. Rusch (Minneapolis: Augsburg Press, 1990) 119–41; Heinrich Holz, ed., *The Church as Communion: Lutheran Contributions to Ecclesiology* (Geneva: The Lutheran World Federation, 1997); George Vandervelde, "*Koinonia* Ecclesiology —Ecumenical Breakthrough?" *One in Christ* 29:2 (1993) 126–42. For a discussion of this theme in various dialogues with the Roman Catholic Church see Susan Wood, "Ecclesial *Koinonia* in Ecumenical Dialogues," *One in Christ* 30:2 (1994) 124–45.

[9] Austin Flannery, gen. ed., *The Basic Sixteen Documents, Vatican Council II: Constitutions and Decrees, A Completely Revised Translation in Inclusive Language* (Northport, N.Y.: Costello Publishing Company, 1996). LG 26.

in and from these that the one and unique catholic church exists. And for that reason each bishop represents his own church, whereas all of them together with the people represent the whole church in a bond of peace, love and unity" (LG 23).

3. Dogmatic Constitution on the Church: "The Church of Christ is really present in all legitimately organized groups of the faithful, which, insofar as they are united to their pastors, are also quite appropriately called church in the New Testament. For these are in fact, in their own localities, the new people called by God, in the holy Spirit and with full conviction (see 1 Thess 1:5). In them the faithful are gathered together by the preaching of the Gospel of Christ, and the mystery of the Lord's Supper is celebrated 'so that, by means of the flesh and blood of the Lord the whole brotherhood and sisterhood of the body may be welded together.' In any community of the altar, under the sacred ministry of the bishop, a manifest symbol is to be seen of that charity and 'unity of the mystical body, without which there can be no salvation.' In these communities, though they may often be small and poor, or dispersed, Christ is present through whose power and influence the one, holy, catholic and apostolic church is constituted. For the sharing in the body and blood of Christ has no other effect than to accomplish our transformation into that which we receive" (LG 26).

4. Decree on the Pastoral Office of Bishops in the Church: "A diocese is a section of God's people entrusted to a bishop to be guided by him with the assistance of his clergy so that, loyal to its pastor and formed by him into one community in the Holy Spirit through the Gospel and the Eucharist, it constitutes one particular church in which the one, holy, catholic and apostolic church of Christ is truly present and active" (CD 11).

According to Vatican II, two things are necessary for a particular church: the Eucharist and a bishop. A particular church is essentially an altar community around its bishop. The statement from the Constitution on the Liturgy presents the liturgical assembly as the place where the church is most manifestly itself. If the Eucharist alone were sufficient for a particular church, the church would be closed in upon itself or at least would have no visible link with other eucharistic communities. We shall see that the presence of the bishop is what brings the particular church into visible communion with the other particular churches.[10] However, these texts also emphasize that this theology of

---

[10] One of the criticisms of this theology is the fact that, given the size of particular churches today, it is practically impossible for all the people to gather around the bishop in a eucharistic celebration. A theology of the presbyterate which interprets

the particular church is not entirely clerical, for the church is manifested in "the full, active participation of all God's holy people," and the Church of Christ is really present "in all legitimately organized groups of the faithful." Thus the ecclesiology of communion builds upon a theology of the people of God.

Definitions and Clarifications

The terms "particular church" and "local church" are often used interchangeably. Most often, Vatican II uses the term "particular church" to refer to the diocese,[11] but this term can also refer to churches in the same region or culture.[12] Henri de Lubac reserves the term "particular church" for the altar community around the bishop. Consequently, the definition of a particular church is sacramental rather than geographic.[13] In contrast, for de Lubac the term "local church" refers to groupings of particular churches which "have their own discipline, enjoy their own liturgical usage, and inherit a theological and spiritual patrimony."[14] These correspond to the churches included within an episcopal conference. Unfortunately, there is no standard practice governing the use of this terminology. In spite of Vatican II's use of the term "particular church," this term has not enjoyed widespread acceptance.[15] Canon law identifies the particular church with a diocese,[16] but

---

a priest as an extension of the bishop represents a partial solution. Unlike many Protestant churches which view the church as the place where the Gospel is truly preached and the sacraments rightly administered, the Roman Catholic Church identifies the basic unit of the church at a more comprehensive level.

[11] CD 11.

[12] AG 22.

[13] For Joseph Komonchak's criticism of this see "The Local Church and the Church Catholic: The Contemporary Theological Problematic," *The Jurist* 52 (1992) 435–6. In his opinion, the particular church seems "to float in mid-air, constituted solely by theological, divine, supernatural elements." Lanne sees this definition as attached to the sanctifying role of the bishop rather than their responsibilities for pastoral governance or responsibility for mission in "L'Église locale et l'Église universelle," 496.

[14] LG 23. Henri de Lubac, "The Particular Churches in the Universal Church," *Homiletic and Pastoral Review* 82 (1982) 13; Henri de Lubac, *The Motherhood of the Church* (San Francisco: Ignatius Press, 1982) 171–211.

[15] Patrick Granfield, "The Local Church as a Center of Communication and Control," *CTSA Proceedings* 35 (1980) 257.

[16] Canon 368: "Particular churches in which and from which exists the one and unique Catholic Church are first of all dioceses; to which unless otherwise evident are likened a territorial abbacy, an apostolic vicariate, an apostolic prefecture, and an apostolic administration which has been erected on a stable basis."

most authors speak of the "local church" in reference to the diocese. Although canon law refers to a diocese in personal and sacramental terms as a "portion of the people of God which is entrusted for pastoral care to a bishop,"[17] it is most often understood territorially and administratively. It thus risks being viewed as a smaller administrative unit of a larger whole which is the universal Church. Hervé Legrand notes that this encourages a false interpretation of catholicity and universalism where one both looks outside the particular church for catholicity and identifies universality with geography.[18] However, as we shall see, particularity and universalism are not opposite terms, and the universal Church has concrete existence only in and through the particular church.

The Eucharistic Center of the Particular Church

A particular church is not a subdivision of the universal Church, but is related to the universal Church as the Eucharist is related to its manifold celebrations: "In each particular church is present, essentially, 'mystically,' the entire universal Church since Christ is there through the Eucharist celebrated by the bishop; but equally, each particular church exists fully only in the 'one, single, and Catholic Church.'"[19] The universal Church is not an idealized concept or simply the sum total of particular churches. It is defined in terms of the Eucharist, which transcends the localized particularity of the eucharistic presence in a specific community. The universal Church subsists in, but is not limited to, each particular church in an analogous way to which Christ is entirely present in, but is not limited to, each eucharistic celebration. We see this relationship in two affirmations: (1) although the Eucharist is a sacrifice, it does not multiply the one sacrifice of Christ, and (2) although the body of Christ is present in many places, there is only one body.[20] In other words, "every local church is nothing but the manifestation of the Body of Christ which is equally present, the same in every place, in all the others."[21] The church is present wherever Christ is, which is wherever the Eucharist is celebrated. Because of this, "the local churches have the whole reality of the church, not merely a parcel cut out of the whole."[22]

[17] Canon 369.

[18] Legrand, "La réalisation de l'Eglise en un lieu," 158.

[19] Henri de Lubac, *De Lubac: A Theologian Speaks* (Los Angeles: Twin Circle Publishing Co., 1985) 20.

[20] Susan Wood, "The Theological Foundation of Episcopal Conferences and Collegiality," *Studia canonica* 22 (1988) 330.

[21] Lubac, *The Motherhood of the Church*, 202, citing Louis Bouyer, *L'Eglise de Dieu* (Paris: Éditions du Cerf, 1970) 488.

[22] Joseph Cardinal Ratzinger, *The Nature and Mission of Theology* (San Francisco: Ignatius Press, 1993) 86.

This said, one must quickly add that although each particular church is wholly Church, no particular church can be the Church of God in isolation.[23] Each particular church bears a responsibility for the whole, which includes proclaiming the gospel to the entire world, collaborating with one another and with Peter's successor, helping the missions, and extending assistance to other churches.[24] The nature of the particular church is to be in communion with the other particular churches.

The universal Church is the *corpus mysticum,* the Mystical Body of Christ, and this is an undivided body which is also present whole and entire in the local eucharistic assembly and the particular church around its bishop. Thus it is evident that the universal Church does not result from an addition or a federation of particular churches. The particular church is the universal Church in the sense that it is the particular, concrete place where the universal is found. The unity between the particular church and the universal Church is not the unity of a plurality of churches, but the unity of the one church which finds concrete, historical objectification in a plurality of particular churches. In speaking of the mutual relations of individual bishops to the universal Church, *Lumen gentium* refers to the Mystical Body as a "body of churches."[25]

Structures of Communion

Diagram 8.1 shows the relationship between the particular churches and the college of bishops.

In Roman Catholicism, when we call the basic unit of the church the "particular church," "an altar community gathered around a bishop," the phrase "altar community" focuses on its particularity in a particular place. Through the episcopacy the particular church is related to the universal since a primary function of the bishop is to represent the particular church in the communion of churches within the episcopal college. This correlation of the particular with the universal is evident in the fact that a Christian becomes bishop only through his admission to the undivided body of the episcopacy.[26] Thus even though the particular church is manifested in its eucharistic worship in a specific place under the leadership of an individual bishop, it exists only in its reference to

---

[23] Jean-Marie R. Tillard, *L'Église locale: Ecclésiologie de communion et catholicité* (Paris: Éditions du Cerf, 1995) 394.

[24] LG 23.

[25] LG 23.

[26] LG 23.

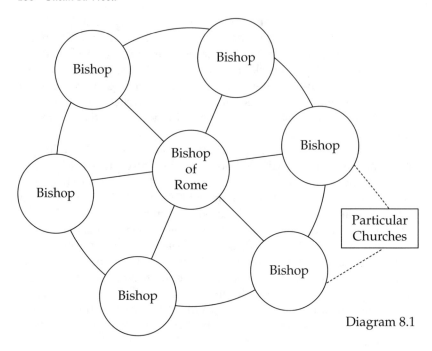

Diagram 8.1

the whole church. The whole church, in its undivided episcopacy, consecrates a bishop. Each bishop has the responsibility to be solicitous for
the entire Church.[27] The universal Church is best characterized as a
"communion of communions," that is, a communion of particular
churches in which there is a relationship of mutual interiority between
the particular church and the universal Church.

There are three analogous relationships between an individual entity and a larger whole: (1) an individual bishop and the episcopal college or body of bishops, (2) a particular eucharistic celebration and the
Eucharist in its unitary character, and (3) the particular church and the
universal Church.[28] According to de Lubac, "the episcopacy is in fact
one: it is not possessed in part."[29] Thus the episcopacy is one, the Eucharist is one, and the Church is one. The bishop can be said to embody
the entire episcopacy, or, conversely, the episcopacy is embodied in
each bishop. The eucharistic body of Christ is present whole and entire
in each eucharistic celebration. The universal Church is present in each

[27] LG 23. In the suggested homily for the ordination rite, the bishop-elect is administered to "have a constant concern for all the churches and gladly come to the
aid and support of churches in need."

[28] Wood, "The Theological Foundation," 331.

[29] Lubac, *The Motherhood of the Church*, 10.

particular church. In each instance, the universal exists in the particular. The universal is not the sum of a number of parts, nor is the particular a part of the whole.

Within this model, ordained ministry is the sacramentalization of ecclesial relationships. This means that the bishops in their relationship of communion within the college of bishops are the visible sign and representation of the communion of the particular churches. Membership in and union with the college of bishops is an essential element within episcopal consecration and arguably represents the "fullness of orders" which sets the episcopacy apart from the other orders.[30] Each bishop represents his particular church and together the episcopal college represents the communion of churches. What is sacramentally signified in episcopal consecration is the collegial nature of the Church as a "communion of communions." The college of bishops symbolizes the unity that exists among the altar communities which each bishop represents in his office. The "order" of the episcopacy truly reflects the ordering among eucharistic communities. The communion of churches is represented in the personal communion of bishops.

This personal dimension of the relationship between church communities functions both synchronically and diachronically, that is, within the communion of churches now throughout the world and within the historical communion of churches in apostolic succession. Thus in Roman Catholicism there is the emphasis on the succession of laying on of hands in apostolic succession (even though this cannot be historically substantiated in the earliest period) and the succession of churches in the apostolic faith. Apostolic succession is both a succession in personal ministry and a succession of communities of faith. In many ways this relationship recalls Cyprian's words, "the bishop is in the church and the church in the bishop."[31]

The Bishop of Rome exercises an important function in working for the unity and communion of all the particular churches, called the "Petrine ministry." In the words of Vatican II: "In order that the episcopate itself, however, might be one and undivided he [Christ] placed blessed Peter over the other apostles and in him he set up a lasting and visible source and foundation of the unity both of faith and communion."[32] This function of Peter continues in the institution of the papacy. This role of the papacy does not diminish the role of the bishops or the autonomy of the local churches, but strengthens them.

---

[30] Susan Wood, "The Sacramentality of Episcopal Consecration," *Theological Studies* 51 (1990) 479–96.

[31] Epist. 66, 8 (*"scire debes episcopum in Ecclesia esse et Ecclesiam in episcopo"*).

[32] LG 18.

The episcopal witness to the unity of particular churches within the episcopal college, as well as the task of being the "visible source and foundation of unity"[33] in his own particular church, are inseparable from a bishop's eucharistic presidency. The liturgical role of the bishop is the sacramentalization of his governing role. The presidency of the bishop over the body of Christ in the Eucharist parallels his governance of the ecclesial body of Christ. Thus the task of witnessing to unity in the church is inseparable from the Eucharist, the sacrament of unity. Just as the Eucharist provides the paradigm of the relationship between particular churches and the universal Church, so does the bishop's eucharistic presidency provide the visible expression of the relationship between a particular church and the communion of particular churches represented sacramentally by the episcopal college. The college of bishops functions as the visible bond between the particular churches. This is reflected in *Lumen gentium*'s statement:

> The individual bishops are the visible source and foundation of unity in their own particular churches, which are constituted after the model of the universal church; it is in these and formed out of them that the one and unique Catholic Church exists. And for that reason precisely each bishop represents his own church, whereas all, together, with the pope, represent the whole church in a bond of peace, love and unity.[34]

Collegiality, Subsidiarity, Diversity

Patrick Granfield has stated that if the universal Church is not primarily a juridical entity, but a communion of local churches, "the principles of collegiality, subsidiarity, and legitimate diversity should be reflected in the administrative life of the universal church."[35] Collegiality is the exercise of responsibility of the worldwide episcopate, in union with the pope, for the Church as a whole. Although the word "collegiality" does not actually occur in the Vatican II documents, two documents, the Dogmatic Constitution on the Church, nos. 22, 23, and the Decree on the Bishops' Pastoral Office in the Church, describe episcopal governance as "collegial" fifteen times and refer to the *"collegium"* of the bishops thirty-seven times.[36] The final report of the

---

[33] LG 23.

[34] LG 23.

[35] Patrick Granfield, "Legitimation and Bureaucratisation of Ecclesial Power," *Power in the Church,* ed. James Provost and Knut Walf (Edinburgh: T. & T. Clark, 1988) 92.

[36] Michael A. Fahey, "Collegiality," *The Harpercollins Encyclopedia of Catholicism,* ed. Richard P. McBrien (San Francisco: HarperSanFrancisco, 1995) 329.

Extraordinary Synod of Bishops in 1985 identified an ecclesiology of communion as the sacramental foundation of collegiality, noting that the theology of collegiality is much broader than its mere juridical aspect.[37] The fullest exercise of collegiality occurs in an ecumenical council. Even though collegiality in the strict and full sense applies to the episcopal college as a whole, partial realizations of collegiality that are manifestations of a collegial spirit include the synod of bishops, episcopal conferences, the Roman Curia, and the *ad limina* visits of bishops to the pope.

It would be a mistake to interpret the principle of collegiality as asserting the authority and power of the bishops over and against that of the pope. The pope is both a member and the head of the college of bishops. Archbishop John R. Quinn observes that "collegial unity is the fundamental paradigm for all the other ways in which the pope is the sign and guarantor of unity."[38] In other words, the pope exercises the Petrine ministry for the union and communion of the Church in a preeminent way with respect to the episcopal college. Some critics argue that papal centrism and the structures of the Curia occasionally hinder the exercise of episcopal collegiality. For example, Archbishop Quinn notes: "There are practical instances which are tantamount to making bishops managers who only work under instructions rather than true witnesses of faith who teach—in communion with the pope—in the name of Christ."[39] The Curia is the arm of the pope and works in the service of the bishops.[40] However, Archbishop Quinn comments that instead of the dogmatic structure of the pope and the rest of the episcopate:

> There emerges a new and threefold structure: the pope, the curia and the episcopate. This makes it possible for the curia to see itself as exercising oversight and authority over the college of bishops. To the degree that this is so and is reflected in the policies and actions of the curia, it obscures and diminishes both the doctrine and the reality of episcopal collegiality.[41]

Examples of actions of the curia which have prevailed over the decisions of episcopal conferences include the rejection of the inclusive English translations of *The Catechism of the Catholic Church* and lectionary.

[37] 2.C.4.

[38] Archbishop John R. Quinn, Lecture June 29, 1996, at Campion Hall, Oxford. "The Exercise of the Primacy: Facing the Cost of Christian Unity," *Commonweal* (July 12, 1996) 13.

[39] Ibid., 15.

[40] Decree on the Bishops' Pastoral Office in the Church, 9.

[41] Quinn, "The Exercise of the Primacy," 15.

A second principle governing the relationship between the local churches and the universal Church is that of subsidiarity. According to this principle larger and higher institutions or collectives do not assume to themselves functions which can be performed and provided for by lesser and subordinate bodies.[42] Since Vatican II the principle of subsidiarity has been applied to the Church. For example, the synod of 1967 voted to apply subsidiarity in the revision of the Code of Canon Law. The synod of 1969 voted in favor of applying it to episcopal conferences. The preface to the 1983 Code of Canon Law states that subsidiarity is one of the important principles which underlies the new law and that it is "a principle which is rooted in a higher one because the office of bishops with its attached powers in a reality of divine law."[43]

Many point to the appointment of bishops as one area where the principle of subsidiarity should be exercised more fully.[44] Historically, Rome rarely intervened in the appointment of bishops outside the papal states until about 1800. Today's practice has its historical roots in the disruption caused by the French Revolution and the withdrawal of the Italian government from the process at the time of the unification. Today the papal nuncio often has more of a role in the choice than the local diocese and the national conference of bishops.

Legitimate diversity in the Church respects the historical heritage and cultural identity of the local church. The model for Church unity is reconciled diversity rather than uniformity. Inculturation, the process by which the gospel is adapted to a particular culture, results in diversity. Essentially, inculturation is simply living the Christian life in a particular context. The Pastoral Constitution on the Church in the Modern World represents the Church's first detailed statement about the relationship of the Church to diverse cultures.[45] It states that "the church has been sent to all ages and nations and, therefore, is not tied exclusively and indissolubly to any race or nation, to any one particular way of life, or to any set of customs, ancient or modern."[46] Inculturation is most often spoken of with reference to the liturgy in terms of use of the

---

[42] Pope Pius XI in *Quadragesimo Anno* (1931) first articulated this principle of modern Catholic social teaching.

[43] *Code of Canon Law,* Latin-English Edition (Washington, D.C.: Canon Law Society of America, 1983) xxi.

[44] See Joseph F. Eagan, *Restoration and Renewal* (Kansas City: Sheed and Ward, 1995) 337–8; Archbishop John R. Quinn, "The Exercise of the Papacy," *Commonweal* (July 12, 1996) 17. For the history of this practice see Tillard, *L'Église locale,* 228–41.

[45] Robert S. Pelton, "Inculturation," *The Harpercollins Encyclopedia of Catholicism* (San Francisco: HarperSanFrancisco, 1995) 660.

[46] Pastoral Constitution on the Church in the Modern World, 58.

vernacular, music, and movement. The observance of liturgical feasts and saints' days represent other examples.

"Universalist" and "Particularist" Tendencies

This relationship between the universal and particular church is not uncontested. Avery Dulles has identified two approaches to communion ecclesiology as "universalist" and "particularist" tendencies. Those who hold a more universalist concept of the Church point out that the Church was originally founded on Peter and the apostles as a universal society and that only subsequently came to be divided into particular regional or local churches.[47] Universalists also see the pope primarily as the successor of Peter and visible head of the whole flock of Christ. He is secondarily Bishop of Rome.[48] This view acknowledges that it is fitting for bishops to be appointed as pastors of dioceses, but maintains that members of the hierarchy who receive no such appointment can still be bishops in the true sense of the term.[49] Within the universalist view, unity is the given and diversity is a matter of accommodation.[50] The primary understanding of communion according to the universalist position is that it is participation in the divine life, achieved through the objective means of grace, notably the sacraments.

"Particularists," on the other hand, point to the diversity of churches represented in the letters in the New Testament. Ecclesial communion consists in the communion of these various communities. The church of Rome enjoys primacy as the site of the martyrdom of Peter and Paul. The primacy of the pope derives from his position as Bishop of Rome. A bishop is primarily the pastor of a diocese and, therefore, in principle it is as pastors of churches that bishops have a voice in the episcopal college. Finally, within the particularist model, diversity is the original situation of the churches, and unity is something to be achieved. Unity is to be required only in necessary models. Consequently, regional differences are characteristic of the Church.

Avery Dulles holds that communion within the particularist model signifies a fellowship of love and intimacy achieved in a local community. This is how he identified the bond of communion within his communion model in his *Models of the Church*.[51] Within Dulles' typology, the

---

[47] Avery Dulles, "The Church as Communion," *New Perspectives on Historical Theology,* ed. Bradley Nassif (Grand Rapids, Mich.: Eerdmans, 1996) 134.

[48] Ibid., 137.

[49] Ibid., 136.

[50] Ibid., 137.

[51] Avery Dulles, *Models of the Church* (Garden City, N.Y.: Doubleday, 1974) 61.

communion model accentuates the personal relationship between the faithful and the Holy Spirit. The emphasis is on the intimate association of believers who are bonded together by "interior graces and gifts of the Holy Spirit, though the external bonds are recognized as important in a subsidiary way."[52]

This view certainly seems to correspond with the type of communion within base Christian communities as articulated by Leonardo Boff in his book *Ecclesiogenesis: The Base Communities Reinvent the Church.* According to Boff, these communities are characterized "by the absence of alienating structures, by direct relationships, by reciprocity, by a deep communion, by mutual assistance, by communality of gospel ideals, by equality among members."[53] The question here is one of ecclesiality. Are base Christian communities churches? In the absence of ordained ministry and the Eucharist, they do not fulfill the definition of a particular church as given in *Lumen gentium.*

I differ from Dulles by identifying communion within the particularist model as a communion among particular churches which is mediated not only by what Dulles identifies as a fellowship of love and intimacy, but also by visible structures. Those who hold a particularist model would not deny communion as also participation in divine life achieved through the sacraments or a mediation of communion through ministerial structures.[54]

Part of the confusion may be due to the two different methodologies represented by Dulles' work *Models of the Church* and by what is now known as communion ecclesiology. In constructing the different models, Dulles emphasized what was distinctive in various concepts of the Church according to whether they emphasized the institutional Church, the sacramental and sign value of the Church, the bonds of communion among members, the evangelical mission of proclaiming the word of God, or the Church's commitment to service and social justice. In other words, the methodology was to divide and separate in order to distinguish. On the other hand, the methodology of communion ecclesiology is more integrative and synthetic. It correlates a number of elements within the Church in order to emphasize connections.

Consequently, in communion ecclesiology, even within a particularist model, there are a number of visible and institutional elements which mediate and facilitate communion. First among these is the papacy, which serves as the focus of ecclesial communion since the Petrine

---

[52] Ibid.

[53] Leonardo Boff, *Ecclesiogenesis: The Base Communities Reinvent the Church* (Maryknoll, N.Y.: Orbis Books, 1986) 26.

[54] See Tillard, *L'Église locale,* 219–91.

ministry is a ministry of unity and communion. Next there is the college of bishops, which represents the communion of particular churches.
Smaller groupings include synods of bishops and national episcopal
conferences. In addition to these ecclesiastical structures, there are, of
course, the sacraments, especially the Eucharist, which effect reconciliation and communion among the People of God and which, as sacraments, are visible bonds of communion. Consequently, it is erroneous
to presume that communion ecclesiology, even within the particularist
model, is devoid of structural and institutional elements of communion.

This concern for visible, ecclesial structures of communion seems to
have been one of the issues that the Congregation for the Doctrine of
the Faith raised in its letter to the bishops of the Catholic Church,
"Some Aspects of the Church as Communion."[55] One of the Congregation's concerns is that ecclesial communion is at the same time both
invisible in grace and visible in church structure. It fears that the rediscovery of a eucharistic ecclesiology may result in a one-sided emphasis
on the principle of the local church in such a way as to render any other
principle of unity or universality inessential. In particular, it fears that a
certain interpretation of communion ecclesiology may insufficiently account for the role of the episcopate and primacy and thus weaken the
concept of the unity of the Church at the visible and institutional level.
In short, it fears that an emphasis on the local church may impoverish
the concept of the universal Church.

In addition, the Congregation for the Doctrine and Faith emphasizes a more universalist view of the Church when it asserts the ontological and temporal priority of the universal Church.[56] The congregation

---

[55] English translation in *Catholic International* 3:16 (1–30 September 1992) 761–7.

[56] Congregation for the Doctrine of the Faith, "Some Aspects of the Church as
Communion." English translation in *Ecumenical Trends* 21:9 (October 1992) 133–4,
141–7. Ratzinger argues this point in *Church, Ecumenism and Politics* (New York:
Crossroad, 1988) 75. He also argued it at the meeting of the College of Cardinals in
1985:

> If on the one hand it must be said that the Church is not a papal monarch, on
> the other hand neither can it be considered a confederation of particular
> churches whose unity results only as something secondary from the addition
> of individual churches, so that the ministry of unity would consist only in
> being a moderator of the agreement of the churches. As in a body the unity of
> the organism precedes and sustains the individual organs, because the or-
> gans could not exist if the body did not, so also the unity of the Catholic
> Church precedes the plurality of particular churches which are born from this
> unity and receive their ecclesial character from it. This temporal order is
> stated in many ways in the New Testament writings. It is enough to cite some
> examples. According to St. Luke's narrative in the Acts of the Apostles, the

wished to avoid a certain horizontalism in conceiving of the Church as the "reciprocal recognition on the part of the particular churches" considered as complete subjects in themselves. The letter notes that such a view weakens the concept of the unity of the Church at the visible and institutional level.

Curiously, two examples at opposite ends of the ecclesial spectrum may be envisaged by this criticism. Within Orthodox ecclesiology, the Church is defined eucharistically in such a way that wherever the Eucharist is celebrated, there is a Church in the full sense of the word. In this instance, ecclesial communion is identified with eucharistic communion. Structures beyond this communion do not represent a completion or increase of ecclesiality.[57] At the other end of the ecclesial spectrum are base Christian communities which may have neither the Eucharist nor ordained ministry.

The Congregation's letter received significant criticism for its claim for the ontological and temporal priority of the universal Church. Such priority seemed to imply the existence of an invisible church which exists apart from its particular, concrete, historical manifestations. A year later an unsigned letter appeared in the 23 June 1993 edition of *l'Osservatore Romano* which both nuanced and explained the text in the *Communionis notio*. This article emphasizes the mutual interiority between the universal Church and the particular churches and summarizes the relationship: "Every particular Church is truly Church, although it is not the whole Church; at the same time, the universal Church is not distinct from the communion of particular Churches, without, however, being conceived as the sum of them." Because of this close relationship, the article affirms that "incorporation into the universal Church is as immediate as is incorporation into a particular Church. Belonging to the universal Church and belonging to a particular Church are a single Christian reality."

Two points may help to clarify this relationship further. First, *Lumen gentium* modified an earlier claim made in Pius XII's encyclical *Mystici*

Church began on the day of Pentecost in the community of Christ's disciples speaking in all languages. Here St. Luke, indeed the Holy Spirit, is intimating that the catholic, universal Church, our mother, existed before the individual churches were born, which arise from this one mother and are always related to her.

"De Romano Pontifice deque collegio episcoporum" (typescript) 3. Cited by Joseph A. Komonchak, "The Local Church and the Church Catholic," 429.

[57] Miroslav Volf, *After Our Likeness: The Church as the Image of the Trinity* (Grand Rapids, Mich.: Eerdmans, 1998) 43, citing Joseph Ratzinger, *Theologische Prinzipienlehre: Bausteine zur Fundamentaltheologie* (Munich: Eich Wewel, 1982) 308.

corporis (1943) that the "Church of Christ is the Roman Catholic Church."
Vatican II nuanced this in its statement, "This church, set up and organized in this world as a society subsists in the catholic church . . ."[58]
Pope John Paul II later extended the concept by saying that the universal Church subsists in the particular churches:

> The Catholic Church herself subsists in each particular church, which
> can be truly complete only through effective communion in faith, sacra-
> ments and unity with the whole body of Christ. . . . It is precisely be-
> cause you are pastors of particular churches in which subsists the
> fullness of the universal church that you are and must always be in full
> communion with the successor of Peter.[59]

Pope John Paul's statement further emphasizes the mutual interiority
of the universal and particular churches.

Second, Joseph Cardinal Ratzinger's emphasis on the universal
Church can be understood from the perspective of his principle that the
Church, in order to be "catholic," must be "from and for the whole."[60]
For him, even though the local church is wholly church, it is not the
whole church. This brings us back to the principle within Roman Catholicism that the fullness of the Church does not reside in the eucharistic community which constitutes the particular church, but in the
communion of particular churches. A particular church cannot be a
church in isolation.

Finally, theological discussion reflects the tension between the local
church and the universal Church present within the conciliar documents themselves. Joseph Komonchak suggests that the persistence of
the question of priority between the local church and universal Church
is due to the ambiguity or transitional character of the council's doctrine on the Church. He points out that the council began its work from
a perspective of a universalist ecclesiology and notes that "its recovery
of an ecclesiology of communion was hesitant and unsystematic."[61] On
the one hand, the statement that particular churches are "formed in the
image of the universal church" gives priority to the universal Church,
while the claim that the universal Church exists in and through the
particular churches gives priority to the particular churches. There is

[58] LG 8.

[59] Address 12 September 1987. The text can be found in *Origins* 17:16 (1 October
1987) 258.

[60] Joseph Cardinal Ratzinger, *Principles of Catholic Theology: Building Stones for a
Fundamental Theology,* trans. Mary Frances McCarthy (San Francisco: Ignatius Press,
1987) 309.

[61] Komonchak, "The Local Church and the Church Catholic," 427.

clearly support for both "particularist" and "universalist" positions in the documents, so that neither position can claim that it exclusively represents the conciliar teaching.

Practical implications resulting from both positions demonstrate the need to maintain a balance between the two. The universalist position protects the Church from falling prey to a narrow nationalism. The expertise and breadth of scope available to the universal Church provide a corrective and balance to the necessarily limited wisdom and skills of a single bishop. On the other hand, more active participation of the laity, greater attention to the social and cultural location of the people in the proclamation of the gospel, and a decentralization of bureaucratic administration are possible with attention to a theology of the local church. Ultimately, it is not a question of one over and against the other, for the universal Church is the communion of the particular churches.[62] The tension remains.

[62] Ibid., 435.

For Further Reading

Granfield, Patrick. "The Church Local and Universal: Realization of Communion." *The Jurist* 49 (1989) 449–71.

The Joint Working Group. "The Church: Local and Universal." *Information Service* #74 (1990) 75–84.

Legrand, Hervé. "La réalisation de l'Eglise en un lieu." *Initiation à la pratique de la théologie.* Ed. B. Lauret and F. Refoulé, 143–345. Vol. III: *Dogmatique 2.* Paris: Éditions du Cerf, 1986.

Lubac, Henri de. *The Motherhood of the Church.* Part Two: Particular Churches in the Universal Church. San Francisco: Ignatius Press, 1982.

Tillard, Jean-Marie. *Church of Churches: The Ecclesiology of Communion.* Trans. R. C. De Peaux. Collegeville: The Liturgical Press, 1992.

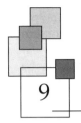

9

The Church as Worshiping Community

Gerard Austin

The best place to begin a discussion on the Church as worshiping community, the Church at prayer, is with baptism. Indeed, baptism is the gateway to the whole spiritual life.[1] It has been traditionally considered "the door which gives access to the other sacraments."[2] Today, however, we are more sensitive to the fact that we can use the term "baptism" in the narrow sense (referring only to the one sacrament) or in the broad sense (referring to all three sacraments of initiation: baptism, confirmation, and Eucharist). The distinction is important in this essay since, while it is correct to say that "baptism is the sacrament by which men and women are incorporated into the Church, built up together in the Spirit into a house where God lives, into a holy nation and a royal priesthood,"[3] still in the Catholic tradition baptism is considered incomplete until its recipients are sealed in confirmation and participate for the first time in the Eucharist. That is why the new Code of Canon Law says: "The sacraments of baptism, confirmation and the Most Holy Eucharist are so interrelated that they are required for full Christian initiation."[4] That is why Pope John Paul II writes: "The participation of the lay faithful in the threefold mission of Christ as priest, prophet and king finds its source in the anointing of baptism, its further development in confirmation, and its realization and dynamic sustenance in the holy eucharist."[5] The three initiation sacraments are thus

[1] Cf. Council of Florence: DS 1314: *vitae spiritualis ianua.*

[2] *Catechism of the Catholic Church* (Washington, D.C.: United States Catholic Conference, 1994) no. 1213.

[3] SC Divine Worship, *Documents on the Liturgy 1963–1979: Conciliar, Papal, and Curial Texts* (Collegeville: The Liturgical Press, 1982) no. 2253. (Henceforth DOL)

[4] Canon 842:2, *Code of Canon Law: Latin-English Edition* (Washington, D.C.: Canon Law Society of America, 1983) 319.

[5] Pope John Paul II, *Christifideles Laici*, 30 December 1988, n. 14, *Origins* 18 (9 February 1989) 567.

best considered as a whole. Each bestows the Holy Spirit, and in that sense each creates the Church, the body of Christ. They operate in a complementary way. While we are baptized but once, confirmed but once, Eucharist is celebrated time after time, Sunday after Sunday, year after year. It is Eucharist that our U.S. Bishops' Committee on the Liturgy called the "repeatable sacrament of initiation."[6]

All the sacraments of the Church are not on the same level, they are not all of equal value. The distinction made by the medieval theologians between the major and the minor sacraments is helpful. The two premiere sacraments of the Church are baptism and Eucharist. Baptism initially incorporates one into the body of Christ, and the role of Eucharist is to gradually bring to completion that initial unity. Baptism and Eucharist are the premiere sacraments of the birth of the Church, symbolized by the water and the blood flowing from the side of Christ on the cross.

Baptized into Christ

By baptism we become Christ. Pope John Paul II writes, "All the baptized are invited to hear once again the words of St. Augustine: 'Let us rejoice and give thanks: We have not only become Christians, but Christ himself. . . . Stand in awe and rejoice: We have become Christ.'"[7] That explains why the baptismal theology of the early Church saw the *alter Christus* to be the baptized woman or man. Only later on, with medieval theology, would the *alter Christus* be used exclusively for the ordained priest, almost forcing into oblivion the importance of the priesthood of all the baptized. By baptism the Christian community is constituted as Church, as bride of Christ, as body of Christ, as People of God. Some scholars believe that the first epistle of Peter represents an early Christian baptismal liturgy. Whether that is literally true or not, it conveys a very early expression of the meaning of Christian baptism. The author says, "You, however, are a 'chosen race, a royal priesthood, a holy nation, a people he claims for his own to proclaim the glorious works' of the One who called you from darkness into his marvelous light."[8] Early baptismal theology viewed the Church as mother, who through the waters of the font gives birth to new Christians. These new members would play different roles in the Church, but baptismal the-

---

[6] *Newsletter: Bishops' Committee on the Liturgy; National Conference of Catholic Bishops* 14 (1978) 111.

[7] Pope John Paul II, *Christifideles Laici*, 30 December 1988, n. 17, *Origins* 18 (9 February 1989) 569. St. Augustine ref.: *In Ioanne. Evang. Tract.*, 21, 8: CCL 36, 216.

[8] 1 Pet 2:9.

ology emphasized what all had in common: communion with Christ. It was based on the teaching of St. Paul that we form with Christ a single body, we are members of this body (Rom 12:3ff.; Eph 4:13, 25ff.; Col 3:15ff.). Indeed, Paul says, "There is neither Jew nor Greek, there is neither slave nor free person, there is not male and female; for you are all one in Christ Jesus."[9] Yves Congar explains that during the apostolic age and the earliest period of Christianity the Church is, in the first place, the body of Christ. He writes:

> This immanence of the living Christ in the Church, his Body, is expressed by St. Paul in two very familiar phrases, each of which, ultimately, indicates the same thing—Christ in us, and us in Christ. The formula, "in Christ Jesus," which, counting equivalent expressions, occurs one hundred and sixty-four times, signifies being under his influence, receiving life and movement from him and, consequently, acting, as it were, under his auspices, performing actions that are really his and belong to the sphere which he animates; it amounts to saying, "in his Body." The corresponding formula, "Christ in us," represents his dwelling in us as our life, as an interior principle of action; it expresses the basis of all the Pauline mysticism of the Christian life as consisting in the imitation of Christ, in having in oneself the sentiments of Christ, the mind of Christ (I Cor.2: 16), and in Christ being formed in us (Gal.4: 19). The two formulas express basically the same reality; what the Christian does as a Christian is an act of Christ, since the Christian is a member of Christ. Christians altogether, animated by the same spirit and acting in the name and under the impulse of the same Lord, form a single whole, the Body of Christ.[10]

This truth is reflected in the new *Catechism of the Catholic Church:*

> Baptism makes us members of the Body of Christ: "Therefore . . . we are members one of another (Eph 4:25)." Baptism incorporates us *into the Church*. From the baptismal fonts is born the one People of God of the New Covenant, which transcends all the natural or human limits of nations, cultures, races, and sexes: "For by one Spirit we were all baptized into one body (I Cor 12:13)."[11]

Baptized into Eucharist

This single body of Christ image was reflected in the celebrations of the Eucharist in the early Church. The accent was placed upon the building up of the body of Christ. The Eucharist was considered to be

[9] Gal 3:28.
[10] Yves Congar, *The Mystery of the Church* (Baltimore: Helicon Press, 1965) 26–7.
[11] *Catechism of the Catholic Church,* no. 1267.

the corporate giving thanks of the community. While the question of the presidency of the Eucharist will greatly dominate later theology, New Testament evidence simply ignores the issue. Raymond Brown writes: "When we move from the Old Testament to the New Testament, it is striking that while there are pagan priests and Jewish priests on the scene, no individual Christian is even specifically identified as a priest."[12]

Still, the early community assembled to celebrate Eucharist under the leadership of one person. Who was that person? Modern scholarship has emphasized that that person presided at Eucharist because he presided over the life of the Church. Put technically, the presidency of the eucharistic assembly was the liturgical dimension of a pastoral charge, the pastoral charge being the upbuilding of the local community. Edward Schillebeeckx writes:

> In the early church there was really an essential link between the community and its leader, and therefore between the community leader and the community celebrating the Eucharist. This nuance is important. It was essentially a matter of who presided over the community. . . . The figure who gives unity to the community also presides in the sacrament of church unity, which is the Eucharist.[13]

This close connection between priest and people was regulated by the prohibition of absolute ordination, that is, the practice of ordaining bishops and presbyters without attachment to any particular church. It was condemned by Canon 6 of the Council of Chalcedon in 451. Thus, the presider at Eucharist was not seen as outside the circle of the community; just the opposite, he operated from within the community as its leader in prayer.

Separation of Priest and Faithful

As time went on, little by little the priest was placed outside that circle, not offering *with* the people but *for* the people, and indeed finally the Mass was considered by many to be his. This happened at different times in different geographic areas. Many predicate the shift as the product of the Carolingian period or even earlier. Still, one finds isolated statements such as the following by as late as the eleventh century: "The priest does not consecrate by himself, he does not offer by

[12] Raymond E. Brown, *Priest and Bishop* (New York: Paulist Press, 1970) 13.
[13] Edward Schillebeeckx, *Ministry: Leadership in the Community of Jesus Christ* (New York: Crossroad, 1981) 49.

himself, but the whole assembly of believers consecrates and offers along with him."[14]

J. A. Jungmann describes the gradual separation of clergy and people:

> Only the priest is permitted to enter the sanctuary to offer the sacrifice. He begins from now on to say the prayers of the Canon in a low voice and the altar becomes farther and farther removed from the people into the rear of the apse. In some measure, the idea of a holy people who are as close to God as the priest is, has become lost. The Church begins to be represented chiefly by the clergy. The corporate character of public worship, so meaningful for early Christianity, begins to crumble at the foundations.[15]

Just why this separation of clergy and people occurred is a very complex issue. According to Cyrille Vogel, little by little the Mass was seen as a "good work" to be performed for one's personal, individual salvation, whether that of the priest who celebrates it or that of the lay-person who requests its celebration. Influential in this view of the Eucharist was St. Isidore of Seville (d. 636). The Eucharist was no longer considered to be the corporate giving thanks of the community but a gift of grace given to the one who celebrates it or has it celebrated, by which one's salvation is effected and assured.[16]

Shift in Ecclesiology

Yves Congar accounts for this loss of the corporate notion of Eucharist by appealing to a shift in ecclesiology. The ecclesiology of the early Church was one of communion. The chief point of reference was what all members of the Church have in common, a share in the priesthood of Christ. It was based on the baptismal unity of head and members within the body of Christ. This ecclesiology of communion was dominant during the first millennium, he says, but it gave way to an ecclesiology of powers, based on the power *(potestas)* given through the sacrament of order whereby one member (the priest or bishop), governed the life of the Church and offered the sacrifice of the Eucharist.[17] Hervé-Marie Legrand asks:

[14] Bl. Guerricus of Igny, Sermon 5; *PL* 185:87.

[15] J. A. Jungmann, *Pastoral Liturgy* (London: Challoner Publications, 1962) 60.

[16] See Cyrille Vogel, "Une mutation culturelle inexpliquée: le passage de l'eucharistie communautaire à la messe privée," *Revue des sciences religieuses* 54:3 (1980) 231–50.

[17] See Yves Congar, "L'ecclesia ou communauté chrétienne, sujet intégral de l'action liturgique," *La Liturgie après Vatican II*, ed. J. P. Jossua and Y. Congar, Unam Sanctam 66 (Paris: Éditions du Cerf, 1967) 241–82.

How did such an evolution occur? It did not happen abruptly. For Congar it is to be explained by a passage from an ecclesiology of communion to an ecclesiology of powers which was effected in the beginning of the thirteenth century. "While for the ancients," Congar writes . . . , "it is existence in the body of the Church which makes it possible to perform the sacraments, after the twelfth century there emerged a theology of self-contained powers: if one personally possesses them, one can posit the sacraments."[18]

This shift in ecclesiology was the result of a number of factors. High on the list of important factors would have been the loss of Christ as mediator, which resulted from the Church's struggle with Arianism. The Arians taught that the Son is less than the Father, and they used as fuel for their argument the prayer of the Church where the approach to the Father was *per Christum,* thus implying for them lack of equality and unity of substance with the Father. To counter this, the mainline Church shifted emphasis from the humanity of Christ to his divinity, lessening and at times even losing Christ's role as mediator. Having lost Christ as mediator, the people began their search for someone to take his place. They found the saints, the Blessed Mother, and finally the priest. Yves Congar, in his classic study of the ecclesiology of the High Middle Ages, states that at the end of the eighth century and then during the course of the ninth century, there were signs of two things: an accentuated distance between the priest and the people, and the role of the priest as mediator.[19] This had the deleterious effect of clericalizing the liturgy and, ultimately, the very notion of Church. Starting with this period the list of witnesses who identify the Church principally with the clergy begins to multiply.[20]

Ecclesiology and Liturgy at Vatican II

This clerical approach to understanding the Church would be reversed during the latter part of the nineteenth century and the twentieth century, culminating in the Second Vatican Council, by a retrieval of baptismal consciousness based on the earlier ecclesiology of communion. Such teaching as Congar's insistence in 1959 that "all are enlightened and active" in the Church would be reflected in the ecclesiology of the Con-

[18] Hervé-Marie Legrand, "The Presidency of the Eucharist According to the Ancient Tradition," *Worship* 53 (1979) 435–6.

[19] See Yves Congar, *L'ecclésiologie du haut moyen-âge* (Paris: Éditions du Cerf, 1968) 96.

[20] Ibid., 98.

stitution on the Sacred Liturgy of Vatican II.[21] Godfrey Diekmann (him-self a *peritus* at Vatican II) writes of the constitution:

> First and perhaps most importantly, is the priority given to the entire people of God as actively and responsively constituting the church, be-fore consideration of the diverse ministries, inclusive of the *diakonía* based on holy orders. . . . Secondly and correlative to this basic con-cept of the church, is the constitution's underscoring of the dignity and role of the laity, based on their sacramental deputation to cult through baptism and confirmation.[22]

Again, Edward Schillebeeckx writes of the effects of the Constitu-tion on the Sacred Liturgy:

> The fundamental gain of this constitution is that it broke the clergy's monopoly of the liturgy. Whereas it was formerly the priest's affair, with the faithful no more than his clientele, the council regards not only the priest but the entire Christian community, God's people, as the sub-ject of the liturgical celebration, in which each in his proper place is given his own particular, hierarchically ordered function—a theological view with all kinds of practical repercussions.[23]

This reflects a theology that sees not just the ordained minister but the Church as the subject of liturgical actions. Congar maintains that this theology is clearly part of the ancient tradition of the Church.[24] The Church is by its very nature priestly. He writes:

> It is not simply a question of a relationship between two terms, the faithful and hierarchical priests: there is a third term, Christ, which en-circles the two others, associating them to himself organically. The whole body is priestly, but it is so in virtue of being the body of the first and sovereign priest, Jesus Christ, who acts in the celebrations of his spouse as the first and sovereign celebrant. It is he first and foremost who offers and the Church offers only because she is his body and fol-lows him faithfully in everything. Jesus offers himself and he offers us; his members, the faithful, offer him in their turn and offer themselves with him.[25]

---

[21] Yves Congar, *Jalons pour une théologie du laïcat,* Unam Sanctam 23 (Paris: Édi-tions du Cerf, 1959) 369ff.

[22] Godfrey Diekmann, "The Constitution on the Sacred Liturgy in Retrospect," *Worship* 40 (1966) 411.

[23] Edward Schillebeeckx, *Vatican II: The Real Achievement* (London: Sheed and Ward, 1967) 27–8.

[24] See Congar, "L'ecclesia ou communauté chrétienne," 241.

[25] Ibid., 255 (my own translation from the French).

This type of intimate connection between ecclesiology and liturgy explains why the Constitution on the Sacred Liturgy calls for "that full, conscious, and active participation in liturgical celebrations called for by the very nature of the liturgy."[26] That participation is a logical consequence of an ecclesiology of communion which gives priority to the entire People of God as actively and responsibly constituting the Church. The Constitution on the Sacred Liturgy began what is called the homogeneous ecclesiology of Vatican II:[27] the starting point is what the members of the Church have in common, a share in the one priesthood of Jesus Christ. That common foundation is prior to one's being cleric or lay. Expressed in terms of concentric circles, the outer circle is the one priesthood of Jesus Christ. Then, within that circle is a smaller circle, the priesthood of the baptized who share in that one priesthood of Christ. Finally, there is a circle within the priesthood of the baptized which is the ministerial priesthood of bishops, deacons, and priests. Thus, it is most accurate to say that the Church baptizes to priesthood, that the Church is a sacerdotal reality at its very core. Medieval theology, with its overemphasis on the role of the ordained in the Church, had clouded this fundamental ecclesiological fact. Aidan Kavanagh summarizes the situation very succinctly: "The association of priesthood with the presbyterate among the Western churches has presbyteralized not only the ministry but the very sacerdotality of the Church as well. . . . Ordination cannot make one more priestly than the Church, and without baptism ordination cannot make one a priest at all."[28]

In Persona Christi[29]

The interaction between the three priesthoods (that of Christ, the baptismal priesthood and the ministerial priesthood) is of paramount importance for a proper understanding of the Church at prayer, especially for the prayer of prayers, the Eucharist. In recent years there has been a growing use of the phrase *in persona Christi* to describe the proper role of the priest at Eucharist. Some argue that only the priest acts *in persona Christi* at the Eucharist, while others argue that it is not

[26] DOL, no. 14.

[27] See J. P. Jossua, "La Constitution sacrosanctum concilium dans l'ensemble de l'oeuvre conciliaire," *La Liturgie Après Vatican II,* 127–56.

[28] Aidan Kavanagh, "Unfinished and Unbegun Revisited: The Rite of Christian Initiation of Adults," *Worship* 53 (1979) 336–7.

[29] See Gerard Austin, "*In Persona Christi* at the Eucharist," *Eucharist: Toward the Third Millennium,* ed. Gerard Austin et al. (Chicago: Liturgy Training Publications, 1997) 81–6.

the ordained but the Church as the body of Christ which first and fore-most acts *in persona Christi*. This tension is reflective of a larger issue: where to begin the search for determining the integral subject of the liturgical action. David Power explains:

> Two positions seem to be at odds with one another. One takes the baptismal priesthood as the foundation of ecclesial sacramental celebration and situates the ordained priesthood within this. For the other, the starting point is the exercise of the ordained priesthood, which is put at the service of the royal priesthood, invited to take part in what is effected by the ordained.[30]

This latter approach is taken by *Inter insigniores,* the 1976 Vatican declaration on Women in the Ministerial Priesthood, when it states: "It is true that the priest represents the church, which is the Body of Christ. But if he does so, it is precisely because he first represents Christ himself, who is the head and shepherd of the church."[31] This whole question is not a new one, and it is related to the more specific question of who offers what at the Eucharist. E. L. Mascall writes:

> What in fact is offered in the Eucharist, and who is doing the offering? Late medieval Catholicism had a quite simple answer: the priest is offering Christ. The Reformers had a quite simple answer too: the worshippers are offering, first their praise and then themselves. It is not Christ that is being offered; he offered himself once for all upon the Cross; all that we can do is remember his offering with gratitude and then offer ourselves. Now what has happened with both these answers is that the unity of Christ with his Church has simply fallen to pieces. St. Augustine could say perfectly naturally, without any sense of incongruity: "The whole redeemed community, that is the congregation and society of the saints, is offered as a universal sacrifice to God through that great Priest, who also offered himself in suffering for us, in the form of a servant, that we might be the body of so great a Head. . . . This is the sacrifice of Christians: *we being many are one body in Christ.* And this also the Church continually celebrates in the sacrament of the altar, so well known to the faithful, that it may be plain to her that *in that which she offers she herself is offered* (De Civ. Dei,X,vi)." Not the priest offering Christ, nor Christians offering themselves, but *the whole Christ,* Head and members, offering *the whole Christ* to the glory of God the Father, this is surely the true conception of the Eucharist.[32]

[30] David N. Power, "Roman Catholic Theologies of Eucharistic Communion: A Contribution to Ecumenical Conversation," *Theological Studies* 57 (1996) 607–8.

[31] *Origins* 6 (3 February 1977) 523.

[32] E. L. Mascall, *The Recovery of Unity: A Theological Approach* (London: Longmans, Green and Co., 1958) 140–1.

This Augustinian sense of Christ living in his Church, being present in his Church, seems to provide an antidote for a theological position that overidentifies the priest with Christ, and thus removes the priest from the body of the faithful as well. It also serves a purpose in avoiding the positing of two actions involved in the Eucharist: the action of Christ and the action of the Church. In fact, there is in reality one action. The action of the Church *is* the action of Christ. Aquinas uses the image of Christ and Church as forming one person.[33] The Church has no self-offering apart from the once-and-for-all offering of Christ. This helps contextualize the search for the interaction of the three priesthoods. Placing the emphasis on the one action would underscore the fact that on the level of sign, it is the liturgical action itself, not the priest, that is *the* sacramental sign. Such an emphasis does not mean that the ordained presider at Eucharist is not necessary, or that his role is not unique. John Paul II states:

> In a primary position in the church are the ordained ministries, that is, the ministries that come from the sacrament of orders. . . . The ministries receive the charism of the Holy Spirit from the risen Christ, in uninterrupted succession from the apostles, through the sacrament of orders: From him they receive the authority and sacred power to serve the church, acting *in persona Christi capitis* (in the person of Christ, the head) and to gather her in the Holy Spirit through the Gospel and the sacraments.[34]

That role of gathering the Church (the baptized) together in the Holy Spirit seems to fittingly describe the role of the ordained at Eucharist. Thus, the baptismal priesthood and the ministerial priesthood are not at odds with one another or in competition, but they join together to bring the Eucharist to completion by entering into the one eternal priesthood of Jesus Christ. In a real sense, each of the priesthoods (the baptismal and the ministerial) is incomplete without the other. They work in tandem. Both operate under the energy of the Holy Spirit. Both reflect a double synergy: one is a joint activity (combined energies) of the Holy Spirit and all the baptized present under the leadership of the ordained minister, and the other is the joint activity of the baptismal priesthood and the ministerial priesthood. This latter synergy is described by David Coffey in terms of "the priesthood of the Church" as

[33] *ST* III, q. 49, a. 1: "Sicut naturale corpus est unum, ex membrorum diversitate consistens, ita tota Ecclesia, quae est mysticum corpus Christi computatur quasi una persona cum suo capite, quod est Christus."

[34] Pope John Paul II, *Christifideles Laici*, 30 December 1988, n. 22, *Origins* 18 (9 February 1989) 571.

a distinct (from baptismal priesthood and ministerial priesthood) category. His distinction has the advantage of underscoring a neglected point: that both the baptismal priesthood and the ministerial priesthood are christological, and both are ecclesiological. He writes:

> It is only when one is brought to see that, while the ordained and the common priesthood can each have a christological reference and in a certain sense a christological nature, each possess properly an ecclesiological nature, that one realizes that the priesthood of the Church consists fully in neither alone but in their integration into a single organic entity. Only this insight enables one to reach a clear understanding of their mutual relationship.[35]

This type of communion ecclesiology both respects the various ministries at work in the Eucharist (unique being that of the ordained presider) and the fact that one single action is effected.

Eucharist as Apex of the Life of the Church

The identification of the Church's action at Eucharist with the action of Christ gets to the very core of the relationship between ecclesiology and liturgy. Karl Rahner writes: "In the sacrifice of the Mass the Church, in obedience to the Lord's express command, offers to God Christ's sacrifice of death on the Cross as its own sacrifice."[36] As Christians we know who we are at various moments of our existence. We know who we are when we give a cup of cold water in the name of Christ. But we know who we are in a unique way, in a privileged way, when we come together to carry out Christ's command to "do this in memory of me." The Constitution on the Sacred Liturgy of Vatican II declares: "The liturgy is the summit toward which the activity of the Church is directed; at the same time it is the fount from which all the Church's power flows."[37] This applies preeminently to the Church at Eucharist. Rahner states this point strongly: "The Church is most manifest, and in the most intensive form she attains the highest actuality of her own nature, when she celebrates the Eucharist. For here everything that goes to form the Church is found fully and manifestly present."[38]

[35] David Coffey, "The Common and the Ordained Priesthood," *Theological Studies* 58 (1997) 225.
[36] Karl Rahner and Angelus Häussling, *The Celebration of the Eucharist* (New York: Herder and Herder, 1968) 85–6.
[37] DOL, no. 10.
[38] Karl Rahner, *The Church and the Sacraments* (New York: Herder and Herder, 1963) 84–5.

This means that the activity of Eucharist is the premiere action of the Church, the body of Christ. That is why both terms (Eucharist and Church) have historically been referred to by the same names: communion, body of Christ. Indeed in some contexts it is difficult to discern whether the author intended the terms to specify "Church" or "Eucharist." The very ambiguity is wrought with meaning.

Thomas Aquinas taught clearly that "the Eucharist is the consummation of the spiritual life, and the goal of all the sacraments."[39] Thus, the Eucharist is the apex of the initiation process, and indeed of the entire life of the Church. The *Rite of Christian Initiation of Adults* states:

> Finally in the celebration of the eucharist, as they take part for the first time and with full right, the newly baptized reach the culminating point in their Christian initiation. In this eucharist the neophytes, now raised to the ranks of the royal priesthood, have an active part both in the general intercessions and, to the extent possible, in bringing the gifts to the altar. With the entire community they share in the offering of the sacrifice.[40]

This sacrifice is most fittingly offered at the Eucharist, but it does not mean that the Church ceases "to be Church" in between moments of celebrating the Eucharist. This is brought out well by noting both the cultic tradition and the testamentary tradition of the Last Supper as described in sacred Scripture. The former approach is in the genre of "liturgical account" and with a historical basis, and is the perspective taken by the Synoptics and Paul. The emphasis is on cult, and it forms the basis of what occurs at the Eucharist. The latter tradition, the testamentary, is in the genre of "farewell meal" and is the perspective taken especially by the Gospel of John. The emphasis is on Jesus' last testament, a life of service and love, and it forms the basis of what occurs in the Christian's everyday life.

Christ mandated his followers to remember him. They do this both by liturgical action and by the lived Christian life. Xavier Léon-Dufour puts it well: "Two *kinds of remembrance* are required of the disciples of Jesus: remembrance by liturgical action and remembrance by an attitude of service. . . . I do not choose between the two but cling to both by establishing a rhythm between them."[41] To put it another way, eucharistic spirituality is not something only for the moments of Mass. It is the hall-

---

[39] *ST* III, q. 73, a. 3.

[40] *Rite of Christian Initiation of Adults: Study Edition* (Chicago: Liturgy Training Publications, 1988) no. 217.

[41] Xavier Léon-Dufour, *Sharing the Eucharistic Bread: The Witness of the New Testament* (New York: Paulist Press, 1987) 283, 288.

mark of the entire Christian life, a life marked by the giving of one's self, in memory of Jesus who gave of himself, who washed the feet of others.

Robert Daly has published widely in the area of the origins of Christian sacrifice. He writes:

> For the New Testament church, Christian sacrifice was not a cultic but rather an ethical idea, an idea that could include prayer and worship in the formal sense, but was not constituted by them. It was centered not in a formal act of cultic or external ceremonial worship but rather in the everyday practical life of Christian virtue, in the apostolic and charitable work of being a good Christian, of being "for others" as Christ was "for us." It was a totally free and loving response, carried out on the practical level of human existence, to Christ's act of self-giving love. That is what Christian sacrifice was for the writers of the New Testament, and, to the extent that we are truly Christian, that is what it must also be for us today. Thus, no matter how similarly or differently we might understand the institutional or ecclesiological ramifications of celebrating the Eucharist, unless we do so with the fully spiritualized (=christologized) dispositions of Christian sacrifice, we call upon ourselves the stern rebuke Paul leveled against the Corinthians: "It is not the Lord's Supper which you celebrate" (I Cor 11:20).[42]

This lived Christian life of love and service is nourished and supported by the Eucharist. When we celebrate the Eucharist we join with Christ in offering to the Father the very same act that brought the Church into existence in the first place—the paschal mystery, that is, Christ's free gift of himself on our behalf to his Father. The Church comes from the act of redemption of Christ, and every time the Eucharist is celebrated that covenant is continued, now with the active involvement of the baptized members. In turn, the baptized leave the Eucharist to return to their ordinary life, to live that same *kenosis* of love in the world. Nathan Mitchell, in describing the characteristics of a liturgical ecclesiology, writes:

> A "liturgical ecclesiology" is thus characterized not only by an emphasis on the Church's cultic activity but also—and more importantly—by its emphasis on the Church as a body of disciples who enflesh Jesus' vision of a new human community based upon justice, mercy, and compassion. The Church is neither "doctrine" simply, nor "doxology" simply; it is a new way of living together.[43]

---

[42] Robert J. Daly, *The Origins of the Christian Doctrine of Sacrifice* (Philadelphia: Fortress Press, 1978) 140.

[43] Nathan Mitchell, "Liturgy and Ecclesiology" *Handbook for Liturgical Studies, II: Fundamental Liturgy,* ed. Anscar J. Chupungco, 113–27 (Collegeville: The Liturgical Press, 1998) 123.

That "new way of living together" is in turn brought back to the Eucharist. The Constitution on the Church of Vatican II states:

> For all their works, prayers and apostolic undertakings, family and married life, daily work, relaxation of mind and body, if they are accomplished in the Spirit—indeed even the hardships of life if patiently borne—all these become spiritual sacrifices acceptable to God through Jesus Christ (cf. I Pet 2:5). In the celebration of the Eucharist these may most fittingly be offered to the Father along with the body of the Lord. And so, worshipping everywhere by their holy actions, the laity consecrate the world itself to God.[44]

This cyclic interaction between cult and lived Christian life is propelled by the synergy, the joint activity, of the Holy Spirit that permeates the energy of human beings and conforms them to Christ. Such a transformation is described by St. Augustine in one of his sermons at Mass: "If then you are the body of Christ and his members, it is your sacrament that reposes on the altar of the Lord."[45]

Conclusion

Ecclesiology and liturgy (the Church at prayer) are so intertwined that they cannot be discussed separately. Every symbol has a twofold function: it represents the reality that it symbolizes, and in turn creates (recreates) that reality. As applied to the worship life of the Church (and in a preeminent way to the Eucharist), this means that what is symbolized is the unity of Christ with his members, the Church. In turn, the very act of symbolizing this unity makes even more one, Christ the head of the body and the members of that body.

Perfect unity will only be achieved, of course, at the end-time. In the meantime, the very source of unity, the Spirit of Jesus, the Holy Spirit, gently gathers all together into the one body of Christ, a living sacrifice of praise.

> Only when "the perfect Man," the total Christ with its full stature, appears in glory (Eph 4:13) will the Bride be able to lift up her eyes and say in her heart: "Who has borne me these? I was bereft and barren,

---

[44] Dogmatic Constitution on the Church, no. 34, *Vatican Council II: The Conciliar and Post Conciliar Documents,* ed. Austin Flannery (Northport , N.Y.: Costello Publishing Co., 1987) 391.

[45] Sermon 272; Latin text: *PL* 38, 1246–8. English trans.: Thomas Halton, *The Mass: Ancient Liturgies and Patristic Texts,* ed. André Hamman (New York: Alba House, 1967) 207.

exiled, turned out of my home; who has reared these? I was left all alone, so where have these come from?" (Is 49:18-21). Then they will say of the Church: "Every one was born there" (Ps 87:5).[46]

[46] Jean Corbon, *The Wellspring of Worship* (New York: Paulist Press, 1988) 107.

For Further Reading

Corbon, Jean. *The Wellspring of Worship.* New York: Paulist Press, 1988.

Kavanagh, Aidan. *On Liturgical Theology.* New York: Pueblo Publishing Co., 1984.

Léon-Dufour, Xavier. *Sharing the Eucharistic Bread: The Witness of the New Testament.* New York: Paulist Press, 1987.

Skelley, Michael. *The Liturgy of the World: Karl Rahner's Theology of Worship.* Collegeville: The Liturgical Press, 1991.

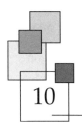

The Ecclesial Dimension of Anthropology

10

Michael J. Scanlon

The modern approach to Christian anthropology found its focus in the individual, or, better, the person who sought to understand the human self in terms of the classical Christian themes of creation, sin, grace, and hope. The paradigm for this Christian self-understanding was, of course, Jesus Christ, the New Adam. The social dimension of anthropology was left implicit or oblique in the notion of person, which implied relationality as essential to the human being. Of course, the classical themes themselves were obviously comprehensive or "social": creation was the world's and humanity's origin; original sin named our universal fallenness; redemptive grace was objectively universal; hope expressed our individual and collective destiny. Premodern theology was characteristically universal in its scope. This is evident in the Christian anthropology of Aquinas wherein the focus is on humanity as such *(natura humana)*. The mitigated realism of the scholastic use of the Platonic "universal ideas" assured this generality of approach— "humanity" was "real" in each human being. But modern thought is distinguished as modern by its novel focus on the individual, which did not in every case imply individualism. Christian thought was protected from this form of reductionism by its heritage of personalism. The individual was not just a particular illustration of the universal. As person, the individual was a singular, unique human being in essential relationship to all other fellow human beings.

I am delighted to have this opportunity to contribute to this volume in honor of my dear friend and colleague of many years, Fr. Patrick Granfield, O.S.B., the esteemed ecclesiologist. My project will be an elaboration of a communal Christian anthropology, or, perhaps better, an ecclesial anthropology. My contention is that our current "postmodern" situation provides new perspectives on understanding the *humanum* that are quite congenial to this project.

First of all, the term postmodern is in need of clarification. According to the philosopher Ludwig Wittgenstein, the meaning of words is found in their use. Given the rapid pace of change in every aspect of our current situation with the increased appearance of neologisms in current writing as a sign of this changing understanding of our world, I concur with those theologians who use postmodern as a synonym for "contemporary." "It is a way of saying 'our time, not some other.'"[1] With the collapse of the secular idea of progress so characteristic of modernity in World War I, the postmodern age, our own age, begins. In the modern period religion was "ignored, tolerated, repressed, and persecuted."[2] I share the hope that our postmodern age may offer a more promising atmosphere for a new religious sensibility.

The Holy Spirit

Our pairing of ecclesiology and anthropology is rooted in the third article of the Nicene-Constantinopolitan Creed: "We believe in the Holy Spirit . . . and in the Holy Catholic Church. . . ." This official Christian anthropology is social or communal—it is identical with the Church. The core of this ecclesial anthropology is the gift of the Spirit, who is the vital source of that "fellowship" (or *communio*) which effects "the People of God." In the form of the theology of grace the whole of Western theology can be summarized as a long commentary (at times quite polemical) on the third article of the Creed.

In the Old Testament the Spirit of God is the symbol of God's universal, vivifying presence in the world. According to the creation story of Genesis God's Spirit or "wind" *(ruach)* swept over the face of the waters, and God breathed the breath of life *(ruach)* into human beings (Gen 1:2; 2:7). These associations of the divine Spirit with power and life remain a constant throughout the Bible. In addition, we note a movement in the usage of Spirit language from the "ecstatic" Spirit who empowers, overpowers, and overwhelms in extraordinary phenomena to the "ethical" Spirit of the prophets and to the "eschatological" Spirit, promised to "all flesh" (Joel 2:28-29). The ethical Spirit empowers the prophet to denounce Israel's infidelity (Mic 3:8) and to promise redemption (Ezek 37:1-14).

---

[1] Paul Lakeland, *Postmodernity: Christian Identity in a Fragmented Age*, Guides to Theological Inquiry (Minneapolis: Fortress Press, 1997) 1.

[2] Hans Küng, *Theology for the Third Millennium: An Ecumenical View* (New York: Doubleday, 1988) 10. Küng reminds us that in our postmodern period the emancipatory "project of modernity" must be retained (7). For the thesis that our postmodern period is also "post-secular," see Phillip Blond, ed., *Post-Secular Philosophy: Between Philosophy and Theology* (New York: Routledge, 1998).

In the resurrection of Jesus Christians perceive the anticipation of the eschatological Spirit. Because of Easter Paul proclaims that the Spirit of God (the Lord and giver of *life*) has become the Spirit of Christ. The ethical Spirit of the prophets is radically focused in Jesus, especially in his Cross, to the extent that Jesus becomes *the* criterion, *the* "yardstick" for Christian discernment of the presence of the Spirit.[3] The spiritual life (life in the Holy Spirit) becomes identical with Christian discipleship. This is the central affirmation of Christian anthropology: God's self-communication to the world in the Spirit of Christ. In the language of the New Testament the Spirit is the power (the *dynamis*) that enables the Christian gradually to approximate the form, the shape *(morphē)* of Christ. But it is the Church, the community *(koinōnia)* of the Holy Spirit (2 Cor 13:13), that provides the "atmosphere" for the Spirit's Christic task. Another name for this "atmosphere" in Catholicism is tradition *(traditio)*, which in its most profound ("pneumatic") meaning is *the lived sense of faith of the People of God.* In Catholicism Spirit, tradition, and Church are cognate terms.

Significant Turns in Recent Thought

This primacy of social anthropology in the creed resonates with much contemporary thought. Postmodern or contemporary thought insists that human beings cannot be understood outside that matrix which we name in different ways—society, culture, history, language— but which constitutes the given point of departure for any particular anthropology. Being human is always being human together; *Dasein* emerges from *Mitsein*.

The modern notion of the self was the "substantial self," the self "in itself," the centripetal self finding its center in its interiority (the mind, the soul, the subject, consciousness). This modern self was dualistic in its self-identification with its "higher" principle, the "spiritual" (in the metaphysical sense of the nonmaterial) as over against its "lower" principle, the body. The Cartesian "ghost in the machine" is its classical illustration, and Descartes was followed by the "transcendental ego" of Kant, and, in general, by the "Universal Reason" of the Enlightenment. This was the modern "flight from the body" so pervasively decried by current trends of thought.

The "modernizing" of Catholic theology was the goal of Karl Rahner —with expressed, painful recognition of the abortive attempts of the

[3] James D. G. Dunn, *Jesus and the Spirit* (Philadelphia: Westminster Press, 1975) 319.

Catholic "modernists," condemned in the first decade of the twentieth century. Reading St. Thomas with Kantian lenses, Rahner "turned to the subject" and gave us "Transcendental Thomism." In a rapid movement from Athens to Jerusalem Rahner unfolded "*the* condition for the possibility" of the *believing* subject as the "supernatural existential" or a universal prevenient grace, echoing the universal divine salvific will (1 Tim 2:4). This prevenient grace was the "Offer" of salvation, identical with the universal presence of the Holy Spirit. Acceptance of this Offer would be the task of a lifetime (the "fundamental option"). The consequence of Rahner's work was a profound advancement in Christian self-consciousness, which left its mark on many of the "optimistic" assertions of the Second Vatican Council. In a short time this modern "turn to the subject" in Catholic theology was complemented by the "sociopolitical turn," which broadened the horizon of the hermeneutical retrieval of the Christian gospel from its Rahnerian focus on personal transformation to a demand for fundamental changes in the *polis* in all of its manifestations and institutionalizations in sociopolitical structures whose *raison d'être* is the flourishing of the world in its natural and historical dimensions. The implications of this second "turn" for ecclesiology, *the* sacramental form of "social grace," are still unfolding.

These two "turns" can be regarded as theological rehearsals of nineteenth-century philosophical developments in German thought (Kant, Hegel, Marx). In our century the dialogue with philosophy continues, and contemporary theology has been deeply affected by the "linguistic turn" in Anglo-American and Continental philosophy. Indeed, the sociopolitical turn which has resulted in political and liberation theologies raises the question: What does Christianity bring to the grand project of "changing the world"? The answer must be that the Christian tradition carries a powerful promise of liberation, and that tradition, like all other traditions, is mediated linguistically.

The linguistic turn is a further specification of that "historical consciousness" which informs contemporary anthropology. Historical consciousness alerts us to the fact that human beings are shaped by and, in turn, shape history, the ongoing "story" of humanity. In broad terms this "being made" by history and "making" history reveals the pragmatics of language (the "action coordinating" function of language) as this historical consciousness discloses the primacy of *praxis* both for persons and for their communities. Personal *praxis,* as Christian discipleship, was the focus of the "turn to the subject" in Catholic theology as that turn is illustrated in the work of Karl Rahner, while social *praxis* is the focus of the "sociopolitical turn" in political and liberation theologies. Both of these turns in theology are concerned with faith, the turn to the subject primarily with personal faith (in technical terms, the *fides qua creditur*), and the sociopolitical turn primarily with the public efficacy of communal, creedal faith (in technical terms, the *fides quae creditur*). With the retrieval of Aristotle's notion of *praxis* came the cognate retrieval of his notion of *phronēsis* as the practical wisdom that guides *praxis*. For Rahner's theology *phronēsis* would be the practical "know how" of the disciple, schooled by the Christian tradition in the Church. Influenced by historical consciousness as it finds articulation in Hegel and Marx, the notions of *praxis* and *phronēsis* receive a political horizon in the sociopolitical turn wherein the gospel is brought to bear on the institutional constructs of humanity's communal life. The "linguistic turn" offers a synthesis of both the personal and the communal turns. The turn to the subject is taken up into the "communal subject" or "the community of *phronēsis*" of the sociopolitical turn, and, similarly, the linguistic turn empowers the sociopolitical turn by providing access to the *fides quae creditur* ("orthodoxy") and accentuating communal *phronēsis* as the *fides quā creditur* ("orthopraxy"). The "we" who constitute the Church are those whose imaginations (the *locus* of *phronēsis* as intersubjective practical wisdom) are formed by Word and Sacrament (both "linguistic" realities) to reproduce "the mind of Christ" in "the Body of Christ."[4] The primary site for this formation would be worship where the "first level" religious language of narrative, metaphor, symbol effects the transmission of the Christian tradition, the living memory of Christ in the Spirit. Theology, as "second level" religious language, has the same "rhetorical" goal as the linguistic pragmatics of worship at a distance of critical reflection on the ramifications of following Christ in today's world.

Contemporary anthropological thinking is in many ways more consonant with the Christian tradition than some of the ahistorical tendencies of the past. The postmodern critique of the Cartesian subject, the disembodied thinking monad, poses an invitation to theology to retrieve its characteristic emphases on human finitude, on our sinful situation, and on the power of God's grace. One way of responding to this invitation is to reflect on the Catholic understanding of "human nature." For Thomas Aquinas "human nature" is a philosophical translation of the biblical understanding of human beings as God's good creatures. Of itself human nature is good *de jure;* it becomes sinful de facto only through human "nurture" in this fallen, albeit redeemed, world. For Aquinas human nature, as "good potential," is the basis for

---

[4] See Phil 2:5 where Paul uses the verbal form of *phronēsis* in his exhortation: "Let the same mind be in you *[touto phroneite]* that was in Christ Jesus."

the "necessity" of grace.[5] Grace is primarily the supernatural perfection of human nature as *capax Infiniti*. The de facto situation of sinfulness is really a "secondary" reason for the necessity of grace. This Thomistic insight into human nature as "potential" can be harmonized fruitfully with current thinking on what might be called the "essential nurturing" of this human potential as it is actualized in the human world. This "essential nurturing" is, of course, always ambiguous, even as it remains "essential" to the emergence of specifically human existence. To be fully human is to be "inducted" into the human community. This "induction" begins for all of us at birth, but the instrument for this actualization of the potential that is human nature is learning language. In radical departure from the Western philosophical tradition which has enthroned ahistorical "reason" as the universal human trait, current thought has broken through to a recognition that what is universally human is language—and there are many languages! In the original Greek of his famous anthropology Aristotle had it right—the human being is the animal that has the *logos* (the word). If language is the basic human attribute for Aristotle, his social anthropology follows—the human is the "political animal."[6] Speech makes intersubjectivity the matrix of personal subjectivity. In his project of retrieving human subjectivity in the wake of the postmodern critique of the monological self philosopher Calvin Schrag explores the notion of the "decentered self" within the context of communicative *praxis*.[7] This "decentered self" is, of course, the Christian ideal. The "self-centered self" is a classical definition of the sinner. In a postmodern approach that refuses simply to jettison human subjectivity the modern question "What is the Self?" is replaced by the question "Who is the Self?"[8] It is the social process that is responsible for the appearance of the self as a kind of "multiple personality."[9] In this process the "who" emerges in its different roles, its different relationships, its different responsibilities. These "different selves" of our different involvements in language and

---

[5] This is the major contribution of St. Thomas to the Catholic understanding of grace; it is later named "elevating grace," the Western form of divinizing grace; see *ST* I-II, q. 109.

[6] On *homo loquens* see Nicholas Lobkowicz, *Theory and Practice: History of a Concept from Aristotle to Marx* (Lanham, Md.: University Press of America, 1967) 17–33; on language and politics see Fred Dallmayr, *Language and Politics* (Notre Dame, Ind.: University of Notre Dame Press, 1984) 1–27.

[7] See Calvin O. Schrag, *Communicative Praxis and the Space of Subjectivity* (Bloomington: Indiana University Press, 1989) 139–57.

[8] Calvin O. Schrag, *The Self after Postmodernity* (New Haven, Conn.: Yale University Press, 1997) 4.

[9] For a fruitful use of this notion see Schrag, *Communicative Praxis,* 148–50.

life against the background of multiple social memories, various customs, habits, and institutional practices revolve around a "responding center," a sphere of interest and concern whence things are said and done. The "who" is a shifting center of initiative and response in the ongoing human "conversation." Thus the decentered self, described by its temporality and its embodiment, acquires its identity in a process of becoming. This description of the decentered self offers a most opportune point of departure for our concern to elaborate the "ecclesial self," implied in some of our central metaphors for describing the Church.

The Pilgrim Church

The intrinsic temporality of the self with other selves renders all of us pilgrims. Pilgrimage is an ancient image for the Church, the people "on the move" through history unto the goal of the kingdom of God. The picture of the Christian as *peregrinus* was central for St. Augustine (one of the first thinkers to reflect on *homo temporalis*) in his rejection of the classical Greek notion of the *polis*. Plato, Aristotle, and the Sophists all held the same fundamental conception of the social order of the *polis* as the essential locus for achieving the good life. While this classical conception of the *polis* makes good sense within the restricted horizon of pagan philosophy, Augustine's Christian faith taught him that people should not "settle in" for the limited, transient values of the "earthly city," since their destiny was a city that ultimately transcends the restrictions of social life in this world. Augustine agreed with the classical understanding of the human being as a "social animal." For a time he was influenced by the "imperial theology" of his mentor, Ambrose of Milan, according to whom the Israelite conquest of Canaan was a mere rehearsal of the Christian conquest of the Roman Empire under Constantine![10] Like Eusebius of Caesarea in the East, Ambrose proclaimed the *tempora christiana*, the establishment of a Christian society on earth. But Augustine's experience of the fall of Rome in 410 rendered this "imperial theology" implausible. His own theology of history in *The City of God* was to be quite different. A common interpretation of Augustine's great work is that he devalued historical society by individualizing, spiritualizing, and supernaturalizing Christian hope for life eternal beyond history.[11] But this interpretation is in need of

[10] For the "imperial theology" of Ambrose and Eusebius see Lloyd Patterson, *God and History in Early Christian Thought* (New York: Seabury Press, 1967) 79–101.

[11] A summary of the interpretation of Langdon Gilkey, *Reaping the Whirlwind: A Christian Interpretation of History* (New York: Seabury Press, 1976) 159–75.

significant nuance. It is important to note that the focus of Augustine's use of the notion of the City of God is not on its heavenly fulfillment but on its temporal "wayfaring on earth" as the Church of Christ. It is this emphasis on the historical pilgrimage of the City of God that makes Augustine a major figure in the history both of ecclesiology and of political philosophy. He portrays an ideal vision of what social life can be when the bonds that unite people are love of God and love of neighbor. For instance, in light of our contemporary sociopolitical value of diversity the following lines are worth quoting:

> So long, then, as the heavenly City is wayfaring on earth, she invites citizens from all nations and from all tongues, and unites them into a single pilgrim band. She takes no issue with that diversity of customs, laws, and traditions whereby human peace is sought and maintained. Instead of nullifying or tearing down, she preserves and appropriates whatever in the diversities of diverse races is aimed at one and the same objective of human peace, provided only that they do not stand in the way of faith and worship of the one supreme and true God.[12]

Instead of proclaiming justice as the supreme value of human society, Augustine dares to go further: love of neighbor can, even now, promote the ideal of a unified humanity which celebrates diversity within the bond of mutual love. How attractive an ideal for us today in the "global village"! Although the City of God, as long as she is in the earthly city, may consider herself a "captive" and an "alien," she must not hesitate to cooperate with all her fellow human beings to secure the necessities of life for all. Indeed, there ought to be "common cause between the two cities in what concerns our purely human living." Citizens of both cities must obey the civil law which governs the details of our common human life. While the City of God cannot share with the earthly city "a common religious legislation," she is bound to share with the latter a common commitment to the pursuit of those political structures which provide the "temporal goods" required by all. The Heavenly City, while wayfaring on earth, "not only makes use of earthly peace but fosters and actively pursues along with other human beings a common platform in regard to all that concerns our purely human life and that does not interfere with faith and worship." Throughout his "political theology" Augustine's favorite metaphor for describing the citizens of the City of God is "pilgrims." These people of faith and hope are pil-

---

[12] St. Augustine, *The City of God,* XIX, 17, trans. Gerald Walsh, Demetrius Zema, Grace Monahan, and Daniel Honan (Washington, D.C.: The Fathers of the Church; Catholic University of America Press, 1950).

grims, wayfarers, wanderers—they are "on the Way" to the ultimate City of eternal bliss. Thus does Augustine "redeem" what seems to be our worst enemy—time, that perpetual loss of whatever goods we achieve. Time can become the way, the path to eternity, to that final, eternal Sabbath, "which we shall be."[13]

The Body of Christ

Contemporary anthropology has begun to overcome the long disparagement of the body in the classical metaphysics (Platonism) and the modern epistemology (Cartesianism) of the Western tradition. The soul with its intellectual powers was understood as the essential core of the human being. The Greeks discovered the mind, and all else, especially the body, seemed of secondary importance. The notion of the "immortality of the soul" claimed that the soul could exist without the body which it inhabited or used as an instrument during our mortal life. There were, however, other anthropological traditions which did not disparage the body. Exemplary was the synthetic anthropology of the Hebrew tradition wherein the body was not a "part" of the human being but its concrete reality. In the New Testament, body *(sōma)* is not a part of the human being together with soul—body is the whole person, as is evident in Christian hope for the "resurrection of the body." For Thomas Aquinas the soul is "the substantial form of the body," an anthropology he derived from the notably less "spiritual" thought of Aristotle. Aquinas's anthropology became defined Church doctrine at the Council of Vienne in 1312: "the rational soul is the form of the human body" (DS 902). One could interpret this official anthropology as rendering the soul as adjectival to the body—the human being is a "living body."[14] Contemporary retrieval of the centrality of the body for a truly Christian anthropology in both its individual and its social dimensions should help us overcome those all too popular misinterpretations of the Christian religion wherein the whole focus of concern is the "soul" with its "interiority." For many modern Western people this

[13] St. Augustine, *The City of God*, XXII, 30.
[14] Wolfhart Pannenberg, *Anthropology in Theological Perspective*, trans. Matthew O'Connell (Philadelphia: Westminster Press, 1985) 523; for further theological reflection on the body see Charles Davis, *Body as Spirit* (New York: Seabury Press, 1976); Elisabeth Moltmann-Wendel, *I Am My Body* (New York: Continuum, 1995); John Sachs, *The Christian Vision of Humanity*, Zacchaeus Studies: Theology (Collegeville: The Liturgical Press, 1991).

"soul" is quite obviously Cartesian in its derivation—"the ghost in the machine." Preachers and teachers of the faith should be very careful when tempted to inveigh against today's "materialism." This all too frequent bromide will confirm people in their "spiritualistic" interpretation of religion. Karl Rahner provides a healthy corrective when he avers that authentic Christian teaching "does lie in the signs of our times because, if we can put it this way, due to their Christian origins our times are *correctly more materialistic* than the pre-Christian Greek age."[15] Maybe "Christian materialism" would be a better way to refer to Christian spirituality. If we must use the word "soul," we should follow the direction of Aquinas's usage as this is nicely captured by Ludwig Wittgenstein's observation: "The human body is the best picture of the human soul."[16]

For contemporary anthropology embodiment together with temporality is an essential characteristic of the "decentered self." Through the emphasis on the linguisticality of human existence the human body is rediscovered as basic symbol. Within and through our intersubjectivity the phenomenon of the decentered self delivers its own embodied presence in the communicative performances of discourse and action. As event and acquisition the decentered subject emerges from and sustains itself within these performances. The body is the self-manifestation, the self-expression of the human spirit, the concrete "medium" through which the human spirit becomes a reality in the world. In the sacramental economy of Catholicism "to express" is "to effect." By bodily self-expression the human being enacts itself in a lifetime. Body is the basic human sacrament through which the human being effects itself in freedom in interdependence with the embodied selves of other human beings in their common commerce with the material world. Metaphoric expansion of the human body to the social level gives us phrases such as "the body politic"—or, in our case, to the Church as the body of Christ. As body of Christ, the Church is the sacrament of Christ in visible, audible, tangible continuation of the salvific role of Jesus in the world. Just as Jesus was the Word incarnate (enfleshed) through whom God has "done himself" definitively for us,[17] the Church continues this divine self-enactment as the sacrament of salvation for the world. A re-

[15] Karl Rahner, *Foundations of Christian Faith*, trans. William Dych (New York: Seabury Press, 1978) 196 (italics added).

[16] Ludwig Wittgenstein, *Remarks on the Philosophy of Psychology*, as quoted in H. Brown, D. Hudecki, L. Kennedy, and J. Snyder, eds., *Images of the Human: The Philosophy of the Human Person in a Religious Context* (Chicago: Loyola Press, 1995) 453.

[17] Karl Rahner, *The Love of Jesus and the Love of Neighbor* (New York: Crossroad, 1983) 38.

trieval of the Greek patristic notion of "divinization" would be apropos here. Following 2 Pet 1:4 (we become "partakers of the divine nature"), the Greek Fathers insisted that grace divinizes the Christian. In this Petrine text "partakers" is a translation of *koinōnoi*, "those in communion with." As we embrace the communion ecclesiology of Vatican II, we must remember that "in the New Testament *communion* stresses not so much the 'horizontal' sharing among Christians but the Christian's 'vertical' sharing with God. The term stresses the relationship between God and the believer, but especially the ongoing activity of the Holy Spirit who vivifies the person for life in the Church."[18] Divinization, grace, sanctification and other terms came to replace this biblical language on communion with God. Thomas Aquinas spoke of this communion as grace, "elevating" the graced person to God's life. Karl Rahner extends this divinization to the whole world. Edward Schillebeeckx can now put a new twist on a famous ecclesial claim: "Outside the *world* there is no salvation."[19]

St. Augustine, the *Doctor gratiae* of Western Christianity, appropriated the theme of divinization from the Greek Fathers. He used it, as they did, to describe the gift of grace, but his more characteristic usage is ecclesial—the Pauline portrayal of the Church as the body of Christ.[20] Commenting on our "Amen" to the Eucharistic minister's "The Body of Christ," Augustine says:

> If you want to understand the body of Christ, listen to the Apostle telling the faithful, *You, though, are the body of Christ and its members* (I Cor 12:27). So if it's you who are the body of Christ and its members, it's the mystery meaning you that has been placed on the Lord's table; what you receive is the mystery that means you. It is to what you are that you reply *Amen*, and by so replying you express your assent. What you hear, you see, is *The Body of Christ*, and you answer, *Amen*. So be a member of the body of Christ, in order to make that *Amen* true.[21]

---

[18] Michael Fahey, "Church," *Systematic Theology: Roman Catholic Perspectives*, ed. Francis Schüssler Fiorenza and John P. Galvin (Minneapolis: Fortress Press, 1991) 2:35.

[19] Edward Schillebeeckx, *Church: The Human Story of God*, trans. John Bowden (New York: Crossroad, 1990) 5.

[20] Henri Rondet, *The Grace of Christ*, trans. Tad Guzie (Westminster, Md.: Newman Press, 1967) 93–4; see also Patricia Wilson-Kastner, "Grace as Participation in the Divine Life in the Theology of Augustine of Hippo," *Augustinian Studies* 7 (1976) 135–52.

[21] *The Works of Saint Augustine: A Translation for the 21st Century*, Sermons, III/7, trans. and notes by Edmund Hill; ed. J. Rotelle (New York: New City Press, 1993) 300.

The Sinful Church

A distinctive theme in traditional Christian anthropology is the doctrine of original sin. Indeed, in Western theology since the time of Augustine hamartiology formed the context for the theology of grace for Catholics and even more so for Protestants. Thomas Aquinas significantly modified this Augustinian heritage when he averred that our basic need for grace is found in our creatureliness rather than our sinfulness. For Aquinas prelapsarian Adam had the same essential need for grace as fallen humanity. Grace is primarily the "elevation" of humanity to an astounding "parity" with God, since grace makes us friends of God and friends are "equal."[22] Nevertheless, in the official teaching of the Catholic Church at the Councils of Carthage (418), Orange (529), and Trent (1546) grace appears in a hamartiological context: sin is discussed first and then grace is presented as God's unowed forgiveness and transformation of the sinner.

In the twentieth century this hamartiological setting for the theology of grace gave way to a broader, far more attractive christological and pneumatological framework for reflection on God's Gift. This marvelous change was due to the great advances in biblical and patristic studies which, in turn, led to major developments in systematic theology beyond the possibilities of neoscholasticism.

Among these developments in systematic theology are new approaches to the doctrine of original sin. Augustine's "biological metaphor" (we are born sinners: *generatione* or *propagatione*) was certainly effective in establishing a universal solidarity of need for redemption. But in light of contemporary thought and sensibility, not to mention the damage its pessimistic fatalism has done over the centuries, it has lost its power to elucidate our obviously sinful condition. With the advent and expansion of historical consciousness theologians today are searching for "historical metaphors" to retrieve the doctrine of original sin. Indeed, historical consciousness offers us a singularly apposite framework for our attempt to clarify the meaning of human sinfulness. To the extent that we understand ourselves as cultural-linguistic constructs we know that we have been formed and "deformed" by history, society, and language. One way to understand the transmission of original sin is to see it as part of our cultural inheritance, appropriated by each one of us as we learn to speak. Biases, prejudices, tendencies

[22] On St. Thomas's theology of grace see Jean-Marie Laporte, *Patience and Power: Grace for the First World* (New York: Paulist Press, 1988) 194–257; Stephen Duffy, *The Dynamics of Grace: Perspectives in Theological Anthropology*, New Theology Series (Collegeville: The Liturgical Press, 1993) 121–70.

toward narrow-mindedness and narrow-heartedness are carried in the language which is the chief instrument in the transmission of our various traditions. A "hermeneutics of suspicion" reveals our sinful situation as our minds are blinded and our hearts are constricted by the language which constructs our consciousness. If "the world as known is language,"[23] our grasp on reality is tainted by our universal situation "after Babel."

In their attempts to retrieve the doctrine of original sin some theologians have turned to the Johannine notion of the "sin of the world." This "original sin" is called "sin" by analogy with personal sin or culpable evil acts. It describes the "situation" in which all human beings find themselves as children of "Adam." As Paul Ricoeur avers, the protological account of the "Fall" in Genesis gives us "an anthropology of ambiguity" in terms of the "before" and "after" the act of disobedience.[24] "Before" this act the sexual relationship between Adam and Eve was part of the goodness of creation—it symbolized openness, fidelity, and trust between human beings. "After" this act they discovered their nakedness with shame and covered their bodies with clothing; this sexual "cover-up" symbolizes the historical plight of all human relationships: mistrust, dissimulation, infidelity. But goodness remains more primordial than evil. Sex remains good in itself, but it now expresses the ambiguity of the human condition. Again, "before" the Fall work is part of the goodness of creation: Adam worked in the garden. But "after" the disobedience the ground is cursed and Adam will live by the sweat of his brow. Work here symbolizes our relationship with the earth, with the world. It remains good as cooperation with the Creator, but it has become for us ambiguous. Our relationships with one another and our relationship with our common home are tainted. All human culture, our human cultivation of creation, is marked with ambiguity, an intransigent mixture of good and evil that will describe us until the end of history. As cultural constructs, we all inherit this mixture and pass it on generation to generation through the tremendous power that is our tongue, "a restless evil, full of deadly poison" (Jas 3:8). We become sinners as we join the "conversation" which is humanity.

We have been describing "social sin." Historical consciousness in its "Hegelian" mode alerts us to the fact that we create all of the institutions which constitute our various sociopolitical arrangements. As our

[23] Hans-Georg Gadamer's fundamental hermeneutical principle: "Being that can be understood is language," *Philosophical Hermeneutics*, trans. David Linge (Berkeley: University of California Press, 1977) 31.

[24] Paul Ricoeur, *The Symbolism of Evil*, trans. Emerson Buchanan (Boston: Beacon Press, 1967) 247.

creations these institutions are always ambiguous. And historical consciousness in its "Marxist" mode alerts us to the fact that these institutional creations of ours in turn create the consciousness of those shaped by these institutions. Evil becomes structural or systemic as dehumanizing forms of injustice are built into our works to wreak havoc on human beings and on the earth. As Gregory Baum instructs us, this "social sin" gains its power over us from the fact that people do not notice it for some time.[25] There is a common blindness to this atmospheric evil, a blindness, however, that is abetted by cultural and religious pseudo-legitimations of the status quo. This ideological function of symbolic "authentication" creates a pervasive false consciousness. People uncritically accept the status quo as right and good.

Hope dawns according to the biblical message when the Spirit of God raises up prophets who discern the covered-up injustices, indict those responsible, and call for change and reform. Here the dialectical relationship between social sin and personal sin becomes clear. The few —the Bible refers to them as the rich, the wise, and the powerful (and they are often in collusion)—make decisions for personal aggrandizement that cause the suffering of the many. If and to the extent that the prophetic call is heeded change for the better occurs. The Church as the community of the Spirit of Christ is called to this prophetic role in society. Christians who are mystics in the everyday sense of the life of faith, hope, and love are called to be prophets, to express their mystical attunement with the Lord and giver of life in word and in deed.

Society with all of its institutional arrangements is a product of human freedom. Since human beings are sinners, their social productions are infected with sin. This infection can be more or less, but no one can escape it. It seems to take on a superhuman form that led in the past to a personification of social sin in a diabolic power—the devil or Satan. To us as well evil continues to seem superhuman in its universal sway, tearing apart (literal meaning of "diabolic") persons and peoples.

No one denies that sin also appears in the Church. There is some disagreement about referring to this sin in the Church as the "sinful Church."[26] A distinction is made between the Church and the members of the Church (sinners) to affirm the Church as mystery indwelt by the Holy Spirit. This does not mean that the "ideal Church" floats like a Platonic idea above the empirical Church. Again, it affirms the Church

[25] Gregory Baum, *Religion and Alienation: A Theological Reading of Sociology* (New York: Paulist Press, 1975) 193–226.

[26] See Richard Lennan, *The Ecclesiology of Karl Rahner* (Oxford: Clarendon Press, 1997) 28–33.

as mystery. It seems to me that this distinction is unnecessary—it too easily evokes the notion of the ideal Church. But the Church is the community of the Spirit of Christ, and that community is made up of sinners (and saints). Thus, the "sinful Church" honestly affirms the reality of the Church as it appears in the world, and this "appearance" is essential to the Church, which, despite sin, is the Sacrament of Christ.

The Grace of the Holy Spirit

We have discussed the traditionally Catholic understanding of grace as divinization and elevation in the section on the Church as body of Christ. We turn now to a consideration of ecclesial grace as "social grace." This contemporary, historically conscious understanding of grace is, once again, characteristically Catholic as we shall see.

In its primary meaning grace is synonymous with the Holy Spirit. Grace is Uncreated Grace in scholastic language. This retrieval of the understanding of grace as fundamentally God's self-gift is the major achievement of theology in this area in the twentieth century. In the context of this achievement we can reclaim another typically Catholic development since the time of St. Thomas—the theology of "created grace." Indeed, in St. Thomas's usage the term grace ordinarily means "created grace." Because Thomas himself did not explicitly clarify the relation between created grace and Uncreated Grace, later theologians came to regard Uncreated Grace as a "formal effect" of created grace.[27]

They held that, if the trinitarian God (the Spirit, Uncreated Grace) were to dwell within the human spirit, the dwelling place would have to be transformed to receive the gift. This position assured a certain primacy—at least temporal—to created grace in Catholic theological textbooks until our time. Any reclaiming of the notion of created grace today must be aware of its secondary character. Historical and ecumenical theology have restored Uncreated Grace to its primacy in the "hierarchy of dogma."

The tradition of created grace, however, points to a genuine Catholic concern that our central belief in the self-gift of God results in a changed situation for its human recipients. It was this concern that inspired St. Thomas to reject Peter Lombard's *identification* of grace with the Holy Spirit.[28] If grace is the Holy Spirit, that would mean that God

---

[27] For a good, ecumenically sensitive discussion of the notion of created grace see C. Moeller and G. Philips, *The Theology of Grace and the Oecumenical Movement*, trans. R. A. Wilson (London: A. R. Mowbray & Co., 1961).

[28] *ST* II-II, q. 23, a. 2.

loves God in the human soul. But Thomas was concerned to affirm that the Holy Spirit transforms us into lovers of God. Thus, grace implies a change in the human recipient. Employing Aristotelian categories for his theological anthropology, Thomas described an entitative elevation of human nature to the supernatural level. Grace raised creatures to the level of the Creator in order that through their divinely human activity they might reach their gratuitous goal, eternal union with their Creator. Thomas did not hesitate to use the category of "merit" to describe the intrinsic relation between graced action and its gracious goal: graced action merits life eternal *ex condigno*.[29] Thus, grace is inchoate glory. This Thomistic theology of merit is ripe for retrieval in our age of historical consciousness.

In terms of the "change" that grace effects Karl Rahner moved its location from the metaphysical notion of human nature to the modern focus on subjectivity or consciousness. For Rahner grace implies a "change" in human consciousness, not a temporal change but a change from what might have been ("pure nature") to what de facto graciously is. In its depths human self-consciousness always is consciousness of grace or "experience of the Spirit." Rahner's contribution to the question of the experience of the Spirit is very important. It overcomes the post-Tridentine theology which held that ordinarily the justified person did not experience the grace, which, however, was really there. Experience of grace was limited to the extraordinary mystics. Rahner renders everyone a "constitutional mystic" on the existential level. The ramifications of this breakthrough for current theologies of religion are obvious.

The contemporary emphasis on "social grace" complements Rahner's "ordinary mysticism" by extending it to prophetic spirituality, the concrete expression of mystical attunement to the Spirit in word and deed. The notion of social grace continues the Catholic tradition that grace always implies a "change."[30] In this case the "change" is not only "interior." It regards the "exterior" cultural and sociopolitical constructions of the "hominized" but not yet fully "humanized" world. The hominized world of cultural or political institutions is always ambiguous, as we have seen. Since we are their creators, they are always tainted by the universal reality of sin. But, where sin abounds, we believe that grace abounds still more.

---

[29] *ST* I-II, q. 114, a. 3. For a recent study of St. Thomas's doctrine on merit see Joseph Wawrykow, *God's Grace and Human Action* (Notre Dame, Ind.: University of Notre Dame Press, 1995).

[30] See Roger Haight, "Sin and Grace," *Systematic Theology*, ed. Fiorenza and Galvin, 2:131–5.

Historical consciousness has broadened our understanding of human freedom. The theology of freedom has been a long commentary on the Pauline teaching that "where the Spirit of the Lord is, there is freedom" (2 Cor 3:17). Pneumatology is the context for understanding freedom as the empowerment to do the good. Free will is a neutral power concerned with choices, but freedom is the hallmark of personhood. In their different ways Augustine, Aquinas, and Luther always attributed freedom as the power to do good to the grace of the Holy Spirit. Historical consciousness enabled Karl Rahner to name the good that we have been freed to do most concretely. Freedom is the power to do oneself, to enact oneself in radical self-determination. For Christian faith love is the "how" of freedom.[31] In response to the secular notion of self-fulfillment through self-assertion, faith holds that freedom is authentic only when it is actualized as self-donation to the Other and to others in love. Again, the paradigm is the freedom of Jesus. Time is the raw material for freedom, and history (the human story) is the realm of freedom.

Historical consciousness alerts us to the fact that we are the makers of history. All of the sociocultural institutions that structure our human world are our creations. We have already assessed these creations from the viewpoint of social sin. We must now balance this indictment with the correlative notion of social grace. Wherever our cultural, social, political, economic institutions serve people with justice, love, and compassion, our eyes of faith discern the efficacy of the grace of the Holy Spirit. Wherever our human institutions mediate the grace of the Lord and giver of life, we see the power of God, the Spirit of Christ. But just as we know that we as individuals and as communities are sinners, we know that all of our "products" carry that sin. Our creations mediate life, and they mediate death—it is always a matter of more or less. This contemporary awareness must intensify our sense of responsibility. The gospel demand that we love our neighbor as ourselves cannot be limited to interpersonal relationships. We are commanded to love everyone, and we now realize that this universal love cannot remain merely a sentiment of our hearts. We can love neighbors we will never meet to the extent that our "communicative *praxis*" really can change our world for the better. In our various competencies we must work with others to "exteriorize" grace in promoting structural changes to serve life. For Catholics this notion of social grace should be most congenial: it is a historically conscious extension of our sacramental

---

[31] For a clear presentation of the Pauline movement from *charis* (grace) to *eleutheria* (freedom) to *agapē* see Jerome Murphy-O'Connor, *Becoming Human Together: The Pastoral Anthropology of St. Paul* (Wilmington, Del.: Michael Glazier, 1982).

imagination. Our contemporary liberation theologies are a superb illustration of social grace at work, changing the world.

For Catholics, again, the Church is perhaps the illustration of social
grace. As the sacrament of Christ, the Church continues the soteriological mission of Jesus. And yet we know that social sin affects the
Church as it affects all of our institutions. It is for us no contradiction to
believe that the Church is the work of the risen Lord or the creation of
the Holy Spirit, and, at the same time, to know that the religious details, the concrete structures and arrangements of Church life, are the
creations of Christians, even as they rightly attribute to the guidance of
the Spirit their pastoral decisions. This is a traditional Catholic understanding of the "interplay" between primary and secondary causality—divine freedom works in and through human freedom. On our
"secondary" level we are responsible for the shape of the Church. The
Church is "always in need of being purified and incessantly pursues
the path of penance and renewal" (LG 8).

The ecclesial "innovation" of Vatican II was the recovery of the *communio* model of the Church. In broad strokes we can say that this model
provided the guiding vision for the Church's first millennium. As a result of the Gregorian Reform of the 1070s the Church came to be practically identified with the hierarchy for the duration of the second
millennium. A clear but theologically deficient distinction was made
between the *Ecclesia docens* (the pope and the bishops) and the *Ecclesia
discens* (the laity). Vatican II significantly nuanced this distinction to the
point of rendering its clarity obsolete. Especially significant here is the
retrieval of the pneumatic notion of the *sensus fidelium* (LG 12), which
demands attention to the theology of "reception." If we can say that the
"material element" of Catholicism is the immanence of grace, then the
"formal element" is reception.[32] In 1985 the Synod of Bishops declared
that "the ecclesiology of communion is the central and fundamental
idea of the Council's documents."[33] In many ways this "idea" has remained an idea or vision of the Church. To render this idea effective
demands significant structural changes in the institutional life of the
Church. The highly developed ecclesiastical structures of the second
millennium have centralized authority in the Church in the direction of
Ultramontanism. To balance the Petrine ministry in the Church, Vatican

---

[32] For further discussion see Michael Scanlon, "Catholicism and Living Tradition:
The Church as a Community of Reception" *Empowering Authority: The Charisms of
Episcopacy and Primacy in the Church Today,* ed. Patrick Howell and Gary Chamberlain
(Kansas City: Sheed and Ward, 1990) 1–16.

[33] Patrick Granfield, "The Church Local and Universal: Realization of Communion," *The Jurist* 49 (1989) 450.

II endorsed the idea of collegiality for the world's bishops, working together as a "college" in church synods or cooperating with one another in their local dioceses. There is obvious tension here between the ideal of collegiality and the offices of the Roman Curia, particularly over the vexed question of the authority of national episcopal conferences.

There are other major issues facing the Church as an institution of social grace. The ecclesiology of communion implies a basic equality among all the members of the Church. The major issue here is the role of women in the Church, given their absence from the structures of authority and their nonordainability to Church office. For many members of the Church this situation exemplifies ecclesiastical sexism. The social evils of sexism, clericalism, and patriarchalism continue to mark the institutional Church.

Ecclesial Anthropology and Hope

There is a general agreement among theologians that Christian eschatology includes both a *now* and a *not-yet* dimension. As the central symbol of the teaching of Jesus the kingdom of God is the fulfillment of God's Name, YHWH, "I am who am" (Exod 3:14). This kingdom was anticipated in the ministry of Jesus and especially in his resurrection from the dead. Easter inaugurates the end-time. Christians believe that we now live in the final age of history. The Spirit has been given to us as the *arrabōn,* the pledge, the guarantee of what is to come.

Historical consciousness has deepened our appreciation of the essentially historical character of human existence. Eternity can no longer mean that we leave history behind and enter into timelessness. Eternity is now anticipated as the fullness of time. For Karl Rahner eternity is the "fruit," the "issue" of time or history (time becomes history when it becomes human time, when human beings can decide how to use their time).[34] The content of eternity is history, and we human beings can create eternity out of time because the eternal Spirit is with us. Hope for life eternal can no longer be dismissed as "opium." Christian hope intensifies Christian responsibility for a redemptive use of time.

If eternity is the fruit of freedom in the Spirit, we may not limit this understanding to the life of the individual. Eternity is also the fruit of that communicative praxis which changes the world in accord with Jesus' portrayal of the kingdom of God. What is done in that love "which has been poured into our hearts through the Holy Spirit that has been given to us" (Rom 5:5) contributes in some way to that ultimate realm of freedom which is the "not yet" of God's kingdom.

[34] Rahner, *Foundations of Christian Faith,* 437.

God's freedom is the key to the meaning of the classical doctrine of the Trinity. As a summary of the story of God's salvific activity in the New Testament, the Trinity expresses God's freedom to become *Deus pro nobis.* There is in God not only the necessity that God be God, but "eternal potentials" for a divine freedom that is narrated throughout the Bible.[35] These "possibilities" are expressed in the Scriptures as God's word *(Logos)* or Wisdom *(Sophia)* and God's Spirit *(Pneuma).* In keeping with this symbolism from the Jewish sapiential literature we could say that the *Logos* or *Sophia* is God's creative plan, God's ordering presence in the world, while God's *Pneuma* is God's creative power to execute this plan. These sapiential symbols of divine presence and agency in the world provided the lofty confessional language of the New Testament's portrayal of the identity of Jesus and his Spirit, later condensed into the doctrine of the Trinity. Given the christological and pneumatological dimensions of ecclesiology, a brief overview of contemporary trinitarian theology as it relates to the Church's and to the world's destiny is in order.

As we have seen some contemporary exegetes translate the tetragrammaton (YHWH) in the future tense. God's Name is God's promise to be with and for God's people. It seems to me that the key to the doctrine of the Trinity is this divine freedom, the attribute of a personal God. For Christians the definitive fulfillment of the Divine Name occurred in Jesus Christ and continues its movement toward ultimate fulfillment in the present activity of the Holy Spirit, an activity focally disclosed in the Church. For St. Augustine, who mediated to the West the biblical understanding of personhood, personhood is ultimately eschatological.[36] It is the result of the completion of our temporal pilgrimage in eternity. Speaking analogically, we can perhaps apply this eschatological understanding of personhood to divine personhood.

Many contemporary trinitarian theologians refer to the implications of "Rahner's rule" for current retrieval of the doctrine of the Trinity: "The 'economic' Trinity is the 'immanent' Trinity, and the 'immanent' Trinity is the 'economic' Trinity."[37] The first part of this rule is essential to Rahner's formulation of the "hierarchy of doctrine"—the gospel is God's self-communication to the world through Christ and in the Spirit.

---

[35] For Rahner, of course, we know of these "potentials" only through their actualization in Christ and in the Spirit.

[36] See Charles Cochrane, *Christianity and Classical Culture* (Oxford: Oxford University Press, 1974) 399–455.

[37] Ted Peters refers to this famous identification of the economic and immanent Trinities as "Rahner's Rule" in his *God as Trinity: Relationality and Temporality in Divine Life* (Louisville: Westminster/John Knox Press, 1993) 96–103.

Rahner did not develop the second part of his rule, but he gave some suggestions for its interpretation. The notion of "person" in the trinitarian formula is analogical. The *Logos/Sophia* is God's "eternal, real possibility" of a historical self-manifestation, and the *Pneuma* is the "eternal, real possibility" of God's becoming the innermost activating principle of the world.[38] Thus, the trinitarian potential in God is the condition for the possibility of a divine freedom or a divine history in which God becomes our God—God becomes concretely trinitarian in history.

The theologian John Mackey does not hesitate to bring Rahner's rule to its logical conclusion. Mackey finds intriguing the suggestion of Jürgen Moltmann that "the economic Trinity completes and perfects itself to immanent Trinity when the history and experience of salvation are completed and perfected."[39] The immanent Trinity is eschatological, when God is all in all. Mackey is aware of the fact that this new understanding of the Trinity is very different from classical Trinitarianism, but he accounts for the traditional distinction between the immanent and economic Trinities in the dualist world view the Fathers of the Church shared with the Platonic religious philosophies they used. Corresponding to the ideal/empirical divisions of their time is the immanent/economic Trinity. Since the immanent Trinity is "not yet," our current trinitarian referents are

> first, the God to whom Jesus prayed, calling him Father, second, Jesus of Nazareth in whom was this same God who was also in the world before Jesus, and who is now so much "in" Jesus (and Jesus in God) as to enable us to say that in and through this human person of Jesus, God experiences a human destiny in the very process of shaping human destiny (saving, revealing), and third, . . . is now the same Jesus-Immanuel, but now as Risen Lord, life-giving Spirit of body in this world. . . .[40]

Again, if Jesus of Nazareth is the second 'persona,' the Church, the body of Christ, is the third 'persona' of the Christian Trinity . . ."[41]

Intriguing, indeed, are these current proposals for trinitarian theology. They are not without foundation in the Christian tradition. Recall

---

[38] Karl Rahner, "Oneness and Threefoldness of God in Discussion with Islam," *Theological Investigations,* vol. 18, trans. Edward Quinn (New York: Crossroad, 1983) 118.

[39] James Mackey, "Are There Christian Alternatives?" *The Christian Understanding of God Today,* ed. James Byrne (Dublin: Columbia Press, 1993) 68.

[40] Ibid., 71.

[41] James Mackey, *Modern Theology: A Sense of Direction* (Oxford: Oxford University Press, 1987) 128.

again the Greek patristic notion of divinization as descriptive of our *communio* with God through Christ in the Spirit, together with the common patristic claim that God became human that human beings might become divine. "For us and for our salvation" the incarnation cannot be simply a "higher realization of God's Self-communication which leaves the rest of the world behind."[42] Indeed, for Rahner christology is a moment in a universal pneumatology.[43] As sacrament of salvation in and for the world the Church is a sign that the world is a world of grace whose destiny is divinization.

An ecclesial anthropology for today must place the emphasis on communal or communicative praxis. If the Church is the People of God, all are called to mission in a centrifugal ecclesiology wherein the Church exists not for itself but for the world Christ has redeemed. God's gift must become our task.

---

[42] Rahner, *Foundations of Christian Faith*, 200.
[43] Ibid., 317.

For Further Reading

Farley, Edward. *Ecclesial Man: A Social Anthropology of Faith and Reality.* Philadelphia: Fortress Press, 1975.

Happel, Stephen, and David Tracy. *A Catholic Vision.* Philadelphia: Fortress Press, 1984.

Hodgson, Peter. *Winds of the Spirit: A Constructive Christian Theology.* Westminster/John Knox Press, 1994.

Linnan, Richard. *The Ecclesiology of Karl Rahner.* Oxford: Clarendon Press, 1997.

Schillebeeckx, Edward. *Church: The Human Story of God.* New York: Crossroad, 1990.

Schrag, Calvin O. *The Self after Postmodernity.* New Haven, Conn.: Yale University Press, 1997.

Tyrrell, George. *Medievalism: A Reply to Cardinal Mercier.* Foreword by Gabriel Daly. Allen, Tex.: Christian Classics, 1994.

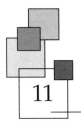

The Ecclesial Dimension
of Spirituality

11

George Tavard

From late Judaism the early Christians inherited a tradition of holiness that was chiefly indebted to the Pharisees' interpretation of Torah. The People of God is holy *(kodesh)* since it has been chosen by God. This holiness had been centered on the Law and the Temple. The purpose of the Law was to protect the holiness of the People of God from contamination by surrounding paganism. The purpose of the Temple was to ensure holy worship, since the Temple was understood, from the books of the prophets Isaiah and Ezekiel, to be the repository of the Glory *(shekinah)* of God. The old prophetic tradition of Elijah and Mount Carmel had itself survived in the conviction that God from time to time calls some among the people to be particularly holy, climbing, as it were, into the chariot *(merkabah)* that took the great prophet to heaven. Because of the destruction of the Temple, the *merkabah* tradition of holiness was given first place at the very moment when the Christians of the second century began to see the implications of their separation from the Judaic matrix.

In a word, all the holiness of Israel was now embodied in Christ, and by extension in "the body of Christ which is the Church." The writings of the New Testament, selected by the Church, preserved, explained, and transmitted to future generations, presented specific starting points for a life of union with God. The light of the Transfiguration of Jesus (Luke 9:28-36) was particularly evocative of a new vision of the *merkabah,* now identified with Christ, while the promise of divine unveiling to those who love him (John 14:21) suggested a new experience of the *shekinah* in the temple of the believing and loving soul.

As had been the case already in late Judaism, Christian believers were taught to choose between two ways of light or darkness, purity or defilement, sanctity or sin. Assisted along the way by the angels of light and goodness, ambushed by the angels of darkness and evil, the disciples find the way of holiness in the example of Christ, and they are enabled to follow it by the grace of the Holy Spirit. Church leaders, bishops and theologians, were so aware of the dimension of the holy in the Christian community that they inserted it in the rule of faith: "I believe . . . in the Holy Spirit, the holy Church, the remission of sins, the resurrection of the flesh, the life everlasting" (Old Roman Creed). Or, in the formulation of the Constantinopolitan Creed (381): "We believe . . . in the Holy Spirit . . . in one, holy, catholic, and apostolic Church." That is, the Holy Spirit is in the Holy Church. Replacing both the Law and the Temple, the Church is the only and also the universal locus of the divine Presence. The *Ecclesia* is *catholica* in this profound sense, even before it has had time to spread through the nations: all the means of salvation are present in it along with the Holy Spirit. As one it is the only way of salvation. As holy it is the sanctified and sanctifying channel of the graciousness of God. As apostolic it is sent to all humankind to bring the way of salvation that is offered in the revelation of the Word made flesh.

However, as the early Christians soon counted more members of pagan origin and culture than of Jewish background, their conception of the holy was profoundly affected. In Greek culture holiness had taken two distinct aspects. An institutional sacredness was attached to the temples in which the gods, imperfect expressions of an unknown yet underlying divinity, were invoked. The great tragedies of Aeschylus, Sophocles, Euripides, had illustrated some of the dramas that could occur in the attempt to discern the rules of the divine games and master the secrets of human destiny. And there was also a sense of interior spirituality, the possibility of a purification of thought, for which seekers and lovers of wisdom found keys in the works of the great philosophers.

As soon as some of the Christians were knowledgeable in Latin and Greek philosophy, they came to realize that if pagan worship was, from the biblical point of view, unholy, the wisdom of Greece pointed to another way of personal holiness as Plato *(The Republic)* and especially Aristotle *(The Ethics to Nichomachos)* analyzed the personal and social virtues that are necessary to ensure a good life for the citizens in a well-organized city. Already Plato *(The Phaedo),* followed and reinterpreted by the Middle Platonists and Neoplatonists, had subordinated the concern for virtues to the desire for union with the ultimate Being, whom Plotinus *(The Enneads)* called the One. Both orientations figured simultaneously in the Mystery cults, the spread of which roughly coincided with the advent of Christianity.

If by spirituality we understand the awareness of the primacy of spirit over flesh, mind over body, the Christian spiritual tradition originated in a conjunction of the holiness strand of the Old Testament with the mystical strand of Middle Platonism and Neoplatonism. Both, however, were reinterpreted in light of the confession of Christ as Lord, Savior, and Redeemer, of a developing knowledge of God as Father, Word, and Spirit, and of a multiform sacramental experience of Christ in worship and liturgy. The primacy of spirit over flesh was found to imply that of faith over human wisdom.

*

During the age of persecution in the Roman Empire (until about 315) the ideal of holiness was identified with readiness to become a martyr for Christ, confessing the faith before pagan tribunals in the face of death, and it was exemplified in the Acts of the Martyrs. Persecutions, however, were not constant and they were rarely universal, so that Christians began to look for other types of holiness even before the official end of persecutions. Given the predominance of pagan cults, the violence of society, and a growing corruption of mores that was bemoaned by pagan philosophers (as in Stoicism) and by Emperor Augustus (who passed laws promoting marriage over concubinage), many Christians of both sexes, following the example of St. Anthony of Egypt (d. 356), sought solitude in deserts and forests, where they could practice meditation unencumbered by worldly cares, reflect on the Gospels and the examples of the saints, and aspire to the contemplation of the true God who was revealed in Jesus Christ and dwells in the heart by faith.

The anachoretic ideal of solitude, however, was not practical for everyone. On the one hand, the cenobitic life, lived in monasteries, began to be highly valued. It was promoted among others by St. Basil of Caesarea and his family, notably his elder sister Macrina the Younger (b. 327–d. 379). It could be viewed as anticipating the eschatological transformation of creation. On the other hand, bishops, who encouraged the formation of communities of men dedicated to the holy life, also exhorted young women to escape the constraints of the world by choosing virginity as a way of life, giving themselves to prayer and good works under episcopal guidance.

It therefore comes as no surprise that the first major syntheses of Christian spirituality gave pride of place to life in common and to virginity for the sake of the kingdom. The community acts as a small Church *(ecclesiola)* modeled on the picture of the early Church that is given in the Acts of the Apostles, when the disciples in the upper room waited for the Holy Spirit (Acts 2:1). Having received the Spirit "They devoted themselves to the teaching of the apostles and to the communal life, to the breaking of the bread and to the prayers" (Acts 2:42); they were "of one heart and mind," sharing all of their goods (Acts

4:32-37). It was out of this spiritual matrix that the apostles went on to preach the gospel to all nations. This double ideal, of the Church gathered in prayer and of evangelism flowing from this common prayer, became central to all Christian spirituality.

Because varieties of temperaments, however, are not overcome by baptism, two aspects of Christian discipleship needed to be properly balanced. The struggle against the world means fighting "sensual lust, enticement for the eyes, and a pretentious life" (1 John 2:16). That is, it requires personal asceticism no less than an ascent of the mind to heavenly realities. In the West an excessively optimistic evaluation of the possibility of perfection by one's own efforts led to the heresy of Pelagius, a Celtic monk who, at the beginning of the fifth century, directed many pious ladies of Roman society in the practice of the ascetic life, assuring them that they could go a long way on their own and that their efforts would be complemented by divine grace. In the East a search for the inner ways of the Spirit in the embodied human soul led to esoteric heterodox conceptions and practices in what is generally called Messalianism. St. Augustine was the chief adversary of the first, and the *Spiritual Homilies* (fourth through fifth centuries) attributed to St. Macarios of Egypt of the second. Thus the search for Christian holiness was inextricably linked with major dogmatic discussions and decisions in the Church at large.

*

Although a full survey of the historical developments of Christian spirituality is not needed, some historical considerations are necessary.

Spirituality is the experience of and reflection on the life of the spirit or soul as distinguished from, though not necessarily opposed to, the life of the body in its individual and social components. As such, spirituality has a universal dimension that is pre-Christian and that could conceivably survive in a post-Christian culture. The life of the soul is of course lived in the body and in society, and society as such is structured around natural and cultural principles that antedate the revelation of Christ. This perspective was not abandoned by the Christian experience of the holy. Rather, the spiritual life was restructured around the theological virtues of faith, hope, and love. Faith is "the realization of what is hoped for and evidence of things not seen" (Heb 11:1). Only by faith can one experience the realities of heaven while living on earth. As St. John of the Cross put it in the sixteenth century, faith is therefore "the only proper and proportionate means of union with God."[1] And it is clear that faith comes to the believers through the

---

[1] *The Ascent of Mount Carmel*, bk. II, ch. 9.

Church. This is true whether one speaks of the faith that believes (*fides qua*) or of the faith that is believed (*fides quae*). The faith that believes is, as the scholastics expressed it, a theological virtue or power infused by the Holy Spirit in baptism; and baptism, the first sacrament of Christian initiation, is the most fundamental of sacraments. Offered to all humans by the Church's preaching and administered by the Church's ministry, the sacraments constitute the necessary framework of Christian spirituality. And the faith that is believed, expressed fundamentally in the articles of the creeds, was formulated by the ecumenical councils. While *fides qua* gives the capacity to relate to Christ as Revealer and Redeemer, *fides quae* indicates the main articulations of piety: worship of the three divine Persons, union to the Word incarnate, solidarity in the holy community, in which two dimensions of the spiritual life emerge as prominent: participation in the grace of the sacraments and anticipation of the kingdom of God. In its public form, this spiritual solidarity has been called, in different times and different places, conciliarity, *sobornost*, collegiality. In its interior form, as it is experienced by the Christian soul, faith flowers forth in hope and in love, in keeping with Augustine's *Enchiridion on Faith, Hope, and Love* (423/424), which the scholastics identified also as theological virtues. Faith provides the principle and the means of holiness. Hope orients radically toward the passing away of the present world and the advent of the heavenly kingdom. Their full flowering is manifest in Christian love or *agape*, the believer's self-gift to God and neighbor.

*

In this common framework one can easily distinguish two main emphases, which may be called Eastern and Western and identified respectively with the heritage of St. Gregory of Nyssa (ca. 330–ca. 390) in Cappadocia and that of St. Augustine (354–430) in North Africa. Gregory of Nyssa may be considered typical of the understanding of Christian spirituality that has prevailed in the Byzantine tradition and the Orthodox Church. Christianity, he wrote, "is the *mimesis* (imitation) of the divine nature."[2] Imitation here is not intended in an extrinsic sense; it is not an imitation of God from the infinite distance (*diastema*) that separates the creature from the Creator. It is a participation by grace in the divine nature, a deification (*theosis*) of the rational creature by the Creator through the assumption of human nature by the *logos* made flesh. By God's action (*energeia*) in the incarnation and the sending of the Holy Spirit the believers are introduced into participation (*metousia*) in the divine nature (*ousia*). This is precisely the purpose of the holy

---

[2] *De Professione christiana* 46:244C.

liturgy: to take the believers out of the conditions of the present world into participation in the eternal kingdom.

This participation was described and celebrated by the great spiritual authors of Byzantium, like, among many others, St. Gregory the New Theologian (949–1022), who was a monk in Byzantium and the author of hymns and homilies on the mystical life, and the layman Nicholas Cabasilas (d. 1371), who wrote *Commentary on the Divine Liturgy* and *Life in Christ*, where God's activity is described in five books and the human response in two books. Litanies and hymns guide the thoughts of worshipers toward the kingdom of God. The greatest hymnwriters, like Romanos the Melode (d. 556), are also profoundly spiritual authors. The *Akathistos Hymn*, composed in thanksgiving for the repulse of an attack on the city of Byzantium by the Avars in 626, is a praise of the Virgin Mary, *Theotokos*, "Bride unbrided," "Key of Christ's Kingdom," "Tabernacle of God and the Logos." Its twenty-four stanzas lead singers and hearers to follow Mary from the annunciation to the birth of Jesus and thus to participate in her mystical share in the incarnation.

Meanwhile, the Eucharist and the icons of Christ, the angels, and the saints, especially of Mary the *Theotokos*, are gates opened on the heavenly realm, through which the devout anticipate the eschatological transformation of the cosmos in the kingdom of God. In this systematically global perspective, the entire process of the ascent to God is profoundly ecclesial.

*

The basis of the Western or Latin approach was established in the struggles of St. Jerome and St. Augustine against Pelagius (ca. 350–ca. 425) and his followers. Augustine could easily see that the Pelagian principles were incompatible with the process of his own conversion, which he had recorded in the *Confessions* (composed between 397 and 401), and he detected in the Pelagian doctrines a downgrading of the indispensable grace of God and the work of the Savior. In opposition he asserted the fundamental incapacity of men and women, affected as they are by the original sin that they have inherited, to access any kind of holiness on their own. The spiritual life implies a struggle against the sinfulness of human nature as well as a total reliance on the grace of Christ to overcome the native corruption of humanity. Out of this "mass of perdition" God chooses the elect and brings them to salvation, a few being led on to perfection. A basic pessimism as to human capacity is corrected by an optimism based on the work of the Savior and the power of the Holy Spirit. Pessimism and optimism, however, are dialectically related as men and women of faith are confronted by a mystery that cannot be fathomed by the human mind, the mystery of the ultimate will of God regarding the eternal destiny of individual persons. As the Church, through the canons of the second Council of Orange (529), pointed to a way between extremes of self-reliance and of self-negation, it directly influenced the believers' spiritual lives. Nothing one can do in the ways of holiness is without the prevenient and accompanying grace that comes to us through the Savior.

It was on this background that the Western ways of spirituality that were emphasized in the Middle Ages and later gave a prominent place to the confession of sins and the sacrament of penance. In so doing they seemed to stress the actions and concerns of individual believers over against the Church as the realm of the holy in which everything natural is transformed to a degree by progressive participation in God. While deification was never denied by the scholastics or even by the Reformers, it was de-emphasized in favor of contrition and sanctification as ongoing processes throughout life, and of justification as God's declaration that in spite of being sinful we are also justified in Jesus Christ by faith and grace.

The individual emphasis of Western spirituality was especially underlined when, taking the example of St. Francis of Assisi (1183–1226) as a norm, the Franciscan movement, while it remained faithful to the institution of the Church and its hierarchy, underlined the uniqueness of individual callings within the Church community. Such individualism was eventually incorporated in the most influential of all spiritual writings, the *Exercises* of St. Ignatius Loyola (1491–1556), composed in 1522. All the meditations of the first week of the exercises are focused on sin and hell. In the second week the participants reflect on the call of the eternal king, our Lord Jesus Christ, and on the choice that has to be made between the standard of Jerusalem, representing the kingdom of Christ, and that of Babylon, standing for the kingdom of Satan. In the third week, the retreatant, having opted for Christ, follows him in the last period of his life on earth as Jesus goes to the passion and suffers it. In the fourth week the participant is faced with the mystery of the incarnation and the internal manifestation of Jesus, the desire to love God and diverse ways of praying. The outcome is the subordination of everything to the will of God and its fulfillment in individual lives. Yet the individualism of this spiritual way is compensated by Ignatius's insistence that the followers of Christ do not live in isolation but are members of the Militant Church. The true disciple of Jesus must learn to discern the spirits in self and in others, and he must leave aside all personal judgment in order to "keep the mind ready and prompt in everything to obey the true Bride of Christ, which is our holy Mother the hierarchical Church."[3] The faithful should always praise what the Church and its hierarchy say and do, especially in everything that relates to prayer, devotion, and sanctity.

*

The ecclesial dimension of the spiritual ways of Christians can be abundantly illustrated from the point of view of the Church as the universal communion of believers led by the successors of the apostles. A number of doctrinal decisions have been directly related to spirituality. Negatively, the Church has condemned what it has found to be mistaken ways of asceticism and mysticism. Already in the second and third centuries the Gnostic sects, especially that of the Valentinians, offered alternative spiritual ways which the Great Church found unacceptable because they departed from the apostolic tradition, in favor of doctrines that St. Irenaeus (d. ca. 200) and others traced back to false prophets.

The decisions of the seventh council (II Nicaea, 781) in defense of the icons guaranteed that, in spite of the necessary ascetic control of the senses, the body played a positive role in the spiritual search for God. As one looks at the images of the saints, bows to them and kisses them, one sees and feels the saints as they have been transfigured by grace and made transparent to the divine light of the *logos*. Although this emphasis was not understood by the Frankish synod of Frankfurt (794), the Western way also promoted the spiritual dimension of the senses: of sight and smell in the liturgy, singing and hearing in hymnody, speaking and articulating in psalmody, touching and feeling the statues of the saints. Walking around in processions and occasionally in liturgical dance, pilgrimaging to near or distant shrines, seeing the consecrated host, pronouncing and hearing the name of Jesus became major aspects of medieval piety and spirituality.

The bodily position for meditation that was favored in the monasteries of Mount Athos provided one of the starting points of the Byzantine controversy around hesychasm, during which St. Gregory Palamas (d. 1359), metropolitan of Salonika, defended the monks and argued for the possibility of seeing the divine light already with the eyes of the body through participation in the "energies" of God. In the East as in the West devotion to the *Theotokos, Dei genitrix,* became a privileged way of spirituality. In the East it involved personal relationship with Mary, participation in her proximity to Christ, tenderness as in the icon of Our Lady of Vladimir, and the determination to follow Christ in his

---

[3] "Rules to think with the Church," *The Spiritual Exercises of St. Ignatius of Loyola,* no. 353.

life and sufferings, as indicated by the icons of Mary *Hodegetria*, pointing the way. The continuing protection of traditional icon piety remained a concern of the Orthodox Church. Thus, after the great fire of
Moscow which had destroyed thousands of icons in 1547, the council
of the Stoglav (1551) insisted that the new icons must not be ruled by
merely artistic imagination or represent living persons or feature new
symbols, but they must show Christ, the *Theotokos*, angels, and saints in
the traditional mode, because such is the way to the divine light. Other
councils in the seventeenth century spoke against icon painters who
wanted to illustrate theological theories or painted images that had
merely didactic value. The councils' basic principle was that the icon
must remain a gate to the spiritual world.

In the West also the hierarchy was concerned to promote true spirituality for the people, as in encouraging and officially promoting certain devotions, such as the evocation of the incarnation with the
Angelus at the ringing of bells three times a day, contemplating Mary
at the annunciation and the visitation in the prayer of the Rosary with
meditation on the joyful, sorrowful, and glorious mysteries of Christ.
Some interventions of the Church have touched on spirituality directly.
Councils and popes have regulated the religious life, approved the
rules of founders, and supervised the fidelity of each community to its
constitutions. It is noteworthy that several of the saints who have been
declared Doctors of the Church are known chiefly for their spiritual
writings: John of the Cross (1542–91), Teresa of Avila (1515–82), Catherine
of Siena (1547–80), Francis of Sales (1567–1622), Thérèse of the Child
Jesus (1873–97). Other predominantly spiritual authors were strongly
supported by the hierarchy in their own life, notably Hildegard of
Bingen (1098–1179) and Brigid of Sweden (1303–73).

It is, however, around various questions of the proper balance along
the spiritual way that the Church has been forced to intervene the most.
There are problems of emphasis between God's grace and human initiative, between the Church as institution and personal awareness of
"the gospel in the heart," between giving witness to Christ in this
world and anticipating the heavenly life, between serving the neighbor
through good works and wishing to be alone with God. In the late thirteenth and the fourteenth century the Spiritual Franciscans, as they
reinterpreted the trinitarian theology of Joachim of Flora (d. 1209),
identified Francis of Assisi as the Angel of the Apocalypse who would
inaugurate the Eternal Gospel and usher in the reign of the Spirit.
Other groups of the late Middle Ages, among them the Brethren of the
Free Spirit, some of the Béguines and Bégards in the Netherlands, and,
in the sixteenth century, the Alhumbrados of Spain, recommended
an attitude of total passivity in regard to the spiritual. In the eyes of

theologians and bishops, however, such a teaching equated reliance on God's grace with annihilation of the self, made it all but impossible to discern the spirits, and diminished the sense of personal responsibility for sin. *Recogimiento* (recollection), not *dejamiento* (abandonment), is the proper attitude in the meditation that prepares for contemplation.

In the process of protecting the faith from being misled by false doctrines or mistaken enthusiasm, however, many perfectly orthodox spiritual authors were suspected of "illuminism." Thus the Augustinian Luis de León (1528–91) spent several years in the prisons of the Spanish Inquisition,[4] John of the Cross was arrested and jailed for nine months by his own confreres, and Teresa of Jesus carefully sought the protection of the apostolic nuncio and of King Philip II as she initiated the reform of the Carmelite Order.

The Reformation did not discuss these questions directly, and Martin Luther (1483–1546) had been sufficiently impressed by an anonymous spiritual writing to have it printed, and to call it *Theologia germanica*, in contrast with *theologia scholastica*. Nonetheless, the Reformers' opponents generally suspected the thesis of Scripture alone of undermining the Church's responsibility to guide the faithful to God, and that of Justification by faith alone of implying that the good works of the justified are of no value before God. It was largely because of anti-Protestant polemics that the Church of the Counter-Reformation paid particular attention to schools of spirituality. "Quietism" was suspect. But there were degrees of quietism. In Spain Miguel de Molinos (1640–97) was condemned as a heretic. In France, however, a sharp controversy opposed Bossuet (1627–1704), bishop of Meaux,[5] to Fénelon (1651–1715), archbishop of Cambrai, over the quietism of Madame Guyon (1648–1717). Fénelon's *Explication des maximes des saints sur la vie intérieure* (1697) was declared by the Holy See to contain erroneous views on the love of God.[6]

*

The ecclesial dimension of spirituality can also be seen from the standpoint of the individual Christians, especially of those who are aware of a call to a special relationship to God in the present life. Bap-

---

[4] He was guilty of publishing a commentary on the biblical Song of Songs in the vernacular; like its medieval commentators, Luis de León treated the Song of Songs as a book of spirituality.

[5] *Instruction sur les états d'oraison*, 1697.

[6] Brief *Cum alias*, 12 March 1699 (DS nn. 2351–74). Jeanne Marie Bouvier de la Motte Guyon was the author of numerous writings on the interior life and the "pure love" of God.

tism, as was taught by St. Thomas Aquinas, implies not only the general gift of sanctifying grace to the baptized, but also the infusion in them of the theological and moral virtues and the seven gifts of the Holy Spirit, which, in the spiritual theology of Aquinas, are the instruments of spiritual progress. Confirmation, the second sacrament of Christian initiation, confers spiritual strength as the faithful prepare for sacramental union with Jesus in the Eucharist.[7] Meanwhile, the Christian child is in principle educated in a progressive knowledge and understanding of the faith in the interlocked circles of family, parish, and, where possible, Christian schools. Attendance at the Eucharistic Liturgy fosters the awareness of Christ the Redeemer who comes to the faithful in his word and in his sacrament. Frequent Communion, which has been highly recommended to all, including children, since Pius X (pope, 1903–14),[8] fosters the sense of the presence of Christ and the wish to follow joyfully where the Holy Spirit leads.

The other four sacraments are given for specific circumstances that directly affect the spiritual life. The sacrament of penance brings God's forgiveness of sins in the name and by the power of Christ. The marriage of husband and wife, blessed by the Church, is a continuing channel of grace. The unction of the sick conveys spiritual comfort to those who struggle with disease. Ordination to the diaconate, the presbyterate, and the episcopate gives the ordinands graces that enable them to labor in the diaconal and priestly service of the faithful. Along with a personal reading of Scripture as word of God, the practice of regular prayer, and the reservation of specific times to meditation in the presence of God, the sacraments contain all that is necessary to the highest spiritual experience. There have even been illiterate Christians, as for instance St. Joan of Arc (1412–31), who traveled the spiritual way and reached the highest sanctity with no other resources than prayer, the sacraments, and whatever spiritual insights God gave them.

The ecclesial structures have been so affected by the search for God in community, especially in the Basilian monasteries of the East and the Benedictine monasteries of the West, that one may speak of the "monasticity" of the Church.[9] The pattern of liturgical prayer, the daily office of diocesan clergy, and the traditional celibacy of deacons and priests in the Latin Church were borrowed from the monastic way of

[7] The widespread delay of confirmation until after first communion, which is often favored for pastoral or educational reasons, is opposed to the tradition, and it is abnormal from the point of view of the proper ordering of the spiritual life.

[8] *Decreta Sacra Tridentina Synodus,* 1905.

[9] See George Tavard, *The Church, Community of Salvation* (Collegeville: The Liturgical Press, 1992) 115–32.

life. Both the Rosary and the Jesus Prayer have adapted concerns and practices of monks or friars to the conditions of lay life. Not only the "third orders" of St. Francis and St. Dominic and the Lay Oblates of monasteries are tied to religious communities, but the entire People of God lives in ecclesial communion with "the apostles and the prophets," teachers and pioneers of the spiritual way. When the churches of the Reformation closed religious communities and abolished the taking of public vows, they did not shed the monasticity that still forms the historical backdrop of their worship, their common prayer, their popularization of *lectio divina*, their revivals. Indeed, the Methodist movement started in the eighteenth century when people in Oxford began to take notice of the quasi-monastic life of prayer, self-examination, and good works that was practiced and spread by John Wesley (1702–91).

*

As humanity approaches the third millennium after the birth of Christ there are aspects of the contemporary Church situation that are particularly relevant to an assessment of the ecclesial dimension of the Christian search for holiness. The seventeenth and eighteenth centuries flourished with new schools of spirituality. Such was the Jesuit school of Louis Lallemant (1587–1635), with a more mystic than ascetic interpretation of the spiritual way of St. Ignatius. The French school, initiated by Cardinal Pierre de Bérulle (1575–1629) with his profound reflections on the states of Jesus, was soon diversified through different orientations among those he inspired. Without being exhaustive one may mention the priestly and sacrificial line of Charles de Condren (1588–1641); the contemplation and imitation of the Hearts of Jesus and Mary of St. Jean Eudes (1601–80); the meditative and studious line of Jean-Jacques Olier (1608–57) and the Sulpicians, who were devoted to the formation of seminarians in the spirit of the Council of Trent; the vow of servitude to Mary of St. Louis Grignion de Montfort (1673–1716), who simplified the Marian line of Bérulle for the ordinary people he encountered in his parish missions; and the missionary spirit of Blessed Jean-Martin Moye (1730–93), devoted to divine Providence.

This blossoming of spiritual schools was put on hold, as it were, by the turmoil of the French Revolution in Europe. It was followed in the nineteenth century by a retrenchment that was due in part to the struggle of the popes with the sequels of the Revolution. Meanwhile, the nineteenth century saw the rebirth of theology in the school of Tübingen, in the works of Matthias Scheeben (1835–88), and in Pope Leo XIII's endorsement of neoscholasticism. This eventually led to a rediscovery of the great Catholic mystics and their writings, notably of St. Bonaventure and of the Carmelite tradition. The "return to the sources" that was operative in the first half of the twentieth century entailed a refocusing of attention on the essential elements of spirituality, that is, on the Church, the liturgy, the reading of Scripture, the basic doctrines of the incarnation and the Trinity. This led to the theological flowering of the Vatican Council II (1962–65), which directly affected the modern understandings and practice of the spiritual life.

This can be illustrated from the documents of the council. Not only did the council promote religious communities as such (decree *Perfectae caritatis* on the renewal and adaptation of religious life), but it also emphasized the spiritual dimension of the Church as a whole. This theme runs through the constitutions *Sacrosanctum concilium* on the holy liturgy, *Lumen gentium* on the Church (especially chs. 5–8 on the Universal Call to Holiness, the Religious, the Church's Eschatological Character, the Virgin Mary in the Mystery of Christ and the Church), *Dei verbum* on divine revelation (notably ch. 6 on Scripture in the Church's life).

The decree *Apostolicam actuositatem* on the lay apostolate teaches that the foundation of this apostolate is found in the sacraments of Christian initiation, especially in baptism as the gate of entrance of the faithful into the Mystical Body of Christ, and in confirmation as their empowerment by the Holy Spirit. The faithful are thus "consecrated as royal priesthood and holy people, so that in all things they may offer spiritual sacrifices, and bear witness to Christ everywhere on earth" (n. 3). Furthermore, the preparation for the lay apostolate requires not only "an integral human formation," but also a "spiritual formation," a "solid doctrinal instruction that will be theological, ethical, philosophical in keeping with diversities of age, condition and intellectual capacity" (n. 29).

The decree *Ad gentes* on the Church's missionary activity describes the trinitarian basis of mission (nn. 2–5) and its nisus toward eschatological fullness, through which "the spiritual temple in which God is adored in spirit and truth grows and is erected on the foundation of the apostles and prophets" (n. 9).

*

In the aftermath of the council, and the turmoil that followed widespread experimentation by enthusiastic partisans of *aggiornamento*, spirituality in the Catholic Church was affected by contradictory orientations that were fed in part by cultural mutations in the last decades of the twentieth century. Such preconciliar cultural movements as the exploration of the unconscious in depth psychology, the investigation of the collective unconscious inspired by Carl Jung, and the use of psychoanalysis as a tool for self-knowledge have been instrumental in fostering confusions between the spiritual and the psychological, between faith and introspection. However, the investigation of the mind for its own sake is not a substitute for the traditional search for God's presence in the depths of the soul. In an opposite direction, the legitimate concern of modern times for the betterment of social conditions have pushed some of the faithful toward downgrading the search for God in favor of a search for the neighbor. A "preferential option for the poor," inspired by the gospel, has at times been mistakenly taken to imply a choice of orthopraxis (right behavior) over against orthodoxy (right doctrine). Hence the sense of urgency that is characteristic of the theologies of liberation has given rise to a certain ambiguity. Action and contemplation, which have been traditionally symbolized by Martha and Mary and treated as naturally going together, have tended to be opposed to each other, action being given primacy in a move that was not unaffected by Marxist philosophy.[10]

*

While these tendencies amplified and strengthened some earlier orientations, the postconciliar period introduced two new factors. The first should have been expected. Most general councils have had a beneficial effect on the Church in the long run, yet also, in the short term, an unsettling effect on many of the Church's members. This again happened in the aftermath of Vatican II, especially where the impression was given that the hierarchy was reluctant to acknowledge the ecclesial responsibilities of women and eager to keep them in roles that are complementary, and by the same token subordinate, to those of men. In the area of spirituality this has had the effect that more and more of the faithful are looking less and less to the Church's hierarchy for spiritual leadership. The institution has lost the trust of many, who therefore look for spiritual inspiration in other areas of experience, as in the plastic arts, in music, in poetry or fiction, and in the amazing new picture of the universe that emerges from contemporary astronomy.[11]

The second factor is due to the change of pace that is affecting communications around the world. The growing facility of immediate in-

[10] Congregation for the Doctrine of the Faith, *Instruction on Certain Aspects of the "Theology of Liberation"* (Washington, D.C.: United States Catholic Conference, 1984); Congregation for the Doctrine of the Faith, *Instruction on Christian Freedom and Liberation* (Washington, D.C.: United States Catholic Conference, 1986).

[11] Anne Primavesi, *From Apocalypse to Genesis: Ecology, Feminism and Christianity* (Minneapolis: Fortress Press, 1991); Briane Swimme and Thomas Berry, *The Universe Story: From the Primordial Flaring Forth to the Ecozoic Era: A Celebration of the Unfolding of the Cosmos* (San Francisco: HarperSanFrancisco, 1992).

formation across countries and continents has introduced interested Christians to spiritual concepts, methods, and practices that have their origin outside of the Judeo-Christian cultural matrix, notably in the great religions of India and East Asia. Writings of Hinduism and Buddhism are now available everywhere. Swamis and gurus have moved to the West, some of them offering simplified versions of Oriental religions.[12] The exile of the Dalai Lama has resulted in the opening of many centers for the study and practice of Tibetan Buddhism. Religious studies at the university level have exposed Christian students to the Upanishads and the *Bhagavad-Gîta*,[13] to Confucian humanism,[14] to Animist religions.[15] "New Age" literature has brought attention to the religious dimension of American Indian lore, to earth spiritualism in Wikka, and to spiritual healing in Shamanism. Religious philosophies have found a new life in the Rose-Croix or the New Acropolis. Creation spirituality has attempted a synthesis of these trends with neglected aspects of the Christian spiritual tradition.[16] Carried to an extreme, some of these orientations have given birth to new sects and cults in the margins of Christianity, which are not without attraction to religious seekers.

Attention has been paid to these movements, both by spiritual authors who have wished to learn from Yoga or Zen and by official organs of the Catholic Church. Negatively, warnings have been given against the lure of sects[17] and against an indiscriminate recourse to non-Christian methods of meditation or contemplation.[18] Positively, serious attempts have been made to build Catholic spiritualities with a Hindu[19] or Buddhist flavor, and to use Oriental symbols in a Christian context.

[12] Thus Transcendental Meditation, Krishna-consciousness, Sokka Gakkai, etc.

[13] There are several English translations of the *Gîta*; reading in non-Christian religions has been facilitated by the publication of anthologies. See Andrew Wilson, ed., *World Scripture: A Comparative Anthology of Sacred Texts* (New York: Paragon House, 1991).

[14] Andrew Chih, *Chinese Humanism: A Religion beyond Religion* (Taiwan: Fu Jen Catholic University Press, 1981).

[15] John S. Mbiti, *Concepts of God in Africa* (London: SPCK Press, 1970).

[16] Matthew Fox, *Original Blessing* (Santa Fe: Bear and Company, 1983).

[17] "Report on the Sects or New Religious Movements: Pastoral Challenge," *Information Service/Secretariat for Promoting Christian Unity* 61:3 (1986) 144–54.

[18] Letter of the Congregation for the doctrine of the faith to the bishops of the Church on "Some Aspects of Christian Meditation," 15 October 1989, *Origins* 19:30 (1989) 492–8.

[19] Jules Monchanin (1895–1957), several essays in *Swami Parama Arubi Anadam: A Memorial* (Tiruchirapalli, India: Saccidananda Ashram, 1959); Jules Monchanin and Henri Le Saux, *A Benedictine Ashram* (Douglas, Isle of Man: Times Press, 1964); Bede Griffiths, *The Cosmic Revelation: The Hindu Way to God* (Springfield, Ill.: Templegate,

These various phenomena within or in the margin of Christian spirituality are in part induced by the ongoing inculturation of the gospel in non-Western civilizations. They may also be due to the crisis of confidence and the loss of nerve that seem to affect modern minds, in which the end of a century is easily perceived as a symbol of the end of the world. The plan of Pope John Paul II to focus attention on the three Persons of the Trinity in the last years of the second millennium presented an opportunity to steer personal spirituality away from fashionable or esoteric idiosyncracies toward the traditional center of the Christian experience of God, which is the indwelling of the three Persons in the soul.

*

The ecclesial dimension of Christian spirituality displays its full scope when both laity and clergy have been properly instructed and educated in Scripture and the Church's spiritual tradition. The frequent absence of such an education, even in Catholic colleges and universities, is one of the shortcomings of our times. The ensuing situation offers a great opportunity to religious communities, from the older monasteries to the newer secular institutes, to make their spiritual charisms better known and their resources and traditions more readily available. Indeed, the diminishing numbers of novices in religious communities may in part be due to ignorance of such resources. In the absence of a public witness to the ways of the Spirit the faithful who are eager for spiritual nurture will naturally be inclined to look elsewhere for guidance and direction. And the laity at large will fail to perceive the radically ecclesial nature of Christian holiness, which is nurtured, like the Church itself, by the testimony of the apostles and the prophets.

1983); Henri Le Saux, *Initiation à la spiritualité des Upanishads* (Sisteron: Editions Présence, 1979); Raymond Panikkar, *The Cosmotheandric Experience: Emerging Religious Consciousness* (Maryknoll, N.Y.: Orbis Books, 1983).

For Further Reading

Dulles, Avery. *Models of the Church.* Expanded edition. Garden City, N.Y.: Doubleday, 1997.

Sanks, T. Howland. *Salt, Leaven, and Light: The Community Called Church.* New York: Crossroad, 1992.

Tavard, George. *The Church, Community of Salvation.* Collegeville: The Liturgical Press, 1992.

_____. *The Pilgrim Church.* New York: Herder & Herder, 1967.

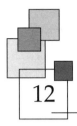

The Evangelizing Mission of the Church

12

Francis A. Sullivan

The purpose of this chapter is to present the modern Catholic Church's understanding of its evangelizing mission. It will be based on five documents in which this mission has been described with the authority of various organs of the Church's magisterium. The documents are: (1) The Second Vatican Council's Decree on the Church's Missionary Activity, *Ad gentes* (AG), 1965; (2) Pope Paul VI's Apostolic Exhortation on the Evangelization of the Modern World, *Evangelii nuntiandi* (EN), 1975; (3) the Final Document of the Third General Conference of the Latin American Episcopate held at Puebla, Mexico: *Evangelization in Latin America's Present and Future* (ELA), 1979; (4) Pope John Paul II's Encyclical Letter on the Permanent Validity of the Church's Missionary Mandate, *Redemptoris missio* (RMis), 1990; and (5) a document issued by the Pontifical Council for Interreligious Dialogue and the Congregation for the Evangelization of Peoples, *Dialogue and Proclamation* (DP), 1991.

While, as one would expect, these five documents have a great deal in common, each has its own distinctive character. They all recognize the complex nature of the Church's evangelizing mission, but each tends to stress some of its elements more than others. A development can be traced in their language, from a more restricted to a more inclusive use of the term "evangelization." The later documents put more emphasis on certain elements of this complex reality than the earlier ones do. It would seem useful, therefore, to begin with a brief account of the modern development of Catholic doctrine on the evangelizing mission of the Church as it is reflected in these five documents.

Development of Catholic Doctrine since Vatican II

Vatican II's *Ad gentes* uses "missionary activity" as an inclusive term which embraces Christian witness and works of charity, preaching the gospel, assembling the People of God, and forming the Christian community (AG 11–18). The stress in this decree, however, is firmly on what is described as "the special end of missionary activity," namely, "evangelization and the implanting of the church among peoples or groups in which it has not yet taken root" (AG 6). Here the term "evangelization" has the specific meaning of preaching the gospel of Jesus Christ to those who have not heard or accepted it.

Pope Paul VI's *Evangelii nuntiandi* was the fruit of the Third General Assembly of the Synod of Bishops, which did not succeed in producing its own document on its topic of evangelization. However, the insistence of many of the bishops at the synod that the Church's evangelizing mission must include participation in the struggle of oppressed people for their liberation had a marked effect on the papal exhortation. For Paul VI, "evangelization involves an explicit message . . . about peace, justice and development—a message especially energetic today about liberation" (EN 29). At the same time, Pope Paul insisted that if the Church links human liberation and salvation in Jesus Christ, the Church never identifies them (EN 35). While the Church has the duty of proclaiming liberation and assisting its birth, "evangelization will always contain—as the foundation, centre and summit of its dynamism, a clear proclamation that in Jesus Christ . . . salvation is offered to all men, as a gift of God's grace and mercy" (EN 27).

Another distinctive contribution of EN is Pope Paul's term "evangelization of cultures." He insisted that "what matters is to evangelize man's culture and cultures. . . . They have to be regenerated by an encounter with the Gospel. But this encounter will not take place if the Gospel is not proclaimed" (EN 20). The final phrase here points to the fact that for Paul VI, evangelization was still identified with the proclamation of the gospel. Despite his insistence on the importance of dialogue in his earlier encyclical *Ecclesiam suam,* he did not recommend interreligious dialogue as a component of the Church's evangelizing mission in EN.

The document of the Puebla Conference differs substantially from the other documents we are considering, all of which see the evangelizing mission of the Church as directed to people who have not yet heard or accepted the message of the gospel. Puebla, on the contrary, focused on the evangelization of Latin America, "where the Gospel has been preached and the general population baptized for almost five hundred years," and where "the work of evangelization must appeal to the 'Christian memory of our peoples.'" In this continent, "the religion of the people must be constantly evangelized over again" (ELA 457).

Looking to the actual situation of most of the people of Latin America, the Puebla Conference stressed the proclamation of "integral liberation" as "an urgent task that belongs to the very core of an evangelization that seeks the authentic realization of the human being" (ELA 480). It insisted on the presence of two inseparable elements in such integral liberation. "The first is liberation from all the forms of bondage, from personal and social sin. . . . The second is liberation for progressive growth in being through communion with God and other human beings" (ELA 482). The distinctive contribution of the Puebla Document is the notion of "liberative evangelization" as the way to achieve "communion and participation."

While the promotion of people's liberation as a component of evangelization is not absent from Pope John Paul II's encyclical *Redemptoris missio*, it received far less attention there than it did in EN or ELA. On the other hand, RMis has brought out some important aspects of the Church's evangelizing mission which had not received much attention in the previous documents. One of these is the relationship between the Church and the kingdom of God. John Paul II insists that the Church is "effectively and concretely at the service of the Kingdom" (RMis 20).

Whereas previous documents had tended to identify "evangelization" with the preaching of the gospel to those who had not heard it, RMis gives this term a broader meaning, including the various aspects of the Church's evangelizing mission. Thus, "the first form of evangelization is witness" (RMis 42). Here, the preaching of the gospel to those who had not heard it is described as "initial proclamation," which "opens the way to conversion" (RMis 44). Whereas EN had spoken of the "evangelization of cultures," RMis speaks of "inculturation, by which the Church makes the Gospel incarnate in different cultures and at the same time introduces peoples, together with their cultures, into her own community" (RMis 52). Perhaps the most distinctive contribution which RMis makes is its recognition of interreligious dialogue as "part of the Church's evangelizing mission." Pope John Paul insists that "dialogue is not in opposition to the mission *ad gentes*," but "is one of its expressions" (RMis 55).

As the title itself indicates, *Dialogue and Proclamation* focuses on two components of the Church's evangelizing mission. Its first part offers the most thorough treatment of interreligious dialogue available in any official document of the Catholic Church. Invoking a term used by Pope Paul VI in *Ecclesiam suam*, it describes the "dialogue of salvation" as an integral element of the Church's evangelizing mission (DP 38). The second part of the document, work of the Congregation for the Evangelization of Peoples, insists that "the Church's mission is to proclaim the Kingdom of God established on earth in Jesus Christ through his life, death and resurrection, as God's decisive and universal offer of salvation to the world" (DP 58). However, it recognizes that "in situations

234 Francis A. Sullivan

where, for political or other reasons, proclamation as such is practically impossible, the Church is already carrying out her evangelizing mission not only through presence and witness but also through such activities as work for integral human development and dialogue" (DP 76).

The final section of DP treats the relationship between interreligious dialogue and proclamation, describing them as "both authentic elements of the Church's evangelizing mission, both legitimate and necessary, and intimately related, but not interchangeable" (DP 77). It observes that "in actual fact, the way of fulfilling the Church's mission depends upon the particular circumstances of each local Church, of each Christian" (DP 78).

Having described the principal contributions which each of these five documents has made to the development of Catholic doctrine on the Church's evangelizing mission, our intent now is to treat each of the major components of that mission in a more systematic way. The documents we have seen will provide the material for this as well, since they offer the most reliable witness to the modern Catholic Church's understanding of its evangelizing mission. As the more recent documents have done, we shall use the term "evangelization" in the inclusive sense, referring to the whole of the Church's missionary activity. This essay will focus on evangelization as it is addressed to "peoples, groups and socio-cultural contexts in which Christ and his Gospel are not known, or which lack Christian communities sufficiently mature to be able to incarnate the faith in their own environment and proclaim it to other groups" (RMis 33). It will not discuss "re-evangelization," which is directed to areas "where entire groups of the baptized have lost a living sense of the faith, or even no longer consider themselves members of the Church, and live a life far removed from Christ and his Gospel" (RMis 33).

Doctrinal Principles

"The Church on earth is by its very nature missionary, since, according to the plan of the Father, it has its origin in the mission of the Son and the holy Spirit. This plan flows from 'fountain-like love,' the love of God the Father" (AG 2). Christ, "whom the Father has consecrated and sent into the world" (John 10:36), said of himself: "The Spirit of the Lord is upon me, because he anointed me; to bring good news to the poor he sent me, to heal the broken-hearted, to proclaim to the captive release, and sight to the blind" (Luke 4:8). "Before freely laying down his life for the world, the Lord Jesus organized the apostolic ministry and promised to send the holy Spirit, in such a way that both would be always and everywhere associated in the fulfillment of the work of salvation" (AG 4). "Rising from the dead, Christ sent his life-giving Spirit upon his disciples and through this Spirit has established his body, the church, as the universal sacrament of salvation" (LG 48). "Having been sent by God to the nations to be 'the universal sacrament of salvation,' the church, in obedience to the command of her founder, and because it is demanded by her own essential universality, strives to preach the gospel to all" (AG 1).

In order to fulfill its role as universal sign of salvation, the Church must strive to become visibly present as a vital Christian community in every place where it has not yet been planted; as universal instrument of salvation the Church must strive to offer the Good News of God's redeeming love to everyone who has not yet heard it.

"It is true that the Church is not an end unto herself, since she is ordered toward the Kingdom of God of which she is the seed, sign and instrument" (RMis 18). The Church on earth is the sign and foretaste of the eschatological kingdom of God; it is likewise the sign and instrument of the present reign of Christ, who "must reign until he has put all his enemies under his feet" (1 Cor 15:25). The essential mission of the Church until the end of time is to manifest and promote the gracious reign of Christ in the world. The Church does this by "establishing and building up communities which make present and active within mankind the living image of the Kingdom" (RMis 19). But the Church also promotes the reign of Christ "by spreading throughout the world the 'Gospel values' which are an expression of the Kingdom and which help people to accept God's plan."

> It is true that the inchoate reality of the Kingdom can also be found beyond the confines of the Church among peoples everywhere, to the extent that they live "Gospel values" and are open to the working of the Spirit who breathes when and where he wills. . . . The Church is the sacrament of salvation for all mankind, and her activity is not limited only to those who accept her message. She is a dynamic force in mankind's journey towards the eschatological Kingdom, and is the sign and promoter of Gospel values (RMis 20).

Presence and Witness

If the Church is going to be in a position to offer the mystery of salvation to people who have never, or barely, heard the gospel message, it must be present to them through those of its members who have been sent to them or who live among them. It must be present to them "in the same way that Christ by his incarnation committed himself in the particular social and cultural circumstances of the people among whom he lived" (AG 10).

> Missionaries who come from other Churches or countries must immerse themselves in the cultural milieu of those to whom they are sent, moving beyond their own cultural limitations. Hence they must learn the language of the place in which they work, become familiar with the most important expressions of the local culture, and discover its values through direct experience. . . . It is not of course a matter of missionaries renouncing their own cultural identity, but of understanding, appreciating, fostering and evangelizing the culture of the environment in which they are working, and therefore of equipping themselves to communicate effectively with it, adopting a manner of living which is a sign of Gospel witness and of solidarity with the people (RMis 53).

"Witness, which involves presence, sharing, solidarity, . . . is an essential element, and generally the first one, in evangelization" (EN 21).

> The first form of witness is the very life of the missionary, of the Christian family, and of the ecclesial community, which reveal a new way of living. The missionary who, despite all his or her human limitations and defects, lives a simple life, taking Christ as the model, is a sign of God and of transcendent realities. . . . The evangelical witness which the world finds most appealing is that of concern for people, and of charity towards the poor, the weak and those who suffer (RMis 42).
>
> The Church is called to bear witness to Christ by taking courageous and prophetic stands in the face of the corruption of political or economic power; by not seeking her own glory and material wealth; by using her resources to serve the poorest of the poor and by imitating Christ's own simplicity of life (RMis 43).

When the situation is

> such that for the time being there is no possibility of directly and immediately preaching the gospel, in that case missionaries patiently, prudently, and with great faith, can and ought at least bear witness to the love and kindness of Christ, and thus prepare a way for the Lord, and in some way make him present (AG 6).

Proclamation

While they recognize that in some areas of the world, presence, witness, and patient dialogue may be the only forms of evangelization possible for the foreseeable future, both Paul VI and John Paul II insist that evangelization is not complete "if the name, the teaching, the life, the promises, the Kingdom and the mystery of Jesus of Nazareth, the Son of God, are not proclaimed" (EN 22). Pope John Paul declares: "Proclamation is the permanent priority of mission. The Church cannot elude Christ's explicit mandate, nor deprive men and women of the 'Good News' about their being loved and saved by God." He then quotes the following statement of Paul VI: "Evangelization will always contain—as the foundation, centre and at the same time the summit of its dynamism—a clear proclamation that in Jesus Christ . . . salvation is offered to all men, as a gift of God's grace and mercy" (RMis 44; EN 27). John Paul continues:

> All forms of missionary activity are directed to this proclamation, which reveals and gives access to the mystery hidden for ages and made known in Christ, . . . the mystery which lies at the heart of the Church's mission and life, as the hinge on which all evangelization turns. In the complex reality of mission, initial proclamation has a central and irreplaceable role. . . . Just as the whole economy of salvation has its centre in Christ, so too all missionary activity is directed to the proclamation of that mystery (RMis 44).

In the document *Dialogue and Proclamation*, the section on proclamation was the work of the Congregation for the Evangelization of Peoples. In describing the "manner of proclamation," the Congregation urged missionaries to remember that

> the Holy Spirit, the Spirit of Christ, is present and active among the hearers of the Good News even before the Church's missionary action comes into operation. They may in many cases have already responded implicitly to God's offer of salvation in Jesus Christ, a sign of this being the sincere practice of their own religious traditions, insofar as these contain authentic religious values. They may have already been touched by the Spirit and in some way associated unknowingly to the paschal mystery of Jesus Christ (cf. GS 22) (DP 68).

Hence, the congregation urges missionaries to be mindful of what God has already accomplished in those addressed, and, in seeking to discover the right way to announce the Good News, to learn from the example given by Jesus himself, and to observe the times and seasons as prompted by the Spirit.

> Jesus only progressively revealed to his hearers the meaning of the Kingdom. . . . Even his closest disciples, as the Gospels testify, reached full faith in their Master only through their Easter experience and the gift of the Spirit. Those who wish to become disciples of Jesus today will pass through the same process of discovery and commitment (DP 69).

Christian Conversion as the Goal of Proclamation

"The proclamation of the word of God has Christian conversion as its aim: a complete and sincere adherence to Christ and his Gospel through faith. . . . Conversion means accepting, by a personal decision, the saving sovereignty of Christ and becoming his disciple" (RMis 46).

> Proclamation only reaches full development when it is listened to, accepted and assimilated, and when it arouses a genuine adherence in the one who has thus received it. . . . In a word, adherence to the Kingdom, that is to say to the "new world," to the new state of things, to the new manner of being, of living in community, which the Gospel inaugurates. Such an adherence, which cannot remain abstract and unincarnated, reveals itself concretely by a visible entry into a community of believers (EN 23).

This "visible entry" is effected sacramentally by baptism. When those who listened to the preaching of the gospel on Pentecost were "cut to the heart" and asked, "What are we to do, my brothers?" Peter answered, "Repent and be baptized, every one of you, in the name of Jesus Christ for the forgiveness of your sins; and you will receive the gift of the holy Spirit" (Acts 2:37-38). "Baptism is not simply a seal of conversion, a kind of external sign indicating conversion and attesting to it. Rather, it is the sacrament which signifies and effects rebirth from the Spirit" (RMis 47). By baptism one enters the Church "as through a door" (LG 14); hence it is by being baptized that those who have come to believe in Christ become members of his body, where they receive the fullness of new life in Christ.

Planting and Building Christian Community

For the Second Vatican Council, "the special end of missionary activity is evangelization and the implanting of the church among peoples or groups in which it has not yet taken part" (AG 6). Pope Paul VI is equally emphatic, declaring: "In its totality, evangelization—over and above the preaching of the message—consists in the implantation of the Church" (EN 28). Some have seen a sign of "ecclesiocentrism" in this insistence on the implantation of the Church as a primary goal of evangelization, but Pope John Paul II has made it clear that he does not share their view. While agreeing that the promotion of human values is at the heart of the Church, he declares that

> such promotion must not be detached from or opposed to other fundamental tasks, such as proclaiming Christ and his Gospel, and establishing and building up communities which make present and active

within mankind the living image of the Kingdom. One need not fear falling thereby into a form of "ecclesiocentrism" (RMis 19).

He insists that the Church serves the kingdom both by spreading "Gospel values" throughout the world and by establishing communities and founding new particular churches, as well as by guiding them to mature faith and charity (RMis 20). Indeed, "to preach the Gospel and to establish new churches among peoples or communities where they do not yet exist, is the first task of the Church, which has been sent forth to all peoples and to the very ends of the earth" (RMis 34).

The evangelizing mission is not complete when a new Christian community has been established; it must continue until the new church has developed to its full maturity.

> This is a central and determining goal of missionary activity, so much so that the mission is not completed until it succeeds in building a new particular church which functions normally in its local setting. . . . Here we are speaking of a great and lengthy process, in which it is hard to identify the precise stage at which missionary activity properly so called comes to an end and is replaced by pastoral activity (RMis 48).

John Paul suggests that the clearest sign that a new church has reached maturity is that it begins to undertake evangelizing activity, first in its own locality, and then elsewhere as part of the Church's universal mission (RMis 49).

In the evangelization of their own locality, "ecclesial basic communities" are playing a key role in many regions of the world. Pope John Paul describes them in this way:

> These communities decentralize and organize the parish community, to which they always remain united. They take root in less privileged and rural areas, and become a leaven of Christian life, of care for the poor and neglected, and of commitment to the transformation of society. Within them, the individual Christian experiences community and therefore senses that he or she is playing an active role and is encouraged to share in the common task. Thus, these communities become a means of evangelization and of the initial proclamation of the Gospel, and a source of new ministries. At the same time, by being imbued with Christ's love, they also show how divisions, tribalism and racism can be overcome (RMis 51).

Inculturation: "Incarnating the Gospel in Peoples' Cultures"

The Final Report of the Extraordinary Assembly of the Synod of Bishops in 1985 described inculturation as "the intimate transformation of authentic cultural values through their integration in Christianity and the insertion of Christianity in the various human cultures" (II, C, 6). Pope John Paul explains:

> Through inculturation the Church makes the Gospel incarnate in different cultures and at the same time introduces people, together with their cultures, into her own community. She transmits to them her own values, at the same time taking the good elements that already exist in them and renewing them from within (RMis 52).

Inculturation will be a task particularly incumbent on the developing Christian communities. They must seek to express their Christian experience in ways that are consonant with their own cultural traditions, provided that those traditions are in harmony with the requirements of their faith. Pope John Paul observes that

> this kind of process needs to take place gradually, in such a way that it really is an expression of the community's Christian experience. . . . In effect, inculturation must involve the whole people of God, and not just a few experts, since the people reflect the authentic *"sensus fidei"* which must never be lost sight of. . . . It must be an expression of the community's life, one which must mature within the community itself, and not be exclusively the result of erudite research. The safeguarding of traditional values is the work of a mature faith (RMis 54).

Interreligious Dialogue

The Second Vatican Council provided the presupposition for the participation of Catholics in interreligious dialogue with its affirmation of the presence, in non-Christian religions, not only of human values but of divine gifts. It described "elements of truth and grace to be found among the nations" as "a sort of secret presence of God" (AG 9). It urged missionaries to make themselves familiar with the national and religious traditions of those to whom they are sent, and "gladly and respectfully to uncover the seeds of the Word which lie hidden in those traditions" (AG 11). In its Declaration on the Relation of the Church to Non-Christian Religions *(Nostra aetate)* the council said:

> The Church therefore has this exhortation for her sons: prudently and lovingly, through dialogue and collaboration with the followers of other religions, and in witness of Christian faith and life, to acknowledge, preserve, and promote the spiritual and moral goods found among these men, as well as the values in their society and culture (NA 2).

Paul VI likewise expressed his respect and esteem for non-Christian religions in EN, saying:

> They are the living expression of the soul of vast groups of people. . . . They possess an impressive patrimony of deeply religious texts. They have taught generations of people how to pray. They are all impregnated with innumerable "seeds of the Word," and can constitute a true "preparation for the Gospel" (EN 53).

However, he did not draw the conclusion that this should lead to interreligious dialogue. Rather, he insisted that respect and esteem for the other religions should not be taken as an invitation to withhold from non-Christians the proclamation of Jesus Christ.

John Paul II is the first pope to recognize interreligious dialogue as a "part" and "expression" of the Church's evangelizing mission.

> In the light of the economy of salvation, the Church sees no opposition between proclaiming Christ and engaging in interreligious dialogue. Instead, she feels the need to link the two in the context of her mission *ad gentes.* These two elements must maintain both their intimate connection and their distinctiveness; therefore they should not be confused, manipulated or regarded as identical, as though they were interchangeable (RMis 55).

John Paul II describes this dialogue as follows:

> It is demanded by deep respect for everything that has been brought about in human beings by the Spirit who blows where he wills. Through dialogue, the Church seeks to uncover the "seeds of the Word," a "ray of that truth which enlightens all men"; these are found in individuals and in the religious traditions of mankind. Dialogue is based on hope and love, and will bear fruit in the Spirit. Other religions constitute a positive challenge for the Church; they stimulate her both to discover and acknowledge the signs of Christ's presence and of the working of the Spirit, as well as to examine more deeply her own identity and to bear witness to the fullness of Revelation which she has received for the good of all (RMis 56).

He further speaks of a "vast field" which

> lies open to dialogue, which can assume many forms and expressions, from exchanges between experts in religious traditions or official representatives of these traditions to cooperation for integral development and the safeguarding of religious values, and from a sharing of their respective spiritual experiences to the so-called "dialogue of life," through

which believers of different religions bear witness before each other in daily life to their own human and spiritual values, and help each other to live according to those values in order to build a more just and fraternal society (RMis 57).

As one would expect, the Vatican document *Dialogue and Proclamation* offers the most detailed explanation "why and in what sense interreligious dialogue is an integral element of the Church's evangelizing mission" (DP 38). Its explanation is based on the goal at which dialogue aims.

Interreligious dialogue does not merely aim at mutual understanding and friendly relations. It reaches a much deeper level, that of the spirit, where exchange and sharing consist in a mutual witness to one's beliefs and a common exploration of one's respective religious commitment. In dialogue Christians and others are invited to deepen their religious commitments, to respond with increasing sincerity to God's personal call and gracious self-gift which, as our faith tells us, always passes through the mediation of Jesus Christ and the work of the Spirit. Given this aim, a deeper conversion of all toward God, interreligious dialogue possesses its own validity (DP 40f.).

This assertion of the validity of a dialogue which aims at the deeper religious commitment of all participants, and not at the conversion of non-Christians to the Christian faith, involves the recognition of the positive role that non-Christian religions can play in the divine economy of salvation. *Dialogue and Proclamation* offers the most positive assessment of this role to be found in any official Catholic document. It says:

Concretely, it will be in the sincere practice of what is good in their own religious traditions and by following the dictates of their conscience that the members of other religions respond positively to God's invitation and receive salvation in Jesus Christ, even when they do not recognize or acknowledge him as their savior (DP 29).

Of course, as the same document insists, "dialogue does not constitute the whole mission of the Church, and cannot simply replace proclamation, but remains oriented toward proclamation insofar as the dynamic process of the Church's evangelizing mission reaches in it its climax and fullness" (DP 82). "The two activities remain distinct, but, as experience shows, one and the same local church, one and the same person, can be diversely engaged in both. In actual fact the way of fulfilling the Church's mission depends upon the particular circumstances of each local Church, of each Christian" (DP 77f.).

Liberative Evangelization

The term "liberative evangelization," used by the Puebla Conference of 1979, expresses the recognition that the evangelization of oppressed people must include taking part in the dynamic process of
their integral liberation from the various forms of bondage that prevent
them from living an authentic human life. The idea had been expressed
five years earlier by the bishops in their final declaration at the synod
on evangelization. They said:

> Among the many matters treated at the Synod we paid particular at-
> tention to the problem of the inter-relation between evangelization and
> integral salvation, or the full liberation of man and peoples. It is a mat-
> ter of considerable importance and we were profoundly at one in reaf-
> firming the close link between evangelization and liberation.[1]

The links affirmed by the bishops between evangelization, liberation, and "integral salvation" were reaffirmed by Pope Paul VI in the
apostolic exhortation which was the fruit of that synod. There he described salvation as "this great gift of God which is liberation from
everything that oppresses man but which is above all liberation from
sin and the Evil One" (EN 9). He declared that "evangelization involves an explicit message . . . about life in society, about international
life, peace, justice and development—a message especially energetic
today about liberation" (EN 29). Referring to the 1974 synod he affirmed:

> The Church, as the Bishops repeated, has the duty to proclaim the lib-
> eration of millions of human beings, many of whom are her own chil-
> dren—the duty of assisting the birth of liberation, of giving witness to
> it, of ensuring that it is complete. This is not foreign to evangelization
> (EN 30).

Paul VI went on to describe the "profound links" between evangelization and liberation: links of the anthropological, theological, and
evangelical orders (EN 31). At the same time, he warned against the
tendency on the part of some to reduce the Church's mission to the dimensions of a purely temporal project. "The Church links human liberation and salvation in Jesus Christ, but she never identifies them . . .
in order that God's Kingdom should come it is not enough to establish
liberation and to create well-being and development" (EN 35). "The
Church strives always to insert the Christian struggle for liberation into
the universal plan of salvation which she herself proclaims" (EN 38).

[1] *Doctrine and Life* 25 (1975) 56.

The Puebla Conference's most distinctive contribution to the development of this notion is its insistence on the presence of two complementary and inseparable elements in liberative evangelization.

> The first is liberation from all the forms of bondage, from personal and social sin, and from everything that tears apart the human individual and society; all this finds its source to be in egotism, in the mystery of iniquity. The second element is liberation for progressive growth in being through communion with God and other human beings; this reaches its culmination in the perfect communion of heaven, where God is all in all and weeping forever ceases (ELA 482).

The basic idea is summed up in the statement: "Authentic liberation frees us from oppression so that we may be able to say yes to a higher good" (ELA 491). This "higher good" is described in the third part of the document as "communion and participation."

The Puebla Conference ascribed an important role in the achievement of such communion and participation to the basic ecclesial communities which have multiplied in many parts of Latin America. United in these small communities,

> Christians strive for a more evangelical way of life amid the people, work together to challenge the egotistical and consumeristic roots of society, and make explicit their vocation to communion with God and their fellow humans. Thus they offer a valid and worthwhile point of departure for building up a new society, "the civilization of love" (ELA 642).

Pope John Paul II speaks of liberation in the chapter of RMis which develops the theme of the kingdom of God. "The liberation and salvation brought by the Kingdom of God come to the human person both in his physical and spiritual dimensions" (RMis 14).

> The Kingdom is the concern of everyone: individuals, society, and the world. Working for the Kingdom means acknowledging and promoting God's activity, which is present in human history and transforms it. Building the Kingdom means working for liberation from evil in all its forms. In a word, the Kingdom of God is the manifestation and the realization of God's plan of salvation in all its fullness (RMis 15).

In the chapter of RMis entitled "The Paths of Mission," in which John Paul II describes the various ways in which the Church's evangelizing mission is carried out, there is no section on "liberation." However, there is one with the heading "Promoting Development by Forming

Consciences." As the heading indicates, the focus is on development and human promotion, but liberation is mentioned twice in connection with it. The section begins by saying: "The mission *ad gentes* is still being carried out today, for the most part in the southern regions of the world, where action on behalf of integral development and liberation from all forms of oppression is most urgently needed" (RMis 58). Later, he spells out the connection between liberation and development:

> Through the Gospel message, the Church offers a force for liberation which promotes development precisely because it leads to conversion of heart and of ways of thinking, fosters the recognition of each person's dignity, encourages solidarity, commitment and service of one's neighbor, and gives everyone a place in God's plan, which is the building of his Kingdom of peace and justice, beginning already in this life (RMis 59).

Ecumenical Collaboration

The Vatican Council II declared that "efforts aimed at restoring Christian unity . . . are very closely connected with the church's missionary endeavor because the division between Christians is injurious to the holy work of preaching the gospel to every creature" (AG 6). Hence, in newly established communities,

> insofar as religious conditions permit, ecumenical activity should be encouraged, so that, while avoiding every form of indifferentism or confusion and also senseless rivalry, Catholics might collaborate with their separated brethren, insofar as it is possible, by a common profession before the nations of faith in God and in Jesus Christ, and by a common, familial effort in social, cultural technical and religious matters, in accordance with the Decree on Ecumenism (AG 15).

Pope Paul VI likewise encouraged

> collaboration with the Christian brethren with whom we are not yet united in perfect unity, taking as a basis the foundation of Baptism and the patrimony of faith which is common to us. By doing this we can already give a greater common witness to Christ before the world in the very work of evangelization (EN 77).

Pope John Paul II expressed confidence that in missionary regions, "ecumenical activity and harmonious witness to Jesus Christ by Christians who belong to different Churches and Ecclesial Communities has already borne abundant fruit." And he added, "It is ever more urgent that they work and bear witness together at this time when Christian and para-Christian sects are sowing confusion by their activity. . . . Wherever possible, and in the light of local circumstances, the response of Christians can itself be an ecumenical one" (RMis 50).

Motives for Evangelization

Until the modern period, a powerful motive for evangelization was provided by the common belief that there was little hope for the salvation of people who lacked explicit Christian faith and membership in the Church. The first Roman pontiff to espouse a more hopeful view of the possibility of salvation for non-Christians was Pope Pius IX, who in 1863 said:

> Those who labor in invincible ignorance concerning our most holy religion and who, assiduously observing the natural law and its precepts which God has inscribed in the hearts of all, and being ready to obey God, live an honest and upright life can, through the working of divine light and grace, attain eternal life.[2]

Vatican II expressed an even more optimistic view about the salvation of those who lack Christian faith through no fault of their own (cf. LG 16). As we have seen above, *Dialogue and Proclamation* goes further, affirming that "it will be in the sincere practice of what is good in their own religious traditions and by following the dictates of their conscience that the members of other religions respond positively to God's invitation and receive salvation in Jesus Christ" (DP 29).

In the light of this modern Catholic optimism about the salvation of non-Christians, and this recognition of the salvific value of what is good in their own religious traditions, it is obvious that motivation for evangelization can no longer be based on the belief that people who lack Christian faith and baptism will not be saved. Pope Paul VI raised this question toward the end of EN: "Why proclaim the Gospel when the whole world is saved by uprightness of heart?" His answer was:

> It would be useful if every Christian and every evangelizer were to pray about the following thought: men can gain salvation also in other ways, by God's mercy, even though we do not preach the Gospel to them, but as for us, can we gain salvation if through negligence or fear or shame—what Saint Paul called "blushing for the Gospel"—or as a

---

[2] *Quanto conficiamur moerore*, Acta Pii IX, I/3, 613.

result of false ideas we fail to preach it? For that would be to betray the call of God, who wishes the seed to bear fruit through the voice of the ministers of the Gospel, and it will depend on us whether this grows into trees and produces its full fruit (EN 80).

For Pope Paul, then, the motive for evangelization is the call which the Church has received from God, to produce the fruit that God wishes it to bear through its ministry. What modern Catholic optimism about the salvation of non-Christians calls for, by way of motivation for evangelization, is a new understanding of what God is calling the Church to do and of the kind of fruit that God wishes it to bear.

Pope John Paul II expressed this new understanding of what God is calling the Church to do when he said: "The Church is not an end unto herself, since she is ordered towards the Kingdom of God of which she is the seed, sign and instrument." He described the fruit that God wishes the Church to bear when he described the Church's mission as that of "announcing and inaugurating the Kingdom of God and of Christ among all peoples" (RMis 18).

This can be summed up by saying that God is calling the Church to promote the reign of Christ in this world. Christ reigns not only where people know and obey him as their Lord, but also where people live according to the values of his gospel of love and justice even without knowing him. This understanding of the mission of the Church provides a motive for evangelization that in no way depends on the idea that people can be saved only by embracing Christian faith and becoming members of the Church. Rather, missionaries can be sure that they are following the call of God and are working to spread God's reign, not only by preaching the gospel to people who had not heard it and forming new Christian communities, but also by their presence and witness, by their preferential option for the poor, by efforts to free people from oppression and promote their human development, and by friendly dialogue with those of other faiths. They have no need to worry if their preaching results in few conversions and baptisms, for the highest authorities of the Catholic Church now assure them that in all of these ways they are following the call of God to be signs and instruments of God's kingdom.

This means that to ask: "Why should Christians engage in the work of evangelization?" is like asking: "Why should Christians be eager to promote the reign of Christ on earth?" The best answer to that is, out of love: love of Jesus Christ and of the people who will be graced by what his reign of love, peace, and justice will bring into their lives.

For Further Reading

Bosch, David J. *Transforming Mission: Paradigm Shifts in Theology of Mission.* Maryknoll, N.Y.: Orbis Books, 1991.

Burrows, William R., ed. *Redemption and Dialogue.* Maryknoll, N.Y.: Orbis Books, 1994.

Eagleson, John, and Philip Scharper. *Puebla and Beyond: Documentation and Commentary.* Maryknoll, N.Y.: Orbis Books, 1979.

Scherer, James A., and Stephen B. Bevans, eds. *New Directions in Mission and Evangelization I: Basic Statements 1974–1991.* Maryknoll, N.Y.: Orbis Books, 1992.

Senior, Donald, and Carroll Stuhlmueller. *The Biblical Foundations of Mission.* Maryknoll, N.Y.: Orbis Books, 1983.

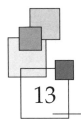

| 13 | Salvation Outside the Church |

John P. Galvin

The question of the possibility of eternal salvation outside the Church, long epitomized in discussion of the controversial ecclesiological axiom *extra ecclesiam nulla salus,* has in recent years receded from the foreground of theological discussion in favor of development of Christian theologies of world religions.[1] In many respects, this development may be welcomed as an antidote to an excessive ecclesiocentrism. Nonetheless, the issue of salvation outside the Church remains an important ecclesiological topic, both in itself and as an example of the range of development which is possible within the framework of Christian understanding of an important doctrinal issue. Over the course of a complex and varied history, conceptions have ranged from an exclusivism, which envisions no possibility of salvation for those outside the Church, through an inclusivism, which remains oriented toward the Church yet allows for the possibility of salvation of those not visibly joined to it, to a pluralistic position which conceives of multiple equally valid paths, Christian and non-Christian, toward one common final destination.[2] In addition to the issues immediately at hand, both the self-conception of the Church and the permanence of the Christian faith over the course of its history are at stake in these discussions.[3]

---

[1] An informative recent treatment of this history has been provided by Bertram Stubenrauch, "Die Theologie und die Religionen," *Fundamentaltheologie—Fluchtlinien und gegenwärtige Herausforderunge,* ed. Klaus Müller (Regensburg: Verlag Friedrich Pustet, 1998) 349–67.

[2] For discussion and classification of the issues involved here, with some variations in terminology, see J. Peter Schineller, "Christ and Church: A Spectrum of Views," *Theological Studies* 37 (1976) 545–66.

[3] This point is rightly stressed by Joseph Ratzinger, "Kein Heil außerhalb der Kirche?" *Das neue Volk Gottes: Entwürfe zur Ekklesiologie* (Düsseldorf: Patmos, 1969) 340.

While investigation of Christian understandings of other religions is beyond the scope of this chapter,[4] this essay will provide a compact account of Catholic thought on the possibility (or impossibility) of salvation outside the Church, with particular attention to modern (nineteenth- and twentieth-century) official statements of Catholic teaching. In view of the nature of the material, a historical presentation is best suited to convey a grasp of the doctrinal and theological issues at stake in the discussion.[5] The chapter will conclude with a brief account of Karl Rahner's conception of anonymous Christianity, one of the more widely discussed ways of articulating a Christian understanding of the possibility of the eternal salvation of non-Christians.

New Testament

It is not surprising that the New Testament, a collection of occasional writings, does not directly address the question of salvation outside the Church. Nonetheless, a number of New Testament passages have a bearing on this issue, and these texts have exerted a strong influence on later theological discussion. From a theological perspective, much of the complexity of the issue derives from the need to do justice to biblical texts and concerns which at least on the surface seem incompatible with each other.

A first group of texts consists of passages which, while not mentioning the Church explicitly, tie salvation closely to baptism, faith, and Christ. Examples include Jesus' reply to Nicodemus, "Amen, amen, I say to you, no one can enter the kingdom of God without being born of water and Spirit" (John 3:5); the risen Lord's instruction of the Eleven that "whoever believes and is baptized will be saved; whoever does not believe will be condemned" (Mark 16:16); and Peter's insistence with regard to Christ that "there is no salvation through anyone else,

---

[4] For a brief introduction to the issues, with particular attention to the question of revelation, see Avery Dulles, *Models of Revelation* (Garden City, N.Y.: Doubleday and Company, 1983) 174–92.

[5] For more extensive treatments of this material see Yves Congar, "No Salvation Outside the Church?" *The Wide World My Parish: Salvation and Its Problems* (Baltimore: Helicon Press, 1961) 93–154; Walter Kern, "'Außerhalb der Kirche kein Heil,'" *Disput um Jesus und um Kirche* (Innsbruck: Tyrolia, 1980) 88–112; Ratzinger, "Kein Heil außerhalb der Kirche?" 339–61; and Francis A. Sullivan, *Salvation Outside the Church? Tracing the History of the Catholic Response* (New York: Paulist Press, 1992). The following presentation draws heavily, though not exclusively, on these works and on Walter Kern's informative and compact "Heilsnotwendigkeit der Kirche," *LTK,* 3d ed. (1995) IV:1346–8.

nor is there any other name under heaven given to the human race by which we are to be saved" (Acts 4:12).[6] Paul's negative description of the state of the human race apart from the gospel (Rom 1:18–3:20) and the reminder in the letter to the Ephesians to the converts it addresses ("You were once darkness, but now you are light in the Lord" [5:8]) fit into the same category. While the expression *extra ecclesiam nulla salus* is not to be found in the New Testament, texts such as these seem clearly to point in the direction of that later formulation.

Yet passages of this sort do not exhaust the relevant New Testament material, for other texts imply that God's salvific will is universal. The Fourth Gospel states with regard to the incarnation that "the true light, which enlightens everyone, was coming into the world" (John 1:9) and insists that "God did not send his Son into the world to condemn the world, but that the world might be saved through him" (John 3:17). In the same letter which contains his unflattering portrait of Gentiles and Jews apart from Christ, Paul concludes a profound meditation on Israel and the Gentiles with the observation that "God delivered all to disobedience, that he might have mercy upon all" (Rom 11:32). Most explicit of all is 1 Tim 2:4, which teaches that God "wills everyone to be saved and to come to knowledge of the truth." The tension between these texts and those cited in the preceding paragraph has provided much grist for the mills of later theologians.

Two additional New Testament passages should also be mentioned here, since they have played a significant role at various later stages of theological discussion: Acts 10 and Heb 11:6. Acts 10 retells the story of Cornelius, a pagan centurion who is visited by an angel and receives the Holy Spirit (Acts 10:3-6, 44) before he is baptized (Acts 10:46-48). While the main point of the narrative concerns the reception of Gentiles into the Church, both the agency of an angelic mediator and the gift of the Holy Spirit prior to reception of baptism proved influential in later discussion of the possibility of salvation outside the Church.

Equally influential was a short passage from the epistle to the Hebrews. According to Heb 11:6, "without faith it is impossible to please him [God], for anyone who approaches God must believe that he exists and that he rewards those who seek him." Later theologians frequently understood this verse as specifying the minimal conditions for achievement of salvation, in the sense that belief in the existence of God and in divine response to human conduct was an indispensable condition for attaining eternal happiness.

---

[6] Historical-critical questions about the origin of these passages are beyond the scope of this essay. In the immediate context, the point at issue is their presence in the canonical text.

Patristic Period

As early as the second century, authors such as Justin and Irenaeus made allowance for the possibility of salvation of both Jews and Gentiles who lived before the time of Christ. In support of this judgment, these Fathers referred to those who had pleased God by living virtuous lives, following either the Mosaic Law or the dictates of reason. In a remarkable passage, Justin even goes so far as to state: "Those who lived by reason are Christians, even though they have been considered atheists. . . . Those who have lived reasonably, and still do, are Christians."[7] As this text indicates, principles invoked to account for the possibility of salvation before the time of Christ may admit of application to the present as well as the past.[8] Our chief concern, however, is with the development of patristic thought on the possibility of salvation for those who live outside the Church in the Christian era.

It is in the third century that the axiom *extra ecclesiam nulla salus* is first found. About the middle of that century, both Origen (in Alexandria) and Cyprian (in North Africa) speak in these terms: Origen writes that "outside this house, that is outside the Church, no one is saved,"[9] and Cyprian insists "there is no salvation outside of the Church."[10] As both Joseph Ratzinger and Francis Sullivan observe, however, authors at this early time used such absolute formulations in pastoral contexts addressing those who refused to enter the Church or who separated

[7] *First Apology* 46 (PG 6:398). Socrates and Abraham are among the names mentioned. The translation is taken from *Writings of Saint Justin Martyr*, Fathers of the Church 6, trans. Thomas B. Falls (New York: Christian Heritage, Inc., 1948) 83–4. For further discussion of Justin and Irenaeus see Sullivan, *Salvation Outside the Church?* 14–16.

[8] Further information on this period is provided by Yves Congar, "Ecclesia ab Abel," *Abhandlungen über Theologie und Glaube,* ed. Marcel Reding (Düsseldorf: Patmos Verlag, 1952) 79–108; and Andreas Bsteh, *Zur Frage nach der Universalität der Erlösung: Unter besonderer Berücksichtigung ihres Verständnisses bei den Vätern des zweiten Jahrhunderts* (Vienna: Herder, 1966).

[9] *In Jesu nave* 3.5 (PG 12:841–2): "*Extra hanc domum, id est extra Ecclesiam, nemo salvatur*"; the text is preserved only in Rufinus' Latin translation. Origen's optimistic eschatological hope that, in the end, all will be saved should, of course, be taken into account in interpreting this statement. For further information on Origen's eschatology see Brian E. Daley, *The Hope of the Early Church: A Handbook of Patristic Eschatology* (New York: Cambridge University Press, 1991) 47–60.

[10] *Epistle 73 (to Jubianus)* 21. The translation is taken from *Fathers of the Third Century: Hippolytus, Cyprian, Caius, Novatian, Appendix,* The Ante-Nicene Fathers 5, trans. Ernest Wallis (New York: Scribner's, 1926) 384. The epistle is numbered 72 in this collection.

themselves from it by apostasy, heresy, or schism.[11] Personal culpability on the part of those condemned was thus presupposed.

In the late fourth and early fifth centuries, Latin and Greek Fathers of the Church such as Ambrose of Milan, Gregory of Nyssa, John Chrysostom, and Jerome adopted a more rigorous position. Convinced that those who have not professed the Christian faith have only themselves to blame, they explicitly applied the principle that "outside the church there is no salvation" to pagans and Jews.[12] At the same time, a traditional symbolic ecclesiology which envisioned the Church as Noah's ark (see Gen 6:5–8:22; 1 Pet 3:20), the only refuge from the destructive flood, pointed ineluctably toward the conclusion that those not on board—for whatever reason—are fated to drown.[13]

The most influential figure in Western thinking on the subject is Augustine (354–430), whose views on this matter were quite rigorous.[14] Despite his recognition of the validity of sacraments among heretics and schismatics, Augustine considered such people excluded from the possibility of salvation, even in the event of martyrdom. Commenting on the status of a Donatist bishop, Augustine wrote:

> Outside the church he can have everything except salvation. He can have honor, he can have sacraments, he can sing alleluia, he can respond with Amen, he can have the gospel, he can hold and preach the faith in the name of the Father and the Son and the Holy Spirit: but nowhere else than in the Catholic Church can he find salvation.[15]

[11] See Ratzinger, "Kein Heil außerhalb der Kirche?" 342–5; Sullivan, *Salvation Outside the Church?* 18–24. Congar ("No Salvation Outside the Church?" 95) and Kern ("'Außerhalb der Kirche kein Heil,'" 89) offer a different interpretation of Cyprian on this point.

[12] For discussion of the chief texts of Ambrose, Gregory, and Chrysostom see Sullivan, *Salvation Outside the Church?* 14–27.

[13] Thus Jerome could write to Pope Damasus, in an ecclesiological context, that "whoever is not in Noah's ark will perish when the flood prevails" (*Epistle* 15, 2 [CSEL 54, 63]; the translation is taken from *The Letters of St. Jerome*, Ancient Christian Writers 33, trans. Charles C. Mierow [Westminster, Md.: Newman Press] 71). Patristic and medieval use of this ecclesiological symbolism is treated at length in Hugo Rahner, *Symbole der Kirche: Die Ekklesiologie der Väter* (Salzburg: Otto Müller Verlag, 1964) 504–47. Both Thomas Aquinas (*Summa Theologiae* III, q. 73, a. 3) and Martin Luther ("The Order of Baptism, 1523," *Luther's Works*, vol. 53: *Liturgy and Hymns*, ed. Ulrich S. Leupold [Philadelphia: Fortress Press, 1965] 97) invoke this imagery in discussing the relationship of Christians to the unbaptized.

[14] On Augustine's ecclesiology see Yves Congar, *L'Église de saint Augustin à l'époque moderne* (Paris: Éditions du Cerf, 1970) 11–24.

[15] *Sermo ad Caesariensis ecclesiae plebem*, 6 (CSEL 53:174–5); the Donatists were schismatics who held that sacraments administered by those who had abandoned the

The relationship of martyrdom is addressed directly in the course of Augustine's treatise on the sacrament of baptism: "'neither does this baptism profit the heretic, even though for confessing Christ he be put to death outside the Church.' This is most true; for, by being put to death outside the Church, he is proved not to have had charity."[16]

Augustine was convinced that salvation was impossible both for those who had heard the gospel and not become Christian and for those who had never had the opportunity to hear the gospel. In his later anti-Pelagian period, he held that the universality of original sin sufficed to justify divine condemnation of all non-Christian adults and also of infants who died without baptism, though "surely the lightest punishment will be for those who added no sin to that which they brought with them originally."[17] In accordance with these harsh positions, Augustine interpreted the "all" of 1 Tim 2:4 quite restrictively: "the 'all' means the many whom He (God) wishes to come to the grace."[18]

Despite Augustine's enormous influence on Western Christianity, later patristic authors differed notably in their reception of his line of reasoning on this subject. Prosper of Aquitaine (ca. 390–ca. 463), a follower but also a critic of Augustine, maintained a milder position by supporting basic elements of Augustine's theology of grace while holding that nations which have not yet heard the gospel continue to receive the general favors of God, though not the abundance of grace now revealed in Christ. Prosper was thus able to maintain both an Augustinian emphasis on the divine initiative in the offer of grace and a firm commitment to the universality of God's salvific will: "Out of the whole world the whole world is chosen, and out of all human beings all human beings are adopted."[19] But other theologians in the Augus-

---

Church in time of persecution were invalid. The translation is taken from Sullivan, *Salvation Outside the Church?* 32.

[16] *De baptismo* 4:17, 24 (CSEL 51:250). The translation is taken from *A Select Library of the Nicene and Post-Nicene Fathers*, vol. 4, ed. Philip Schaff (Buffalo, N.Y.: Christian Literature Company, 1887) 458; a printing error has been corrected. The passage cited by Augustine is from Cyprian (*Epistle* 73).

[17] *Enchiridion* 23:93 (CCL 46:99). The translation is from *The Writings of Saint Augustine*, vol. 4, *Fathers of the Church* 2, trans. Bernard M. Peebles (New York: Fathers of the Church, 1947) 446.

[18] *Contra Julianum* 4:8, 44 (PL 760). The translation is taken from *Saint Augustine: Against Julian*, Fathers of the Church 35, trans. Matthew A. Schumacher (New York: Fathers of the Church, 1957) 206.

[19] *Pro Augustino responsiones ad capitula obiectionum Gallorum* 2, 8 (PL 51:172); my translation. Shortly before this passage, Prosper observes that one "who says that God will not have all men to be saved but only the fixed number of the predestined,

tinian tradition moved in the opposite direction. Fulgentius of Ruspe
(468–533), for example, taught that God

> willed to save those to whom he gave knowledge of the mystery of sal-
> vation, and he did not wish to save those to whom he denied the
> knowledge of the saving mystery. If he had intended the salvation of
> both, he would have given the knowledge of the truth to both.[20]

In accordance with this reasoning, Fulgentius insisted: "Most firmly
hold and never doubt, that not only all pagans but also all Jews and all
heretics and schismatics who finish this present life outside the Catholic Church, will go into the 'eternal fire which has been prepared for the
Devil and his angels.'"[21] Centuries later, in 1442, this extreme statement
was cited authoritatively by the Council of Florence in its Decree for
the Jacobites (DS 1351).

Middle Ages

Over the course of the Middle Ages, scholastic theologians gradually introduced distinctions in their understanding of the eternal fate of
those who die outside the Church. Because of original sin, all the unbaptized suffer from the lack of the beatific vision, the face-to-face vision of God which is constitutive of eternal bliss (1 Cor 13:13). Only
those culpable of serious actual sins, however, undergo the pains of
hell. While this differentiation draws attention to the relevance of personal guilt, theologians in this period nonetheless maintained a pessimistic attitude toward the possibility of salvation for adults dying
outside the Church in the Christian era.[22] While allowance must be
made for differences among theologians, some observations of Thomas
Aquinas (1224/25–74) will illustrate the state of the question in theological discussion in that period.[23]

---

speaks more harshly than we should of the depth of the unsearchable grace of God"
(*Prosper of Aquitaine: Defense of St. Augustine*, Ancient Christian Writers 21, trans. P.
de Letter [Westminster, Md.: Newman Press, 1963] 159).

[20] *De veritate praedestinationis* 3:16–18 (PL 65:660–1). The translation is taken from
Sullivan, *Salvation Outside the Church?* 42.

[21] *De fide, ad Petrum* 38 (81) (PL 65:704); the citation is from Matt 25:41. The translation is taken from *Fulgentius: Selected Works*, Fathers of the Church 95, trans.
Robert B. Eno (Washington: Catholic University of America Press, 1997) 104.

[22] For a brief discussion of major authors prior to Aquinas, see Sullivan, *Salvation
Outside the Church?* 44–7.

[23] For another expression of medieval thinking see Dante's description of the first
circle of hell in Canto IV of the *Inferno*.

Like other medieval theologians, Thomas Aquinas recognized the possibility of salvation for those who lived before the gospel had been preached. In pre-Christian times explicit faith in the existence and salvific providence of God (Heb 11:6) could suffice for salvation, as did, in cases like that of Cornelius (Acts 10), an explicit or implicit desire for the sacraments. Nonetheless, he also held that, now that the gospel has been promulgated, explicit faith in Christ and participation in the sacramental means of salvation are necessary. Those who had heard the gospel but failed to accept it were presumed culpable. As far as those to whom the gospel had not been preached were concerned, Aquinas' opinion appears to have changed over the course of his life. At least for some time, he taught that God would provide in some way (by an angel, a preacher, or a revelation by inner inspiration) for what Thomas seems to have considered the rare case of a person who had heard nothing of Christ. His final treatment of the matter, however, does not mention these possibilities, but points instead to inherited original sin as sufficient reason to justify denial of divine aid to some people.[24] In one particularly strong and historically important formulation, Aquinas even expressed the necessity of belonging to the Church by stating that "being subject to the Roman Pontiff is of necessity for salvation."[25]

Despite Aquinas' pessimistic view of the possibility of salvation outside the Church, other aspects of his thought provided resources for future theologians to mine in seeking more nuanced understandings of *"extra ecclesiam nulla salus."*[26] Such developments took place, however, centuries later, under the impact of changed historical conditions. Official formulations from the late Middle Ages, which appear to presuppose personal guilt on the part of adults outside the Church, reflect an undifferentiated negative position. Two texts are of particular importance.

The first example is provided by Pope Boniface VIII's bull *Unam sanctam,* which was issued in 1302 at a time of severe conflict with King Philip IV of France. Having professed belief in "one, holy, catholic and apostolic Church . . . outside of whom there is neither salvation nor remission of sins," Boniface concluded: "Furthermore, we declare, state

[24] *Summa Theologiae* II-II, q. 2, a. 5, ad 1. The chief texts of Thomas on this subject are drawn together and analyzed by George Sabra, *Thomas Aquinas' Vision of the Church: Fundamentals of an Ecumenical Ecclesiology* (Mainz: Matthias-Grünewald-Verlag, 1987) 158–69; and Sullivan, *Salvation Outside the Church?* 44–62.

[25] *Contra errores Graecorum*, pars. 2, cap. 32; my translation. On the unusual circumstances which led to the composition of this text see James A. Weisheipl, *Friar Thomas D'Aquino: His Life, Thought and Works* (Garden City, N.Y.: Doubleday, 1974) 168–71.

[26] This point is stressed by Sullivan, *Salvation Outside the Church?* 62.

and define that it is absolutely necessary for salvation for every human creature to be subject to the Roman Pontiff."[27] The solemn formulation of the final sentence, which seems to exclude all non-Catholics from any possibility of salvation, has figured prominently in later discussion of papal teaching authority and papal infallibility.[28]

A second text, equally uncompromising in maintaining the necessity of belonging to the Catholic Church, is to be found in the Decree for the Jacobites, issued in 1442 by the Council of Florence in an ultimately unsuccessful attempt to reestablish communion with a Monophysite church. Citing Fulgentius of Ruspe, this decree contains the following affirmation (DS 1351):

> [The holy Roman Church] . . . firmly believes, professes and preaches that all those who are outside the catholic church, not only pagans but also Jews or heretics and schismatics, cannot share in eternal life and will go *into the everlasting fire which was prepared for the devil and his angels,* unless they are joined to the catholic church before the end of their lives; that the unity of the ecclesiastical body is of such importance that only for those who abide in it do the church's sacraments contribute to salvation and do fasts, almsgiving and other works of piety and practices of the christian militia produce eternal rewards; and that nobody can be saved, no matter how much he has given away in alms and even if he has shed his blood in the name of Christ, unless he has persevered in the bosom and the unity of the catholic church.[29]

Despite the apparent clarity and authority of this profession of faith by an ecumenical council, the axiom *extra ecclesiam nulla salus* was to be interpreted with significant qualifications in the centuries to follow.

---

[27] DS 870, 876. The translation (slightly amended) is taken from *The Christian Faith in the Doctrinal Documents of the Catholic Church,* ed. J. Neuner and J. Dupuis (Westminster, Md.: Christian Classics, 1975) 210–1.

[28] This final sentence of *Unam sanctam* is clearly based on Aquinas' *Contra errores Graecorum,* but its meaning in the papal document is disputed. In Aquinas, the statement affirms the need to belong to the Roman Catholic Church. Most interpreters find the same meaning in *Unam sanctam,* but George Tavard ("The Bull *Unam Sanctam* of Boniface VIII," *Papal Primacy and the Universal Church,* ed. Paul C. Empie and T. Austin Murphy, Lutherans and Catholics in Dialogue V [Minneapolis: Augsburg Publishing House, 1974] 105–19) interprets the sentence in context as a claim to papal supremacy over civil rulers. In Tavard's judgment, no part of the bull meets the criteria of Vatican I for infallible exercise of the papal magisterium. For further discussion and additional literature, see Congar, *L'Église,* 275–7.

[29] Translations of all conciliar texts are taken from *Decrees of the Ecumenical Councils,* ed. Norman P. Tanner, 2 vols. (Washington, D.C.: Georgetown University Press, 1990). The italicized words are a citation of Matt 25:41.

Later Scholastic Theologians

Beginning in the sixteenth century, theologians introduced significant qualifications into their understanding of the axiom *extra ecclesiam nulla salus*. Influenced by the discovery of America and newly alert to the existence of vast numbers of people unaware of the gospel through no fault of their own, Spanish Dominican theologians such as Francisco de Vitoria (1493–1546), Melchior Cano (1505–60), and Domingo Soto (1524–60) devoted new attention to the issue. Vitoria postulated invincible ignorance on the part of the natives of America, and held that they had no (subjective) obligation to believe in the gospel until the faith had been presented to them persuasively and effectively (as it had not been by the *conquistadores*).[30] Cano took the halfway step of holding that implicit faith in Christ could suffice for justification but not for eternal salvation, while Soto judged eventually that the implicit faith which Aquinas had recognized as sufficing for salvation in pre-Christian times should also be recognized as sufficient for all who inculpably lack explicit Christian belief. While such reflections were not universal, the Flemish theologian Albert Pigge (1490–1542) also spoke of the possibility of salvation of those inculpably lacking explicit faith in Christ, and argued that Muslims might well fall into this category.

Comparable considerations are to be found among Jesuit theologians of the period, especially Francisco Suarez (1548–1619) and Juan de Lugo (1583–1660). Suarez envisioned the possibility that a desire for faith (or implicit faith) in Christ could suffice for salvation of non-Christians, while Cardinal de Lugo explicitly extended the possibility of salvation despite invincible ignorance to heretics, Jews, and Muslims. Responding to objections based on *Unam sanctam* he wrote:

> The possibility of salvation for such a person is not ruled out by the nature of the case; moreover, such a person should not be called a non-Christian, because, even though he has not been visibly joined to the church, still, interiorly he has the virtue of habitual and actual faith in common with the church, and in the sight of God he will be reckoned with the Christians.[31]

A position similar on the main points at issue was later held by the Jesuit theologian Giovanni Perrone (1794–1876), whose thought influenced the teaching of Pope Pius IX. In a similar vein, the German theologian Heinrich Klee (1800–40) concluded his treatment of the necessity

---

[30] For a brief assessment see Congar, "No Salvation Outside the Church?" 115–6.

[31] *De libero hominis arbitrio et divina gratia libri* X (Cologne, 1542) fol. 180, v. 181 r; cited according to Sullivan, *Salvation Outside the Church?* 96.

of the Church for salvation by observing that "only those who remain outside the church through crass and affected ignorance, through indifference to God's truth, will and grace, are excluded from her and from her salvation."[32] In the second half of the nineteenth century, this widespread theological opinion would make its way into papal teaching.[33]

Pope Pius IX

In the evolution of official Catholic teaching on the possibility of salvation outside the Church, Pope Pius IX (1846–78) occupies a decisive position. In two important texts he combined rejection of indifferentism in religious matters with explicit acknowledgment that invincible ignorance makes lack of Church membership inculpable. Because of the historical significance of these statements, they deserve to be cited at length.

The first text is taken from *Singulari quadam*, an allocution which Pius IX delivered in 1854 to bishops assembled in Rome for the definition of Mary's Immaculate Conception. After an emphatic condemnation of indifferentism in matters of religion, the Pope added:

> It must, of course, be held as a matter of faith that outside the apostolic Roman Church no one can be saved, that the Church is the only ark of salvation, and that whoever does not enter it will perish in the flood. On the other hand, it must likewise be held as certain that those who live in ignorance of the true religion, if such ignorance be invincible, are not subject to any guilt in this matter before the eyes of the Lord. But then, who would dare to set limits to this ignorance, taking into consideration the natural differences of peoples, lands, native talents, and so many other factors?[34]

Nearly a decade later, in 1863, Pius IX offered similar observations in *Quanto conficiamur moerore*, an encyclical letter addressed to the bishops of Italy (7–8):

---

[32] *Katholische Dogmatik*, vol. 1: *Generaldogmatik*, 2d ed. (Mainz: Kirchheim, 1839) 150; my translation. That Klee contributed to the revival of the patristic notion of the Church as sacrament is worth noting in this context; see Leonardo Boff, *Die Kirche als Sakrament im Horizont der Welterfahrung: Versuch einer Legitimation und einer strukturfunktionalistischen Grundlegung der Kirche im Anschluß an das II. Vatikanischen Konzil* (Paderborn: Verlag Bonifacius-Druckerei, 1972) 115–7.

[33] With the exception of Klee, the theologians noted in this section are treated at greater length in Sullivan, *Salvation Outside the Church?* 69–102.

[34] *Acta Pii IX* 1/1, 626; the translation is taken from *The Christian Faith*, 217.

> It is again necessary to mention and censure a very grave error entrapping some Catholics who believe that it is possible to arrive at eternal salvation although living in error and alienated from the true faith and Catholic unity. Such belief is certainly opposed to Catholic teaching. There are, of course, those who are struggling with invincible ignorance about our most holy religion. Sincerely observing the natural law and its precepts inscribed by God on all hearts and ready to obey God, they live honest lives and are able to attain eternal life by the efficacious virtue of divine light and grace. Because God knows, searches and clearly understands the minds, hearts, thoughts and nature of all, his supreme kindness and clemency do not permit anyone at all who is not guilty of deliberate sin to suffer eternal punishments. Also well known is the Catholic teaching that no one can be saved outside the Catholic Church. Eternal salvation cannot be obtained by those who oppose the authority and statements of the same Church and are stubbornly separated from the unity of the Church and also from the successor of Peter, the Roman Pontiff.[35]

While passages of this nature cannot be considered definitive teaching, these words of Pope Pius IX mark official adoption of a position which had been defended for several centuries by respected theologians, but which had not previously received papal approbation. From this time on, official Catholic teaching has understood the axiom *extra ecclesiam nulla salus* as referring only to those culpably outside the Church. However, the limitations of the text should not be overlooked. No distinctions are made between baptized non-Catholics and other non-Catholics, and the remarks are confined to the possible salvation of individuals seen as such, without regard for the churches or other religious communities to which they may belong.

Pius XII

The next important stage in the development of official Catholic teaching on salvation outside the Church comes with the teaching of Pope Pius XII (1939–58), especially in his encyclical *Mystici corporis* (1943). Having equated the Roman Catholic Church and the Mystical

---

[35] *Acta Pii IX* 1/3, 613; the translation is taken from *The Papal Encyclicals 1740–1878*, ed. Claudia Carlen (Wilmington, N.C.: McGrath Publishing Company, 1981) 370. The importance of these teachings of Pius IX is stressed by Karl Rahner, "Membership of the Church According to the Teaching of Pius XII's Encyclical 'Mystici Corporis Christi,'" *Theological Investigations*, vol. 2 (Baltimore: Helicon Press, 1963) 38–40; the essay was originally published in 1947.

Body of Christ (13), Pius XII states with regard to Church membership (22):

> Actually only those are to be included as members of the Church who have been baptized and profess the true faith, and have not been so unfortunate as to separate themselves from the unity of the Body, or been excluded by legitimate authority for grave faults committed. . . . It follows that those who are divided in faith or government cannot be living in the unity of such a Body, nor can they be living the life of its one Divine Spirit.

Despite the apparent implications of the final line of this section, a later portion of the encyclical (103) explicitly allows for the possibility of salvation outside the Catholic Church. Speaking of "those who are not yet members of the church," Pius XII writes:

> We ask each and every one of them to correspond to the interior movements of grace, and to seek to withdraw from that state in which they cannot be sure of their salvation. For even though, by an unconscious desire and longing they have a certain relationship with the Mystical Body of the Redeemer, they still remain deprived of those many heavenly gifts and helps from Heaven which can only be enjoyed in the Catholic Church.[36]

This passage, which provoked intense theological discussion, draws on the thinking of sixteenth-century theologians to allow for the possibility of salvation of nonmembers of the Church who are related to it by at least an unconscious desire. Like the texts of Pius IX, however, it makes no reference to other possible relationships to the Church, and takes no account of the ecclesiological implications of Catholic recognition of baptism outside the Catholic Church.

Further clarification of Pius XII's teaching on the necessity of the Church for salvation was provided in 1949 by an important letter of the Holy Office to Archbishop Richard Cushing of Boston.[37] This letter is a result of prolonged controversy surrounding the rigorous interpretation of the axiom *extra ecclesiam nulla salus* by Rev. Leonard Feeney, s.j., in the sense that no one outside the Roman Catholic Church could be saved. While appealing explicitly to *Mystici corporis*, the letter explains the issues in more detail:

[36] DS 3802, 3821. The translation of these passages is taken from *The Papal Encyclicals 1939–1958*, ed. Claudia Carlen (Wilmington, N.C.: McGrath Publishing Company, 1981) 41, 58.

[37] DS 3866–72. The Latin text and an English translation were published in the *American Ecclesiastical Review* 127 (1952) 308–15.

To gain eternal salvation it is not always required that a person be incorporated in reality *(reapse)* as a member of the Church, but it is required that he belong to it at least in desire and longing *(voto et desiderio)*. It is not always necessary that this desire be explicit, as it is with catechumens. When a man is invincibly ignorant, God also accepts an implicit desire, so called because it is contained in the good dispositions of soul by which a man wants his will to be conformed to God's will.

In keeping with this explanation, the letter maintains that "no one who knows that the Church has been divinely established by Christ and, nevertheless, refuses to be a subject of the Church or refuses to obey the Roman Pontiff, the vicar of Christ on earth, will be saved" (DS 3867). Echoes of medieval formulations are unmistakable, but so too are the new qualifications.

Taken together, these texts represent the state of official Catholic teaching on the subject prior to the Second Vatican Council. Further development would depend on the council's reexamination of other aspects of ecclesiology.

Vatican II

The final stage in this brief account of Catholic teaching on salvation outside the Church is represented by the Second Vatican Council (1962–65). Only the major relevant texts can be considered here.

While the early drafts of the text eventually adopted as a Dogmatic Constitution on the Church under the title *Lumen gentium* contained material derived from the teaching of *Mystici corporis* and the 1949 Letter of the Holy Office to Archbishop Cushing, important modifications were introduced during the course of the council's deliberations.[38] First, instead of teaching that the Church of Christ is the Roman Catholic Church, the council teaches that the

church, set up and organized in this world as a society, subsists in the catholic church, governed by the successor of Peter and the bishops in communion with him, although outside its structure many elements of sanctification and of truth are to be found which, as proper gifts to the church of Christ, impel towards catholic unity (LG 8).

Second, and as a result of this differentiation, the council refrains from stating that only Catholics are really members of the Church. Instead, it

[38] The history of the text of *Lumen gentium* may conveniently be traced by consultation of *Synopsis historica constitutionis dogmaticae Lumen Gentium*, ed. Giuseppe Alberigo (Bologna: Istituto per le Scienze Religiose, 1975).

discusses the issue in terms of degrees of incorporation and relationship to the People of God (LG 14–16). This procedure makes possible both distinct treatment of other Christian churches and ecclesial communities and separate references to different groups of non-Christians.[39] As far as salvation outside the Church is concerned, the following texts are especially important.

First, speaking of the necessity of the Church in conjunction with the necessity of faith and of baptism, the council teaches that "those cannot be saved who refuse to enter the church or to remain in it, if they are aware that the catholic church was founded by God through Jesus Christ as a necessity for salvation" (LG 14). In substance, this teaching repeats the position of the 1949 Letter of the Holy Office.

Second, the council affirms the salvific function of other Christian churches and ecclesial communities. Here the clearest text is to be found in the Decree on Ecumenism, *Unitatis redintegratio* (3):

> Our separated brothers and sisters also celebrate many sacred actions of the christian religion. These most certainly can engender a life of grace in ways that vary according to the condition of each church or community, and must be held capable of giving access to that communion in which is salvation.
>
> It follows that the separated churches and communities as such, though we believe them to be deficient in some respects, have by no means been deprived of significance and importance in the mystery of salvation. For the Spirit of Christ has not refrained from using them as means of salvation whose efficacy comes from that fullness of grace and truth which has been entrusted to the catholic church.

But the council does not limit the possibility of salvation to Christians. After speaking in specific positive terms of Jews and Muslims, *Lumen gentium* (16) explicitly affirms the possibility of salvation on an even wider basis:

> There are those who without any fault do not know anything about Christ or his church, yet who search for God with a sincere heart and, under the influence of grace, try to put into effect the will of God as known to them through the dictate of conscience: these too can obtain eternal salvation. Nor does divine Providence deny the helps that are necessary for salvation to those who, through no fault of their own, have not yet attained to the express recognition of God yet who strive, not without divine grace, to live an upright life.

[39] For further information see the informative commentary of Aloys Grillmeier in *Commentary on the Documents of Vatican II*, ed. Herbert Vorgrimler (New York: Herder and Herder, 1967) 1:146–85.

In a similar manner, the Pastoral Constitution on the Church in the
Modern World, *Gaudium et spes,* teaches that "since Christ died for
everyone, and since the ultimate calling of each of us comes from God
and is therefore a universal one, we are obliged to hold that the holy
Spirit offers everyone the possibility of sharing in this paschal mystery
in a manner known only to God" (22). While grace is absolutely indispensable for salvation, the possibility of salvation is universally available.

The teaching of Vatican II, which is clearly influenced by the council's understanding of the Church as the "universal sacrament of salvation" (LG 48) or "instrumental sign of intimate union with God and of
the unity of all humanity" (LG 1), is thus marked by a high degree of
optimism with regard to salvation. In view of earlier history, it is not
surprising that Karl Rahner, in a lecture originally delivered in 1971,
called this optimism regarding salvation "one of the most noteworthy
results of the Second Vatican Council" and suggested that the council's
assertions on this subject "marked a far more decisive phase in the development of the Church's conscious awareness of her faith" than
other important doctrinal developments at the council.[40]

Karl Rahner

Among the better known, though also more controversial, theological explanations of the possibility of salvation outside the Church is
Karl Rahner's theory of anonymous Christianity. Here as elsewhere,
the starting point of Rahner's thought lies in his theology of grace.

Convinced of the universality of God's salvific will, the necessity of
grace for salvation, and the universal mediation of salvation by Jesus
Christ, Rahner argued in numerous works that God's free self-gift in
grace tends of its own nature toward visible manifestation in Christ
and the Church. As a kind of sacrament, the Church is the visible sign
and instrument of the grace which is offered to all human beings. In
order to express simultaneously both the possibility of salvation outside the Church and the objective Christian ecclesial character of salvation, Rahner proposed that those non-Christians whose lives (unknown
to them) constitute a positive response to God's free self-gift in grace
may appropriately be termed anonymous Christians. Ultimately identifiable only by God, they are *Christians* (in a certain sense of the word)
because the grace which they have received and accepted is in fact intrinsically linked to Christ; they are *anonymous* Christians because this

[40] Karl Rahner, "Observations on the Problem of the 'Anonymous Christian,'"
Theological Investigations, vol. 14 (New York: Seabury Press, 1976) 284.

dimension of their own real situation remains unrecognized (and perhaps unrecognizable) by them.

Rahner's theory of anonymous Christianity is intended neither as a comprehensive Christian interpretation of other religions nor as a vocabulary which non-Christians themselves should be encouraged to adopt. Its purpose is rather to express in a brief formulation some consequences of Christian understanding of the multidimensional divine offer of salvation. From a pastoral perspective, it seeks in part to prevent the Church from succumbing to a sect-like mentality in assessing its position in the world.[41]

While supported by numerous theologians, Rahner's conception has also been subjected to criticism from various sides.[42] His views have been accused of both underestimating the need for explicit Christian faith in its historical particularity (and thus undermining the Church's missionary endeavors) and as an imperialistic Christian assimilation of non-Christians, lacking in respect for the legitimate autonomy of other religions.[43] It must be noted, however, that many critics of Rahner on this point differ from him more in terminology

---

[41] For Rahner's own presentation of his thought see his works: "Anonymous Christians," *Theological Investigations,* vol. 6 (Baltimore: Helicon Press, 1969) 390–8; "Anonymous Christianity and the Missionary Task of the Church," *Theological Investigations,* vol. 12 (New York: Seabury Press, 1974) 161–78; and "Observations on the Problem of the 'Anonymous Christian,'" 280–94. The foundational ecclesiological reflections of "Membership of the Church According to the Teaching of Pius XII's Encyclical 'Mystici Corporis Christi'" (1–88) should also be consulted.

[42] The most thorough analysis is Nikolaus Schwerdtfeger, *Gnade und Welt: Zum Grundgefüge von Karl Rahners Theorie der "anonymen Christen"* (Freiburg: Herder, 1982); a more compact account has recently been provided by Albert Raffelt, "'Anonyme Christen' und 'konfessioneller Verein' bei Karl Rahner: Eine Bemerkung zur Terminologie und zur Frage der Interpretation seiner frühen Theologie," *Theologie und Philosophie* 72 (1997) 565–73. For more general accounts of Rahner's ecclesiology, including discussions of anonymous Christianity, see Leo J. O'Donovan, ed., "A Changing Ecclesiology in a Changing Church: A Symposium on Development in the Ecclesiology of Karl Rahner," *Theological Studies* 38 (1977) 736–62; and Richard Lennan, *The Ecclesiology of Karl Rahner* (Oxford: Clarendon Press, 1995).

[43] For examples see the anonymous article, "A Modern Conception of the Salvation of Infidels Which Hampers Apostolic Zeal according to Father Karl Rahner," *Christ to the World* 8 (1963) 421–8; Hans Urs von Balthasar, *The Moment of Christian Witness* (Glen Rock, N.J.: Newman Press, 1968) 60–8; and Hans Küng, *On Being a Christian* (Garden City, N.Y.: Doubleday, 1976) 97–8, 125–6. But note also Hans Urs von Balthasar, *Dare We Hope "That All Men Be Saved"? With a Short Discourse on Hell* (San Francisco: Ignatius Press, 1988); and Küng, *On Being a Christian,* 447; in these texts, each author adopts a position quite close to the substance of Rahner's conception.

than in substance, and that some criticisms are based on distorted accounts of Rahner's conception. While developed before the Second Vatican Council and presented in a distinctive terminology, the substance of his theory would seem amply supported by the Church's teaching on the relevant issues.

Conclusion

As the history of discussion of the possibility of salvation outside the Church makes clear, answers to this complex question have ranged widely between pessimistic and optimistic positions. Yet, while more optimistic positions are characteristic of modern theology and recent Church teaching, the history of the discussion is too complex to be summarized accurately as a linear movement from a negative to a positive answer to an unchanging question. The history reflects instead an effort to maintain simultaneously both the universality of God's salvific will and what Francis Sullivan has expressed as "the belief that God has assigned to the church a necessary role in the accomplishment of his plan for the salvation of humanity."[44]

At various times in the course of history, one or the other of these poles (usually God's universal salvific will) has receded almost to the point of disappearance. The success of future efforts to address this question and related issues in the theology of religions may well depend on their ability to incorporate into their conceptions both of these important elements of the Church's faith.

---

[44] Sullivan, *Salvation Outside the Church?* 12; see also 204.

For Further Reading

Congar, Yves M.-J. "No Salvation Outside the Church?" *The Wide World My Parish: Salvation and Its Problems.* Baltimore: Helicon Press, 1961, pp. 93–154.

Conway, Eamonn. *The Anonymous Christian—A Relativised Christianity? An Evaluation of Hans Urs von Balthasar's Criticism of Karl Rahner's Theory of the Anonymous Christian.* Frankfurt: Peter Lang, 1993.

Rahner, Karl. *Theological Investigations.* Vols. 1, 5, 6, 12, 14, 16. New York: Crossroad. Articles on the salvation of non-Christians and anonymous Christianity.

Sullivan, Francis A. *Salvation Outside the Church? Tracing the History of the Catholic Response.* New York/Mahwah, N.J.: Paulist Press, 1992.

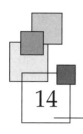

14

The Social Mission of the Church: Its Changing Context

T. Howland Sanks

When the Roman Catholic Church in solemn council declared that the Church was in solidarity with and in service to all humanity (GS 3), it was the culmination of almost one hundred years of teaching about the social mission of the Church. This is frequently noted as beginning with Pope Leo XIII's encyclical *Rerum novarum* (1891), but the roots of the self-understanding of the Church as having a mission in the social, political, and economic spheres to pursue justice and peace can be found very early in the Christian tradition, including both the Hebrew and Christian Scriptures. In this chapter, we will briefly review those roots, look at the modern development of this social mission, then examine some current examples. I will argue, with J. Bryan Hehir, that "'the right and competence' of the church to address political, legal, social, and economic issues is rooted in the nature of the church."[1] Finally, I will suggest that the social mission of the Church is always specified by its local social and historical context, but that this contextualization is now complicated by the phenomenon of globalization.

Scripture and Early Christianity

"Characteristic of all strands of Israel's traditions," says noted biblical scholar John R. Donahue, "is concern for the widow, the orphan, the poor and the sojourner in the land."[2] Citing Exodus, "You shall not

---

[1] J. Bryan Hehir, "The Right and Competence of the Church in the American Case," *One Hundred Years of Catholic Social Thought: Celebration and Challenge,* ed. John A. Coleman (Maryknoll, N.Y.: Orbis Books, 1991) 55.

[2] John R. Donahue, "Biblical Perspectives on Justice," *The Faith that Does Justice: Examining the Christian Sources for Social Change,* ed. John C. Haughey (New York: Paulist Press, 1977) 73.

wrong a stranger or oppress him. You shall not afflict any widow or orphan. If ever you wrong them and they cry out to me, I will surely hear their cry" (Exod 22:21-22), and Deuteronomy ". . . and also the alien, the orphan and the widow who belong to your community, may come and eat their fill; so that the LORD, your God, may bless you in all that you undertake" (Deut 14:29; 15:7). Donahue argues that this is not just a command to promote social harmony, but it is the nature of YHWH to be defender of the oppressed.

This same theme is found in the prophetic literature as represented by Amos, Jeremiah, and Isaiah. One of the strongest texts is Amos 5:21, 24:

> I hate, I spurn your feasts,
> I take no pleasure in your solemnities; . . .
> then let justice surge like water,
> and goodness like an unfailing stream.

And Jeremiah, "Thus says the LORD: Do what is right and just. Rescue the victim from the hand of his oppressor. Do not wrong or oppress the resident alien, the orphan, or the widow, and do not shed innocent blood in this place" (Jer 22:3). One of the strongest passages in the Old Testament for equating true religion with the doing of justice is the conclusion of the same passage:

> Woe to him who builds his house on wrong,
> his terraces on injustice;
> . . . .
> Did not your father eat and drink?
> He did what was right and just,
> and it went well with him.
> Because he dispensed justice to the weak and the poor,
> it went well with him.
> Is this not true knowledge of me?
> Says the LORD (Jer 22:13, 15-16).

Donahue concludes that the doing of justice is not just an application of religious faith, but its substance.[3] After acknowledging the differences between our social world and that of the Old Testament and the consequent need for interpretation, Donahue suggests that some constants remain: "The expression of religious faith by confrontation with the evils which destroy the social fabric of society is no new phenomenon but as old as the eighth-century prophets."[4]

[3] Ibid., 76.
[4] Ibid., 78.

Although the New Testament may not be as clear or strong as the Old Testament prophetic literature, the roots of the Church's social mission can be found there as well. In proclaiming the advent of the kingdom of God in his own ministry and mission, Jesus is also implying the advent of God's justice since the kingdom has all the overtones of establishing God's justice that it has in the Old Testament. Again, Donahue says, "The Kingdom and therefore the justice of God . . . are to be manifest in history no less than the proclaimer of the Kingdom, Jesus, was incarnate in history."[5] Further, by his actions, his table fellowship, and close association with sinners and tax collectors Jesus makes present the justice and mercy of God to those who were outcasts from the social structures of his time. Those he called to discipleship were also expected to continue his mission of compassion and mercy, of active involvement with their social world.

The scene of the final judgment as presented in Matt 25:31-46 indicates what is demanded of Jesus' followers, what justice is, but also where justice is to be located: in the neighbor. Donahue points out that Luke is the evangelist who is most interested in "social justice," and the Lukan Jesus is a prophet in the Old Testament model. In the Magnificat, "Jesus is proclaimed as the one who is to show the saving mercy and justice of God; he will put down the mighty and will exalt the lowly and fill the hungry with good things. This prophetic motif is taken up by Jesus in his inaugural sermon (Lk 4:18-19)."[6] The Gospel of Luke is also the most critical of wealth; wealth is portrayed as incompatible with the gospel.

Although it would be anachronistic to speak of the "social teaching" of the Fathers, issues concerning the origin, accumulation, and distribution of wealth continued in the early Church. After surveying the Fathers—from the Apostolic Fathers through the Cappadocians, Chrysostom, and Augustine—Justo L. Gonzalez concludes that "not one major Christian leader held that issues of faith and wealth should be kept separate."[7] They considered the Christians' relationship to and participation in the economic and social order to be part and parcel of following Jesus.

There were some themes that were constant throughout the patristic period and which we will see developed in the modern social teaching of the Church. There was general agreement that material goods in themselves were good since everything was created by God. Gonzalez

---

[5] Ibid., 87.

[6] Ibid., 106.

[7] Justo L. Gonzalez, *Faith and Wealth: A History of Early Christian Ideas on the Origin, Significance, and Use of Money* (San Francisco: Harper & Row, 1990) 225.

says that "in a church beset by gnostic notions about the evil of material creation, it was important to insist that all things, including those that are usually counted as wealth, are good."[8] It was not things in themselves but the unnecessary and superfluous accumulation and inordinate attachment to wealth that was evil.[9] Rather, the Christian should be detached from material goods since they all ultimately belong to God. Our ownership is only temporary; it always ends with death.[10] The wealthy only exercise stewardship of material goods.

Second, wealth is to be used for the good of all. A notion frequent among early theologians is that in creation God intended all things to be common, but that private property exists because of our fallen condition. Private property, according to Ambrose, is the result of usurpation. The Fathers do take the existence of private property for granted. However, they place drastic limitations on its use, though they differ on the criteria to determine proper use. Some thought that owners could only use what was necessary to meet their own needs; others argue that wealth should not be spent on useless things or for ostentation. The Fathers generally embraced the principle that wealth is meant to be shared and that the intended use of wealth is the common good.[11]

Hence, the necessity and obligation of almsgiving. If some were wealthy, it was in order that they might take care of others. As the Christian community grew in numbers and diversity, the commonality of goods extolled in Acts (though this may have lasted well into the second century) shifted to almsgiving. "By almsgiving, however, the writers of the first four centuries do not mean the practice of giving loose change to beggars. On the contrary, the criterion they most often use is that one should keep for oneself only what is necessary and give the superfluous to the needy."[12]

Part of the reasoning behind giving to the poor was the common theme of the identification of the poor with Christ. Matthew 25:31-46 was just as important a text for the Fathers as it is in our time for the liberation theologians.[13] John Chrysostom was particularly strong on this identification, going so far as to suggest that the rich should actually invite the poor to live in their homes, fixing up a room for them called

---

[8] Ibid., 226.
[9] Ibid.
[10] Ibid., 228.
[11] Ibid., 228–9.
[12] Ibid., 227.
[13] William J. Walsh and John P. Langan, "Patristic Social Consciousness: The Church and the Poor," *The Faith that Does Justice: Examining the Christian Sources for Social Change*, ed. John C. Haughey (New York: Paulist Press, 1977) 130.

Christ's cell.[14] Finally, the early Christian writers were unanimous in their condemnation of usury, which meant any loan on interest.[15]

It is important to emphasize that the early Church was not concerned with reforming the social structures of the Roman Empire. They did, however, think that followers of the Way should have different values and modes of behavior in the social and economic spheres of life than the surrounding pagan world. Hence, their teachings about material goods, wealth, its use, accumulation, and distribution were directed to other Christians. They did not understand Christianity to be merely a private or individual form of discipleship. Following Christ had social consequences and, hence, the Church had a social mission. The kingdom of God was their utopian symbol for a just and peaceful social order and their mission was to announce its presence, though not its fulfillment, among humans.

Modern Development of the Social Mission

It is not the purpose of this chapter to trace the entire historical development of the Church's self-understanding of its social mission, but we should note the context and the forces that occasioned its modern formulation. Foremost amongst these was the process of industrialization that took place, in England first and then on the continent, in the latter part of the eighteenth and nineteenth centuries. This was accompanied by a population explosion and a mass migration from rural areas to the newly expanding industrial cities. Josef L. Altholz comments that "the vast and rapid transformation from an agrarian to an industrial society dislocated traditional social relationships and produced an entirely new class, the urban proletariat. Rootless and restive, living at the level of bare subsistence, the proletariat was only superficially a part of the civilization of the age."[16]

Industrialization, of course, was driven by new developments in technology. As Paul Misner points out,

> The construction, purchase, and use of steam engines and iron forges, both dependent upon coal, gave the monied bourgeoisie and the rich nobility who did not disdain to do business with them a decisive breakthrough to societal power and influence. Henceforth two new industrial classes would take shape: those who owned the machines and

[14] Ibid., 132.

[15] Gonzalez, *Faith and Wealth*, 226.

[16] Josef L. Altholz, *The Churches in the Nineteenth Century* (New York: Bobbs-Merrill, 1967) 137.

those who worked them—the bourgeois entrepreneurs and the wage earners in their direct employ—capitalists and the laboring class.[17]

In this newly emerging system, factory workers labored for twelve- or fourteen-hour work days under brutal and pitiless conditions. Women and children were even worse off. It became not just a question of rich and poor as in early Christianity, but of a "newly dominant mode of production that . . . redounded to the benefit of the few . . . and to the social and economic decline or exploitation of a great number."[18] Thus did this new system provide the context for the so-called "labor question" or the "social question."

In the early phases of this process there was a variety of Christian responses to these conditions, most of them charitable but paternalistic. The St. Vincent de Paul Society, for example, founded in 1833 by Frederic Ozanam, was intended to be "exclusively charitable and spiritual" and to alleviate the needs of the poor and suffering, but not to initiate social reform.[19] Other forms of organization were formed not of or by the workers, but for them with similar charitable intentions. Traditional confraternities for explicitly religious purposes, when formed for members of a specific trade or skill, took on the features of the old trade corporations or guilds which had been suppressed in France in 1791. Some vocational groups formed fraternal or benevolent organizations which became labor organizations, such as the Fraternal Weavers and Spinners of Ghent (1857). A third form of outreach to workers was the *patronage*, an organization for the education and moral betterment of workers, best exemplified by Maurice Maignen in France. Finally, there were experiments with the so-called "Christian factory," such as the Harmel Freres of Val-des-Bois in France.[20] All of these types of organization were initiated by upper-class or aristocratic leadership and with explicitly religious sponsorship. For the most part they shared a "Romantic glorification of the Middle Ages" and the corporatist model of social unity and harmony. The Roman Catholic Church could not accept the emerging divisions along the new class lines.

The beginning labor organizations that did exist were socialist in orientation and very anticlerical. After the Revolution of 1848, the Church in France identified with the restoration of order in the political realm and the repression of workers' organizations. Misner observes

---

[17] Paul Misner, *Social Catholicism in Europe: From the Onset of Industrialization to the First World War* (New York: Crossroad, 1991) 25.

[18] Ibid., 39.

[19] Ibid., 59.

[20] Ibid., 123–6.

that "Anti-clericalism entered into a new phase and became inextricably connected with the self-image of the working class," and any possibility of a "Christian socialism" vanished. By the time the First International Workingmen's Association formed in London in 1864, Marxism in one form or another was the dominant ideology of the European working class.[21]

Only gradually did the leaders of the Catholic Church in Europe begin to see that the plight of the industrial proletariat was going to demand more than almsgiving and charitable works. One of the most influential precursors of Leo XIII was Wilhelm Emmanuel von Ketteler, bishop of Mainz from 1850 until 1877. Although his programmatic work *The Labor Problem and Christianity* (1864) still thought in terms of Christian charity and interclass cooperation, he began to recognize the need for some state intervention and, in 1869, endorsed the British trade-union model. He supported the demands of labor organizers for a substantial increase in wages to be gained by strikes if necessary, for reduction in work hours, for more days off (especially Sundays), and for the elimination of the need for women in factory work.[22]

As Catholic social thought progressed, so did the frustration of the factory workers. Strikes and riots proliferated. A series of them in March and April of 1886 "starting from the Liege region and spreading throughout industrialized Belgium, lent a new social urgency to the deliberations of the Congress of Liege in September of the same year," and strikes multiplied in Germany and Britain around 1890.[23] Thus, it was more than the gradual development of Catholic social thought that prompted Leo XIII to write *Rerum novarum*.

Rerum novarum

Although we have seen the roots of the Church's social mission in the beginnings of Christianity, *Rerum novarum* really does mark the beginning of its modern formulation. The primary concern of the encyclical is the condition of the worker—"the question of the hour." The "right and competence" of the Church to speak out on these issues of social justice is simply asserted since "no good solution to the problem can be found without recourse to religion and the Church" (RN 14).[24]

[21] Ibid., 114–6.

[22] Ibid., 142.

[23] Ibid., 191.

[24] References in the text are from Pope Leo XIII, *Rerum Novarum, Proclaiming Justice and Peace: Papal Documents from* Rerum Novarum *through* Centesimus Annus, ed. Michael Walsh and Brian Davies (Mystic, Conn.: Twenty-Third Publications, 1991).

The Pope feels it is his responsibility to speak out: "continued silence on our part would be seen as neglect of duty." The Church's mission is, drawing on the gospel, to set out the principles which should govern a solution. But, further, "Not content with merely pointing out the way to set things right, the Church herself takes reform in hand" (RN 26). Still the emphasis is on the Church's teaching mission in social matters.

Briefly summarized, the major themes of the encyclical are: the condemnation of socialism (RN 3, 12, 13); affirmation of the absolute right to private property rooted in nature (RN 5–8, 47); rights and obligations of both property owners and the unpropertied workers (RN 17–20); the right of workers to form "associations," but preferably including employers and exclusively Catholic (RN 48–53); the limited right and necessity of state intervention, but only to the extent necessary, an adumbration of the principle of subsidiarity (RN 33–7); the desire that the classes gradually come closer together (RN 47); that all material goods are for the common good of all members of society (RN 20–2); the call for a "just wage" for workers in keeping with their basic human dignity (RN 45); God's preference for the poor and weak (RN 23).

The earlier paternalism is still echoed in the encyclical as the Pope praises those "eminent men" who have taken up the workers' cause (RN 54), and there is a harkening back to the medieval guild system (RN 48). There is also a frank recognition of the Church's loss of the working class, noting that many workers "now either altogether despise the Christian faith or live contrary to its requirements" (RN 58.1).

Reaction to the encyclical varied. Altholz remarks that "contemporaries were impressed, even stunned, by the vigor with which Leo proclaimed the need for justice for the working class. He had clearly rejected the doctrine of laissez-faire and asserted the propriety of state intervention in the economic sphere."[25] More recently, David O'Brien opines that "it was a reformist, not a radical document . . . evenhandedly condemning both socialism and laissez-faire liberalism."[26] It was also, as O'Brien and others remark, a document of the Ultramontane church. The Pope wanted Catholics to participate in Catholic organizations under clerical control, and winning workers for the Church was as important as defending their rights. Nonetheless, *Rerum novarum* marks a new understanding of the Church's mission in the social order.

Concerned as was the early Church with the use and distribution of wealth, now avarice and greed are understood as stemming not only

---

[25] Altholz, *The Churches in the Nineteenth Century*, 152.

[26] David J. O'Brien, "A Century of Catholic Social Teaching: Contexts and Comments," *One Hundred Years of Catholic Social Thought: Celebration and Challenge*, ed. John A. Coleman (Maryknoll, N.Y.: Orbis Books, 1991) 16–17.

from the sinfulness of individuals but from the new economic system itself. It is the structure which is causing the conditions of the working poor. And almsgiving, Christian charity, will not of itself remedy the situation. It is a matter of justice and structural reform. The Church must teach the Christian principles that should guide such reform, but also help to initiate it by founding appropriate institutions.

From *Rerum novarum* to Vatican II

Between 1891 and the Second Vatican Council the understanding of the Church's social mission was further developed and clarified in the great social encyclicals. It is not our purpose to survey all these documents, but let us point out some themes that continue and some significant developments.

Forty years later, Pope Pius XI commemorated the publication of *Rerum novarum,* calling it the Magna Carta on which "all Christian activity in the social field ought to be based" (QA 39).[27] By 1931, the political and economic situation had changed considerably. The world was in the midst of a worldwide depression and liberal capitalism seemed a complete failure. Russia had become the Soviet Union and was an existing example of a socialist-communist state. Now the "question of the hour" was not so much the condition of workers, but the real alternative and threat to the ideal of a Christian social order posed by Communism. The socialism so strongly condemned in *Rerum novarum* had split into two sections—the violent one of Communism which had "laid waste vast regions of eastern Europe and Asia" (QA 112), and a more moderate Socialism "which inclines toward and in a certain measure approaches the truths which Christian tradition has always held sacred" (QA 113). Nonetheless, both are inimical to Christian teaching. Pius XI continues to defend the right to ownership of private property but acknowledges not only individual ownership but also social ownership for the common good (QA 45–9).

Although *Rerum novarum* had said that the state should not "swallow up either the individual or the family" (RN 37), the principle of subsidiarity was first clearly stated in *Quadragesimo anno* (QA 79–80). This has remained a fundamental principle of Catholic social teaching, although the Church has been reluctant to apply it internally. Pius XI follows his predecessor in urging those in the same industry or profession to "form guilds or associations" and avoid forming separate classes divided into "battle lines" (QA 83–8).

[27] References in the text are from the version of *Quadragesimo anno* in *Proclaiming Justice and Peace.*

The Pope also points out changes that have occurred since 1891—the "'capitalist' economic regime has spread everywhere" and is pervading economic and social life even beyond its own orbit (QA 103), and there has been a concentration of "immense power and despotic economic dictatorship . . . consolidated in the hands of a few" (QA 105). The other significant change, already mentioned, was the rise of actually existing Communist states.

O'Brien observes that "the keynote of *Quadragesimo anno* was *social justice*, a term introduced in this document and specifying the directive principle of social institutions, not competition but the common good."[28] Another significant difference was that in *Quadragesimo anno* the Pope had to argue, not merely assert, the right and duty of the Church to speak on economic and social matters. He based this on the "duty of disseminating and interpreting the whole moral law" from which the economic order is not distinct or alien (QA 41–3). O'Brien comments that both popes, Leo XIII and Pius XI, "saw and denounced the rampant inequalities of modern life, but never made their own the idea that ordinary people have the right to share responsibility for the life of their communities." They played a critical but not a constructive role.[29]

The context and situation were quite different when the next major developments in the Church's understanding of its social mission were articulated by Pope John XXIII in his two major social encyclicals, *Mater et magistra* (1961) and *Pacem in terris* (1963). The communist world—the Soviet Union, Eastern Europe, and China—were engaged in a Cold War with the democratic West. The nuclear age and the age of space exploration had dawned. The problems in the social, political, and economic arenas which the Church faced were no longer only those of industrialized Western Europe. These two encyclicals constitute a marked break with the past and are the background for *Gaudium et spes*.

The most outstanding characteristic of these two encyclicals is their international perspective. The "social questions" are not merely between labor and capital, nor between individuals and corporations or individuals and states, but the problems are worldwide, between state and state, and concern the whole human community. Pope John XXIII understood himself to be the "father of all peoples" (MM 158; PT 117)[30] and the Church to be the "Mother and teacher of all nations." The Church's concern for human temporal welfare and prosperity is based, not only on the moral law, but on the teaching of and imitation of Christ

[28] O'Brien, "A Century of Catholic Social Teaching," 19.

[29] Ibid., 21.

[30] References in the text are from the versions of *Mater et magistra* and *Pacem in terris* in *Proclaiming Justice and Peace*.

himself who "multiplied bread to alleviate the hunger of the crowds" (MM 3–4).

Although John XXIII continues the teaching of his predecessors concerning the right to private ownership of property (MM 109, 121; PT 21), the just and living wage (MM 71), and the principle of subsidiarity (MM 53, 152), the primary focus of both encyclicals is on the international problems caused by recent developments—discovery of nuclear energy, lack of balance between agriculture and industry in the economy, the disparity of wealth possessed by different countries, and the end of colonialism and the political independence of peoples of Asia and Africa (MM 47–50).

Mater et magistra says that "probably the most difficult problem today concerns the relationship between political communities that are economically advanced and those in the process of development" (MM 157). It also calls for the collaboration and cooperation among nations to eliminate these discrepancies. This is based on the solidarity of the human race, "which binds all men together as members of a common family." This theme of the interdependence of nations, the need for them to work together, is cited in dealing with the population problem and the need for international aid (MM 161ff., 185ff.).

Pacem in terris focuses on human rights (PT 11–20), but also on the rights and duties of nations (PT 91–2). Attention is given to the rights of ethnic minorities (PT 94–5) and the rights of refugees (PT 103–5). Repeatedly, the Pope speaks about the "common good of the entire human family" and the universal common good (PT 98, 100). He also applies the principle of subsidiarity to the relations between the public authority of the world community and that of individual nations (PT 140). In pursuing this universal common good, John XXIII explicitly encouraged Catholics to cooperate with other Christians and even non-Christians who are "reasonable men, men of moral integrity" (PT 157) —a far cry from Leo XIII. These themes from John XXIII's two encyclicals greatly influenced the Second Vatican Council's Pastoral Constitution on the Church in the Modern World, *Gaudium et spes.*

Gaudium et spes

The social mission of the Church took stage front and center at Vatican II. Though not included in the preparatory schema drafted before the council, this document, under the leadership of Cardinal Suenens, emerged from the council floor and went through a series of revisions before being finally approved at the last session in 1965. It was intended to complement the Dogmatic Constitution on the Church, *Lumen gentium,* which dealt with the Church *ad intra* by treating the Church *ad extra,* or in relation to the world.

In keeping with the international perspective of John XXIII, this document is addressed to the whole of humanity and expresses the Church's "solidarity with the entire human family" (GS 2, 3, 10).[31] The Church's purpose is "to foster the brotherhood of all men" in keeping with the work of Christ himself who "entered this world to give witness to the truth, to rescue and not to sit in judgment, to serve and not to be served" (GS 3). The Church is in service to all humanity because it continues the mission of Christ himself. Thus, the Church's social mission is rooted in its very nature as the body of Christ continuing his work.

In describing "The Situation of Men in the Modern World," the council recognizes the Church's "duty of scrutinizing the signs of the times," a phrase frequently used by John XXIII. The council acknowledges a true social and cultural transformation and that science and technology have transformed the face of the earth. It asserts that the "destiny of the human community has become all of a piece" and "has passed from a rather static concept of reality to a more dynamic, evolutionary one" (GS 5).

Among the changes that have taken place in the world, the council notes the spread of the industrial type of society leading some nations to great affluence, and the increase in urban living. There is frequent mention of increased social bonds among humans and of the interdependence of humans on one another and on society (GS 23–5). As a result of this interdependence, the common good "takes on an increasingly universal complexion and consequently involves rights and duties with respect to the whole human race" (GS 26). This notion of a single world community, of human solidarity, pervades the document and is one of the most significant developments in the Church's understanding of its social mission.

The council further argues that "merely individualistic morality" is no longer sufficient. Because of the solidarity of the human race, one must "count social necessities among the primary duties of modern man" and seek to become "artisans of a new humanity" (GS 30). Chapter III recognizes the "autonomy of earthly affairs . . . which enjoy their own laws and values," and therefore genuine scientific investigation "never truly conflicts with faith" (GS 36). Although the council carefully distinguishes earthly progress from the growth of the kingdom, "Nevertheless, to the extent that the former can contribute to the

[31] References in the text are to the version of *Gaudium et spes* in *The Documents of Vatican II,* ed. Walter M. Abbott (New York: Crossroad, 1989).

better ordering of human society, it is of vital concern to the kingdom of God" (GS 39).

The council, thus, clarifies the Church-world relationship. The Church "serves as a leaven and as a kind of soul for human society" (GS 40). Though the Church has "no proper mission in the political, economic, or social order," nevertheless from her religious mission comes a "function, a light, and an energy which can serve to structure and consolidate the human community according to the divine law." In certain circumstances the Church "can and indeed should initiate activities on behalf of all men," particularly the needy (GS 42). At the same time, the council makes clear that "in virtue of her mission and nature, she is bound to no particular form of human culture, nor to any political, economic, or social system." The council thus walks a fine line between describing the mission of the Church as a religious one and encouraging the pursuit of a just social order as a consequence of the gospel spirit.

The relationship, however, is not only *from* the Church *to* the world —"the Church herself knows how richly she has profited by the history and development of humanity," even "from the antagonism of those who oppose or persecute her" (GS 44). Thus, the Church-world relationship is one of dialogue and mutual cooperation. The Church recognizes itself as embedded in the world and the world is embedded in the Church. The alienation of the Church from the modern world, so characteristic of the nineteenth and early twentieth centuries, is over and the right and competence of the Church to speak for and actively promote a just social order is well established. Popes Paul VI and John Paul II can speak in their social encyclicals with the whole Church behind them.

After the Council

Fifteen months after the council, Pope Paul VI, continuing his predecessors' and the council's concern with justice in the international social order, issued his encyclical *Populorum progressio* (1967). Its focus is on the disparity and inequality between rich and poor nations, not merely on the rights and obligations of individuals. The obligations, based on the "human and supernatural brotherhood of man," fall foremost on the wealthy nations. They are obliged to provide mutual solidarity, social justice in trade relations, and universal charity (PP 44).[32] But the development of all peoples is not just a matter of economic growth alone—"To be authentic, it must be well rounded; it must foster

---

[32] Citations in the text are based on the version in *Proclaiming Justice and Peace.*

the development of each man and of the whole man" (PP 14–21). The pope, citing Pius XI, condemns the evil consequences of unbridled liberal capitalism but also the "dangers of a planned economy which might threaten human liberty" (PP 33). He calls for mutual cooperation among nations based on their equal dignity. He condemns two "major obstacles to the creation of a more just social order and world solidarity: nationalism and racism" (PP 62). Paul VI addressed his appeal to Catholics, other Christians, and, finally, to all men of good will.

The social mission of the Church in the modern world was confirmed again by the 1971 meeting of the Synod of Bishops on the topic of "Justice in the World." In one of the strongest statements on the theological basis for this social mission, the synod said, "Action on behalf of justice and participation in the transformation of the world fully appear to us as a constitutive dimension of the preaching of the gospel, or, in other words, of the Church's mission for the redemption of the human race and its liberation from every oppressive situation" (JW 6).[33] The Church's "right, indeed the duty, to proclaim justice on the social, national and international level, and to denounce injustice" is based on the mission the Church received from Christ to preach the gospel message which includes "universal brotherhood and a consequent demand for justice in the world" (JW 36). The document uses the language of the "liberation of the oppressed," apparently influenced by the teaching of the bishops of CELAM II at Medellín in 1968. Also, for the first time the synod speaks of justice within the Church itself, examining its "modes of acting and [of] the possessions and life-style" and calling for the participation of laypersons, especially women, in the administration and decision making in the Church (JW 40–6).

Since John Paul II was elected pope in 1978, he has issued a series of encyclicals on the social mission of the Church, most notably *Laborem exercens* (1981), *Sollicitudo rei socialis* (1987), and *Centesimus annus* (1991), the last to commemorate the hundredth anniversary of *Rerum novarum*. Since this last encyclical touches all the themes of the others, we will deal only with it, and briefly. It also summarizes the continuity and development of the Church's social teaching over the century since 1891.

The encyclical looks back to *Rerum novarum*, looks around at the "new things" of our own time, and looks to the future of the already glimpsed third millennium (CA 3). In Leo XIII's time the "right and duty" of the Church to speak out on social issues was "far from being commonly admitted," but today the "validity of the approach" can be assumed (CA 5). Then, the social question was the "condition of the worker," but today "the center of the social question [has shifted] from

[33] Citations in the text are from *Proclaiming Justice and Peace*.

the national to the international level" (CA 21). Then, the type of private property considered was primarily land and later accumulated capital, but "today the decisive factor is increasingly man himself, that is, his knowledge, especially his scientific knowledge, his capacity for interrelated and compact organization as well as his ability to perceive the needs of others and satisfy them" (CA 32).

The pope reemphasizes the principle of subsidiarity but adds the principle of solidarity which he had developed at greater length in *Sollicitudo rei socialis* (CA 10, 15). He considers the collapse of communism in Eastern Europe to be a vindication of Leo XIII's earlier condemnation of socialism (CA 12). But those social ideologies which sought to respond to Marxism, such as the national security state or the consumer society, are equally unacceptable (CA 19). One of the consequences of the fall of Marxism has been the highlighting of the interdependence among peoples (CA 27). The Pope reiterates the right to private ownership as well as the limits on its use proposed by his predecessors (CA 30), but in our time "there exists another form of ownership which is becoming no less important than land: the possession of know-how, technology and skill" (CA 32). The encyclical is concerned with the problem of poverty and underdevelopment in the Third World and the issue of the foreign debt of the poorer nations, suggesting that the burden needs to be lightened or even canceled (CA 35). In connection with the "responsibilities and dangers" in our phase of history, the Pope points to consumerism and the ecological question (CA 36–8).

While the encyclical rejoices in the collapse of Marxist socialism, it does not give unequivocal approval to an unbridled free market economy (CA 42–3). Indeed, it is very specific in asserting that the "church has no models to present," but that the appropriate models "can only arise within the framework of different historical situations" (CA 43). The Church, however, "values the democratic system" and the balance of powers (CA 44–7). Finally, it should be noted that John Paul II uses the term "preferential option for the poor" several times. Although he cites his own previous use of the term, the term itself originated with the Puebla documents of 1979, indicating their influence on his thinking.

It should be clear from this survey of the official Church's understanding of its social mission that there has been both continuity and development. As the context has changed so has the social teaching, for there are always "new things." Principles that emerged in particular contexts, such as the principle of subsidiarity, have been extended even to the international situation, and new principles, such as the principle of solidarity, have developed. The right and duty of the Church to speak on social, political, and economic matters has been affirmed by an ecumenical council and is firmly established in the Catholic tradition. But how that social mission is concretized always depends on specific historical and cultural contexts. We will briefly examine three different situations.

Reading the Signs of the Times Today

Since Vatican II, we take it for granted that "scrutinizing the signs of the times" is an ongoing and continuous task. Social and cultural contexts are dynamic, constantly and rapidly changing. Sometimes these changes are sudden and dramatic, as in the case of the collapse of communism in Central and Eastern Europe or the end of apartheid in South Africa. Other times the changes are gradual, subtle, and more difficult to discern, as with the recent process of globalization. The Christian community must be ever on the alert to adapt its social mission to the changing contexts, always guided by the principles developed over the past century. I want to briefly illustrate how this has been happening in three diverse contexts—Latin America, South Africa, and the United States.

Latin America

By the end of the Second Vatican Council, the Latin American bishops realized that the social, historical, and cultural context of their continent was quite different from the situation of the Church in Western Europe which had shaped much of the agenda of the council. In Latin America, they were concerned not with the *nonbeliever*, but with the *nonperson*.[34] When they convened for the second meeting of the Council of Latin American Episcopacies (CELAM) in Medellín in 1968, they analyzed their situation in terms of massive poverty and oppression. At that time on the continent, most countries were under repressive military regimes. They were class-structured societies with a wide gap between the elite or oligarchy and the vast majority of the people and almost no middle class. A small percentage of the population controlled the vast majority of the land and invested wealth. Some countries had large indigenous populations that were exploited and/or ignored, treated as less than human. The economies of most countries were dependent on the fluctuation of prices of raw materials they exported. Decisions were made by multinational corporations in the First World that determined their fate and their future.

---

[34] Gustavo Gutiérrez, *The Power of the Poor in History* (Maryknoll, N.Y.: Orbis Books, 1983) 57.

The bishops at Medellín recognized that the Church on that continent had been identified for centuries with the upper classes and had neglected the poor who were the vast majority. Hence, they called for the Church to focus its mission and ministry on the poor. Guided by some liberation theologians such as Gustavo Gutiérrez and using some Marxist analysis and the dependency theory then in vogue, Medellín saw the mission of the Church as striving for "integral human development and liberation." The "Document on Justice" said "We do not confuse temporal progress and the kingdom of Christ; nevertheless, the former 'to the extent that it can contribute to the better ordering of human society, is of vital concern to the kingdom of God,'" and, "In the search for salvation we must avoid the dualism which separates temporal tasks from the work of sanctification."[35] In this view, the social mission of the Church is integral and essential to its overall mission—witnessing to and building up of the kingdom of God. Granted that the coming of the kingdom is always a gift of God and is ultimately eschatological, nonetheless human work for the kingdom in the here and now is a necessary but insufficient condition for its coming.

The third CELAM conference in Puebla (1979) specified the Church's mission further by professing the "preferential option for the poor."[36] The "poor" were not just those without material goods, but all the marginalized, the voiceless, those who were not subjects of their own history. In short, as Gustavo Gutiérrez put it, "The poor are those who die before their time." This pervasive extreme poverty, the bishops said, "is not a passing phase. Instead it is the product of economic, social, and political situations and structures . . . and calls for personal conversion and profound structural changes. . . ."[37] The underdevelopment of the continent of Latin America was also seen as due to "the exploitation caused by the organizational systems governing economics and international politics . . . which can grow worse and even become permanent."[38] Thus, the "social question" with which the church in Latin America must deal is also an international issue. The universalization

[35] Second General Conference of Latin American Bishops, "The Church in the Present-Day Transformation of Latin America in the Light of the Council," *Liberation Theology: A Documentary History*, ed. Alfred T. Hennelly (Maryknoll, N.Y.: Orbis Books, 1990) 99.

[36] "Evangelization in Latin America," Final Document of the Third General Conference of the Latin American Episcopate, *Puebla and Beyond: Documentation and Commentary*, ed. John Eagleson and Philip Scharper (Maryknoll, N.Y.: Orbis Books, 1979) 264–7.

[37] Ibid., 128.

[38] Ibid., 279.

of the Church's social mission which we saw began with John XXIII continues even in a particular regional context.

By the time of the fourth general meeting of CELAM in Santo Domingo in 1992, the political, social, and economic situation in Latin America had changed. Politically it had changed for the better since the military regimes in the majority of Latin American countries had been replaced by at least formal democracies between 1979 and 1990. The murder, torture, and disappearances that had terrorized the population ended. The civil wars in Nicaragua, El Salvador, and Guatemala were over. Economically, however, the situation worsened. The bishops wrote: "The growing impoverishment in which millions of our brothers and sisters are plunged—to the point where it is reaching intolerable extremes of misery—is the cruelest and most crushing scourge that Latin America and the Caribbean are enduring" (nn. 179–80).[39] Thus, the conference reaffirmed the preferential option for the poor of Medellín and Puebla (180, 296).

Among the "new signs of the times" the conference noted an increased awareness of human rights and their violations among the poorest groups in society, especially small farmers, indigenous people, and African Americans (164–8); greater attention to the gravity of the ecological crisis (169–70); the tenure, administration, and utilization of the land in Latin America and the Caribbean (174–7); the prevalence of neoliberal policies which have widened the gap between rich and poor (179–81); the continuing importance of the dignity of work (182–5); the sharp increase in migration both to the North and within the continent (186–9); the deterioration in some countries of a democratic common life (190–3); the tendency to absolutize the free market economy and the problem of the foreign debt (194–203); and, finally, the need for greater integration, interdependence, and solidarity of the Latin American nations (204–9). In addition, they noted the problems associated with increased and rapid urbanization. All of these are issues which the Church's social mission should address.

Perhaps because these social, economic, and political issues were integrated within the overall theme of the conference, the "new evangelization," or perhaps because the meeting was so dominated by the Vatican, the clarion call of Medellín for the Church to identify with and act in solidarity with the poor seemed muffled in the laundry list of Santo Domingo. The social mission of the Church was not as clear in 1992 as it had seemed in 1968.

[39] Citations in the text are from "Conclusions: New Evangelization, Human Development, Christian Culture," *Santo Domingo and Beyond: Documents and Commentaries from the Fourth General Conference of Latin American Bishops,* ed. Alfred T. Hennelly (Maryknoll, N.Y.: Orbis Books, 1993).

Today, the conditions that gave rise to the preferential option for the poor at Medellín remain, but it is not clear what actions the Church should take to implement that commitment. Speaking about the current state of liberation theology which had been the guiding voice at Medellín and Puebla, Robert Schreiter, an astute observer of the Latin American scene, suggests that there is need for a new social analysis that does not place such a heavy emphasis on the external factors such as global capitalism, the United States, or the IMF, but looks at the internal factors that can account for the poor voting for the right, the growth of Pentecostalism, and the materialism and consumerism of the youth.[40] Citing others, he also suggests that "this is not a time for grand visions. One should concentrate instead upon building up the intermediate structures of society, strengthening neighborhoods, urban zones, trade unions, and political parties."[41] In countries like Peru and El Salvador, the Church must contribute to the reconstruction of civil society by fostering mediating structures like clubs, associations, and voluntary organizations. In Lima, such organizations as *clubes de madres, comedores populares,* and *Vaso de Leche,* led mostly by poor women, are bringing the Church's social mission to life on a more local level. Thus, the principles of subsidiarity and solidarity are being implemented in the present juncture. In any case, it should be clear that as the social, economic, and political situation in Latin America has changed over the past thirty years, so has the social mission of the Church. Reading the signs of the times is an ongoing necessity.

South Africa

The church in South Africa provides a clear and dramatic example of how the social mission changes as the context changes. The state system of apartheid established in 1948 was a clear case of the oppression of the black majority by the white minority. It was denounced as a sin and a heresy by the Christian churches. Under such a regime, the social mission of the Church was clearly one of denunciation and resistance. A prophetic stance was called for. This was vividly expressed by a group of 150 theologians in *The Kairos Document: Challenge to the Church* (1985). They wrote:

> The time has come. The moment of truth has arrived. South Africa has been plunged into a crisis that is shaking the foundations and there is

---

[40] Robert J. Schreiter, *The New Catholicity: Theology between the Global and the Local* (Maryknoll, N.Y.: Orbis Books, 1997) 106.

[41] Ibid., 108.

> every indication that the crisis has only just begun and that it will
> deepen and become even more threatening in the months to come. It is
> the *kairos* or moment of truth not only for apartheid but also for the
> Church and all other faiths and religions.[42]

They called for a prophetic theology that would include a reading of
the signs of the times, a call for repentance, conversion, and change, as
well as to announce hope for the future.[43] "Either we have full and
equal justice for all or we don't. . . . Prophetic theology therefore faces
us with this fundamental choice that admits of no compromise."[44]

The Kairos Document was a version of liberation theology; it used the
biblical language of oppressor and oppressed. Like Medellín, it was a
clear prophetic denunciation of an unjust social and political structure.
The social mission of the churches (it was an ecumenical effort) was
clearly that of resistance in a variety of forms, such as boycotts, economic pressure, and civil disobedience.

When the South African government in a major policy reversal,
under the leadership of President F. W. De Klerk and the inspiration of
Nelson Mandela, began to dismantle the structure of apartheid in 1990
and began negotiations for a new constitution leading to free elections
in 1994, the whole social, political, and cultural context changed
rapidly and dramatically. The churches, under such leaders as Archbishop Desmond Tutu and Archbishop Denis E. Hurley of Durban, had
contributed significantly to the change. Now, the churches had to re-
define their social mission.

Like the church in Latin America, though more suddenly, the church
or churches in South Africa currently find the social mission less clearly
defined or definable. According to theologian Charles Villa-Vincencio:
"The challenge now facing the church is different. The complex options
for a new South Africa require more than resistance. The church is
obliged to begin the difficult task of saying 'Yes' to the unfolding process of what could culminate in a democratic, just and kinder social
order."[45] He believes it is the essence of the theological contribution to
social reconstruction to "keep alive a social vision of what society ought
to become," while not allowing theology to be used for "sectarian political purposes" as has happened so often in the past.[46] The churches

[42] *Kairos: Three Prophetic Challenges to the Church,* ed. Robert McAfee Brown
(Grand Rapids, Mich.: Eerdmans, 1990) 26.

[43] Ibid., 49–50.

[44] Ibid., 54.

[45] Charles Villa-Vincencio, *A Theology of Reconstruction: Nation Building and Human
Rights* (Cambridge: Cambridge University Press, 1992) 7.

[46] Ibid., 13, 20.

must develop a theology of reconstruction and he suggests a postexilic church is a good metaphor for the current situation.

The Special Assembly for Africa of the Synod of Bishops held in Rome in 1994, speaking now not only of South Africa, rejoiced in the democratic process that has begun in many countries (especially in South Africa) and encouraged "all Christians who are so gifted to become engaged in the political field, and we invite all without exception to educate themselves for democracy."[47] Education for the common good as well as respect for pluralism is a pastoral priority for our time, they said. Directing their remarks to the Northern Hemisphere, the synod also called for a halt to arms sales to groups in conflict in Africa and asked for "at least a substantial, if not a total, remission of debt" and the "formation of a more just international economic order."[48] It should be clear again that the changing social context calls forth a changing social mission of the Church. It is also clear that achieving social justice in South Africa involves a more just international economic order.

United States

In the United States, the changing understanding of the Church's social mission has been due not only to the changing social, political, and economic context, but also to the changing social location of the Catholic Church in the United States. Predominantly an immigrant and outsider Church in the nineteenth century, it was preoccupied with the preservation of the faith and the adaptation of its people to the Protestant host culture. But early in the twentieth century, under the leadership of Fr. John A. Ryan, the Church began to adapt and apply the teachings of *Rerum novarum* to the U.S. scene. American Catholic historian Jay Dolan notes:

> The genius of Ryan was his ability to merge Catholic social thought with the American current of reform. The basis for this merger was the natural law tradition. . . . From this basic principle of the natural law flowed Ryan's emphasis on a living wage, the importance of labor unions, and the need of the state to intervene and effect change in the social order.[49]

---

[47] "Message of the Synod," *The African Synod: Documents, Reflections, Perspectives,* comp. and ed. the Africa Faith and Justice Network (Maryknoll, N.Y.: Orbis Books, 1996) 79.

[48] Ibid., 81.

[49] Jay P. Dolan, *The American Catholic Experience: A History from Colonial Times to the Present* (New York: Doubleday, 1985) 343.

Ryan's thought was embraced by the American hierarchy in their "Bishops' Program of Social Reconstruction" published by the National Catholic Welfare Council in 1919. Ryan became head of the Social Action Department of the NCWC and, during the 1930s, "a cheerleader for Roosevelt and the New Deal." He continued his leadership of the Catholic "social gospel" until his death in 1945.[50] Thus, the social mission of the Catholic church in the United States was very much in line with *Rerum novarum* and *Quadragesimo anno*. It was primarily educational and implemented by a series of National Catholic Social Action Conferences and labor schools involving a large number of laity.

Without tracing the whole history of the Catholic Church in the United States, World War II was a watershed for its social location in U.S. society. After the war, the Church moved into the mainstream of the culture, with a boom in population and a rapid rise in its educational and economic level. It became a middle-class Church, self-confident and expansive.[51] Its articulation of its place in American society was epitomized by the work of John Courtney Murray who made, according to historian David O'Brien, "the most important contribution to clarifying the public responsibilities of the American church since the work of John A. Ryan."[52] Murray focused on issues of Church and state, believing that the "American proposition" of equality, inalienable rights, and limited government was quite compatible with Catholic social teaching. Religious liberty, rather than the more traditional teaching of the establishment of the Catholic religion wherever possible, proved, in the American experience, to be beneficial to the Church. After considerable opposition in the 1950s and early '60s, his position was vindicated by Vatican II's Declaration on Religious Freedom (1965).

Also in the 1960s and '70s, the Church was involved in the civil rights crusade, the peace movement, and the war on poverty. Priests, nuns, and laity all participated, along with Protestants and Jews, in marches in Selma, Washington, and Chicago. The bishops supported President Johnson's War on Poverty in 1965, and the following year launched their own Campaign for Human Development.[53] Partly as a result of the peace movement and partly because of the escalating nuclear arms race, the Catholic bishops issued a major pastoral letter in 1983, *The Challenge of Peace: God's Promise and Our Response*. By introducing moral analysis into the discussion of nuclear strategies, the pas-

---

[50] Ibid., 402.

[51] Wade Clark Roof and William McKinney, *American Mainline Religion: Its Changing Shape and Future* (New Brunswick, N.J.: Rutgers University Press, 1987) 15–16.

[52] David O'Brien, *Public Catholicism* (New York: Macmillan, 1989) 225.

[53] Ibid., 237ff.

toral letter had a major impact on policy discussions in the United States.

A similar letter in 1986, *Economic Justice for All*, introduced moral issues into discussions of the U.S. economy and, again, provoked widespread responses, including some from conservative lay Catholics who disagreed with the bishops' positions. Once again, they disputed the bishops' right and duty to speak on such matters. The message and significance of these two pastoral letters was recalled by similar statements on the tenth anniversary of the respective letters. Commemorating *The Challenge of Peace*, the bishops said, "The 'challenge of peace' today is different, but no less urgent. Although the nuclear threat is not as imminent, international injustice, bloody regional wars and a lethal conventional arms trade are continuing signs that the world is still marked by pervasive violence and conflict."[54] A similar statement on the tenth anniversary of the pastoral on the economy noted that the moral dimensions apply now to the global economy.[55] Thus, the social mission of the church in the United States continues to develop with the changing context.

Globalization

The three examples above illustrate how the social mission of the Church is always specified or concretized by the local—regional or national—context in which it is carried out. But concomitant with this localization of the social mission has been its increasing internationalization and the interdependence of regional churches. The Latin American churches have made it clear that their situation of massive poverty and oppression is due *in part* to decisions made by governments and multinationals in the Northern Hemisphere. Apartheid in South Africa was dismantled *in part* due to the economic and social boycott of the free world democracies. And in the United States, our free market economy and technological and cultural hegemony help or hinder social justice around the world.

In recent years this phenomenon has been referred to as "globalization." "Globalization as a concept refers both to the compression of the world and the intensification of consciousness of the world as whole."[56]

---

[54] "The Harvest of Justice Is Sown in Peace," *Origins* 23:26 (December 9, 1993) 451.

[55] "A Catholic Framework for Economic Life," *Origins* 26:23 (November 21, 1996) 370–1.

[56] Roland Robertson, *Globalization: Social Theory and Global Culture* (London: Sage Publications, 1992) 8.

The phenomenon is perhaps most obvious in the economic sphere, but it is increasingly manifested in the political, cultural, and social domains. Schreiter suggests three major contributing factors: the move from a dipolar political arrangement (Soviet Union–United States) to a multipolar political world, the global spread of neoliberal capitalism, and new communication technologies.[57] It has resulted in the extension of the effects of modernity throughout the entire world, e.g., modern science and medicine are global, as well as the compression of our sense of time and space (by some estimates, if space is measured by time, the world is now one-fifth the size it was in 1900).

Our purpose here is not to elaborate all the implications of the phenomenon of globalization, but merely its effects on the Church's social mission. Basically, it means that the pursuit of justice and peace will have to be carried out amidst the interplay of the local and the global, of the particular and the universal. Robertson argues that in the late twentieth century we are in a "massive, twofold process involving the *interpenetration of the universalization of particularism and the particularization of universalism.*"[58] Both things are happening concomitantly. As we saw with the Synod on Africa, social justice on that continent demands a change in the international economic order, and any change in the international economic order effects the possibility of social justice there, or not. Further, it implies that the free market economic model, as it spreads globally, will be particularized, that is, it will take a different form in Latin America than in the United States. It may also happen, as it did at the 1997 Synod of the Americas, that bishops from Latin America and bishops from North America will have a similar moral evaluation of neoliberalism. Thus, the carrying out of the social mission of the Church in any one locale will entail the cooperation and collaboration of other particular churches. The particular social missions will give rise, perhaps, to a new universal social mission.

Summary

As we have seen that from its inception, the Church has understood itself to have a mission to pursue peace and justice in all spheres of human activity because it must continue the mission of Jesus, the preaching of and witnessing to the kingdom of God. Its understanding of this mission has developed over the centuries and has come to fuller development in the last one hundred years or so, culminating in the

[57] Schreiter, *The New Catholicity*, 5–8.
[58] Robertson, *Globalization*, 100.

Constitution on the Church in the Modern World of Vatican II. Recent popes and synods have seen this social mission as directed to all humanity, non-Christian as well as Christian. That mission, however, is always made specific by the particular social and historical context in which it is carried out, as we have seen in some examples. Today, that particularization is complemented and complicated by the phenomenon of globalization. Among all the historical developments and local specifications, the Church continues to follow the injunction to care for the widow, the orphan, and the stranger, to feed the hungry, clothe the naked, and shelter the homeless. It is constitutive of the Church's life as the People of God.

For Further Reading

Coleman, John A., ed. *One Hundred Years of Catholic Social Thought.* Maryknoll, N.Y.: Orbis Books, 1991.

O'Brien, David. *Public Catholicism.* New York, Macmillan, 1989.

Schuck, Michael. *That They May Be One: The Social Teaching of the Papal Encyclicals, 1740–1989.* Georgetown: Georgetown University Press, 1991.

Walsh, Michael, and Brian Davies, eds. *Proclaiming Justice and Peace: Papal Documents from* Rerum novarum *through* Centesimus annus. Mystic, Conn.: Twenty-Third Publications, 1991.

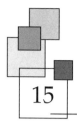

| 15 | Ministries in the Church |

John Ford

This chapter treats the following aspects of ministries in the Church: (1) terminology; (2) the ministry of Jesus and the apostles; (3) ministries in the early Church; (4) the Second Vatican Council: episcopate and presbyterate; (5) the Second Vatican Council: laity and permanent diaconate; (6) ecumenical convergence on ministry; (7) education for ministry, and (8) reflections. A select bibliography is provided at the end of this chapter.

Terminology

The word "ministry" in English is derived from the Latin *ministerium,* which means "service." Ministry in English has a variety of meanings; for example, in the political world ministry often refers to service in a nation's cabinet that consists of a prime minister along with ministers responsible for various governmental agencies. Similarly, in the diplomatic world, envoys from one country to another are sometimes called ministers. For example, an ambassador with special powers may be called a minister plenipotentiary.

This secular usage has parallels in the religious world, where a minister is a person who conducts some type of religious service or provides some service based on religious motives. The use of the term in Christianity stems from the New Testament, where "ministry" translates the Greek word *diakonia,* which was used to describe various types of "service" in the first Christian communities. *Diakonia* (service) is one of the principal commitments of the Church, along with *leitourgia* (worship) and *martyria* (witness). Correspondingly, a person providing such service is a *diakonos,* which can be translated as "servant," "assistant," or "deacon."

In the United States prior to Vatican II, "minister" was commonly used to describe a member of the clergy in Protestant churches, while the word "priest" was customarily used to designate the celebrant of the Eucharist in Roman Catholic and Orthodox churches. Nonetheless, "minister" was also used in Roman Catholic sacramental theology and canon law in a technical sense to distinguish between "ordinary" and "extraordinary" ministers of the sacraments; for example, the ordinary minister of confirmation is a bishop, its extraordinary minister is a priest with appropriate authorization.

In general, the different uses of the term "ministry" reflect the multiplicity of forms that ministry has taken in the twenty centuries of Christianity. Underlying the variety in usage of the term, the reality represents a fundamental aspect of Christian belief and life: ministry is service for others in imitation of Christ.

The Ministry of Jesus and the Apostles

Jesus is the prime exemplar of ministry in the New Testament; from the earliest days of Christianity his followers have sought to imitate Jesus' example of loving service for others. However, instead of a single portrait of Jesus and his "public ministry," the New Testament presents various vignettes of Jesus, each with its special resonance with the Old Testament and the Judaism of his day. For example, the Gospel of Matthew (5:1-12) portrays Jesus teaching the Beatitudes on a mountainside in a prophetic manner resembling Moses receiving the Commandments from God on the mountaintop. In the Gospel of Luke (4:14-22) Jesus is described as initiating his ministry of preaching with a reading from the prophet Isaiah:

> The Spirit of the Lord is upon me,
>   because he has anointed me to bring glad tidings to the poor.
> He has sent me to proclaim liberty to captives,
>   and recovery of sight to the blind, to let the oppressed go free (4:18).

In the Gospel of John (10:1-21) Jesus is identified as the Good Shepherd who "lays down his life for the sheep" (10:11). Later in the same Gospel (13:1-17), Jesus washed the feet of his disciples as an example of the service his followers were to give one another: "If I, therefore, master and teacher, have washed your feet, you ought to wash one another's feet" (13:14). In contrast to this picture of Jesus as humble servant, the letter to the Hebrews describes Christ as "high priest of the good things that have come to be," because he entered into the sanctuary, "not with the blood of goats and calves but with his own blood, thus obtaining eternal redemption" (9:11-12). This salvific role was realized at the crucifixion when Jesus was designated "King of the Jews" in the inscription placed on the cross by his Roman executioners.

Thus, the New Testament portrays Jesus as a minister in a variety of ways; eventually, it became customary to synthesize these different portraits around three titles: prophet, priest, and king. The New Testament provides numerous examples of each of these ministerial roles: Jesus as prophet, teaching people through parables in word and in deed and continuing to guide the Christian community after his ascension; Jesus as priest, healing his contemporaries of their ills, both physical and spiritual, and ultimately sacrificing his own life for the salvation of all; Jesus as king, rejecting the legalism of his contemporaries and ascending into heaven to sit in judgment at the right hand of the Father. Each of these ministerial titles has a historical dimension during the lifetime of Jesus, a theological dimension for the Church through the centuries, and an eschatological dimension for the communion of saints. Thus, these three titles have provided the basis for distinguishing three different types of ministry: prophetic or teaching, priestly or sanctifying, kingly or governing.

The Gospels describe not only the public ministry of Jesus, but also his selection of followers entrusted with assisting in his ministry. Jesus selected a core group of twelve, who were his closest companions during his life and later constituted the leadership of the first Christian community. Yet for all their importance as assistants of Jesus, the portraits of the apostles in the New Testament are fragmentary: Peter and John, along with Judas Iscariot, are the most prominent; others like Thomas, Matthew, Philip, James, Andrew, and Bartholomew have cameo roles; while the three with duplicate names, Simon, James, and Judas, receive only passing mention. The apostles were chosen from a larger group of disciples, described by Luke as "seventy[-two] others" who were sent by Jesus "in pairs to every town and place he intended to visit" (10:1). Aided by a set of instructions about the way that they should conduct themselves (10:2-16), this mission of the disciples was apparently successful (10:17-20). Finally, prior to the ascension, the Gospel of Matthew concludes with the final commissioning of the "eleven disciples": "Go, therefore, and make disciples of all nations" (28:19).

Humanly speaking, the continuation of the mission and ministry of Jesus after his ascension depended on the efforts of his apostles. Originally the group of twelve as witnesses of the Lord's life and resurrection was considered so significant that a replacement for Judas Iscariot was immediately selected (Acts 1). Yet the subsequent history of the apostles as a group is surprisingly vague. On the one hand, the privileged position of the apostles as witnesses to the ministry and resurrection of Christ was unique and could not be transmitted to others, and so ended with the death of the last of the Twelve. On the other hand, the title of apostle was claimed by Paul, even though he did not know Christ during his public ministry. In fact, the title apostle was sometimes given to others, including people about whom little is known beyond their names.

In any case, the title apostle soon faded out of ordinary usage for ministers in the Christian community. Although the apostles occasionally assembled as a group when important decisions needed to be made (Acts 15), the Twelve apparently dispersed to do missionary work outside Jerusalem. In any case, with the destruction of Jerusalem in 70 C.E., the Twelve could hardly have continued as the leadership group of the early Christian community.

One important decision of the Twelve was the creation of new ministries in light of new needs in the growing Christian community. One specific situation that prompted a new type of ministry was a complaint by Greek-speaking Christians that their widows were being neglected in the daily distribution of food, as compared with the widows of those who spoke Hebrew (Acts 6:1). In response, the Twelve decided to appoint "seven reputable men, filled with the Spirit and wisdom" (6:3), as their assistants in this *diakonia.* After the selection of these assistants by the community, the apostles "prayed and laid hands on them" (6:6).

This event has several important implications for ministry: first, while all Christians are called to be witnesses to the message of Jesus, some are commissioned by the leaders of the Christian community to exercise specific ministries. Second, prayer and laying on of hands have been used from apostolic times to the present to commission people for ministry. Third, ministry is a gift of the Spirit to share in the mission of Christ. Fourth, the Twelve chose to share their own apostolic ministry with others. On the one hand, the apostles devoted themselves to the task of evangelization; on the other hand, they recognized the need for various services within the community and commissioned assistants for such tasks as caring for widows and orphans, healing the sick, and administering the temporal goods of the Christian community. In the early Church, evangelization was frequently an itinerant ministry, while charitable service was usually a residential ministry. Subsequently, both types of ministry developed in the Church: those who witness to Christ by proclaiming the gospel, particularly in missionary situations, and those who serve in an established Christian community in a particular place.

During apostolic times, a plurality of ministries was recognized. Paul, for example, speaks of different spiritual gifts and ministries: "Some people God has designated in the church to be, first, apostles; second, prophets; third, teachers; then, mighty deeds; then gifts of healing, assistance, administration, and varieties of tongues" (1 Cor 12:28). This list includes ministries that are charismatic in the sense that they are special graces given to a specific person, as in the case of prophets and miracle workers. Yet this list also includes ministries that are institutional in the sense that the Christian community can assign these responsibilities, as in the case of assistants and administrators.

In fact, the New Testament indicates not only a variety of ministries within a specific local church, but also variations in ministries from one church to the next. For example, at Jerusalem the Christian community was first governed by the Twelve, who soon appointed seven assistants. Yet later this same community was administered by James and other elders. At Corinth the Church was led by a variety of ministers, some apparently assigned, others apparently recognized for their charisms or gifts of grace. In the Apostolic Church, ministerial roles included: presiders and leaders, prophets and teachers, pastors and presbyters, etc. Paul, for example, describes himself as "a minister of Christ Jesus to the Gentiles" (Rom 15:16) and also commends the ministry of Phoebe, "who is [also] a minister of the church of Cenchreae" (Rom 16:1).

In sum, the question "What is the nature of ministry in the New Testament?" does not have a simple answer. On the one hand, one must be cautious about retrojecting contemporary notions of ministry on a situation that was in the process of development. On the other hand, there are a few constant characteristics: ministry in the New Testament is linked to the person and example of Christ; all ministries, whether charismatic or institutional, are considered service on behalf of the Christian community.

Ministries in the Early Church

Although the organization of the first Christian communities varied from place to place, three basic patterns can be discerned: (1) a congregational model, represented by "house churches" where the local Christian community met in the home of one of its members; (2) a presbyteral model, where the local church was supervised by *presbyteroi* or "elders"; (3) an episcopal model, where the local church was governed by a bishop with the assistance of *presbyteroi* and/or *diakonoi*. By the middle of the second century, however, a threefold hierarchy of bishops, presbyters, and deacons prevailed as the dominant pattern of ministerial leadership.

Thus, the ordained ministries in the Church were hierarchically structured with bishops assuming administrative authority in major cities and their surrounding areas. However, the process that resulted in episcopally structured churches seems to have emerged at different times in different places. For example, in the *(First) Letter of Clement*, written in Rome at the end of the first century, the terms "presbyter" (elder) and "bishop" seem to be used interchangeably. In contrast, at Antioch the three-tiered ministry of bishop, presbyters, and deacons was already in place early in the second century.

The word "bishop" is the English translation of the Greek *episkopos*, meaning "supervisor" or "superintendent." And while bishops are described as successors of the apostles, the evolution of their ministry of leadership took time and varied from place to place. Nonetheless, the need for episcopal leadership seems to have been widely recognized in the early Church, where the principal ministry of a bishop was to preside over a local church and to maintain communion between that church and other churches.

Bishops were usually assisted by *presbyteroi* (the Greek *presbyteros*, from which the English word "priest" is derived, means "elder"—not necessarily in age, but in responsibility). The relationship between *episkopoi* and *presbyteroi* varied: sometimes, presbyters were assistants to a bishop in his church; at other times, presbyters presided over nearby communities by preaching the word, celebrating the sacraments, and exercising pastoral leadership and care.

In the early Church, the *presbyteroi* eventually came to be identified as "priests." This usage contrasts with the New Testament, which did not use the word "priest" to designate any ordained minister but spoke of the unique priest, Jesus Christ, and the "royal priesthood" of all the baptized (1 Pet 2:9). During the Middle Ages, priests came to be viewed primarily in terms of their sacramental role, particularly in celebrating the Eucharist and hearing confessions. In medieval times, a priest was often seen as a sacred person, vested with sacramental, even supernatural, powers: "another Christ." Whatever its other merits, such a view effectively placed a priest on a pedestal and led to a separation between priests and people that persisted until the Second Vatican Council (1962–65).

In the early Church, the *diakonoi* usually served as assistants to the bishop in two major ways: first, they had liturgical responsibilities, such as assisting at the celebration of baptism and the Eucharist; second, they were entrusted with charitable works, such as dispensing alms to the needy. In the medieval Church, deacons sometimes managed the temporal affairs of a diocese—a function that often made them powerful officials. In fact, as late as the nineteenth century, there were some deacons who were ordained to serve primarily as ecclesiastical administrators. Yet, for the most part, the ministry of deacon in the

Western Church gradually became a transitional step on the way to the priesthood. Although such transitional deacons continued to have a liturgical function at least for solemn ceremonies, in other respects their *diakonia* (service) was considerably diminished. With Vatican II came a restoration of the diaconate as a permanent type of ordained ministry.

In the early Church some women served as deaconesses; their primary responsibilities included assisting and anointing women at baptism, caring for widows and orphans, and ministering to sick women. However, once infant baptism became the norm, there was no longer a need for deaconesses to assist at adult baptisms; consequently, by the eleventh century deaconesses had disappeared in the Western Church, though they continued to serve in some Eastern churches. In the nineteenth century, some Anglican and Protestant churches reinstituted the order of deaconess to serve in such ministries as education and health care.

In sum, in the early Church, there was a plurality of ministries that varied according to the needs of the local church. In addition to such ministries as teachers, evangelists, virgins, widows, and penitents, there was even a ministry of grave diggers—an occupation not to be taken lightly during times of persecution when these *fossores* were apparently responsible for obtaining and burying the bodies of Christian martyrs. However, as situations changed over time, there was a process of institutionalization that resulted in the disappearance of some ministries and the development or modification of others. For example, the "minor orders" of lector, acolyte, porter, and exorcist, which at one time had been separate ministries in the Church, became transitional steps en route to ordination to the priesthood.

The Second Vatican Council: Episcopacy and Presbyterate

In the decades after the First Vatican Council (1869–70) with its emphasis on the primacy and infallibility of the Roman pontiff, ecclesiologists tended to image the Church as a pyramid with the pope at the summit, with bishops at the upper reaches, with priests at midlevel, and with the laity at the base. Such a view of the Church implied a correlative understanding of the ministries of the person(s) at each level. For example, the pope was sometimes characterized as a supreme judge, who definitively decided all cases brought to him from lower levels; bishops were often viewed as vicars or delegates of the pope, who implemented his decisions in their dioceses. Priests in turn were considered representatives of their bishop, who were responsible for carrying out his decisions in their parishes. The laity in such a schema were often assigned a passive role, expected to receive the sacraments and support the Church, but accorded little voice in its operation. Accordingly, when popes and bishops in the early part of the twentieth century encouraged the laity to join various movements of "Catholic Action," lay participation was usually described as "collaboration in the mission of the hierarchy."

Nonetheless, in the decades prior to Vatican II, new ecclesiological views were emerging which envisioned the Church not as a pyramid, but as a communion or community. While such ecclesiologies did not consider the Church a democracy, they did favor a less institutional and more sacramental and spiritual view of the Church. For example, communion ecclesiology sometimes depicted the Church as a series of concentric circles with the pope at the center and bishops and priests in the middle, surrounded by the laity. This image stresses cooperation among all people in the Church: like a wheel in motion with the interplay of centrifugal and centripetal forces, ideas and initiatives not only flow in different directions but are necessary for the vitality of the Church.

Communion ecclesiology backdrops much of the teaching of Vatican II on ministries: the pope and bishops are seen as members of an apostolic college with the ministry of governing the Church; priests are seen as members of a presbyterate cooperating with their bishop in his ministry as pastor of a diocese; the laity are seen as empowered for ministry at baptism and gifted with graces for service in the Church.

In contrast to the First Vatican Council, whose ecclesiological teaching focused on the papal office and its prerogatives, the Second Vatican Council's Dogmatic Constitution on the Church began with a consideration of "the Mystery of the Church," followed by a treatment of "the People of God" that affirmed that the "baptized, by regeneration and the anointing of the Holy Spirit, are consecrated to be a spiritual house and a holy priesthood" (LG 10). While maintaining that the difference between "the common priesthood of the faithful and the ministerial or hierarchical priesthood" is one of essence and not only degree, the council insisted that each Christian "shares in the one priesthood of Christ" (LG 10). Such an affirmation was nothing less than astounding, given the earlier subordination of the laity to the hierarchy, as well as a hesitancy about speaking of the "priesthood of the laity" because of the long-standing use of the term in Protestantism.

Yet even more surprising was the council's assertion of the role of the laity in regard to doctrine:

> The whole body of the faithful who have an anointing that comes from the holy one (cf. 1 Jn. 2:20 and 27) cannot err in matters of belief. This

characteristic is shown in the supernatural appreciation of the faith *(sensus fidei)* of the whole people, when, "from the bishops to the last of the faithful" they manifest a universal consent in matters of faith and morals (LG 12).

Given this conciliar emphasis on the "priesthood of the laity," it was inevitable that new understandings of the ministries of bishops, priests, deacons, and lay people would develop in the postconciliar Church.

First, in regard to the episcopacy, Vatican II steered away from those preconciliar ecclesiologies that had reduced bishops to being delegates of the pope. Instead, Vatican II saw episcopal ordination as the sacramental incorporation of a bishop into a body or college of bishops: "One is constituted a member of the episcopal body in virtue of the sacramental consecration and by the hierarchical communion with the head and members of the college" (LG 22). The council viewed the college of bishops, including the pope, as collectively inheriting the ministry of leadership once exercised by the apostles: "The order of bishops is the successor to the college of the apostles in their role as teachers and pastors, and in it the apostolic college is perpetuated" (LG 22). However, speaking of bishops as "successors of the apostles" does not necessarily mean that the apostles were bishops in the modern sense of the term, nor that the apostles ordained bishops in the same way as the present.

By viewing the episcopacy as an authentic development of apostolic ministry on behalf of the universal Church, Vatican II set the stage for a number of important developments: since it is impractical for thousands of bishops to meet regularly in a general council, Vatican II's Decree on the Pastoral Office of Bishops in the Church authorized the establishment of an international synod of bishops, "representative of the whole Catholic episcopate," to meet periodically to consider problems affecting the universal Church (CD 5). In addition, since bishops as a college share responsibility for ministry in the whole Church, they are called upon to provide personnel and resources for needy churches in other parts of the world (CD 6). In fact, since Vatican II many clergy and laity have gone to minister in other countries.

Another manifestation of the collegial ministry of bishops is the establishment of episcopal conferences "in which the bishops of a certain country or region exercise their pastoral office jointly in order to enhance the Church's beneficial influence on all men, especially by devising forms of the apostolate and apostolic methods suitably adapted to the circumstances of the times" (CD 38). Episcopal conferences have been able to provide ministries to meet needs that many individual dioceses would otherwise be unable to afford; among these are such diverse services as the Campaign for Human Development, the National Plan for Hispanic Ministry, and the Military Ordinariate.

Second, in treating the priesthood in its Decree on the Ministry and Life of Priests, Vatican II acknowledged that "a most important and increasingly difficult role is being assigned to this order in the renewal of the Church" (PO 1). Characterizing priests as "promoted to the service of Christ the Teacher, Priest, and King" (PO 1), Vatican II considered the primary task of priests as "ministers of God's Word" to be "co-workers of the bishops to preach the Gospel of God to all men" (PO 4). Vatican II described "the purpose for which priests are consecrated by God . . . is that they should be made sharers in a special way in Christ's priesthood" (PO 5). Then, in signaling priests as "rulers of God's people," Vatican II pointed out: "For the exercise of this ministry, as for the rest of the priests' functions, a spiritual power is given them, a power whose purpose is to build up" the Church (PO 6).

Vatican II envisioned the relationship between priests and their bishop in terms of collegiality: since "all priests share with the bishops the one identical priesthood and ministry of Christ," each diocese should have a representative "group or senate of priests" that "by their advice could effectively help the bishop in the management of the diocese" (PO 7). Simultaneously, priests "should unite their efforts with those of the lay faithful" by "giving lay people charge of duties in the service of the Church, giving them freedom and opportunity for activity and even inviting them, when opportunity occurs, to take the initiative in undertaking projects of their own" (PO 9).

The council recognized that the exercise of the threefold priestly ministry both demands and fosters holiness. Central to priestly spirituality is the celebration of the Eucharist, which "is an act of Christ and the Church even if it is impossible for the faithful to be present" (PO 13). Vatican II also listed "special requirements" for priestly ministry, including humility, obedience, celibacy, and voluntary poverty. While acknowledging that celibacy "is not demanded of the priesthood by its nature," Vatican II considered celibacy a means for priests "to dedicate themselves more freely . . . to the service of God and of men" (PO 16). While recognizing the need for appropriate remuneration for priests, Vatican II encouraged priests "to manage ecclesiastical property . . . with the help, as far as possible of gifted laymen" (PO 17).

The Second Vatican Council:
Laity and Permanent Diaconate

In discussing "the laity's special and indispensable role in the mission of the Church," Vatican II's Decree on the Apostolate of the Lay

People asserted that "it is hard to see how the Church could make her presence and action felt without the help of the laity" (AA 1). Since the "laity are made to share in the priestly, prophetical and kingly office of Christ" (AA 2), the laity have "the noble obligation of working to bring all men throughout the whole world to hear and accept the divine message of salvation" (AA 3). For this apostolate, "each one has received suitable talents" that should be cultivated along with "the personal gifts" that each one has received from the Holy Spirit (AA 4).

Since the mission of the Church is "not only to bring men the message and grace of Christ but also to permeate and improve the whole range of the temporal" (AA 5), laypersons need to be witness of Christ in the workplace; indeed, laypersons have "countless opportunities for exercising the apostolate of evangelization and sanctification" (AA 6) that are not available to clerics. In addition to direct Christian witness, "laymen ought to take on themselves as their distinctive task this renewal of the temporal order" (AA 7). In so doing, the council encouraged lay people to collaborate with all people of good will.

Thus, the lay apostolate "is exercised both in the Church and in the world" (AA 9). In the Church, the laity participate "in the function of Christ, priest, prophet and king" by such activities as catechetical instruction, pastoral care for others, and administering the resources of the Church (AA 10). In a special way, Vatican II encouraged the laity to engage in "the family apostolate" through such activities as

> adopting abandoned children, showing a loving welcome to strangers, helping with the running of schools, supporting adolescents with advice and help, assisting engaged couples to make a better preparation for marriage, taking a share in catechism-teaching, supporting married people and families in a material or moral crisis, and in the case of the aged, not only providing them with what is indispensable but also procuring for them a fair share of the fruits of economic progress (AA 11).

In the world at large, the council encouraged the laity "to infuse the Christian spirit into the mentality and behavior, laws and structures of the community in which one lives" (AA 13). Sometimes, such witness will take the form of an "individual apostolate"; at other times, the laity will have greater effectiveness by working together in group apostolates. While insisting that "the laity have the right to establish and direct associations, and to join existing ones" (AA 19), Vatican II also presumed the continuation of "Catholic Action," which was the major avenue for the "collaboration of the laity in the hierarchical apostolate" in Europe prior to the council.

Yet, Vatican II recognized that if such apostolic work is to be efficient and effective, lay people must be afforded appropriate training. Indeed, the council felt that "training for the apostolate should begin from the very start of a child's education" (AA 30). Later, "schools and colleges and other Catholic educational institutions should foster in the young a Catholic outlook and apostolic action" (AA 30). On the one hand, "training for the apostolate cannot consist in theoretical teaching alone" (AA 29); on the other hand, "different types of apostolate require their own appropriate method of training" (AA 31). Yet ultimately, "every single lay person should himself actively undertake his own preparation for the apostolate" (AA 30).

Thus, the Second Vatican Council stressed the multiple ways in which lay people share in the mission of the Church. First, their apostolate in the Church is derived from their baptismal incorporation into the prophetic, priestly, and kingly roles of Christ. Second, the laity are called upon to be "leaven in the world" by living the gospel in their family and by witnessing the gospel in the world. While the council continued to speak of the "lay apostolate," it effectively set the stage for the development of numerous lay ministries in the postconciliar Church.

Some aspects of this postconciliar development of lay ministries have been the result of official decisions. For example, in his apostolic letter *Ministeria quaedam* (August 15, 1972), Pope Paul VI revised ordained ministries in a notable way. Among these revisions, the "minor orders," which previously had been preparatory stages en route to the priesthood, were reclassified as "ministries" and reduced to two: lector and acolyte. Moreover, these two ministries were no longer reserved to candidates for the priesthood—laymen could be "installed" in these ministries. However, most lay people who read or serve at the liturgy are chosen in less formal fashion.

A second example was the reestablishment of the permanent diaconate, which Pope Paul VI described in his apostolic letter *Ad Pascendum* (August 15, 1972): "the diaconate flourished in a wonderful way in the Church, and at the same time gave an outstanding witness of love for Christ and the brethren through the performance of works of charity, the celebration of sacred rites, and the fulfillment of pastoral duties." Subsequently, thousands of married laymen have been ordained permanent deacons and exercise such responsibilities as preaching the gospel, presiding at baptisms, weddings, and funerals, and exercising a variety of other ministries.

However, thousands of other lay men and women are involved in a multitude of ministries in the Church. Some of these are full time, such as ministers of music, religious education, and parish administration, teachers of theology, and even canon lawyers. Countless lay people serve as volunteers in other ministries in the Church, ranging from traditional roles such as ushers and sacristans, to more recent roles such as eucharistic ministers and parish home visitors. On the one hand, such lay participation represents a much needed infusion of labor to replace priests and religious, whose numbers have notably declined since the council. On the other hand, this dramatic increase in lay participation represents a restoration of the long neglected "priesthood of the laity."

Ecumenical Convergence on Ministry

The Faith and Order Commission of the World Council of Churches in a plenary session at Lima, Peru, on January 12, 1982, approved a statement on *Baptism, Eucharist and Ministry* (BEM) that received the approval of participants representing a broad spectrum of Christian confessions. This convergence is remarkable insofar as theological convergence on these three topics had been the subject of international ecumenical discussion for over half a century. In issuing this document the commission requested churches to prepare official responses indicating to what extent this report represented the faith of the Church throughout the ages, as well as the implications of this statement for the responding church itself.

Nearly two hundred churches from all parts of the world prepared official responses; nearly all gave the Lima Report a basically favorable reception. A primary reason for this widespread acceptance is due to the fact that the report was deliberately written in language taken from the Bible and the early Church—thus from a time before the major divisions in Christianity occurred—not in the systematic language of any particular theological tradition, which as often as not has been controversial, even polemical. This is not to say that the Lima Report resolved all ecumenical problems concerning baptism, Eucharist, and ministry; however, it did express much of the teaching common to Christian churches throughout the world. As might have been anticipated, some churches (for example, those of the Reformed tradition) felt that the Lima Report went further than what they were prepared to acknowledge; other churches (for example, the Roman Catholic and Orthodox) felt that the statement did not go far enough.

The chapter on ministry in the Lima Report begins with a treatment of "the Calling of the Whole People of God," which emphasized the diversity of gifts given to people in the Church:

> The Holy Spirit bestows on the community diverse and complementary gifts. These are for the common good of the whole people and are

manifested in acts of service within the community and to the world. They may be gifts of communicating the Gospel in word and deed, gifts of healing, gifts of praying, gifts of teaching and learning, gifts of serving, gifts of guiding and following, gifts of inspiration and vision. All members are called to discover, with the help of the community, the gifts they have received and to use them for the building up of the Church and for the service of the world to which the Church is sent (M 5).

The Lima Report then described ministry as "the service to which the whole people of God is called, whether as individuals, as a local community, or as the universal Church" (M 7b). This description of ministry "in its broadest sense" was contrasted with ordained ministry, described as service by "persons who have received a charism and whom the church appoints for service by ordination through the invocation of the Spirit and the laying on of hands" (M 7c). The Lima Report described the role of ordained ministers as follows: "The chief responsibility of the ordained ministry is to assemble and build up the body of Christ by proclaiming and teaching the Word of God, by celebrating the sacraments, and by guiding the life of the community in its worship, its mission and its caring ministry" (M 13). While acknowledging that the New Testament does not explicitly indicate who is to preside at the Eucharist, the Lima Report commented that "very soon however it is clear that an ordained ministry presides over the celebration"; and addressing those churches which allow people who are not ordained to preside at the Eucharist, the report proposed: "If the ordained ministry is to provide a focus for the unity of the life and witness of the Church, it is appropriate that an ordained minister should be given this task" of presiding at the Eucharist (M C14).

Before discussing "the forms of the Ordained Ministry," the Lima Report emphasized that "the Church must discover the ministry which can be provided by women as well as that which can be provided by men" (M 18). The report pointed to the fact that while an "increasing number of churches have decided that there is no biblical or theological reason against ordaining women," still "many other churches hold that the tradition of the Church in this regard must not be changed" (M 18).

Next, while acknowledging that "there is no single New Testament pattern" of ministry, the report suggested that "the threefold ministry of bishop, presbyter and deacon may serve today as an expression of the unity we seek and also as a means for achieving it" (M 22).

The Lima Report also gave generic descriptions of the functions of each of the three ordained ministries:

Bishops preach the Word, preside at the sacraments, and administer discipline in such a way as to be representative pastoral ministers of oversight, continuity and unity in the Church (M 29). . . .

Presbyters serve as pastoral ministers of Word and sacraments in a local eucharistic community (M 30). . . .

Deacons represent to the Church its calling as servant in the world (M 31). . . .

While these ministries "serve permanent needs in the life of the community" (M 32), the report also recognized that "in the history of the Church there have been times when the truth of the Gospel could only be preserved through prophetic and charismatic leaders" (M 33).

The report also treated the ecumenically divisive issue of "Succession in the Apostolic Tradition" which was defined as follows:

Apostolic tradition in the Church means continuity in the permanent characteristics of the Church of the apostles: witness to the apostolic faith, proclamation and fresh interpretation of the Gospel, celebration of baptism and the eucharist, the transmission of ministerial responsibilities, communion in prayer, love, joy and suffering, service to the sick and the needy, unity among the local churches and sharing the gifts which the Lord has given to each (M 34).

Accordingly, the "primary manifestation of apostolic succession is to be found in the apostolic tradition of the Church as a whole" (M 35). Therefore, the succession of bishops is important, but only one of the ways "in which the apostolic tradition of the Church was expressed." Thus, episcopal succession is understood "as serving, symbolizing and guarding the continuity of the apostolic faith and communion" (M 36). Episcopal succession is then "a sign, though not a guarantee, of the continuity and unity of the Church" (M 38).

The report noted that by ordination of "certain of its members for the ministry in the name of Christ by the invocation of the Spirit and the laying on of hands," the Church "seeks to continue the mission of the apostles and to remain faithful to their teaching" (M 39). While allowing for different interpretations of ordination, the report stated that "ordination denotes an action by God and the community by which the ordained are strengthened by the Spirit for their task and are upheld by the acknowledgment and prayers of the congregation" (M 40). The report also recognized the permanent nature of ordination, so that "ordination to any one of the particular ordained ministries is never repeated" (M 48).

The final and most neuralgic issue addressed at Lima was "the mutual recognition of the ordained ministries." Recognizing apostolic succession as a pivotal issue, the report suggested: "Churches which have preserved the episcopal succession are asked to recognize both the apostolic content of the ordained ministry which exists in churches which have not maintained such succession and also the existence in these churches of a ministry of *episkopé* in various forms" (M 53). A comparable request was made of churches without episcopal succession: "These churches are asked to realize that the continuity with the Church of the apostles finds profound expression in the successive laying on of hands by bishops and that, though they may not lack the continuity of the apostolic tradition, this sign will strengthen and deepen that continuity" (M 53). Indeed, the report suggested that such churches "may need to recover the sign of the episcopal succession" (M 53). Finally, the report noted that "the mutual recognition of churches and their ministries implies decision by the appropriate authorities and a liturgical act from which point unity would be publicly manifest" (M 55).

Since responses to the Lima Report were requested from the highest level of authority in the responding churches, the official response of the Roman Catholic Church was issued by the Vatican Secretariat for the Promotion of the Unity of Christians on July 21, 1987, after a lengthy process of consultation with the ecumenical offices of episcopal conferences throughout the world. The Vatican statement was basically favorable, characterizing the Lima text as "perhaps the most significant result of the [Faith and Order] movement so far." While acknowledging that the Lima Report and Roman Catholic doctrine converged on many points, the Vatican noted that some passages expressed opinions incompatible with Roman Catholic teaching.

In the case of ministry, the Vatican noted that the Lima Report seemed unclear about whether the threefold ministry of bishop, presbyter, and deacon is an essential element of the Church or a historically conditioned aspect. Nonetheless, the Vatican acknowledged that the Lima Report, while not describing ordination as a sacrament, effectively treated it as such. However, insofar as ordained ministry requires sacramental ordination by a bishop in apostolic succession, the Vatican felt that the Lima proposals for mutual recognition of ministries were insufficient.

In sum, *Baptism, Eucharist and Ministry* is a significant ecumenical accomplishment that reflects a theological convergence about ministry in the Church. Foremost among these agreements is the conviction that all Christians are called to ministry in virtue of their baptism. Equally important is the recognition that while a variety of ministries is evident in the New Testament, the Church and the churches would be well served by a renewal of the threefold ordained ministry in apostolic succession.

Education for Ministry

Since the Council of Trent in the sixteenth century, preparation for ordination to the priesthood has usually taken place in seminaries, where students have studied philosophy and theology as their principal courses. Until Vatican II, courses on practical preparation for ministry tended to be marginal to the main curriculum in Scripture, systematic theology, moral theology, and canon law. When taught in more than an anecdotal fashion, courses on pastoral ministry tended to follow a speculative approach that presumed that seminarians who were well versed in the theology of the priesthood would be able to apply their theoretical knowledge to the concrete situations that they would encounter in their priestly ministry.

Such an approach had obvious limitations: sooner or later, most priests encountered situations for which their theological training had not prepared them; real-life situations did not always fit the theoretical categories that they had learned in the seminary. New approaches were needed and in fact came into Roman Catholic seminary programs largely from the pastoral training offered by Protestant seminaries in the United States. This pedagogical change resulted from two intertwined aspects of Vatican II: first, the council led to the recognition that a more pastoral orientation was needed in seminary formation; second, the ecumenical climate fostered by the council facilitated the incorporation of approaches to pastoral training that had gained acceptance in many Protestant schools of theology.

By the time of Vatican II, many Protestant seminaries had incorporated clinical pastoral education (CPE) into their curriculum. Such clinical education has two major components: (1) experience: seminarians are assigned field placements as student ministers, usually in hospitals or parishes; (2) theological reflection: each student's experiences in a placement are subsequently analyzed in terms of such factors as pastoral approach, cultural dimensions, theological assumptions, and personal implications for faith. Thus, in contrast to preconciliar courses in pastoral theology that tended to be theoretical, deductive, and sometimes impersonal, clinical pastoral education uses an approach that is practice-oriented, inductive, and personally interactive. For example, instead of attempting to apply abstract theological principles to concrete cases, the clinical model uses actual ministerial experiences as a springboard to train a student to use pastoral techniques appropriate to each situation, to increase a student's awareness of the cultural dimensions of ministry, to discern the implicit theologies of both the student and the other person(s) involved in the situation, and to reflect on the student's own faith-stance and spirituality. In the process of theological reflection, a student is expected to consider options for pastoral practice that take into account both the needs of the situation and the pertinent teachings of Scripture and the Church.

Roman Catholic seminaries have significantly updated their curricula in the decades since Vatican II. Many seminaries now describe themselves as "schools for ministry" and admit not only students preparing for the priesthood, but also lay people involved in other ministries in the Church. Thus, many lay people today receive training for ministry comparable to that of seminarians preparing for ordination. In some schools of ministry, lay people constitute the majority of students. Many of these lay men and women are preparing themselves for full-time ministry in such areas as religious education, youth ministry, music and worship, parish administration, retreat work, ecumenical dialogue, etc. Unfortunately, however, only a small percentage of lay ministers are currently receiving the comprehensive preparation appropriate for their ministries, partly because of the very limited amount of funding available to lay people for pursuing such programs on a full-time basis.

Much more common at the local and diocesan level are short-term programs for preparing lay ministers for specific ministries. Typical in many parishes are courses intended to prepare lay people to be eucharistic ministers or lectors at Mass. Often this training consists of one or more sessions in practical techniques with little treatment of the theology of lay ministry in general or the theological implications of a particular ministry. In response to the Second Vatican Council's insistence that lay people need to receive appropriate training for ministry, better programs are needed, particularly for those laypersons involved in such ministries as the religious education of young people and the preparation for the reception of baptism, First Communion, and confirmation.

However, intensive long-term programs are available on the diocesan level for men preparing for ordination to the permanent diaconate. Such programs, usually extending over several years, tend to treat many of the topics covered in academic theological programs, though sometimes in a truncated way. Special attention is usually given in these programs to the theology of the diaconate and its pastoral exercise.

While much has been accomplished in theological education for ministry in the United States in the decades since Vatican II, much more remains to be done, particularly in the training of lay ministers for the many ministries that they exercise in thousands of parishes throughout the country.

Reflections

Much more could be said about "ministries in the Church." Indeed each section of this chapter could easily be the topic for a book of its own; some of the books that background each section are listed in the bibliography. In fact, in doing a computer search of recent bibliographical materials for this chapter, there were nearly a thousand references on "ministry": far too many to list, but indicative of the widespread interest in and discussion about "ministries" in the Church today.

Part of that discussion involves theological problems left unresolved by Vatican II. For example, what is the relationship between the sacramentality of the priesthood and that of the episcopacy? What is the difference in the way that a priest and a layperson participate in the priestly, prophetic, and kingly role of Christ? What sacramental powers are conferred by ordination to the diaconate? To these and other *quaestiones disputatae* must be added a host of practical problems that have emerged in implementing the teaching of Vatican II. For example, what role should the presbyterate have in diocesan decision-making? Why have vocations to the priesthood and religious life decreased so drastically in the decades since Vatican II? What is distinctive about the diaconate, if lay ministers perform many of the same ministries as do deacons? What ministries should be open to women in the church? The list of both theological and practical questions is long and has produced much debate in the contemporary Church—debates that will likely continue in the future.

Thus, the topic of "ministries in the Church" is one that still has many open questions. But are there any conclusions? Perhaps the most important conclusion to this chapter is the recognition of the variety of ministries, past and present. If, for example, the New Testament does not provide a systematic theology of ministry, it does suggest that the first Christians engaged in numerous ministries as witnesses to the Lord and in service to their neighbor. Thus, from the beginning, ministry or *diakonia* has been an important part of the commitment of each Christian.

If some types of ministry proved to be transitional and disappeared, other ministries have become permanent. If some ministries are intramural, centered on the life and worship of the Church itself, others are ecumenical, reaching out to serve people in need, including those outside the boundaries of the Christian community. Some ministries are charismatic, dependent on the natural endowments of, and the graces divinely given to, a particular person in the Church. Other ministries are institutional, established by the Church to serve particular needs on behalf of the Christian community. Some ministries are bestowed by ordination with prayer and the laying on of hands. Other ministries are conferred by an installation or commissioning. Yet whatever their nature, all ministries are linked to Christ through the Holy Spirit.

The Church is richer for this multiplicity and variety of ministries. The Church needs this multiplicity if it is to be universal and catholic. The Church needs this variety for its vitality. Sometimes this multiplicity and variety are a source of tension within the Church, yet tension can be either destructive or creative, depending on how it is managed. Suffice it to say that using tension in a healthy, creative way is also a much needed ministry in the contemporary Church and world. But where do all these reflections leave the reader of these lines? While this chapter may be read simply as an academic survey of "ministries of the Church," hopefully all readers will be encouraged to ask where, when, and how they can exercise the ministry to which they are called by both baptism and charism.

For Further Reading

Related Chapters in This Book

For background on ministries in the New Testament see Matera, Frank J. "New Testament Theology of the Church."

For background on ministries in the early Church see Plumer, Eric. "The Development of Ecclesiology: Early Church to the Reformation."

For further treatment of episcopacy see Pottmeyer, Hermann J. "The Episcopacy."

For further treatment of the laity see Nilson, Jon. "The Laity."

For further treatment of the Second Vatican Council see Komonchak, Joseph A. "The Significance of Vatican II for Ecclesiology."

For further treatment of communion ecclesiology see Wood, Susan K. "The Church as Communion."

For further treatment of recent developments in ecclesiology see Himes, Michael J. "The Development of Ecclesiology: Modernity to the Twentieth Century."

Documents of the Vatican Council II

Since Vatican II was a "pastoral council," all its documents were concerned in some way with various aspects of "ministries in the Church"; however, particularly important in this regard are the following:

Lumen gentium (LG), The Dogmatic Constitution on the Church, 21 November 1964.

Christus Dominus (CD), Decree on the Pastoral Office of Bishops in the Church, 28 October 1965.

Apostolicam actuositatem (AA), Decree on the Apostolate of Lay People, 18 November 1965.

Presbyterorum ordinis (PO), Decree on the Ministry and Life of Priests, 7 December 1965.

References

Among the hundreds of works on "ministries in the Church" that have appeared since Vatican II, the following have been particularly helpful:

Baptism, Eucharist and Ministry. Faith and Order Paper 111. Geneva: World Council of Churches, 1982.

Baptism, Eucharist & Ministry, 1982–1990: Report on the Process and Responses. Faith and Order Paper 149. Geneva: World Council of Churches, 1990.

Barnett, James M. *The Diaconate: A Full and Equal Order.* New York: Seabury Press, 1981; rev. ed., Valley Forge, Pa.: Trinity Press International, 1995.

Baranowski, Arthur R. *Creating Small Faith Communities: A Plan for Restructuring the Parish and Renewing Catholic Life.* Cincinnati: St. Anthony Messenger Press, 1988.

Boff, Leonardo. *Ecclesiogenesis: The Base Communities Reinvent the Church.* Maryknoll, N.Y.: Orbis Books, 1986.

Brown, Raymond. *Priest and Bishop: Biblical Reflections.* Paramus, N.J.: Paulist Press, 1970.

Cooke, Bernard. *Ministry to Word and Sacrament: History and Theology.* Philadelphia: Fortress Press, 1976.

Cozzens, Donald B., ed. *The Spirituality of the Diocesan Priest.* Collegeville: The Liturgical Press, 1997.

Deck, Allan Figueroa, Yolanda Tarango, and Timothy Matovina, eds. *Perspectivas: Hispanic Ministry.* Kansas City, Mo.: Sheed and Ward, 1995.

Kinast, Robert. *Let Ministry Teach: A Guide to Theological Reflection.* Collegeville: The Liturgical Press, 1996.

O'Gara, Margaret. *The Ecumenical Gift Exchange.* Collegeville: The Liturgical Press, 1998.

O'Meara, Thomas. *Theology of Ministry.* New York: Paulist Press, 1983.

Power, David. *Gifts That Differ: Lay Ministries Established and Unestablished.* New York: Pueblo, 1980.

Schillebeeckx, Edward. *The Church with a Human Face: A New and Expanded Theology of Ministry.* New York: Crossroad, 1985.

_____. *Ministry: Leadership in the Community of Jesus Christ.* New York: Crossroad, 1985.

Whitehead, James D., and Evelyn E. Whitehead. *Method in Ministry.* New York: Seabury Press, 1980; rev. ed., Kansas City, Mo.: Sheed and Ward, 1995.

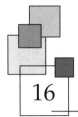

| 16 | The Papacy |

Richard P. McBrien

It is a special privilege for me not only to contribute to this *Festschrift* in honor of Patrick Granfield, but to write the chapter on the subject that has been central to his own work as a theologian. Father Granfield has been justly praised for his two monographs on the papacy: *The Papacy in Transition*[1] and *The Limits of the Papacy: Authority and Autonomy in the Church*.[2] The former work assumes, and argues for, a papacy that is "in transition" from a monarchical to a collegial model. The latter identifies four factors in the Church that generate "limits" on papal authority: the pope's collegial relationship with the worldwide episcopate; the existence of local churches as churches in their own right and not simply as administrative subdivisions of the universal Church; the *sensus fidelium*, which places limits upon what the pope can teach; and the very existence of other Christian churches, which generates implicit (and sometimes explicit) pressures to promote certain limits on papal authority in order to make the office more effective (and, therefore, more acceptable) as a truly Petrine ministry in the service of the unity of the whole Church.[3]

[1] *The Papacy in Transition* (Garden City, N.Y.: Doubleday, 1980). A revised and expanded edition subsequently appeared in German translation, *Das Papsttum: Kontinuität und Wandel* (Münster: Aschendorff, 1984).

[2] *The Limits of the Papacy: Authority and Autonomy in the Church* (New York: Crossroad, 1987). A revised and expanded edition subsequently appeared in Spanish translation, *Los Limites del Papado* (Bilbao: Desclée de Brouwer, 1991).

[3] Pope John Paul II, in fact, invited non-Catholic Christian pastoral leaders and theologians to offer suggestions on how the exercise of the papal office might be improved. See his 1995 encyclical, *Ut unum sint* (That All May Be One), in *Origins* 25 (June 8, 1995) 49, 51–72, especially nn. 95–6. For an excellent response to the pope's invitation, see *May They All Be One: A Response of the House of Bishops of the Church of England to* Ut Unum Sint (London: Church House Publishing, 1997).

This chapter begins with a general consideration of the papacy, addressing two subquestions: (1) What does the papacy have to do with Peter (the pope as the successor and Vicar of Peter)? and (2) What does the papacy have to do with Rome (the primacy of Rome and the pope as Bishop of Rome)? Second, it provides a selective ecclesiological overview of the history of the papacy, mindful always of the striking contrast between the papacy of the first Christian millennium and that of the second. Finally, it identifies the magisterial sources and explains the theological meaning of the Church's two dogmatic teachings on the papacy: primacy and infallibility.[4]

What Is the Papacy?
Its Petrine and Roman Connections

The papacy is the office of, and the jurisdiction exercised by, the Bishop of Rome, who is known more popularly as the pope.[5] The word "pope," "*papa*" in Italian, means "father." In the earliest centuries of the Christian era the title was applied to every bishop in the West. In the East it was also used by priests, but was a special title of the patriarch of Alexandria. In 1073 Pope Gregory VII formally restricted its use to the Bishop of Rome.

The pope has several other formal titles in addition to Bishop of Rome, which is the primary one. He is also known as Vicar of Jesus Christ (a title limited to the pope by Eugenius III [1145–53] in the mid-twelfth century), Successor of the Chief of the Apostles (the more succinct title is Vicar of Peter), Supreme Pontiff of the Universal Church, Patriarch of the West, the Primate of Italy, Archbishop and Metropolitan of the Roman Province, Sovereign of Vatican City State, and Servant of the Servants of God (first used by Pope Gregory the Great [590–604]).

Of these various titles, the two that are most commonly applied to the pope, by Catholics as well as the media, are Vicar of Christ and Supreme Pontiff. Ironically, the latter title (in Latin, *Pontifex Maximus*, "supreme bridge-builder") is of imperial and, therefore, pagan origin. It was accorded to the emperors in their role as head of the college of

---

[4] Since, at this writing, I had recently completed an ecclesiological and historical study of the papacy, I rely throughout this chapter on the research done in connection with that book, *Lives of the Popes: The Pontiffs from St. Peter to John Paul II* (San Francisco: HarperSanFrancisco, 1997).

[5] For a compressed statement on the nature of the papacy, see Jean-M.R. Tillard, "The Papacy," *The HarperCollins Encyclopedia of Catholicism*, ed. Richard P. McBrien (San Francisco: HarperCollins, 1995) 953–5.

(pagan) priests of Rome, and then was assumed by the popes themselves from the late fourth century. The former title, Vicar of Christ, is actually less traditional as a papal title than is Vicar of Peter, which was commonly accepted by popes, also from the end of the fourth century. The Second Vatican Council taught that all diocesan bishops are "vicars of Christ" (Dogmatic Constitution on the Church, n. 27). The pope is a vicar of Christ insofar as he is a bishop, not insofar as he is a pope. The title Vicar of Peter, on the other hand, emphasizes the point that the pope does not replace Peter, but rather is his substitute. In that role of vicar, or substitute, the pope continues Peter's mission to serve the unity of the whole Church and to strengthen the faith of the brethren (Luke 22:32), meaning the pope's brother bishops.[6]

What Does the Papacy Have to Do with Peter? *The Question of the Petrine Ministry*[7]

According to traditional Catholic belief, the papacy was directly established by Jesus Christ when he said to Peter at Caesarea Philippi:

> And so I say to you, you are Peter, and upon this rock I will build my church, and the gates of the netherworld shall not prevail against it. I will give you the keys to the kingdom of heaven. Whatever you bind on earth shall be bound in heaven; and whatever you loose on earth shall be loosed in heaven (Matt 16:18-19; see also Luke 22:31-32; and John 21:15-19).

The fact that Jesus' naming of Peter as the "rock" occurs in three different contexts in three separate Gospels has raised a question for biblical scholars about the original setting of the incident itself. They are not certain if it occurred before or after the resurrection, although the majority of scholars argues for a postresurrectional setting.[8] If that is the case, the account found in Matthew 16 would be a subsequent retrojection into Jesus' earthly ministry. Moreover, while the conferral of the power of the keys of the kingdom suggests an imposing measure of authority, given the symbolism of the keys, there is no explicit indication that the authority was meant to be exercised over others or that it be

---

[6] See Tillard, "Vicar of Christ" and "Vicar of Peter," *The HarperCollins Encyclopedia of Catholicism*, 1310–1.

[7] See Tillard, "Petrine Ministry" and "Petrine Succession," *The HarperCollins Encyclopedia of Catholicism*, 995–6. Also, Jerome Neyrey, "St. Peter," *The HarperCollins Encyclopedia of Catholicism*, 990—3.

[8] See Raymond E. Brown, *An Introduction to the New Testament* (New York: Doubleday, 1997) 221.

monarchical in character—a type of authority that developed especially in the Middle Ages and thereafter. On the contrary, Peter is portrayed as consulting with the other apostles and is even sent by them (Acts 8:14). And Paul "opposes him to his face" (Gal 2:11) for his inconsistency and hypocrisy in drawing back from table fellowship with Gentile Christians in Antioch because of pressure from newly arrived Jewish Christians from Jerusalem.

Nevertheless, there is a significant trajectory of biblical images that lays a foundation for the Church's traditional claims about the Petrine primacy. He is the fisherman (Luke 5:10; John 21:1-14), the shepherd of Christ's sheep (John 21:15-17), the Christian martyr (John 13:36; 1 Pet 5:1), an elder who addresses other elders (1 Pet 5:1), a proclaimer of faith in Jesus as the Son of God (Matt 16:16-17), the receiver of a special revelation (Mark 9:2-8; 2 Pet 1:16-18; Acts 1:9-16; 5:1-11; 10:9-16; 12:7-9), the guardian of the true faith against false teaching (2 Pet 1:20-21; 3:15-16), the rock on which the Church is to be built (Matt 16:18), and the repentant sinner (Mark 14:72) who becomes once again a source of strength to others (Luke 22:32). This trajectory of images continued into the life of the postbiblical Church: missionary preacher, great visionary, destroyer of heretics, receiver of the new law, gatekeeper of heaven, helmsman of the ship of the Church, and co-teacher and co-martyr with Paul.[9]

The Catholic Church considers Peter the first pope, but the first succession lists, prepared by Irenaeus (d. ca. 200) and the historian Hegesippus (d. ca. 180) and later attested to by Eusebius of Caesarea (d. ca. 339), identified Linus, not Peter, as the first pope, because popes were, in the understanding of the early Church, the successors of Peter. Peter was not regarded as himself a pope until the late second or early third century. Nevertheless, for almost all of its history the Catholic Church has, in fact, regarded Peter as the first pope, not only because of the special commission he received from Christ but also because of the unique status he enjoyed and the central role he played within the college of the twelve apostles. He was the first disciple called by Jesus (Matt 4:18-19), served as a spokesman for the other apostles (Mark 8:29; Matt 18:21; Luke 12:41; John 6:67-69), was the first to whom the Lord appeared after the resurrection (although Mary Magdalene is the primary witness in the tradition of Matthew, John, and the Marcan appendix), and was the one most frequently commissioned to preach the gospel following the Easter event.

[9] See *Peter in the New Testament: A Collaborative Assessment by Protestant and Roman Catholic Scholars,* ed Raymond E. Brown, Karl P. Donfried, and John Reumann (Minneapolis: Augsburg Publishing House; New York: Paulist Press, 1973) 157–68.

According to Catholic teaching, the pope continues Peter's distinctive ministry on behalf of the universal Church. For that reason, the service which the pope renders to the Church is called the Petrine ministry, which Jesus is believed to have conferred upon Peter at the Last Supper: "I have prayed that your own faith may not fail; and once you have turned back, you must strengthen your brothers" (Luke 22:32). It is essentially the same ministry of pastoral leadership that Peter is described as exercising in the first part of the Acts of the Apostles, involving the witnessing to the faith, overseeing the manner in which the local churches preserve and transmit the faith, providing assistance and encouragement to other pastoral leaders in the proclamation and defense of the faith, speaking in the name of other pastoral leaders and their local churches when the need arises, and articulating the faith of the Church on behalf of the whole communion of local churches.

In a very real sense, however, every bishop is a successor of Peter. Cyprian of Carthage (d. 258) held this, and so, too, did Hilary of Poitiers (d. 367), for whom all bishops are "successors of Peter and Paul." Nevertheless, it is a matter of Catholic doctrine that Petrine succession, like apostolic succession, is a development guided by the Holy Spirit and, therefore, of divine institution (Dogmatic Constitution on the Church, LG 18).[10]

What Does the Papacy Have to Do with Rome?
The Question of the Roman Primacy and of the Pope as the Bishop of Rome

The pope is, first and foremost, the Bishop of Rome.[11] If he is also the successor of Peter, would it not logically follow that Peter himself was the first Bishop of Rome? There are at least two difficulties with this assumption. First, there was already a thriving Christian community in Rome almost two decades before Peter arrived there. Second, there is no evidence that Rome even had a monoepiscopal form of ecclesiastical governance before the middle of the second century.

It is generally agreed by historians and biblical scholars alike that Christianity arrived in Rome in the early 40s, while Peter was still in Jerusalem. Therefore, Peter could not have been the original missionary to Rome or the founder of its local church. The best evidence is provided

[10] The Second Vatican Council follows the teaching of the First Vatican Council's First Dogmatic Constitution on the Church of Christ, *Pastor aeternus*, 2.

[11] The most important study in this regard is Jean-M.R. Tillard's *The Bishop of Rome*, trans. John de Satgé (Wilmington, Del.: Michael Glazier, 1983). On the question of the primacy, see Tillard, "Primacy, Papal," *The HarperCollins Encyclopedia of Catholicism*, 1051–3.

by Paul's letter to the Romans (written in 57/58), which makes no mention at all of Peter's presence in Rome. Most scholars agree that Peter probably did not come to Rome until the early 60s, but there are no available sources to permit us to determine when exactly he arrived in Rome, what he did there, and whether he exercised any kind of leadership within the Roman community.[12]

Although Peter did exercise an important role in the church at Jerusalem, neither is there any evidence that he functioned as the leader of that community (which should have been the case if he had been recognized, from the beginning, as the one chosen by Christ to be the first pope or the earthly head of the universal Church). On the contrary, it was James, not Peter, who presided over the so-called Council of Jerusalem in 49/50, described in Acts of the Apostles 11–15. Nevertheless, there is increasing agreement among historians and biblical scholars that Peter did go to Rome and was martyred there sometime after the year 60, during the reign of Nero. The North African theologian Tertullian (d. ca. 225) testified to Peter's having been crucified, as did the historian Eusebius of Caesarea in his *Ecclesiastical History* (2.25.5, 8), and there is a tradition that Peter asked to be crucified upside down, because of his unworthiness to endure the same form of death that the Lord had suffered. The Roman leader Clement (d. ca. 101), traditionally regarded as the third successor of Peter, described Peter's trials in Rome (*1 Clement* 5:4) and referred to both Peter and Paul as the "twin pillars" of the Roman church (5:2-7). Irenaeus of Lyons also assumed that Peter and Paul jointly founded the church of Rome and inaugurated its succession of bishops (*Against Heresies* 3.1.2; 3.3.3). But, again, there is no evidence that Peter actually served the church of Rome as its first bishop, or that Rome even had a monoepiscopal form of church governance until the middle of the next century. Although Ignatius of Antioch (d. ca. 107) is traditionally regarded as the first major witness to the primacy of Rome, having referred to it in the opening greeting of his *Letter to the Romans* as "foremost in love," it is significant that this letter is the only one of his seven letters to the churches of the ancient Mediterranean world that makes no mention of a local bishop.

Why, then, did Rome come to occupy so central a place in the life of the Church and particularly in the papal scheme of things? First, because of the city's political importance as the center of the Roman Empire and thus of the Gentile world to which the mission of the Church was increasingly directed. Second, because of the tradition that Peter

[12] See Raymond E. Brown and John P. Meier, *Antioch and Rome: New Testament Cradles of Catholic Christianity* (New York: Paulist Press, 1983), and Raymond E. Brown, *The Churches the Apostles Left Behind* (New York: Paulist Press, 1984).

and Paul were martyred and buried there. Third, because the Roman church regarded Peter and Paul as its "twin pillars" (*1 Clement* 5, again) and began in its letters to manifest care for other churches in the Roman Empire.[13] Indeed, it would have been extraordinary if Rome had *not* been singled out for a special role and position of authority in the early Church.

Not until the middle of the third century, with the pontificate of Stephen I (254–56), did any Bishop of Rome appeal to the classic "You are Peter . . ." text in Matt 16:18, and the correlation between Peter and the Bishop of Rome did not become fully explicit until the pontificate of Leo the Great (440–61), who insisted that Peter continued to speak to the whole Church through the Bishop of Rome. Indeed, when Leo intervened from afar in the great christological debates at the Council of Chalcedon (451), the bishops there proclaimed that it was the voice of Peter speaking through Leo.

In the end, is it absolutely essential that the successor of Peter be the Bishop of Rome rather than of some other local church? No, but the primacy of the see of Rome is so deeply rooted in Catholic tradition that the connection between Peter and its bishop could only be changed for the gravest of reasons.

How Has the Papacy Evolved Historically?[14]

This section is not intended as a compressed history of the papacy, but as an ecclesiological reflection on some of the most significant

[13] Brown, *An Introduction to the New Testament*, 221.

[14] Included among the classic histories of the papacy are: Erich Casper, *Geschichte des Papsttums von den Anfängen biz zur Höhe der Weltherrschaft*, 2 vols. (Tübingen: Mohr, 1930–33); Horace K. Mann, *The Lives of the Popes in the Early Middle Ages*, 18 vols. (London: Kegan Paul, Trench, Trübner, 1902–32); Ludwig von Pastor, *The History of the Papacy from the Close of the Middle Ages*, 40 vols. (St. Louis: Herder, 1899–1933); Franz Xaver Seppelt, *Geschichte der Päpste von den Anfängen bis zur Gegenwart* (Munich: Kösel, 1964). One of the most important sources for the history of the early popes is the *Liber Pontificalis*, ed. and trans. Raymond Davis, *The Book of Pontiffs* (Liverpool: Liverpool University Press, 1989). Other works include: Paolo Brezzi, *The Papacy: Its Origins and Historical Evolution* (Westminster, Md.: Newman Press, 1958); Robert B. Eno, *The Rise of the Papacy* (Wilmington, Del.: Michael Glazier, 1990); and Bernhard Schimmelpfennig, *The Papacy*, trans. James Sievert (New York: Columbia University Press, 1992). There are several excellent encyclopedias and dictionaries of the papacy, including: J.N.D. Kelly, *The Oxford Dictionary of Popes* (New York: Oxford University Press, 1986); and Philippe Levillain, ed., *Dictionnaire historique de la papauté* (Paris: Fayard, 1994). More recent historical commentaries include:

aspects of that history. Indeed, a deficient ecclesiology is almost always a function of a deficient sense of history. As Pope John XXIII, himself an accomplished historian, once pointed out, history is "the teacher of life."[15] The reader should be advised that some of the theses listed below have a decidedly critical edge to them. There is surely no intention here to engage in any kind of theological deconstruction of the papacy, an office which the Catholic Church formally teaches to be essential to the nature and structure of the Church. On the other hand, there are few topics in Catholic theology which have been so frequently distorted when viewed through the twin lenses of piety and institutional loyalty. The main reason for that distortion is the failure to examine and then to understand the historical contexts in which the papal office has taken root, evolved, and developed. This section is intended to serve, in part at least, as a corrective of that lack of critical historical comprehension. It is a concern, one might add, that Patrick Granfield himself has addressed with clarity and courage in his two books on the papacy, mentioned at the beginning of this chapter.

Peter can be considered a pope, indeed the first pope, but only in the most extended and accommodated sense of the word; and so, too, his immediate successors.

If we understand the papacy as an institutional vehicle of the Petrine ministry, that is, as a ministry dedicated to the unity of the universal Church and to the strengthening of the faith of its principal pastoral leaders, the bishops, then Peter can be regarded as a pope, and indeed as the first pope. We have already seen above that Peter exercised such a ministry. At the same time, there is no evidence that Peter himself established the church in Rome or served as its first bishop. Moreover, there is no evidence that there was even a monoepiscopal form of ecclesiastical governance in Rome until the middle of the second century, beginning perhaps with the pontificate of Pius I (ca. 142–ca. 155).[16] Before that time, the Roman community seems to have had a

---

Eamon Duffy, *Saints & Sinners: A History of the Popes* (London: Yale University Press, 1997); and Michael Walsh, ed., *The Papacy* (London: Weidenfeld & Nicolson, 1997). Duffy's book contains a number of useful bibliographies.

[15] "Pope John's Opening Speech to the Council," *The Documents of Vatican II*, ed. Walter M. Abbott, trans. Joseph Gallagher (New York: America Press, 1966) 712.

[16] J.N.D. Kelly agrees that the monarchical episcopate was a reality in Rome by this time. See his *The Oxford Dictionary of the Popes*, 10. Others place the beginning of the monoepiscopacy in Rome with the pontificate immediately following Pius I's, namely, that of Anicetus (ca. 155–ca. 166). See W.H.C. Frend, "The Origins of the Papacy: c. 33–440," *The Papacy*, ed. Michael Walsh, 26; and Duffy, *Saints & Sinners*, 9.

corporate or collegial form of pastoral leadership. Those counted among the earliest popes may very well have been the individuals who presided over the local council of elders or presbyter-bishops, or were simply the most prominent pastoral leaders of that community, or, like Clement (ca. 91–ca. 101), acted as the official representative of the Roman church in its correspondence with other churches throughout the ancient Mediterranean world.

The popes of the first four centuries, that is, until the watershed pontificate of Leo the Great (440–61), functioned with relatively limited authority outside of Rome and its immediate environs.

Sylvester I (314–35) seems to have exercised no influence over the first ecumenical council held at Nicaea in 325, a council that defined the divinity of Jesus Christ. So, too, Damasus I (366–84) had no role in convening or presiding over the First Council of Constantinople in 381, a council that defined the divinity of the Holy Spirit and gave us the Nicene-Constantinopolitan Creed that is recited to this day during the Sunday Eucharist and on great feasts. Likewise, Celestine I (422–32) played no role in the Council of Ephesus (431) that defined that there is only one divine person in Jesus Christ.

When the Donatist schismatics in North Africa appealed to the emperor Constantine to overturn a decision of Pope Melchiades (311–14), the emperor summoned a council of representatives from all of the western provinces to meet at Arles on August 1, 314. In doing so, he clearly signaled that he did not regard the pope's decision as final. Moreover, the pope himself took no exception to the emperor's action. And when the aforementioned Celestine I rehabilitated a presbyter who had been excommunicated by the African bishops, his brother bishops chastised him for failing to respect their autonomy.

The first pope to attempt to assert his authority beyond Rome and its neighboring dioceses (known as the suburbicarian sees) was Victor I (189–99). However, when he presumed to excommunicate those who disagreed with his ruling on the proper date for the celebration of Easter, he was rebuked by Irenaeus of Lyons, who pointedly reminded Victor that all of his predecessors had been indulgent toward the diversity of practice and had not dared to resort to the ultimate spiritual weapon of excommunication.

The first major turning-point in the history of the papacy was the pontificate of Leo the Great (440–61), in that he was the first to claim a universal and supreme authority for the office.

Leo I was the first pope to claim to be Peter's heir, which, according to Roman law, meant that all rights and duties associated with Peter lived on in Leo. Previous popes had spoken of their succession to Peter's chair or appealed to his martyrdom and burial in Rome as the basis of their authority. In his sermon given on the fifth anniversary of his election to the papacy, Leo insisted that "the stability which 'the Rock' himself received from that rock which is Christ, he conveys also to his heirs." Thereafter, popes increasingly regarded themselves as standing in the place of Peter, exercising authority not only over all of the faithful but over all of the other bishops as well. Leo himself exercised firm control not only over the bishops of Italy, including Milan and the northern regions, but also over Spain, North Africa, and southern Gaul. The East, however, was much less disposed than the local churches of the West to accept Leo's claims. And in spite of his powerful influence on the Council of Chalcedon (451), through his famous *Tome* on the humanity and divinity of Christ, he was unable to have that council held in Italy, with his own representatives presiding over it. He later objected in vain to the council's canon 28, granting Constantinople the same "prerogatives" and ecclesiastical dignity in the East as Rome enjoyed in the West. In fact, Leo was so opposed to this canon that he withheld his endorsement of the council's proceedings for two and a half years—and he never approved the canon itself.

Leo the Great's electoral principle, "He who is in charge of all should be elected by all," has been more honored in the breach than in the practice, particularly in the election of a pope.

One of Pope Leo's greatest legacies is his electoral principle, "He who is in charge of all should be elected by all" *(Letter 10)*. Nowhere has this principle been more blatantly neglected than in the election of a pope. From the time that the monoepiscopal form of ecclesiastical governance took root in Rome, its bishops were elected by the clergy and laity of that local church, in accordance with the custom in force throughout the universal Church. In the sixth and seventh centuries, the clergy and bishops of the suburbicarian dioceses (Ostia, Palestrina, Porto-Santa Rufina, Albano, Velletri-Segni, Frascati, and Sabina-Poggio Mirteto) took a more prominent part in electing the Bishop of Rome. Important civil and military officials as well as other influential laypersons also began to exercise a greater role than ordinary citizens, although the approval of the general populace was always regarded as necessary. Then, from the time of the Byzantine conquest of northern and extreme southern Italy and Sicily in 535–53 until the waning of their power with the ascendancy of the Lombards in the early eighth century, the Eastern emperors exercised an unhealthily decisive influence over papal elections. Those elected as Bishop of Rome could not be consecrated unless and until the Byzantine emperor had formally approved. It is important to remember that the pope is pope only insofar as he is the Bishop of Rome. Until 882 (with the election of Marinus I), every individual elected as pope was not yet a bishop. Consequently, during this period when the emperor had the authority to withhold permission for a pope-elect to be consecrated a bishop, he also had, in effect, the authority to decide who could and could not be pope. In almost all cases, however, that authority served only to delay the consecration of a newly elected pope, not to prevent it entirely. Benedict I (575–79), for example, had to wait eleven months from the day of his election. The last pope to seek the Byzantine emperor's approval for his consecration was Gregory III (731–41).

The role of the laity in the election of the Bishop of Rome was even further restricted in 769 when Stephen III decided, with the acquiescence of a Roman synod, that henceforth only clergy could vote. The laity's role was to be one of subsequent acceptance of their newly elected bishop. Emperor Louis the Pious (Charlemagne's successor) restored the role of the laity when he promulgated a Roman constitution in 824. However, the constitution also stipulated that before being consecrated, a newly elected pope had to take an oath of loyalty to the Carolingian emperor in the presence of the imperial legate.

The character of papal elections changed for the worse in the tenth century when the aristocratic families of Rome (the Theophylacts, the Crescentii, and the Tusculans) overwhelmed not only the voice of the laity but that of the clergy as well. Following the death of the notoriously corrupt John XII (a creature of the Theophylacts) in 964, the Holy Roman Emperor Otto I controlled the next three papal elections. But after Otto's death the powerful Crescentii family of Rome emerged as the new dominant force. That family's influence continued even into the eleventh century, when the Tusculans came to the fore, engineering the election of three successive (and generally undistinguished) laymen in 1012, 1024, and 1032.

The power of the German emperor-kings reasserted itself later in the eleventh century with the election of four successive German popes. Upon the election of a French pope, Nicholas II, in 1058 the qualifications of papal electors changed yet again. Nicholas decreed that henceforth only cardinal-bishops could vote. That provision was modified more than a century later when Alexander III included cardinal-priests and cardinal-deacons as papal electors, and also required for the first time a two-thirds majority for election. The clergy and laity of Rome were simply to give their subsequent assent to the election. The emperor would be notified of the result, but would no longer have the right of confirmation. The only major exception to this new electoral arrangement (which has held to this day) was in the election of Martin V at the Council of Constance in 1417. Because of the turmoil created by the Great Schism of 1378–1417, during which there were as many as three concurrent claimants to the papal throne, Martin was elected by twenty-two cardinals and thirty other prelates, six from each of the five major nations represented at the council (Italy, France, Spain, Germany, and England).

In 1945 Pius XII modified the ancient two-thirds rule established by Alexander III and stipulated that the required majority needed for election would be two-thirds plus one. In 1970 Paul VI decreed that only cardinals under the age of eighty would be eligible to vote in papal elections, with the maximum number of electors set at 120. Finally, in 1996 John Paul II negated Pius XII's modification of the two-thirds rule and dropped his plus-one amendment.[17] (In 1998 he also exceeded Paul VI's limit in his appointment of new cardinals under the age of eighty. However, several deaths almost immediately thereafter brought the number of eligible electors once again below 120.)

Throughout almost the entire second Christian millennium, however, the clergy and laity of the see of Rome were denied any voice in the election of their bishop. But, alas, their situation was and is no different from any other diocese in the Catholic Church, in direct violation of Leo the Great's principle, "He who is in charge of all should be elected by all."

Centralization of authority in the papacy has not only diminished the legitimate pastoral autonomy of the worldwide episcopate, but has also served to spread the effects of papal deficiencies beyond Italy to the worldwide Church.

Although some historians refer to the ninth and tenth centuries as the nadir of the papacy because of papal corruption in the form of simony, nepotism, concubinage, and even violent behavior, the worldwide Church beyond the Italian peninsula did not suffer so great a harm as one might otherwise have expected. Indeed, the Anglo-Saxon Church experienced a period of vigorous revival and reform. Lacking a strong central government and an efficient system of international communication, the Church of this time was more like a loose federation of local churches, which were themselves synodal federations of monarchical sees. But once the monarchical papacy was clearly established in the pontificate of Gregory VII (1073–85), this situation changed—sometimes for the better (as in the case of the dissemination of needed reforms) and sometimes for the worse (as in the case of the

[17] "Apostolic Constitution *Universi Dominici Gregis*," *Origins* 25 (March 7, 1996) 617, 619–30. For a historical overview of papal elections, see McBrien, *Lives of the Popes*, 403–10.

Church's deep involvement in political conflicts in Europe and beyond).

Indeed, it was one of the greatest theologians of the twentieth century
and perhaps the greatest ecclesiologist of all time, Yves Congar, who argued that "the great turning point in ecclesiology is the eleventh century. The turning point is, of course, embodied in the person of Gregory
VII."[18] Congar acknowledged, as any historian must, that Gregory VII
faced overwhelming internal and external problems when he was
elected, as a reformer, in 1073. Unfortunately, in a good-faith effort to
amass the kind of legal support he felt he needed to combat these problems, Gregory created a new kind of papacy. As Congar pointed out, by
seeking to rely on legal precedents for the exercise of what should be only
spiritual authority, Gregory VII "ended up by making the Church itself
into a legal institution," with "papal power as the basis of everything."[19]
Gregory VII thereby launched the second-millennial papacy as a legalistic, monarchical office—a concept foreign to the first-millennial
Church and the whole of the East. (It is perhaps not entirely coinciden-
tal that it was Gregory VII who decreed in 1073 that the title of "pope"
should thereafter be restricted to the Bishop of Rome. It had been applied previously to every bishop in the West, and even to priests in the
East.) The Roman Curia was established soon after Gregory VII's pontificate, by Urban II (1088–99), but it did not become fully organized
and operational until 1588, under Sixtus V (1585–90).

*Although the papal office is one of the principal means of unifying the
Church, it has also functioned as a principal cause of division in the Church, as
in the case of events leading up to the Protestant Reformation.*

The Second Vatican Council's Decree on Ecumenism acknowledges
that the divisions in the Church occasioned by the East-West Schism
and the Protestant Reformation were the responsibility of "people on
both sides" (n. 3). The Reformation in particular was the product of a
series of tragic mistakes and even corrupt actions on the part of the papacy itself, a ministry designed to maintain unity in the universal
Church.

The fourteenth and fifteenth centuries were among the worst in the
history of the Church in the West. The monarchical papacy, unwittingly
launched by Gregory VII in the latter part of the eleventh century, became a bloated bureaucracy too often marked by greed and a lust for
power. The Avignon papacy (1305–78) and then the Great Schism

[18] *Fifty Years of Catholic Theology: Conversations with Yves Congar,* ed. Bernard Lauret
(Philadelphia: Fortress Press, 1988) 40.
[19] Ibid., 42.

(1378–1417) so diminished the papacy's standing in the Church that the Councils of Constance (1414–17) and Basel (1431–49) sought to replace the pope as earthly head of the Church by a general, or ecumenical, council. The situation became so deteriorated that many of the cardinal-electors elicited solemn promises from papal candidates to work for reform if elected. Unfortunately, those promises were broken more often than not.

The chair of Peter was occupied in the century just before the Reformation by two of its most corrupt incumbents in history, Callistus III (1455–58) and his nephew Alexander VI (1492–1503). The two popes who served just prior to its outbreak were Julius II (1503–13), who won election through bribery, spent much of his time as pope in military armor, and sold indulgences to help raise funds for the new St. Peter's Basilica, and Leo X (1513–21), who sold Church offices as well as indulgences to pay off debts incurred through personal extravagances, military campaigns, and the construction of St. Peter's. His response to the growing call for reform in the Church was to excommunicate Martin Luther.

By the time those in the papal office realized the seriousness and staying power of the Reformation, the proverbial horses had already bolted from the barn. Some of the popes did make good-faith efforts to repair at least some of the damage. Paul III (1534–49) convened the Council of Trent in 1545, which initiated the Catholic Counter-Reformation. Unfortunately, this Counter-Reformation also bore the seeds of its own excesses. Paul IV (1555–59) strengthened the Inquisition, established the Index of Forbidden Books, and confined Jews to a ghetto in Rome and required them to wear a distinctive headgear. But there were other true reformers in the papacy besides Paul III. Pius IV (1559–65) reconvened the Council of Trent after a ten-year suspension. Pius V (1566–72) enforced its decrees, published the Roman Catechism, and reformed the Roman Missal and the Divine Office; unfortunately, he also excommunicated Queen Elizabeth I, thereby placing English Catholics in mortal danger. Gregory XIII (1572–85) continued to support the reformist decrees of Trent, reconstructed and endowed the old Roman College (now the Gregorian University), and reformed the Julian calendar (the new version being the Gregorian calendar still in use today).

When the papacy engages the world rather than simply opposing it in a single-minded countercultural fashion, the office can be an effective force for justice and peace.

Four of the most effective modern popes in their dealings with the wider world have been Leo XIII (1878–1903), John XXIII (1958–63), Paul VI (1963–78), and John Paul II (1978–present).

Leo XIII was least like his immediate predecessor, Pius IX (1846–78), in his understanding of the relationship between Church and society as well as his general openness to scholarship and the intellectual life. He opened the Vatican archives to scholars, declaring that "the Church has nothing to fear from the truth," gave tentative recognition to democracy in his encyclical *Diuturnum illud* (1881), and, in his watershed encyclical *Rerum novarum* (1891), insisted on the social responsibility of property-owners and on the rights of workers to form labor unions and to earn a just wage in a safe and humane work environment. He also secured a revision of the anticlerical laws passed in Germany during the *Kulturkampf,* reached diplomatic accommodations with Belgium and Russia, and secured the withdrawal of anticlerical legislation in Chile, Mexico, and Spain.

In spite of some mistakes, like his forbidding Catholics from participating in Italian elections, his censuring of what was misleadingly labeled as Americanism, and his intransigent stand against recognizing the validity of Anglican orders, Leo XIII brought a new measure of international prestige to the papacy after long years of reactionary and separatist papal attitudes and policies toward the emerging modern world, at once pluralistic and increasingly democratic.

John XXIII, more than any other pope in history, earned the admiration, respect, and affection of the world beyond the Church. He proclaimed the fundamental dignity of every human being and radiated a sense of warmth, inclusiveness, and love for all. His opening address to the Second Vatican Council in October 1962 embodied the vision and spirit of his relatively brief pontificate. In that address he placed himself in direct opposition to leading figures in the Roman Curia who held to a more authoritarian, defensive, and punitive concept of the Church.

> In the daily exercise of our office we sometimes have to listen, much to our regret, to voices of persons who, though burning with zeal, are not endowed with too much sense of discretion or measure. In these modern times they can see nothing but prevarication and ruin. They say that our era, in comparison with past eras, is getting worse, and they behave as though they have learned nothing from history, which is, nonetheless, the teacher of life. They behave as though at the time of former councils everything was a full triumph for the Christian idea and life and for proper religious liberty. We feel we must disagree with those prophets of gloom, who are always forecasting disaster, as though the end of the world were at hand. In the present order of things, Divine Providence is leading us to a new order of human relations which, by our own efforts and even beyond our very expectations, are directed toward the fulfillment of God's superior and inscrutable designs. And

everything, even human differences, leads to the greater good of the Church.[20]

His agenda was captured in one Italian word, *aggiornamento,* an "updating" of the Church. He also employed the metaphor of a closed window suddenly thrust open "to let some fresh air in." We are not born to be "museum keepers," he once said, "but to cultivate a flourishing garden of life."

Beyond the council itself—clearly his greatest achievement—John XXIII's openness to the world was conveyed through his several encyclicals. *Mater et magistra* (1961) updated Catholic social teaching on property, the rights of workers, and the obligations of government. *Pacem in terris* (1963) insisted that the recognition of human rights and responsibilities is the foundation of world peace. Earlier, during the Cuban missile crisis of 1962, he had broadcast a message over Vatican Radio to heads of state, urging both sides to exercise caution. The next day the Soviet newspaper *Pravda* carried a quotation from the address in a banner headline: "We beg all rulers not to be deaf to the cry of humanity." Commentators have pointed out that John XXIII's appeal made it possible for the Soviet premier Nikita Khrushchev to back down without losing face. The event also encouraged the Pope to write *Pacem in terris.* He was awarded the Peace Prize of the International Balzan Foundation in 1962, and posthumously the U.S. Presidential Medal of Freedom in 1963.

The most ecumenically-minded pope in history, John XXIII was mourned in death like no other Bishop of Rome before him. Even the Union Jack was lowered to half-mast in the bitterly divided city of Belfast.

Paul VI chose his papal name as a sign that he, like the apostle to the Gentiles, was determined to reach out to the modern Gentiles, that is, to the whole world. One of the high points of his pontificate was his historic visit to the United Nations on October 4, 1965, to plead for peace. His speech, delivered in French, contained the powerful and memorable words, *"Jamais plus la guerre! Jamais plus la guerre!"* ("Never again war!"). His first encyclical, *Ecclesiam suam* (1965), insisted that the Church must always be in dialogue, not only with other religious bodies but with the world at large. In 1967 he published his *Populorum progressio,* an encyclical that highlighted and deplored the gap between rich and poor nations and which reminded readers that the goods of the earth are intended by God for everyone. His apostolic exhortation *Evangelii nuntiandi* (1975) linked evangelization with the Church's abiding concern for social justice, human rights, and peace. In 1968 he

---

[20] *The Documents of Vatican II,* 712–3.

instituted an annual observance of World Day of Peace on January 1. In the minds of many Catholics, the only significant blemish on his pontificate was his encyclical *Humanae vitae* (1968), which declared that every artificial means of birth control is always seriously sinful. So taken aback was he by the negative reaction to the pronouncement from within the Catholic Church itself that he vowed never again to publish an encyclical. And he did not.

John Paul II, elected in 1978, became the most traveled pope in history. He has been generally credited with accelerating the downfall of the Soviet Empire by his astute and persistent support of the Solidarity movement in Poland. His first encyclical, *Redemptor hominis* (1979), emphasized the dignity and worth of every human person, deplored the "exploitation of the earth" and the destruction of the environment, and condemned the accumulation and misuse of material goods by privileged social classes and rich countries, the arms race for diverting essential resources from the poor, and the violation of human rights around the globe. In 1981, a few months after the attempt on his life in St. Peter's Square, he published *Laborem exercens* (1981), an encyclical that viewed human work as a form of collaboration in the creative work of God and, therefore, of infinite dignity. He also condemned what he called a "rigid" capitalism that exaggerates the rights of private ownership over the common good and the common use of goods. In 1987 he published yet another social encyclical, *Sollicitudo rei socialis,* which emphasized the obligations of rich and developed nations toward poor and undeveloped countries, and also the "preferential option for the poor" as a guideline for moral action. The goods of the earth, he insisted, are destined for all. In 1991, on the hundredth anniversary of Leo XIII's *Rerum novarum,* he released yet another major social encyclical, *Centesimus annus,* which reaffirmed the principle that the individual human person is at the heart of the Church's social message and of its "preferential option for the poor," and it referred positively to democratic systems for ensuring the participation of citizens in a nation's political life. John Paul II also published encyclicals of a more conservative nature: *Veritatis splendor* (1993), which was critical of moral relativism, and *Evangelium vitae* (1995), which reaffirmed the Church's condemnation of contraception, euthanasia, and abortion. The encyclical also condemned capital punishment, insisting that there are, for all practical purposes, no sufficient reasons ever to justify it.

Given the subject of this chapter, perhaps his most remarkable encyclical, also issued in 1995, was *Ut unum sint,* which acknowledged that, while the Petrine office belongs to the essential structure of the Church, the manner in which the papal office is exercised is always subject to criticism and improvement. As pointed out above, he invited

pastoral leaders and theologians of other Christian churches to enter
into dialogue with him about the manner in which his office is exercised and to recommend ways by which its exercise might conform
more faithfully to the gospel.

What Does the Church Teach about the Papacy?

Papal Primacy[21]

The first major conciliar teaching on the primacy of the pope was
formulated by the Council of Florence in its Decree for the Greeks
(1439), a document that would be cited more than four hundred years
later by the First Vatican Council:

> We also define that the holy apostolic see and the Roman pontiff holds
> the primacy over the whole world and the Roman pontiff is the succes-
> sor of blessed Peter prince of the apostles, and that he is the true vicar of
> Christ, the head of the whole church and the father and teacher of all
> Christians, and to him was committed in blessed Peter the full power of
> tending, ruling and governing the whole church, as is contained also in
> the acts of ecumenical councils and in the sacred canons.[22]

Vatican I taught that the pope enjoys "a primacy of jurisdiction over
the whole Church of God," and not only a "primacy of honor," and that
this primacy was conferred upon him by Christ "immediately and directly" (First Dogmatic Constitution on the Church [*Pastor aeternus*],
1).[23] Moreover, this primacy is permanent and is passed on to each of
Peter's successors (2).[24]

> So, then, if anyone says that the Roman pontiff has merely an office of
> supervision and guidance, and not the full and supreme power of juris-
> diction over the whole church, and this not only in matters of faith and
> morals, but also in those which concern the discipline and government

[21] The most recent comprehensive study of the primacy is Klaus Schatz's *Papal Primacy: From Its Origins to the Present*, trans. John A. Otto and Linda M. Maloney (Collegeville: The Liturgical Press, 1996). The most important ecumenical study is *Papal Primacy and the Universal Church: Lutherans and Catholics in Dialogue V*, ed. Paul C. Empie and T. Austin Murphy (Minneapolis: Augsburg Publishing House, 1974).

[22] *Decrees of the Ecumenical Councils*, vol. 1: *Nicaea I to Lateran V*, ed. Norman P. Tanner (London: Sheed and Ward; Washington, D.C.: Georgetown University Press, 1990) 528.

[23] *Decrees of the Ecumenical Councils*, vol. 2: *Trent to Vatican II*, ed. Norman P. Tanner (London: Sheed and Ward; Washington, D.C.: Georgetown University Press, 1990) 812.

[24] Ibid., 813.

of the church dispersed throughout the whole world; or that he has only the principal part, but not the absolute fullness, of this supreme power; or that this power of his is not ordinary and immediate both over all and each of the churches and over all and each of the pastors and faithful: let him be anathema (*Pastor aeternus*, 3).[25]

On May 14, 1872, Otto von Bismark, chancellor of Germany, issued a document in which he maintained that the teaching of Vatican I concerning the immediate and universal jurisdiction of the pope made bishops into mere executive organs of the pope. Early in 1875 (January–February) the German bishops issued their own Collective Declaration which insisted that the episcopate also has divinely instituted rights and duties and that the pope has "neither the right nor the power to change them." The bishops directly rebutted Bismark's view that, by reason of the council's teaching on the primacy, episcopal jurisdiction has been absorbed into the papal, and that the pope has, in principle, taken the place of each individual bishop, who is now no more than a tool of the pope. In a subsequent apostolic brief, issued on March 6, 1875, Pope Pius IX gave his full approval to the German bishops' Collective Declaration.[26]

The Second Vatican Council reaffirmed the teaching of Vatican I on "the institution, the permanence, the nature and the force of the sacred primacy of the Roman Pontiff," but explicitly situated the primacy in a collegial context, insisting that all the bishops "together with Peter's successor . . . govern the house of the living God" (Dogmatic Constitution on the Church, 18; also 22), albeit "never apart from him" (22). At the same time, the bishops are not to be regarded as "vicars of the Roman Pontiff; for they exercise a power which they possess in their own right" (27). The nineteenth-century German bishops who responded to Bismark would have been pleased.

Papal Infallibility [27]

Infallibility means literally "immunity from error." Theologically, it is a negative charism of the Holy Spirit in that it protects the Church from fundamental error when it solemnly defines a matter of faith or morals. Papal infallibility is a dimension of the Church's infallibility,

[25] Ibid., 814–5.

[26] "Collective Declaration by the German Hierarchy (1875)," *The Christian Faith in the Doctrinal Documents of the Catholic Church,* ed. Jacques Dupuis, 6th ed. (New York: Alba House, 1996) 298–9.

[27] The classic historical study is Brian Tierney's *Origins of Papal Infallibility, 1150–1350: A Study on the Concepts of Infallibility, Sovereignty and Tradition in the*

not vice versa. The pope's infallibility is the same infallibility as that "with which the divine redeemer wished to endow his church" (Dogmatic Constitution on the Church, 25). Papal primacy and papal infallibility are conceptually distinct. The one does not essentially require the other. In Catholic teaching, however, they inhere in the same office. At the same time, infallibility is not to be confused with indefectibility. The latter ensures that the Church will remain faithful to the teaching of Christ over the long course of history, in spite of many individual errors in non-infallible teaching; the former ensures that in a particular teaching of its own, and given the appropriate conditions, the Church will not, and indeed cannot, deviate from Christ's teaching. Those conditions for the exercise of papal infallibility are: (1) that the pope be teaching as earthly head of the universal Church, that is, *ex cathedra* (Latin, "from the chair"); (2) that the teaching be a matter of faith or morals; and (3) that the pope clearly intend to bind the whole Church.[28]

The essence of the Church's teaching on papal infallibility was given in the First Vatican Council's *Pastor aeternus*, 4:

> We teach and define as a divinely revealed dogma that when the Roman pontiff speaks *ex cathedra*, that is, when, in the exercise of his office as shepherd and teacher of all Christians, in virtue of his supreme apostolic authority, he defines a doctrine concerning faith or morals to be held by the whole church, he possesses, by the divine assistance promised to him in blessed Peter, that infallibility which the divine Redeemer willed his church to enjoy in defining doctrine concerning faith or morals. Therefore, such definitions of the Roman pontiff are of themselves *[ex sese]*, and not by the consent of the church *[non autem ex consensu ecclesiae]*, irreformable.[29]

Papal infallibility, however, is not a personal prerogative. The pope is empowered with the charism of infallibility only when he is in the act of defining a doctrine of faith or morals as earthly head of the uni-

---

Middle Ages (Leiden: E. J. Brill, 1972). The book was reprinted in 1988 with a new postscript. The most significant dissenting view is that of Hans Küng, *Infallible? An Inquiry* (New York: Doubleday, 1971). The most important ecumenical study is *Teaching Authority and Infallibility: Lutherans and Catholics in Dialogue VI*, ed. Paul C. Empie, T. Austin Murphy, and Joseph Burgess (Minneapolis: Augsburg Publishing House, 1980). See also John T. Ford, "Infallibility," *The HarperCollins Encyclopedia of Catholicism*, 664–5.

[28] If there is any reasonable doubt about the pope's intention to teach infallibly and to bind the whole Church thereby, the definition in question is not to be regarded as infallible. "No doctrine is understood to be infallibly defined unless it is clearly established as such" (Code of Canon Law, Can. 749.3).

[29] *Decrees of the Ecumenical Councils*, vol. 2, 816.

versal Church and on its behalf. When Vatican I declared that papal definitions are "irreformable" of themselves and not by the consent of the Church, it did not mean that the pope is above the Church. The phrasing was added to the definition in order to exclude the tendency of some Gallicans to regard subsequent approval by the bishops to be necessary to establish the final authority of an infallible teaching.[30] But the consent of the whole Church can never be lacking, according to Bishop Vincenz Gasser, the floor manager of the document. Similarly, irreformability does not mean that infallible teachings are perfect as they stand and, therefore, immune to change. They are formulations written in human language and are historically conditioned. As such, they are subject to revision. According to the Congregation for the Doctrine of the Faith's *Mysterium ecclesiae* (1973), even infallibly defined dogmas are affected by the limits of human knowledge and by the situation in which they are framed, by the specific concerns that motivated the definitions, by the changeable conceptions (or thought categories) of a given epoch, and by "the expressive power of the language used at a certain point of time."[31]

Insofar as papal infallibility concerns the faithful proclamation of the gospel and the unity of the Church, it will remain a matter of some theological and pastoral importance and debate. However, when it is disengaged from conventional exaggerations of papal authority and is placed in the wider context of collegiality and the nature of the Church as the People of God, the dogma of papal infallibility becomes a much less serious ecumenical problem than it was in the past.

Conclusion

At Pope John XXIII's coronation Mass in St. Peter's Basilica on November 4, 1958, the senior cardinal-deacon, in keeping with a millennium-long custom, carefully placed an imperial tiara on the new pope's head, at the same time reciting the ancient formula: "Know that you are the father of princes and kings, pontiff of the whole world and Vicar of Christ on earth." Given the extraordinarily humble and self-effacing persona that John XXIII would almost immediately disclose to

[30] Gallicanism was a movement that claimed for the Church in France an independence from papal intervention. It regarded a general, or ecumenical, council as superior to the pope and insisted that papal pronouncements are subject to subsequent episcopal approval. The movement was essentially dissolved with the French Revolution, although it was revived in some form after the restoration of the monarchy in the nineteenth century.

[31] Full text in *Origins* 3 (July 19, 1973) 97, 99, 100. For pertinent excerpts, see my *Catholicism: Completely Revised and Updated* (San Francisco: HarperCollins, 1994) 1209–10.

the world, that whole scene, in retrospect, could not have been more in-congruous.

From the moment the tiara was placed on his head, and much to the consternation of the conservative cardinals around him, he signaled that he would be a very different kind of pope from those who had pre-ceded him in the office: a servant rather than a sovereign, a pastor rather than a patrician, a priest rather than a prelate. He sounded the keynote for his pontificate in the homily of the Mass which, contrary to tradition, he delivered himself. He would not be "the father of princes and kings," but a Good Shepherd, after the pattern of Jesus himself. "There are those," he pointed out, "who expect the pontiff to be a statesman, a diplomat, a scholar, the organizer of the collective life of society, or someone whose mind is attuned to every form of modern knowledge" (in other words, a pope just like his predecessor, Pius XII). Such a profile, John XXIII insisted, "was not fully in conformity with [the papacy's] true ideal." Indeed, those qualities, he said, cannot "sub-stitute for being the shepherd of the whole flock."

That is what the papacy is all about.

For Further Reading

Brown, Raymond E., ed. *Peter in the New Testament.* Minneapolis: Augsburg Publishing House; New York: Paulist Press, 1973.

Duffy, Eamon. *Saints & Sinners: A History of the Popes.* London: Yale University Press, 1997.

Granfield, Patrick. *The Limits of the Papacy: Authority and Autonomy in the Church.* New York: Crossroad, 1987.

_____. *The Papacy in Transition.* Garden City, N.Y.: Doubleday, 1980.

LaDue, William. *The Chair of St. Peter: A History of the Papacy.* Maryknoll, N.Y.: Orbis Books, 1999.

McBrien, Richard P. *Lives of the Popes: The Pontiffs from St. Peter to John Paul II.* San Francisco: HarperSanFrancisco, 1997.

Schatz, Klaus. *Papal Primacy: From Its Origins to the Present.* Trans. John A. Otto and Linda M. Maloney. Collegeville: The Liturgical Press, 1996.

Tillard, Jean-M. R. *The Bishop of Rome.* Trans. John de Satgé. Wilmington, Del.: Michael Glazier, 1983.

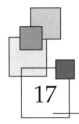

17   The Episcopacy

Hermann J. Pottmeyer

The Conceptual, Structural, and Pastoral Renewal of the Church through Vatican II

Whoever wishes to speak of the ministry of the episcopacy must speak first of the mystery of the Church. Because the ministry of the episcopacy has its roots in the mystery of the Church, it belongs to its historical form and must serve the reality of the Church in the world.

It is in this way that Vatican II speaks of the episcopacy. No other council has treated in such detail the mystery of the Church and the ministry of the episcopacy. With the renewal of the Church, the council also wanted to renew the ministry of the episcopacy. Today—more than thirty years after the closing of the council—we are still on the way to the renewal the council wanted and initiated. This journey has been marked by progress and regress. At any rate, Vatican II's teaching represents the current dogmatic understanding of the Catholic Church on the episcopacy.

With its reform of the Church, Vatican II was pursuing a pastoral goal: "That the kingdom of God may come and the salvation of the human race may be accomplished" (GS 45). The council recognized that the Church can fulfill its divine mission, which is to be the universal sacrament of God's kingdom and its coming, only by renewing itself "at once manifesting and actualizing the mystery of God's love for humanity" (GS 45; cf. LG 1). In order to rediscover God's original will for his Church, the council took inspiration from the Bible and the early tradition and praxis of the Church. To be exact, the council had a threefold renewal of the Church in mind: a conceptual, structural, and pastoral renewal.

At the center of the conceptual renewal stand three biblical metaphors corresponding to the threefold being and action of God: the Church as the People of God the Father, as the body of Christ, and as

communio or communion in the Holy Spirit. The doctrine of the Church
as the People of God affirms that all believers, on account of their baptism and confirmation, are bound together by the same dignity of the
children of God and bear responsibility for the common mission of the
whole People of God. The doctrine of the Church as the body of Christ
affirms that Jesus Christ is the head and shepherd of the Church; the
body of the glorified Christ consists of many members who all contribute to the life and growth of the Church according to their vocations
and gifts. The doctrine of the Church as *communio* in the Holy Spirit
affirms that the Holy Spirit gives the members of the Church various
gifts and charisms with which they can live out their vocations; it is the
same Holy Spirit who brings the many members into the one community.

With the structural renewal the council kept before its eye the
communio-structure and *communio*-praxis of the early Church in which
the biblical concept of Church first took form. The early Church understood itself as the community of the sisters and brothers of Christ,
whom God has taken as his children *(communio fidelium)*. The community was gathered by Jesus who is present in the word of the gospel and
in the celebration of the Eucharist as well as other sacraments. Because
the preaching of the gospel and the celebration of the sacraments are
carried out in each local church or diocese, each particular church is
truly Church. However, the only true Church is that which is in communion with the other particular churches. Hence, according to its
structure, the universal Church, the body of Christ, is a communion of
local churches *(communio ecclesiarum)*. The rediscovery of this fundamental structure of the Church is one of the most important results of
Vatican II.

The Holy Spirit is the life principle of *communio*. Just as the Spirit
binds the believers in each particular church into a community, so the
Spirit leads the particular churches into the communion and unity of
the universal Church together. The role of the Holy Spirit as the life
principle of the Church as *communio* and the role of charisms as contribution to the life of the Church are likewise one of the greatest rediscoveries of the last council. These rediscoveries were grounded not
only in the return to the Bible and the early tradition of the Church, but
also in the recognition that the *communio*-structure of the Church is in
many respects more challenging and endangered than a centralizing
and one-sided hierarchical structure. All the members of the Church
must therefore be aware that they have need of the gifts of the Holy
Spirit in order to build up and form the Church as *communio*.

The basis of the pastoral renewal which Vatican II had in mind is
the comparison of the Church with a sacrament. The Church—so

teaches the council—is in Christ and in the power of the Holy Spirit as it were the sacrament of the kingdom of God, that is, for the *communio* of humans with God and among themselves. This fruitful idea, of course, has deep roots in the biblical and early tradition; however, expressed in this form, it is a peculiar contribution of Vatican II. The council characterizes the Church as a sacrament because it is called to be the sign and instrument of the coming of the reign of God. Both functions are important. The Church must be a credible sign for people to be able to recognize in it what the kingdom of God is and brings. Many things make up the nature of the Church as sign: the witness of each individual Christian, that of the community, and that of the whole Church. Because the kingdom of God means the *communio* of humans with God and with one another, it is above all through the witness of this *communio* that the Church becomes a credible sign of the reign of God and its coming, be it in its structural form or in its praxis. Through its witness the Church becomes an instrument of God by means of which God realizes his reign. It belongs to the economy of salvation, to which God is committed, that God will bring about the kingdom through the saving incarnation in Jesus Christ and through the ministry of the Church.

It is in the context of this project of threefold renewal of the Church and ecclesiology that a conceptual renewal of the episcopacy came about. Indeed, Vatican II even saw in it one of the most important building blocks of its whole reform project. For the reform of the episcopacy the council returned likewise to the Bible and the early tradition and praxis of the Church.

In order to obtain a correct understanding of Vatican II's teaching on the episcopacy, it is necessary to take a brief overview of the history of this doctrine. Only in the light of this history can it be explained in which respects the doctrine of the episcopacy was renewed and deepened by the last council. In addition, it is necessary to pay particular attention to the origin of the episcopal office, since the opinion that monoepiscopacy belongs to the binding structure and the divinely willed constitution of the Church is not shared by all Christians. The dissenting opinion is based above all on three grounds. The first sees monoepiscopacy as a later and nonbinding development, since, according to the witness of the Bible, there were originally other forms of community leadership. The second holds that monoepiscopacy and the monarchical bishop to be a contradiction of the teaching of Jesus and the *communio*-character of the Christian community which requires a brotherly and sisterly organization. The third maintains that monoepiscopacy is an outdated patriarchal structure belonging to a past social and cultural age.

Origins and Changing Theological
Concepts of the Episcopacy

Three factors have contributed to the rise and formation of the episcopacy: the theological self-understanding of the Christian community
or churches, the form or model of the apostle, and, finally, the influences of the cultural and social world.

The first communities described themselves as *ecclesia Dei*. In connection with the Jewish *qahal Jahweh* or People of God, they understood
themselves as the community that was chosen by God from all peoples
and nations of those who believe in Christ. The name *"ecclesia Dei"* or
"Church of God" designates both the local church and the universal
Church. The most important ground for this self-understanding is the
Church's consciousness of being called together by God. Strictly tied
with this understanding is the awareness that God has convoked the
Church, the people of the end-time, through Jesus Christ. Indeed, it is
the gathering presence and power of the risen Lord that is experienced
in the Church; the risen one is identical with the Jesus who before Easter
had sent out his disciples to gather together the people of the end-time.
That is why Jesus Christ was for the first communities the shepherd
and head of the Church, and the Church was the body of the glorified
Christ. This fundamental characteristic of the *ecclesia Dei*—to be called
together by God through Christ—must express itself in all the institutions within the Church: in preaching, in the celebration of the Eucharist and other sacraments, in service *(diakonia)*, and in church offices.
The services and offices of the Church must be grounded in the will of
God and Christ.

The second factor was the form and model of the apostle. The pre-
Easter Jesus as well as the risen one had sent out his disciples and invested them with his power. Through their preaching they founded
communities, established overseers as Paul did, and invested them
with their power. In Jerusalem, James was an example of how the form
of an overseer in the circle of elders (presbyters) was shaped. In the
Pauline communities Paul exercised his authority, supported by his
collaborators. For other communities Peter, the first among the apostles,
was the prototype of overseer; in other communities it was the figure of
John. In the succeeding generation the communities considered their
overseers as successors of the apostles and their ministries. Through
their services Jesus Christ continues to be effective as the living shepherd of the Church.

The third factor is made up of the influences of the cultural and
social world. Thus, the community of Jerusalem and other Jewish-
Christian communities were led by the college of *presbyteroi* or elders—

a form of leadership originating from Jewish synagogues (Acts 15:22). As imitators of Christ, "the shepherd and guardian of your souls" (1 Pet 2:25), they must serve the community as shepherds (Acts 20:17, 28; 1 Pet 5:1, 4). In Pauline communities there was a plurality of charisms, among which there was that of serving the upbuilding of the community (1 Cor 12:28); furthermore, Paul also mentions the service of overseer (1 Thess 5:12ff.; 1 Cor 16:16). For the first time, in Phil 1:1, the dual offices of "bishops and deacons" are mentioned—expressions that came from the Hellenistic world. In the beginning the services were grounded in charisms, which later evolved into definite offices. In the *Didache* (in Syria, ca. 100 c.e.) the two offices of bishops and deacons are seen as taking the place of stationary or traveling charismatics (*Didache* 15:1ff.).

At about the same time in Rome and Corinth the two offices of presbyter and bishop began to merge into each other. According to the information given by *1 Clement* (in Rome, ca. 96 c.e.), both churches were led by a college of presbyters who were also called bishops. In addition there were deacons. Here too began the theological grounding of offices and their order: just as God sent Christ, so Christ sent the apostles; these in turn established bishops and deacons, and determined that after their deaths, tried and tested men should take over their ministries (*1 Clement* 42:1, 4ff.; 44:1ff.). In this justification the theological self-understanding of the Church came to the fore: because the Church is the Church of God, these Church orders also reached back to God, who has established them through Christ. Among the tasks of the presbyter-bishop, *1 Clement* mentions the "bringing of the sacrifice," which can be interpreted as referring to the Eucharist (*1 Clement* 44:4). Insofar as the presbyter presides over the Eucharist, he is called bishop and is compared to the high priest and his functions in the Old Testament temple worship. Hence it may be concluded that the liturgical role of the bishop as presider of the eucharistic celebration has contributed to the rise of monoepiscopacy. We have here, however, not a structural but only a functional monoepiscopacy.

The same picture emerged in the somewhat later canonical pastoral letters of 1 and 2 Timothy and Titus. They speak of bishops, presbyters, and deacons, but do not distinguish between bishops and presbyters. Their offices were taken over by the imposition of hands by the apostles or the presbyters. Through the imposition of hands the charism of God is transmitted (1 Tim 4:14; 2 Tim 1:6). The men receiving the imposition of hands must be proven (1 Tim 3:2, 7). Their most important task is to preserve the teaching of the apostles and protect the community from errors (2 Tim 4:3ff.). We have here therefore clearly determined offices which are transmitted through sacramental ordination. Their foundation corresponds to the theological self-consciousness of the Church:

The office of leadership can be exercised on the basis of a charism given by God, and these offices go back to Christ through the apostles and their successors. The free charisms became office charisms because God himself leads his Church.

The first witness to this structural monoepiscopacy and a hierarchically ranked organization of bishop, presbyters, and deacons is the letters of the bishop-martyr Ignatius of Antioch (ca. 110 or 160 C.E.). The theme of Ignatius was the unity and harmony of the communities which he saw as grounded in the heavenly order and harmony. The bishop stands in the place of God, the Bishop of all (*Magnesians* 6:1); hence, the bishop is a copy of the Father (*Trallians* 3:1). Just as Christ submits to the Father, and the apostles to Christ, so must the deacons, the presbyters, and the whole community submit to the bishop (*Magnesians* 2ff.; *Ephesians* 5:3; *Smyrnians* 8:1). Baptism, Eucharist, and *agape* ought to be celebrated only under his leadership (*Smyrnians* 8:1ff.). The one bishop, who presides over the eucharistic celebration, surrounded by the presbyters, the deacons, and the community, is the sacramental sign through which the unifying power of the heavenly liturgy and hierarchy effects the unity of the community (*Philadelphians* 4; *Ephesians* 20:2). Even this typological grounding of offices and their ordering shows itself to be molded by the theological self-understanding of the Church as the Church of God.

The notion that bishops are the successors of the apostles was already present in *1 Clement* and the pastoral letters. But it was not until 185 C.E. that we encounter for the first time in Irenaeus of Lyons a succession list in which the names of individual bishops since the founding apostles are mentioned. This list traces the line of the bishops of Rome back to Linus, who was established as the first Bishop of Rome by Peter and Paul (*Adversus Haereses* III, 3:3). Such lists were intended to show against the Gnostics that the teaching of the apostles had not been transmitted falsely in one church. In any case, these lists show that in the meantime the bishop has become responsible for the correct faith of his particular church. Being a successor of the apostles—this became in the West the properly theological grounding of the episcopal office and the monoepiscopacy.

With monoepiscopacy—the system of only one bishop in each church—also the monarchical character of the episcopal office was developed, that is, the hierarchy of one bishop and the priests and deacons. The church order contained in *Traditio Apostolica* (in Rome, ca. 210 C.E.) and transmitted under the name of Hippolytus is an impressive witness of this fact. In the prayer of consecration of bishops (*Traditio Apostolica* 3), it is expressed that a priestly spirit *(pneuma)* or gift of the Spirit and a kingly spirit are transmitted to the bishop through the imposition of hands. Only one bishop was made through the imposition of hands. In connection with the consecration, the bishop celebrates the Eucharist with the community. The leadership of the community and the presidency over the celebration of the Eucharist now belong together, just as the priestly and kingly spirits do. With the office of shepherd and high priest the bishop is given the apostolic power of forgiving sins. The episcopal office and the ordering of the Church are grounded theologically in the divine world order; a line was drawn from Abraham through the Old Testament kings and high priests and the apostles to the episcopal office of the Church. Furthermore, the future bishop ought to be chosen by the whole people (*Traditio Apostolica* 2).

The development of the monarchical episcopacy was closed in the first half of the third century. This is witnessed by the Syrian *Didascalia Apostolorum* for the East and Bishop Cyprian of Carthage for the West. Whereas in the *Didascalia* the typological grounding predominates, Cyprian grounds the episcopal office in Christ's promise to Peter (Letter 3:1; 66:8) and in the empowering by the apostle (Letter 69:11; 73:7).

That the institution of monoepiscopacy was formed both in East and West in so short a time is an astounding course of events, since there was no central authority demanding or guiding this development. As the biblical and extrabiblical sources show, the Church saw the rise of a ministry of *episcope,* an office of guardian or shepherd in the Church, as a work of God. It was always presupposed that God guides the Church through Christ, and Christ is the shepherd and head of the Church. But Christ takes into his service humans who would represent him as shepherds. The Christians are admonished to obey God by accepting and listening to those whom Christ sends to them (Matt 10:40; Luke 10:16). Insofar as they listen to their shepherds, the believers follow Christ (Phil 2:29; 4:9; Heb 13:17).

The fact that monoepiscopacy and the form of monarchical episcopacy developed out of the originally collegial form of community leadership is attributed today to different historical causes. Obviously, this form proved itself in the struggle against erroneous doctrines in order to preserve the unity of the Church. A role was also played by the typological interpretation which sees in the one bishop the representative of God and of Christ, and the view that the bishop is the successor of the apostles. Whether the rise of monoepiscopacy was due to these interpretations or whether there had been a prior supplementary theological legitimation cannot be determined with certainty.

A significant influence on the development of monoepiscopacy was exercised by the view of the community as the household of God (*domus Dei*), which was formulated for the first time in 1 Tim 4:15.

Many communities had their origin in families that had converted to Christianity. These families made their houses available as meeting places for the community. These house communities played an important role in the mission of the apostle Paul, and he named many women and men who took care of them. As the number of such house communities increased, it was natural that the whole community understood itself as the household of God and regarded the bishop as the father of the family *(pater familias)*. The corresponding analogy was the position of the father in Jewish and Roman families. The bishop became the "ruler of the household of God" (Titus 1:7).

Although Paul also mentioned women among those who made their houses available or cared for the house communities, the patriarchal structures of the contemporary society could have played such a role in shaping the view of the bishop as the father of the family that in the long term only men were appointed as overseers. Also the typological interpretation and the view that the bishop is the successor of the apostles could have facilitated such a development.

As time went on, the bishops acquired an increasingly greater responsibility over the universal Church through councils and synods. The slowly developing claim of the Roman bishop to a juridical primacy over the universal Church met with opposition until the First Vatican Council (1869–70). Many considered this claim to be irreconcilable with the responsibility of each bishop for his church and with the responsibility of the college of bishops for the universal Church. In modern times the position and responsibility of individual bishops were weakened both by political powers and Roman centralism.

In the first millennium, the episcopacy was considered to be a proper and indeed the highest rank of order or the sacrament of consecration. Since the fourth century, however, there were isolated theologians who saw no difference between the episcopacy and the presbyterate. The most important representative of this "presbyteral" view was Jerome. On the basis of the New Testament he taught that the distinction between the episcopacy and the presbyterate was not of divine institution but depended on the decision of the Church (Letter 146:6; *Commentary on the Letter to Titus,* 1:5, esp. 69:3).

Since the ninth century this view gained increasing acceptance by the theologians of the early Middle Ages. With other theologians, Peter Lombard expressly excludes the episcopacy from the number of orders; he characterizes the episcopacy as a special dignity or ministry within the priestly order *(Sententiarum* IV 24:14). Many theologians no longer considered the episcopacy as a sacrament, but as a sacramental. This development was supported by the fact that the priesthood was now defined as the power to consecrate the eucharistic body of the

Lord; with regard to this power, there is no difference between the priest and the bishop. With few exceptions, however, it was still maintained that only the bishop can confer the holy orders. Among canonists, however, the opinion still prevailed that the episcopacy constitutes a rank of the orders.

Among the theologians of the High Middle Ages there was a variety of views. While Albert the Great grants the bishop only a higher juridical power (*Sententiarum* IV a. 39), Thomas Aquinas distinguishes two meanings of the word *"ordo"*: *ordo* as sacrament and *ordo* as office. In the first meaning the episcopacy is not an *ordo*, since the bishop possesses no higher power over the eucharistic body of the Lord than the priest. As office, however, the episcopacy is an *ordo* because the bishop has power over and beyond the priest with regard to the Mystical Body of Christ, that is, the Church, insofar as only he can confirm and ordain. Hence, the higher power of the bishop is not only a higher juridical power but also a higher consecratory power (*Sententiarum* IV d. 24, q. 3, a. 2, sol. 2 = *Supplementum* q. 40, a. 5). John Duns Scotus also expressed reservations about the prevailing view that the episcopacy was not a rank of the orders. Were the episcopacy simply a higher juridical power, he argued, then it could be taken away by the pope; the autonomy and indestructibility of the episcopacy could be maintained only if it is a proper rank of the orders, distinct from the priesthood (*Ordinatio* IV d. 24, q. 11, a. 2). Pope Pius XII was the first officially to determine, in his apostolic constitution *Sacramentum ordinis* (1947), that the episcopacy, the presbyterate, and the diaconate constitute each a proper rank of the sacrament of orders (DS 3857–61).

A fateful development in the theology of the episcopacy occurred in the scholastic understanding which placed the bishop's shepherding tasks of teaching and leadership outside the sacrament of orders. His pastoral ministry, detached from his sacramental power, became a mere power of jurisdiction. Consequently, ministry became a juridical rule. This juridical concept is often connected with the canonical theory according to which the bishop's jurisdiction is not bound with his episcopal office conferred sacramentally, but is a concession from the pope. This theory is at the heart of Roman centralism, which treats bishops as mere vicars of the pope.

It would be a mistake to regard the Roman attempt to make bishops dependent on the pope as merely Rome's will to power. Rather, behind this attempt were also Rome's efforts to remove the bishops from their dependence on the political powers under which they found themselves in many countries. It is no exaggeration to speak of a centuries-long "Babylonian Captivity" of the episcopacy which became the pawns of the interests of nobles, princes, and national governments.

The Conceptual Renewal of the Episcopacy Through Vatican II

The conceptual renewal of the episcopacy was one of the most important elements of Vatican II's reform project. The relevant documents are the third chapter of the Dogmatic Constitution on the Church (LG 18–29) and the Decree on the Pastoral Office of Bishops in the Church *Christus Dominus.*

The Episcopacy as Sacrament

At the center of the conceptual reform of the episcopacy stands the affirmation of its sacramental character. The episcopal office is not just a special power of jurisdiction but the fullness of that ministry which Christ has given to the apostles and therefore is properly a rank of the sacrament of orders.

> The holy synod teaches, moreover, that the fullness of the sacrament of Orders is conferred by episcopal consecration, that fullness, namely, which both in the liturgical tradition of the Church and in the language of the Fathers of the Church is called the high priesthood, the acme of the sacred ministry. . . . In fact, from tradition, which is expressed especially in the liturgical rites and in the customs of both the Eastern and Western Church, it is abundantly clear that by the imposition of hands and through the words of the consecration, the grace of the Holy Spirit is given, and a sacred character is impressed in such wise that bishops, in a resplendent and visible manner, take the place of Christ himself, teacher, shepherd and priest, and act as his representative (LG 21).

At first sight the sacrament seems to place the bishop above the community of believers. That would be the case only if the episcopal office is viewed as a special power of jurisdiction. In reality the sacrament integrates the bishop into the community of Christ's brothers and sisters. All the believers participate in the common priesthood and the mission of the Church which they have received in the sacraments of baptism and confirmation. That the bishop receives a sacrament for his ministry does not separate him from the rest of the believers.

However, insofar as the bishop has received a special charge to serve the community as teacher, shepherd, and priest, he is distinguished from the Church. That this charge is communicated to him through a sacrament makes it clear that his charge neither is the outcome of a personal preference nor grants him a personal honor. Rather, this commission comes to him from Christ alone. The sacrament also implies that the bishop ought not to feel that he himself is the teacher, shepherd, and priest of the community, but rather it is Christ himself that he must make present as teacher, shepherd, and priest. Therefore, he should not take the place of Christ. It is through his service and not through his person that the bishop represents Christ. Indeed, this service challenges the whole person of the bishop, and is not just a job.

All this would not be evident if the episcopal office were based only on human choice and commissioning. When, as occurred in the early Church, the community elected the bishop, it only made the decision as to whether the candidate would be fit for the office. The commissioning itself was given through the sacramental ordination.

In announcing the word of God, celebrating the sacraments with the believers, and caring for the unity of the body of Christ, the bishop makes Christ present through his service. That the bishop makes Christ present sacramentally is repeatedly emphasized by the council:

> In the bishops, to whom the priests render assistance, the Lord Jesus Christ, supreme high priest, is present in the midst of the faithful. Though seated at the right hand of God the Father, he is not absent from the assembly of his pontiff; on the contrary indeed, it is above all through their signal service that he preaches the Word of God to all peoples and administers without cease to the faithful the sacraments of faith (LG 21).

The council grounds the existence of the episcopal office in the sending and empowerment of the apostles by Jesus and the risen one. It supports its teaching that the apostles' mission continues, according to God's will, in the ministries of the bishop, the priest, and the deacon with quotations from the Bible and the early Church given in the preceding paragraphs (LG 18–20). "The sacred synod consequently teaches that the bishops have by divine institution taken the place of the apostles as pastors of the Church, in such wise that whoever listens to them is listening to Christ and whoever despises them despises Christ and him who sent Christ (cf. Lk. 10:16)" (LG 20). The early Church saw the living presence of Christ in the Church and in particular in the sacraments as grounded in the work of the Holy Spirit. This conviction remains stronger in the Eastern tradition than in the Western. Vatican II takes up this old tradition and grounds the sacramentality of the episcopacy both in the action of Jesus and in that of the Holy Spirit.

> In order to fulfill such exalted functions, the apostles were endowed by Christ with a special outpouring of the Holy Spirit coming upon them (cf. Acts 1:8; 2:4; Jn. 20:22-23), and, by the imposition of hands (cf. 1 Tim. 4:14; 2 Tim. 1:6-7), they passed on to their auxiliaries the gift of the Spirit, which is transmitted down to our day through episcopal consecration (LG 21).

When it is the question of a special gift of the Spirit for a particular ministry, the bishop is no exception. In fact, the council also teaches that the believers are all given a charism of the Spirit for their own mission.

Moreover, the renewed strengthening of the sacramental character of the episcopacy is part of the council's teaching on the sacramentality of the Church. The Church is said to be "the universal sacrament of salvation" through the witness of its members (LG 48). Hence, this witness which the bishop gives through his ministry also takes part in the sacramentality of the Church. The sacramentality of the episcopacy is an expression of the sacramentality of the Church and of the ministry of witness by all its members.

Episcopacy as Service

It is not only through its sacramental character that the episcopacy is integrated into the community of Christ's sisters and brothers. It is so no less through a further characteristic of the episcopacy according to the council's teaching. In contrast to the one-sided understanding of the episcopal office as a power of juridical rule, the council strongly emphasizes its nature as a brotherly service within the People of God. "That office, however, which the Lord committed to the pastors of his people, is, in the strict sense of the term, a service, which is called very expressively in sacred scripture a *diakonia* or ministry (cf. Acts 1:17 and 25; 21:19; Rom. 11:13; 1 Tim. 1:12)" (LG 24). Hence, the bishop is exhorted to keep "in mind that he who is greater should become as the lesser, and he who is the leader as the servant (cf. Lk 22:26-27)" (LG 27). The character of the episcopal office as service is strictly connected with its sacramental character. Only by exercising his office as service does the bishop represent Christ as the shepherd and head of the Church, who in turn represents the Father as the housefather of the family of God.

> Sent as he is by the Father to govern his family, a bishop should keep before his eyes the example of the Good Shepherd, who came not to be waited upon but to serve (cf. Mt. 20:28; Mk. 10:45) and to lay down his life for his sheep (cf. Jn. 10:11) (LG 27).

The Threefold Office of the Episcopacy

The tasks which the council attributes to the bishop emerge likewise out of the concept of the sacramental representation of Christ. Jesus Christ is present in the Church in three ways: in his word, in the sacraments, and in the unity and communion of his Mystical Body which is the Church. Hence, there are three classical tasks of the bishop by which he represents Christ as teacher, priest, and shepherd in the Church: the ministry of preaching, the ministry of the sacraments, and the ministry of leadership.

In contrast to the medieval theologians who thought that only the priestly office of the bishop was grounded in his consecration, the council emphasizes that with the episcopal consecration the offices of teaching and leadership are also conferred. "Now, episcopal consecration confers, together with the office [*munus*] of sanctifying, the duty [*munus*] also of teaching and ruling, which, however, of their very nature can be exercised only in hierarchical communion with the head and members of the college" (LG 21). The council distinguishes therefore between the three offices which are conferred by the sacramental consecration and the *exercise* of these offices which must occur only in unity and communion with the episcopal college and the pope. That the exercise of these offices must be done "in hierarchical communion" is grounded "in their nature." In fact, it is assumed by the council that the apostles were not sent out by Jesus as individuals but as a group. "These apostles (cf. Lk. 6:13) he constituted in the form of a college or permanent assembly, at the head of which he placed Peter, chosen from amongst them (cf. Jn. 21:15-17)" (LG 19). On the basis of this concept the council seeks to solve one of the most difficult problems of ecclesiology and Church order: how to bind together the responsibility of each bishop for his church, his insertion into the episcopal college, and his subordination to the pope, without jeopardizing any one of them. The council distinguishes between the threefold office or *munus*, which is conferred by sacramental consecration, and the exercise of this same threefold *munus*. In the Preliminary Explanatory Note, which Pope Paul VI ordered to be attached to the constitution, the difference is explained as follows: While sacramental consecration gives "an ontological share" in the threefold *munus*, its exercise requires a "canonical or juridical determination through hierarchical determination" with which such power is ordered to action: "A determination of this kind can come about through appointment to a particular office or the assignment of subjects, and is conferred according to norms approved by the supreme authority" (Preliminary Explanatory Note, 2).

Compared with the theory according to which the authority of the bishop is grounded only in the assignment of the power of jurisdiction by the pope, this teaching of the council no doubt represents a step forward. The council seeks to bind together the sacramental and juridical basis of the episcopal office by showing how both elements belong together. The sacramental consecration does not isolate the bishop; on the contrary, it inserts him into the collegial *communio* with the other bishops and the pope—relationships that require a juridical regulation. The council chooses formulations that are open to various legal regulations.

More difficult to handle in the bishops' investiture is the relationship between the authority of the bishop and that of the pope with regard to the ordinary exercise of the bishop's power of leadership. The council explains:

> This power [to govern, as vicars and legates of Christ, the particular Churches assigned to them], which they exercise personally in the name of Christ, is proper, ordinary and immediate, although its exercise is ultimately controlled by the supreme authority of the Church and can be confined within certain limits should the usefulness of the Church and the faithful require that. In virtue of this power bishops have a sacred right and duty before the Lord of legislating for and passing judgment on their subjects, as well as of regulating everything that concerns the good order of divine worship and of the apostolate (LG 27).

These explications of the council speak in favor of a consistent application of the principle of subsidiarity in the formulation of Church laws. This would create more room for the pastoral authority of individual bishops as well as for the legislation for each region by national or continental episcopal conferences. Moreover, it would be in line with the reforming efforts of the council to have the bishops participate in the enactment of laws for the universal Church.

Episcopacy and Collegiality

The affirmation of the collegial character of the episcopacy and the ancient doctrine of the episcopal college as well as the bishop's responsibility for the universal Church is a further element of the conceptual renewal of the episcopacy undertaken by Vatican II. The definition of papal primacy by Vatican II and the growing centralism since have pushed this doctrine into the background. However, Vatican I had no intention whatsoever to deny it. The majority of the fathers at Vatican II requested the renewal of this doctrine so as to bring centralism to an end and to make it clear that the universal Church represents a communion of churches. Hence, this teaching of the council:

> The order of bishops is the successor to the college of the apostles in their role as teachers and pastors, and in it the apostolic college is perpetuated. Together with their head, the Supreme Pontiff, and never apart from him, they have supreme and full authority over the universal Church (LG 22).

The affirmation of the sacramental character of the episcopacy also had great significance for the doctrine of collegiality. The council explains that the sacrament of episcopal consecration, together with the recognition by the other bishops and the pope, makes the bishop a member of the episcopal college. "One is constituted a member of the episcopal body in virtue of the sacramental consecration and by the hierarchical communion with the head and members of the college" (LG 22). The collegial co-responsibility for the universal Church is therefore an essential and intrinsic element of the episcopacy. As members of the episcopal college, the pope and the bishops are bound together in their responsibility for the universal Church.

The frequent emphasis on the special authority of the pope found in the council's texts shows that the council was aware that the relationship between the common authority of the pope and the bishops and that of the pope cannot be easily brought into balance with each other. This is also a lesson of Church history. Since the last council, criticism has been voiced that the collegial co-responsibility of the bishops for the universal Church has been given too little room and that centralism has not been broken.

The episcopal synod, whose establishment has been suggested by the council, is an organ for the collegial co-responsibility of the bishops. Even though the concrete form which Pope Paul VI gave it did not meet the expectations of many council fathers, it is still a first and important step in the direction toward a greater participation of the episcopacy in the governing of the universal Church.

Episcopal collegiality, however, is not only in its origin grounded in the college of the apostles, but it is also an expression of the structural character of the universal Church as communion of particular churches. "It is in these [particular Churches] and formed out of them that the one and unique Catholic Church exists. And for that reason precisely each bishop represents his own Church, whereas all, together with the pope, represent the whole Church in a bond of peace, love and unity" (LG 23). Also the relationship between the particular churches and the whole Church and the connection among the particular churches to each other still require a more convincing realization and formation. Not only the pope and the bishops are bearers of *communio,* but the rest of the members of the Church are as well.

Because the Church is structured through the interpenetration of the universal Church and the particular churches, a double duty is incumbent upon the bishop. He must both represent the universal Church to his particular church and represent his particular church and its members to the universal Church and its authorities. In the image of the body of Christ the bishops with their duty of double solidarity are characterized as the joints binding together the whole body with its members.

The Conceptual Renewal of the Episcopacy— Decisive Element of the Renewal of the Church

In retrospect, the conceptual renewal of the episcopacy may be seen as a fruit of the conceptual, structural, and pastoral renewal which Vatican II wanted to bring about for the Church as a whole. At the same time, the conceptual renewal of the episcopacy was and is also an important element of the reform of the Church.

On the conceptual level, it is the sacramental character of the episcopal office that integrates the bishops and their ministries into the Church as People of God, body of Christ, and unity in the Holy Spirit. "Presiding in God's stead over the flock of which they are shepherds" (LG 20), the bishops lead the People of God on their way to the kingdom of God. As representatives of Christ, they make present through their ministry Christ as the head of the body of Christ and as the shepherd of the Church, for "in the bishops . . . the Lord Jesus Christ, supreme high priest, is present in the midst of the faithful" (LG 21). In the sacramental consecration, the bishops receive for their ministry the gifts of the Holy Spirit "who, being one and the same in head and members, gives life to, unifies and moves the whole body" (LG 7).

For the structural renewal of the Church the affirmation of the proper authority and responsibility of the bishop for his own particular church and his collegial responsibility for the universal Church plays a decisive role. The proper responsibility of the bishop corresponds to the teaching of the council that each particular church is truly Church, insofar as in it the Church realizes itself as the community of believers *(communio fidelium)*. The collegial responsibility of the bishops for the whole Church corresponds to the structure of the universal Church as communion of churches *(communio ecclesiarum)*.

To the pastoral renewal of the Church, which is the universal sacrament of salvation, the bishops bring their contribution insofar as they "devote themselves to their apostolic office as witnesses of Christ to all [persons] . . . , so that ultimately all human beings may walk 'in all goodness, justice and truth' (Eph. 5:9)" (CD 11).

—*Translated from the German by Peter C. Phan*

For Further Reading

Anciaux, Paul. *The Episcopate in the Church.* Dublin: Gill and Sons, 1965.

Groupe des Dombes. "The Episcopal Ministry." *One in Christ* 14 (1978) 267–88.

Lawler, Michael G. *A Theology of Ministry.* Kansas City, Mo.: Sheed and Ward, 1990.

Moore, Peter, ed. *Bishops but What Kinds? Reflections on Episcopacy.* London: SPCK, 1982.

National Conference of Catholic Bishops. *The Ministry of Bishops: Papers from the Collegeville Assembly.* Washington, D.C.: United States Catholic Conference, 1982.

O'Meara, Thomas F. *Theology of Ministry.* New York: Paulist Press, 1999.

Ratzinger, Joseph. "The Pastoral Implications of Episcopal Collegiality." *The Church and Mankind.* Ed. Edward Schillebeeckx, 39–67. Glen Rock, N.Y.: Paulist Press, 1965.

Suenens, Léon Joseph. *Coresponsibility in the Church.* New York: Herder & Herder, 1986.

Swidler, Arlene, and Leonard Swidler, eds. *Bishops and People.* Philadelphia: Westminster Press, 1970.

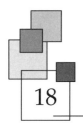

| 18 | **The Teaching Office of the Church** |

John P. Boyle

The Church as Sacrament of God's Saving Presence

Chapter one of the Second Vatican Council's Constitution on the Church, *Lumen gentium,* describes the Church as a mystery or sacrament, a sign of the saving presence in the world of God Father, Son, and Holy Spirit. An innovation of the council in *Lumen gentium* was the introduction of Jesus' threefold offices as prophet, priest, and king as a way of understanding the threefold *munera* given by Jesus to his Church.[1]

The Church is composed of those who also form the People of God (LG 2), and it is this People of God which has priestly, prophetic, and kingly/pastoral roles to perform. I will not repeat here what is said of the Church in *Lumen gentium* 1–2 and discussed elsewhere in this book. This chapter will focus on the teaching of the Catholic Church about its own teaching function and authority. I will, however, draw attention to the implications this Catholic doctrine has for ecumenical relations. It is well known that many Christian churches and communities do not accept the claims of the Catholic Church to teach authoritatively.[2]

My attention in this chapter is on the prophetic function as understood in the Catholic Church. The council points out that the whole people exercises its prophetic role by its witness to Christ. Moreover, it

---

[1] For what follows see Francis Sullivan, *Magisterium: Teaching Authority in the Catholic Church* (New York: Paulist Press, 1983); Hans Küng, *Infallible? An Inquiry,* trans. Edward Quinn (Garden City, N.Y.: Doubleday, 1971); Richard Gaillardetz, *Teaching with Authority: A Theology of the Magisterium in the Church* (Collegeville: The Liturgical Press, 1997).

[2] The importance of this problem was pointed out by Cardinal Edward Cassidy, president of the Pontifical Council for Promoting Christian Unity in a sermon preached in July 1998 to the Lambeth Conference meeting in Canterbury. *Origins* 28 (1998) 174–6.

continues, the whole people, in virtue of its anointing by the Holy One, cannot err in matters of belief. This people possesses a supernatural appreciation of the faith called the *sensus fidei* (sense of the faith), when the whole people manifests a universal consent in matters of faith and morals.

This People of God is made holy not only by the sacraments and other ministrations of the church but also by the gifts which the Spirit distributes as he will among them (see 1 Cor 12:7). These are gifts to be used for the needs of the Church, and it is the duty of those in charge of the Church to judge the genuineness and proper use of such gifts.

Bishops as Authoritative Teachers

After setting out the belief of the Church about the Church as mystery and People of God, the Second Vatican Council declares it to be the faith of the Church that Christ set up a variety of offices which aim at the good of the whole body. The apostles designated by Christ made provision for successors to continue their leadership of the Church in the persons of the bishops of the various local churches.

Lumen gentium draws a parallel between the college of apostles with Peter at its head and the college of bishops headed by the Bishop of Rome, Peter's successor. It is to this college of bishops headed by the pope that the government of the Church has been confided. The bishops succeed not only to the pastoral and priestly roles of the apostles but also to their role as teachers.

Bishops, as successors of the apostles, are authoritative teachers in the Church in virtue of their ordination and the power of the Holy Spirit invoked upon them. The collegial nature of the episcopacy appeared very early in the tradition of the Church in such customs as having several bishops participate in the ordination of a new bishop and in the custom which grew up early in the church of having major questions decided by a meeting or council of the bishops of a region. When the Roman persecutions of the Christian Church ended, the whole episcopate (at least in principle) gathered in "ecumenical" or general councils. The decisions of such councils, approved by or at least accepted by the Bishop of Rome, came to be recognized as exercises of the supreme teaching authority of the Church, protected from error by the assistance of the Holy Spirit. The First Vatican Council defined that this supreme teaching authority can also be exercised by the Bishop of Rome alone, acting as the successor of St. Peter as head of the college. When the pope does exercise this supreme authority, his definitions in matters of faith and morals enjoy that infallibility with which Christ wished to endow his Church (DS 3074). The various kinds and levels of authoritative teaching and the assent owed to it were further elaborated in the Profession of Faith published by the Congregation for the Doctrine of Faith (CDF) in 1989.[3]

The Magisterium

Vatican II and many councils before it have placed the first responsibility for the Church's teaching of the Word of God upon those who have succeeded to the place of the apostles, the bishops. Vatican II declares:

> Among the more important duties of bishops that of preaching the Gospel has pride of place. For the bishops are heralds of the faith, who draw new disciples to Christ; they are authentic teachers, that is, teachers endowed with the authority of Christ, who preach the faith to the people assigned to them, the faith which is destined to inform their thinking and direct their conduct; and under the light of the Holy Spirit they make that faith shine forth, drawing from the storehouse of revelation new things and old (cf. Mt. 13:52); they make it bear fruit and with watchfulness they ward off whatever errors threaten their flock (cf. 2 Tim. 4:14) (LG 25).

This paragraph is an important one because it defines the distinction between the prophetic tasks proper to the hierarchy, the bishops in particular, and those which belong to the People of God generally. The bishops are "authentic," that is, "authoritative" teachers whose teaching is done under the light of the Holy Spirit. The term commonly used in the contemporary church for this authoritative teaching office of the bishops is magisterium. The word has come to mean both the authoritative teaching office and those who hold that office.[4]

---

[3] See the Congregation for the Doctrine of the Faith (hereafter CDF), *Mysterium ecclesiae, AAS* 65 (1973) 396–408; CDF, "Profession of Faith and Oath of Fidelity to Be Made by Those Undertaking an Office to be Exercised in the Name of the Church," *AAS* 81 (1989) 104–6; English translation in *Origins* 18 (1989) 661–3.

[4] Joseph Fuchs traced the development of this terminology and its meaning in an unpublished dissertation in 1941 which was summarized by Yves Congar in "Origines d'une trilogie ecclésiologique à l'époque rationaliste de la théologie," *Revue des sciences philosophiques et théologiques* 53 (1969) 185–211; see also J. Fuchs, "Weihesakramentale Grundlegung kirchlicher Rechtsgewalt," *Scholastik* 16 (1941) 496–520; Yves Congar, "A Semantic History of the Term 'Magisterium'" and "A Brief History of the Forms of the Magisterium and Its Relations with Scholars," *Readings in Moral Theology*, vol. 3, ed. Charles E. Curran and Richard A. McCormick (New York: Paulist Press, 1982) 297–313 and 314–31. On the term "ordinary magisterium" see J. Boyle, *Church Teaching Authority: Historical and Theological Studies* (Notre Dame, Ind.: University of Notre Dame Press, 1995) 10–29 and 30–42.

The task of the bishops is therefore to proclaim the Word of God, to see to its proper interpretation and concrete application to the times and places where Christians must live out the gospel. The bishops have as well a task of vigilance, of identifying and correcting errors when they arise.

The Teaching Role of Bishops' Conferences

Since the conclusion of the Second Vatican Council and the organization of bishops' conferences urged by the council and Pope Paul VI, a discussion has continued on the role and authority of bishops' conferences in teaching. Issues arose about the relationship of the conferences to the teaching authority of the pope and of the body of bishops assembled in council, and of the relationship of the various conferences and their teaching to one another. A fundamental question persisted about the authority relationship of individual bishops of the local churches and the bishops assembled in their conference. Some bishops felt that the conferences were intruding into matters which were the duties and responsibilities of individual bishops. There was a lingering question of the relationship of the modern bishops' conference to the tradition of provincial and plenary councils, perhaps especially in places like the United States, where such councils played an important role from the time of John Carroll to the 1890s. The Extraordinary Synod of 1985 summoned by Pope John Paul II asked that a study be made of the conferences. A first attempt at such a study was circulated to the bishops in 1988 and received a barrage of criticism.

But on July 22, 1998, the Vatican released an apostolic letter dated May 21, 1998. The papal letter is entitled *Apostolos suos* and deals with "the theological and juridical nature of episcopal conferences." The letter is presented as the response by the Holy See to the request of the Extraordinary Synod of 1985 for clarification of the role and authority of bishops' conferences.

In short, *Apostolos suos* simply denies that the bishops possess conjoint teaching authority. Taking its cue from the CDF's 1992 letter *Communionis notio*,[5] on the Church as communion, the pope's letter asserts that there are only two levels of authority: that of the worldwide episcopal college (exercised "with and under Peter") and that of the individual bishops. Consequently, in order to exercise magisterial authority, the bishops sitting as an episcopal conference must either unanimously approve a proposed teaching document, thus employing their individual teaching authority simultaneously for all their dioceses, or the bish-

[5] CDF, *Communionis notio*, May 19, 1992; text in *Origins* 22 (1992) 108–12.

ops must approve the teaching document by at least a two-thirds majority of the member bishops who have a deliberative vote and then seek the Roman *recognitio* (approval) of the document. If it is approved by the pope's primatial authority, it is clothed with the authority of the whole college of bishops. Therefore, the *recognitio* becomes a sort of deputation from the college of bishops acting through its head, the pope, and the Roman Curia.[6]

There is a most important theological issue here: in Roman teaching only the universal Church and the local church exist, with no locus of authority between them. The tradition of synodical governance in the Church and the theology which underlies it are declared simply irrelevant.

Church Teaching and the Assent It Commands

Lumen gentium 25 declares that the Church teaches with varying degrees of authority. At times the teaching mission of the college of bishops is exercised in its fullness by the head of the college, the pope. To the papal magisterium as well as to the magisterial[7] pronouncements of diocesan bishops individually to their own people is owed a religious assent of intellect and will, an *obsequium mentis et voluntatis*. The nature and extent of this assent has been much discussed in the wake of the publication of the 1968 encyclical letter *Humanae vitae* on contraception by Paul VI and the brief encyclical letter *Ordinatio sacerdotalis* on restricting priestly ordination to males by John Paul II in 1994. The first of several recent doctrinal statements was the publication in 1989 of a revised formula for the Profession of Faith which canon 833 requires in certain instances.[8]

The new formula begins, as had earlier ones, with a profession of faith in the doctrines set out in the Nicene Creed. Then there are three added paragraphs specifying additional doctrines more generally included in the Profession of Faith. It should be noted that the Profession of Faith of the Council of Trent (1564; DS 1862–70) also included a number of additions after the Nicene Creed, specifying doctrinal points defined by the Council of Trent against the Reformers. Additional points were

---

[6] See *Apostolos suos*, nn. 12, 13, 20–4, and the attached "complementary norms" in *Origins* 28 (1998) 152–8.

[7] The apostolic letter *Ad tuendam fidem* introduced into the Code of Canon Law an "appropriate penalty" *(iusta poena)* for denying doctrines in the second category of the Profession of Faith. But it is only in the much less authoritative commentary from the CDF that specific examples of such doctrines are provided.

[8] See note 2 above.

added after Vatican I, including the doctrines of papal primacy and infallibility defined by the council.

The 1989 Profession of Faith replaced a more general formula published in 1967 by Pope Paul VI and distinguishes three types of Church teaching and the assent each demands. The three types are based on *Lumen gentium* 25 and have been repeated in all major Roman statements on Church teaching authority since 1989.

The first paragraph of the 1989 Profession of Faith deals with "all those things which are contained in the word of God either written or handed down and which the church has definitively proposed to be believed *(definitive credenda)* either by a solemn judgment or by its ordinary and universal magisterium." The believer professes belief in all of these things with firm faith, the *obsequium fidei*.[9]

The second added paragraph deals with all those things pertaining to faith or morals which have been proposed definitively by the Church *(definitive tendenda)*, even if they are not taught as divinely revealed: One professes to embrace and hold firmly all such teachings *(firmiter . . . amplector ac retineo)*. It is that profession with respect to this category of doctrine that has provoked recent papal statements and even a revision of the Code of Canon Law.

The third added paragraph has to do with those teachings which either the Roman pontiff or the college of bishops (including the pope) has declared when they exercised their authoritative magisterium even if they did not intend to declare those teachings by a definitive act. The believer professes to adhere with a religious assent of will and intellect to such teachings *(religioso voluntatis et intellectus obsequio . . . adhaereo)*.

The first thing one notes about the 1989 Profession of Faith is that it distinguishes kinds of teaching and the authority with which they are taught much more precisely than did the 1967 Profession of Faith.

The distinctions introduced in 1989 relate to different ways in which the authoritative teachers in the Church exercise their teaching authority. It is apparent that the teaching activity of the Church is carried on constantly. The bishops themselves teach personally through their preaching and writing, often interpreting the meaning of traditional teaching as their people confront new situations. But the bishops also work with their priests and many other persons, both lay and religious, who carry on the work of instruction and formation in the gospel under the supervision of the bishop.

This day-to-day activity of the Church's authoritative teachers has come to be called the ordinary magisterium. The term distinguishes day-to-day teaching from more solemn teaching events such as a coun-

[9] See Sullivan, *Magisterium*, 79ff.

cil in which the college of bishops, with the pope at its head, gathers and publicly exercises the fullness of the Church's teaching authority, the *extraordinary magisterium*. The distinction is an important one. Much Church teaching, even on matters of importance, has not been solemnly taught, much less defined, by a council or by the pope. But such teaching may well be contained in the day-to-day teaching of persons officially authorized by the pope or the bishops or in books such as liturgical texts, the *Catechism of the Catholic Church*, or other manuals or instructional materials approved by the bishops. The teaching of the ordinary magisterium thus ranges over a great deal of Christian belief and practice which it proposes with varying degrees of authority.

It should also be emphasized that this ordinary teaching of the Church carries the authority of the magisterium of the Church and thus calls for an assent proportionate to the authority with which it is taught. When the whole college of bishops, in communion with the pope as head of the college, proposes definitively a matter of faith or morals as revealed by God and thus to be believed by all the faithful, that teaching is owed the assent of faith. There are no prescribed formalities for teaching in this way, so there remains the question of how to establish that the whole college of bishops indeed teaches a particular doctrine and that it teaches it definitively as a matter of revealed faith or morals.[10]

This common teaching by the college of bishops, the *ecclesia per orbem dispersa* ("the church scattered throughout the world"), was named by the First Vatican Council the "ordinary and universal magisterium" to distinguish it from the teaching authority of the pope alone. Such teaching by the college of bishops (always including the pope) in matters of faith and morals carries the same authority as a more formal act of the extraordinary magisterium, of the Church in *concilio congregata* (gathered in council), or of the head of the college of bishops, the pope, acting *ex cathedra*, that is, in his official capacity.

These distinctions have become increasingly important in the years since Vatican II published its Constitution on the Church, *Lumen gentium*, where most of the distinctions are found. Arguments about such matters as contraception and the restriction of priestly ordination to men often center on what the authority and reformability of Church teaching on those matters is. Much of that teaching has been done over a long period of time and by the day-to-day activity of the ordinary

---

[10] One possibility was the consultation of the bishops by Popes Pius IX and Pius XII prior to their definitions of the doctrines of the Immaculate Conception and the Assumption of Our Lady respectively. The bishops were asked whether their people in fact held that the doctrines were revealed. But the definition of the doctrines was by papal authority alone.

teaching activity of popes and bishops. The arguments have turned on whether or not that teaching (1) was about matters of faith and morals, (2) was based on divine revelation, and (3) was indeed definitive and therefore irreformable or instead merely reflected the changeable expectations of the times.

The response of Pope John Paul II to dissenters from Church teaching on contraception and the ordination of women has been to emphasize the definitive character of the teaching on each issue by the universal and ordinary magisterium of the bishops in communion with the pope. The same is true of the Church's teaching on the sacredness of human life, which John Paul II addressed in the encyclical *Evangelium vitae*.[11] But here the procedure of the Pope is different—and more formal: he sent a letter to all the bishops of the Church asking whether their local church held as definitive the teaching of the Church on several aspects of the sacredness of human life. The Pope found that the churches hold that the life of an innocent person can never be deliberately taken—a teaching in agreement with that of the popes. Then, Pope John Paul, in solemn words, declared that the Church through the ordinary and universal magisterium of the college of bishops had taught definitively the inviolability of every innocent human life (EV 57). In the encyclical the Pope reports the unanimous condemnation of abortion under the sanction of excommunication, and adds:

> Given such unanimity in the doctrinal and disciplinary tradition of the church, Paul VI was able to declare that this tradition is unchanged and unchangeable. Therefore, by the authority which Christ conferred upon Peter and his successors, in communion with the bishops—who on various occasions have condemned abortion and who in the aforementioned consultation, albeit dispersed throughout the world, have shown unanimous agreement concerning this doctrine, *I declare that direct abortion, that is, abortion willed as an end or as a means, always constitutes a grave moral disorder,* since it is the deliberate killing of an innocent human being. This doctrine is based upon the natural law and upon the written word of God, is transmitted by the church's tradition and taught by the ordinary and universal magisterium (EV 62).

What the Church Teaches

Catholic theology[12] has long distinguished primary and secondary objects of authoritative, and in some cases infallible, Church teaching. Similarly, Catholic theology has distinguished different grounds for

---

[11] Text in *Origins* 24 (1995) 689–727; n. 5 regarding life, and n. 62 on abortion.

[12] For what follows see Sullivan, *Magisterium,* 119–52.

holding various categories of Church teaching. By adding the three paragraphs to the creed to further define Catholic faith, the Profession of Faith published in 1989 drew attention to diverse categories of Church teaching and also to the diverse forms of assent owed to each.

The first added paragraph in the Profession of Faith identifies what has long been called the "primary object" of Church teaching and the assent of faith that is owed to it. The primary object of faith is God's revelation proposed as such by the Church. The proper response to divine revelation proposed by the Church is an act of faith in the God who reveals, the assent of faith *(obsequium fidei)*. It should be noted too that to deny teachings which the Church[13] proposes as divinely revealed is to commit the crime of heresy (defined at Can. 751 along with apostasy and schism), which brings automatic excommunication upon the person denying the teaching (Can. 1364/1). However, the 1983 code had no penal canon corresponding to canon 752, which sets out the obligation to accept Church teaching about the secondary objects of revelation.

The difference between the teachings described in the first paragraph added to the profession of faith and those in the second is important. The teachings revealed by God and proposed by the Church as divine revelation to be believed definitively *(definitive credenda)* must be accepted by a firm act of faith *(firma fide)*.

The teachings in the second added paragraph are not proposed as divinely revealed, but they are proposed to be held definitively *(definitive tendenda)*. Of this category of teaching Pope John Paul writes in *Ad tuendam fidem:*

> Yet this second clause of the Profession of Faith is of great importance because it refers to truths necessarily connected with divine revelation. Such truths manifest the particular inspiration of the divine Spirit given to the church in the exploration of Catholic doctrine and in the church's deeper understanding of some truth concerning faith or morals. The truths definitively stated and the truths revealed are intimately linked either for historical reasons or through logical connection (n. 3).[14]

Although the pope offers no examples in the text of the apostolic letter, some examples are given along with further elaboration of the teaching in a document published simultaneously by the CDF and signed by its prefect, Cardinal Joseph Ratzinger, and its secretary, Archbishop Tarcisio Bertone.[15]

---

[13] See *Dei verbum,* nn. 1–5.

[14] *Ad tuendam fidem,* n. 3.

[15] The authority of the document is not clear. *Ad tuendam fidem* appears in *Origins* 28 (1998) 113, 115–6, and the commentary in the same issue, 116–9. Copies of the

The CDF document offers several examples of teachings which fall in the second category: the first examples are corollaries of the defined doctrines of papal primacy and infallibility. The CDF document says that prior to Vatican I the primacy of the successor of Peter was held as revealed, but there was dispute over whether the concepts "jurisdiction" and "infallibility" were to be considered an intrinsic part of revelation or only as logical consequences. Moreover, although the doctrines of papal primacy and infallibility were defined at Vatican I, the CDF authors believe that the doctrines about the primacy and infallibility of the pope were already definitively taught in the period before the council. And they continue: "History clearly shows, therefore, that what was accepted into the consciousness of the church was considered a true doctrine from the beginning and was subsequently held to be definitive; however, only in the final stage—the definition of Vatican I—was it also accepted as a divinely revealed truth" (n. 11). The authors see a parallel in the contemporary question of the reservation of priestly ordination to men. They report that Pope John Paul did not wish to make a dogmatic definition on this question, but he did wish to insist that the teaching be held definitively:[16] "Since, founded on the written word of God, constantly preserved and applied in the tradition of the church, it has been set forth infallibly by the ordinary and universal magisterium." And they continue: "As the prior example illustrates, this does not foreclose the possibility that in the future the consciousness of the church might progress to the point where this teaching could be defined as a doctrine to be believed as divinely revealed" (n. 11).

The CDF document goes on to mention other teachings which its authors believe have been definitively taught, even if there has been no claim to infallibility for the teachings. They mention the Church's teaching on euthanasia from *Evangelium vitae,* cited above, arguing that even though Scripture does not know the concept of euthanasia, the relationship of faith and reason becomes apparent in this case because "Scripture, in fact, clearly excludes every form of the kind of the self-

commentary were sent to bishops with a cover letter which also was published in *Origins* 28 (1998) 163–4. The letter gave additional explanation of the congregation's reasons for preparing the commentary, especially as an explanation of the Profession of Faith in response to objections raised by certain theologians.

The commentary carries no indication of papal approval and is therefore a document of the congregation itself. In fact it reflects usefully theological views that might be found in many texts in ecclesiology prior to Vatican II. The inclusion of the canonization of saints and the judgment of Leo XIII against the validity of Anglican orders among things to be held definitive has provoked questions.

[16] See the letter *Ordinatio sacerdotalis, Origins* 24 (1994) 50–2, and the CDF's subsequent *Responsum ad dubium, Origins* 25 (1995) 401 and 403.

determination of human existence that is presupposed in the theory and practice of euthanasia" (n. 11). Finally, the CDF mentions the Church's condemnations of prostitution and fornication as definitively taught by the ordinary and universal magisterium, even if there is no claim that the teaching is revealed.

A second category of doctrines is said to be definitively taught because they are linked to revelation by "historical necessity," even if there is no claim that they are revealed. The CDF mentions the legitimacy of the election of a pope or of the celebration of an ecumenical council, and the canonization of saints—all of which fall in the category of "dogmatic facts." So does their other example, the 1896 declaration by Pope Leo XIII that holy orders administered in the Anglican communion are invalid.[17]

The Reception of Church Teaching

In the several documents published since Vatican II which deal especially with the magisterium there is little explicit discussion of the reception by the Church of the teaching of the magisterium.

However, in *Lumen gentium,* discussing the doctrinal definitions of the pope or of the college of bishops with the pope, the council teaches: "The assent of the church can never be lacking to such definitions on account of the same holy Spirit's influence, through which Christ's whole flock is maintained in the unity of the faith and makes progress in it" (n. 25). An echo of this teaching is found in canon 750, which deals with those things that must be believed with the assent of faith: "It [the assent of divine and catholic faith] is manifested by the common adherence of the Christian faithful under the leadership of the sacred magisterium." And the canon adds a line inspired by the First Vatican Council's Dogmatic Constitution on the Catholic Faith (DS 3045): "Therefore, all are bound to avoid any doctrines whatever which are contrary to these truths."

The doctrine of reception had a very juridical caste in pre-Vatican II theology. The hierarchy constituted the *ecclesia docens* (the teaching Church) and the rest of the faithful were the *ecclesia discens* (the learning Church). The relationship between the two put those who were not ordained in a very passive position summed up in the cynical dictum that the role of the laity in the Church was to "pray, pay, and obey." In 1859 the very title of John Henry Newman's book *On Consulting the Faithful in Matters of Doctrine* was enough to create a furor that cost Newman the editorship of *The Rambler*—and much grief. Newman's

---

[17] See DS 3315–9 for excerpts from Pope Leo XIII's papal letter *Apostolicae curae.*

suggestion that the laity had given lessons in fidelity to true doctrine to the bishops during the Arian controversy was simply not acceptable. In a time of much controversy, that was the dominant notion: the learners were not to be teachers of their teachers. But the period since the end of Vatican II is another matter. Never in modern times have papal teachings been so publicly refused reception by many in the Church as were Paul VI's *Humanae vitae* (1968) and the numerous pronouncements of John Paul II on contraception.[18] More recently, the stand of John Paul II on the restriction of priestly ordination to males noted above has also encountered public contradiction, even in the face of declarations by the pope and the CDF that the doctrine has been taught definitively. Such a situation of apparent nonreception of papal and/or episcopal teaching poses serious and difficult theological questions which have serious implications for the unity of the Church.

Church Teaching, Assent and Dissent

From what we have seen thus far from the teaching documents of the Church, it is clear that the expected response to the teaching of the magisterium is assent of mind and will (the *obsequium intellectus et voluntatis*). We have noted from the Profession of Faith various forms this assent might take. They range from the assent of faith to doctrine proposed by the Church as divinely revealed to an assent short of the act of faith which nonetheless accepts the definitive teaching of the Church on a matter of faith or morals. Finally, there is the religious assent owed to the teaching of the magisterium, even if the teaching is not definitive or is not a matter of faith and morals, though its acceptance is necessary for the integral truth of revelation to be presented and defended.

But could there be a case in which, even after careful consideration of the teaching of the magisterium and the fact that the Holy Spirit assists the Church, a conscientious believer might find assent impossible? Might a theologian after careful study find it impossible to give assent? This is a possibility considered by the CDF in its "Instruction on the Ecclesial Vocation of the Theologian" dated May 24, 1990.[19]

[18] Pope John Paul II's numerous writings in support of *Humanae vitae* can be represented here by the postsynodal apostolic exhortation *Familiaris consortio*, an extended response to the Synod of Bishops meeting in 1980. Text in *Origins* 11 (1981) 28, 29, 437–68.

[19] CDF, "Instruction on the Ecclesial Vocation of the Theologian" (Vatican City: Libreria editrice Vaticana, 1990). I have discussed the instruction at length in *Church Teaching Authority*, ch. 8, "The 1990 Instruction *Donum veritatis* On the Role of the Theologian," 142–60. On dissent from authoritative teaching, see 155–9.

First of all, the congregation puts great emphasis on the divine assistance given to the Church's teaching, even when the issue is not a matter of revelation. Christ is the source of all the Church's teaching activity. Great deference is therefore owed to the Church in any event.

But the congregation cautiously concedes that over time some Church pronouncements appear to be less than wholly satisfactory. But it rejects the notion that the magisterium is habitually mistaken in the prudential judgments it makes, including those on moral issues which bind the consciences of believers. The emphasis on the passage of time follows up statements in the 1973 declaration *Mysterium ecclesiae*, which conceded that expressions, even of Church dogma, are the products of their times and can at a later time require modification. But an underlying loyalty and respect for the Church and the divine assistance at work in it should appear in a fundamental attitude of acceptance of the Church's teaching even in the face of difficulties in particular cases.

The instruction also offers some definition of *obsequium religiosum voluntatis et intellectus* when it says: "This kind of response cannot be simply exterior or disciplinary but must be understood within the logic of faith and under the impulse of the obedience of faith" (n. 23). And: "The willingness to submit loyally to the teaching of the Magisterium on matters per se not irreformable must be the rule" (n. 24).

The curious use of the double negative suggests that the believer should expect that Church teaching is generally correct even if not irreformable, as dogmatic definitions or other forms of definitive teaching are according to the Profession of Faith. The instruction says plainly that the believer must be willing to suffer when questions and problems arise in the confidence that ultimately the truth will prevail (n. 31).

With these cautions, the instruction does see the possibility that assent to some nondefinitive magisterial pronouncement might be withheld. The reluctant theologian is told for example that she or he should enter into a dialog with Church authorities in an effort to resolve problems about a doctrine or the way in which it is expressed. The instruction also sees the possibility of publishing discreetly questions about magisterial teaching so that one's peers in theology might evaluate both the teaching and their colleagues' problems and suggestions.

Much of this is quite traditional, even if it has not received emphasis in recent statements issued in a time of contestation. It also helps to define what the congregation means when it speaks of "dissent" rather than the personal or theological problems the theologian has with a particular nondefinitive Church teaching.[20]

---

[20] The instruction discusses only the problems of theologians with magisterial teaching—and of course theologians are the theme of the instruction. The theologian,

"Dissent," as the instruction understands it, means something more than personal, occasional theological difficulties with particular Church teachings. Dissent implies an attempt to bypass the authoritative teaching of the Church in favor of private opinions or even opinions widely held for which the claim is made that they represent the *sensus fidelium.* Dissent may also arise "from hostile and contrary feelings" (n. 25). Dissent implies organized attempts to change Church doctrine employing methods borrowed from political pressure groups, including the use of the media. In sum, the methods would create a second teaching authority on an equal footing with the Church's official magisterium. As we have seen, many recent statements from Pope John Paul and the CDF have strongly criticized such dissent.

The Obedience of the Judgment

How is it possible for the believer to give the response of an *obsequium mentis et voluntatis* to Church teaching which contradicts beliefs commonly held in today's culture? Francis Sullivan discusses this question in his book *Magisterium* in a section devoted to the "obedience of the judgment."[21] The "obedience" (i.e., *obsequium*) in question is discussed by Catholic theologians like Thomas Aquinas in their treatment of the virtue and the act of faith. Aquinas discusses faith and the interaction of the intellect and will in making the act of faith in the *Summa Theologiae* II-II, q. 2. Aquinas is following a theological tradition which has its roots in the New Testament, which speaks of the "obedience of faith." Medieval commentators on the *Sentences* of Peter Lombard often cite the saying of Paul in 2 Cor 10:5 that "[we] take every thought captive in obedience [obsequium] to Christ." Faith, in this tradition, is an affirmation of the truth of the Christian revelation, but it is an act of the intellect under the command of the will. Like other virtues, faith is a habit, a kind of instinct, which inclines the understanding to affirm the truth of God's revelation. Sullivan is therefore following a long established theological tradition in writing of the act of faith as "obedience of the judgment." As a virtue infused by God, faith inclines the believer to recognize acceptance of God's self-revelation as a good to be willed but also as a good to be acquired by affirming in a judgment a truth that is revealed by God and therefore to be believed. Religious belief,

---

who has professional training and has been granted a canonical mission or mandate to teach has at least a presumption of competence that others may not be able to claim.

[21] See Sullivan, *Magisterium,* 162–6. For further discussion, see J. Boyle, *Church Teaching Authority,* 63–78, 79–94.

the embrace of God's self-revelation, is therefore an act of obedience to God, a judgment that accepting God's revelation is a good but also a judgment that what God reveals must also be true precisely because God reveals it.

The theological tradition has little difficulty in affirming that what God reveals is true and therefore deserving of faith. That is reflected in the first paragraph added to the creed in the 1989 Profession of Faith.

But what of those things definitively taught by the Church which are not taught as divine revelation—those things in the second paragraph added to the Profession of Faith? On what grounds does one hold the teaching of the Church on contraception or the restriction of ordination to the priesthood to males?

In the instruction *Donum veritatis* the CDF wrote:

> One must therefore take into account the proper character of the Magisterium, considering the extent which its authority is engaged. *It must also be borne in mind that all acts of the Magisterium derive from the same source, that is, from Christ, who desires that his People walk in the entire truth. For this same reason, magisterial decisions in matters of discipline, even if they are not guaranteed by the charism of infallibility, are not without divine assistance and call for the adherence of the faithful* (n. 17, emphasis added).

And later it adds: "When the Magisterium proposes 'in a definitive way' truths concerning faith and morals, which, even if not divinely revealed, are nevertheless strictly and intimately connected with Revelation, these must be firmly accepted and held" (n. 23).

Sullivan[22] points out that this formulation paraphrases the usual definition of the secondary objects of infallibility.

The Hierarchy of Truths

Finally, note the important statement of the council in its Decree on Ecumenism at n. 11 that there is a hierarchy of truths among Catholic doctrines. The council says: "When comparing doctrines with one another, they [Catholic theologians and separated brothers and sisters] should remember that in catholic doctrine there exists an order or 'hierarchy' of truths, since they vary in their relation to the foundation of the christian faith."

The "foundation of Christian faith" mentioned here clearly refers to the central doctrines of Christianity such as the Trinity, the incarnation, the atonement, and the like. By contrast, other doctrines may be less

[22] In Francis A. Sullivan, *Creative Fidelity: Weighing and Interpreting Documents of the Magisterium* (New York: Paulist Press, 1996) 15.

central to Christian belief—a fact that has important implications for dialogue not only with other Christians but with members of the other world religions as well. I cannot develop this notion here, but the importance of this distinguishing of central doctrines from others lower in the hierarchy of beliefs is apparent.

For Further Reference

Documents of the Vatican Council I

Dogmatic Constitution on the Catholic Faith *(Dei Filius)*, DS 3000–45. *Documents of Vatican Council I.* Ed. J. F. Broderick. Collegeville: The Liturgical Press, 1971.

First Dogmatic Constitution on the Church *(Pastor aeternus)*, DS 3050–75. *Documents of Vatican Council I.* Ed. J. F. Broderick. Collegeville: The Liturgical Press, 1971.

Pius XII. Allocutions *Si diligis* and *Magnificate Dominum mecum. AAS* 46 (1954) 313–7 and 666–77.

_____. Encyclical Letter *Humani generis. AAS* 42 (1950) 561–78.

Documents of the Vatican Council II

Decree on Ecumenism *(Unitatis redintegratio)*, 1964. *Vatican Council II: Constitutions, Decrees, Declarations.* Ed. Austin Flannery, 452–70. Revised ed. Northport, N.Y.: Costello Publishing Co., 1996.

Dogmatic Constitution on the Church *(Lumen gentium)*, 1964. *Vatican Council II: Constitutions, Decrees, Declarations.* Ed. Austin Flannery, 350–426. Revised ed. Northport, N.Y.: Costello Publishing Co., 1996.

Dogmatic Constitution on Divine Revelation *(Dei verbum)*, 1965. *Vatican Council II: Constitutions, Decrees, Declarations.* Ed. Austin Flannery, 750–65. Revised ed. Northport, N.Y.: Costello Publishing Co., 1996.

Books and Articles

Boyle, John P. *Church Teaching Authority: Historical and Theological Studies.* Notre Dame, Ind.: University of Notre Dame Press, 1995.

Catholic Theological Society of America. *Cooperation between Theologians and the Ecclesiastical Magisterium.* Ed. Leo J. O'Donovan. Washington, D.C.: Canon Law Society of America, 1982.

_____. *Report of the Catholic Theological Society of America Committee on the Profession of Faith and the Oath of Fidelity.* Chicago: Catholic Theological Society of America, 1990.

Congar, Yves. "A Semantic History of the Term 'Magisterium'" and "A Brief History of the Forms of the Magisterium and Its Relations with Scholars." *Readings in Moral Theology.* Vol. 3: *The Magisterium and Morality.* Ed. Charles E. Curran and Richard A. McCormick, 297–313 and 314–31. New York: Paulist Press, 1982.

Fahey, Michael. "Church." *Systematic Theology: Roman Catholic Perspectives.* 2 vols. Ed. F. Fiorenza and J. Galvin, 2:1–74. Minneapolis: Fortress Press, 1991.

Galliardetz, Richard R. *Witnesses to the Faith: Community, Infallibility, and the Ordinary Magisterium of Bishops.* New York: Paulist Press, 1992.

_____. *Teaching with Authority: A Theology of the Magisterium of the Church.* Collegeville: The Liturgical Press, 1997.

Küng, Hans. *Infallible? An Inquiry.* Trans. Edward Quinn. Garden City, N.Y.: Doubleday, 1971.

Örsy, Ladislas. *The Church: Learning and Teaching: Magisterium, Assent, Dissent, Academic Freedom.* Wilmington, Del.: Michael Glazier, 1987.

_____. *The Profession of Faith and the Oath of Fidelity: A Theological and Canonical Analysis.* Wilmington, Del.: Michael Glazier, 1990.

Sanks, T. Howland. *Authority in the Church: A Study in Changing Paradigms.* AAR Dissertation Series, 2. Missoula, Mont.: AAR and Scholars Press, 1974.

Sullivan, Francis A. *Creative Fidelity: Weighing and Interpreting Documents of the Magisterium.* New York: Paulist Press, 1996.

_____. *Magisterium: Teaching Authority in the Catholic Church.* New York: Paulist Press, 1983.

Zapelena, Timotheus. *De ecclesia.* 2 vols. Rome: Gregorian University Press, 1950–54.

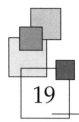

| 19 | The Church and the Law |

Thomas J. Green

Introduction

The last three decades of the twentieth century have witnessed an extraordinary outburst of legislative activity in the Catholic Church following the Second Vatican Council, the defining ecclesial event of the century. First one should note the January 1983 promulgation by John Paul II of the Code of Canon Law for the Latin Church[1] after a decade and a half preparation process.[2] Subsequently, in June 1988 John Paul II promulgated the apostolic constitution *Pastor bonus*,[3] reforming the Roman Curia and following through on the initial postconciliar curial reform efforts of Paul VI (1967).[4] Finally, in October 1990 John Paul II

---

[1] *Code of Canon Law, Latin-English Edition*, New English Translation (Washington, D.C.: Canon Law Society of America [CLSA], 1998). See especially the apostolic constitution *Sacrae disciplinae leges*, xxvii–xxxii.

[2] For a brief overview of the process leading to the 1983 Latin code see John A. Alesandro, "General Introduction," *The Code of Canon Law: A Text and Commentary*, ed. James A. Coriden et al. (hereafter *CLSA Commentary*) (New York/Mahwah, N.J.: Paulist Press, 1985) 4–8. Also John A. Alesandro, "The Revision of the Code of Canon Law: A Background Study," *Studia Canonica* 24 (1990) 91–146.

[3] The Roman Curia is a complex of dicasteries (departments) assisting the pope in exercising his ministry to the universal Church. For an unofficial translation of *Pastor bonus* see *Code of Canon Law Annotated*, ed. Ernest Caparros and others (Montreal: Wilson and LaFleur, 1993) 1166–279. For a helpful overview of the competencies of the curial dicasteries see "The Roman Curia," *Official Catholic Directory 1999* (New Providence, N.J.: Kenedy, 1999) A29–A31.

[4] See apostolic constitution *Regimini Ecclesiae universae*, August 15, 1967. English translation in *The Canon Law Digest* 6, 324–57.

promulgated the Code of Canons of the Eastern Churches[5] after a lengthy preparation process beginning in 1972.[6]

Both the conciliar enterprise and the aforementioned significant legislative initiatives are designed to enable the Church to be a more vital pastoral instrument of God's salvific presence in an ever-changing world at the turn of the millennium. As in other periods of noteworthy ecclesial renewal, recent popes among others have recognized that a revitalization of the Church's mission in part presupposes a reform of its institutional structures.

John Paul II, who continued contemporary papal legislative reform initiated especially by John XXIII, has viewed the revised codes as significant efforts to translate the breadth of conciliar doctrine into canonical language. This is true despite the difficulty of such an undertaking and the inadequacy of legal forms in expressing the richness of ecclesial life and doctrine. This is especially the case regarding our understanding of the complex mystery of the Church itself. The conciliar teaching on the Church, expressed especially in *Lumen gentium*, must be a constant frame of reference for understanding the aforementioned codes. There is a profound complementarity between the council documents and the codes, which notably depend on the former documents.

The key ecclesiological themes of the council must serve as significant criteria for interpreting and implementing the codes in practice. This is true not simply for canonists, but for theologians, other scholars, and pastoral ministers who daily implement the law in serving the Church's mission at various levels.

There are probably as many different ways of conceptualizing such themes as there are authors who have attempted to do so. However, in his apostolic constitution *Sacrae disciplinae leges* promulgating the Latin code, John Paul II emphasized the following key ecclesiological themes as underlying the code: the Church as the People of God; hierarchical authority as service; the Church as a communion with its wide-ranging implications for universal Church-particular church relationships and primacy-episcopacy relationships; the participation of all the faithful in the threefold functions *(munera)* of Christ with its profound implica-

---

[5] *Code of Canons of the Eastern Churches*, Latin-English Edition (Washington, D.C.: CLSA, 1990). A revised translation of this document is currently being prepared and should be available in the near future. See especially the apostolic constitution *Sacri canones*, xi–xix.

[6] See J. Faris, "The Codification of the Eastern Canon Law," *The Eastern Catholic Churches: Constitution and Governance according to the Code of Canons of the Eastern Churches* (New York: St. Maron Publications, 1992) 67–106; T. Green, "Reflections on the Eastern Code Revision Process," *The Jurist* 51 (1991) 18–37.

tions for their fundamental rights and duties; and, finally, the importance of the Church's ecumenical commitment.[7]

An extraordinary richness characterizes the liturgical, theological,
spiritual, and disciplinary patrimony not only of the Latin Church but
also of the twenty-one *sui iuris* or self-governing Eastern Churches.[8]
However, limitations of space make it imperative that we focus primarily on the Latin code since it probably affects most of the readers of this
festschrift.[9] Nevertheless, occasionally cross references will be made to
the Eastern code (CCEO) for comparative reflection purposes.

If the Latin code is to be genuinely helpful in realizing the Church's
multifaceted mission, it must be implemented creatively and responsibly. And this is a task not simply for canonists but also for theologians
and especially pastoral ministers functioning at every level of the Church.
Only serious and sustained interaction among them will assure that the
code contributes appropriately to the Church's legal-pastoral life and
does not become prematurely obsolescent due to insufficient attention
to significant and shifting theological-pastoral realities.

A concern to foster such an exchange within the Church prompted
the author in 1979 to reflect on theological aspects of the revision of the
1917 code.[10] At that time the Latin code revision process was in its last
stages. The reflections were basically twofold in character: an *exposition*
of significant stages in the revision of the 1917 code and key components of the drafts of proposed legislation and a *critical* appraisal of
some significant theological concerns identified in the drafts. Similar

[7] This last ecumenical theme was highlighted more prominently in the apostolic
constitution *Sacri canones* promulgating the Eastern code than in *Sacrae disciplinae
leges,* since ecumenical concerns were more notably emphasized in preparing that
code than in its Latin counterpart.

[8] For a thoughtful overview of all the Eastern Churches, including those not in
full communion, see Ronald Roberson, *The Eastern Catholic Churches,* 6th ed. (Rome:
Edizioni Orientalia Christiana, 1999). For a commentary on the whole Eastern code
see Victor Pospishil, *Eastern Catholic Church Law,* 2d ed. (Staten Island, N.Y.: St.
Maron Publications, 1996). For helpful reflections on the governance structures in
the Eastern code see Faris, "The Codification of the Eastern Canon Law." For pertinent bibliography on the Eastern code see Warren Soule, *Eastern Canon Law Bibliography,* 2d ed. (Staten Island, N.Y.: St. Maron Publications, 1994).

[9] Latin Church law is a much broader reality than the 1983 code. It includes also
liturgical law, the occasional laws passed by episcopal conferences (such as the
NCCB), diocesan legislation, and the proper law governing religious institutes and
societies. However, given the centrality of the 1983 code, it is the author's nearly exclusive focus in this article.

[10] Thomas J. Green, "The Revision of Canon Law: Theological Implications,"
Theological Studies 40 (1979) 593–679.

preoccupations motivated a 1986 article critically examining selected aspects of the 1983 code to determine to what extent the aforementioned concerns had been addressed.[11]

Similar concerns underlie the current article. While a canonist and not a theologian, the author is increasingly aware that theological (and especially ecclesiological) issues are central to the healthy evolution of canon law in service to the People of God.[12] There had been a certain pre-conciliar tendency to view Church law in ways quite comparable to civil law. This tendency in turn embodied an overly juridicized ecclesiology understanding the Church as a so-called perfect society like the state with its own independent law and governance structures. Church law was to function like law in any society, keeping the peace, serving justice, preserving institutional values, protecting rights, etc. While these purposes of law are indeed quite laudable, canon law needs to be seen in the broader theological perspective of the mystery of the Church (TO 16).

Increasingly there is a consciousness that theology (the Church contemplative) is to seek to understand and articulate the inexhaustible mystery of Christ (faith seeking understanding). However, canon law (the Church active) is to embody that mystery ecclesially, fashioning appropriate structures and ordering ecclesial relationships in service to the Church's mission as a light to the nations (faith seeking action).[13]

The Church, simultaneously divine and human, is incomplete and unfinished; it must grow and expand in history. It needs to reach out for authentic values, that is, good things that can perfect the community and support its life. Theology attempts to help the community understand those values, while canon law attempts to assist it in appropriating them in practice.

In his aforementioned articles the author explored certain aspects of contemporary Latin Church canonical development in light of selected principles of institutional reform. These principles, initially articulated

---

[11] Thomas J. Green, "The Revised Code of Canon Law: Some Theological Issues," *Theological Studies* 47 (1986) 617–52.

[12] See John Huels, "The Role of Canon Law in Light of *Lumen Gentium*," *The Ministry of Governance*, ed. James Mallett (Washington, D.C.: CLSA, 1986) 98–120.

[13] Perhaps no author on the American scene has done more to clarify the theology-law relationship than Ladislas Orsy. See his *Theology and Canon Law: New Horizons for Legislation and Interpretation* (Collegeville: The Liturgical Press, 1992). During the post-conciliar period the work of the CLSA has frequently been interdisciplinary in character precisely because of such concerns. See Thomas Green, "The Canon Law Society of America and the Revision of the Code: Historical Reflections and Continuing Concerns," *The Jurist* 53 (1993) 1–21.

by Austrian pastoral theologian Ferdinand Klostermann,[14] embodied key conciliar ecclesiological values. The principles overlap at times, and occasionally it is difficult to differentiate sharply their ecclesiological and canonical dimensions. Nevertheless, they may help to focus the following observations.

In light of the aforementioned principles the author wishes to offer a few general reflections on the relationship between ecclesiology and canon law. Secondly, he proposes to orient the reader to the 1983 Latin code, highlighting certain key ecclesiological concerns underlying the canons. Given limitations of space, his focus is basically expository rather than critical in character. The author does not pretend to offer a comprehensive introduction to the code,[15] much less detailed comments on the individual canons.[16] Rather, his purpose is much more modest: to express certain general ecclesiological themes that are particularly relevant to contemporary canonical reform. Hopefully this will motivate the reader to study Church law somewhat more carefully and integrate it more appropriately in continuing theological reflection and pastoral practice.

Church-Law Relationship: Selected Themes

Following the order of his aforementioned articles, the author will deal with the Church-law relationship according to the following principles of institutional reform: (1) historicity, (2) pneumatic-charismatic, (3) fundamental Christian equality and co-responsibility, (4) collegiality,

---

[14] Ferdinand Klostermann, "Reform of Church Structures," *Rethinking the Church (La fine della Chiesa come società perfetta)*, ed. M. Cuminetti and F. V. Johannes (Dublin: Gill and Macmillan, 1970) 142–93, esp. 142–56.

[15] See James A. Coriden, *An Introduction to Canon Law* (New York/Mahwah, N.J.: Paulist Press, 1991). See also a useful collection of articles and case studies on various canonical issues: Jordan T. Hite and Daniel Ward, ed., *Readings, Cases, Materials in Canon Law: A Textbook for Ministerial Students*, rev. ed. (Collegeville: The Liturgical Press, 1990).

[16] The author especially recommends the following canon-by-canon commentary on the Latin code: James A. Coriden and others, eds., *The Code of Canon Law: A Text and Commentary Commissioned by the Canon Law Society of America* (New York/Mahwah, N.J.: Paulist Press, 1985). While it comprehensively examines the canons of the code, this work is currently being thoroughly revised in light of post-1983 code developments. See also Gerard Sheehy and others, eds., *The Canon Law Letter and Spirit* (Collegeville: The Liturgical Press, 1995); Ernest Caparros and others, eds., *Code of Canon Law Annotated* (Montreal: Wilson & LaFleur Limitée, 1993). This last work is an English translation of a Spanish work prepared at the University of Pamplona in Navarra, Spain.

(5) dialogue, and (6) subsidiarity. Each principle will be briefly expressed and its key implications for canonical reform noted.

Principle of Historicity [17]

The conciliar emphasis on the Church as the People of God[18] clarifies both its continuity with the people of the Old Testament and the Church's immersion in human history. We live in a time of tension between the first breakthrough of the kingdom of God and its final flowering. This flowering is to be fostered by a pilgrim Church, which serves the realization of the kingdom amid a changing human situation. Despite being graced by the Spirit, the Church contains sinners and hence always needs purification and renewal. Since this is true, there is a certain provisional, relative character to much of the Church's life, of which we are especially conscious at the turn of the millennium.

An older, more institutionally oriented ecclesiology failed to do justice to the above aspects of the Church and overly stressed its unchanging aspects, thereby leading to canonical formulations, liturgical rites, and creeds that were unduly rigid and unbending. However, the Church must constantly clarify and distinguish the changing from the unchanging dimensions of its life, what is absolute and what is relative. Otherwise we tend to overemphasize historically contingent formulations of values without due sensitivity to changes in our understanding of them.

One possible reason for continuing tensions in the Church is the fact that the legal system has not been adequately adapted to changing circumstances. Change has come upon us too suddenly in terms of a new cultural situation and the newer theological-pastoral insights of Vatican II, and our structural forms have not always been appropriate for the task of mediating such insights. Given the rapidity of societal change today, the legal order should be duly open to the shaping of new institutional forms and the development of new ministerial approaches in response to the signs of the times.

Such openness to change has somewhat characterized the postconciliar period, although it seems to have been more true in the pre-1983 code period, since the code crystallized certain lines of institutional

---

[17] See Green, "The Revision of Canon Law," 628–30; Green, "The Revised Code of Canon Law," 623–5; Huels, "The Role of Canon Law in Light of *Lumen Gentium*," 102–6; Klostermann, "Reform of Church Structures," 143–5.

[18] This motif is an especially significant organizing principle for the Latin code. For example, Book II (cc. 204–746) is entitled "The People of God." The abbreviation c. (cc.) refers to the canons of that code.

development. A certain institutional stability is undeniably indispensable for the welfare of the community, certainty regarding one's substantive and procedural rights. However, the Church must be equally open to the legitimate demand for change—an ongoing task if it is to fulfill its teaching, sanctifying, and serving mission responsibly. A continuing concern in this regard is the absence of institutional forms at the universal Church level to provide for systematic updating of the code. However, at other levels of Church life such institutional forms are available, such as diocesan synods (cc. 460–8; CCEO 235–42) and chapters of religious institutes and societies (cc. 631–3; CCEO 511–2).

Pneumatic-Charismatic Principle [19]

The primary principle of unity and life within the Church is the Spirit, who freely distributes charisms and gifts to all within the community, not just to those in official hierarchical positions.[20] The Church is constituted by and lives from those charisms and gifts and is accordingly enabled to remain in fidelity to the apostolic faith. A respect for those gifts and the dignity of all believers requires a receptivity to the contribution of all believers to institutional reform.

There may well be a conflict between the requirements of Church law, the exigencies of individual freedom and dignity, and the individual's judgment about how best to fulfill the will of the Lord. An ever-present challenge is harmonizing these vital aspects of community life; official Church law should not stifle but rather leave ample room for the workings of the Spirit, whose activity in unifying and energizing brothers and sisters in Christ is to be facilitated.

Of their very nature Church law and structures should have a serving character, be person-centered, and be somewhat modest in their expectations. Above all Church law should be viewed in relationship to the more basic goals it serves: fuller personal growth and corporate vitality in the achievement of Church purposes.

Christ is the basic authority figure in the Church, and its various ministries bear witness to his presence and meaning for people. Therefore, those exercising authority in virtue of some particular office are geared primarily to serving the needs of the community and the spiritual

---

[19] See Green, "The Revision of Canon Law," 630–2; Green, "The Revised Code of Canon Law," 625–33; Huels, "The Role of Canon Law in Light of *Lumen Gentium*," 107–8; Klostermann, "Reform of Church Structures," 145–6.

[20] The Latin Church (code) has been less sensitive to this vital ecclesial dimension than the Eastern Churches (code).

welfare of individuals; ideally there is no room for dominating, manipulating, or controlling persons.

Law can at times be substituted as a goal instead of those more basic ecclesial realities. This can happen if we press too closely the analogy between civil and Church law and do not recognize the basic differences between the Church and the state. Church law must be as open to continual critique as well as other ecclesial institutions in terms of their contribution to the Church's mission. Gospel values and priorities, especially the spiritual welfare of persons, are primary considerations in this continuing examination, which was not a significant priority during the preconciliar period.

At the very heart of the Church's life is service to people. Law can do much to facilitate or impede the interrelationships between different members of the community as it organizes and shapes the patterns of service appropriate to different circumstances.

Church law operates within the context of a community of individuals freely believing and called to an ever deeper realization of that faith. The primary concern of Church law is not primarily external order as seems to be true with civil law, prescinding from intent or motivation. The freedom of believers should be restricted only where necessary to foster community life and integrity. Furthermore, Church law should articulate clearly the fundamental substantive human and ecclesial rights of believers[21] and provide appropriate procedural protections for their responsible exercise. Fostering an environment of respect for such rights is indispensable if the Church is credibly to proclaim the value of justice in the world.[22]

Law is necessarily concerned with general community needs, hence it cannot reasonably deal with all possible contingencies. There may be conflict situations where one must depart from the letter of the law; in such situations one must care for the well-being of the community, make an honest effort to discern the law's purpose, and have a prevailing reason for departing from the norm.

---

[21] See, for example, cc. 208–23 (CCEO 12–26). The articulation and protection of fundamental Christian rights have been central postconciliar canonical concerns. Principles 6–7 guiding the preparation of the 1983 code highlight the importance of this issue. See Hite and Ward, "Principles Which Govern the Revision of the Code of Canon Law," *Readings, Cases, Materials in Canon Law,* 89–91. See also *Protection of Rights of Persons in the Church: Revised Report of the Canon Law Society of America on the Subject of Due Process* (Washington, D.C.: CLSA, 1991).

[22] 1971 synod of bishops, declaration *Convenientes ex universo: Acta Apostolicae Sedis* 63 (1971) 433 (hereafter AAS).

Principle of Fundamental Christian Equality and Shared Responsibility [23]

This principle is closely linked to the preceding one. It poses a continuing issue at the heart of postconciliar institutional reform: the need to transcend the sharp clerical-lay distinctions and overly stratified ecclesiology of the 1917 code and its unduly hierarchical, minimally communitarian governance patterns.

Lumen gentium 9 and 32 strongly emphasized the basic equality of all believers regarding certain primary realities in ecclesial life: common baptism, destiny, Lord, mission (c. 208; CCEO 11). This equality is prior to any sacramentally based structural differences within the community (ordained ministry: c. 207, §1), which are geared to fostering the spiritual welfare of individuals and the community's corporate mission. In structuring appropriate relationships between the ordained and the nonordained, Church law must take the value of fundamental equality as seriously as the legitimate functional diversity rooted in sacred orders.

The primary aspect of ecclesial life is the fact that the Church is a communion in the Spirit. God's salvific work is inescapably communal in character. A key ecclesiological motif reaffirmed at Vatican II was the Pauline image of the head and members of the Mystical Body of Christ. The profound unity of all such believers in Christ is symbolized most powerfully and deepened anew at the Eucharist. And yet this communion is not an undifferentiated one but rather a hierarchically structured one. The diversity of roles operative during the eucharistic celebration is paradigmatic for the diversity of ecclesial relationships in the ongoing realization of the Church's mission.

A major continuing canonical task is fashioning corporate structures to foster the informed contributions of all members to the Church's mission. Canon law helps the Church be and do what it is meant to be and do. In other words, it helps the Church proclaim the life and mission of Christ, be a communal witness to the loving presence of God, and serve the world of today. This principle implies that different segments of the community are to be involved in the processes of continually renewing Church law and shaping new institutional structures. Understandably, certain aspects of legal reform at all levels require the specialized input of experts in law. Yet in dealing pastorally with the needs of people to which the law must respond, Church authorities and canonists need to call upon a wide range of Christians for their

[23] See Green, "The Revision of Canon Law," 641–8; Green, "The Revised Code of Canon Law," 633–9; Huels, "The Role of Canon Law in Light of *Lumen Gentium*," 104–7; 109–12; Klostermann, "Reform of Church Structures," 146–9.

experiences and insights. Presumably where there is genuine consultation during the decision-making process,[24] legal change and other institutional developments (e.g., modifications of parish structures) will be
received more willingly and will enrich the community in pursuing its
mission.

There is a growing realization that the viability of Church structures
depends greatly on the consensus of the community, however it be expressed.[25] The postconciliar creation of councils at various levels[26] concretely recognizes the need for opportunities for communication and
collaboration among Christians as they deepen their experience of life
together. Such sustained and serious communication is indispensable if
the community is to be self-renewing and not a stagnating group. The
community constantly must assess its life and mission to provide ever
wider areas of shared responsibility and concern.

Principle of Collegiality [27]

A central conciliar ecclesiological theme with broad canonical ramifications is episcopal collegiality. In a broad sense collegiality refers to
the spirit of collaboration and fraternal interaction that should charac-
terize relationships among the bishops in their service of the particular
churches and the universal Church. In a more proper sense collegiality
means that the bishops united in hierarchical communion to the pope
and to one another are the subjects of supreme and full power in governing the Church (c. 336).

Three significant factors are especially operative in assuring the
unity of the Church and the fruitfulness of its teaching, sanctifying, and
serving mission: interiorly the life-giving presence of the Spirit of the
risen Christ and exteriorly the apostolic ministry of the college of bishops and the central and indispensable Church-unifying role of the
Bishop of Rome within it.

There is a mysterious dynamic at work in the interrelationship between the pope and his brother bishops. His primacy is always to be

[24] On the complexities of ecclesial decision-making and the need for broad input
in that enterprise see Robert Kennedy, "Shared Responsibility in Ecclesial Decision-
Making," *Studia Canonica* 14 (1980) 5–24.

[25] See James A. Coriden, "Canonical Doctrine of Reception," *The Jurist* 50 (1990)
58–82.

[26] In this connection one might point to the diocesan pastoral council (cc. 511–4;
CCEO 272–5), the parish pastoral council (c. 536; CCEO 295), and the parish finance
council (c. 537; CCEO 295).

[27] See Green, "The Revision of Canon Law," 648–51; Green, "The Revised Code of
Canon Law," 639–43.

viewed as a primacy within the college and not apart from it or above it. The Church is governed by the episcopal college in such a way that the pope is not merely an instrument of the college, nor is the college merely his executive organ. The pope is not an absolute monarch, nor are the bishops simply his delegates. Rather, they all have their distinctive divine law-based pastoral governance competencies to be exercised in a spirit of mutual respect.

The supreme and full power to govern the Church in the pursuit of its mission has been conferred upon the whole college. Although such power is exercised in different modes and forms, it is radically one and the same power for the service of the kingdom. The pope determines the modality of its exercise in response to the concrete needs of the Church.

These brief comments can hardly do justice to the complexity of papal-episcopal relationships. Appropriately structuring such relationships canonically in fidelity to the conciliar data has been an especially difficult postconciliar enterprise. This was one of the central theological-canonical issues during the code revision process. Relatively new legal institutes such as the synod of bishops (cc. 342–8) and episcopal conferences (cc. 447–59) have contributed notably to enhancing episcopal ministry and fostering more effective papal-episcopal relationships in the postconciliar period. Yet questions continue to be raised about the canonical adequacy of such institutes. For example, does their present canonical status and functioning tend to overemphasize the value of papal primacy, however foundational, while insufficiently recognizing the important governance role of the college of bishops and individual bishops?[28]

While it is not technically collegiality in the proper sense, the issue of bishop-presbyter relationships in a diocese might be noted here. This is because such sacramentally based relationships are integral to adequate pastoral service of the People of God in the diocese (cf. c. 369).

Vatican II highlighted the importance of the presbyterate as a corporate reality and called bishops to view presbyters as their assistants and advisers in pastoral governance (PO 7; c. 384). The presbyteral council is one institutional embodiment of this joint pastoral concern (cc. 495–501; CCEO 264–70). Significant progress has been made in

---

[28] The lack of a properly deliberative role for the synod of bishops (c. 343) and the gradually diminished legislative role of episcopal conferences (c. 455) during the code revision process were among the issues posed in this connection. For two recent works that thoughtfully examine the exercise of papal primacy see: Michael Buckley, *Papal Primacy and the Episcopate* (New York: Crossroad, 1998); and Phyllis Zagano and Terrence Tilley, eds., *The Exercise of the Primacy: Continuing the Dialogue* (New York: Crossroad, 1998).

fostering more effective pastoral relationships within dioceses through such councils. However, there needs to be continuing attentiveness to the legal-pastoral demands of ensuring ever more genuinely collaborative bishop-presbyter relationships.[29]

Principle of Dialogue [30]

Since Vatican II there has been a renewed commitment by the Catholic Church to various forms of dialogue (e.g., reflection, prayer, and Christian witness) with other religious traditions, especially other Christians who are not in full Catholic communion (c. 205). The council recognized the presence of the Spirit in the efforts of other religious traditions to foster deeper unity among themselves and with the Catholic communion. In fact the council positively welcomed the insights of other religious traditions and invited certain of their members to participate in the conciliar deliberations as observers—an especially significant role in shaping documents such as the decrees on ecumenism and the Eastern Catholic churches.

It seems fitting that, following the conciliar pattern, systematic provision be made for eliciting input from those not fully in communion with regard to various ecclesial decisional processes, e.g., the reformulating of Church law at various levels.[31] Such provisions would reflect a realistic consciousness of our interdependence in various ways and of the impact of our policies on other communions.

If deeper communion is to be fostered among the churches (UR 5), Church structures cannot be parochial or sectarian but must fully respond to the task of implementing various aspects of the Church's ecumenical engagement.[32] Church law must be regularly evaluated to determine if it facilitates or impedes the realization of the Church's ecumenical objectives.

[29] See National Conference of Catholic Bishops (NCCB), "United in Service: Reflections on the Presbyteral Council," *Origins* 21/26 (December 5, 1991) 409; 411–21.

[30] See Green, "The Revision of Canon Law," 651–2; Green, "The Revised Code of Canon Law," 643–6; Klostermann, "Reform of Church Structures," 155.

[31] See, for example, c. 443, §6, on possible ecumenical guests at particular councils (e.g., provincial councils) and c. 463, §3, on such observers at diocesan synods. Canon 844, §5, calls for consultation with the leaders of other Christian churches before norms on sacramental sharing are finalized.

[32] For detailed provisions on various aspects of that ecumenical engagement see Pontifical Council for Promoting Christian Unity, *Directory for the Application of Principles and Norms on Ecumenism,* March 25, 1993 (Washington, D.C.: USCC, 1993).

Principle of Subsidiarity [33]

A profound conciliar ecclesiological datum with significant canonical ramifications is the teaching that the Church is not a monolithic organization but rather a vital communion of churches *(communio ecclesiarum)* brought together in a dynamic unity by the Spirit. In a certain sense Church history has been characterized by efforts at balancing various significant theological values, e.g., a respect for the integrity of the particular churches and the status of their bishops (apostolicity) and the need to honor appropriately the primatial role of the Bishop of Rome in fostering the unity of the ecclesial communion (catholicity).

The inescapable tension involved in balancing those values must be dealt with creatively by theologians, canonists, and pastoral leaders. Particularly since the council there has been a renewed recognition of the need to respect the diverse traditions of the particular churches even while striving to avoid tendencies that would seriously fracture the Church's unity and impair the quality of its mission. A respect for such diversity in geography, history, race, culture, spiritual and liturgical traditions seems to be a prerequisite for the appropriate development of the different gifts and charisms of the Spirit (LG 23; OE 2).

Besides a healthy theological, liturgical, and ascetical pluriformity there must be room for a genuine canonical pluriformity in structuring the life and ministry of the various particular churches. Despite continuing tensions the perennial need to incarnate the Church in various cultures is better understood today than in the immediately preconciliar period with its emphasis on institutional uniformity and notably centralized patterns of governance. The various millennium-related special synods have borne varied but constant testimony to this continuing legal-pastoral imperative.

Such an incarnation presupposes greater freedom of initiative for pastoral leaders in the various particular churches. While it may be easy to affirm this principle theoretically, working out the practical implications of appropriately decentralized governance patterns has been one of the most difficult postconciliar canonical challenges.

The principle of subsidiarity seems to mean in part that legal-pastoral decisions should be made at the most appropriate level, and frequently (but not always) that seems to mean the lowest possible level. The

---

[33] See Green, "The Revision of Canon Law," 656–68; Green, "The Revised Code of Canon Law," 646–52; Huels, "The Role of Canon Law in Light of *Lumen Gentium*," 112–7; Klostermann, "Reform of Church Structures," 155–6. While questions were raised at the 1985 extraordinary synod about the ecclesial relevance of the principle of subsidiarity, it was principle five approved by the 1967 synod to guide the revision of the code. See Hite and Ward, *Readings, Cases, Materials in Canon Law*, 87–9.

principle also seems to imply that lower level governmental authorities (e.g., diocesan bishops or episcopal conferences) should have the maximal freedom to shape the life and ministry of their particular churches with minimal curtailment of such initiatives by the Holy See. The principle also means that at times the resolution of certain issues needs to be reserved to higher level authorities for the Church's unity and advantage. Structuring a healthy balance between the various levels of governance in the Church continues to be a constant challenge that requires ongoing reflection on our legal-pastoral experience.

It is difficult to balance the conflicting demands for unity within a worldwide Church and a respect for legitimate diversity. This makes imperative constant communication between the bishops (representing their own communities and the principle of diversity) and the pope (representing the universal Church and the principle of unity).

As far as Church law is concerned, while it is necessary that there be certain general principles of Church order applicable to all the churches, there must also be ample room for institutional adaptation to regional and local diversity.

An Overview of the 1983 Code:
Some Noteworthy Ecclesiological Themes[34]

Before offering a brief overview[35] of the pastorally relevant issues addressed in the various books of the 1983 code, it seems useful to comment briefly on its basic organization vis-à-vis the 1917 code. The 1752 canons of the seven books of the 1983 code[36] are organized in a way partly similar to its 1917 predecessor and in a way notably different from it, which reflects certain important conciliar themes.[37] This illustrates both the continuity and the discontinuity characterizing the relationship of the two Latin codes.

There are certain points of continuity in the organization of the codes: Book One of the 1983 code is entitled "General Norms," as it is in the 1917 code. Book Six of the present code is entitled "Sanctions in the Church," comparable to Book Five of its predecessor. Book Seven of

[34] In preparing this brief overview of the 1983 code, the author has found especially helpful Alesandro, *CLSA Commentary,* 8–10, 14–20. See also Coriden, *An Introduction to Canon Law,* passim. Cross-references will also be made to the Eastern code (CCEO).

[35] Such an overview focuses especially on parts of the code that seemingly are most pertinent to the readers of this *festschrift.*

[36] The 1546 canons of the Eastern code are organized not in seven books, but in thirty titles following the Eastern canonical tradition.

[37] See Alesandro, *CLSA Commentary,* 21.

the present code is entitled "Processes," comparable to Book Four of the prior code.

However, there are interesting points of discontinuity regarding the organization of the codes: Book Two on the "People of God" reflects a central conciliar ecclesiological motif, unlike its 1917 predecessor. In keeping with the conciliar emphasis on the Church's call to fulfill the threefold *munera* or functions of Christ, Book Three is entitled "The Teaching Office of the Church." Similarly Book Four is called "The Office of Sanctifying in the Church." Book Five is called "The Temporal Goods of the Church." The 1917 code lacked a separate book on temporalities, which were addressed in a widely criticized, somewhat comprehensive, yet undifferentiated Book Three called "On Things." It also dealt with the magisterium and the sacraments among other ecclesial realities.

Conciliar ecclesiology does not seem to influence significantly the structuring of Book One on general norms (cc. 1–203).[38] It clarifies the persons, offices, and legal instruments comprising the Church's canonical system. Book One initially defines general rules about ecclesiastical laws and the binding legal force of custom and general decrees. Then it treats of general executory decrees, instructions, and other administrative provisions (e.g., dispensations) lacking the force of law but rather geared to implementing the existing law.

After the code clarifies certain factors affecting the canonical status of physical persons (e.g., domicile) and the notion of juridic persons (somewhat like civil corporations), a still extensively discussed canon 129 describes clerics as those capable of exercising the power of governance and laity as eligible to cooperate in its exercise. Subsequently the code briefly refers to such governance as legislative (making laws), judicial (resolving conflicts), and executive (implementing laws) in character, while focusing somewhat more notably on the latter. Book One devotes numerous canons to clarifying how one can acquire or lose an ecclesiastical office, i.e., any function stably established by divine or Church law for a spiritual purpose (c. 145, §1) in service of the Church. The book closes with some brief comments on calculating time.

[38] See CCEO 1488–539; 909–19; 27–41; 920–35; 979–95; 936–78; 1540–6. The order in which the Eastern code treats the various issues frequently differs from the overall Latin code organization. The aforementioned cross-references and the subsequent ones will roughly follow the organization of the Latin code. However, some Latin code provisions are not found in the Eastern code, for example, synod of bishops (cc. 342–8); and some Eastern code provisions are not found in the Latin code, for example, patriarchal churches (CCEO 55–150). See also Alesandro, *CLSA Commentary*, 14–15; Coriden, *An Introduction to Canon Law*, 147–62.

Perhaps Book Two on the People of God (cc. 204–746),[39] the longest book in the code, is most notably affected by Vatican II ecclesiology and the corresponding "new way of thinking canonically" *(novus habitus mentis)* regularly emphasized by Paul VI.

This book is subdivided into three main parts, somewhat reflecting the structuring of *Lumen gentium* itself, which discussed all believers first in chapter two on the People of God, then dealt with the hierarchy in chapter three, and later treated the laity in chapter four and religious in chapter six. Book Two deals first with the sacramentally based legal status of all the members of the Christian faithful, then with the Church's hierarchical constitution at various levels, and finally with the charismatically based canonical status of institutes of consecrated life and societies of apostolic life.

Part one on the Christian faithful (cc. 204–329) in turn is subdivided into five titles, which clarify various ways in which different members of the faithful participate in the Church's life and ministry. An extraordinarily significant initial title (cc. 208–23) affirms the fundamental baptismal equality of all believers. It articulates certain sacramentally based human and ecclesial rights and obligations corresponding to that sacramental status, e.g., spiritual nourishment in word and sacrament, Christian education, defense of rights. A brief title (cc. 224–31) explicates certain ecclesial rights and obligations somewhat proper to the laity, e.g., in virtue of their married status and secular involvement.

The largest title of this part of the code addresses the legal status of sacred ministers or clerics given their noteworthy, though hardly exclusive, ministerial commitment rooted in sacred orders (cc. 232–93). After discussing in some detail the intellectual, spiritual, and pastoral formation of clerics (cc. 232–64), the code specifies their incardination or inscription in a particular diocese or religious institute/society for ecclesial service. Provisions for certain clerical obligations (e.g., residence) and rights (e.g., support) are followed by several norms on the loss of the clerical state through declaration of the invalidity of orders or dismissal (rarely), or laicization (somewhat more common).

After a brief title on personal prelatures (cc. 294–97), the code illustrates certain other implications of the basic Christian right to associate and assemble by providing certain norms on various associations of the faithful (cc. 298–329). Such groupings of the faithful for various spiritual purposes are de facto, private, or public depending on the extent of the official Church commitment in their establishment, governance, and continuing existence.

---

[39] See CCEO 7–26; 399–409; 323–98; 573–83; 42–322; 410–572. See also Alesandro, *CLSA Commentary,* 15–16; Coriden, *An Introduction to Canon Law,* 53–99.

The largest part of Book Two is part two on the Church's hierarchical constitution (cc. 330–572), which structures the exercise of its threefold mission at various levels. While certain canons govern Church organization at the universal level or at other levels above the diocese (e.g., episcopal conferences like the NCCB), most of the canons focus on the organization of the diocese and the parish, the latter of which affects most Catholics on a daily basis.

An initial section (cc. 330–67) deals with supreme Church authority, that is, the college of bishops with the pope as its head. While the college may exercise its supreme and full authority solemnly in an ecumenical council, the pope exercises such authority on a daily basis to unify the Church either personally or, more likely, through the cardinals, other bishops, and other members of the faithful.

After some initial canons on the pope and the ecumenical council, this part of the code treats of various institutes assisting him in serving the communion of churches. This includes the synod of bishops, a representative group of bishops occasionally advising the pope on pastoral issues, and the College of Cardinals, who assist the pope corporately (e.g., consistories) or individually (e.g., heading Roman Curia agencies). The code here also briefly mentions the Roman Curia, a complex of agencies enabling the pope to govern the Church,[40] and papal legates who represent him throughout the world.

A second more extensive section of part two of Book Two (cc. 368–572) primarily considers particular churches, especially dioceses, and significantly focuses on bishops and other leadership figures such as pastors who sanctify, teach, and govern the People of God. However, a relatively small title (cc. 431–59) regulates groupings of such dioceses (e.g., provinces) or their bishops (e.g., episcopal conferences) to foster better pastoral care.

After a few initial canons pertinent to all bishops, most of the provisions on authority in the particular churches regulate the rights and duties of diocesan bishops (i.e., those heading dioceses), especially their threefold pastoral governance role (legislative, executive, and judicial). Subsequently the code deals with coadjutor or auxiliary bishops, who assist diocesan bishops in exercising their office.

The rest of the canons on the diocese illustrate how other believers participate in the Church's mission. For example, a diversified group of the faithful may assist the bishop in creating diocesan laws (diocesan synod). The diocesan curia is a complex of persons (clerics and laypersons) and institutes assisting the bishop especially in exercising his executive (e.g., vicars, chancellor, and finance officer) or judicial roles

---

[40] See note 3 above.

390 Thomas J. Green

(e.g., judges and defender of bond). As a result of the conciliar call for more collaborative decision-making, two new diocesan consultative bodies are also envisioned, one mandatory (presbyteral council) and one elective (diocesan pastoral council).

The parish is described in personalistic terms as a community of the Christian faithful entrusted to a pastor for pastoral care under the bishop's supervision (c. 515, §1). The fundamental legal-pastoral reality is the pastoral care of the faithful which may be provided in various ways. Most canons highlight the sanctifying, teaching, and governing functions of the priest pastor or the other leadership figure functioning in place of the ordinary priest pastor-parish relationship. This might be a team of priests or perhaps a deacon, layperson, or group of laypersons functioning under the supervision of a priest, who is not technically the pastor. Several canons also provide for a priest parochial vicar to assist the pastor in discharging his pastoral responsibilities. The aforementioned concerns about collaborative ministerial patterns also underlie provisions for a parish pastoral council (elective) and a parish finance council (mandatory). Finally, a dean (vicar forane) may function as a pastoral coordinating figure for a group of parishes.

Part three of Book Two governs institutes of consecrated life/societies of apostolic life (cc. 573–746). After some general norms on all such institutes (cc. 573–606), the code differentiates between religious institutes (cc. 607–709) and secular institutes (cc. 710–30). Both groups profess the evangelical counsels of poverty, chastity, and obedience in some public fashion (e.g., public vows). However, members of religious institutes live a common life and are somewhat distanced from the world, whereas secular institute members are noted for their secularity and generally do not live common life. Subsequently, the code addresses societies of apostolic life (cc. 731–46) whose primary focus is their commitment to the apostolate and common life, although they do not make public vows. Numerous canons on the governance of religious institutes are applicable *mutatis mutandis* to secular institutes and societies of apostolic life, e.g., basic governance structures, admission and formation of candidates, rights and obligations, apostolate, separation from the institute/society. One particularly noteworthy illustration of the principle of subsidiarity is the extensive provision for the proper law of institutes/societies to regulate their life and mission within the broad parameters of the code.

Book Three on the Church's teaching office (cc. 747–833)[41] somewhat reflects the new conciliar communitarian perspectives while embody-

---

[41] See CCEO 595–606; 896–908; 607–26; 584–94; 627–66. See also Alesandro, *CLSA Commentary,* 16–17; Coriden, *An Introduction to Canon Law,* 101–11.

ing certain hierarchical features. While respecting the bishops' authoritative teaching office, it also provides for the diversified involvement of the faithful in proclaiming the gospel to all nations. Such involvement is based on their sacramentally based sharing in Christ's prophetic office.

After some initial canons on different levels of authoritative teaching, infallible and otherwise, the code briefly describes the involvement of bishops, other clerics, religious, and the laity in the Church's teaching mission. A significant title on the ministry of the word (cc. 756–80) highlights the primary leadership role of the bishop regarding the ministries of preaching and catechetics, but also envisions the necessary involvement of other clerics, such as pastors, and of laity, such as parents and catechists. A new title on missionary action calls for broad ecclesial engagement in evangelization under the leadership of the bishops (cc. 781–92).

The varied dimensions of Catholic education at different levels are treated in a somewhat lengthy title (cc. 793–821), which, however, hardly does justice to the complexity of the pertinent issues. This title is subdivided into schools (primary and secondary education), Catholic universities and other institutes of higher studies, and ecclesiastical universities and faculties. In the latter two instances legislation outside the code is especially relevant, e.g., the August 1990 apostolic constitution of John Paul II *Ex corde ecclesiae* on Catholic universities.[42] Finally, two brief titles regulate the instruments of social communications (especially books) (cc. 822–32) and the profession of faith binding certain officeholders and teachers (c. 833).

Book Four on the Church's sanctifying office (cc. 834–1253)[43] notably embodies the newer conciliar ecclesiological and liturgical horizons. While highlighting the central cultic leadership role of bishops and other clerics, it also calls for diversified involvement of the faithful in the Church's life of prayer. Moreover, more than in any other area of the code, significant components of sacramental and liturgical law are found outside the code itself, especially in the liturgical books.

Like Book Two, this book is also divided into three main parts, the most important part dealing with the sacraments while other parts treat of other acts of divine worship and sacred places and times.

Some initial canons clarify certain key aspects of liturgical celebrations: the diversity of roles, their communal character, the centrality of faith, and the primary educational role of the Church's ministers. Subsequently part one of Book Four (cc. 840–1165) deals with the seven

---

[42] *AAS* 82 (1990) 1475–509. English translation in *Origins* 20 (1990) 265–76.
[43] See CCEO 667–895. See also Alesandro, *CLSA Commentary*, 17–18; Coriden, *An Introduction to Canon Law*, 113–46.

sacraments in seven titles. The actual sacramental celebration is a primary legal concern in five sacraments; the legislator also focuses on the minister, the recipient, and the registration and proof of such a celebration.

While the canons on orders (cc. 1008–54) and marriage (cc. 1055–165) are clearly concerned about the liturgical celebration, both focus much more on the legal-pastoral factors surrounding such celebrations. In orders this concerns the various steps necessary to determine the candidate's suitability, e.g., testimonials and dimissorials.

In light of the complex issues surfacing throughout our legal-pastoral tradition, marriage is the sacrament most extensively discussed in the code. Among the issues addressed are preparation for its celebration, certain impediments barring one from such, factors adversely affecting proper marital consent and possibly giving rise to annulments, ecumenical marriages, the separation of the spouses, and the possible convalidation of an initially invalid marriage.

Part two on other acts of divine worship (cc. 1166–204) recognizes the fact that the Church's sanctifying office is broader than sacramental celebration. It deals with such religious realities as sacramentals, the liturgy of the hours, funerals, veneration of the saints, vows, and oaths.

Finally, part three on sacred places and times (cc. 1205–53) initially regulates such liturgically significant realities as churches and other worship spaces, altars, and cemeteries. It subsequently offers general principles on feast days and penitential practices.

The organization of Book Five on the Church's temporal goods (cc. 1254–310),[44] the shortest book of the code, does not seem to reflect Vatican II significantly. Those goods are basically ordered to the service of divine worship, the support of the clergy and other ministers, and the pursuit of apostolic and charitable works especially toward the poor. After a few introductory canons, four titles deal with various aspects of the basic concern to use such goods wisely for the aforementioned ecclesial purposes. The legislator is concerned especially about the acquisition, administration, and alienation (transfer of ownership) of such goods, as well as the proper monitoring of pious wills and foundations in the interests of ecclesial accountability.

While the Church is a graced community empowered by the Spirit, occasionally the attitudes of its sinful members contradict the faith, or their behavior is seriously contrary to its discipline. Accordingly the community must take certain measures to protect the integrity of its faith, communion, and service while reconciling such members with their fellow believers.

---

[44] See CCEO 1007–54. See also Alesandro, *CLSA Commentary*, 18; Coriden, *An Introduction to Canon Law*, 163–9.

Book Six on sanctions in the Church (cc. 1311–99),[45] which largely provides such measures, seems minimally influenced by Vatican II in its basic structure, although it notably simplifies the 1917 code. Book Six is divided into two main parts, the first of which (cc. 1311–63) articulates certain general principles on establishing, applying, and remitting penalties, while the latter (cc. 1364–98) indicates penalties for specific ecclesiastical offenses organized according to certain categories, e.g., offenses against religion and church unity. A final canon 1399 indicates the extraordinary conditions for penalizing someone, although no law or precept prohibits the behavior in question.

Although ecclesial disputes should ideally be resolved without recourse to formal procedures, the vindication of Christian rights at times requires the availability of such conflict-resolution procedures. The lengthy Book Seven on processes in the Church (cc. 1400–752),[46] which provides a variety of such procedures, also seems minimally influenced by Vatican II in its basic structuring. Realistically speaking, the vast majority of cases before church tribunals at various levels involve the adjudication of claims of marital nullity.

Book Seven is divided into five parts, the first four of which largely deal with judicial issues while the fifth treats of certain administrative matters. After stating general principles on Church procedures and those involved in them (part one: cc. 1400–500), the code specifies elaborate rules on so-called contentious procedures (part two: cc. 1501–670) and provides special rules for certain particular cases such as marriage nullity actions (part three: cc. 1671–716). Subsequently, part four contains some pertinent norms on applying penalties administratively or especially judicially (cc. 1717–31).[47] Finally, part five regulates the taking of recourse against allegedly illegitimate administrative decisions (cc. 1732–9) and the removal or transfer of unwilling pastors (cc. 1740–52).

The salvation of persons is the Church's supreme law (c. 1752). Hopefully, the preceding reflections on the relationship between the Church and its law will assist those interpreting and applying it pastorally. Accordingly the Church may be ever more truly a light to the nations—a goal served so well by our honoree Dr. Patrick Granfield, O.S.B.

---

[45] See CCEO 1401–67. See also Alesandro, *CLSA Commentary*, 18–19; Coriden, *An Introduction to Canon Law*, 171–9.

[46] See CCEO 1055–400. See also Alesandro, *CLSA Commentary*, 19–20; Coriden, *An Introduction to Canon Law*, 181–8.

[47] See CCEO 1468–87.

For Further Reading

Primary Sources

Code of Canon Law Latin-English Edition. Washington, D.C.: Canon Law Society
of America, 1983.

Code of Canons of the Eastern Churches Latin-English Edition. Washington, D.C.:
Canon Law Society of America, 1990.

Commentaries and Other Secondary Sources

Alesandro, John A. "The Revision of the Code of Canon Law: A Background
Study." *Studia Canonica* 24 (1990) 91–146.

Beal, John P., et al., eds. *New Commentary on the Code of Canon Law.* New York/
Mahwah, N.J.: Paulist Press, 2000.

Coriden, James A., et al., eds. *The Code of Canon Law: A Text and Commentary.*
New York/Mahwah, N.J.: Paulist Press, 1985.

_____. *An Introduction to Canon Law.* New York/Mahwah, N.J.: Paulist Press,
1991.

Green, Thomas J. "The Canon Law Society of America and the Revision of the
Code: Historical Reflections and Continuing Concerns." *The Jurist* 53
(1993) 1–21.

_____. "The Revised Code of Canon Law: Some Theological Issues." *Theologi-
cal Studies* 47 (1986) 617–52.

_____. "The Revision of Canon Law: Some Theological Implications." *Theo-
logical Studies* 40 (1979) 593–679.

Mallett, James, ed. *The Ministry of Governance.* Washington, D.C.: Canon Law
Society of America, 1986.

Orsy, Ladislas. *Theology and Canon Law: New Horizons for Legislation and Interpretation.* Collegeville: The Liturgical Press, 1992.

Sheehy, Gerard, et al., eds. *The Canon Law Letter & Spirit.* Collegeville: The Liturgical Press, 1995.

20 | The Laity

Jon Nilson

Introduction[1]

Some years ago, a friend of mine, a moral theologian with a reputation as a superb lecturer, was invited to give some workshops in Canada. One of his hosts was a bishop whose diocese was spread over thousands of square miles near Hudson Bay. This bishop did not have nearly enough priests, so he had appointed a married couple in each town and village who would gather all the area Catholics together each week and lead them in Scripture reading, reflection, and prayer. Then the couple would distribute the Eucharist, which had been consecrated during the last visit of a priest. Once a year these leader-couples would meet for two weeks of planning and continuing formation with their bishops and the priests. Moral theology workshops were part of the two-week process.

Saying good-bye at the end of his stint, my friend asked him, "Bishop, don't you sometimes wish that you had a priest for every community in your diocese and you didn't have to rely on these lay leaders?"

"Sometimes I do," the bishop admitted. "But then I think, if I did have enough priests, the people might forget that it's their Church."

A Church without enough priests to preside at the Sunday Eucharist must become the laity's Church in order to survive. Yet the Eucharist is central to the Church's life, as Vatican II's Constitution on the Sacred Liturgy affirmed. A community that lives without the eucharistic celebration may be Christian, but in what sense is it Roman Catholic? On the other hand, could the ministry provided by laity like these

[1] I am thankful for this opportunity and means of expressing my gratitude to Patrick Granfield. His scholarship and teaching have enriched Catholic theology worldwide and his friendship has greatly enriched my own life and work.

Canadians be one place among many where a new vision of the Church is being born?

The dearth of priests is one of the indicators that the clergy-laity paradigm that has reigned for hundreds of years is dying. Its death rattle can also be heard in the contention that the very terminology obscures a central teaching of Vatican II and impedes the healthy changes underway in the Church since the council.[2] While the grounds and causes of this death may be clear, its practical and theological implications are not. The Divine Sculptor seems to be fashioning a new form of the Church for the new millennium, but that form is still hidden in the rock.

A Historical Sketch[3]

While the earliest Christian communities were counterculturally egalitarian (Gal 3:28 is, of course, the classic text) and all its members were expected to help build up the Church by means of their own gifts (see, for example, 1 Corinthians 12), they were never without authoritative leadership. While the terminology used for the offices in the early Church might have been fluid, used in different ways by different communities,[4] the bishop-presbyter-deacon structure is evident in the larger churches by the mid-second century. Nonetheless, the people played a major role in choosing these servant-leaders of theirs.

Gradually, however, a sort of class structure emerged in the Church. When a bishop died, communities were sometimes eager to elect a proven leader as their new bishop, whether or not he was a seasoned Christian. The wisdom of probationary periods soon became clear. A Christian should serve as a lector, acolyte, deacon, and presbyter to prove his commitment to Christ and the Church before he was ordained a bishop. Punishment for clerical malfeasance was often "reduction" to the state of the ordinary Christian, marking it as a less desirable Christian condition. Thus, the notions of a ranking among the ministries and an ascent through them developed in the Church.

---

[2] For example, "I am convinced that the term laity is now theologically dead. . . . The word now has many theologically erroneous positions attached to its normal everyday meaning and use, and so it seems to concretize within itself the history of our mistakes." Leonard Doohan, *The Lay-Centered Church: Theology and Spirituality* (Minneapolis: Winston Press, 1984) 23.

[3] What follows depends heavily on Alexandre Faivre, *The Emergence of the Laity in the Early Church*, trans. David Smith (New York: Paulist Press, 1990).

[4] Kenan B. Osborne, *Ministry: Lay Ministry in the Roman Catholic Church, Its History and Theology* (New York: Paulist Press, 1993) 160–1.

As the communities grew in number and size and bishops remained the chief administrators of their resources, the office became more influential. Once Christianity became the established religion of the empire, bishops, priests, and deacons often acquired a civil status and importance above that of the ordinary Christian. When dioceses became aligned with the Roman Empire's jurisdictional boundaries, some bishops became remote figures who governed their flocks through delegates, that is, presbyters and deacons. The ruling of Nicaea I in 325 that bishops could not be "translated" from diocese to diocese was sidestepped when important dioceses needed leadership that could not be found among local candidates.

Monasticism greatly fostered the sense of a class structure in the Church. Monks were regarded as "super Christians," wholly devoted to Christ by their poverty and celibacy. Other Christians, ordained or not, whose lives were occupied with the terrestrial and transitory realities of family and civic life, stood on lower rungs. The role of the ordinary Christian was to support those who served them by contemplation and prayer, that is, the monks and those who presided over them, the ordained.

The clergy/laity distinction with its connotations of superior/inferior, active/passive in matters spiritual became deeply inculcated in the Western Church with the forced baptisms of the illiterate European tribes in the ninth and tenth centuries.

> *De facto,* the church in northern Europe had to be constituted from the top down. Bishops had the primary responsibility for turning young boys into churchmen, and deputing these ordained churchmen to watch over and minister to the baptized masses who were seldom evangelized or catechized. *De facto,* "the Aeropagite's" [sic] top-down thinking about the working of the Holy Spirit through the sacramental mediation of the ordained matched medieval western ecclesial experience.[5]

This distinction is expressed in Gratian's twelfth-century codification of law that regulated Church life until the first Code of Canon Law appeared in 1917: *"Duo sunt genera Christianorum,"* that is, there are two kinds of Christians.[6]

The continental Reformation was in part a protest against the clericalization of the Church and the relegation of the laity to passive objects of the clergy's ministrations and governance. Instead, Luther and others maintained the "priesthood of all believers," the fundamental

---

[5] Mary Collins, "Liturgy for a Laity Called and Sent," paper privately printed for the Salt and Light for the World Conference, Mundelein, Ill., (May 7–8, 1998) 9.

[6] *Corpus Juris Canonici,* causa 12, q. 1, c. 7, in J. P. Migne, *Patrologia Latina* 187:884.

equality of every member and condition in the Church. For most of the Reformers, Church office was a temporary function, not a distinct condition or higher status, discharged by certain Christians. Ministers were chosen and given by God to the Church, but the structure of bishop-priest-deacon was a human construction, not a reflection of the divine will. Therefore, it could be changed. The Council of Trent reacted by teaching that the sacrament of orders was instituted by Christ and by it a certain permanent "character" was impressed *(imprimitur)*.[7]

Yet the laity's role in the post-Tridentine Church was not simply reduced to the (in)famous triad, "pray, pay, and obey." Spiritualities, such as that of St. Francis de Sales, urged and helped them to find sanctity amid their worldly duties. Influential laypersons, male and female, emerged in every country to enrich the life and thought of the Church.[8] Yet these factors did not dethrone the established sense of a dual status in the Church. Canon 107 of the 1917 code held that "by divine institution clergy are distinct from laity in the Church, though not all clerics are of divine institution; however, both can be religious"; it also cited canon 4 of Trent's decree on holy orders on the "character" imprinted by ordination.[9] Thus, St. Pius X was simply expressing the dominant mentality in 1906 by declaring

> the Church is by essence an unequal society, that is, a society comprising two categories of persons, the pastors and the flock, those who occupy a rank in the different degrees of the hierarchy and the multitude of the faithful. . . . The one duty of the multitude is to allow themselves to be led, and, like a docile flock, to follow the pastors.[10]

Thus, leadership and governance belonged to the ordained alone. Lay initiatives, activities, and organizations were to be supervised by the ordained since these were understood as forms of collaboration in the proper mission of the hierarchy. Movements that were led or dominated by the laity made the bishops nervous. So, for instance, the leader of the American hierarchy, James Gibbons, worked behind the scenes to undermine the lay Catholic congresses in the late 1800s.[11]

[7] DS 1764, 1767, 1774.

[8] Jan Grootaers, "The Roman Catholic Church," *The Layman in Christian History*, ed. Stephen Charles Neill and Hans-Ruedi Weber (London: SCM Press, 1963) 298–336.

[9] Osborne, *Ministry*, 41–2.

[10] Quoted in Aurelie A. Hagstrom, "The Vocation and Mission of the Laity: Historical and Conciliar Perspectives," paper privately printed for the Salt and Light for the World Conference, Mundelein, Ill., (May 7–8, 1998) 7.

[11] James Hennesey, *American Catholics: A History of the Roman Catholic Community in the United States* (New York: Oxford University Press, 1981) 190–1.

About a century ago, however, the Church's tectonic plates began to shift. A key factor in the revolution in ecclesiology was the discovery —or, better—the rediscovery of the laity. European nations had become more secularized. In the United States and France especially, the Church's influence on the state decreased drastically. Society became more "compartmentalized" with the rise of industrialization. Church leaders in most denominations began to realize that the laity were indispensable if the Church was to exercise any significant influence on "the world." Later, the trauma of World War II would show them that "the real world of men [sic] was much more remote and foreign to the faith than we had thought after so many searchings."[12] The churches' choice became stark: either a committed and trained laity carries out the Church's mission in the world or the Church fades into ineffectual invisibility.

The laity were therefore on the agenda of the First Assembly of the World Council of Churches at Amsterdam in 1948. Its Second Assembly at Evanston in 1954 created a department on the laity alongside its foundational units, such as faith and order.[13] In 1961 this department put out a bibliography containing over fourteen hundred publications that had appeared since 1948 in Protestant and Orthodox circles.[14] Academies were established, such as the Ecumenical Institute at Bossey, Switzerland, to provide laity with the resources for their mission in the world.

Similar ideas had become central to the Catholic understanding of evangelization long before Vatican II had urged "the apostolate of like toward like."[15] The particular demands of Christian outreach to laborers, office workers, industrialists, and students could be understood and carried out only by Christian laborers, office workers, industrialists, and students. Hierarchical control was, however, still being emphasized in "Catholic Action." Although St. Pius X (1903–14) was the first pope to use the term, his successor Pius XI (1922–39) was its most vigorous papal promoter.[16] For both popes, however, it meant the structured apostolic activity of lay people under the control of the hierarchy

---

[12] Yves M.-J. Congar, "My Path-Findings in the Theology of Laity and Ministries," *The Jurist* 32:2 (Spring 1972) 172.

[13] Hans-Ruedi Weber, "The Rediscovery of the Laity in the Ecumenical Movement," *The Layman in Christian History,* ed. Neill and Weber, 379.

[14] Ibid., 391, n. 2.

[15] Vatican II, Decree on the Laity *(Apostolicam actuositatem)*, 13. Unless otherwise noted, quotations from Vatican II are taken from *The Documents of Vatican II,* ed. Walter M. Abbott and Joseph Gallagher (New York: America Press, 1966).

[16] Hagstrom, "The Vocation and Mission of the Laity," 8–10.

and understood as auxiliary to the proper mission of the bishops. Pius XII (1939–58), whose initiatives showed his desire to enhance the Church's influence on the modern world, promoted further reflection on the laity with his encyclicals on the Church as the Mystical Body of Christ (1943) and on the Liturgy (1947). During the preconciliar period, lay movements such as the Young Christian Workers and the Young Christian Students flourished. Major conferences on the laity were held in Rome in 1951 and 1957.

No wonder, then, that a Roman Catholic bibliography on the laity published in 1957 contained more than 2200 entries,[17] the most influential of which was Yves Congar's *Jalons pour une théologie du laïcat.*[18] During this period emerged others like Rahner, Lonergan, Schillebeeckx, Murray, and Küng, who helped to dismantle the neoscholastic paradigm in theology. So Vatican II was able to draw upon a wealth of reflection and research when the bishops there turned their attention to the laity. As John Paul II observed, "The Council, in particular, with its rich doctrinal, spiritual and pastoral patrimony, has written as never before on the nature, dignity, spirituality, mission and responsibility of the lay faithful."[19]

Vatican II

Vatican II became the "Council of the Laity" in virtue of three major decisions.

First, the bishops rejected the Preparatory Commission's draft schema on the Church, since it was largely a summary of the juridical and hierarchical approach which characterized preconciliar ecclesiology. The bishops wanted, instead, a text that would present a renewed vision of the Church, informed by contemporary biblical studies, historical research, and ecumenical openness.

Second, the bishops placed the chapter on "the hierarchical constitution of the Church" after the chapters on "The Mystery of the Church" and "The People of God" in the Dogmatic Constitution on the Church, *Lumen gentium.* Since the fundamental reality of the Church is primar-

[17] Weber, "The Rediscovery of the Laity," 391, n. 2.

[18] Yves Congar, *Jalons pour une théologie du laïcat* (Paris: Éditions du Cerf, 1953). ET: *Lay People in the Church,* trans. Donald Attwater (Westminster, Md.: Newman Press, 1957).

[19] John Paul II, *The Vocation and the Mission of the Lay Faithful in the Church and in the World (Christifideles laici)* (Washington, D.C.: United States Catholic Conference, 1989) no. 2.

ily communion with God and with one another, every member of the Church shares a basic equality, dignity, and call which are grounded in baptism, confirmation, and Eucharist. Thus, chapter four on the laity begins, "Everything which has been said so far concerning the People of God applies equally to the laity, religious, and clergy."[20]

Their third decision was to devote a separate document to the laity in order to affirm and enhance the life of the "ordinary Catholic." Yet implementing this decision turned out to be difficult. Their new appreciation for the lay role had already permeated the bishops' thinking so much that the laity had already been treated extensively in previous documents. The council fathers had realized that they could not discuss Church without *ipso facto* discussing the laity. The mission and nature of the Church were the mission and nature of the laity, too. Note 3 of the Decree on the Apostolate of the Laity, therefore, indicates the places in other council documents where the laity are also the focus of attention.

Who then are the laity, according to the council?

> The term laity is here understood to mean all the faithful except those in holy orders and those in a religious state sanctioned by the Church. These faithful are by baptism made one body with Christ and are established among the People of God. They are in their own way made sharers in the priestly, prophetic, and kingly functions of Christ. They carry out their own part in the mission of the whole Christian people with respect to the Church and the world (LG 31).

This is not a minimal or negative description, as if the laity were simply the nonordained and the nonvowed in the Church, since "*everything* which has been said so far concerning the People of God applies equally to the laity, religious, and clergy" (emphasis added).

In place of the superiority/inferiority, active/passive distinction between clergy and laity, Vatican II declares their complementarity: "In the Church, there is diversity of ministry but unity of mission" (AA 2; translation amended). While the ordained and the laity differ, each is necessary to the mission of the Church and so they must cooperate with one another, indeed, serve one another for the good of the Church and the world (LG 32; see also AA 25). The mission of the Church does not rest on the shoulders of the ordained alone (LG 30).

---

[20] Dogmatic Constitution on the Church *(Lumen gentium)*, 30. Unless otherwise noted, the quotations from Vatican II are drawn from *The Documents of Vatican II*, ed. Walter M. Abbott and Joseph Gallagher (New York: America Press, 1966). In the following, the council documents will be cited in parentheses in the text using the abbreviations cited at the beginning of this book.

While both clergy and laity participate in Christ's roles of prophet, priest, and king, they do so differently (AA 2, 10; LG 31). Christ conferred the duty of teaching, sanctifying, and ruling in his name and power on the apostles and their successors alone. The common priesthood of the faithful and the "ministerial or hierarchical priesthood" differ "in essence and not only in degree,"[21] although the council itself did not specify what this difference was. Yet it resonates in the adjective "sacred" that often modifies the noun "pastors" in the conciliar texts; for example, in LG 30. Furthermore, the council affirms that the mission of the Church "is done mainly through the ministry of Word and of the sacraments, which are entrusted in a special way to the clergy" (AA 6). The bishops and their assistants, the priests, are to order and coordinate the various ministries and apostolates of the laity (AA 23–4; LG 32). To them belong the tasks of discerning, judging, and ordering the charisms given by the Spirit (LG 12, 23–4; AA 3).

Accordingly, the laity have no official role in the governance of the Church. Without the sacrament of orders they are unable to exercise jurisdiction, as the 1983 Code of Canon Law maintains (c. 129, no. 2). In councils and synods, their participation and vote is consultative, not legislative (c. 443, nos. 4, 5). The bishop is the only legislator in a diocesan synod (c. 466). In this respect the Roman Catholic Church differs from other churches where the laity do exercise constitutionally established power.

Still, the laity can exercise power in the Church in other ways. For instance, they can make their opinions about the good of the Church known to their pastors by reason of their competence, as the council urges and even obliges them to do (LG 37); they can utilize the Spirit's gifts for the unity of the Church and the vitality of its mission (AA 3); their study, contemplation, and experience contribute to the development of tradition in the Church (DV 8); they are united with Christ in his perfect offering to the Father (SC 7) and their "full, conscious, and active participation in liturgical celebrations" (SC 14; see also LG 34) enhances the effectiveness of the Church's worship.

The laity exercise their power most characteristically in their mission to the world, for only through them can the Church truly be the "salt of the earth" (LG 33). As the classic conciliar text states, "The laity by their very vocation seek the Kingdom of God by engaging in temporal affairs and ordering them according to the plan of God" (LG 31; see also AA 2, 7; GS 43). Vocation, of course, designates a summons from God to a distinctive way of life that fosters the good of the indi-

---

[21] "Essentia et non gradu tantum differant," LG 10. On the issues raised by this formula, see Osborne, *Ministry*, 547–55, 580–1.

vidual and of the community at the same time. This summons comes to a layperson in baptism, is strengthened by confirmation, and is sustained by the Eucharist (LG 33, 11; AA 3). Thus, "The laity derive the right and duty with respect to the apostolate from their union with Christ their Head. . . . They are assigned to the apostolate by the Lord himself" (AA 3) and not by the hierarchy, as the teaching of Pius XI and Pius XII had it. The laity's apostolate is a "participation in the saving mission of the Church itself" (LG 33).

While the council described the laity in terms of their vocation in and for the world, it did not mark out the world as the realm of the laity and the Church as the realm of the ordained in any hard and fast way, as, for example, LG 1, AA 9, and GS 43 make clear. This is a description, not a definition, of the laity. Even those who are not ordained for the service of the Church can still have important functions within it, such as catechesis, liturgy, pastoral care (AA 24), and even Church administration (AA 5, 10); they can fulfill other Church functions "for a spiritual purpose" as well (LG 33).

But the council's emphasis on the world as the laity's proper sphere is clear. "Temporal affairs" are the realm of their vocation (LG 31; AA 2, 5, 7) and their role is to order them according to the plan of God. This demands collaborative efforts within the various sectors of culture to foster the increase of justice, charity, and peace. Here the laity are the experts and they ought not to expect that the clergy have the answer to every question which their mission to the world might raise (LG 43).

The lay vocation constitutes a whole way of life. Lay spirituality should therefore be shaped by the distinctive circumstances of that way of life (AA 4, 16, 29). Charity remains the heart of this apostolate (AA 16), as it remains the heart of every truly Christian endeavor, and it is nourished by the same means as those utilized by clergy and religious: the liturgy, prayer, and meditation.

Since "in the Church there is diversity of ministry but unity of mission" (AA 2; see also LG 13, 32) and the laity are assigned to the apostolate by Christ himself (AA 3), the ordained have obligations to the laity. The latter have the right "to receive in abundance from their sacred pastors the spiritual goods of the Church, especially the Word of God and the sacraments" (LG 37).[22] Since the laity have the right and duty to express their views on matters relating to the good of the Church, the clergy must establish the means for them to do this (LG 37; see GS 62). Bishops and priests must be aware of lay rights and responsibilities and strive to support and encourage them in their apostolic

[22] The argument that many of the laity are being deprived of this right on account of the requirement of celibacy for priests is well known.

endeavors (AA 25). Priests are to offer light and support, but not an answer to every problem that arises in the apostolate, for that is not their duty and mission (GS 43; see also 33).

Since the Church considers the "conjugal partnership" as the origin and basis of human society, and "the family has received from God its mission to be the first and vital cell of society" (AA 10), the council highlights marriage and family life. "The family is, so to speak, the domestic Church" (LG 11, 35). Thus, marriage and family life constitute an apostolate of their own and some families might well consider their life together to be the chief focus of their mission. Yet a strong family can also extend its positive influence outside the home in many ways—AA 11 gives some examples—and in so doing help to fulfill the council's dream of a vital laity. John Paul II echoes and emphasizes this point in *Christifideles laici* 40.

Vatican II's "last word" on the laity, AA 6, underlines the necessity of education and formation to prepare the laity for the demands of their vocation. It challenges the Church to provide the resources for the lay apostolate. Sunday Mass alone is not enough to equip the laity to fulfill their demanding role.

The Council's Aftermath

Vatican II did not initiate all the structural reforms necessary to implement its vision of a laity vigorously collaborating with the clergy in the Church and carrying out its mission in the world. Its aims were to be furthered by a Council of Laity established on an experimental basis in 1967 by Paul VI. In 1976 he enhanced its status by making it the Pontifical Council on the Laity. Since the Pontifical Council is administered largely by clerics, however, many hold that it has not been particularly effective in advancing the role of the laity in the Church. In its present form, it does not and cannot serve as a truly representative voice for the laity in the Church's administration.[23]

Canon 204 of the 1983 Code of Canon Law states:

> The Christian faithful are those who, inasmuch as they have been incorporated in Christ through baptism, have been constituted as the people of God; for this reason, since they have become sharers in Christ's priestly, prophetic and royal office in their own manner, they are called to exercise the mission which God has entrusted to the

---

[23] Kathleen Walsh, "The Apostolate of the Laity *(Apostolicam Actuositatem),*" *Modern Catholicism: Vatican II and After,* ed. Adrian Hastings (New York: Oxford University Press, 1991) 153.

Church to fulfill in the world, in accord with the condition proper to each one.[24]

What is proper to the laity, however, excludes them from participation in the governance of the Church in their own right, since the code links governance to the sacrament of orders. According to canon 129, the ordained are able *(habiles)* to exercise power, while the laity may only cooperate in the exercise of power in the Church *("cooperari possunt in exercitio potestatis")*. As James Coriden notes, this restriction is not a matter of divine law but of mutable, human law in the Church.[25]

While the new code gives a listing of rights (cc. 208–23 on the rights of all the baptized; cc. 224–31 on the rights of the laity; cc. 298–9, 321–9 on the right to form associations), many hold that the structures, policies, and procedures needed to implement these rights are still woefully underdeveloped in the Church. Postconciliar institutional structures have been encouraged and developed, such as diocesan synods and parish pastoral councils, and lay people were urged to form associations to advance their mission and to collaborate with the clergy. Yet ecclesiastical jurisdiction has remained a prerogative of the ordained and the lay role remains purely advisory. At a diocesan synod, the bishop is the only legislator, as noted above. A parish pastoral council must be headed by the ordained pastor and can make no binding decisions of itself; the final decision rests with him (cc. 514, 536). Consequently, some hold that

> The total absence of laity from leadership roles, even from those Church organizations specifically for laity, is an extremely unhealthy dimension of the Church. Power in the Church is linked to office, not to competence, and even non-sacramental jurisdiction is granted only to the cleric. . . . The laity, then, participate less in the structures of today's Church than they do in those of civic life.[26]

Hopes and expectations were raised by the announcement of a Synod of Bishops to examine the condition of the laity since the close of the council. Preparatory consultations were held all over the world. In the United States, around 250,000 Catholics participated in such consultations on various levels.[27] The bishops' Committee on the Laity

---

[24] As quoted in Osborne, *Ministry,* 534.

[25] James A. Coriden, "Church Authority in American Culture: Cases and Observations," privately published paper prepared for meeting of the Common Ground Initiative (March 6–8, 1998) 10.

[26] Doohan, *The Lay-Centered Church,* 30–1.

[27] Margaret O'Brien Steinfels, "The Bishops' Right-Hand Woman: An Interview With Dolores Leckey," *Commonweal* 125:10 (May 22, 1998) 17.

sponsored several meetings between lay leaders and the bishops who were going to the synod. In these gatherings, radical and realistic issues were raised and questions posed about various dimensions of lay Catholic life.

Yet the synod (held October 1–30, 1987) turned out to be a lost opportunity for deeper understanding and vigorous enhancement of the laity's role. Its working paper was bland and the results of the bishops' preparatory consultations that had been sent to Rome ahead of time were kept secret. The Catholic world received only summaries of the debates and discussions within the synod itself. Its most notable result, John Paul II's apostolic exhortation *Christifideles laici,* did not grapple with the radical questions raised in the consultations and seemed too concerned about regulating and controlling the level of lay activity within the Church itself.

The Holy Father reaffirms that laity may be commissioned "to exercise the ministry of the word, to preside over liturgical prayers, to confer Baptism, and to distribute Holy Communion," but only in cases of necessity.[28] These are activities conceded to the laity in virtue of need, not in virtue of the competence which they might have from their incorporation into Christ and their particular gifts. Moreover, their work must always be exercised under the control of the ordained. Since *Christifideles laici* reaffirms the exclusion of women from the priesthood (see CL 49) based on their complementarity, and maintains that the pope and the Curia have the primary role in the formation of the laity (see CL 61, 30), its formal address, "To Bishops, To Priests and Deacons, To Women and Men Religious, and to All the Lay Faithful" seemed to replicate the official Church's priorities nearly perfectly.

Since the council, the traditional distinction between clergy and laity has been reasserted, even as that distinction has become more and more problematic, both theologically and practically. Though the word itself is not used, lay submission to the ordained is the ideal and norm. In these documents, the authority of the ordained is always framed as "service" in accordance with Vatican II's texts, but how authentic can this service be when those who are served have no say in deciding who is to serve them or how they are to be served? In the process of appointing a bishop to a diocese or a pastor to a parish, there may be some consultation. The fact remains that the laity have no official say in these important matters, as they do in other churches, such as the Episcopal Church in the United States, which have a constitutionally established role for the laity in the governance of the church. Declarations of equality and communion among all the members of the Church ring

[28] CL 23, citing canon 230.

hollow when one class has so little voice and role in the ecclesial decisions that profoundly affect them.

Meanwhile, the lack of priests indirectly highlights the gifts of the nonordained in the Church. Vatican II did not foresee all the lay roles and ministries that would emerge since the council; indeed, "lay ministry" is largely a postconciliar term and phenomenon. Lay chaplains, parish administrators, DREs (whose acronym really means not "Director of Religious Education," but "Does Really Everything," according to a DRE friend of mine), and campus ministers manifest their talents and charisms in preaching, administration, spiritual direction, and catechesis.[29] Their vocations are evident not only in their inner experience of a call but also in the testimonies of their communities. When their charisms, developed through education and formation, are exercised more consistently and effectively in their communities than the ministry of the ordained, people begin to question the nature of ordination and the notion of sacred powers. They lose a sense of that "difference in essence, not only in degree" (LG 10) between the ordained ministry and the ministry exercised by lay people and experienced as "graceful" by their communities.

> When a lay person conducts a Communion service, sometimes you get people saying, "I like Sister's Mass," said a church official. . . . If the lay minister convokes the people to worship, leads the prayers, does everything else and then just steps off the stage while the priest performs the consecration, people can end up asking, "What do we need the priest for?"[30]

It is thus ironic that efforts to maintain the distinctiveness of the ordained ministry via a sharpened differentiation between a clerical mission to the Church and a lay mission to the world, the retention of the celibacy requirement for priests, and the stress upon the theology of an ontological difference conferred by ordination should foster a functionalist view of orders.

The Vatican has viewed developments like these with concern and issued an Instruction in response.[31] The document was prompted by the conviction that "true communion" in the Church is being damaged

---

[29] As I write this, one of my lay graduate students and I cannot find a good time to meet on account of her engagement to give two eight-day retreats.

[30] John L. Allen Jr., "Lay Ministry Emerges as a New Vocation," *National Catholic Reporter* 34:10 (January 9, 1998) 7.

[31] Eight Vatican Offices, "Some Questions Regarding Collaboration of Nonordained Faithful in Priests' Sacred Ministry," *Origins* 27:24 (November 27, 1997) 398–409.

today by a blurring of the lines between the ordained and the non-ordained. It presents the current situation not only as a threat to communion but as a masking of the hierarchical constitution of the Church "imprinted on it by Christ."

So it stresses the difference between the "common priesthood of all the faithful" and the ministerial priesthood which is "rooted in the apostolic succession and vested with *potestas sacra*."[32] The latter's essence is thus the "exercise of the *munus docendi, sanctificandi, et regendi*."[33] The ordained are "ontologically configured to Christ," but modernity obscures this truth of faith.[34] We are dealing here with a mystery that escapes our reductionist categories.

The specific difference of the laity lies in their secular vocation and in their own mode of participating in the priesthood of Christ.[35] The council's description of the laity's secular character seems hardened into a normative definition here, whereby the Church becomes the realm of the ordained and the "world" the realm of the laity, even though, as we have seen, Vatican II makes no such hard and fast distinction.[36] The dicasteries charge the bishops to enforce thirteen specific norms (e.g., lay people may distribute the Eucharist only in cases of genuine need, parish councils are to be advisory only) and disavow any intention of simply reinforcing clerical privileges in this instruction.

Instead of recognizing that theology and church life today are surfacing questions that strain the traditional categories, the document seeks to reassert the increasingly problematic understandings and practices. It resists the reduction of ordained ministry to a function, but it does not offer a fresh and credible reading of the "ontological difference" that it reaffirms so strongly.

Three Priorities

Given the council's teaching and developments in the nearly four decades since its end, certain priorities for action suggest themselves.

First, enhance consultation of the laity. The issue of the legitimation of Church power is real, complex, and demanding today, as Patrick

---

[32] Ibid., 401.

[33] Ibid.

[34] "The Instruction: An Explanatory Note," *Origins* 27:24 (November 27, 1997) 409.

[35] Ibid., 401.

[36] See also Osborne, *Ministry*, 561–3, on fluid ministerial boundaries.

Granfield himself has noted.[37] Bare assertions and problematic exercises of clerical power can foster a dangerous alienation between the ordained and the nonordained. Yet the consultative and collaborative possibilities are many and would require no change in official Church teaching. Many have long been calling for wider and more public consultation in the process of choosing bishops for dioceses and priests for parishes. Likewise, lay people could have a real voice in selecting candidates for ordination, not simply the echo of power in the ordination rite when the bishop asks if there are any objections to ordaining a candidate. Parish councils and diocesan synods could be enhanced by delegating real jurisdiction to them, although this would require changes in canon law. Greater consultation and collaboration may make administration more cumbersome for an impatient bishop or priest, but how else will their governing role be experienced as true service to the laity?

Likewise, there is a role for the laity in the development of tradition and the formulation of Church teaching, as DV 8 makes clear. Unfortunately, the consultative processes that led to the U.S. bishops' pastoral letters on peace and on the economy remain the exception, not the rule. There is resistance to the notion that bishops should be listeners in order to be more effective teachers, but if they are to speak in the name of the Church and express its faith, consultation must be the rule, not the exception.

Second, develop new methods and models for lay education and formation. Retreats, spiritual direction, and continuing education courses do not fit well into the lives of most laity. The average Catholic must rely on the resources of the parish for missional inspiration and empowerment. Is the Sunday liturgy enough? Not according to Vatican II and John Paul II. How can the laity be stimulated and strengthened to understand and to live out their baptismal calling?

Despite the repeated emphasis on the need for lay formation, education, and spiritual direction,[38] there are still relatively few resources committed to the development of lay spirituality and education for lay mission. Critics have contrasted this situation with the money spent to educate just one man for priestly ordination. Since a budget reveals the real values of a group, many have questioned the seriousness of the Church's emphasis on the lay role in the Church and world. One seasoned observer, Gregory Pierce, sums it up in this way: "The institutional church does not know how to support the lay role in the world,

---

[37] Patrick Granfield, "Legitimation and Bureaucratisation of Ecclesial Power," *Power in the Church* (*Concilium* 197), ed. James Provost and Knut Walf (Edinburgh: T. & T. Clark, 1988) 86–93.

[38] See, for example, CL 5.

doesn't prepare people for that role and doesn't demand that the laity accept their role."[39]

If the parish is and will remain the center of Catholic life for the foreseeable future, perhaps we ought to begin with a new image for the parish. Imagine, suggests Pierce, that the parish is not so much a family or a community but a campaign headquarters, which exists primarily to encourage, direct, support, and strengthen the lay mission in the world.[40] Such a parish would constantly plan and evaluate with a single priority in mind: How do our parish activities and projects and organizations advance the kingdom of God in this place? Then the development urged by AA 4, that lay spirituality grow out of the circumstances of lay life, would accelerate and nourish the parish's liturgy. The result would be ritual language and action that expresses the heart of what it means to be a disciple such that the people would recognize it as truly liturgy, that is, the people's work.

Third, continue reflection on women's issues, as John Paul II has urged.[41] Again and again, the essentialist anthropology of complementarity that characterizes the official Church's teachings about women and their roles has been questioned and critiqued, but it remains central to those teachings. Each time it is reaffirmed, more women who are crucial to the effectiveness of its mission are alienated from the Church. It is not an overstatement to say that concern for the Church's future must include concern for women's issues.

Toward a New Paradigm

The lack of priests and the record of lay people committed to and living out ministry in the Church and in the world has transformed "lay ministry." No longer the oxymoron it was prior to Vatican II, it is a defining characteristic of the contemporary Church. As laity too teach, sanctify, and even govern in a fashion, roles that were formerly the exclusive preserve of the ordained, a crisis has emerged in the Church that goes to the heart of its self-understanding. For centuries the Church has viewed itself as a hierarchical institution, established in that particular way by the will of Christ himself. Office in the Church

[39] Robert McClory, "Laity Seek Vocation Amid Noise, Crowds," *National Catholic Reporter* 37 (February 6, 1998) 6.

[40] Cited in Juan L. Hinojosa, "The Mission of the Laity: Some Current Issues," paper privately printed for the Salt and Light for the World Conference, Mundelein, Ill. (May 7–8, 1998) 7–8.

[41] CL 50.

has not been understood and lived as a human construction to meet particular and pragmatic needs, but, rather, as a mirror of Jesus' will and the continuation of his ministry.

Yet, if Vatican II teaches that all the members of the Church are summoned and empowered to mirror and continue the ministry of Jesus as prophet, priest, and king, in what ways is the ministry of the ordained materially distinct from that of the nonordained? There is as yet no theological consensus about a specific dimension of Jesus' ministry that requires ordination and expression in the language of ontological difference or configuration. "The Church is a community built up by a great number of modes of service. It is no longer the layman [sic] who stands in need of definition but the priest. . . . Priests have been asking not only what their precise place is but even who exactly they are."[42]

Of course, servant leadership has always existed among Christ's followers. The Church has always chosen people from among its members to serve the community in special ways and regarded its choices as manifestations of God's, too. What is questioned today is not the necessity of servant leadership but its articulation in the conceptuality of "ontological difference" conferred in the sacrament of orders, which in turn becomes the ground for the exercise of juridical power in the Church by the ordained alone.

Indeed, it is not the laity but the ordained who are problematic here, as the laity resume their rightful role and place *as* the Church, not simply *in* the Church. The fundamental reality is discipleship. Then the theological question concerns the ordained, since they are the special, unique case.

> As one enters into the Jesus community through the sacrament of initiation [baptism-confirmation-Eucharist] a person is not thereby a lay person. Baptism-eucharist is not the sacramental initiation into lay status in the Church. Rather, some new name needs to be developed, one which does not have any of the implications of klerikos/laikos, but rather a name through which the fundamental reality of Christian discipleship can be expressed.[43]

Lay ministers are so necessary to the life of the contemporary Church that some have suggested that they be recognized by conferring upon them something like the preconciliar "minor orders" or by commissioning ceremonies to give them an official status. Then they would be clearly authorized and therefore more credible than they are now.

[42] Congar, *Jalons pour une théologie du laïcat*, 182.
[43] Osborne, *Ministry*, 537–8.

Catholics and non-Catholics alike would take them more seriously. While this might solve a practical problem, it would surely intensify the theological issue of the nature of orders. Lay ministry would continue to pose questions to the traditional theology since lay people would continue to do nearly everything that the ordained with their "sacred power" do. Their vocation and activities would keep pointing to the need for a new paradigm.[44]

What is now needed is nothing less than a new theology and language for those who are still called "laity" and a new praxis in the Church that reflects this renewed theology. Let the final word, then, come from *Commonweal,* the most prominent lay Catholic journal of opinion in the United States, a reflection that was prompted by the events surrounding the Synod on the Laity in 1987:

> When Congar wrote *[Lay People in the Church]* in the fifties the question of the laity seemed almost an exotic interest, even to many lay people. Thirty years later, with the issues barely advanced beyond Congar's treatment, the laity, though critical to the future of the church, remain peripheral to its theological self-understanding and to its decision-making. Early in the next century the church will flourish or wither depending not only on how vigorously laity have come to understand and take up their responsibilities as Christians, but on how prudently Vatican officials understand and exercise theirs. If we are now working in the dark, it's because someone keeps dimming the lights.[45]

[44] David Coffey explains the teaching in LG 10 that the ordained priesthood differs from the common priesthood in essence because it is a charism given by the Holy Spirit to serve as an official witness to Christ. The nonordained also witness to Christ, but not in an official manner. The incarnational/pneumatological grounding is crucial to his proposal. See also his note 28 for a reconception of the "sacramental character" conferred in orders. "The Common and the Ordained Priesthood," *Theological Studies* 58:2 (June 1997).

[45] "Lecturing (Sigh!) the Laity," *Commonweal* 116:5 (March 10, 1989) 133.

For Further Reading

Congar, Yves M.-J. *Lay People in the Church.* Trans. Donald Attwater. Westminster, Md.: Newman Press, 1957.

Dulles, Avery. "Can the Word 'Laity' Be Defined?" *Origins* 18:29 (December 29, 1988) 470–5.

John Paul II. *The Vocation and the Mission of the Lay Faithful in the Church and in the World (Christifideles laici).* Washington, D.C.: United States Catholic Conference, 1989.

Klostermann, Ferdinand. "Decree on the Apostolate of the Laity." *Commentary on the Documents of Vatican II,* vol. 3. Ed. Herbert Vorgrimler, 273–404. New York: Herder and Herder, 1969.

Osborne, Kenan B. *Ministry: Lay Ministry in the Roman Catholic Church, Its History and Theology.* New York: Paulist Press, 1993.

Thils, Gustave. *Les laïcs dans le nouveau Code du droit canonique et au IIe Concile du Vatican.* Cahiers de le revue Théologique de Louvain, 10. Louvain-la-neuve: Librarie Peeters, 1983.

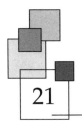

| 21 | Women and the Church |

Sara Butler

At the close of the Second Vatican Council in 1965, Pope Paul VI and the council fathers addressed special words of encouragement to various groups of people: rulers, intellectuals and scientists, artists, the poor and the sick, workers, youth, and "women."[1] Their intention, no doubt, was to acknowledge publicly the special contributions of women in all states of life (girls, wives, mothers, widows, consecrated virgins, women living alone) and to exhort them to share responsibility for humanity's future. This warm salute, however, remains symbolic of an important ecclesiological question of our time: What is the relationship between women and "the Church"? Why was no comparable message addressed to "men" (identified as boys, husbands, fathers, etc.)?

What causes this difficulty? In part it is the fact that although the Church is comprised of both women and men, only men are authorized to speak for the Church as pastors and teachers. The pastors, then, are perceived as men addressing women, rather than as pastors addressing a particular segment of the community. Second, often the pastors are speaking about women and their role to everyone, not just to women or to Catholic women. Third, women are generally presumed to constitute a "class" united by a common "nature" in a way that men are not. Men are regarded either as identical with humankind or as members of subgroups differentiated on some basis other than sex.

A chapter on women *and* "the Church" must be alert to this asymmetry and report on both official Catholic teaching regarding women's status, vocation, and mission and the situation of women in the Church. Since it is the emergence of modern feminism which gives rise to these questions, that too must be factored in. The following survey attempts to illuminate Catholic teaching regarding women by placing it in dialogue

[1] Walter Abbott, ed., *The Documents of Vatican II* (New York: Guild Press, 1966) 732–4.

with the chief expressions of feminism (Socialist, Liberal, Cultural, and Radical)[2] in relation to its two historical phases or "waves," and with the experience of Catholic women.

The "First Wave" of Modern Feminism

The nineteenth-century "women's movement" can in general be identified with efforts to improve women's situation with respect to education, work, marriage and family life, and participation in the Church and in public life. During the first wave, the magisterium responded to feminist proposals chiefly in light of their effects on the family; it came to support women's participation in public life only gradually.[3] Some of its ambivalence can be traced to the fact that the various expressions of feminism had different theoretical foundations.

Socialist Feminism and the Church's Response

Socialist feminism saw economic liberation as the key to women's liberation: earning their own wages sets women free from dependence on their fathers and husbands. The state, which had a vested interest in their economic productivity, would undertake to "free" women from responsibility for their homes and families by providing collectivized childcare, kitchens, housing, etc., and to help them gain control of their fertility so that they could compete on an equal basis with male workers.

The Church realized that Marxist-socialist feminism was a grave threat to the social order. The magisterium addressed the status of women indirectly, by defending the family, the basic unit of society. It saw that once the authority of the father-headed family was denied, individual workers were at the mercy of the state. Pope Leo XIII (1878–1903) defended woman's "place" in the home as wife and mother over against the Marxist socialism which would value her primarily for her contribution to the economy, and he affirmed the duty of Christian wives to be submissive to their husbands—the "heads" of their families—over against the feminist theory that free love, legal abortion, and the right to divorce guaranteed women's emancipation.

---

[2] See Maria Riley, *Transforming Feminism* (Kansas City, Mo.: Sheed and Ward, 1989) 46–63.

[3] See Robert Harahan, *The Vocation of Women: The Teaching of the Modern Popes from Leo XIII to Paul VI* (Rome: Pontificia Universitatis Laterensis, 1983); William B. Faherty, *The Destiny of Modern Woman in the Light of Papal Teaching* (Westminster, Md.: Newman Press, 1950). For papal texts see Monks of Solesmes, eds., *The Woman in the Modern World* (Boston: St. Paul Editions, 1959).

Liberal Feminism and the Church's Response

Liberal feminism embraced the Enlightenment doctrine of egalitarianism and worked to gain for women the inalienable rights that men took for granted. It had ideological roots in philosophical liberalism, but also in the gospel, and—at least at its beginning in the United States—was closely identified with the abolitionist movement. Liberal feminism had practical goals: to secure for women equal access to education; admission to the professions; and civil rights, especially the right to participate in public life (suffrage) and—for married women— to hold property, control their earnings, make contracts, and bring suits. The formation of the Catholic Women's Suffrage Society of England (now the St. Joan's International Alliance) in 1911 stands as an important, if somewhat isolated, testimony to interest in liberal feminism on the part of Catholic women.

At first the magisterium also addressed the goals of liberal feminism only indirectly, for example, by demanding equal pay for women workers, opposing the exploitation of their labor, and warning of the moral dangers that women faced in the workplace. For decades there was no explicit Catholic position on, much less encouragement of, women's suffrage. The popes rejected the liberal feminist ideal of the autonomous woman, freed from dependence upon and obedience to her husband. They inveighed against changes in women's dress and deportment that endangered their virtue and betrayed their dignity, denounced contraception, discouraged married women from entering the workforce, and extolled—often in highly romantic terms—the dignity of motherhood and of women's irreplaceable contribution in the home.

Confronted with multiple shifts in the social, political, economic, scientific, and cultural landscape, Pope Pius XII took up the challenge of liberal feminism more directly. Speaking on "Woman's Duties in Social and Political Life," he examined the feminist movement, distinguished its good from its bad aspects, and called upon Catholic women to join it and to take an active role in establishing Christian principles in modern culture, economy, and politics. Like his predecessors, Pius XII presupposed a feminine identity based on woman's roles as wife and mother, but he explicitly extended the scope of his concern to include the vocations of women religious and single women. He taught that women and men have equal dignity but diverse and mutually complementary roles. The authentic promotion of women, therefore, had to include respect for their dignity, their rights, and their unique feminine prerogatives—in other words, their own "nature." Though he initially identified motherhood as the source of feminine dignity, his later teaching opened the way to the discovery of its deeper source in personhood.

Cultural Feminism and the Church's Response

Cultural feminism extolled the moral superiority and the "special gifts" of women. Its objective was to bring a feminine influence to bear on the social order. Feminists motivated by this spirit organized to promote temperance, oppose prostitution, and campaign against the exploitation of women and children in the workplace. The magisterium, and Catholic thinkers like Gertrud Von le Fort and Edith Stein who addressed the "woman question," favored this direction. At the urging of Popes Pius X, Benedict XV, and Pius XI many Catholic women were educated and mobilized in national and international Catholic Women's Leagues and in the Catholic Action movement. They promoted the Catholic vision of woman's dignity and her role in the family.

In the period before Vatican II, then, the popes defended women's prerogatives in the family unit: their *place* in the home and their proper work in the family circle. As women succeeded in gaining access to public life, the popes encouraged their participation in the Church's mission as agents of social change and supported their entry into the political process. They did not examine presuppositions about women's "proper" *role* (motherhood, physical or spiritual) or their subordinate status vis-à-vis their husbands (within the family) and clerics (within the Church). Women's equal dignity was defended, but their vocation and rights as *persons* were yet to be explored.[4] In 1965, when the Fathers of Vatican II claimed with pride that the Church had liberated women, most Catholics agreed with them on the grounds that the gospel had overturned the double standard in sexual morality, sanctified the marriage bond, and prohibited divorce, and that for centuries the Church had encouraged the consecrated life for women.

The "Second Wave" of Modern Feminism

In the 1960s—just as Vatican II got underway—feminism received a new impulse and emerged once again as a profoundly influential social movement. At the outset of this wave, many Catholics continued to see the Church as a champion of women on account of the council's strong defense of human rights. Before long, however, disagreement over what justice for women requires in practice—a divergence based on different philosophical and theological understandings of human na-

---

[4] Harahan, *The Vocation of Women*, traces this progression.

ture and the meaning of human sexuality—led to divisions among feminists, among Catholic women, and between some Catholic women and their pastors.

Liberal Feminism Revived

The revival of liberal feminism can be traced to the civil rights movement and interest in political activism, a general awakening to the demands of social justice, and government and organizational initiatives. Betty Friedan's *The Feminine Mystique* (1963) gave popular impetus to women's demand for a life and an identity of their own. Contributing to these aspirations were women's changed social circumstances (in the "first world," at least): the experience of working outside the home during World War II, a greatly increased life expectancy, relief from household duties brought about by new technologies, and the capacity to regulate fertility with effective methods of birth control. Women began entering the workforce in large numbers, postponing marriage, having smaller families, and combining marriage and career. They claimed the rights of self-definition, self-affirmation, and self-determination, that is, the right to assert themselves as *persons* in every sphere.

Liberal feminists rejected the sex-role stereotyping that limited women's access to public life by appeal to their roles as wives, mothers, and homemakers or to their innate "feminine gifts" or "character traits." Refusing to be defined by men, and analyzing their experience as victims of sex discrimination, they developed critical feminist theories in order to identify systemic causes of discrimination and the structural changes needed to abolish them. Liberal feminists first emphasized legal rights, equal pay for equal work, and equal access to education, the professions, and the workplace. Next they campaigned for women's "reproductive rights"—access to family planning services, the right to a legal abortion, and the right to bear a child (apart from marriage). The latter they viewed as essential to preserving personal autonomy, sexual freedom, "rights over one's own body," and equal opportunity for career advancement. Most liberal feminist organizations adopt a "pro-choice" agenda.

Many Catholics in the liberal feminist movement endorse the first part of its social agenda, but reject—or have grave reservations about—most of the second. They raise critical questions about Church teachings and about their equal status in the Church. Some see the prohibition of contraception (and abortion) and the exclusion of women from ministerial priesthood as expressions of a "sexist" refusal to acknowledge women as equals—as moral agents with respect to their own sexuality, as participants in shaping moral teaching that affects them, and as persons competent to function in ordained ministry. If they did not initially imagine "justice" in the Church to require the ordination of women as deacons and priests, this topic was added to the agenda after the initial meeting of the Women's Ordination Conference (1975), the Episcopal Church's decision to ordain women priests (1976), and the promulgation of the Vatican Declaration *Inter insigniores*[5] (1977). Widespread advocacy for women's ordination and the publication of scholarly studies critical of the declaration's premises and of its reasoning followed. By 1978, Catholic feminists were divided into liberals who sought to serve the Church in a "renewed priestly ministry" and radicals who sought to reform Church structures.

During this same period many women's religious institutes, claiming the right to self-determination in matters of corporate renewal, disputed with the Vatican officials whose approval was needed for their revised constitutions. These prolonged struggles fanned the flames of liberal feminism among their number. In general, these developments revealed that "feminism" could no longer simply be equated with the belief that women and men are equal in dignity as human beings.[6]

The Church and Liberal Feminism

At first liberal feminists claimed the Church as an ally in their struggle on account of the council's commitment to human rights, and its uncompromising affirmation that "with respect to the fundamental rights of the person, every type of discrimination, whether social or cultural, whether based on sex, race, color, social condition, language, or religion, is to be overcome and eradicated as contrary to God's intent." This principle was, in fact, illustrated by reference to the case of a woman "denied the right and freedom to choose a husband, to embrace a state of life, or to acquire an education or cultural benefits equal to those recognized for men."[7] The council located the question of women's rights in the context of its reflection on the vocation and dignity of the person created in the divine image. Attention to women as the subjects of personal rights and responsibilities opened the way to the Church's first direct engagement with the central concern of feminism, namely, women's desire to be regarded and valued as persons in their own right.[8]

[5] See "Vatican Declaration: Women in the Ministerial Priesthood," and Commentary in *Origins* 6 (February 3, 1977).
[6] For the range of opinions among Catholic women, see *Origins* 14 (March 21, 1985) and 15 (October 3, 1985).
[7] GS 29. See also GS 9, 60; AA 9; and PT 41.
[8] See Harahan, *The Vocation of Women*, ch. 6.

Pope Paul VI advocated the social advancement of women in his apostolic letter A Call to Action (1971) and in several addresses in connection with the United Nation's International Women's Year (1975). His program is summed up in his exhortation to Catholic jurists "to labor everywhere to have discovered, respected, and protected the rights and prerogatives of every woman in her life—educational, professional, civic, social, religious—whether single or married."[9] Pope Paul VI's encyclical *Humanae vitae* underlines the council's teaching on the equal personal dignity of husband and wife. It does not support the view that a wife must accede to unreasonable demands on the part of her husband or that she is responsible for the regulation of the couple's fertility. *Humanae vitae* presents marriage as a special form of friendship engaging a reciprocal, personal gift of self on the part of each partner. It maintains that the prohibition of contraception defends the human dignity of both husband and wife, and in a particular way of the wife.[10]

Pope John Paul II has continued this program of advocacy for women's equal rights. Addressing all the women of the world on the occasion of the Fourth World Conference on Women (1995), for example, he reaffirms the Church's desire to promote and defend women. Justice for women, he writes, requires "equal pay for equal work, protection for working mothers, fairness in career advancement, equality of spouses with regard to family rights and the recognition of everything that is part of the rights and duties of citizens in a democratic state."[11] In his apostolic letter On the Vocation and Dignity of Women he applies to women the council's teaching on the dignity of the *person:* a person, made in the divine image, is "the only creature on earth willed by God for its own sake."[12] A woman, no less than a man, is a person, endowed with intelligence and freedom and capable of self-determination. Every human person is a subject; therefore, the victimization of women by a mentality that considers a human being as an "object"—to be used, bought and sold, as an instrument for selfish pleasure—is especially deplorable. The pope firmly reasserts, in this connection, the Church's prohibition of contraception and abortion.[13] He presses Catholic teaching on women's equal dignity in marriage to new conclusions. Taking into account both Jesus' example as reported

[9] "Women/Disciples and Co-Workers," *Origins* 4 (May 1, 1975).

[10] See *Humanae vitae*, nos. 13, 17, 18, 20.

[11] "Letter to Women," *Origins* 25 (July 27, 1995); see also the collection *The Genius of Women* (Washington, D.C.: United States Catholic Conference, 1997).

[12] See the apostolic letter MD 6–7 for a development of this theme from GS 24.

[13] See FC 28–33 and EV 11–14.

in the Gospels and the key text from Galatians (3:28), he affirms the "Gospel innovation," that is, "the awareness that in marriage there is mutual 'subjection of the spouses out of reverence for Christ,' and not just that of the wife to the husband." By extension, he says, this innovation requires the more general emancipation of women from unilateral subjection to men.[14]

The equal dignity of women and men *in the Church* is a related, though distinct, question. According to Vatican II, all of the baptized

> share a common dignity of members from their rebirth in Christ. They have the same filial grace and the same vocation to perfection. They possess in common one salvation, one hope, and one undivided charity. Hence, there is in Christ and in the Church no inequality on the basis of race or nationality, social condition or sex.[15]

Together with Vatican II and the 1971 Synod of Bishops, Paul VI taught that women's advancement in social order must have as its counterpart their fuller integration into the Church's life and mission. The Study Commission on Women in Society and in the Church, convened in response to the synod, addressed women's inclusion in Church advisory bodies at all levels, access to theological education and to nonordained ministries, and participation in some forms of ecclesiastical jurisdiction. It published its recommendations in 1976.[16]

Does Paul VI's teaching on women in ministry contradict the principle of full baptismal equality? The pope did reserve installation into the lay ministries of lector and acolyte to men, "in accord with the venerable tradition,"[17] but since laypersons (therefore, women) can receive a temporary deputation to exercise identical functions this restriction is not based on a feminine "incapacity." *Inter insigniores* does uphold the constant tradition of reserving the ministerial priesthood to men, but the Church does not regard access to priesthood as a "justice" issue. Two points are noteworthy: (1) the declaration appeals to the example of Jesus to confirm and advance women's equal dignity with men, and (2) it omits explanations, frequently used in the past, based on women's subordinate status. The fundamental reason given for this tradition is the will of Christ, made known by his choice of men to belong to the Twelve. Traditional practice contradicts neither Gal 3:28 nor the Church's

---

[14] MD 24.

[15] LG 32; the passage ends with Gal 3:28.

[16] *Crux [of the News] Special* (September 20, 1976). See also *International Women's Year 1975: Study Kit* (Washington, D.C.: United States Catholic Conference 1975) and *Marialis cultus*, nos. 34–5; 37.

[17] *Ministeria quaedam* (1972), norm 7.

teaching about baptismal equality, the declaration argues, for "priesthood does not form part of the rights of the individual" and in the body of Christ "equality is in no way identity."

During the pontificate of John Paul II the council's teaching on the baptismal equality of women with men has been confirmed and developed in the 1983 Code of Canon Law and in the postsynodal apostolic exhortation *Christifideles laici* (1988). The basis for distinctions among the Christian faithful in the new code is not sex but "condition and function" (c. 208). Women now have the same juridic status—equal rights and obligations[18]—as lay men. Canons that discriminated on the basis of sex have been omitted or adjusted; in addition, certain functions and offices previously reserved to the ordained have now been opened to the laity, and therefore to women.[19] Laypersons may now serve as chancellors and censors and as defenders of the bond and collegiate judges in Church tribunals; they can be authorized to preach (though not the homily) in church, cooperate in the pastoral care of a parish, exercise the ministries of lector and acolyte, administer sacramentals, and—in cases of necessity and as substitutes—confer baptism, lead liturgical services, and witness marriages. *Christifideles laici* (no. 51) notes the possibility of women's participation in parish and diocesan pastoral councils, diocesan synods, and particular councils. Women may be consulted and involved in the process of coming to decisions, in transmitting the faith not only in the family but as theologians, and in the evangelization of culture. In his 1994 apostolic letter on the ordination of women, *Ordinatio sacerdotalis*,[20] the Pope teaches that the Church does not have the authority to change the tradition of reserving the ministerial priesthood to males. Again, the reason given is not women's incapacity but that holy orders is a sacrament—a sacred sign—instituted by Christ. The Pope recalls Jesus' freedom from cultural constraints in his dealing with women, and maintains—appealing to the case of the Blessed Virgin—that this tradition does not compromise the equal dignity of women, who share the apostolic mission of the whole People of God and exemplify the holiness of the whole Church to which the ministerial priesthood is ordered.

Together with *liberal feminism*, then, the Church defends and promotes the equal dignity and rights of women with men in society and in the Church. Unlike liberal feminism, the magisterium acknowledges that justice sometimes allows or even requires differential treatment on the basis of sex.

[18] See cann. 208–22 and (for the laity) cann. 224–31.

[19] See Rose McDermott, "Women in the New Code," *The Way Supplement* 50 (Summer 1984) 27–37.

[20] "Apostolic Letter on the Ordination of Women," *Origins* 24 (June 9, 1994).

Cultural Feminism Revived

Modern "cultural" (also "romantic" or "relational") feminists affirm the equal dignity of women and men, but they contend that women have "special gifts" to contribute. Unlike liberal feminists, they accept the theory of sex complementarity. They want to influence the social order *as women*, and when they defend "women's rights" they envision a social order that acknowledges the contribution of women who are mothers and makes provision for their needs and responsibilities. They refuse to purchase equality with men at the expense of conforming to a masculine norm. Cultural feminists value women's virginity and their unique capacity for motherhood. They argue that premarital sex, the "right" to abortion, and no-fault divorce enslave women to the illegitimate demands of men under the pretext of "liberating" them. While for many liberal feminists (like the National Organization for Women) the right to abortion has become a litmus test for inclusion, for "pro-life feminists" abortion—like rape, incest, and wife abuse—is a form of violence against women.

The Church and Cultural Feminism

Papal teaching consistently upholds both the equal dignity of the sexes and their "effective complementarity" as something willed by God. It holds that sexual identity affects the human person "on the biological, psychological, and spiritual levels"; woman and man are complementary from an ontological point of view.[21] Pope Paul VI warned that "an equalizing of rights must not degenerate into an egalitarian and impersonal leveling" which would undermine feminine dignity.[22] Motherhood is more than a "reproductive role specialization"; it is a woman's proper and personal vocation which must be respected if women are to obtain justice. He also affirmed the "irreplaceable contribution" women make to the Church's mission by fulfilling their vocation as mothers, bringing their gifts to the work of evangelization, and serving as reconcilers and peacemakers.

Pope John Paul II likewise affirms both the equal dignity and the complementarity of the sexes and cautions women against seeking equality with men by imitating them. Women's equal dignity, he grants, fully justifies their access to public functions, but their true advancement requires that their maternal and family role be properly

[21] Congregation for the Doctrine of the Faith, *Persona humana*, no. 1, and Pope John Paul II, *Letter to Women*, no. 7.

[22] "Women/Balancing the Rights and Duties," *Origins* 5 (February 19, 1976) 552.

recognized and valued.[23] The Pope's doctrine of sexual complementarity is grounded in a personalist philosophical-theological reflection.[24] Every human person exists either as a man or a woman and is called to fulfill himself or herself through a sincere gift of self. This vocation to love—to interpersonal communion with God and neighbor—is realized for both women and men in two specific ways: marriage and virginity or celibacy. Man and woman are made for *mutual* help and are equally responsible for humanity, for the earth, for history and culture. Neither sex is superior to the other, yet their equality is not undifferentiated, for each contributes something "original."

The original and specific gift or "genius" of women is rooted in the vocation to motherhood; it belongs to their psychophysical and personal structure and to the "gift of self" by which they are fulfilled. In a particular way, God entrusts the human being to the woman. Women's unique contact with the mystery of life in its beginning makes them "more capable than men of paying attention *to another person.*"[25] On this account, the Church anticipates that women as protagonists in the public sphere will bring a humanizing influence to the world of culture, leisure, the intellectual life, science, ecology, and politics. Similarly, although they have not been lacking in the past, the Church will be enriched as women's charisms and example of holiness are expressed in new forms.

Together with *cultural feminism,* then, the Church accepts a theory of complementarity and values women's specific vocation with its gifts, tasks, and "original" contributions. It views motherhood as the vocation of a person, asymmetrical with that of father because of the nature of women's investment in childbearing. Still, according to John Paul II, the values and specific gifts of both femininity and masculinity need further study.[26]

Socialist Feminism Revived

Contemporary feminism has been defined as "a comprehensive ideology which is rooted in women's experience of sexual oppression, engages in a critique of patriarchy as an essentially dysfunctional system, embraces an alternative vision for humanity and the earth, and actively seeks to bring this vision to realization."[27] Socialist and radical

[23] FC 23; MD 10; and "Letter to Women," nos. 7–8.
[24] See MD 6–7.
[25] MD 18, 30; CL 51.
[26] CL 50.
[27] Sandra M. Schneiders, *Beyond Patching: Faith and Feminism in the Catholic Church* (New York: Paulist Press, 1991) 15.

feminism fit this description particularly well. Socialist feminism traces patriarchy to its roots in an economic system and defines it as a set of social relations among men achieved by means of control over women. It aims to eradicate patriarchy by changing the economic system which grounds the classist social order. Equality before the law is unable to remedy this apart from a social reform in which women gain control of their reproductive lives, men assume their share of childcare, the state takes more responsibility for children's well-being, and the workplace is reorganized to provide equal opportunity for women.

Some Catholic feminists find this analysis compelling; others are committed only to some of its practical goals, which they see as responding to the "feminization of poverty." Some favor them because they choose to work outside the home not only to supplement the family income but also to express themselves and to contribute to society at large. Many working women, on the other hand, want marriage and motherhood and long for stable family life. They feel overburdened at work and frustrated in their aspirations to establish a harmonious and nurturing home environment. Economic independence is not a priority for them.

The Church's Response to Socialist Feminism

Because the popes teach that the family—not the individual—is the basic unit of society, they qualify their support for women's economic independence. Pope John XXIII defended the right of mothers to working conditions favorable to their family duties, and *Gaudium et spes* affirmed that productive work should be accommodated to the needs of the human person and domestic life so that workers, including mothers of families, should not be enslaved to the economy.[28] Paul VI acknowledged that both parents must collaborate, but also insisted that the woman's role is essential. Or, he asks, is contributing to the formation of human personalities and preparing the coming generations an unworthy task?[29]

Pope John Paul II draws the connection explicitly in his encyclical *Laborem exercens*. Women's unpaid work in the family benefits both the economy and the common good. He calls for

> *a social reevaluation of the mother's role*, of the toil connected with it, and of the need that children have for care, love and affection in order that they may develop into responsible, morally and religiously mature and

[28] See PT 19; GS 67.
[29] "Women/Balancing Rights and Duties," *Origins* 5 (February 19, 1976) 551.

psychologically stable persons. It will redound to the credit of society to make it possible for a mother—without inhibiting her freedom, without psychological or practical discrimination, and without penalizing her as compared with other women, to devote herself to taking care of her children and educating them in accordance with their needs, which vary with age.

Justice requires that remuneration given to an adult who is responsible for a family be sufficient for its maintenance and future security. This may be achieved by paying a "family wage" to the worker or by other social measures (e.g., family allowances, grants to full-time mothers).[30] His point is that "society must be structured in such a way that wives and mothers are *not in practice compelled* to work outside the home." He deplores "the mentality which honors women more for their work outside the home than for their work within the family."[31]

The Church, then, rejects socialist feminism's theory—which attacks the family—without rejecting all of its practical remedies. Its great flaw is its failure to recognize the social and economic value of women's work in the home.

Radical Feminism

Radical feminism views patriarchy—the social system of father-rule—as the root and paradigm of all forms of social domination, especially of all hierarchical (i.e., divinely sanctioned) relationships. Some radical feminists, characterized as "gynocentric" ("woman centered"), theorize about patriarchy from the vantage point of gender but—by contrast with liberal feminists—explicitly claim their power *as women*, celebrating feminine superiority even to the point of separatism, including an ideological lesbian separatism. The "gynocentric" expression of radical feminism takes cultural feminism to its extreme, universalizing women's experience and rejecting men, heterosexual marriage, and traditional family relationships as oppressive. Other radical feminists have abandoned the "binary gender system" as the chief point of reference for feminist theory. They identify patriarchy (or "kyriarchy")[32] as ideologically interconnected with all other forms of domination, so they reject not only "hierarchy" but all "dichotomous dualisms"[33] (e.g., classism, racism, clericalism, colonialism, heterosexism,

---

[30] *Laborem exercens*, no. 19.

[31] FC 23.

[32] Elisabeth Schüssler Fiorenza's term for the "rule of the emperor/master/lord/husband/father over his subordinates."

[33] Schneiders, *Beyond Patching*, 26.

ageism, humanocentrism) in favor of egalitarianism. Their goal is a feminist future of cooperation and sharing, dialogue and consensus building, participative decision-making, inclusion, and respect for the earth.

Among the varieties of feminism, radical feminists are most concerned about the responsibility of religion for the oppression of women. In their view, Christianity and the Church justify and promote sexism in both theory and practice. It seems to them that patriarchy originates in or at least draws support from the religious symbol of God as Father, and that the identification of God with maleness—and of the male with God—is reinforced by the doctrine of the incarnation of God's Son as a male. When Catholics among them read the theological argument from "fittingness" in *Inter insigniores*—namely, that the ministerial priesthood is reserved to males because the sacrament of holy orders requires the "natural resemblance" of gender between the priest and Christ—they began to claim that the gospel itself had suffered a "massive distortion" at the hands of men.[34] Finding evidence of this in the Scriptures (Eve is blamed for the Fall, St. Paul commands women to be silent and submit to their husbands) and in the theological tradition, they adopted the "feminist critique" of Christianity and began to examine the evidence for themselves, assuming the double role of critics and apologists with respect to the Catholic faith.[35]

Some Catholics had raised critical questions about the Church's responsibility for sexism from the outset of the "second wave,"[36] but many others made the move to radical feminism in response to *Inter insigniores*. The litmus test for most radical Catholic feminists remains, perhaps only for symbolic purposes, a woman's right to "ordination." They hold that the genuine liberation of women requires the conversion of the patriarchal, hierarchically structured Church into a "discipleship of equals" and the reconstruction of a Christian symbol system favorable to the "full flourishing of women" by means of feminist theology.[37] Feminist theology has been accompanied by feminist spiritual-

[34] Their objection rests on a mistake: they take this supporting argument to be the foundation of the tradition.

[35] See Anne E. Carr, *Transforming Grace: Christian Tradition and Women's Experience* (San Francisco: Harper and Row, 1988).

[36] See Mary Daly, *The Church and the Second Sex* (San Francisco: Harper and Row, 1968); Albertus Magnus McGrath, *Women and the Church* (Chicago: Thomas More Association, 1972).

[37] "Discipleship of equals" is Elisabeth Schüssler Fiorenza's term. See Catherine Mowry LaCugna, ed., *Freeing Theology: The Essentials of Theology in Feminist Perspective* (San Francisco: Harper, 1993) for essays exemplifying feminist theology.

ity—an effort to reclaim female ritual authority, create an alternative space for theological reflection, and project a feminist future.[38] The development of feminist spirituality is largely carried on outside the "institutional church" (e.g., in "Women-Church"). Certain of its issues, for example, the use of "inclusive language" for God in catechetical, biblical, liturgical, and hymn texts, have become questions for the rest of the community.

The Church's Response to Radical Feminism

Pope John Paul II clearly had the objections of radical feminism in mind when he prepared his apostolic letter *Mulieris dignitatem*. Two major lines of his response may be sketched out here. First, he distinguishes the order of the Fall from the orders of creation and redemption in order to insist that sexism and the patriarchal oppression of women by men do not belong to the divine plan; they are the consequence of sin. In the beginning, God created both man and woman in his image and likeness. Sharing an identical human nature, they are made "for" each other, that is, to become "one flesh" through the gift of self in love, and to transmit life to their children. Their interpersonal communion of love bears a certain likeness to the communion of love in the Trinity.

Because of sin, which, despite the distinction of roles, is charged to both of the "first parents," the likeness to God is obscured and the original relationship between the sexes disturbed. In place of a sincere gift of self, the man dominates the woman (Gen 3:16); their mutual relationship is affected by concupiscence (1 John 2:16) in a way that lays a special burden on the woman, not only in marriage but in other spheres of life. Scripture confirms the existence of this disorder ("patriarchy"), identifies its cause, and proclaims the need for conversion.

The promise of the New Covenant foretells victory over sin (Gen 3:15). The end of the mutual opposition between the sexes is signaled by the fact that the New Covenant begins with a woman, Mary: in Christ "there is neither male nor female" (Gal 3:28). The redemption restores God's original plan in the New Eve when the Son of God, the New Adam, takes our humanity from her. The Lord Jesus reveals the dignity of women as persons in his teaching (for example, his teaching on divorce) and in his dealings with them. Women respond to him with lively faith and love, following him even to the Cross. They are the first to find the empty tomb and announce his resurrection. Jesus promotes and confirms women's "gospel" equality with men in all that has to do

---

[38] See Schneiders, *Beyond Patching*, 72–112.

with the gift of the Holy Spirit and prophetic witness to the "mighty works of God." Unity in Christ Jesus does not cancel out diversity: both "sons" and "daughters" prophesy (Acts 2:11). It does, however, end the antagonism between the sexes and establish the possibility of living according to the "Gospel innovation."[39]

Second, the Pope comments on the theological significance of maleness. If we are "like" God, God is also "like" us; this accounts for the anthropomorphic language of the Bible. (Still, analogy has its limits. God is more "unlike" than like us.) Scripture, he notes, ascribes both masculine and feminine attributes to God, indirectly confirming the creation of both sexes in the divine image. It compares God's love to a mother's as well as to a husband's and a father's. Jesus' custom of calling God "Father" establishes a norm for Christian prayer, but this fatherhood—which belongs to God's inner life—must be understood in "an ultra-corporeal, superhuman and completely divine sense."

Nevertheless, there is a profound value in the biblical revelation of God in masculine images. Here, masculinity speaks not of sinful domination and subjugation but of self-gift and communion of life. The harmony of the maleness of Christ with the economy of salvation is discovered through an appreciation of the covenant as a "nuptial mystery."[40] From the time of the prophets forward, the compassionate love of God for Israel is depicted as the love of a husband. The Chosen People, in turn, is called to a loving, "spousal" union with God as his beloved bride. This motif is carried forward in the New Testament: the Word made flesh establishes the New Covenant in his blood. He is the bridegroom; the Church, his bride. The fullest expression of this image is found in Eph 5:21-32. The "great mystery" (Eph 5:32), or "great analogy," compares a man's love for a woman to Christ's love for the Church. In his gift of self on the cross, Jesus accomplished the New Covenant (Eph 5:25): his "headship" is expressed in laying down his life. God's redeeming love is revealed as spousal love.

The magisterium cannot, of course, endorse radical feminism, or subscribe to the "feminist critique" insofar as it rejects biblical revelation or suggests that the Church has betrayed the gospel from post-apostolic times. It cannot approve radical feminist alternatives to Christianity or alternative feminist "liturgies" and communities like Women-Church. The critique, however, must be addressed, and feminist theologians have contributed some helpful clarifications and "retrieved" many valuable historical materials. But insofar as Catholic

---

[39] See above, p. 422.
[40] See *Inter insigniores*, no. 5; MD 23.

radical feminists are ideologically opposed to hierarchy on principle, and make women's interpreted experience a norm for faith—in place of Scripture read within the tradition and authentically interpreted by the magisterium—their feminist theological reconstructions remain in some tension with—if not opposition to—Catholic doctrine.[41]

The "New Feminism"

In his "Letter to Women," Pope John Paul II continues the tradition in which "the Church" thanks women—mothers, wives, daughters, sisters, women who work, consecrated women—for their contributions and "for the simple fact of being a woman"! Addressing all the women of the world, he proclaims the power of the gospel to emancipate them and uphold their dignity and rights. This letter is not just a rosy tribute coupled with an exhortation, however, for it goes on to spell out the ways women have experienced discrimination and the injury this has caused them and the human community. The Pope offers an apology for the way members of the Church may have contributed to this and calls the whole Church to renewed fidelity to the gospel vision. He praises women "who have devoted their lives to defending the dignity of womanhood by fighting for their basic social, economic, and political rights." The process of women's liberation he describes as "difficult," "complicated," and "unfinished," but "substantially positive."

The Pope calls for an end to discrimination so that humanity can benefit from the contribution women will make—a spiritual, cultural, sociopolitical, and economic contribution—to the solution of contemporary problems in the life of societies and nations. In the encyclical *The Gospel of Life* (1995) he writes that it depends on women to promote a "new feminism" which can transform culture so that it supports life.[42]

Many women are issuing the same call. What they want and need is stronger social support for child-raising families, better day care, more flexibility in the workplace, and better protection of women from the hazards of divorce, abandonment, and sexual violence. Some charge that "the official feminists"—e.g., NOW leaders—have lost touch with the reality of ordinary women's lives. Women of color, working-class women, and poor women protest that the feminist agenda favors the

---

[41] See Francis Martin, *The Feminist Question: Feminist Theology in the Light of Christian Tradition* (Grand Rapids, Mich.: Eerdmans, 1994).

[42] *The Gospel of Life*, no. 99.

goals of the elite at their expense.[43] This call is also heard from within the feminist ranks.[44]

Many Catholic women, unwilling to be excommunicated as "anti-feminists" by radical feminists, are also calling for and putting into practice a "new feminism." They wish to identify what constitutes women's well-being in ways that include—along with the usual goals— the values of premarital chastity, marriage, motherhood, unpaid work in the home, volunteerism, and solidarity with the poor. Having learned the feminist lesson of self-definition, they are claiming their own vision of women and men as partners in the human enterprise who have a common stake in a civilization of love.

[43] African-American women speak of contributing a "womanist" perspective which takes their experience of double discrimination into account; Hispanic women identify "mujerista" concerns.

[44] See Mary Ann Glendon, "A Glimpse of the New Feminism," *America* 175 (July 6–13, 1996) 10–15; Elizabeth Fox-Genovese, *Feminism without Illusions: A Critique of Individualism* (Chapel Hill: University of North Carolina Press, 1991); Elizabeth Fox-Genovese, *Feminism Is Not the Story of My Life* (New York: Doubleday, 1996).

For Further Reading

Ashley, Benedict M. *Justice in the Church: Gender and Participation.* Washington, D.C.: The Catholic University of America Press, 1996.

Butler, Sara. "Women's Ordination and the Development of Doctrine." *The Thomist* 61 (October 1997) 501–24.

Congregation for the Doctrine of the Faith. *From "Inter Insigniores" to "Ordinatio Sacerdotalis": Documents and Commentaries.* Washington, D.C.: United States Catholic Conference, 1998.

Glendon, Mary Ann. "What Happened at Beijing." *First Things* 59 (January 1996) 30–6.

Hinsdale, Mary Ann, and Phyllis H. Kaminski, eds. *Women and Theology.* Maryknoll, N.Y.: Orbis Books, 1995.

John Paul II. "Apostolic Letter on Ordination and Women." *Origins* 24 (June 9, 1994).

_____. *The Genius of Women.* Washington, D.C.: United States Catholic Conference, 1997.

_____. "On the Dignity and Vocation of Women *(Mulieris Dignitatem).*" *Origins* 18:17 (October 1988) 261–83.

_____. *The Theology of the Body: Human Love in the Divine Plan.* Foreword by John S. Grabowski. Boston: Pauline Books & Media, 1997.

Moll, Helmet, ed. *The Church and Women: A Compendium.* San Francisco: Ignatius Press, 1988.

National Conference of Catholic Bishops. "Strengthening the Bonds of Peace." *Origins* 24 (December 1, 1994).

Range, Joan A. "Women and Canon Law." *Review for Religious* 58 (May–June 1999) 266–85.

Riley, Maria. *Transforming Feminism.* Kansas City, Mo.: Sheed and Ward, 1989.

Ross, Susan A., and Mary Catherine Hilkert. "Feminist Theology: A Review of Literature." *Theological Studies* 56:2 (June 1995) 327–52.

Schneiders, Sandra M. *Beyond Patching: Faith and Feminism in the Catholic Church.* New York: Paulist Press, 1991.

Schumacher, Michele M. "The Prophetic Vocation of Women and the Order of Love." *Logos* 2 (Spring 1999) 147–92.

Tavard, George H. *Woman in Christian Tradition.* Notre Dame, Ind.: University of Notre Dame Press, 1973.

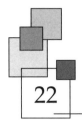

22

Mary and the Church

Frederick M. Jelly

The intimate relationship between the mysteries of Mary, the Mother of Christ, and of the Church, the Mystical Body of Christ, has come to be an important part of Catholic teaching during this final century of the second millennium. This is found in the teaching of Vatican Council II, which met in several public sessions over a period of four years (1962–65). Its Marian doctrine was included as chapter eight in the Dogmatic Constitution on the Church *(Lumen gentium)*. The truths that it teaches about Mary's unique place in her Son's body the Church are based upon the best in our Catholic tradition. Although it represented a significant development in the doctrines about Mary and devotion to her, the teaching of Vatican II about the Mother of God the Son made flesh for our salvation is solidly rooted in sacred Scripture and the tradition of the Church in which it has unfolded over the centuries. From the great Fathers and Doctors of the Church such as SS Ambrose, Augustine, Jerome, Pope Gregory I, etc., in the West, and SS Athanasius, Epiphanius, Cyril of Alexandria, John Damascene, etc., in the East, through the outstanding medieval theologians such as SS Albert the Great, Bonaventure, Thomas Aquinas, Blessed Duns Scotus, etc., to the many more modern and even contemporary scholars of our faith, there has been a continuous testimony to Mary's unparalleled role in salvation history that has been articulated in the Church's magisterium or teaching authority culminating in Vatican II and postconciliar developments.

In light of the above introduction, this essay may be outlined in the following five sections: Mary and the Church (1) in the teaching of Vatican II, (2) in the revelation of the New Testament, (3) in the dogmatic developments of the Catholic tradition, (4) in the contemporary characteristics of Marian doctrine and devotion, and (5) in prospects of future progress.

Mary and the Church in the Teaching of Vatican II

Before we actually examine the conciliar teaching about Marian doctrine and devotion, it will be helpful to analyze the discussion that led to the decision that this teaching appear as part of LG, the council's teaching about the mystery of the Church, and not in a separate document about the mystery of Mary. During the debate on the floor which took place on October 24, 1963, Cardinal Santos of Manila spoke in favor of making the Marian *schema* or draft an independent document, and Cardinal König of Vienna represented those who wished to see it become a section of the *schema* on the Church. At the outset of the debate it was clearly stated that the differences of opinion in the matter had nothing to do with the very special devotion and veneration which all the conciliar fathers gave to the Blessed Virgin Mary.

Cardinal Santos argued that: (1) Mary's great dignity and unique role in the Church would be made more apparent in a separate document; (2) her preservative redemption as the Immaculate Conception, her singular cooperation in bringing about the very existence of the Church as the Mystical Body of Christ, and her intimate relationship with our redemption through her Son's saving grace made her so preeminent and distinctive from the rest of us in the Church that these truths could not be suitably treated in the *schema* on the Church; (3) although there is a very close connection between Mary and the Church, she also has close connections with Christ and salvation, and so the Mariology of Vatican II ought not to be reduced to ecclesiology; and (4) to insert the teaching about Mary into the already complicated structure of the proposed document on the Church would be awkward and unclear as well as send the wrong signal to the faithful that the council intended to lessen her most honorable place among the redeemed members of the Church.

In response Cardinal König began his address in the debate on the floor by clearly stating that he was in no way about to contradict the assertions made by Cardinal Santos, either doctrinally or devotionally. He reminded the conciliar fathers of the abundant supernatural fruit that the Marian Movement of the previous century, starting in the mid-nineteen century, had brought forth under the inspiration of the Holy Spirit. He also called their attention to the fact that six hundred of them had submitted petitions for further explanation of Marian doctrine at Vatican II. And these had been recommended for both theological and pastoral reasons. He also pointed out that, at the meeting of the theological commission on October 9, 1963, the majority expressed their wish that the council's teaching about Mary be integrated into the *schema* on the Church. König intended to give the theological, historical, pastoral, and ecumenical reasons behind this majority opinion. Among the theological reasons were: (1) the Church is the central theme of the second session of the council as well as of Vatican II as a whole, so placing its Marian teaching with that on the Church would both provide a more prominent setting for Mariology and, at the same time, avoid separating it from the rest of theology which led to some excesses in the past; (2) it would create the erroneous impression that Vatican II intended to define a new Marian dogma which had been repeatedly denied; (3) contrary to the argument advanced by Santos, the insertion of the council's Mariological doctrine within the document on the Church would be beneficial to both Mariology and ecclesiology, e.g., the Church as the communion of saints in union with the heavenly Church and Mary's glorious assumption and her intercessory role for us in the pilgrim Church on earth; (4) as the Immaculate Conception uniquely redeemed by her Son and as medatrix of his graces to us, Mary is the archetype of the Church as both the redeemed body of Christ and also his redeeming body endowed with the means of mediating salvation to the world; and, finally, (5) the proper balanced understanding of the mystery of the Church as both redeemed and redeeming would avoid putting at odds a Mariology emphasizing Mary's relationship to the Church with a Mariology accentuating her relationship with Christ. This most important point will be explained further later in the essay.

In addition to his five theological reasons why the council's teaching about Mary ought to be integrated into that on the Church, König gave three historical reasons: (1) devotion to Mary in our Catholic tradition has arisen out of a contemplation of the Church as mother, e.g., all the titles attributed to Mary in the litanies of Our Lady were originally given to the Church so that her privileges were portrayed in an ecclesiological perspective, which seems to favor treating her in LG; (2) in a homily on October 11, 1963, Pope Paul VI insinuated the close relationship between the Church and the Mother of God; and (3) the international Mariological-Marian Congress held at Lourdes in 1958 was devoted to "Mary and the Church," showing the special interest and concern with the topic.

From this observation emerged König's pastoral reason: that relating Mary more clearly to Christ and his body the Church will nourish the devotional life of the faithful regarding the essentials about the incarnation and redemption and Mary's unique role in these mysteries of the Church.

The ecumenical reason for inserting the Marian teaching in LG concluded the debate presentation by König. He argued that it would enhance Mary's role as *Theotokos* or God-Bearer, which would help our dialogue with the Orthodox Churches of the East and the Protestants would be more receptive to a biblical portrait of Mary according to which she is prefigured as a type of the Church as in John 19:25 (the woman at the foot of the cross) and Revelation 12 (the woman clothed in the sun).

The actual voting took place on October 29, 1963, after the long weekend following the debate. Some of the observers and most of the other Christian churches in the West favored an integrated *schema* on Mary and the Church. Before the voting, Cardinal Agagianian, the moderator, assured the conciliar fathers that the issue before them was indeed not Marian doctrine and devotion as such and that the writing of a new text, if necessary, would be done under the direction of the doctrinal commission. Of the 2,193 votes cast, 1,114 were in favor of integrating the Marian *schema* into that on the Church, 1,074 were in favor of a separate schema on Mary, and 5 votes were spoiled. The difference was less than 2 percent, so the required majority was reached by only 17 votes to spare! By far it was the narrowest majority in the history of Vatican II. One wonders how the hand of the Holy Spirit may have been working in this very close vote. Was it perhaps a warning that in this and comparable matters there had to be very careful implementation of the real meaning and intent of the council's decision and teaching? I firmly believe so!

In the perception of most Catholic Mariologists or theologians of Mary, the decision has proven to be providential. Although it has often been misinterpreted, as though Vatican II were minimizing Mary's role in the Church, the results have generally been salutary. Doctrinally it has helped place the truths of our faith concerning the dogmas about Mary in their proper perspective, that is, in intimate relationship with the mystery of Christ and the Church. Devotionally, the portrait of a contemporary Madonna in LG 8 has helped attract Catholics away from a "privilege-centered" Mariology toward one that is more "sharing-oriented." In other words, instead of seeing Mary's special graces and privileges as isolating her from us, we behold them as revealing what God intends ultimately for all who have been redeemed by Christ. Ecumenically this decision to make their conciliar teaching about Marian doctrine and devotion an integral part of that on the Church has helped convince our sisters and brothers in the other Christian churches that we Catholics really do not virtually make Mary a substitute for Christ and the Holy Spirit in our salvation and sanctification. But a Mariology that tended to place Mary at the side of Christ looking down upon us did distort her proper relationship both to him and to us. Making her a member of his body the Church, even though a preeminent and uniquely favored member, is much less likely to appear to attribute to her prerogatives and functions that can belong only to her Son as the one mediator of redemption between God and us and to the Holy Spirit as the sanctifier in the Holy Trinity.

We have gone into some detail about the debate leading to the decision to make Vatican II's teaching about Mary chapter eight of LG so that you can appreciate the sound reasons behind that balanced teaching with its fruitful effects for the Catholic faithful and for the members of other churches. The very title of that chapter, "The Blessed Virgin Mary, God-Bearer, in the Mystery of Christ and of the Church," conveys the complete complementarity of a christocentric and an ecclesiotypical Mariology. All authentic teaching about Mary, as well as any true devotion to her, is based upon her unique relationship with Christ. And, just as Christ cannot be properly understood and revered apart from the ecclesial body or Church that he received through his redemptive activity, so neither can Mary be properly contemplated and venerated as though she were not in solidarity with that same body. After all, she is the first fruits of her Son's redeeming love, and so the prototype or primary example of faithful discipleship in her Son's Church.

Yves Congar, the outstanding Dominican theologian who had such a profound influence as a *peritus* or expert at Vatican II, particularly on LG, observed that the tiny preposition "in" that related Mary so nicely to Christ and his Church in the title of chapter eight of LG really spoke volumes about a balanced Marian doctrine and devotion.

In light of this historical and theological background, let us now consider the actual teaching of Vatican II about Mary and the Church in the context of LG. The following outline is a synopsis of the document as a whole:

T			ch. 1: Church as mystery
H	as it *is*	in its *totality*	ch. 2: Church as People of God
E			ch. 3: Hierarchy
C		in its *parts*	ch. 4: Laity
H			ch. 5: Universal call to holiness
U			
R		in *pilgrimage*	ch. 6: Religious
C	as it is *called*		
H	*to be* HOLY		ch. 7: Church's eschatological nature
		in *consummation*	ch. 8: Mary, archetype of the Church

As the concluding chapter of LG, therefore, the main teaching of the council (or its *magna carta* as it has been called) about Mary enters the picture in the context of the mystery of the Church as called to share in the perfect holiness of Jesus Christ and the triune God in heaven. In a certain sense the Church has already reached this perfection in the glorious assumption of our Blessed Mother who is the "sign of certain hope and comfort for the pilgrim People of God" (LG 68) or for all of us upon earth who are still striving to share in the glory of our risen Lord through the glorious resurrection of our own bodies. And so it is of the utmost importance that we study LG as a whole, especially chapter five on the call of us all to holiness and chapter seven on the Church's eschatological nature or our intimate relationship with the heavenly Church, if we are to grasp the meaning of Mary's relationship to us in the pilgrim Church on earth as well as to the dearly departed souls in purgatory.

Chapter eight of LG, "The Blessed Virgin Mary, God-Bearer, in the Mystery of Christ and of the Church," is itself divided into the following sections: (1) Preface (52–4), which considers Mary's relation to Christ in the divine plan of the redemptive incarnation (52), Mary's place in the Church closest to God and to us after Christ (53), and the declaration of the council's intention to describe Mary's role in the mystery of the Incarnate Word (55–9) and of the Church (60–5), as well as our duties to her as Mother of Christ and of the human race (66–7) without attempting to give a complete doctrine on Mary; (2) The Role of the Blessed Virgin in the Economy of Salvation (55–9), contemplating how it was foretold in the Old Testament (55), how Mary accepted the calling to be the Mother of God's Son incarnate at the annunciation (56), how Mary was united to her Son in his work on earth from the virginal conception to his death in the hidden life (57) and his public ministry (58), as well as after his ascension into heaven (59); (3) The Blessed Virgin and the Church (60–5), reflecting upon her effective salutary influence on the Church or her maternal intercession and care (60–2) and her exemplarity as type and model of the Church (63–5); (4) Devotion to the Blessed Virgin in the Church (66–7), teaching about the Church's special veneration of Mary (66) and the practical norms for a true devotion to her (67); and (5) Epilogue: Mary, Sure Sign of Hope and Solace for the Pilgrim People of God, proclaiming her as the gloriously assumed body and soul in heaven to be the beginning of the Church as it will be on the Lord's day or Second Coming of Christ (68) and concluding with the prayer that Mary intercede for the entire People of God (69).

Much of what has been outlined here concerning the contents of Vatican II's Marian doctrine about the mystery of Mary and the Church as well as about authentic devotion to her will be discussed in the following sections of this essay. Suffice it to point out here that the title "Mother of the Church" for Mary was proclaimed by Pope Paul VI in his closing address to the third session of Vatican II on November 21, 1964. He had received numerous requests from the conciliar fathers that the maternal role of the Blessed Virgin Mary be given very special attention. In proclaiming Mary "Mother of the Church," Pope Paul VI carefully pointed out the close connection between Mary's motherhood of Christ and her maternal relationship to the Church:

> Mary is the Mother of Christ who, as soon as he assumed human nature in her virginal womb, took to himself as Head his Mystical Body, which is the Church. Mary, therefore, as Mother of Christ is to be considered as Mother also of all the faithful and pastors, that is of the Church.

This title was received by the majority of the conciliar fathers with joyous approval even though it did not appear in LG 8 since the theological commission decided that it was better to express its meaning in equivalent terms: "The Catholic Church, taught by the Holy Spirit, honors her with filial affection and devotion as a most beloved mother" (LG 53).

Mary and the Church in the Revelation of the New Testament

With the teaching of Vatican II as our guide, let us now glance at some significant passages in the New Testament, particularly at Luke/ Acts and the Johannine Writings, to gain a clearer understanding of the scriptural basis for contemporary Catholic Marian doctrine and devotion.[1] The composite picture of Mary revealed in the New Testament is both christocentric ("Mother of God's Son Incarnate) and ecclesiotypical ("Mary as the Perfect Disciple of Christ," i.e., the most excellent example or the archetype of belonging to his body the Church). While the Gospels according to Mark and Matthew seem to be mainly concerned with the christocentric emphasis, Luke's Gospel, including his reference in Acts 1:14, where Mary is at the center of the believing community persevering with one mind in prayer awaiting Pentecost nicely combines both emphases. John's Gospel, on the other hand, along with Revelation 12, seems mainly interested in portraying the ecclesiotypical

[1] Raymond E. Brown et al., eds., *Mary in the New Testament* (New York/Mahwah, N.J.: Paulist Press, 1978); Frederick M. Jelly, *Madonna: Mary in the Catholic Tradition* (Huntington, Ind.: Our Sunday Visitor, 1986) 26–68.

emphasis with his "woman at Cana," "woman at the foot of the cross," and "woman clothed in the Sun." For the purposes of this essay, we shall focus our attention upon Luke/Acts and the Gospel and book of Revelation attributed to John the apostle and evangelist. Even though neither had that much to say about Mary in terms of length, what they did write as inspired Scripture has had a profound influence upon developments regarding Mary in the Catholic tradition right up to our own time as we begin the third millennium or celebrate the two-thousandth birthday of Mary's Son.[2]

First of all, let us recall that there were three stages in the formation of the four Gospels: (1) the historic deeds and words that formed the basis of the narrative in each account of the Good News; (2) the oral traditions about these events based upon the interpretations of the early Christians, especially by the apostolic preaching some of which found its way into fragmentary writings; and (3) the third and final stage as the work of the four evangelists who were special individuals called to become a part of the process of selecting those words and deeds of the Lord and his closest disciples, including Mary, that were discerned as having the utmost importance for their spiritual lives and ministries. These four accounts are called the final redaction of the previous stages and are handed down to us in the Church as part of the canon or inspired books of the New Testament. As believers in the Catholic tradition, we are called to preserve and nourish our faith in finding the sources about Mary or any other Christian mystery in these inspired Gospels.

Each one of the four Gospels gives us a distinctive portrait of Christ, of Mary, of the twelve apostles, and any of the prominent personalities in their narratives according to the special theological purpose of each evangelist. It is well to note that there is a basic unity amidst this diversity so that the various images do not conflict with each other but are complementary in conveying the infinite richness of the revealed mysteries that are expressed. We should also be aware of the fact that the Gospels are not primarily apologetic documents inspired to be written in order to make converts to Christianity from the Jews and pagan Gentiles, but are confessional documents composed by men of faith to nourish the faith of Christian believers or members of the apostolic Church. Luke was inspired to write primarily for Gentile converts to Christianity in order to deepen their conviction that the salvation of all is centered upon Christ, seen in relationship to the triune God's merciful love for his people in the past and to what he continues to accomplish through his Holy Spirit in the Church. Luke/Acts attributes to

---

[2] Jelly, *Madonna*, 69–147.

Mary a very special role in God's loving plan of universal salvation. Other theological themes of these two New Testament books are the favored place of women, the joy of those who hear the word of God and keep it, the demands of discipleship, the blessedness of the poor, the spirit of prayer, and the Good News about the Pentecostal Spirit in the Church. And all these themes embellish his portrait of the Madonna. Luke's infancy narrative is a good illustration of the close continuity between the Gospel and Acts which constitute more a single volume rather than two books. The first two chapters of each parallel the birth of Christ and the birth of the Church. What the Holy Spirit accomplished definitively in Christ is continued until the end of time through his active presence in the Church for the salvation of the world. We shall consider this in some detail at the conclusion of our summary of Mary in Luke's Gospel and in Acts.

Let us begin with a meditation upon the annunciation scene in Luke's infancy narrative (1:26-38), the first joyful mystery of Mary's Rosary. In their pastoral letter on Mary, *Behold Your Mother—Woman of Faith* (BYM), our American Bishops teach: "The chapter on Mary in the Dogmatic Constitution on the Church may be regarded as an extended commentary on her consent at the Annunciation" (BYM 28). The literary structure of the dialogue between Gabriel and Mary is based upon the annunciation patterns of the Old Testament and was already used by Luke in the angelic annunciation to Zechariah about the birth of John the Baptizer (1:11-20) as well as by Matthew in the message of the angel of the Lord to Joseph in a dream (1:20ff.). Parallels in the Old Testament are the messages delivered to Hagar (Gen 16:7-15), to the wife of Manaoh (Judg 13:3-20), and to Gideon (Judg 6:1-24). The basic pattern is: (1) the appearance of an angel of the Lord or the Lord himself since God always takes the initiative in the dialogue; (2) a reaction of fear, which is sometimes met with "Do not be afraid"; (3) an announcement about the birth of a son; (4) an objection or a difficulty raised by the recipient of the announcement; and (5) the giving of a sign to reassure the recipient, who accepts the message with enough understanding before the episode ends.

Gabriel's greeting to Mary, "Hail, full of grace," may also be translated, "Hail, favored one!" (Luke 1:28). The latter translation brings out more clearly the great joy prophetically promised to the "Daughter of Sion" (Zeph 3:14-17), and also the fact that Mary's great holiness is the fruit of God's special love freely bestowed upon her. But how could Mary possibly be "greatly troubled" over such a greeting of joy and hope? She is perplexed because it has not yet been revealed to her why she has been so fully favored by God. Immediately Gabriel reassures her and announces God's special calling, her unique vocation in salvation history to be the mother of the Son of the Most High (see Isa 9:6). Depending upon her free and willing acceptance of this divine calling, God will make his own Son hers also if she utters her *fiat,* her "yes." At this point in the annunciation pattern, Mary brings up a difficulty in her dialogue with Gabriel: "How can this be, since I have no relations with a man?" (Luke 1:34). This question must not be misinterpreted as a negative reply from Mary, but as the reasonable question of an intelligent believer. Apparently her "yes" to Gabriel would mean that she would be with child at once, which was naturally impossible in the circumstances since she and Joseph, her betrothed, had not yet come together. This inquiry by Mary set the stage for Gabriel's revelation of the virginal conception: "The holy Spirit will come upon you, and the power of the Most High will overshadow you. Therefore the child to be born will be called holy, the Son of God" (Luke 1:35).

It is helpful to note here that the language in which Luke has Gabriel reveal how the child is to be conceived by the power of the Holy Spirit has come to be called "conception christology" in the New Testament. It is an expression of the faith of the Church after the resurrection that Jesus Christ was truly divine as well as really human from the first instant of his conception in Mary's virginal womb. This will prove to be an important New Testament basis for the definition of the dogma that Mary is *Theotokos* or God-Bearer at the Ecumenical Council of Ephesus (431).

The annunciation episode comes toward a conclusion with the sign given by the angel of the Lord to Mary. Appropriately that sign was the pregnancy of Mary's older relative Elizabeth who was considered to be sterile. She has come to be with child, "for nothing will be impossible for God" (Luke 1:37). How fitting that the sign points to the conception of John the Baptizer called to be the forerunner of the Messiah! Also our American Bishops remind us: "When Abraham was told that Isaac was to be born, God strengthened him with the reminder that all things are possible to God (Gen. 18:14)" (BYM 32). Mary, the "Daughter of Abraham," our father in faith, is about to become our mother in faith. Mary's response to the heavenly messenger is really a reply to God's calling: "Behold, I am the handmaid of the Lord. May it be done to me according to your word" (Luke 1:38). And thus Luke introduces Mary to us as the very first to hear the Good News, and the foremost disciple in believing it and carrying out her ministry of sharing her Son with all who also believe it.

Now let us turn to the second joyful mystery of Mary's Rosary, the Visitation when Mary "traveled to the hill country in haste" to help Elizabeth prepare for the birth of John the Baptizer (1:39-45). She walked the four-day journey from Nazareth as impelled by the Spirit to bring the child Jesus in her own womb to sanctify the child conceived in Elizabeth, who bore witness that he "leaped for joy" when she heard Mary's greeting. She humbly praises the faith of her younger kinswoman who is the mother of her Lord, and acknowledges her unworthiness to receive her as a guest in her home. What an inspiration it is to ponder the joyful encounter between these two holy women of God! How can anyone believe this joyful mystery and not be "pro-life" in favor of the dignity and rights of the preborn child created to the image and likeness of the Holy Trinity and recreated or redeemed by Jesus Christ?

Luke has his Madonna respond to the praise and blessing of her older relative, singing in her Magnificat that all the glory is due to God (1:46-45). This canticle has been sung daily over the centuries in the tradition during evening prayer of the Church's Liturgy of the Hours. Mary begins her song of true liberation or authentic redemption by joyfully praising and thanking God for blessing her, and through her, all of Israel (1:46-50). The second half of the canticle switches from what God has accomplished for Mary, the individual person, to his mighty deeds on behalf of all his people through her (1:51-55). Mary's Magnificat places her on the boundary of the Old Testament and the New Testament. Summing up and surpassing the best of the old, and anticipating the greatest of the New, she represents the *Anawim* or "poor of Yahweh" who completely rely upon the saving power of God and not on one's own resources.

In the third joyful mystery, the birth of Christ, we behold once again the theme of lowliness and poverty surrounding the entire life of Christ and those closest to him as his mother. According to early tradition Jesus was born in a cave, perhaps one used as a stable portrayed by the Christmas crib. Appropriately enough in the Gospel of Luke poor shepherds nearby hear about the Good News of Christ's birth first through the message of an angel (2:9-12). Luke points out that "Mary kept all these things, reflecting on them in her heart" (2:19) when the shepherds came to pay homage to her child and then shared the glad tidings of great joy with others. Here we behold the Lukan Madonna as the perfect disciple in her contemplative character as she ponders over and over again the mystery of her Son unfolding before her. We might say that this was Mary's "Rosary" coming to be as she meditated upon the mighty deeds of our salvation in the events of Christ's life from the joyful mysteries through the sorrowful unto the glorious.

As we meditate *with* Mary as well as *about* her in the fourth joyful mystery, the presentation of Jesus in the Temple, we receive a prophetic premonition of the sorrowful mysteries that lie ahead from the words of Simeon to Mary: "Behold, this child is destined for the fall and rise of many in Israel, and to be a sign that will be contradicted (and you your-self a sword will pierce) so that the thoughts of many hearts may be re-vealed" (2:34-35). One interpretation of these words that seems most acceptable in light of recent biblical scholarship may be summarized in this way. The basic reason why Mary's Son "is destined for the fall and rise of many in Israel" is that his preaching, teaching, and whole way of life will demand a decision. No one can remain neutral before him, but must either accept or reject his calling. This will mean suffering for all involved: for Jesus, the Suffering Servant of Yahweh; for Mary, both as an individual who must pay the price of discipleship, and as the "Daughter of Sion" representing all of Israel which will be divided by the sword of God passing through the land (see Ezek 14:17). For Luke, it seems that the "sword" is the revealing word of God which chal-lenges all to make a decision for or against Mary's Son and which di-vides the wicked from the faithful remnant. At the same time this interpretation can include Mary's heart, the heart of a mother who pon-dered her mysterious Son over and over again and which would be so deeply wounded by his suffering.

The fifth joyful mystery, the finding of Jesus in the Temple, is a fur-ther revelation of the sacrifices that Mary would be called upon to make if she is to be his disciple as well as his natural mother. When Mary said, "Son, why have you done this to us? Your father and I have been looking for you with great anxiety," how are we to understand Jesus' pronouncement in his reply: "Why were you looking for me? Did you not know that I must be in my Father's house?" (2:48-49). If it is a rebuke at all, I do not believe that it was a sharp one. Luke sees fit to tell us once more that "his mother kept all these things in her heart" (2:51) after pointing out that his parents did not understand him (2:50). Their closeness to Christ and holiness did not exempt them from walk-ing by faith with all of its obscurity amidst the light of believing. In fact, one who is called to live so profoundly in divine mystery, as were Mary and Joseph, is called to a deeper faith. They had to learn how to "let go" so that their child could carry out his messianic mission according to the will of his heavenly Father. And yet they would continue to carry out their own calling of being his parents to whom he would be subject until the start of his public ministry.

Luke is the only evangelist to narrate the following incident during the public ministry of Jesus: "While he was speaking, a woman from the crowd called out and said to him, 'Blessed is the womb that carried you and the breasts at which you nursed.' He replied, 'Rather, blessed are those who hear the word of God and observe it'" (11:27-28). Is Jesus here in any way refusing to accept the woman's great praise of his mother? The translation "rather" which is usually an adversative in our idiom can be misleading in making the proper interpretation of this text. Perhaps a clearer word to translate the New Testament Greek would be "moreover," so that the sense of Christ's reply to the woman might be something like this paraphrase: "Yes, but let me tell you why my mother is so deserving of your praise. Of all my disciples she has heard the word of my heavenly Father most prayerfully and has kept it most carefully." For Luke, apparently, it would be inconceivable that Mary be the mother of the Messiah without also being his perfect disciple, the model of his Church.

Now we arrive at the last mention of Mary in Luke/Acts: "All these devoted themselves with one accord to prayer, together with the women, and Mary the mother of Jesus, and his brothers" (Acts 1:14). Luke's portrait of Mary as the perfect disciple is now completed. From the annunciation at her home in Nazareth to the upper room or cenacle in Jerusalem, Mary's spiritual journey has been a "pilgrimage of faith" (LG 58). In the midst of her Son's Church about to be born of the Holy Spirit on that first Pentecost, she was leading her fellow disciples in prayerful preparation. There seems to be a certain parallelism between the birth of Christ in the infancy narrative of Luke's Gospel and the birth of his Mystical Body the Church in Acts 1–2. This must be more than a mere coincidence because Luke evidently was convinced that the life of Christ was incomplete without the story of his Church to continue his mission until the end of time. It has been proposed, therefore, that there is a special relationship between Mary and the Holy Spirit according to both accounts. In the Gospel at the annunciation the Holy Spirit comes upon Mary and inspires her to visit Elizabeth and to sing the Magnificat during the visitation. What the Holy Spirit did for Mary alone according to Luke's Gospel, that same Spirit accomplished for her together with her Son's nascent Church on Pentecost. The Holy Spirit came upon Mary and all of the disciples of Christ in the upper room in the form of tongues of fire, inspiring them to sing out in praise with the gift of tongues and moved them, particularly Peter, to preach the Good News that would reach the very ends of the earth. The Mariology inspired by Luke/Acts carefully contemplates Mary as both christocentric and ecclesiotypical, since her unique relationship with Christ as his mother has united her intimately with us as mother of the Church.

At this point we turn to consider very briefly the New Testament revelation regarding Mary and the Church in the Johannine Writings of the Fourth Gospel and the book of Revelation. Most likely composed sometime after 85 C.E., it presupposes both the Synoptic tradition of Mark, Matthew, and Luke/Acts and a Christian audience able to reflect upon that tradition for a generation. Consequently, he could choose from the events of the life of Christ already familiar to his hearers and interpret them in accord with his own special theological purposes. He seems to have written primarily for a community of Christians who were deeply rooted in the Jewish traditions of liturgical feasts. The Gospel attributed to John is profoundly ecclesiological, showing that the kingdom of God initiated by Christ finds its realization upon earth in the Church. Whether or not the evangelist is to be identified with the apostle John, that member of the Twelve seems to have had a definite influence upon it, the three epistles, and the book of Revelation that constitute the Johannine corpus in the New Testament. He wishes to convince the Christian hearers of his message that the spiritual realities experienced by the disciples of Christ during his time on earth are to be found in the Church. And so his Gospel message is also deeply sacramental, particularly in reference to baptism and the Eucharist, as we are about to see in the Cana scene.

This introductory episode of the wedding feast at Cana (John 2:1-11) is rich in symbolism which is characteristic of the Fourth Gospel as a whole. In fact there seem to be several layers of meaning in his symbols helping his hearers to penetrate to the divine intention behind the historical events in the messianic mission of Christ. Of course this fact may be seen especially in the Book of Signs or chs. 1–12 (1:19–12:50) of the Fourth Gospel in which he calls "signs" what the Synoptics name "miracles." Thus he concludes his narrative about the wedding feast at Cana with: "Jesus did this as the beginning of his signs in Cana in Galilee and so revealed his glory, and his disciples began to believe in him" (2:11). For John the miraculous works of Christ were more than manifestations of the divine power acting through him. They were signs or symbols of spiritual realities given through him during his ministry on earth, and also given to the members of his Church through that same faith in the risen Lord who sends them his Holy Spirit.

Let us keep these comments in mind as we interpret the special role of Mary in her encounter with her Son at the wedding feast of Cana. When she informs him "they have no wine," apparently with the wish that he will do something about the embarrassing situation, Jesus does not seem to want to satisfy her seeking a sign from him. In fact his reply comes across to us as definitely a refusal: "Woman, how does your concern affect me? My hour has not yet come" (John 2:4). We must grasp the Johannine symbol of his "hour" before interpreting this passage, particularly what it symbolizes about Mary. It really symbolizes the "hour" of his suffering and death upon the cross, or the hour of his glorification, according to John's "theology of the cross," when the Father accepts his Son's perfect sacrifice of atonement for our sins, and glorifies his human nature and sends the Pentecostal Spirit to give birth to the body of Christ, the Church. Only then will the glory of our Lord and Savior be fully revealed. But at his mother's request of faith in him he will anticipate that final revelation of his glory on the cross by manifesting a glimpse of it in the sign of changing water into wine through which his first disciples began to believe in him. As in the case of each sign Christ works the miraculous deed in response to a faith that is confirmed and deepened by the sign. This prepares for the perfect faith in him revealed in the "Book of Exaltation" (13:1–20:31) when his glorification on Calvary, which includes the entire paschal mystery of passion, death, resurrection, ascension, and sending of the Pentecostal Spirit, will be accomplished according to John's Gospel. At the same time as responding to his mother's faith in him, he also reveals to her that this is the time of beginning his public ministry when his relationship to the Father and the accomplishment of his will by redeeming us must take precedence over everything else including his relationship to her as his natural mother, that the family of his disciples has priority over the natural family. Bearing all this in mind, we might distinguish at least three layers of symbolism in the sign of his changing the water into wine: (1) the transformation of the "water" of the Jewish rites of purification to represent ancient Israel into the "wine" of the New Israel or the Church which is an ecclesial symbolism; (2) a sacramental symbolism of the new creation in the "wine" of the Eucharist as a fulfillment of the many prophetic types and figures of the Messiah in the Old Testament by the Real Presence of Christ himself; and (3) a Marian symbolism in which Mary herself is changed from a type of the synagogue, the daughter of ancient Sion, into a figure of the Church, the new People of God (see BYM 36). The polyvalent symbolism of the sign at Cana, therefore, is a rich source in the New Testament revelation of the developments in the Catholic tradition that have come to contemplate in faith the close relationship between Mary and the Church.

The "woman at Cana" must be interpreted in the context of the "woman at the foot of the cross." The key text is: "When Jesus saw his mother and the disciple there whom he loved, he said to his mother, 'Woman, behold your son.' Then he said to the disciple, 'Behold, your mother.' And from that hour the disciple took her into his home" (John 19:26-27). In the setting of John's Gospel as a literary whole, Mary and the beloved disciple represent perfect faith in Jesus who is much more than a miracle worker, but is the risen Lord who continuously, with the Father, sends the Holy Spirit to animate his Mystical Body the Church. The symbolism of the scene extends well beyond the wish of Jesus that the beloved disciple look after his mother as her only child about to die. According to the evangelist they are indeed models of the perfect faith that the Lord wills for all the members of his Church and for the apostolic

Johannine community in particular. Since the symbolism of the Fourth Gospel seems to have had a profound influence upon the developments of Marian doctrine and devotion in the Catholic tradition, we may also reflect that the emphasis on the disciple-son's care of the disciple-mother has shifted in that tradition to Mary's care of "him" and all of us faithful disciples in the Church represented by him. This has become a biblical basis for her title "Mother of the Church," and of her "spiritual motherhood" of us all "in the order of grace" (see LG 61, 62) so clearly taught by Vatican II in explaining her role of heavenly intercession and mediation of her Son's saving grace.

As a very brief final reflection in this section on the New Testament revelation regarding Mary, let us turn to "the woman clothed in the Sun" found in Revelation 12. There we read: "A great sign appeared in the sky, a woman clothed with the sun, with the moon under her feet, and on her head a crown of twelve stars. She was with child and wailed aloud in pain as she labored to give birth" (12:1-2). Most likely the story of how the dragon was unable to destroy the child of the woman indicates that the primary symbolism of "woman" here personifies both ancient Israel, the Church of Christ coming to be during the Old Covenant, and the new Israel, that very Church of the New Covenant after the birth of the messianic child. This does allow, however, for a secondary symbolism in reference to Mary. Here, in the wider canonical context of the "woman at Cana" and the "woman at the foot of the cross," the "woman clothed with the sun" can be extended to embrace Mary precisely as she is a corporate personality representing the holy mother the Church.

Mary and the Church in the Dogmatic Developments of the Catholic Tradition

After the New Testament portraits of Mary, the earliest image of the Mother of Christ and his Church is the "New Eve" or the "Second Eve." It draws a comparison between Mary and Eve, Adam's "helpmate" (Gen 2:18) and the "mother of all the living" (Gen 3:20). In fact, it is more a contrast than a comparison which emerged from the woman at Cana, on Calvary, and clothed with the sun in the Johannine Writings of the New Testament, and has come to be called an "antithetical parallelism" since what distinguishes Mary and Eve is more significant than whatever similarities there were between them. At the time of the temptation in the Garden of Eden (Genesis 3) and of the annunciation at Nazareth, both were virgins. However, that image is far outweighed by the fact that Eve's unbelief and disobedience succumbed to the fallen angel's (serpent's) temptation, while Mary's faith and obedience inspired her to say "yes" to God's word as communicated to her by the good angel. In recent years this symbolism or typology has shed considerable light upon the Mary-Church analogy as we have seen in the ecclesiotypical Mariology of Vatican II: "For in the mystery of the Church, which is itself rightly called mother and virgin, the Blessed Virgin stands out in eminent and singular fashion as exemplar of both virgin and mother" (LG 63). The teaching of our American Bishops adds: "Even more anciently, the Church was regarded as the 'New Eve.' The Church is the bride of Christ, formed from his side in the sleep of death on the cross, as the first Eve was formed by God from the side of the sleeping Adam" (BYM 41). As Cardinal König pointed out in his debate with Cardinal Santos on the council floor, the U.S. bishops teach that gradually some of the motherly characteristics of the Church were seen in Mary.

The three ancient writers who gave the earliest testimony to the Eve-Mary typology are St. Justin Martyr (d. ca. 165), St. Irenaeus (d. after 193), and Tertullian (d. after 220). Their writings together form a witness to the faith of the universal Church concerning Mary during the latter part of the second century. St. Irenaeus developed it in greatest detail in his polemical work *Against Heresies,* particularly the Gnostic Marcionites, who held that the Old Testament was the product of the devil. He defended the basic unity of salvation history principally by his meditation on the Bible, showing that the evil perpetrated by the serpent-devil, Eve, Adam, and the tree of the knowledge of good and evil in the Fall, was undone at the annunciation by the good of the archangel Gabriel, Mary, and Christ the New Adam (as St. Paul called him in Romans 5), who overcame sin on the tree of the cross. This Eve-Mary typology is still current in the Church's tradition as indeed indicated by the Marian teaching of Vatican II following upon its brilliant usage in the writings of Cardinal Newman.

This most ancient image of Mary after the New Testament revelation leads us into a summary of the development of the dogma of her virginity in the tradition. There are three aspects to this mystery: (1) her virginal conception of Christ by the power of the Holy Spirit at the annunciation, often referred to as the "virgin birth," (2) her virginal parturition, or remaining a virgin in bearing Christ on the first Christmas in the stable cave, (3) and her perpetual virginity, or remaining a virgin for her entire life. Certainly the virginal conception and the virginal parturition are clearly revealed by Matthew and Luke in the infancy narratives of their Gospels. Patristic witness to Mary's virginal conception of Christ came as early as the Apostolic Father, the martyr St. Ignatius of Antioch (d. ca. 110). The Fathers of the Church and other ancient Christian writers such as those who used the New Eve typology also gave early and decisive testimony to this truth in the tradition. The aspect of the virginal parturition developed more slowly since it seemed to give some basis to the heresy of those Gnostics who were Docetists in holding that Christ did not really become one of us in the incarnation. They considered all matter, including human flesh, to be unworthy of God, so they considered him to appear to have a body but really be a phantom who passed through Mary's womb as though it were a tunnel. But gradually her virginal parturition came to be held as a matter of faith by the Fathers of the Church. Those in the West emphasized their understanding of the mystery as the infant Jesus passing from Mary's womb as he did through the rock of the enclosed tomb at his resurrection. The Fathers of the Eastern Church, on the other hand, emphasized its meaning as the indescribable joy of Mary in giving birth to the Son of God made flesh through her. Since the revealing word of God does not seem to deal with such matters as genetic details, I prefer the approach of interpreting this aspect of Mary's virginity in accord with the Eastern Fathers so that the rhetoric of the Western Fathers need not be understood literally. She is the woman who brought forth the child on that first Christmas filled with the messianic joy of her faith. Frequently the Fathers of the Church were fond of saying that she conceived Christ in her heart through faith before doing so physically in her womb. Belief in her perpetual virginity in the tradition of the Church coincided with the call of the Holy Spirit to consecrate oneself to a life of virginity for the sake of the kingdom of God, thus becoming an expression of the Church as the bride of the risen Lord.

Even though the New Testament revelation makes reference to the "brothers" and "sisters" of the Lord (see Mark 6:3), St. Jerome, the outstanding authority on the sacred Scriptures among the Fathers and Doctors of the Church (ca. 347–420), refuted those who misinterpreted such New Testament texts as referring to blood brothers and sisters of Jesus as other children of Mary and Joseph born in the natural way, showing that they were cousins of the Lord. According to a current hypothesis they were probably cousins who were raised with Jesus at Nazareth, perhaps the children of Joseph's widowed sister. The expression that Mary is "ever-virgin" became very popular after the middle of the fourth century and has been used traditionally in the Roman Canon or first Eucharistic Prayer.

Throughout the Catholic tradition the reasons of theological fittingness for Mary's virginity from SS Augustine through Thomas Aquinas until today have never been based upon any attitude of negativity toward the sexual expression of conjugal love between spouses in marriage. On the contrary, they have been founded upon such reasons as asserting that, if Joseph had been the natural father of Jesus, the fact that he has only one Father, the First Person of the most Holy Trinity, would have been obscured, which is intimately connected with the mystery of the incarnation. Similarly Mary's perpetual virginity is appropriately associated with her calling to be the archetype of the Church who is also a virginal mother in her spiritual generation of the members of Christ's body through baptism and her ministries of word and sacrament generally.

Now let us trace the development of the dogma about Mary as *Theotokos* or the birth-giver of God. This is her most glorious title that relates her uniquely and most intimately to Christ and his Church. Its use goes back as early as the Council of Nicea (325) and probably even a century before that, as evidenced by the most ancient prayer to Mary, "We fly to thy protection," still popular in our own time among the faithful. The name seems to have developed from two New Testament christologies: the "conception christology" found in the annunciation according to Luke and the "preexistence christology" most clearly revealed in the prologue of John's Gospel where Christ as the Word was explicitly called "God" from all eternity who became flesh of Mary in time. So, even though it is not a New Testament term as such, *Theotokos* or God-bearer as a name of Mary is firmly rooted in the Gospel. Historically it became necessary to define it as a matter of divine revelation and so of faith because Nestorius, who was made the patriarch of Constantinople in 428, rejected its usage since it seemed to make a goddess out of the Mother of Jesus. His heresy was essentially christological since he thereby denied that Christ was divine as well as human from the first instant of the incarnation or of his conception in Mary's virginal womb. The conciliar fathers at the ecumenical council held in Ephesus (modern Turkey) during 431 were mainly concerned with safeguarding the revealed truth about the mystery of Jesus Christ who was always true God and true man. In order to accomplish this, it was necessary to defend this title of Mary as truly the Mother of God, a mystery that we celebrate today on January 1, the octave of Christmas Day, which is the restoration of an ancient feast in the early tradition. In his *Summa Theologiae*, St. Thomas Aquinas explains in what sense Mary is truly the Mother of God, and not just in some metaphorical sense. As a theologian, he reasons in the light of divine faith that, since motherhood is predicated of the woman who conceives and bears a child as a person, and because the person conceived and born of Mary is none other than the Second Person of the blessed Trinity or the Son and Word of God made flesh of her, then she is really and truly the mother of a divine person in his human flesh as true man (*ST* III, q. 35, a. 4).

The other two Marian dogmas, her Immaculate Conception and glorious assumption body and soul into heaven, took a long time to develop in our Catholic tradition. They are to be understood in close connection with the dogmas of her virginity and motherhood of God. Neither one can be found as explicitly revealed in sacred Scripture. Their dogmatic development, however, is to be considered in light of certain insinuations divinely inspired in the Scriptures. In the setting of the hierarchy of truths (see Vatican II's Decree on Ecumenism, 11), the Immaculate Conception according to which Mary was preserved from original sin by reason of the foreseen merits of her Son's redemption links that dogma with the central truths of incarnation and redemption, since it made Mary a worthy mother of God, thanks to her Son's saving grace. In our relatively detailed exegesis of Luke's account of the annunciation, we saw that Gabriel's greeting of her as "full of grace" was proven to be a suggestion in the inspired word of God which led gradually through the New Eve image to its fuller meaning *(sensus plenior)* in the tradition, especially by the devotion of the faithful celebrated in the liturgy, to its dogmatic definition by Pope Pius IX in 1854. Similarly the dogmatic definition of her glorious assumption by Pope Pius XII in 1950 sprang gradually from the same biblical sources that helped inspire the New Eve typology. How fitting that she who was closely associated with Christ in his redemptive activity of overcoming sin and death for the human race was the first to receive the fruits of his redeeming love by being preserved from all sin, original and actual or personal, as well as from the power of death insofar as we firmly believe that she has been perfectly reunited with her Son the risen Lord and does not have to await the resurrection of the glorified body on the Day of Judgment.

Pope Pius XII left open the question of whether or not Mary actually died before being taken up body and soul or was taken into heaven in her complete human personhood. And so theologians are still free to discuss the matter. The stronger tradition has been that she did experience death, certainly not as a result of sin but as a condition of passing over to an entirely transformed way of living beyond space and time. Even in a general survey of Mary and the Church such as this essay, it is significant that we know just what we are committed to believe as revealed truth with our divine Catholic faith and how the dogmas should influence our own spiritual lives as disciples of Christ in our own day and culture. Even the unique privilege of Mary's Immaculate Conception contains a profound meaning for us sinners. It helps impress upon us that, even though we have been conceived in original sin, we are born into a world where grace has priority over guilt and the mystery of good is infinitely more powerful than that of evil. Thanks to the grace of Mary's Son we begin to share in his life through the saving waters of baptism. Then like our spiritual mother Mary we become what Christ is by nature, the adopted children of the heavenly Father. Unlike Mary we remain wounded by the consequences of original sin, particularly tempted by the unruly passions of concupiscence. She alone among all of us redeemed was a completely undivided personality, totally uninhibited in her love of God and neighbor. But one day we sinners in the Pilgrim Church upon earth hope to be completely victorious over sin and death in heaven through the special intercession of our gloriously assumed mother Mary who continuously mediates to us her Son's saving grace.

Contemporary Characteristics of Marian Doctrine and Devotion

In this very short section of the essay, we might do well to summarize some of the points already mentioned and reflect upon them a bit.[3] This will be done mainly by commenting upon the distinguishing features characterizing teaching about Mary and devotion to her during our own time as we enter the third millennium or twenty-first century celebrating the two-thousandth anniversary of the birth of Christ. As this essay has shown, contemporary Mariology may be described as biblical, patristic, and liturgical in its sources. The magisterial teaching of Vatican II as well as postconciliar documents such as Paul VI's apostolic exhortation on renewing devotion to Mary (1974), John Paul II's encyclical letter for the Marian Year, Mother of the Redeemer, and our American Bishops' pastoral letter (1973), all start with the biblical portrait of Mary. Unlike a tendency of the past when Mariologists too often searched for "proof texts" to show the foundations for Marian doctrines, in more recent years the Scriptures are listened to attentively as speaking for themselves. Likewise the writings of the Fathers of the Church as the pioneers of bearing witness to the apostolic faith and of developing it in the Catholic tradition have come to be interpreted in their proper context. They indeed preached and taught the fundamentals of our faith with great fidelity to the Scriptures and the apostolic traditions. And, although their testimony to the development of the Marian dogmas of faith and other doctrines about her as well as the proper devotion due to her in the Church took place quite gradually, it did provide a solid foundation for the doctrines and piety that eventually emerged over the centuries. Their presentation of Mary was particularly as the

[3] Jelly, *Madonna*, 1–18, 148–203.

woman of faith and perfect disciple of her Son in complete accord with the New Testament revelation. As a source, the liturgy has been especially effective and influential in the development of Marian dogmas. The sense of the faithful was manifested most consistently in the liturgical worship of the Church, e.g., the ancient feast of Mary's dormition gradually led to the celebration of her glorious assumption body and soul into heaven.

Two of three other characteristics of contemporary Mariology, namely christocentric and ecclesiotypical, have already been sufficiently considered in this essay. The third is pneumatological or more intimately relating Mary to the Holy Spirit, which is a more recent characteristic in the Western Church where it still requires much more development in terms of presenting the content about Mary. While the teaching of Vatican II on Mary and the Church did much to relate Mariology with christology and ecclesiology, it only launched us in the right direction of relating Mary more intimately to the Holy Spirit. We are in a much better position to see her as the masterpiece of the new creation in the Spirit. There will be a few more comments on this matter in the concluding section of this essay about future prospects.

The third and final set of three characteristics have to do with the effects of Marian doctrine and devotion in our time. They are spiritual, pastoral, and ecumenical. As with any part of theology, if its implications for and applications to the spiritual life of members of the Church are neglected, it is incomplete and truncated even as an intellectual discipline. This is especially true of Mariology, where all the truths of our faith about Mary are designed to inspire a deeper devotion to her and through it a more faithful following of her Son. This has really always been a Catholic conviction, even if at times it was not implemented in a very balanced way in practice. The characteristic of a more pastoral Mariology may be seen in the spirit of her Magnificat or song of true liberation from the slavery of sinful injustice. Like her Son, Mary's spirit was always one of serving others whether at the visitation or at Cana or as spiritual mother in the cenacle at Pentecost. Finally, the ecumenical character of contemporary Marian doctrine and devotion has been shown in the fact that the Church-dividing issues regarding Mary have become an important part of the dialogues between the Roman Catholic and other Christian communions. In particular her mediation has been clarified so as not to be misconstrued as interfering with the unique mediatorship of Christ, the sole mediator of redemption, but as enhancing it through the mediation of her intercession on our behalf along with that of all the saints in heaven.

Mary and the Church in the
Prospects of Future Progress[4]

Ecumenically there still remains much further dialogue leading toward consensus concerning the development of the Marian dogmas of the Immaculate Conception and assumption. This will require more conversation with the other churches and ecclesial communions about the organic and interdependent relationship between Scripture and tradition in face of the *sola scriptura* principle of the Protestant Reformation. Similarly, the Catholic devotional practices of invoking the saints and Mary must be more clearly manifested as not really opposed to the *solus Christus* principle according to which Christ alone is the mediator of the triune God's redeeming love for us. Nor is Mary's *fiat* at the annunciation, freely uttered with the fullness of divine grace, to be understood as contradicting the *sola fides* of the Protestant Reformation, holding that we are justified not by any merits of our own but by the grace of faith in Jesus Christ, which has reached considerable agreement. Along with these remaining challenges to Christian unity regarding Mary are the signs of hope derived from common scholarly studies of the Scripture such as *Mary in the New Testament*, more serious attention paid to the Fathers' witness to tradition in the undivided Church of the first six or seven centuries of Christianity, and the realization that Luther, Calvin, and Zwingli actually did retain significant beliefs about the mother of Jesus.

As previously pointed out, there are good prospects also for developing further the intimate relationship between Mary and the Holy Spirit. Some efforts in this regard have especially concentrated upon the theological reflections in both pneumatology and Mariology, which seem to meet most intimately in ecclesiology. The theology of the Holy Spirit helps to keep that of Mary clearly in christocentric perspective and, at the same time, an ecclesiotypical Mariology provides criteria whereby we can more clearly discern the workings of the Spirit, particularly in the liberation movements of our time regarding racial justice, feminism, etc. Where are they truly inspired by the Holy Spirit and where are they distorted by demonic spirits of sinful enslavement rather than authentic liberation? As the contributions of Fr. Patrick Granfield's scholarly work in ecclesiology have amply demonstrated over the years, such criteria can be founded only on a balanced theology of the Church. This essay has attempted to show how in many ways Mariology in close connection with the ecclesiology inspired by

---

[4] Ibid., 196–203; Frederick M. Jelly, "Pneumatology and Mariology: Orthodoxy and Orthopraxis in Dialogue," 1980 Proceedings of CTSA Annual Convention.

Vatican II, with emphasis upon the mystery of the Church as a community of life in Christ, should be further developed to promote the ecumenical movement and the many liberation movements toward greater peace and justice in our world.

For Further Reading

Anderson, H. George, et al. *The One Mediator, the Saints and Mary: Lutherans and Catholics in Dialogue.* Vol. 8. Minneapolis: Fortress Press, 1992.

Brown, Raymond E., et al. *Mary in the New Testament.* New York/Mahwah, N.J.: Paulist Press, 1978.

Cantalamessa, Reniero. *Mary, Mirror of the Church.* Collegeville: The Liturgical Press, 1992.

Jelly, Frederick M. *Madonna: Mary in the Catholic Tradition.* Huntington, Ind.: Our Sunday Visitor, 1986.

John Paul II. *Mother of the Redeemer.* Encyclical Letter for the Marian Year. Washington, D.C.: United States Catholic Conference, 1988.

Marian Studies. Proceedings of the Thirty-Seventh National Convention of the Mariological Society of America. Dayton, Ohio: Marian Library at the University of Dayton, 1986.

Shaw, Russell, ed. *Our Sunday Visitor's Encyclopedia of Catholic Doctrine.* Huntington, Ind.: Our Sunday Visitor, 1997.

Stacpool, Alberic, ed. *Mary and the Churches.* Collegeville: The Liturgical Press, 1987.

Tavard, George H. *The Thousand Faces of the Virgin Mary.* Collegeville: The Liturgical Press, 1996.

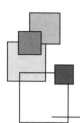

PART III

A North American Ecclesiology: The Theological Achievement of Patrick Granfield

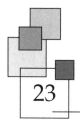

Patrick Granfield:
A Biographical Essay

23

David Granfield

Having lived with my brother for most of my life, I find writing about him to be pleasant to do, but somewhat difficult. I know him so well that I may lack the distance that a friend or colleague might easily possess. It may be harder for me to put him in context, to look objectively at one whose life I have shared for so long. Fortunately, the fact that I am writing about him for a volume in his honor enables me to focus my thoughts on his life as a theologian. I shall consider him mainly as a teacher and writer, one who has shared his ideas, especially on the Church, with his fellow theologians and with generations of students.

Patrick was born in Springfield, Massachusetts, on March 8, 1930, the third child of Patrick Edward and Mabel Fitzgerald Granfield. He attended Our Lady of Hope Grammar School and Cathedral High School. Those twelve years of education by the Sisters of St. Joseph were a major influence in his young life. In his own words: "I have always been deeply impressed by the Sisters, their deep faith, their loyalty to the Church, and their commitment to skillful teaching. My gratitude to them is enormous. For me, they were models of Christian ministry."

Even in his early years, his mind and heart were touched periodically by a yearning for the priesthood. Hence the reason for our more or less continuous living together—both of us became Benedictine monks. As his older brother, I entered St. Anselm's monastery in Washington, D.C., first. Patrick, though eight years my junior, joined me there a year later, in 1948, when he graduated from high school. Richard was his baptismal name; on joining the Benedictines he took the name Patrick, after our father, who was born on St. Patrick's Day. Incidentally, our mother was born on St. Valentine's Day.

After his time as a novice and two years as a student at The Catholic University of America, in 1951 Patrick was kindly sent by the prior,

Alban Boultwood, o.s.b., to pursue his philosophical studies in Rome at the Pontifical Institute of Saint Anselm. His years there, with his classes and examinations in Latin and his occasional summer visits to monasteries in Europe, helped develop his knowledge of several foreign languages. These proved valuable in his later career as a theologian. Of great importance, too, were the lifelong friends that he made during his Roman sojourn of three years.

In 1958 he earned his doctorate in philosophy (Ph.D.) with a dissertation entitled "Behavioral Semiotic: A Critique." In 1962 he earned his doctorate in theology (S.T.D.) at The Catholic University of America, writing on "The Theological Development of the Defendant's Obligation to Reply in a Civil Court." These two degrees were not directly on the theology of the Church, but they did significantly shape his intellectual life, affording him a solid structure in philosophy and theology and an excellent start in the journey that would lead to his work as an ecclesiologist.

Patrick has had a long and consistent publishing career. Apart from his two dissertations, he has written or edited eight books and some one hundred scholarly articles and book reviews.

Publishing began for him before his two doctorates. His first work, in 1954, was an article for the *American Benedictine Review* entitled "Blessed Placid Riccardi." The piece appeared on the occasion of his beatification, which was thirty-nine years after his death. Placid lived in troublesome nineteenth-century Italy and died at seventy years of age in 1915. He was a monk of deep prayer, pastoral commitment, and perfect obedience—a fine model for Patrick.

This article is important from our perspective; it reveals already present the characteristics of Patrick's writing style: order, clarity, and concreteness. Both in his lecturing and in his writing he preserves order, not just logical order but psychological order as well; he adjusts his words well to the mind of his reader or listener. Moreover, because he writes clearly one easily grasps what he says and can remember it. Finally, he writes concretely, something we all should do but most of us do not. This skill is especially difficult to realize in complex theological work. Patrick's writing is always intelligent and readable, well-attuned to his subject matter and to his reader. A superb memory makes him meticulous about details and concrete facts. His subsequent writings and lectures all manifest that gracious style.

One aspect of his personality should not be overlooked: Patrick has a friendly sense of humor. He laughs easily and responsively, yet remains seriously aware of the incongruities of life, even the intellectual life. His humor sharpens his sense of reality without diminishing his Christian appreciation of that reality.

By 1962 he began his teaching career at The Catholic University of America. Whatever else he taught—and there were many other subjects over the years—he always offered a course on the Church. There were no interruptions. As time passed he went through the various promotional stages, until he became a full professor in 1980. In 1991 the Alumni Association of The Catholic University of America gave him a well-deserved award for "Outstanding Achievement in Research and Scholarship." In September 2000 he was named the Shakespeare-Duval Professor of Systematic Theology.

The same year that he began teaching he also became part of *The American Ecclesiastical Review*. This was a hectic but satisfying job. He stayed on the editorial staff for eight years (1962–70), becoming an associate editor, the managing editor, and, finally, the editor-in-chief. During his work with the journal he edited twelve issues a year. His responsibilities extended to all phases of the publication process, including planning issues, soliciting articles, frequently corresponding with authors, giving detailed evaluations, and, of course, editing articles. In addition, there was the unending and overlapping series of jobs— sending material to the printer, checking galley sheets, and reading page proofs. Occasionally, unpredictable mishaps complicated these three sets of tasks which were repeated every month of the year. It was a very stressful time but Patrick enjoyed it.

In 1963 Patrick joined The Catholic Theological Society of America. After giving many talks and serving on several committees, he was elected president for the 1984–85 term. A few years later, in 1989, the Society honored him with The John Courtney Murray Award for Distinguished Achievement. The award citation noted the following: "Our honoree has devoted his professional life to teaching and research. He is a recognized authority in the field of ecclesiology who has given special attention to issues in Church government today. His books, his articles, and his service to Catholic ecclesiology constitute truly distinguished achievement." The same year, he received the Benemerenti Medal from John Paul II.

During these years of teaching and working he was busy writing his books and articles. His first book, *Theologians at Work* (1967), which stemmed in part from his exposure to the contacts made through *The American Ecclesiastical Review* and The Catholic Theological Society of America, was a series of interviews with well-known theologians. It proved extremely popular and was a "Book of the Month" selection by the Thomas More Association. He interviewed foreign writers Christopher Butler, Markus Barth, Yves Congar, Piet Franzen, Henri de Lubac, and Karl Rahner, as well as American writers Barnabas Ahern, John C. Bennett, Robert McAfee Brown, Francis J. Connell, Abraham J.

Heschel, George Lindbeck, John Meyendorff, Reinhold Niebuhr, Jaroslav Pelikan, and Johannes Quasten. Published in 1967 right after the Second Vatican Council, it caught the flavor and substance of the post-Vatican II theological spirit. His questions touched upon a variety of topics which the Church faced as it moved into a new age. It was for Patrick an experience that brought him into proximity and friendship with some of the great thinkers of the theological world. The book introduced many of them personally to American Catholics.

A continuation of this international rapport was the two-volume work edited by Patrick Granfield and Josef Jungmann entitled *Kyriakon: Festschrift Johannes Quasten* (1970). A tribute to a famous patrologist, the work contained contributions from eighty-one authors with articles in English, French, German, Italian, and Spanish. The *Tabula Gratulatoria* was immense, many times the number of the contributors. All in all, it was a major accomplishment for a young theologian to plan and edit such a large work dedicated to his teacher, colleague, and friend, Johannes Quasten.

By the time Patrick was forty he had already attuned himself to the wide world of theology, yet his focus still remained on the Church. His subsequent books reflect this direction. The second took a theme close to his Ph.D. dissertation; not semiotics, however, but cybernetics. The title, *Ecclesial Cybernetics: A Study of Democracy in the Church* (1973), was a formidable one, though it caught precisely the underlying processes of the Church. Distinguishing between open and closed systems, he analyzed the Church as it operates primarily as an open system but inevitably with certain closed aspects. His detailed focus on the output-input-feedback loop brought the question of democratization into play. Creativity and growth were revealed as participatory modalities of Christianity, especially of the Roman Catholic Church of the current era.

His next book, *The Papacy in Transition* (1980), was also published in England and later in Germany as *Das Papsttum: Kontinuität und Wandel* (1984). It was a "Book of the Month" selection of the Catholic Book Club and it won the "Book of the Year" award from the College Theological Society. He began it in 1978, "the year of the three Popes"—the year when Paul VI and John Paul I both died and when John Paul II was elected. The book focused concretely on the transition that the post-conciliar Church was undergoing as papal leadership gradually moved from an authoritarian to a more collegial exercise of authority. Patrick viewed the pope from many viewpoints: as monarch, fellow bishop, ecumenical pastor, and elected leader. With nuanced appreciation, he noted the shifts in these areas of development and finished his analysis by discussing the ultimate stages: the loss of the papacy through resignation and deposition. The book assessed the dynamics of the Church in a changing era, seeking to discern the perennial principles, the temporary modes, and the flawed expedients.

Pushing further in a following book, Patrick confronted, as the title indicates, *The Limits of the Papacy: Authority and Autonomy in the Church* (1987)—the things that the pope cannot do or should not do. It was the named "Book of the Month" by the Catholic Book Club and the Clergy Book Service, and was given an award by the Catholic Press Association. He observed that limits may be guidelines rather than barriers, they may truly be channels to fulfillment. A study of limits, however, requires a delicate assessment of the multifaceted context of power in the Church. Patrick's attempt was not to diminish the papacy but to reveal the special balance between authority and autonomy that best enables the Church to flourish. In more legal terms, he sought out the balance between the pope's legitimate decision-making power and the local church's relative autonomy. The principle of collegiality is seen as a flexible guide not a rigid one. Since the council, it has taken on a sharper visibility, though on occasion it is treated more as an abstract truth than a practical solution. But things move slowly. Patrick has successfully weighed the delicate and generally ongoing harmony that is ever emerging as a part of the life of the body of Christ.

As a practical, scholarly contribution to the study of the Church, in 1985 Patrick, together with Avery Dulles, S.J., wrote *The Church: A Bibliography*. It was considerably revised in 1999 and entitled *The Theology of the Church: A Bibliography*. It is a valuable asset for anyone studying or writing about the Church.

In 1994 Patrick edited *The Church and Communication*, which he introduced with an important article of his own on "The Theology of the Church and Communication." The opening sentence reminds us of Patrick's own training: "The Church is a religion of communication." He appropriately quoted the words from the epistle to the Hebrews:

> At various times in the past and in various different ways, God spoke to our ancestors through the prophets, but in our own time, the last days, he has spoken to us through his Son, the Son that he has appointed to inherit everything and through whom, he made everything there is (Heb 1:1-2).

I mention this sentence and the scriptural quotation because they summarize so much of Patrick's work, the work of communicating the truths of the Church and also the role of the magisterium in preserving and developing these truths. Patrick ended his article with the following words: "Our goal is to understand better the relationship between communication, the Church, and ecclesiology. It is an attempt to read 'signs of the times' as Vatican II taught us." To this he added the statement of the council: "The Church has always had the duty of reading the signs of the times and of interpreting them in the light of the Gospel" (GS 4). That task, as it has its center in the Church, has constituted the personal and professional life of Patrick Granfield.

Patrick's books, however, are not his only scholarly communication. He has been teaching at The Catholic University of America since 1962. He has also taught summer school at St. Michael's College, Winooski, Vermont; St. Joseph's College, West Hartford, Connecticut; and St. Norbert's College, De Pere, Wisconsin. In addition, he has offered courses at two schools that are members of the Washington Theological Consortium: Virginia Theological Seminary and Wesley Theological Seminary. Significant, too, are the multitude of professional experiences apart from his university and college teaching: many lectures, interviews, seminars, workshops, colloquia, retreats, and evaluation teams. He has participated in many international conferences, such as the meetings sponsored by the Istituto Paolo VI held in Italy since 1980.

Three areas in particular reveal Patrick's ecclesiological ministry: his work with the National Conference of Catholic Bishops (NCCB), his participation in diocesan continuing education programs, and his involvement in ecumenism.

First, he has worked with the NCCB on several projects. For example, he was a member of the planning committee and a participant in the colloquium on "Scholarship in the Church" organized by the NCCB and the Joint Committee of Catholic Learned Societies and Scholars (1978). He also was a consultant to the NCCB's Joint Committee on Lay Pastoral Ministry (1988–90). Finally, as a consultant to the Bishop's Committee on Priestly Life and Ministry of the NCCB in their study on presbyteral councils, he wrote the draft text of the document "United in Service" (1990–91).

Second, he has given workshops and conferences to priests, permanent deacons, and religious educators in such dioceses as Albany, Baltimore, Portland (Maine), Providence, Rochester, and Wheeling-Charleston.

Third, his commitment to the cause of Christian unity is revealed not only in his teaching and research but also by his work on several ecumenical projects. He lectured at a meeting of Episcopal and Catholic Diocesan Officers (1987). As a member of the international Task Force of the Joint Working Group—comprised of representatives of the Faith and Order Commission of the World Council of Churches and the Secretariat for the Promotion of Christian Unity—he helped draft the document "The Church: Local and Universal" (1988). On the national level, he was a member of the Lutheran–Roman Catholic Coordinating

Committee (1994–96) and is presently a member of the Lutheran–Roman Catholic Dialogue in the United States.

In short, Patrick is neither a radical nor a reactionary. He adheres faithfully to the magisterium but is ready to push beyond the past to see whether there are new ways of understanding the faith and of communicating it. He strives to express the perennial truths of the Church by using the language of the present. Not caught up in the myth that theologians know all the answers, he puts his questions in the context of what is actually known. Grounded solidly on established doctrine, he progresses creatively toward true growth in the theology of the Church.

In the book *The Limits of the Papacy,* Patrick ended with words that catch his own feelings about the Church and his responsibility in writing about the Church. He said: "What is important is that all members of the Church be open to Christ, who through his Spirit 'bestows on it the various hierarchical and charismatic gifts, and adorns it with his fruits and leads it to all truth and to perfect union in communion and ministry' (LG 4)."

A North American Ecclesiology:
24 The Achievement of Patrick Granfield

Peter C. Phan

If a scholar's doctoral dissertation is a reliable prediction of the area of his or her future professional expertise, then Patrick Granfield defies the received wisdom. His dissertation in philosophy deals with the behavioral semiotic as expounded by Charles W. Morris (1901–79), whose lifelong goal was to relate American pragmatism, especially the insights of Charles Peirce and George Herbert Mead, to logical positivism and whose division of semiotic into syntactics, semantics, and pragmatics has been widely accepted in contemporary philosophy. Granfield's dissertation in theology studies the historical development of the privilege against self-incrimination, or to use the common expression of theologians, the right to silence, in relation to the defendant's obligation to reply in a civil court. From these doctoral works one would expect Granfield to pursue contemporary philosophy or moral theology or canon law as his scholarly specialization, but, of course, the name of Granfield is today associated not with these fields but with ecclesiology and especially the teaching on papal ministry.

Not that these philosophical and canonical studies are unrelated to or did not have an impact upon Granfield's later writings, as we shall see below, but as the citation of The John Courtney Murray Award for Distinguished Achievement, which the Catholic Theological Society of America bestowed on him in 1989, makes clear, the field in which Granfield has achieved international reputation and in which this *festschrift* is dedicated to him is the theology of the Church: "He is a recognized authority in the field of ecclesiology who has given attention to issues in Church government today. His books, his articles, and his service to Catholic ecclesiology constitute truly distinguished achievement."

In this essay I will first examine Granfield's contribution to philosophy and theological scholarship in general. Then attention will be turned to his contribution to ecclesiology, in particular to the theology of the papal ministry. The last part will situate Granfield's achievement in the context of contemporary ecclesiology.

From the Philosophy of Sign to the Theology of the Right to Silence

Philosophy of Sign and Language

As was mentioned earlier, Granfield's doctoral dissertation in philosophy discusses the semiotic of Charles Morris.[1] It is not our intention here to evaluate Granfield's presentation of Morris's semiotic or the accuracy of his critique of the Morrisean system. Granfield takes Morris to task for his confusing use of terms and words, his overlapping classification of the modes of signifying, his deficient understanding of the nature of sign and its causality, his exclusive use of behaviorism as a method to analyze signs, and finally his insufficient understanding of the nature of human language.[2]

Apart from Granfield's contribution to the scholarly debate on semiotic as it was formulated in the late fifties, what is of interest to us here is the underlying philosophical position which Granfield adopts and in the light of which he critiques Morris's semiotic as well as his basic methodological approach. Both his philosophical stance and his method are, as we will see, characteristic of his later theology and in particular his ecclesiology. Philosophically, Granfield stands within the Thomistic tradition, and in epistemology, within what has been described as "the moderate realism of St. Thomas" which, for him, is "best expressed in the formula that our ideas are *fundamentaliter in rebus et formaliter in mente.*"[3] In his critique of Morris's behavioral semiotic, Granfield acknowledges that his "most important criterion is the fact that man does have universal ideas, that he does know abstract realities as well as concrete ones, and that, as a rational animal, he can rise above merely empirical experiences."[4] It is this philosophical realism and "centrism" that will prevent Granfield from moving to either

---

[1] Patrick Granfield, "Behavioral Semiotic: A Critique" (Ph.D. dissertation, Pontifical Athenaeum of St. Anselm's, Rome, 1958). An excerpt of the dissertation appeared as "Behavioral Semiotic: A Critique," *The Thomist* 24 (1962) 495–536. Henceforth, references will be made to this article, not to the dissertation.

[2] See Granfield, "Behavioral Semiotic," 507–33.

[3] Ibid., 504. For Granfield, moderate realism avoids the errors of idealism, empiricism, and nominalism.

[4] Ibid., 505.

the extreme right or the extreme left, especially during the turbulent post-Vatican II period.

Also characteristic of Granfield's thinking is his openness to and willingness to learn from contemporary currents of thought, indeed, as he puts it, "to seek truth no matter where it may be found."[5] Though highly critical of the Morrisean semiotic, he is able to write: "It is most beneficial for scholastics to read Morris and to examine this modern contribution to semiotic. A thoughtful and clear examination of modern semiotic helps the scholastic to re-examine his own position and to seek truth no matter where it may be found."[6] It is this openness, I submit, that allowed Granfield to move beyond the more conservative ecclesiology of his colleagues such as Joseph Clifford Fenton.[7]

Though Granfield never returned to semiotic as a scholarly specialization, his early study of the theories of sign had a lasting impact on his theology. One of the ecclesiological themes that will be the focus of his later research is precisely the problem of communication and control in the Church.[8] Even though he criticizes Morris' behavioral semiotic for not offering a satisfactory account of human language as an intentional and interpretative act, Granfield commends him for having developed the three dimensions of semiotic: semantics, syntactics, and pragmatics. In particular, he notes the importance of Morris's elaboration of pragmatics in which, in the footsteps of George Mead, Morris treats the social aspects of sign, that is, the origin, use, effect, and social environment of the sign.[9] Given this appreciation of sign as communication, it

[5] Ibid., 536.

[6] Ibid.

[7] On Joseph Clifford Fenton, see the brief but informative essay by Joseph Komonchak, "Fenton, Joseph (1906–69)," *The Encyclopedia of American Catholic History,* ed. Michael Glazier and Thomas J. Shelley, 505–6 (Collegeville: The Liturgical Press, 1997). Of Fenton, Komonchak writes:

> Not an original scholar, he was a passionate advocate of traditional methods and positions and promoter of the papal magisterium with vigor and little nuance not only against outsiders but, especially in the years between the Second World War and the Second Vatican Council, against the slightest tinge of liberalism and the threat of a revival of Modernism in the Church (505–6).

One of the theologians Fenton sought to have condemned by Rome is John Courtney Murray. Fenton was the editor of *American Ecclesiastical Review* (henceforth *AER*) from 1944 to 1970. Granfield was associated with *AER* from 1962 to 1971. He succeeded Fenton as editor in 1968.

[8] We will discuss below Patrick Granfield's book *Ecclesial Cybernetics: A Study of Democracy in the Church* (New York: Macmillan, 1973) and the book he edited *The Church and Communication* (Kansas City, Mo.: Sheed and Ward, 1994).

[9] See Granfield, "Behavioral Semiotic," 534–5.

is not surprising to read Granfield's following, much later, statements: "Christianity is the religion of communication" and "To be human means to communicate."[10]

"The Right to Silence"

Granfield completed his theological studies with a doctoral dissertation on the right to silence or the privilege against self-discrimination ("pleading the fifth") at The Catholic University of America.[11] After a thorough investigation of the historical development of this right to silence, from Roman law to our times, with special focus on Thomas Aquinas, John de Lugo, some key magisterial texts, and representative contemporary theologians, the dissertation summarizes four possible positions with regard to the right to silence: (1) the right to silence is founded on the natural law (the consensus of theological opinion); (2) the positive law has unlimited power to restrict the right to silence for the sake of the common good (Thomas Aquinas, Cajetan, Billuart, St. Alphonsus, etc.); (3) the positive law has a limited power to limit the right to silence for the sake of the common good (Abbas Panormitanus, de Lugo, etc.); and (4) the positive law has no power under any circumstances to restrict the right to silence for the sake of the common good (opinion held by no theologian).[12]

Granfield himself is inclined to the first and third positions. Again what interests us here is not his legal and moral reasoning in favor of these positions and against the others.[13] Rather, what is important is that, though it is in itself a dissertation in moral theology and legal philosophy, the work adumbrates in significant ways its author's later theological development. First of all, it illustrates one key feature of Granfield's theological method, namely, its emphasis on careful historical analysis. This was done not only on individual theologians but also,

---

[10] Granfield, ed., *The Church and Communion*, 1 and 2 respectively.

[11] Patrick Granfield, "The Theological Development of the Defendant's Obligation to Reply in a Civil Court" (S.T.D. dissertation, The Catholic University of America, 1962). The director was John J. Shinners, and the two readers were John J. Abbo and Joseph C. Fenton. It was defended in 1962. Out of his dissertation Granfield wrote two essays, both of which were published by *Theological Studies* as "The Right to Silence." Since both have the same title, we will refer to them by their title followed by the year of publication, 1965 for the first and 1966 for the second.

[12] See Granfield, "The Right to Silence," 1965, 284–9; 293–6.

[13] Granfield presents five arguments for the natural-law position: (1) the right to secrecy, (2) the right to reputation, (3) the rare duty to perform a heroic act, (4) the legitimate love of the self, and (5) the dignity of the human personality. See Granfield, "The Right to Silence," 1965, 289–93.

and especially, on magisterial documents.[14] This close attention to historical development will be seen in Granfield's later works on the papacy.

Second, connected with this historical "archaeology" is Granfield's important insight into dogmatic development. As a result of his study of magisterial teaching on the right to silence, Granfield is able to conclude that "on the magisterial level, no evidence of an organic development of the right to silence appears in the documents. . . . Rather we discover a sudden, abrupt change."[15] On the other hand, Granfield also notes that "on the theological level . . . there is a genuine development which was possible only because many theologians considered the magisterial documents as directive, not prescriptive."[16] In addition, Granfield notes that one of the elements that provoked the change in the Church's teaching is, besides persistent contrary theological position, something outside the Church, that is, a change in civil law:

> The right to silence did develop, but not, at least on the official magisterial level, by a gradual, organic process. The Church's recognition of this right was sudden and long overdue. It was the presence of a persistent contrary theological opinion and a dramatic change in the civil law that finally influenced the Church.[17]

Third, in his evaluation of the grounds for the right of silence, Granfield already discloses his overriding preference and profound respect for democracy, a theme he will exploit to great advantage in his work on ecclesial cybernetics. Distinguishing between "minimal public order" and "maximal public order," the former consisting in the security of the state and the latter being "the full prosperity of a society in which public and private good are in harmony,"[18] Granfield grants that

[14] See Granfield, "The Right to Silence," 1966, 402–16.

[15] Ibid., 416.

[16] Ibid., 417.

[17] Ibid., 420. Three things deserve highlighting here. First, Granfield does not deny the possibility of an organic, homogeneous development of doctrine, such as in the christological dogmas, as he himself has noted (420). But he has pointed out that an important fact the theory of homogenous development of dogma tends to overlook is the reality of sudden reversal of positions in magisterial teaching. Second, the role of "persistent contrary theological opinion" in dogmatic development, which today may be framed in terms of "theological dissent," not in the sense of public, organized opposition, but of well-reasoned arguments contrary to nondefinitive teaching of the magisterium. Third, the role of non-ecclesial and nontheological opinions and practices in theological development, which is often neglected in historical accounts of the development of doctrines.

[18] Granfield, "The Right to Silence," 1965, 296.

sometimes the right to silence may be curtailed for the sake of the minimal public order. But he hastens to add:

> Maximal public order, however, seeks more than mere peace. It looks to the perfect fulfilment of man's potential. It attempts to create an atmosphere in which men can truly live well in accord with the highest aspirations of their nature. This kind of public order can be realized only if the state respects the human and civil rights of its citizens. It must allow its citizens, for example, the right to legitimate assembly, the right to worship, the right to free speech, and not least of all, the right to silence. In principle, then, maximal public order is not possible unless the state recognizes and protects the individual's privilege against self-incrimination.[19]

Theological Commentator and Editor

Before moving on to Granfield's ecclesiology it is necessary to pause and take note of another side of his scholarly career which, had it been sedulously pursued, might have earned him if not the Pulitzer Prize for theological journalism at least the title of eminent social and theological commentator. We have already alluded to Granfield's association with the *American Ecclesiastical Review* of which he was successively associate editor, managing editor, and editor-in-chief.[20] From August 1962 to August 1964 (issues 147–51 of *AER*), Granfield wrote a column (a total of twenty-five) entitled "Comment" which he himself initiated. "Comment" is a capacious umbrella under which Granfield could deliver his opinion on practically anything that struck his fancy, from lives of notable ecclesiastics and theologians (e.g., Louis Billot, Francis J. Connell, Henry Denzinger, Reginald Garrigou-Lagrange) to controversial books (e.g., John A. T. Robinson's *Honest to God*) to liturgical and theological trends (e.g., healing services, African liturgy, glossolalia, cursillos), to activities of the Second Vatican Council.

Not rarely did Granfield try to lighten such weighty subjects with comments titled "travel—Irish style," "fashions in fasting," and "sarto-

---

[19] Ibid., 297.

[20] On the history of *AER* see Joseph Hubbert, *"American Ecclesiastical Review,"* *The Encyclopedia of American Catholic History,* ed. Glazier and Shelley, 91–2, and Hubbert's three-volume dissertation: "'For the Upbuilding of the Church': The Reverend Hermann Joseph Heuser, D.D., 1851–1933" (Ph.D. dissertation, The Catholic University of America, 1992). Granfield has written a short history of the review: "Seventy-five Years of the American Ecclesiastical Review," *AER* 150 (January 1964) 18–32. Granfield was editor of the journal from 1968 until 1970, when he was succeeded by James P. Clifton who held this post until 1975 when the journal ceased publication.

rial style." Granfield's splendid style and dry wit are in abundant display in the following gems:

> Mortification, like clothes, has its styles. It too changes with the times. In the twelfth century, for example, a Flemish mystic was revered by all her contemporaries for her fast of seven years on nothing but bread—and beer.[21]
>
> Men's fashions change slowly. Yet whatever happened to the Chesterfield coat, spats, derbies, vests, and double-breasted suits? Clerical styles reflect the average U.S. male's apathy to change in clothes. Around the turn of the century clerics wore the *infra genua* coat and the derby. Pants gradually became less baggy and jackets shorter and more tailored, until now the majority of priests in this country wear a suit that is known in the trade as the American classic. The military collar rabbat seems to be more popular style than the full Roman collar and who can say whether the L.B.J. hat will catch the clerical fancy?[22]

In addition to his hectic editorial work, Granfield managed to conduct a series of interviews with practically all the who's who in the theological orbit of the early seventies.[23] Of course, these interviews cannot replace the perusing of these theologians' works themselves, but as lively, comprehensive, and clear introductions to their life, work, and thought, Granfield's biographical and theological vignettes cannot be improved upon. However, our interest does not lie in the substance of these interviews itself, but in how they foreshadow Granfield's later theological development. First, there is his broad ecumenical concern. The sixteen interviewees belong to different denominations and even religions: Catholic (Johannes Quasten, Karl Rahner, Piet Fransen, Francis Connell, Henri de Lubac, Barnabas Ahern, Christopher Butler, and Yves Congar), Protestant (Robert McAfee Brown, Reinhold Niebuhr, Jaroslav Pelikan, George Lindbeck, John C. Bennett, and Marcus Barth), Orthodox (John Meyendorff), and Jewish (Abraham Heschel).[24]

[21] *AER* 148 (February 1963) 135.

[22] *AER* 150 (April 1964) 300.

[23] These interviews were later published in book form as Patrick Granfield, *Theologians at Work* (New York: Macmillan, 1967), which was selected as "Book of the Month" by the Thomas More Association.

[24] To these theologians must be added Hans Küng, whom Granfield interviewed in 1965. The interview is published under the title "The Spirit of Change in the Church," *The Homiletic and Pastoral Review* 65 (1965) 17–21. In 1962 Granfield had given a short report on how "this young [34-year-old] priest is causing considerable stir in theological circles from the green hills around the Bodensee to the shores of

Second, these interviews evidence the breadth and depth of Granfield's theological knowledge. As he himself has put it:

> Preparation for the interviews was extensive. My "homework" consisted of reading some biographical material and whatever books and articles of these theologians that I had not yet read. I tried to immerse myself in their theology, to develop a sense of rapport, so that I would feel at home when I met them personally.[25]

Third, these interviews reveal Granfield's understanding of the complex task of theology in the contemporary world. In an illuminating passage he describes what theology should be and how it should be done today:

> Theology has to be in every instance a response to what Latourelle calls "the first fact, the first mystery, the first category"—the revelation of God to man. This is the basis of all theology. Once one believes that God has spoken to man, then there arises the exigency of understanding this communication. . . .
>
> In theology, faith develops in a properly human way according to the laws and resources of reason. Through the centuries, these resources have been employed in various ways. In the past, art, philosophy, and history influenced the development of theology. Today, our theology must also take into account psychology, phenomenology, existentialism, sociology, and literature. The theologian must avail himself of the insights of all the various sciences if his theology is to be dynamic. This means that the theologian must wear many hats. He cannot be the "encapsulated man." He has to be a *specialist* in one field, but at the same time he has to be a *generalist*, at home in several other disciplines.[26]

The complex challenges the last quarter of the twentieth century poses to theology (and, one may add, these challenges will only increase and intensify in the next century) require, according to Granfield, that the theologian develop "a sense of community and a sense of tradition." First,

---

the tawny Potomac." In a remark that reveals much of his theological temper, Granfield writes of Küng's then-celebrated book *The Council, Reform and Reunion:*

> Father Küng develops his central theme with precision and with a candor that American Catholics rarely see in print. His book is provocative, yet many will undoubtedly take offence at its severe critical appraisal and will feel that the prudence of such an attitude, at times annoying, is of dubious value.

See "Comments," *AER* 147 (1962) 137.

[25] Granfield, *Theologians at Work,* xi.

[26] Ibid., xv.

> the modern theologian must be *communitarian.* He must operate *in, for,* and *through* the *koinonia*—the community of love and worship that is God's people. . . . Theology is a quest within the community for the genuine understanding of God's Word in all its purity and clarity. . . . The theologian is a *diakonos,* a servant of the community.[27]

In this community, two kinds of theologians are needed: the theologian-scholar who is dedicated to serious research, and the theologian-prophet who can recognize God's working in history and is able to interpret it for his or her contemporaries.[28] Second, the theologian must work with the *traditum.* But tradition, Granfield warns, must be identified neither with the past nor with the present:

> Tradition, for the theologian, cannot be equated solely with the past or the present. It is both the past and the present and will continue into the future. . . . Theological tradition is a tradition of growth, and the theologian stands at the outer periphery of the "growing edge" of tradition. He must study theology in terms of the evolutionary development of doctrine that is a sober evaluation of the past and the present. This is historical orthodoxy and relevant theology at its best.[29]

Lastly, as a genre, these interviews represented at the time something of a novel way of writing on theology. It was no doubt Granfield's intentional response to the situation of Catholic theology in the late sixties which, as he notes, "faces an information explosion of its own."[30] Because theology has moved into the market place, Granfield laments the practice of an "ivory tower," "artificial," "lifeless," "parasitic" theology, "an ineffectual subculture of the ecclesiastical society with its own jargon, customs, and methods that are totally unreal and unrelated to the community."[31] By presenting theologians "live" as it were and by asking probing questions about their lives and works, Granfield not only has overcome the image of theology as a bloodless enterprise but also develops his earlier interest in language as communication.[32]

[27] Ibid., xvii.
[28] See ibid., xx–xxii.
[29] Ibid., xxv. When these comments on tradition are placed in their historical context (1967), when Granfield was editor-in-chief of *AER,* it is clear that they represent their author's radical departure from his predecessor Joseph Fenton, who had unabashedly used *AER* as a forum for his anti-Modernist ideas.
[30] Ibid., vii.
[31] Ibid., xviii.
[32] In this connection it is appropriate to mention another effort of Granfield to "communicate" theology through his mammoth two-volume *festschrift* entitled

From "Ecclesial Cybernetics" to
"the Limits of the Papacy"

Practicing his own counsel about the need for theologians to become a specialist in one field and a generalist in several other disciplines, Granfield has moved since the early seventies to carve out for
himself a niche in ecclesiology in general and in the theology of the papacy in particular. It is in these two fields that he has made an important and lasting contribution.

Ecclesial Cybernetics

Granfield's first break away from the traditional mold of ecclesiology took the form of a thorough application of the cybernetic theory to
the understanding of the Church.[33] In line with his dictum that contemporary must make use of resources other than philosophy, Granfield
applies the communication model proposed by Norbert Wiener and
others to the Church.[34] The science of cybernetics, Granfield notes, has
been widely applied to electronics, neurology, engineering, telecom-
munications, political science, and economics. Its application to the

---

Kyriakon (Münster: Verlag Aschendorff, 1970), which he edited with Josef Andreas
Jungmann in honor of Johannes Quasten. Eighty-one authors from around the
world contributed to this work. Granfield's journalistic talents are again on display
in an extremely informative and colorful *tour d'horizon* he gave on the German theological scene in the late sixties. Here too wit is not absent. After noting the high
standards of doctoral studies in German universities, Granfield writes:

> We should not, however, idealize the German university student. He should
> not be pictured as a pale, pathetic, bespectacled individual chained to a small
> table and working far into the night amid dusty tomes. . . . Like students
> the world over, he likes to relax. The number of *Bierstuben* and cafés in the
> university cities of Germany is a graphic example of the supply and demand
> theory. It is a favorite student pastime to spend endless hours in discussion
> over beer and coffee.

See "The German Theological Scene," *Thought* 43:170 (1968) 331. Finally, in the category of *instrument de travail* is to be mentioned the extremely useful bibliography on
ecclesiology which Granfield (in collaboration with Avery Dulles) has made available to scholars, *The Theology of the Church: A Bibliography* (New York: Paulist Press,
1999).

[33] His first writing on ecclesial cybernetics was published as an essay in "Ecclesial
Cybernetics: Communication in the Church," *Theological Studies* 29 (1988) 662–78.
Granfield later developed this theory in the book-length work *Ecclesial Cybernetics,*
mentioned above.

[34] See Norbert Wiener, *Cybernetics; or Control and Communication in the Animal and
the Machine* (New York: John Wiley, 1949), and Norbert Wiener, *The Use of Human*

Church is now a necessity because "an understanding of the problem of communication and control in the Church is basic to its future maintenance and development."[35]

Granfield begins with a brief explanation of cybernetics. He quotes Wiener's understanding of the purpose of cybernetics as "to develop a language and techniques that will enable us to attack the problem of control and communication in general, but also to find the proper repertory of ideas and techniques to classify their particular manifestations under certain concepts."[36] These concepts include: (1) the system, (2) the environment, (3) the negative entropy, and (4) the information-conversion process. A "system" is the basic unit of control and communication in cybernetics. It is an undivided whole with a multiplicity of interdependent and interacting parts. A system can be "closed," that is, static because it is isolated from its environment; or it can be "open," that is, dynamic because it is in constant interaction with its environment. Systems that are able to resolve to their advantage the tension between stability and change by adapting to their environment are called "ultrastable systems."

The "environment" is whatever that is not part of the system and with which open systems interact. Interaction with the environment enables the open system to achieve two related goals: homeostasis (its ability to maintain steadiness) and evolution (its ability to improve itself).

"Negative entropy" is the characteristic of open systems. Contrary to closed systems which move inexorably to self-destruction, open systems avoid entropy or organizational dissolution by performing anti-entropic functions, that is, interacting with the environment for self-maintenance and self-development.

Anti-entropic functions are performed through an "information-conversion process" which is composed of input, output, and feedback. An "input" is a unit of information that modifies the system in some way. Inputs flow within the system and act as determinants of behavior. There are two major kinds of input: demands and supports. The former are stressful messages directed to authorities demanding positive or negative decisions. The latter are positive messages providing

---

Beings (New York: Doubleday Anchor Books, 1954). Other scholars referred to by Granfield include: A. Rosenblueth, J. Bigelow, Claude E. Shannon, Warren Weaver, W. Ross Ashby, John von Neumann, David Easton, Karl W. Deutsch, and others. For the works of these authors, see Granfield, *Ecclesial Cybernetics*, 2–3.

[35] Granfield, *Ecclesial Cybernetics*, xii. It has been mentioned above that Granfield's earlier interest in the philosophy of sign finds further development in his study of the dynamics of communication elaborated in *Ecclesial Cybernetics*.

[36] Ibid., 2. Wiener's statement is taken from his *The Use of Human Beings*, 17.

the system with continuity. An "output" is a unit of information emanating from the system, normally from its authorities, and directed to the subordinate part of the system or its environment in response to the "input," particularly to its demands, in light of the compatibility of the demands with the goals of the system, the availability of resources, and the feasibility of implementation.

The "feedback" is any unit of information that is returned to the system in reaction to antecedent output. It can be positive or negative, consisting again of demands and supports. This circular process of input and output, aptly described by the expression "feedback loop," functions in open systems continuously, repeating itself again and again.[37]

On the basis of the contemporary democratic experience with its stress on participation in decision-making and on the co-responsibility of all citizens for the common good and of Vatican II's teaching on freedom, collegiality, and the role of the laity in the Church, Granfield proposes that "the Church needs cybernetic reform through democratization."[38] That the Church is an open cybernetic system functioning in the manner described above, through interacting with its environment by way of a feedback loop of inputs and outputs, is taken as a given by Granfield. What is important for us is that through an analysis of the present structure of the Church, both at the universal level (the papacy, the College of Cardinals, the Roman Curia, and the college of bishops) and the local level (the bishop, the diocesan curia, the synod and council, the clergy and laity), Granfield comes to two conclusions. First, "the Church is clearly susceptible of cybernetic analysis." Second, "this cybernetic analysis of the Church indicates an imbalance in its role structure. Authoritative outputs are almost solely within the exclusive competence of the hierarchy, with little significant participation by the lower clergy or the laity. . . . In the modern Church there is little democratization."[39]

---

[37] For Granfield's description of cybernetics see his "Ecclesial Cybernetics," 663–7 and *Ecclesial Cybernetics*, 5–33.

[38] Granfield, *Ecclesial Cybernetics*, xii.

[39] Ibid., 58. Granfield goes on to illustrate these two conclusions by examining the feedback loop occurring in the debate of four concrete issues, two doctrinal— the slavery question and the birth control debate—and two disciplinary—the ecumenical movement and the requirement of priestly celibacy. See *Ecclesial Cybernetics*, 59–125. Granfield ends his survey with four conclusions:

> First, all input is important, even that coming from outside the ecclesial system. Secondly, Catholics are involving themselves more and more in ecclesial decisions, even though their contribution is only on the level of input. Thirdly, even minor success in influencing decision-making increases the quantity of input. Fourthly, since Vatican II and its emphasis on liberty and collegiality, the move for participation in decision-making has intensified (125).

Democratization in the Church?

But *may* the Church function democratically? Is not democracy contrary to the Church's hierarchical constitution? Has the Church ever functioned democratically, at least in some instances, in the past? Is there any theological foundation for "democratization" in the Church?

Before answering these questions Granfield makes some important observations about democracy and the nature of the Church. As far as the Church and the application of sociological theories to ecclesiology are concerned, Granfield makes three important points. First,

> any discussion of the Church's communication structure must take into consideration the unique nature of the Church. It is multidimensional, with paradoxes, conflicts, and tensions, but it is one. It is divine and human, invisible and visible, pneumatic and institutional. Although here we are concentrating on its human, visible, and institutional aspects, we are not prescinding from its spiritual side. . . . Although we focus to some extent on the organizational Church, we are also fully cognizant of the Church as the sacramental presence of Christ in the world, as the entire people moving as a pilgrim on the way to final glory. In a word, we view the Church as a mystery filled with the hidden presence of the divine.[40]

Second, Granfield highlights and accepts a critical difference between the Church and human social systems, namely, the fact that the Church owes its origin and existence to God's self-revelation in Christ: "Therefore, the validity of any ecclesiological conclusions about the nature of the Church is determined primarily by its fidelity to the kerygma. Unlike human societies with their man-made constitutions, the Church is founded on the communication of God to man."[41]

Third, another factor that distinguishes the Church from purely human societies, Granfield points out, is "the Church's indefectibility": "This faith-affirmation means that the Church will remain in existence and will never be destroyed by the forces of evil and error. . . . This indefectibility of the Church is forged from that intimate union of Christ and the Church."[42]

These conclusions bring us back to Granfield's study of the factors influencing the change in magisterial teaching on the right to silence.

[40] Granfield, "Ecclesial Cybernetics," 667–8.

[41] Ibid., 668.

[42] Ibid. I dwell on these three points to correct the uninformed critique made by Clare Watkins of Granfield when she writes: "Granfield does not appear to emphasize sufficiently the distinctiveness of the Church's activity. . . . Nowhere does Granfield take up the issues in which the Church might be critical of secular changes;

With regard to democracy Granfield recognizes that "direct democracy, with its rapid conversion of feedback, is no longer feasible on a large scale."[43] In its place, there is "indirect democracy" in which instead of a continuous participation of the people in the direct exercise of power, there is a system of limitation and control of power.[44] For a democratic system to be established and flourish, two principles must be accepted by all its members: "that all members share a common human dignity and that the government exists for the people and not vice versa."[45] Granfield goes on to note three aspects of democracy: the principle of majority rule, the need for leadership, and the value of decentralization.[46]

---

nor does he highlight the significance of the fact that the Church's identity is grounded in revelation." See her "Organizing the People of God: Social-Science Theories of Organization in Ecclesiology," *Theological Studies* 52 (1991) 699. One cannot see how on earth such an opinion can be justified in light of Granfield's remarks quoted above. Elsewhere Granfield faces the problem of adopting some democratic elements for Church organization head-on: "Can the Church incorporate some democratic elements into its governmental system? We know that the Church is not simply another political entity but a unique religious society. An application, therefore, of democracy to the Church has to take into account this uniqueness" (*Ecclesial Cybernetics*, 138). At any rate, Watkins's scruples will be permanently laid to rest by perusing Granfield's essay "The Mystery of the Church," *AER* 160 (January 1969) 1–19 in which Granfield, anticipating Avery Dulles' *Models of the Church*, discusses the nature of the Church in relation to the Trinity and as the kingdom, the body of Christ, the People of God, and sacrament.

[43] Granfield, *Ecclesial Cybernetics*, 131.

[44] The distinction between direct and indirect democracy is taken from Giovanni Sartori, *Democratic Theory* (New York: Praeger, 1965) 252.

[45] Granfield, *Ecclesial Cybernetics*, 133.

[46] Here again, after reading Granfield's discussion of these three aspects of democracy it is hard to see how Clare Watkins's accusation that Granfield is unaware of the possibility of "'the management' winning the day precisely through the use of democratic structures" is justified. See her "Organizing the People of God," 700. Nor is her remark that Granfield ignores the "tendency to mass apathy in all human organization" well founded. Witness:

> Renewal does not take place automatically. It happens because people want it to happen and work toward it. No plan for renewal, cybernetic or not, can succeed if there is apathy. . . . Renewal in the Church is impossible without the concomitant spiritual revitalization of individual believers. The two complement one another. Unless the Gospel message permeates the life of the faithful, even the best program for reconstruction is destined to failure (*Ecclesial Cybernetics*, 214).

See also Granfield's strong emphasis on the need of "commitment to community" for reform programs to succeed in *Ecclesial Cybernetics*, 236–8.

But may the Church adopt even this indirect democracy in its structure? Are the democratic ideals of majoritarianism and decentralization compatible with the hierarchical structure of the Church? True to his method, which he has used to immense advantage in his study of the right to silence, Granfield formulates his answer to these questions by looking back at Church history, from the New Testament to the emergence of conciliarism. We do not need to tarry over his historical analysis here. Suffice it to note his conclusion: "Ecclesial democracy is not a new thing. It has its deep roots in Christian tradition. Evidence of democratic elements in the open system which is the Church appears primarily in the selection of office holders."[47]

Following his historical investigation Granfield builds the theological foundation for "ecclesial democracy" on the egalitarian aspect of the ecclesial system. This egalitarian character of the ecclesial community is elaborated in terms of Vatican II's teaching on the laity's participation in the threefold mission of Christ as priest, prophet, and king and on the principle of subsidiarity. Granfield is well aware that equality in the ecclesial system is not absolute since the Church is established by Christ as a hierarchical structure. To show how ecclesial democracy is compatible with the hierarchical constitution of the Church, Granfield distinguishes between the "vesting of ecclesial authority" and the "structure of ecclesial authority." With respect to the former, the official Church has taught that bishops do not receive their authority from the community but from Christ and, ultimately, from God. In *this* sense, the Church is not a democratic system, that is, not an organization in which the community itself possesses authority over its leaders and delegates its power to them. However, with regard to the structure of ecclesial authority, Granfield points out that the Church needs not and should not function as a monarchy, but in the model envisaged by the two teachings of Vatican II, that is, collegiality and the charismatic aspect of the Church. Granfield concludes:

> Theologically, power in the Church is held to come directly from God and not from the people. But nothing prevents the designation of the

---

[47] Granfield, *Ecclesial Cybernetics,* 139. Granfield takes the practice of election of the bishop by the people as well as decision-making by consensus in the early church as the most convincing evidence of ecclesial democracy. See his "Episcopal Elections in Cyprian: Clerical and Lay Participation," *Theological Studies* 37:1 (1976) 41–52 and "Concilium and Consensus: Decision-Making in Cyprian," *The Jurist* 35 (1975) 397–408. For Granfield's discussion of papal election see *The Papacy in Transition* (Dublin: Gill and Macmillan, 1980) 124–50. In this context he proposes that there be a greater participation by a more representative electorate and that there be a fixed term of office or retirement at a fixed age.

decision-makers by the members of the Church. Moreover, this same type of decision-making could function in other areas, excepting, of course, the special prerogatives of the Pope and the college of bishops.[48]

How, in practice, can the Church be reformed cybernetically through democratization? Granfield is keenly aware of the difficulties facing the task of reform in the Church which can be miscarried by the immobility, ineffectuality (encouraged by inadequate selection process, ambition, and incompetence), and isolation of Church leaders as well as by the lack of competence and control among the laity. To promote and facilitate such a cybernetic renewal, Granfield suggests several "techniques of ecclesial democracy," all the while conscious that because the Church is a complex, "non-linear, multiple-loop-feedback system with variable elements,"[49] no single and simple solution is adequate to all the interconnected problems facing the Church. Among these techniques, Granfield highlights commitment to community,[50] the exercise of minority power by means of protests and pressure groups,[51] the use of communication media,[52] the use of study commissions,[53] and the election of bishops either by a general plebiscite or by an elected committee.[54]

[48] Granfield, *Ecclesial Cybernetics*, 209.

[49] Ibid., 235.

[50] Granfield points out that intense commitment to large communities, e.g., parishes of several thousand people, is difficult if not impossible. He is therefore in favor of smaller communities.

[51] Granfield realizes that protests and pressure groups can be counterproductive, but says:

> Protests and pressure groups are valuable in the ecclesial community. Through their efforts, they bring to light sensitive issues and stimulate discussion about them. Important matters can move from a theoretical level to a practical one in a short time. Feedback, if adequately publicized, can at least force those in authority to listen. Well-organized and reasonably conducted protest has the best chances of success (*Ecclesial Cybernetics*, 241).

Granfield will discuss the possibility of dissent from Church teaching at length in *The Limits of the Papacy* (New York: Crossroad, 1987) 158–62.

[52] Granfield makes three recommendations in the use of communication media: sound professional training, broadening of the horizon of the Catholic press, and institutional support. See *Ecclesial Cybernetics*, 144.

[53] Granfield supports the use of public opinion polls not "as an infallible index of public sentiment, but as one of the many ways for the Church to determine more accurately the *consensus fidelium*" (*Ecclesial Cybernetics*, 246).

[54] Granfield is inclined to the latter method, since "the election of bishops by general plebiscite does seem, on balance, to have so many disadvantages as to be prohibitive" (*Ecclesial Cybernetics*, 250).

A New Form of Papal Ministry:
From the Monarchical to the Collegial Model

Granfield's conviction that some form of participatory democracy, cybernetically and theologically sound, is the most effective way for the Church to achieve its mission in the modern world is put to the test by one of the most intractable and controverted ministries in the Church: the papacy. With the election of John Paul I and especially of John Paul II in 1978, the papacy, Granfield notes, is "clearly in transition." This transition is "from a monarchical to a collegial self-understanding" of the papacy.[55] Granfield believes that co-responsibility, which is one of the foundational principles of ecclesial democracy, does not render the papacy obsolete but rather requires the papal ministry, of course in new forms.

To promote this papal renewal Granfield typically reviews the crucial transitions of the papacy from the fourth century to the present. In a magisterial overview, he highlights the basic influences that shaped the institutional form of the papacy as it moved from century to century, and notes the seven critical phases of the development of the papacy in particular: the Edict of Milan, the donation of Pepin, the Hilderbrandine reform, the Great Western Schism, the Protestant Reformation, Vatican I, and Vatican II. Granfield's conclusion from this historical survey is that "the papacy must always function for a living constituency and to do so effectively must always be a papacy in transition."[56]

A papacy "in transition" is therefore not simply one that has de facto continuously changed in response to historical pressures but also one that *in principle* must be in constant reform in order to be true to its mission. However, before appropriate reforming measures can be suggested, it is necessary to understand why objections have been voiced against the papacy. Granfield enumerates several complaints against the papacy: that it is "nonscriptural," "anachronistic," "imperialistic," "too Italian," "remote," "antitheological," "too liberal," and "not credible."[57]

In Granfield's view, however, the basic difficulty against the papacy is its monarchism, which reached its doctrinal apogee in Vatican I. An

---

[55] Granfield, *The Papacy in Transition*, x. This book was named Most Significant Book of the Year by College Theology Society. In expounding Granfield's ecclesiology in this section, I will collate his ideas expressed in *The Papacy in Transition* as well as in its sequel, *The Limits of the Papacy*.

[56] Granfield, *The Papacy in Transition*, 14.

[57] See ibid., 20–33. Granfield writes: "In conclusion, the case against the papacy reveals that the papacy is not what it once was. It is in the process of transition. There is a widespread feeling among many Christians today that the papacy needs to be reformed" (33).

effective reform of the papacy must come to terms with this form of the papacy that dominated the Church until recent times. Again, true to his method, Granfield reviews the historical development of papal absolutism, from Leo I to Vatican I, and the theological arguments in support of it.[58] While acknowledging the truth of Vatican's definitions of papal primacy and infallibility, Granfield makes a distinction between "the essence of the papacy" and "its exercise." He sees the emergence of a "new ecclesiological consciousness" according to which "the papacy should recover its deep pastoral character and eliminates those legalistic qualities that limit its effectiveness. What is needed, then, is a transition from a monarchical papacy to a collegial one."[59]

For Granfield, the recent transition of the papacy from the monarchical to the collegial model is its most radical transformation. Or as Granfield puts it, "perhaps the single most important aspect of the papacy in transition, one that determines whether the Pope will be a monarch or a pastor, is the relationship between the Pope and the bishops."[60] This relationship is encapsulated by the description of the pope as "a true fellow bishop." Inherent in this description is the concept of "collegiality." Negatively, collegiality implies that there are limits to papal primacy and infallibility. Theologically, it is based on the concept of the Church as *communio*, especially as it is applied to the relationship between the Church of Rome and the local church. Organizationally, it calls for ecclesiastical structures to implement episcopal collegiality in an effective way. Let us see how Granfield develops these three aspects in turn.

Limits of the Papacy

As a precondition to an adequate understanding and exercise of episcopal collegiality it is necessary to affirm that there are limitations to the pope's primatial authority. Granfield distinguishes four kinds of limitations: official, legal, dogmatic, and practical. *Official* limits are those that emerge from the office of the papacy itself. They are of two types. The first type flows from the nature of the Church as a mystery and a social institution. The papacy, whose existence is to serve the Church, is limited in its function by the purpose or the "directing idea"

---

[58] A historical overview of the papacy as a monarchy and the claim of papal primacy is given in Granfield, *The Papacy in Transition*, 34–61, and *The Limits of the Papacy*, 32–50.

[59] Granfield, *The Papacy in Transition*, 61.

[60] Ibid., 62.

of the Church as a social institution.[61] Because the "directing idea" of the Church is the Christ event, the mandate of the Bishop of Rome is "to make the directing idea of the Christ event a living reality" and "to maintain and safeguard the visible unity of the Church and to show solicitude for all the local Churches that belong to the *communio*."[62] The second type of limitations flows from the way in which the papacy must be exercised, namely, to "build and not destroy the Church": "Any exercise of papal authority that does not contribute to the good of the Church but leads to its destruction is reprehensible."[63]

The *legal* limits are those that are connected with natural law, divine positive law, and, to a lesser extent, ecclesiastical law, all of which the pope is bound to obey. For example, the pope cannot command things contrary to natural laws, nor can he abolish the sacraments or the entire episcopacy because these are divinely established. Granfield notes that even if the Church is called a monarchy (which he rejects), it "is not hereditary nor absolute but constitutional."[64]

Dogmatic limits are those built into the way papal teaching authority must be exercised. Granfield calls to mind the fact that "in exercising his teaching ministry, the Pope is limited by revelation. He cannot reject the 'deposit of faith' and repudiate everything in Scripture and tradition."[65] The pope is therefore bound to adhere to the dogmatic canons of the councils and to all previous dogmatic articulations of the faith. Furthermore, Vatican I, in defining papal infallibility, attaches stringent conditions to the valid exercise of such an act. Finally, there is the possibility of the deposition of popes for heresy and moral crimes.[66]

---

[61] For Granfield's explanation of the Church as an institution, that is, as a stable communion of persons sharing ideas and operations for the development and integration of values flowing from the Christ event, see his "The Church as Institution: A Reformulated Model," *Journal of Ecumenical Studies* 16 (1979) 431–46.

[62] Granfield, *The Limits of the Papacy*, 59.

[63] Ibid., 61.

[64] Ibid., 62. See also Granfield, *The Papacy in Transition*, 59.

[65] Granfield, *The Limits of the Papacy*, 68.

[66] Granfield discusses at length the possibility of the loss of the papal office through resignation and deposition. See Granfield, "Papal Resignation," *The Jurist* 38 (1978) 118–31; Granfield, *The Papacy in Transition*, 151–74; and Granfield, *The Limits of the Papacy*, 71–3. With characteristic realism Granfield writes:

> Papal resignation and deposition are unusual and unsettling events in the Christian community. A fixed term of office or a fixed age limit for the Pope would presumably reduce the possibility of such drastic actions. Nevertheless, in the absence of such norms, it seems preferable for the conclusion of a papal reign to be left to the wisdom of Divine Providence. . . . In short, the

Lastly, there are *practical* limits derived from the personal qualities of the pope himself, the complex nature of the papal office that cannot be fulfilled except through the assistance of others, and the social context within and outside the Church that can limit the efficacy of the papacy through a hostile or indifferent attitude. In addition, the pope can also voluntarily limit his power through resignation, delegation, or negotiation.[67]

The Church as Communio: *Papal Primacy and Collegiality*

Granfield distinguishes two dimensions in *communio (koinonia)*, the vertical and the horizontal:

> The vertical aspect of communion refers to participation and sharing through grace in the life of the Father through Christ in the Holy Spirit. Communion is a gift, the fruit of the Paschal Mystery that establishes a new relationship between God and ourselves. The horizontal aspect of communion is the relationship among believers that is possible because of our relationship to God.[68]

With respect to horizontal communion, Granfield believes that Vatican II has given a charter for a pastoral papacy with its doctrine of collegiality with which it seeks to promote the unity and collaboration between the papal and episcopal offices. Collegiality in turn rests on the doctrine of the Church as *communio,* that is, "a united people participating in God's saving grace in Christ and celebrating his presence most visibly at the Eucharist. The universal Church is a *communio ecclesiarum,* a fraternity of local communities joined together by the one Spirit."[69] Church communion, Granfield points out, is grounded in a twofold relationship: "one that exists between the individual bishop and the members of the local church, and the other, which is a binding

---

peace and unity of the Church may, in the meantime, be best served by reliance on that final deposition that is death (*The Papacy in Transition,* 174).

[67] See Granfield, *The Limits of the Papacy,* 73–6.

[68] Patrick Granfield, "The Collegiality Debate," *Church and Theology: Essays in Memory of Carl Peter,* ed. Peter C. Phan (Washington, D.C.: The Catholic University of America Press, 1995) 92–3.

[69] Granfield, *The Papacy in Transition,* 63. A somewhat fuller definition of *communio* is found in Granfield's *The Limits of the Papacy:* "The Church is a *communio*—a people united in faith, sharing the grace of God in Christ and the Spirit, and celebrating this unity most visibly through the eucharist" (82). For Granfield's further discussion of the Church as *communio* see "The Church Local and Universal: Realization of Communion," *The Jurist* 49 (1989) 449–71, and "The Concept of the Church as Communion," *Origins* 28:44 (1999) 754–8.

together of the local churches and their bishops into a larger unity."[70] Because of this double relationship, *communio* protects the unity of the universal Church as well as the individuality of the local church.

Of the two relationships Granfield focuses almost exclusively on that between the bishops and the pope, and therefore on episcopal collegiality. He distinguishes between *effective* and *affective* collegiality. Effective collegiality "refers to the world-wide solidarity of the bishops who, through their sacramental consecration and hierarchical communion with one another and with their head, the Pope, possess full and supreme authority in relation to the universal Church. The fullest expression of this kind of collegiality is an ecumenical council."[71] By affective collegiality is meant "mutual cooperation, collaboration, and fraternal interaction among the bishops and the Pope on the national, regional, and international levels."[72]

Of episcopal collegiality Granfield highlights three principles. First, it is "primarily a theological and evangelical reality and not a juridical structure."[73] It is rooted in *communio* and is based on sacramental ordination. Hence, bishops receive their threefold office of teaching, sanctifying, and governing from God in their sacramental ordination, and not from the pope, even though they need a canonical mandate from the pope to exercise their office in a particular church.

Second, collegiality has "both a theoretical and practical dependency on the papacy."[74] On the theoretical level, the college of bishops cannot exist without the pope, since he is both fellow member and head. Here arises the question of how to understand the relationship between the pope as the supreme head of the Church and the episcopal college also as the supreme head of the Church. Over against the opinion that there are two inadequately distinct subjects of supreme authority in the Church, i.e., the pope as head of the Church and the pope as the head of the episcopal college, Granfield holds that there is only one subject of supreme authority in the Church: "the episcopal college under papal leadership which can operate in two ways: through a

---

[70] Granfield, *The Papacy in Transition*, 63.

[71] Granfield, *The Limits of the Papacy*, 78.

[72] Ibid. Granfield discusses these two forms of collegiality at length in "The Collegiality Debate," 94–7. For him, affective collegiality plays an important role: "The collegial spirit or disposition should never be absent, since it is at the heart of all forms of collegiality. The collegial attitude of collaboration and cooperation among bishops is essential in the process of transmitting the Word of God and strengthening the unity of the *communio ecclesiarum*" ("The Collegiality Debate," 97).

[73] Granfield, *The Limits of the Papacy*, 82.

[74] Ibid., 84.

strictly collegial act or through a personal act of the Pope as head of the college. Thus every primatial action is collegial."[75]

On the practical level, collegiality is also dependent on the pope since the latter, at least from the canonical point of view, is not required to act collegially, for example, to convoke an ecumenical council or a synod of bishops.

Third, collegiality is "essentially dialogic."[76] Dialogue, Granfield points out, is rooted in God's inner trinitarian life, that is, the community of the Father, Son, and Spirit. Collegiality challenges bishops and believers to enter into dialogue with each other and with the pope. Such a dialogue is a "two-way street." Granfield suggests that sometimes individual bishops or a conference of bishops may have no choice but

> to react negatively—though with respect and charity—to what they consider to be misapprehensions or misguided efforts on the part of Rome. The dialogic interaction, a kind of mutual fraternal correction, between the Pope and the bishops may be the critical test of the collegial principle, demanding wisdom and courage as well as tact and creativity.[77]

One helpful way to understand how *communio* and episcopal collegiality should work out practically in the life of the Church is to investigate the relationship between the Church of Rome and the local or particular church.[78] Granfield approaches this theme in three steps. First, he outlines the broad principles undergirding the meaning of the local and universal Church. He begins by noting how the model of Church as "perfect society," that is, Church as "a society that is complete and independent in itself and possesses all the means necessary

[75] Ibid., 85.

[76] Ibid., 86.

[77] Ibid., 87. For Granfield's further reflections on papal primacy and episcopal collegiality see his works: "The Church Local and Universal: Realization of Communion," *The Jurist* 49 (1989) 449–71; "Cum Petro et Sub Petro: Episcopacy and Primacy," *The Jurist* 54 (1994) 591–604; and "The Priority Debate: Universal or Local Church?" *Ecclesia Tertii Millennii Advenientis: Omaggio al P. Angel Antón,* ed. F. Chica, S. Panizzolo, and H. Wagner (Casale Monferrato: Piemme, 1997) 152–61.

[78] By "local" or "particular" church is meant (1) in the strict sense "that community of Christians called together by the Holy Spirit; under the leadership of the bishop, priests, and other ministers, it preaches the Word of God, celebrates the eucharist and other sacraments, and manifests the redemptive work of Christ in the world" (Granfield, *The Limits of the Papacy,* 110); (2) in the broad sense, "the parish, the domestic Church or family, and other Christian assemblies" (Granfield, *The Limits of the Papacy,* 111).

to attain its proposed end," encouraged the development of a juridical view of the Church, discouraged ecumenical dialogue, and, with reference to our present concern, fostered a universalist ecclesiology that left little room for a theology of the local church.[79] In opposition to this perfect-society ecclesiology, Vatican II proposes a communion ecclesiology in which the universal Church is not "a mere collection or external union of many local Churches, but the communion of Churches. The universal Church comes to be out of the mutual reception and communion of the local Churches united in faith and the Holy Spirit."[80] Thus, local churches are not simply administrative units of the universal Church; rather, they are "concrete realizations, admittedly of varying degrees, of the entire mystery of the Body of Christ which is one."[81] Concretely, then, the universal Church realizes itself only in the local churches that are united in the bond of communion.

Second, Granfield recalls the doctrine that diocesan bishops are not "mere functionaries of the Pope; they possess proper, ordinary, and immediate power that they exercise in the name of Christ."[82] However, diocesan bishops do not possess an unlimited and independent power; they are subject to the pope. But, Granfield hastens to add, "the Pope is also limited: he cannot impose uniformity as if the whole world were the Diocese of Rome."[83] He sees the role of the pope as the "principle" (not "source") or center of unity and the promoter of diversity for the universal Church: "The Pope has the responsibility to protect both unity and diversity. The ideal is the complementarity of diversities and not simply uniformity. . . . The papal charism is to evaluate valid diversity and to allow it to enrich the unity of the entire Church."[84]

Third, Granfield points out that the principle of subsidiarity must be made to function effectively in the relationship between the Church of Rome and local churches: "The Pope should not do for all other local Churches what they can well do for themselves."[85] The principle of subsidiarity rejects uniformity, resists centralization, and mandates legitimate diversity in the Church. It means that the pope should interfere in the affairs of a diocese only for the most serious reasons: "when grave conflicts are unresolved, when other solutions have failed, or when a bishop is unwilling or unable to settle a matter. The ultimate

[79] Granfield, *The Limits of the Papacy,* 109.
[80] Ibid., 112–3.
[81] Ibid., 112.
[82] Ibid., 117.
[83] Ibid., 121.
[84] Ibid., 122.
[85] Ibid., 123.

reason is the unity and good of the Church."[86] Against doubts as to whether the principle of subsidiarity, which has a sociopolitical connotation, is applicable to the Church, Granfield argues that even though it is applied only analogically to the Church, the principle in its essence— the protection of the rights, functions, and responsibilities of small groups vis-à-vis larger social units—can and must be applied to the Church and is not contrary to papal primacy. It will also discourage the harmful practice of bypassing the local bishop and the episcopal conference and going directly to Rome with complaints.

Structures of Episcopal Collegiality

In addition to ecumenical councils,[87] there are two other structures established to implement episcopal collegiality that have attracted Granfield's attention: The Synod of Bishops and the episcopal conference. Established by Pope Paul VI in 1965, the Synod of Bishops has met with serious discussion with regard to its nature as a collegial structure. Granfield is inclined to the view that

> the only subject of a true collegial act is the entire *ordo episcoporum* and not a part of it. Thus, the synod cannot perform a strict collegial act, because individual bishops cannot delegate the supreme and full authority of the College of Bishops to those few bishops who are selected as representatives to the synod.[88]

To improve the efficacy of the Synod of Bishops, Granfield makes a number of proposals: better process of consultation, relaxing the rule of secrecy, expansion of its membership, conferral of a deliberative vote, clarification of its role vis-à-vis the Curia, and a longer meeting.[89]

[86] Ibid., 130.

[87] For Granfield's discussion of ecumenical councils, see *The Papacy in Transition,* 79–85. He discusses in particular two issues: their membership and frequency. With regard to the former, he suggests the inclusion of the laity and non–Roman Catholic Christians. Concerning the latter, he writes: "There does not seem any immediate urgency to convoke an ecumenical council at the present time—Vatican II still reverberates strongly—but by the end of the century, the situation in the Church and the world may well demand another conciliar gathering" (*The Papacy in Transition,* 85). It would seem that Granfield's prediction has been partially fulfilled. Though John Paul II has not convoked a council, he has organized special synods of bishops of the five continents in preparation for the third millennium of the Church.

[88] Granfield, *The Limits of the Papacy,* 91–2. See also Granfield, "The Collegiality Debate," 99–100.

[89] See Granfield, *The Papacy in Transition,* 85–8; Granfield, *The Limits of the Papacy,* 92–7; and Granfield, "The Collegiality Debate," 100.

The episcopal conference, mandated by Pope Paul VI in 1966, is another expression of collegiality. Despite several criticisms against this intermediate organization between the diocesan bishop and the Holy See,[90] Granfield is persuaded of its theological basis: "Episcopal conferences . . . are legitimate theological expressions of the ministry of bishops and valid applications of the spirit of collegiality."[91] He is also convinced that episcopal conferences do have teaching authority, distinct from the papal and universal episcopal magisterium, even though they "can never exercise an infallible magisterium."[92]

The Sensus Fidei *and Dissent*

Intimately connected with the teaching function of the Church are the *sensus fidei* or *sensus fidelium* and reception/dissent. By *sensus fidei* is meant the "subjective quality—a supernatural gift, graced sensitivity, or instinct—given to all believers, enabling them to perceive the truth of the faith."[93] The *sensus fidelium (communis sensus fidei, sensus Ecclesiae, sensus Christi)* refers to the objective quality, "the corporate presence of the *sensus fidei* in the community of believers, the objective mind of the Church—what the faithful believe."[94] While deeply convinced of the irreplaceable role of both the *sensus fidei* and the *sensus fidelium* in the formulation of the doctrines of the faith, especially when there is unanimous agreement *(consensus fidelium)*, Granfield warns that they should not be overestimated or viewed in an uncritical or romantic way, especially if this *sensus fidelium* is determined by the use of polls. The reasons are that not every position held by the faithful is necessarily a true expression of the *sensus fidelium,* that the *sensus fidelium* itself is not self-sufficient but must be related to the hierarchical magisterium, that the magisterium and the *sensus fidelium* are complementary and not opposing realities, and that broad consultation should be part of the process by which doctrines are formulated.[95]

With regard to the reception of the Church's teachings, Granfield insists that it is not an action that confers validity upon a conciliar declaration or doctrinal decree but "a sure sign that an infallible judgment is a true and binding expression of the faith."[96] Furthermore, the process

[90] For the seven criticisms often voiced against the episcopal conference see Granfield, "The Collegiality Debate," 102–3.

[91] Granfield, *The Limits of the Papacy,* 100.

[92] Granfield, "The Collegiality Debate," 108.

[93] Granfield, *The Limits of the Papacy,* 135.

[94] Ibid., 136.

[95] See ibid., 140–4.

[96] Ibid., 150.

of reception is not automatic but takes time and involves the entire People of God. Full reception involves "the official promulgation of a doctrine by the Church, its communication, its reflection in the liturgy, its presence in the spiritual and moral life of the faithful, and its articulation by theologians."[97]

Concerning the possibility of nonreception or dissent, Granfield adopts the usual distinctions of the various kinds of objects of Church teachings and their required correlative kinds of assent: infallible teachings on "primary objects" which demand the irrevocable and unconditional assent of divine and Catholic faith; definitive teachings on "secondary objects" which require the absolute assent, internal and external, though not necessarily of divine and Catholic faith; and authoritative but noninfallible teachings on "tertiary objects" which require a religious submission of mind and will. Of course, dissent is possible only in the third kind of teachings. Granfield distinguishes between "private" and "public" dissent. Private dissent refers to the "internal dissent by one who has tried honestly, conscientiously, and with docility to make a sincere assent to the ordinary teaching of the Church, but is unable for good reasons to do so."[98] Such dissent is, for Granfield, in principle admissible but ought to be an exception. Public dissent refers to "open nonconformity or disagreement with a Church teaching, which is communicated publicly in a spoken or written manner." This kind of dissent is possible only when expressed "in theological journals and conferences," where "provisional and hypothetical conclusions that differ from Church teaching may be properly submitted to other theologians and to Church officials for critique. This kind of public dissent may be more correctly called nonassent or withholding of assent."[99] But for Granfield, even this so-called scholarly dissent has its limits and must take into account such factors as "the degree of opposition to current magisterial teaching, the seriousness of the matter, the forum of the dissent, and the subsequent polarization of the faithful."[100]

In sum, Granfield proposes four models according to which theologians interact with the teachings of the magisterium. The "free-market model" brings all theological opinions, including the teachings of the Church, into the public arena and lets the public determine their truth status by a sort of majority vote of laity, theologians, and hierarchy, Catholic and non-Catholic, religious and secular. The "peer-review model" restricts the voting public to professional theologians who will

[97] Ibid., 148.
[98] Ibid., 159.
[99] Ibid., 160.
[100] Ibid., 161.

determine the truth of a teaching by debate and consensus. The "open-season model" replaces public consensus with the teaching authority of the magisterium who does not argue but imposes its teaching and sanctions those who disagree with it. Granfield finds all three models unacceptable, the first two for devaluing the teaching authority of the Church, and the third for its failure to learn from theologians and its lack of openness to the Holy Spirit. The last model, called "the court-of-last-resort model," replaces authoritarianism with "due process." It acknowledges the magisterial role of the Church but this role is exercised "through dialogue and a shared concern for unity" and with "sensitivity to the *sensus fidelium*."[101] In this model, which Granfield favors, "sanctions are not the norm but may function, when necessary, as the public promulgation of a magisterial decision. Even in noninfallible matters, the magisterium is the court of last resort; its primary mandate is not to punish but to bring guidance to all of the faithful."[102]

The Papacy in the Ecumenical Context

The last issue of Granfield's ecclesiology that needs our attention is the papacy in the ecumenical context or, as he puts it, the pope as ecumenical pastor. It is often recognized that the Roman Catholic doctrines about papacy are one of the greatest obstacles to ecumenical unity. Granfield notes, however, that in recent ecumenical dialogues there has been a growing acceptance by non-Roman Catholics, especially the Orthodox, the Lutherans, and the Anglicans, of the Petrine office and of the Bishop of Rome as the best person to fulfill this office.[103] On the other hand, he also points out, papal doctrines such as the divine institution,

---

[101] Ibid., 166.

[102] Ibid. In this context Granfield makes a number of useful corrections to the *Ratio agendi,* the procedure for doctrinal investigations of theologians made public by the Sacred Congregation of the Doctrine of the Faith (SCDF) in 1971:

> The theologian should be informed of the charges and, if relevant, the names of the accusers; time limits should be reasonable; the theologian should have access to the full record; the procedures for the colloquium (the meeting of the theologian with representatives of the SCDF) should be published; the theologian should be able to have counsel present at the colloquium; appeal procedures should be more clearly indicated; and, finally, members (hierarchical and staff) of the SCDF should not comment publicly on the positions of the theologian before the investigation is completed (*The Limits of the Papacy,* 167).

[103] See Granfield, *The Papacy in Transition,* 97–9; and Granfield, *The Limits of the Papacy,* 171–7.

primacy, and infallibility have received much more nuanced and less legalistic interpretations at the hands of Catholic theologians.[104]

To promote a more realistic chance for ecumenical reunion, Granfield suggests a number of strategies by which Church government and teaching function can be shared among Christians of different denominations, such as participation in the World Council of Churches, summit meetings, membership in the Curia extended to non-Roman Catholics, and formation of an institution comprising all the Christian churches.[105] As for models of reunion, Granfield examines the Uniate model and the federal model, and tends to favor the second, despite its many difficulties.[106]

In addition, Granfield also suggests that to facilitate the reunion of all Christian churches, the pope may voluntarily restrict the exercise of his legal authority which he rightly possesses in order to preserve and foster a legitimate diversity among the churches, to act in a collegial manner as much as possible, even in his teaching function. With regard to the papal teaching function, Granfield observes that some theologians suggest that first, the Catholic Church should not require other Christians to accept all its dogmas if they wish to unite with Rome, especially the two Marian dogmas and the two papal dogmas, and, second, that non-Catholics should be allowed to share in the teaching task of the Catholic Church.[107]

An Ecclesiology in the North American Context

Even though Granfield has not produced a comprehensive ecclesiology, he has undoubtedly made an important and lasting contribution to this theological theme. This last part of the essay does not intend to offer a detailed evaluation of all of Granfield's writings on the Church but only to comment on his most significant approaches and ideas from the perspective of the North American context in which he lives and works.

---

[104] See Granfield, *The Papacy in Transition,* 100–6.

[105] See ibid., 106–17. With regard to the last strategy, Granfield proposes an important idea of "institution." For him, an institution is "a stable communion of men in an idea for the shaping and sharing of values through a pattern of practices" (*The Papacy in Transition,* 116). The *idée directrice* is of course the Christ event. In this institution intimate participation in the directive idea is more important than rules and structures. In it the pope "will be more a symbol than a ruler, more charismatic than juridical, a principle of unity whose strength resides in the convictions of others, rather than on his own political power" (*The Papacy in Transition,* 117).

[106] See ibid., 117–23.

[107] See Granfield, *The Limits of the Papacy,* 179–92.

An Empirical Approach to Ecclesiology

In a rare autobiographical remark Granfield describes his ecclesiology as a "functional ecclesiology with an emphasis on communication and control, information and power."[108] As we have seen, Granfield's interest in sign and language as communication dated from his philosophical studies on American behavioral semiotic. Quite likely this concern for effective communication, now extended from language, especially the social aspects of sign (pragmatics) to societal structures, has determined his approach to ecclesiology. This approach can be characterized as "empirical," not only in the sense that it prefers to focus on structural and organizational issues rather than the more theological aspects of ecclesiology.[109] More importantly, it is also empirical in the sense that it makes extensive use of empirical sciences such as cybernetics in the study of the Church.

It is this empirical character of Granfield's approach that some commentators have missed in their evaluation of his work on ecclesial cybernetics. *Pace* Clare Watkins, for instance, it cannot be said that Granfield has neglected the "theological" aspect of the Church or that he has not taken into account the differences between the Church and a purely secular society. Rather, as Sabbas Kilian has correctly noted, "cybernetic analysis is concerned with the proper functioning of this human element, not with the entire ecclesial reality. It was, therefore, no oversight on Granfield's part not to treat the supernatural aspect of the Church. For him, it was a methodological necessity."[110]

Of course, in standing at the border between cybernetics and ecclesiology and in trying to apply the insights of the former to the latter, Granfield risks displeasing practitioners of both disciplines. On the one

---

[108] Granfield, *Ecclesial Cybernetics*, 3. This statement, I submit, is true not only of the book in which it occurs but also of Granfield's ecclesiology as a whole.

[109] For instance, in comparison with his colleague Avery Dulles, whose works he often cites, Granfield's writings evince a much less "theological" perspective, not in the sense that they are not inspired and undergirded by a profound ecclesiology, but in the sense that he does not treat *in extenso* (except in essay form) such issues as the Church as mystery, body of Christ, communion, and the like. It is interesting to note that Granfield acknowledges that he does not make use of "a strict 'models approach'" (*The Papacy in Transition*, 33, n. 38).

[110] Sabbas J. Kilian, review of *Ecclesial Cybernetics* in *Theological Studies* 35 (1974) 196. In spite of this remark, Kilian betrays his interest in pneumatology when he continues: "Yet this reader is convinced that, even from the viewpoint of input, output, and feedback, more attention should have been paid to the operational role of the Spirit" (196). How the Spirit can be made to fit into cybernetics remains a mystery to me.

side of the spectrum, for those coming from a more congregationalist background, for example, Granfield's attempt to bring democratization into Church structures may be news to Roman Catholics but can hardly be exciting to them.[111] On the other hand, Roman Catholics with a more conservative bent will strenuously object to his attempt at democratizing the Church, while those with a more liberal orientation will find his proposals not radical enough. On the other side of the spectrum, there are those (e.g., social scientists) who would question the applicability of system analysis to human communities.[112] Whatever position one takes on this issue, it is indisputable that Granfield's interdisciplinary approach to ecclesiology remains an important contribution to Catholic ecclesiology which often runs the risk of remaining at the abstract level, especially when it discusses such topics as episcopal collegiality, papal primacy and infallibility, the role of the laity, and the like.

This does not mean that Granfield's use of cybernetics is unproblematic or cannot be improved. One commentator has rightly suggested that he should have studied the Church as a social system first, "with cybernetic and political analysis as subordinate to this more general framework, as in Talcott Parsons' *Politics and Social Structure.*"[113] Had Granfield proceeded in this way, he would have given a greater appreciation to the role of ad hoc and voluntary associations in the transformation of the Church and would have distinguished more clearly between "authority" (conferred by one's official position in the hierarchy) and "power" (one's actual influence on Church members).

Furthermore, a study of the Church as a social system would have enabled Granfield to highlight the oppressive and discriminatory char-

---

[111] See, for instance, Bernard Reardon's review of *Ecclesial Cybernetics* in *Expository Times* 85 (1974) 123–4. Reardon writes: "The problem is one, the non-Roman reader will reflect, already tackled in a radical way by many Christians over four centuries ago, but that Catholics themselves have now at last, after an era of Vatican absolutism, come to grips with a challenge that, after all, can no longer be resisted is a heartening thought" (124).

[112] For instance, Richard L. Means asks: "The author does not seem in the least troubled by the question of whether cybernetic vocabulary is applicable to historically derived human communities. . . . Is anything gained by shifting sociological analysis out of its traditional categories (Weber's study of bureaucracy, for instance) and into the vocabulary of system analysis?" See his review in *Christian Century* (March 1974) 345–6. Of course, the answer is: the proof of the pudding is in the eating! It has to be shown that Granfield's cybernetic analysis has not shed light on how democratization can be introduced into the structures of the Roman Catholic Church to the advantage of the Church itself.

[113] See B. David Delahanty in his review of *Ecclesial Cybernetics* in *Journal of Ecumenical Studies* 11 (1974) 149.

acter of some of its structures more clearly than he has done.[114] In this context it is interesting to note that despite his interest in how power is exercised in the Church, Granfield has not engaged in print in an extensive way with the ecclesiology of liberation theologies, whether of the feminist or Latin American types, in which the question of power is a central concern.[115]

Finally, how Granfield's use of cybernetics can be extended and improved may be shown by comparing his work with two more recent books, one more sociological and the other more theological. In his *Church and Organization*[116] Joseph F. McCann, making extensive use of recent sociological studies (much more than Granfield could have done), offers a richer classification of organization: In addition to the "open system theory school" (which Granfield uses), there are the "classical or scientific management school" and the "human relations school." Furthermore, he is able to present a more complete typology of organizational structures (i.e., the hierarchy, the clan, the collegium, and the arena) and take into account the three crucial variables of any organization, i.e., the environment, membership, and technology. With these sociological categories McCann is able to carry his analysis of how the Church functions as an organization in much greater detail

---

[114] Granfield is of course aware that problems in the Church do not arise only from personal defects and sins but also from imperfect structures (which the use of cybernetics tries to improve). For example, in proposing that the electoral college for the papacy be expanded, his arguments include not only the possible personal limitations of the cardinal-electors but also the insufficient representation in the current system. Similarly, in arguing for a term limit and retirement at a fixed age for the papacy, he does not simply point out the possibility of a pope who "through a long and difficult pontificate, might easily become complacent, intransigent, or simply exhausted," but also emphasizes the advantages of the structure of term limit and mandatory retirement: "A set term of office for the Pope would have several advantages. Such a practice would facilitate the regular circulation of fresh ideas, energy, and talent within the papacy; introduce a greater sense of urgency in the direction of the Church; and prevent an ineffective Pope from causing spiritual harm to the Church" (*The Papacy in Transition,* 149). However, Granfield has not explored the oppressive and exploitative nature of certain systems or parts of a system.

[115] I use the words "in print" because there is no doubt Granfield is quite familiar with liberation theologies and has engaged with it in other forums. He regularly teaches a graduate course on liberation theology at Catholic University and has directed or served as reader for several theses and dissertations on liberation theologians, such as Juan Luis Segundo, Leonardo Boff, Gustavo Gutiérrez, Jon Sobrino, and Choan-Seng Song.

[116] Joseph F. McCann, *Church and Organization: A Sociological and Theological Enquiry* (Scranton: University of Scranton Press, 1993).

and sophistication, in terms of the eight "regimes": fief, bureaucracy, familia, guild, team, professional organization, coalition, and market. My brief discussion of McCann's work is no criticism of Granfield's method, which was conditioned by sociological studies of organization available when he carried out his cybernetic analysis of the Church. Rather, it may be said that it is his pioneering use of cybernetics in ecclesiology that enables authors such as McCann to carry out their work.

The second work is Johannes A. van der Ven's *Ecclesiology in Context*.[117] The comparison of this work with Granfield's is particularly interesting since it focuses explicitly on the Roman Catholic Church, especially as it functions at the local level (the micro [the local and regional] as distinguished from the meso [the national and continental] and the macro [the interglobal and global level]), and makes use of the semiotic approach in which the religious images are conceived as codes. Placing the Church as a denomination and association in the social context of modernization and taking the general function of the Church as religious communication, van der Ven proceeds to analyze the four core functions of the Church—identity, integration, policy, and management—and the three functions of religious codes—communicating religious information (the cognitive aspect), expressing religious emotions and attitudes (the emotive aspect), and orienting toward transformative action (the conative aspect). By combining the four core functions of the Church with its four religious codes, that is, identity with Church as Church and Jesus movement, integration with Church as body of Christ, policy with Church as building of the Spirit, and management as Church of the poor, van der Ven is able to bring semiotics and ecclesiology into a much more complete and harmonious synthesis. Once again, my reference to van der Ven does not invalidate Granfield's work but serves to indicate how and where his application of cybernetics to ecclesiology can be extended and improved.

Democracy in the Church

Not only is Granfield's use of the social sciences characteristic of the North American ethos, but his sympathies for democracy as well. Such sympathies, as has been shown above, are pronounced in his study of the right to silence which he maintains must be defended and protected for the "maximal public order" of the society. It is these democratic impulses, I suggest, that inspire his later attempts at democratizing Church structures through cybernetic analyses and his rejection of the

---

[117] Johannes A. van der Ven, *Ecclesiology in Context*, originally published in Dutch in 1993 (Grand Rapids, Mich.: Eerdmans, 1996).

monarchical model of the papacy and his analysis of the limits of the papacy.

Of course, Granfield's ecclesiology is theology and not mere sociology of religion or Church.[118] His proposals concerning the democratization of the functioning of Church offices and structures are always firmly rooted in a careful and nuanced analysis of the history of Church practices and theological concepts such as Church as *communio* and episcopal collegiality. But it is no discrediting of Granfield's ecclesiology to say that it is also inspired by sociopolitical and democratic ideals. For example, in defense of the need of the papacy as a symbolic center of unity, even for the Church of today, he correctly notes: "From a sociopolitical perspective every large organization needs a symbolic center to provide co-ordination, communication, and direction. Without leadership capable of overseeing the whole, an organization can easily fall victim to stagnation, confusion of goals, and disastrous fragmentation."[119] But if the necessity of the papacy can be demonstrated from the perspective of the social sciences, then its exercise can and should be determined not only by theological but also sociopolitical considerations.[120] As Granfield has explicitly stated, the inspiration for his work on ecclesial cybernetics is twofold:

> First, the contemporary democratic experience with its stress on participation in decision-making and on the co-responsibility of all citizens for the common good; and second, the vision of the Church suggested by Vatican II with its principles of liberty and collegiality and its recognition of the charismatic role of all members of the Body of Christ.[121]

It is this balance in the use of social sciences and theology, between viewing the Church as a social institution and viewing it as a mystery of faith that is characteristic of Granfield's work. As he puts it concisely:

> To focus solely on the human and social aspects of the Church is to reduce the Church to just another social group. To focus solely on the divine and spiritual qualities of the Church is to exaggerate its supernatural aspects and to overlook the crucial fact that its members are human beings living in the world. The Church is a human society, albeit unique because of its divine foundation, guidance, and goal.[122]

---

[118] Yves Congar overstated his case in his review of *The Papacy in Transition* in *Revue des Sciences Philosophiques et Théologiques* (1980) 589.

[119] *The Papacy in Transition*, 99.

[120] J. R. Villar has minimized the importance of the social sciences for ecclesiology in his review of *The Limits of the Papacy* in *Scripta Theologica* 22 (1990) 263.

[121] Granfield, *Ecclesial Cybernetics*, xii.

[122] Granfield, ed., *The Church and Communion*, 7.

Of course, one can agree with Granfield's democratizing project and yet disagree with any of his specific proposals. However, it is undeniable that—with his philosophical study of semiotic, his theological defense of the right to silence, his generous service as editor, his use of interviews as a way of theologizing, his skillful combination of historical research with systematic speculation, his pioneering use of cybernetics in ecclesiology, his comprehensive investigations into the papacy, and his dynamic correlation of communication with ecclesiology— Granfield has made an important and lasting contribution to theology and the life of the Church.

For Further Reading

McCann, Joseph F. *Church and Organization: A Sociological and Theological Enquiry.* Scranton: University of Scranton Press, 1993.

Van der Ven, Johannes A. *Ecclesiology in Context.* Grand Rapids, Mich.: Eerdmans, 1993.

Orna, Mary Virginia. *Cybernetics, Society and the Church.* Dayton, Ohio: Pflaum Press, 1969.

Gill, Robin. *Prophecy and Praxis: The Social Function of the Churches.* London: Marshall, Morgan and Scott, 1981.

Thung, Mady. *The Precarious Organization: Sociological Explorations of the Church's Mission and Structure.* The Hague: Morton, 1976.

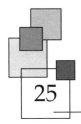

Bibliography of
Patrick Granfield

25

Compiled by David Granfield

1954

"Blessed Placid Riccardi." *American Benedictine Review* 5 (Winter 1954–55) 299–305.

1955

Review of *The Nihilism of John Dewey* by Paul K. Crosser. *American Benedictine Review* 6 (Winter 1955–56) 465–7.

Review of *Points for the Meditations and Contemplations of St. Ignatius Loyola* by Franz von Hummelauer. *The American Ecclesiastical Review* 133 (1955) 284–5.

Review of *The Spirituality of St. Ignatius Loyola* by Hugo Rahner. *The American Ecclesiastical Review* 133 (1955) 284–5.

1956

Review of *Does God Exist?* by A. Mazzei. *The Catholic Standard.* Washington, D.C., Nov. 2, 1956.

Review of *Neglected Saints* by E. I. Watkin. *The American Ecclesiastical Review* 135 (1956) 359–60.

Review of *St. Francis Solanus: Apostle to America* by Franchon Royer. *American Benedictine Review* 7 (Autumn 1956–57) 315–6.

1957

"Blessed Contardo Ferrini: Model of Virtue and Scholarship." *The American Ecclesiastical Review* 137 (1957) 105–12.

Review of *Worship and Work* by Colman J. Barry. *The American Ecclesiastical Review* 136 (1957) 213–4.

1958

"Behavioral Semiotic: A Critique." Ph.D. dissertation, Pontifical Athenaeum of
St. Anselm, Rome, 1958.

Review of *Abbot Extraordinary: A Memoir of Aelred Carlyle, Monk and Missionary,
1874–1955* by Peter F. Anson. *American Benedictine Review* 9 (Autumn–
Winter 1958–59) 252–3.

Review of *Nor Scrip Nor Shoes* by John H. McGoey. *American Benedictine Review*
9 (Spring–Summer 1958) 139–40.

1960

Review of *The Holy Rule* by Hubert van Zeller. *The American Ecclesiastical Review*
142 (1960) 357–8.

1961

Review of *Before His Face* by Gaston Courtois. *The American Ecclesiastical Review*
145 (1961) 141–2.

Review of *It Stands to Reason* by Rudolf Harvey. *The American Ecclesiastical Review* 145 (1961) 358–9.

1962

"Behavioral Semiotic: A Critique." *The Thomist* 24 (1962) 495–536. (Excerpt from
Ph.D. dissertation.)

"Comment." *The American Ecclesiastical Review* 147 (1962) 135–9.

"Comment." *The American Ecclesiastical Review* 147 (1962) 206–8.

"Comment." *The American Ecclesiastical Review* 147 (1962) 273–6.

"Comment." *The American Ecclesiastical Review* 147 (1962) 351–5.

"Comment." *The American Ecclesiastical Review* 147 (1962) 426–9.

"The Theological Development of the Defendant's Obligation to Reply in a
Civil Court." S.T.D. dissertation, School of Sacred Theology at The
Catholic University of America, 1962. Published in *Studies in Sacred
Theology*, 2d series, no. 138 and Ann Arbor, Mich.: University Micro-
films, Inc., 1963, no. 63–1911.

1963

"Book Notes." *The American Ecclesiastical Review* 148 (1963) 215.

"Book Notes." *The American Ecclesiastical Review* 148 (1963) 358.

"Book Notes." *The American Ecclesiastical Review* 149 (1963) 70.

"Book Notes." *The American Ecclesiastical Review* 149 (1963) 357–8.

"Comment." *The American Ecclesiastical Review* 148 (1963) 60–4.

"Comment." *The American Ecclesiastical Review* 148 (1963) 135–9.

"Comment." *The American Ecclesiastical Review* 148 (1963) 205–9. Translated in part in *Nouvelles de Chrétienté* 393 (May 9, 1963) 28.

"Comment." *The American Ecclesiastical Review* 148 (1963) 277–80.

"Comment." *The American Ecclesiastical Review* 148 (1963) 350–4.

"Comment." *The American Ecclesiastical Review* 148 (1963) 420–4.

"Comment." *The American Ecclesiastical Review* 149 (1963) 59–62.

"Comment." *The American Ecclesiastical Review* 149 (1963) 135–9.

"Comment." *The American Ecclesiastical Review* 149 (1963) 208–11.

"Comment." *The American Ecclesiastical Review* 149 (1963) 281–3.

"Comment." *The American Ecclesiastical Review* 149 (1963) 344–7.

"Comment." *The American Ecclesiastical Review* 149 (1963) 437–40.

1964

"Answers to Questions." *The American Ecclesiastical Review* 150 (1964) 296–7.

"Comment." *The American Ecclesiastical Review* 150 (1964) 91–2.

"Comment." *The American Ecclesiastical Review* 150 (1964) 153–5.

"Comment." *The American Ecclesiastical Review* 150 (1964) 217–21.

"Comment." *The American Ecclesiastical Review* 150 (1964) 298–302.

"Comment." *The American Ecclesiastical Review* 150 (1964) 375–7.

"Comment." *The American Ecclesiastical Review* 150 (1964) 440–3.

"Comment." *The American Ecclesiastical Review* 151 (1964) 57–61.

"Comment." *The American Ecclesiastical Review* 151 (1964) 133–8.

"The Nature of Theology: St. Thomas and Karl Barth." *The American Ecclesiastical Review* 150 (1964) 256–66.

Review of *Peter and the Church: An Examination of Cullmann's Thesis* by Otto Karrer. *The Catholic Historical Review* 50 (1964) 213.

"Seventy-five Years of the AER." *The American Ecclesiastical Review* 150 (1964) 18–32.

1965

"An Interview: Karl Rahner—Theologian at Work." *The American Ecclesiastical Review* 153 (1965) 217–30. (Appeared later in *Theologians at Work*, 1967.)

"The Right to Silence." *Theological Studies* 26 (1965) 280–98. (From S.T.D. dissertation.) In digest form as "Derecho al Silencio." *Selecciones de Teologia* 20 (1966) 310–3.

"The Spirit of Change in the Church: An Interview with Hans Küng." *The Homiletic and Pastoral Review* 65 (1965) 17–21.

1966

"Diakonia and Salvation History: Piet Fransen Interviewed." *The Clergy Review* 51 (1966) 332–49. (Later in *Theologians at Work*, 1967.)

"An Interview—Robert McAfee Brown: The Ecumenical Venture." *The American Ecclesiastical Review* 154 (1966) 1–19. (Later in *Theologians at Work*, 1967.)

"An Interview with Reinhold Niebuhr." *Commonweal* 85 (1966) 315–21. (Later in *Theologians at Work*, 1967.) Also translated into Dutch as "In Gesprek mit Reinhold Niebuhr." *De Maand* 10 (1967) 307–16.

"Paul VI." *Britannica Book of the Year* 1966. Chicago: Encyclopaedia Britannica, Inc., 1966.

"The Right to Silence: Magisterial Development." *Theological Studies* 27 (1966) 401–20. (From S.T.D. dissertation.)

1967

"An Interview with Abbot Butler." *Review for Religious* 26 (1967) 46–9. (Also in *Theologians at Work*, 1967.)

"An Interview with Father Connell." *The American Ecclesiastical Review* 57 (1967) 74–82. (Also in *Theologians at Work*, 1967.)

"An Interview with Yves Congar." *America* 116 (1967) 676–80. (Also in *Theologians at Work*, 1967.)

Theologians at Work. New York: Macmillan, 1967. Book of the Month selection by Thomas More Association.

1968

"Ecclesial Cybernetics: Communication in the Church." *Theological Studies* 29 (1968) 662–73. Also translated into Hungarian as "Egyhaz es Kibernetika." *Merlag* 5 (1969) 139–50.

"The German Theological Scene." *Thought* 43 (1968) 325–47. Received from the Catholic Press Association an award of Honorable Mention "for the best piece of analytical and interpretive reporting among all Catholic magazines of the Catholic Press Association."

1969

"Malcom Boyd: An Interview." *The Catholic World* (February 1969) 208–13.

"The Mystery of the Church." *The American Ecclesiastical Review* 160 (1969) 1–20.

1970

Kyriakon—Festschrift Johannes Quasten. Ed. Patrick Granfield and J. A. Jungmann. 2 vols. Münster: Aschendorff, 1970.

1972

Review of *The Once and Future Church.* Ed. James A. Coriden. *The Jurist* 32 (1972) 301–2.

1973

Ecclesial Cybernetics: A Study of Democracy in the Church. New York: Macmillan, 1973.

Review of *Christ and the Church* by René Latourelle. *The Jurist* 33 (1973) 94–5.

1974

Review of *The Community Called Church* by Juan Luis Segundo. *The Jurist* 34 (1974) 232–3.

Review of *Frontiers for the Church Today* by Robert McAfee Brown. *The Thomist* 38 (1974) 394–5.

1975

"Concilium and Consensus: Decision-Making in Cyprian." *The Jurist* 35 (1975) 397–408.

"Contemporary Prophecy: The Solzhenitsyn Case." *Thought* 50 (1975) 227–46.

1976

"Episcopal Elections in Cyprian: Clerical and Lay Participation." *Theological Studies* 37 (1976) 41–52.

"Shared Responsibility." *Stewardship of Time and Talent.* Ed. Francis A. Novak, 18–19. Washington, D.C.: National Catholic Stewardship Council, 1976.

1977

"The Pope." *Catholic Charismatic* 2 (June–July 1977) 22–5.

1978

"Papal Resignation." *The Jurist* 38 (1978) 118–31.

1979

"The Church as Institution: A Reformulated Model." *Journal of Ecumenical Studies* 16 (1979) 425–47.

"The Church as *Societas Perfecta* in the Schemata of Vatican I." *Church History* 48 (1979) 431–46.

1980

"Authority: The Petrine Ministry." *Exploring the Faith We Share*. Ed. Glenn C. Stone and Charles LaFontaine, 88–106. New York: Paulist Press, 1980.

"The Ecumenical Significance of the Charismatic Movement." *Ecumenical Trends* 9 (1980) 97–9.

"The Local Church as a Center of Communication and Control." *Proceedings of the Catholic Theological Society of America* 35 (1980) 256–63.

The Papacy in Transition. Garden City, N.Y.: Doubleday, 1980. Book of the Month Selection by Catholic Book Club. Most Significant Book of the Year Award from College Theology Society.

Review of *Faith and Freedom: Toward a Theology of Liberation* by Schubert M. Ogden. *Religious Studies Review* 6 (1980) 47.

Review of *Päpstliche Primat und Autorität der Allgemeinen Konzilien im Spiegel der Geschichte* by Georg Schwaiger. *The Catholic Historical Review* 66 (1980) 435–6.

"The *Sensus Fidelium* in Episcopal Selection." *Electing Our Own Bishops*. Concilium 137. Ed. Peter Huizing and Knut Walf, 33–8. New York: Seabury Press, 1980. (Also translated into French, Italian, Dutch, German, Spanish, and Portuguese.)

1981

"John Paul's Spiritual Vision: A Study in Complexity." *National Catholic Reporter* (October 16, 1981) 16–17.

The Papacy in Transition. Dublin: Gill and Macmillan, 1981.

Review of *Ecclesiastical Office and the Primacy of Rome: An Evaluation of Recent Theological Discussion on First Clement* by John Fuellenbach. *The Thomist* 45 (1981) 641–2.

Review of *The Pope's Divisions: The Roman Catholic Church Today* by Peter Nichols. *National Catholic Reporter* (November 6, 1981) 23.

1982

"Ein Theologe bei dem Arbeit: Gespräch mit Dom Patrick Granfield." *Karl Rahner im Gespräch.* Ed. Paul Imhof and Hubert Biallowons. Band I: 1964–77. Munich: Kösel, 1982. (Originally published in *Theologians at Work,* 1967.)

Intervention at International Colloquium of Istituto Paolo VI, Rome, October 24–26, 1980. Published in *Ecclesiam Suam: Première lettre encyclique de Paul VI,* 182–4. Brescia: Istituto Paolo VI, 1982.

Review of *The Family and the Fellowship: New Testament Images of the Church* by Ralph P. Martin. *The Virginia Seminary Journal* 34 (1982) 48.

Review of *The Mind of John Paul II: Origins of His Thought and Action* by George Huntston Williams. *Religious Studies Review* 8 (1982) 292.

"The Rise and Fall of *Societas Perfecta.*" *May Church Ministers Be Politicians? Concilium* 157. Ed. Peter Huizing and Knut Walf, 3–8. New York: Seabury Press, 1982. (Also translated into French, Italian, Dutch, German, Spanish, and Portuguese.)

"Theological Evaluation of Current Procedures." *Cooperation between Theologians and the Ecclesiastical Magisterium.* A Report of the Joint Committee of the Canon Law Society of America and the Catholic Theological Society of America. Ed. Leo J. O'Donovan, 117–43. Washington, D.C.: Canon Law Society of America, 1982.

"What Does It Mean To Be Church?" *Proceedings of the Sixteenth Assembly of the National Conference of Vicars for Religious* 16 (1982) 7–13.

1983

Review of *Concern for the Church* by Karl Rahner. *The Virginia Seminary Journal* 35 (1983) 34–5.

Review of *Der Kennzeichen der Kirche* by Peter Steinacker. *Religious Studies Review* 9 (1983) 362.

Review of *L'ecclesiologia del Vaticano II: Dinamismi e prospettive.* Ed. Giuseppe Alberigo. *Religious Studies Review* 9 (1983) 249.

1984

"Changes in Religious Life: Freedom, Responsibility, Community." *America* (September 15, 1984) 120–3.

Contribution to "Doctrinal Responsibilities: Procedure for Promoting Cooperation and Resolving Disputes between Bishops and Theologians." A joint project by committee of the Catholic Theological Society of America and Canon Law Society of America. Published in *Proceedings of the Catholic Theological Society of America* 39 (1984). Granfield's contribution is on 209–13, 230–2. Also published in *Proceedings of the*

Forty-Fifth Annual Convention of the Canon Law Society of America. Washington, D.C.: Canon Law Society of America, 1984. Granfield's contribution is on 261–5 and 281–3.

Das Papsttum: Kontinuität und Wandel. Trans. Siegfried A. Schulz. Münster: Aschendorff, 1983. (Revised and expanded edition of *The Papacy in Transition.* Garden City, N.Y.: Doubleday, 1980.)

1985

The Church: A Bibliography. Co-authored with Avery Dulles. Wilmington, Del.: Michael Glazier, 1985.

Intervention at International Colloquium of Istituto Paolo VI, Milan, September 23–25, 1983. Published in *Giovanni Battista Montini, Arcivescovo di Milano e il concilio ecumenico Vaticano II—preparazione e prima periodo,* 342–6. Brescia: Istituto Paolo VI, 1985.

Review of *Discovering the Church* by Barbara Brown Zikmund. *Religious Studies Review* 11 (1985) 51.

Review of *Initiation à la pratique de la théologie* by Bernard Lauret and François Refoulé. *Religious Studies Review* 11 (1985) 179–80.

Review of *The Ministry in the Church* by the Roman Catholic and Lutheran Joint Commission. *Religious Studies Review* 11 (1985) 273.

"The Uncertain Future of Collegiality." *Proceedings of the Catholic Theological Society of America* 40 (1985) 95–106. Presidential address.

1986

"A Theologian at Work" (an interview with Karl Rahner). *Karl Rahner in Dialogue.* Ed. P. Imhof, H. Biallowons, and H. D. Egan, 11–22. New York: Crossroad, 1986. (From *Theologians at Work,* 1967.)

1987

"Church Historian Sees Synod Sparking Dialogue." Interview on the 1987 Synod on the Laity in *Gathering* (Summer 1987) 10.

"Johannes Quasten: 1900–1987." *Focus* 1 (November 1987) 3.

"John Paul II, Pope." *Academic American Encyclopedia,* 11:425–6. Danbury, Conn.: Grolier, 1987.

The Limits of the Papacy: Authority and Autonomy in the Church. New York: Crossroad, 1987. Selected as Book of the Month by the Catholic Book Club and the Clergy Book Service. Award from the Catholic Press Association (1988). Published in England: *The Limits of the Papacy.* London: Darton, Longman and Todd, 1987.

"Papacy." *Encyclopedia of Religion,* 11:171–83. New York: Macmillan, 1987.

"Pope." *New Dictionary of Theology*, 779–84. Wilmington, Del.: Michael Glazier, 1987.

Review of *The Church Renewed: The Documents of Vatican II Reconsidered.* Ed. George P. Schner. *Toronto Journal of Theology* 3 (1987) 175–6.

Review of *Unity of the Churches: An Actual Possibility* by Heinrich Fries and Karl Rahner. *Horizons* 14 (1987) 161–2.

1988

"Ecclesiological Reflections." *Whither the Wind: A Telltale of Authority.* Publication of Standing Committee of EDEO-NADEO—Episcopal Diocesan Ecumenical Officers (Episcopal) and National Association of Diocesan Ecumenical Officers (Roman Catholic), 43–6.

"Legitimation and Bureaucratisation of Ecclesial Power." *Power in the Church.* Concilium 197. Ed. James Provost and Knut Walf, 86–93. Edinburgh: T. & T. Clark, 1988. (Also translated into Dutch, French, German, Italian, Spanish, and Portuguese.)

1989

"The Church Local and Universal: Realization of Communion." *The Jurist* 49 (1989) 449–71.

"Ecclesiology." *New Catholic Encyclopedia.* Vol. 18, Supplement 1978–1988, 128–31. Palatine, Ill.: Jack Heraty and Associates, in association with the Catholic University of America, 1989.

Review of *Authority and Leadership in the Church: Past Directions and Future Possibilities* by Thomas P. Rausch. *National Catholic Reporter* (August 11, 1989) 21.

"Two Specific Ecclesiological Points." Intervention at International Colloquium of Istituto Paolo VI, Brescia, September 19–21, 1986. Published in *Paolo VI e i problemi ecclesiologici al concilio*, 395–8. Brescia: Istituto Paolo VI, 1989.

1990

"John Paul II, Pope." *Academic American Encyclopedia*, 11:425–6. Danbury, Conn.: Grolier, 1990. Updated version of 1987 contribution.

The Limits of the Papacy: Authority and Autonomy in the Church. New York: Crossroad, 1989. Paperback edition.

Review of *Ministry and Authority in the Catholic Church* by Edmund Hill. *The Thomist* 54 (1990) 738–41.

Review of *Teología de la Iglesia particular. El tema en la literatura de lengua francesa hasta el Concilio Vaticano II* by José R. Villar. *The Jurist* 50 (1990) 671–3.

1991

"American Theologians, 'Dignitatis humanae,' and Paul VI." Delivered at International Colloquium of Istituto Paolo VI, Rome, September 22–24, 1989. Published in *Paolo VI e il rapporto chiesa-mondo al concilio*, 194–204. Brescia: Istituto Paolo VI, 1991.

"In Remembrance of Reverend Carl J. Peter." *Focus* 9 (1991) 2.

Los limites del papado. Autoridad y autonomia en la Iglesia. Bilbao: Desclée De Brouwer, 1990. (Revised and expanded version of *The Limits of the Papacy*, 1987.)

Review of *The Church We Believe In: One, Holy, Catholic and Apostolic* by Francis A. Sullivan. *The Jurist* 51 (1991) 521–2.

1992

Review of *The Emergence of the Laity in the Early Church* by Alexandre Faivre. *The Catholic Historical Review* 78 (1992) 433–4.

1994

The Church and Communication. Ed. Patrick Granfield. Kansas City, Mo.: Sheed and Ward, 1994.

"Cum Petro et Sub Petro: Episcopacy and Primacy." *The Jurist* 54 (1994) 591–604.

Review of *Ecclesia unum et plura. Riflessione teologico-canonica sull'autonomia della chiese locali* by Franceso Lopéz-Illana. *The Jurist* 54 (1994) 773–4.

Review of *Il primato del vescovo di Roma nel primo millennio. Ricerche e testimonianze* by Michele Maccarrone. *The Catholic Historical Review* 80 (1994) 546–8.

"Theology of the Church and Communication." *The Church and Communication.* Ed. Patrick Granfield, 1–18. Kansas City, Mo.: Sheed and Ward, 1994.

1995

"The Collegiality Debate." *Church and Theology: Essays in Memory of Carl J. Peter.* Ed. Peter C. Phan, 88–110. Washington, D.C.: Catholic University of America Press, 1995.

"The Commitment of Paul VI to Collegiality." Intervention at International Colloquium of Istituto Paolo VI, Brescia, September 25–27, 1992. Published in *Paolo VI e la collegialità episcopale*, 367–9. Brescia: Istituto Paolo VI, 1995.

"Discussion Summary" (with Scott Huber). *Religious Liberty: Paul VI and Dignitatis Humanae*, 165–8. Brescia: Istituto Paolo VI, 1995.

"Un papa latinoamericano?" *Vision. La revista latinoamericana* (April 1–15, 1995) 18–19.

Review of *Church and Justification: Understanding the Church in the Light of the Doctrine of Justification* by the Lutheran–Roman Catholic Joint Commission. *The Jurist* 55 (1995) 450–2.

Review of *S. Pietro unico titolare del primato: A proposito del decreto del S. uffizio del 24 Gennaio 1647* by Adriano Garuti. *The Jurist* 55 (1995) 432–3.

Review of *Théologie des conferences épiscopales. Une hermeneutique de Vatican II* by François Guillemette. *The Jurist* 55 (1995) 435–6.

1997

"Comments on 'Church and Justification.'" *One in Christ* 33 (1997) 35–46.

"Jesus Christ and the Millennium." *The Word Among Us* (June 1997) 6–9.

"The Priority Debate: Universal or Local Church?" *Ecclesia Tertii Millennii Advenientis: Omaggio al P. Angel Antón.* Ed. F. Chica, S. Panizzolo, and H. Wagner, 152–61. Casale Monferrato: Piemme, 1997.

Review of *Papal Primacy: From Its Origins to the Present* by Karl Schatz. *Theological Studies* 58 (1997) 565–6.

"Vatican II: A New Pentecost." *The Word Among Us* (January 1997) 4–11.

1998

"Ecumenism: The Journey Toward Unity." *The Word Among Us* (January 1998) 4–9.

"The Holy Spirit and the Millennium." *The Word Among Us* (June 1998) 16–21.

Review of *That All May Be One: Hierarchy and Participation in the Church* by Terence L. Nichols. *Theological Studies* 59 (1998) 533–4.

"Some Ecclesiological Reflections on 'Evangelii Nuntiandi.'" Intervention at International Colloquium of Istituto Paolo VI, Brescia, September 22–24, 1995. Published in *L'esortazione apostolica di Paolo VI "Evangelii Nuntiandi." Storia, contenuti, recezione,* 311–5. Brescia: Istituto Paolo VI, 1998.

1999

"The Concept of the Church as Communion." *Origins* (April 22, 1999) 753, 755–8.

"God the Father and the Millennium." *The Word Among Us* (June 1999) 16–21.

The Theology of the Church: A Bibliography. Co-authored with Avery Dulles. New York/Mahwah, N.J.: Paulist Press, 1999.

"Three Ecumenical Pioneers." *The Word Among Us* (January 1999) 63–7.

2000

Review of *Hans Küng. Breaking Through: The Work and Legacy* by Hermann Häring. *The Catholic Historical Review* 86 (2000) 144–5.

"The Oneness of the Future Church." *The Word Among Us* (January 2000) 16–21.

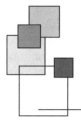

Contributors

GERARD AUSTIN, O.P., teaches at the Rice School for Pastoral Ministry in the Diocese of Venice, Florida. He taught for thirty years at the Catholic University of America. A past-president of the North American Academy of Liturgy, he has published widely about the sacraments of initiation and ministry.

JOHN P. BOYLE is professor emeritus in the School of Religion at the University of Iowa. He received his B.A. degree in philosophy from St. Ambrose College and his S.T.B. and S.T.L. degrees from the Gregorian University. He completed his Ph.D. at Fordham University with a dissertation on the ethics of Karl Rahner and Bernard Lonergan directed by Gerald McCool, S.J. He is the author of *Church Teaching and Authority: Historical and Theological Studies* (Notre Dame, Ind.: University of Notre Dame Press, 1995).

SARA BUTLER, M.S.B.T., S.T.L., Ph.D., is associate professor of systematic theology at Mundelein Seminary of the University of St. Mary of the Lake. She teaches courses in christology, mariology, ecclesiology, and Christian anthropology. She has studied the question of women's status in the Church for the past three decades, and has lectured and published on questions related to the ordination of women. Since 1991 she has been a member of the Anglican–Roman Catholic International Commission.

AVERY DULLES, S.J., Laurence J. McGinley Professor of Religion and Society, Fordham University, and professor emeritus in the Catholic University of America, is an internationally known theologian and lecturer and author of twenty books and over six hundred articles on theological topics. His latest books are *The Theology of the Church: A Bibliography* (in collaboration with Patrick Granfield;

New York: Paulist Press, 1999) and *The Splendor of Faith: The Theological Vision of Pope John Paul II* (New York: Crossroad, 1999). Past-president of both the Catholic Theological Society of America and the American Theological Society, Father Dulles has served on the International Theological Commission and as a member of the United States Lutheran/Roman Catholic Coordinating Committee. He is presently a consultor of the Committee on the Doctrine of the National Conference of Catholic Bishops.

MICHAEL FAHEY, S.J., is the Emmett Doerr Professor of Catholic Systematic Theology at Marquette University, where he also serves as editor-in-chief of the journal *Theological Studies*. A former dean in the faculty of theology, St. Michael's College, University of Toronto, he did his graduate studies in philosophy at the University of Louvain and completed doctoral studies at the University of Tübingen. His principle interests are in ecclesiology and ecumenism, especially with the Eastern Orthodox Church.

JOHN FORD, C.S.S., is professor of theology at the Catholic University of America, where he teaches in the areas of revelation and faith, American ecumenism, nineteenth-century European theology, and Hispanic/Latino theology and ministry. He is a graduate of the University of Notre Dame, received a master's degree in theology from Holy Cross College, Washington, D.C., and both a licentiate and doctorate from the Gregorian University of Rome, Italy.

JOHN GALVIN, professor of theology at the Catholic University of America, received his doctorate in theology from the University of Innsbruck. A priest of the Archdiocese of Boston, he is the co-editor (with Francis Schüßler Florenza) of *Systematic Theology: Roman Catholic Perspectives* (2 vols.; Minneapolis: Fortress Press, 1991).

DAVID GRANFIELD earned a B.A. from College of the Holy Cross, an LL.B. from Harvard Law School, and an M.A. in philosophy and an S.T.D. from the Catholic University of America. He is professor emeritus at the Catholic University of America School of Law. He has written many articles and books, including *Domestic Relations* with Philip Ryan (Brooklyn, N.Y.: Foundation Press, 1963), *The Abortion Decision* (Garden City, N.Y.: Doubleday, 1969), *The Inner Experience of Law: A Jurisprudence of Subjectivity* (Washington, D.C.: Catholic University of America Press, 1988), and *Heightened Consciousness* (New York: Paulist Press, 1991).

THOMAS GREEN is professor of canon law at the Catholic University of America. He received S.T.L. and J.C.D. degrees from the Gregorian University of Rome. He has published articles in various canonical journals and served the Canon Law Society of America in several capacities. He also served as an editor of the 1985 CLSA Commentary and of the forthcoming new edition of that commentary.

MICHAEL J. HIMES is professor of theology at Boston College. Among his books are *Ongoing Incarnation: Johann Adam Möhler and the Beginnings of Modern Ecclesiology* (New York: Crossroad, 1997) and *Fullness of Faith: The Public Significance of Theology* (New York: Paulist Press, 1993), both co-authored with Kenneth R. Himes. He is the translator and editor of J. S. Drey's *Brief Introduction to the Study of Theology* (Notre Dame, Ind.: University of Notre Dame Press, 1994).

FREDERICK JELLY, O.P., S.T.D., S.T.M., S.T.Lr., is the recipient of the 1993 Patronal Medal bestowed by the Catholic University of America for his special scholarly contributions to mariology, particularly in relationship to ecumenism on three national dialogues. He is the past-president of the Mariological Society of America and also an associate of the International Pontifical Marian Academy in Rome. He is one of the co-founders of the Ecumenical Society of the Blessed Virgin Mary (ESBVM) in America and has served on the faculty and board of the International Marian Research Institute at the University of Dayton for the past twenty years. He is professor of systematic theology at Mount St. Mary's Seminary in Maryland.

JOSEPH A. KOMONCHAK is a priest of the Archdiocese of New York. Since 1977 he has taught theology in the Department of Religion and Religious Education at the Catholic University of America, where he now holds the John C. and Gertrude P. Hubbard Chair in Religious Studies. Editor of *The New Dictionary of Theology* (Wilmington, Del.: Michael Glazier, 1987) and of the English-language edition of the *History of Vatican II* (Maryknoll, N.Y.: Orbis Books, 1995), he has published widely in the areas of ecclesiology and twentieth-century Catholic theology.

FRANK MATERA is a priest of the Archdiocese of Hartford and professor of New Testament at the Catholic University of America, where he is presently chair of the Department of Theology. He is the author of *Galatians* in the Sacra Pagina Series (Collegeville: The

Liturgical Press, 1992), *New Testament Ethics: The Legacies of Jesus and Paul* (Louisville, Ky.: Westminster John Knox Press, 1996), and *New Testament Christology* (Louisville, Ky.: Westminster John Knox Press, 1999).

RICHARD MCBRIEN is the Crowley-O'Brien-Walter Professor of Theology at the University of Notre Dame and former chair of the department. A priest of the Archdiocese of Hartford, he is the author of some twenty books, including *Catholicism* (rev. and updated; San Francisco: HarperSanFrancisco, 1994) and *Lives of the Popes: The Pontiffs from St. Peter to John Paul II* (San Francisco: Harper-SanFrancisco, 1997), and was general editor of the *HarperCollins Encyclopedia of Catholicism* (New York: HarperCollins, 1995). He is a past-president of the Catholic Theological Society of America and winner of its 1976 John Courtney Murray Award "for outstanding and distinguished achievement in theology."

JOHN NILSON is associate professor of theology at Loyola University, Chicago. He studied in the Chicago archdiocesan seminaries and received his Ph.D. from the University of Notre Dame. He has taught at Benedictine College, the University of Dallas, and the General Theological Seminary, New York. He is a Catholic member of the Anglican–Roman Catholic Consultation in the United States. In addition to his articles and essays, he is the author of *Nothing Beyond the Necessary: Roman Catholicism and the Ecumenical Future* (New York: Paulist Press, 1995).

PETER C. PHAN is the Warren-Blanding Distinguished Professor of Religion and Culture in the Department of Religion and Culture at the Catholic University of America. He holds an S.T.D. from the Salesian Pontifical University, Rome, and a Ph.D. and a D.D. from the University of London. He has authored 6 books and over 150 articles, and edited some 20 volumes. His recent scholarly interests focus on missiology and intercultural theology. He is slated to serve as president of the Catholic Theological Society of America.

ERIC PLUMMER holds degrees in theology from Oxford University and the University of Notre Dame. In addition to teaching for many years at Oxford and Notre Dame, he was visiting assistant professor of early Church history at the Catholic University of America in 1997–98. His book on Augustine's commentary on Galatians is forthcoming from Oxford University Press.

HERMANN J. POTTMEYER is professor of fundamental theology in the Department of Catholic Theology of the University of Bochun, Germany. He was visiting professor at the Gregorian University, Rome (1989), and at the University of Notre Dame (1991, 1999). A member of the International Theological Commission in Rome since 1992, he was honored with the 1991 Johannes Quasten Award by the Catholic University of America and with an honorary doctorate of theology by the Pontifical Theological Academy in Krakow, Poland, in 1998. His latest book is entitled *Towards a Papacy in Communion: Perspectives from Vatican Councils I and II* (New York: Crossroad, 1998).

PEDRO RODRÍGUEZ is ordinary professor of dogmatic theology at the University of Navara. He holds doctorates in theology and canon law and is the author of numerous monographs, including *Das Amt des Bischofs* (1972), *Iglesia y ecumenismo* (1979), *El Catecismo Romano: Fuentes e historia del texto y de la redacción* (1982), *Particular Churches and Personal Prelatures* (1986). In 1985 he discovered the manuscript of the Roman Catechism in the Vatican Library and published a 1378-page critical edition (1989). In addition, he is a member of the Pontifical Academy of St. Thomas and serves as consultant on many committees of the Catholic Church in Spain.

T. HOWLAND SANKS, S.J., is professor of historical and systematic theology at the Jesuit School of Theology at Berkeley and Graduate Theological Union. He has written, among other titles, *Authority in the Church: A Study in Changing Paradigms* (Missoula, Mont.: Scholars Press, 1974) and *Salt, Leaven, and Light: The Community Called Church* (New York: Crossroad, 1992). His teaching and research interests include ecclesiology, theological method, liberation theology, and ecumenical theology.

MICHAEL J. SCANLON, O.S.A., is a past-president of the Catholic Theological Society of America and currently holds the Josephine C. Connelly Chair of Christian Theology at Villanova University, where he is the chair of the graduate committee in the Department of Theology and Religious Studies. He received an S.T.D. from the Catholic University of America. He has taught and published in the areas of fundamental theology, systematic theology, and Augustinian studies. His most recent writings are on Christian anthropology and ethics and the postmodern debate. He is the co-editor (with John D. Caputo) of *God, the Gift, and Postmodernism* (Bloomington: Indiana University Press, 1999).

FRANCIS SULLIVAN, S.J., is professor emeritus of the Pontifical Gregorian University, where he taught ecclesiology from 1956 until 1992. He is now teaching as an adjunct professor in the Department of Theology at Boston College.

GEORGE H. TAVARD, A.A., professor emeritus of theology at the Methodist Theological School in Ohio, is the author of *The Church, Community of Salvation: An Ecumenical Ecclesiology* (Collegeville: The Liturgical Press, 1992).

SUSAN K. WOOD, S.C.L., associate professor of theology at St. John's University, Collegeville, Minnesota, is the author of *Spiritual Exegesis and the Church in the Theology of Henri de Lubac* (Grand Rapids, Mich.: Eerdmans, 1998) and *The Sacrament of Order in the Liturgy and Life of the Church* (Collegeville: The Liturgical Press, 2000), as well as a number of articles. She is a member of the U.S. Lutheran/Roman Catholic Dialogue and is an associate editor of *Pro Ecclesia*.

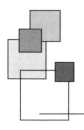

Index